TURMOIL IN NEW MEXICO
1846–1868

Turmoil in New Mexico

William A. Keleher

with a new introduction by
Lawrence R. Murphy

UNIVERSITY OF NEW MEXICO PRESS
Albuquerque

Library of Congress Cataloging in Publication Data

Keleher, William Aloysius, 1886–1972.
   Turmoil in New Mexico, 1846–1868.

   Reprint. Originally published: Santa Fe, N.M.:
Rydal Press, 1951, c1952.
   Bibliography: p.
   Includes index.
   1. New Mexico—History—1848.   2. Arizona—History—To
1950.   3. Frontier and pioneer life—New Mexico.   4. Frontier and
pioneer life—Arizona.   I. Title.
F801.K355   1982   978.9'04   82–11113
ISBN 0–8263–0631–4
ISBN 0–8263–0632–2 (pbk.)

"*The iniquity of oblivion scattereth her poppy and deals with the memory of men without distinction to merit and perpetuity . . . who knows whether the best of men be known, or whether there be not more remarkable men forgot, than any that stand remembered in the known account of time.*"

Sir Thomas Browne, 1686.

CONTENTS

BOOK 4 - THE LONG WALK

INTRODUCTION*
Lawrence R. Murphy

Few eras in the history of any American region surpass in drama, in excitement, or in historical significance the first quarter-century during which New Mexico fell under United States rule. In a third the lifespan of a single individual, a vast section of northern Mexico was integrated into an Anglo-dominated political scheme, survived the tumult of Civil War, and initiated experiments in the pacification of Native Americans. In the process, pioneering Southwesterners began to transform a hostile, arid, largely unpopulated expanse into a modern agricultural, mineral, and commercial society. Here the forces of nationalism and localism confronted one another amidst complexities resulting from ethnic, religious, political, and economic differences. Indeed, the years between 1846 and 1868 in New Mexico provide a complex pattern of people and issues eminently worthy of historical discussion. No writer had attempted a serious, detailed tracing of these important developments, however, until amateur historian William A. Keleher published *Turmoil in New Mexico* in 1952. Although dozens of monographs and articles published since have added detail to Keleher's story, no one has fully surpassed him in describing this critical era.

I

Despite a lack of formal historical training, William A. Keleher was well qualified to write about pioneer New Mexico. Like many of those whose accomplishments he portrayed, Keleher himself was

*Portions of this essay originally appeared in the author's "Dedication to the Memory of William A. Keleher," *Arizona and the West* 23, no. 2 (1981): 105–8 and are used with permission.

born far from the arid deserts and panoramic vistas of the Southwest. Born November 7, 1886, in Lawrence, Kansas, he was the third of seven children of David and Mary Ann (Gory) Keleher. In 1888, David Keleher followed the route of the Santa Fe Trail traversed by General Stephen Watts Kearny to Albuquerque, New Mexico, to work as a tinsmith in the Atlantic & Pacific railway shops. As a youngster, Will observed firsthand the growth of frontier Albuquerque only a generation removed from the events he later described. Here Italian, German, and Irish immigrants—many of whose children became prominent Southwestern businessmen and political leaders—settled alongside Hispanic, Indian, and Anglo-American residents.

Will Keleher was not quite fourteen and had completed only eight years of parochial education when his father's deteriorating health forced him to quit school to help support the family. Starting as a messenger boy, he became manager of Western Union's Santa Fe office by 1902. Hard work at such a young age, however, undermined young Will's strength. In 1906, a doctor recommended that he turn to outdoor occupations, so the next year he worked as a surveying chainman, bridge inspector, and surveyor for the Atlantic & Pacific. In the process, he began travels throughout the Southwest that nurtured a lifelong fascination with the land and its people.

Eventually, Keleher's natural aptitude for more bookish activities led him to another desk job, this time as a school bookkeeper and clerk. The post had the advantage of providing easy access to the school library next to his office, from which he devoured books on a wide variety of subjects. When, in 1908, Thomas E. Sherman—a Jesuit priest whose father was Gen. William Tecumseh Sherman—delivered a series of lectures in Keleher's parish church, Will submitted reports of the speeches to the *Albuquerque Journal*. His literary skill impressed the paper's editor, who hired Keleher as a reporter; within two years he became city editor.

As he covered local court cases, Keleher developed an intense interest in law. He studied with Albuquerque attorneys and through a correspondence course, but he found the required reading so "dull, monotonous, and even exasperating" that he soon abandoned the effort. There being no law school in New Mexico, in 1913 the twenty-six-year-old Keleher traveled east to enroll at Washington and Lee University in Lexington, Virginia, which he chose because it was highly respected by Southwestern attorneys and was known for its unusual receptiveness of older-than-usual students. Perhaps because of his limited and haphazard preparatory education, Keleher's academic career was erratic. He did find Franklin L. Riley's American history course rewarding, and he may have developed his first interest in the Civil War (which he often termed the "War Between the States" as it is known in the South) in the town where both Robert E. Lee and "Stonewall" Jackson were buried. He graduated in 1915 with a Bachelor of Laws degree. Nearly forty years later, following a distinguished career, Keleher was honored by Washington and Lee with membership in Phi Beta Kappa. He also received honorary degrees from the University of New Mexico and the College of St. Joseph (later known as the University of Albuquerque).

For more than half a century Keleher was one of the most successful practicing attorneys in New Mexico as well as devoting energy to public service and political activities. He served as Albuquerque city attorney from 1916 to 1918 and was prominent in the state bar association. The state Democratic Party elected him chairman in 1928, and he headed the regents of New Mexico A & M (now New Mexico State) University in 1941–42. He was a member of the powerful New Mexico Finance Board in the 1930s and 1940s, helped reorganize the bankrupt First National Bank of Albuquerque, and settled a bitter strike in the Gallup coal fields.

Extensive travel, a natural curiosity about the past, and a fascination with the personalities of a number of historic persons stimulated Keleher's interest in New Mexico's colorful heritage. He had personally heard stories from such legendary figures as Elfego Baca and George Curry and spent many weekends and vacation periods with his family exploring historic haunts. In his law practice, Keleher discovered the value of historic perspective and knowledge in understanding complex legal circumstance. His first substantial historical effort resulted from an examination of one of the most significant aspects of New Mexico real estate law, land grants. He delivered a paper on the "Law of the New Mexico Land Grant" at a meeting of the Texas Bar Association in 1929. The study was a pioneering investigation of a topic of immense legal and historical interest not only in New Mexico, but in other borderlands areas as well. Drawing on a wide variety of primary and secondary sources, Keleher was typically forthright in injecting his own opinions. He noted, for example, how lucrative land grant cases had been to lawyers "of the old school," and expressed his view that New Mexico would have been "more fortunate" had the Treaty of Guadalupe Hidalgo voided all grants. The address subsequently appeared in printed form in both the *Texas Law Review* (September 1929) and the *New Mexico Historical Review* (October 1929).

Keleher's interest in land grants was no passing hobby. He spent more than a decade undertaking the necessary writing and research to expand his original paper into a book-length study, *The Maxwell Land Grant* (1942). It was the first extensive treatment of one of the most colorful, controversial, and historically complex Mexican grants; and the volume remains a standard reference forty years after its first appearance.

What came to intrigue Keleher most about the history he studied were the colorful personalities of individuals from the past. Perhaps encouraged in part by his original work on land grant entrepreneur Lucien Maxwell, he started collecting stories about other memorable people. The sketches he wrote constituted his second book, *The Fabulous Frontier* (1945). The volume included chapters on nine important figures in New Mexico history, plus essays on Lincoln County, land controversies, and pioneer writers. Keleher had known several of those about whom he wrote. In the case of Oliver Lee, he interviewed the subject himself; for the others he delved into what printed sources were available and talked with relatives and friends.

Keleher's first two books provided him with ample opportunity to develop methods of historical research and analysis. His basic approach at first—as we might expect—was that of an attorney: identify witnesses, collect their testimony, and verify it wherever possible from other testimony or written records. In studying Maxwell, for example, he traveled to the rancher's last home at Fort Sumner to interview those descendants and servants who were still alive. Except for the occasional use of legal documents or a stray newspaper clipping, written materials served primarily to buttress what could be learned from witnesses. In his use of oral history, Keleher was well in advance of most professional historians. He also discovered, however, the drawbacks of too great a dependence on personal testimony. In researching historical events from the distant past, the difficulty of finding living participants increased and their reliability declined. In several instances encountered while preparing *The Fabulous Frontier,* for example, written documents which he located demonstrated that traditional oral accounts were inaccurate or at least highly exaggerated. Keleher's use of such historiographical conventions as footnotes and bibliography was also unsophisticated in his earliest writings. And he could have used the professional editorial assistance that might have been available from larger publishers. Keleher learned from each of his literary efforts, probably consulted either professional historians or books on proper methodology, and depended on his sister, Julia, a professor of English, for literary suggestions. As a result, his knowledgeability, technical expertise, and writing excellence increased until, by the publication of *Turmoil in New Mexico,* they had reached near full development.

II

Turmoil in New Mexico is without doubt a study of truly professional quality, reflecting the investigative skills Keleher acquired through legal schooling and practice, his increasingly sophisticated historiographic techniques, and his intense love of the subject matter. The challenges Keleher faced in completing the volume were enormous. Instead of focusing on a single locale or a handful of interesting people, he now spread his canvas to include a complex series of events covering the western United States and northern Mexico and encompassing dozens of major and hundreds of minor characters. Before commencing the project, Keleher spent three weeks visiting the locations about which he intended to write. Horseback forays were required to reach isolated areas of the Navajo Reservation; he also explored what remained of the principal army installations in the state.

Keleher's research techniques now underwent a substantial change. No living witnesses were available to provide firsthand testimony, so he was forced into more conventional use of written records. In an era before microfilm or photocopying were generally available, collecting evidence required days poring over materials at the University of New Mexico and Museum of New Mexico libraries. His own collection of New Mexicana grew substantially. Where efforts to find sufficient materials from local sources proved inadequate, he contacted distant depositories. A longtime friend, Commissioner of Indian Affairs Frank A. Brophy, helped him acquire Indian-related materials which would not otherwise have been available, while a librarian at the State Historical Society of Wisconsin aided in finding information about Judge Joseph Knapp. Keleher had first met George P. Hammond when the latter was dean of the Graduate School at the University of New Mexico; now Hammond directed the Bancroft

Library at the University of California, Berkeley, and gave Keleher continued assistance.

Keleher's search for materials extended beyond traditional libraries and archives. In seeking materials about Santa Fe trader James Magoffin, he contacted New Mexico Senator Carl A. Hatch, who enabled him to acquire copies of Magoffin papers from the State Department for use in the book. A distant relative of Gen. E. R. S. Canby collected information from family papers, while Mrs. Olive S. Arnold in Atlanta, Georgia, provided details about James S. Calhoun, New Mexico's first governor. Years later, Keleher felt most satisfied in having been able to track down information about the New Mexico activities of Dr. Jonathan Letterman, the pioneering army physician. Two of Letterman's daughters who had settled in Albuquerque furnished him manuscript materials which, as he later explained, "enabled me to write in an authentic way about their father." He ultimately obtained their permission to give the doctor's original commission to officials at Letterman General Hospital in San Francisco, where it was framed for display in the reception area. Keleher also traveled extensively to find appropriate illustrations: the search for a likeness of Manuel Armijo led him to the home of court reporter Edward Baca of Socorro, who provided the portrait inserted between pages 10 and 11 of the printed book.

Keleher organized his book around four principal events that shaped the years 1846 to 1868: the American conquest of the region from Mexico and the subsequent occupation, the struggle between Union and Confederate troops for the territory during the Civil War, the trek of Gen. James H. Carleton's California Column to New Mexico, and the government's attempts to relocate Navajos on the Bosque Redondo reservation. These events paralleled each other in several ways. All involved military activities, the federal government played a preeminent role in the execution of all four, and all represented attempts to integrate the unique social, cultural, and ethnic characteristics of New Mexico within the larger Anglo-oriented United States. Each also had peculiar characteristics and, most important, its own cast of actors.

No one before Keleher had described in such detail the role of New Mexico in the Mexican War. While for general background he utilized such classic studies as Justin Smith's *The War With Mexico* (1919), Keleher's work was much more circumscribed. He chose not to emphasize the causes of the war (with which New Mexico was only peripherally associated) or to try to assess blame. Instead, his emphasis here as elsewhere throughout the volume is on presenting a readable narrative which describes what happened from the perspective of a person living in the Southwest. Especially compared with most other Anglo historians, Keleher's portrayal of Mexican leaders Manuel Armijo and Antonio Jose Martinez is remarkably sympathetic. He pays greater attention, however, to the activities of officers who led United States troops into the territory. Keleher finds Gen. Stephen Watts Kearny especially impressive and quotes liberally and approvingly from his declarations on arriving in the Southwest. Sterling Price, Alexander Doniphan, and other American soldiers receive similar treatment. Keleher devotes special attention to James W. Magoffin, whom he defends against charges of malfeasance and whose frustrating efforts to recover expenses incurred while helping the U.S. Army are sympathetically chronicled. The war Keleher describes is strangely humane; he deemphasizes such barbarous events as the Taos Uprising (which is omitted except in the notes), ignores the ill-treatment of Mexicans and Indians by United States soldiers, and neglects to mention that racism and anti-Catholicism often characterized the attitudes of Anglos toward Hispanic New Mexicans. Perhaps from his perspective as a leader of modern New Mexico, Keleher deemed it unwise to open old wounds.

Some of Keleher's strongest praise is reserved for Governor James S. Calhoun, the first civilian territorial governor of New Mexico. In part this may have occurred because plentiful information was available from Calhoun's published correspondence, his annual gubernatorial messages and Indian Affairs reports, and the materials provided Keleher by his Georgia descendants. It is clear that Keleher agrees with most pioneer New Mexicans' conviction that attacks by Indians required strong punitive action as he describes in detail Calhoun's efforts to pacify the natives of the territory, as well as his difficulties in dealing with military officials and in establishing a functional government. Ill health eventually forced Calhoun's departure from Santa Fe a short time before his death on the plains.

Like an attorney presenting his case, Keleher allows his characters to speak for themselves wherever possible. Lengthy quotations from letters, speeches, reports, and other primary documents follow one after the other, often with less explanation or interpretation than other writers might provide. Keleher's selections are excellent, however; many quotations constitute extremely effective narrative, and several contain memorable phrases.

Nearly as important as the chapters themselves are the "Notes and Profiles" at the end of each Book. Their primary purpose is not to cite sources, although they serve that purpose too, but to provide added details about people, places, and events mentioned in the text. Keleher's abiding interest in personalities becomes evident in the sketches he has prepared of major and minor characters. Book One, for example, includes lengthy biographies of Governor Armijo, Father Martinez, "Kit" Carson, and James S. Calhoun. Frequently, these sketches were the most detailed available at the time. All are carefully researched, succinct, and well written. The notes also contain what personal opinions and asides Keleher allowed himself to interject. In the notes for Book One we learn that Governor Armijo's handwriting was "very legible," as well as that there is "no evidence" to support the theory that Magoffin bribed Armijo in order to assure the peaceful conquest of New Mexico. Other asides include a publishing history of John T. Hughes's history of *Doniphan's Expedition* and brief histories of places as varied as Santa Fe, Valverde, and Bernalillo. In 1929, Keleher further notes, writer Eugene Manlove Rhodes wrote New Mexico Governor R. C. Dillon to characterize Governor Calhoun as "the most interesting figure" he had encountered "in all history." "If ever a man was sent to make ropes of sand," Rhodes added, "Calhoun was that man."

Skipping lightly over the last half of the 1850s, Book Two turns to Confederate attempts to take over New Mexico. There are no villains or heroes in Keleher's portraits of Union and Confederate leaders, only human beings attempting to make difficult decisions under trying circumstances. He describes with obvious compassion, for instance, the tribulations of Southern-born officers forced to decide whether or not to resign their commissions to join the Confederate Army and, if so, whether or not to take their men with them. In describing the military campaigns that follow, Keleher relies primarily on the voluminous correspondence included in *The Official Records of the War of Rebellion,* along with rare published recollections and contemporary newspaper articles. The important battle of Valverde, the capture of Fort Fillmore, the fall of Albuquerque and Santa Fe, and the ultimate Union triumph at Apache Cañon–Glorieta Pass are all carefully described. Keleher's familiarity with local geographical conditions, his frequent use of firsthand descriptions from both sides, and the excellence of his battle descriptions all add to the value of this section.

Readers who neglect the "Notes and Profiles" will be deprived of much of Keleher's knowledge and wisdom. Besides lengthy sketches of major participants, the author relates how one of Gen. Canby's descendants, Henry S. Canby, chairman of the editorial board of the

Saturday Review, had corresponded with Keleher about the general's reputation. Later he notes from a personal visit that "Fort Fillmore today is little more than a name place. The one-time adobe walls of the fort have crumbled to dust; the grounds are thickly covered with cacti and mesquite brush" (p. 196). Mesilla, he adds later, "sleeps lazily in the sun today, dreaming of its one-time grandeur and significance in the life of the Southwest" (p. 196). Sometimes Keleher uncovers such interesting tales that he wants to share them even if they are not wholly relevant to his main thrust. "There is temptation," he admits, "to follow a side path and tell of the efforts of Sibley and his officers to get concessions in the states of Chihuahua and Sonora, Mexico, but such a narrative would be too far afield" (p. 198). He proceeds anyway to describe these activities with a long quotation.

The scene in Book Three shifts from the Rio Grande Valley to the deserts of Arizona and the fertile valleys and rugged coastlines of California. Keleher's principal objective is to describe the march of Gen. James H. Carleton's California Column to New Mexico. Along the way, readers learn about California during the Civil War and disputes among military commanders, while encountering such interesting personalities as Capt. Sherod Hunter and mining promoter Sylvester Mowry. Keleher's attitude toward Carleton is revealed, as usual, not in any high-flown rhetoric of his own but by reprinting the General's own boastful claims: "I worked hard with our California boys," Carleton had written from Santa Fe, "and got them safely through the desert." The "toils and privations" had been terrible, he continued, and "a single mistake would have been a horrible disaster. . . ." "I assure you," he concludes at the end of the Book, "that I would not encounter the same anxiety again for ten major generals' commissions" (pp. 258–59).

Nearly half of *Turmoil in New Mexico* is devoted to Book Four, titled "The Long Walk." Today the agonies of the Navajo and Apache nations in being forcibly relocated across New Mexico are well known, but in the early 1950s little had yet been written about Indian history generally, and no detailed study of the Bosque Redondo experiment had ever appeared. In fact, except for Clyde Kluckhohn and Dorothea Leighton's *The Navaho* (1947), almost nothing was known of the tribe or its history. Thus, more so than any other portion of his work, this section ploughed new, fertile ground.

Fortunately for Keleher, the federal government had prepared, collected, and published a great deal of Navajo-related material. In addition to wartime correspondence found in the *Official Records of the War of Rebellion,* Keleher used the annual reports of the Commissioner of Indian Affairs, several special Congressional reports, contemporary newspapers, and territorial documents. Like all historians writing about Native Americans, Keleher suffered from the fact that nearly all these sources were written by Anglos and represented their perspective.

Whereas Keleher's earlier descriptions had made the Mexican and Civil wars seem almost benign and his approach had been scrupulously evenhanded, the horrible brutality of the Navajo wars quickly became evident and there was no doubt where Keleher's sympathies lay. The drama of the story also evoked his most poignant prose. Fighting began, in Keleher's view, not because of any real threat from the Indians, but because General Carleton needed some activity to "capture the imagination and challenge the abilities" of his restless troops. "With no Confederates on the horizon, Carleton's active mind fastened on the idea of fighting Indians" (p. 278). From the initiation of the campaign, the outgunned and outmaneuvered Apaches and then the Navajos were doomed to defeat. Few sections of the book are as memorable as that describing Navajo captives ready to be moved: ". . . their appearance cadaverlike, their clothing mostly rags, the Navajo prisoners were indeed objects of pity. . . . And poor creatures they were indeed," he continues. "Their wheat fields had been laid waste; their fruit trees had been chopped down and burned; their means of livelihood had been taken away" (pp. 318–19).

The agony was just beginning, for the Indians were forced more than 400 miles to a remote reservation along the Pecos River. The men, wrote Keleher, "walked in funeral-like procession, in twos and fours, silent, grim and gloomy. Small wonder the Navajos walked along as if on their way to the grave" (p. 319). Once they arrived at the Bosque Redondo, fright exacerbated physical suffering. "Now in their new environment," he writes, "even the bravest of the Navajos were dazed and cowed. Ignorant of what the future might hold for them, they dreaded the uncertainty as a frightened child dreads the dark of night. . . . A stoic and silent people, the Navjos were stunned when at long last they were prisoners, and in an alien land" (p. 320).

The failure of the Bosque Redondo experiment soon became apparent to everyone except General Carleton and those of his sycophants whose commitment to the project blinded them to reality.

While throughout *Turmoil* Keleher carefully avoids praise or con-
demnation for the individuals and events he describes, his dislike
of Carleton's Indian policies is never disguised. His was "a program
of violence . . . which had no precedent in recorded New Mexico
history" and violated "many of the rules of civilized warfare," writes
Keleher (p. 440). But even in Carleton's case, bad luck and timing
rather than a character flaw produced disaster. "It was Carleton's
misfortune," he concludes, "to become commander of the Department of New Mexico at a most inopportune time." Anywhere and
anytime else he would have "won honor and renown"; instead, he
"blundered" into Indian campaigns "with results that were disastrous
to the Indians, and unfortunate for the government." Only Carleton's
removal from office under heavy local pressure led to a recognition
of his failure and the ultimate release of the Indians from "bondage"
(p. 458). Still, Keleher's ultimate appraisal of government-Navajo
relations was sorrowful: "there are those who will argue, with much
to sustain their views," he writes at the end of the Book, "that the
plight of the Navajo today is infinitely worse than it was on that
fateful day in 1846 when General Kearny . . . assumed responsibility for the welfare of the Indians of New Mexico" (p. 480).

Perhaps because he recognized that readers would be distressed
by an unbroken litany of Indian tragedy, Keleher interspersed Book
Four with asides revealing other aspects of contemporary New Mexico
history. Readers are introduced, for example, to Capt. James "Paddy"
Grayton and Dr. J. M. Whitlock, whose duel at Fort Stanton resulted
in the deaths of both, and to Paula Angel, who, having been convicted of murdering her lover, became the only woman ever hanged
in the territory. To counter the negative picture of Carleton, Keleher
devotes a chapter to Dr. Michael Steck, a Pennsylvania-born physician whose activities as a civilian Indian agent were characterized
by honesty and dedication. Another of Keleher's heroes is Judge
Joseph G. Knapp, who defied Carleton's order that everyone (even
federal judges) carry a travel permit from the army. Other sections
describe the creation of Arizona Territory and the development of
New Mexico newspapers during and immediately after the Civil
War.

Completion of such a major writing project consumed nearly all
Keleher's free time over several years. He had decided never to allow
his historical work to interfere with his law practice. "Compliance
with and obedience to the rule," he later recalled "had made it
necessary for me to do the research and writing . . . outside office

hours, at night, on Sundays and holidays. Working late at night, getting to sleep late, and starting to work on the books soon after daybreak, made it possible for me to accomplish a great deal." Once when a friend, U.S. Judge Colin Nesbitt, asked how the work was going, Keleher voiced his desire to have a hideaway somewhere in which to pursue his writing. The judge responded that he seldom used his Albuquerque office and handed Keleher the key. Such "kindness," explained the author, "afforded me the seclusion I needed and speeded up completion of the book" (*Memoirs,* pp. 273–74).

Several final touches added to the quality of the volume. Taos artist Ernest L. Blumenschein prepared an original drawing of the Navajos' long walk for use as a frontispiece; together with portraits of the major people and places in the book, it was hand tipped into the published volume. (The Blumenschein drawing is not included in this edition.) In addition, the first page of each Book bore a drawing appropriate to the subject prepared by Taos artist Oscar Berninghaus. Thomas H. Tutt drew an original map of New Mexico in 1859 which, reversed to white on black, was used for the endpapers. To print the book, Keleher turned to the Rydal Press in Santa Fe, which had issued his two previous publications. A simple, elegant design complemented by a red, black, and gold binding resulted in an attractive book, although the press lacked promotion or distribution capabilities that might have led to wider distribution. "Respectfully submitted" by Keleher in mid-August 1951, *Turmoil in New Mexico* was available early the next year at a price of $6.00.

Perhaps in part because the book had been issued by a printer rather than a publisher, it never received deserved notice. Even though a portion of Book One appeared in the January 1947 issue .as an article entitled "The Year of Decision," the *New Mexico Historical Review* failed to review *Turmoil in New Mexico.* Nevertheless, the book was reviewed in local and regional newspapers and soon came to the attention of serious historians; citations to it began to appear in other studies of the period, and it is listed in the bibliography of nearly every monograph or textbook about the nineteenth-century Southwest. It has now been out of print for nearly a quarter-century. Republication will make it available to those who failed to obtain copies of the first edition as well as to a whole new generation whose interest in the Southwest postdates its publication.

III

Completion of *Turmoil in New Mexico* did not end Keleher's interest in New Mexico history. His final historical work explored the Lincoln County War. He became so obsessed with finishing the project that for once he abandoned his legal practice to devote full time and attention to historical endeavors. Initially, his interest had been sparked by what he termed "the 'Billy the Kid' puzzle." He quickly discovered, however, that the Kid's role had been greatly exaggerated. What made the subject so interesting was not William Bonney's legend but the complexity, mystery, and intrigue of the affair. Keleher traveled to Governor Lew Wallace's home in Indiana to uncover important materials, while New Mexico Senator Clinton P. Anderson helped him acquire State Department records. Other new information came from local archives or interviews. Publication of *Violence in Lincoln County* in 1957 symbolized the recognition which *Turmoil in New Mexico* had won for Keleher. Instead of having the book issued by a private printer (probably on a subsidized basis), Keleher now submitted his work to the University of New Mexico Press, which aided in preparing the manuscript and, just as important, facilitated wider distribution. While once critics had questioned Keleher's reliance on oral testimony and challenged him to utilize more traditional historiographical techniques, his accuracy and care now won considerable praise from professional historians.

Violence in Lincoln County was Keleher's last major historical publication. In the fifteen years before his death in Albuquerque on December 18, 1972, poor health and the demands of his successful legal practice prevented further investigations. These last years also allowed him to spend more time with his wife, Loretta Barrett Keleher, whom he had married in 1932, and his children—Mary Ann, Keleher's daughter by his deceased first wife Mae J. Kelly, and his four sons, William Barrett, Michael Lawrence, John Gorry, and Thomas Franklin. He published a memorial to longtime friend Erna Fergusson in the *New Mexico Historical Review*, and he contributed frequent reviews to historical journals. He also devoted considerable time to completing his *Memoirs* (1969).

Keleher became known in these later years for his willingness to assist young historians probing the history of New Mexico. "He would give freely of his ideas and knowledge when it was apparent that they were sincerely desired," Victor Westphall recalls, "and his mind was a storehouse of information that came from him in detailed and orderly way." After himself adding so much to historical knowledge about his beloved Southwest, Will Keleher must have taken great pride in seeing historians trained in ways which were never available to him delving into many of the topics he found so fascinating. Surely many of them looked upon him as a sterling example of the significance of the amateur historian in exploring new fields of history and presenting them to both professional and nonscholarly audiences.

Lawrence R. Murphy
Central Michigan University

FOREWORD

The writer has attempted to tell in this book the stories of the American Occupation of New Mexico in 1846; of the Confederate invasion of New Mexico by Texans in 1861; of the march of California troops into New Mexico in 1862, and of the exile during Civil War years of the Navajo Indians at Bosque Redondo, on the Pecos River in New Mexico, known in tribal history as "The Long Walk."

To all intents and purposes, New Mexico became United States territory on Aug. 18, 1846, following the Occupation of Santa Fe by American troops, under the command of General Stephen Watts Kearny. New Mexico was organized as a Territory of the United States in 1850. At the time of the American Occupation, New Mexico was a Department of Mexico. The Mexican government ruled New Mexico for twenty-five years, from 1821 to 1846. Santa Fe, the capital of New Mexico, was some fifteen hundred miles in distance, and months away in time, from the Mexican national capital. For hundreds of years before the Mexican revolution of 1821, New Mexico was governed by remote control from Seville, Madrid and Mexico. Despite overwhelming obstacles, New Mexico retained political identity and continuity of a kind, and its people survived countless hardships during the period from 1598, the year of the first extensive occupation by the white man, and 1846, the year of the American Occupation.

After New Mexico became American territory, the United States government assumed the burden of attempting to solve problems inherited from Mexico pertaining to control of the wild Indians. In 1846 some forty thousand Ute, Apache and Navajo Indians roamed the vast region between the Arkansas, Pecos and Colorado rivers, and the present day Mexican border.

Whether under Spanish, Mexican or American rule, the people of New Mexico clamored for many years for a war to exterminate the wild Indians. After the Occupation of 1846 the United States built and maintained a string of forts in New Mexico, (which then embraced most of present day Arizona,) and waged intermittent wars against the Indians. Each campaign ended in a stalemate, bringing death and desolation nevertheless to soldier and Indian alike.

New Mexico had barely recovered from the shock incident to American Occupation days, when its people were subjected to a new and entirely unexpected experience. In 1861, only fifteen years after General Kearny had conquered New Mexico for the United States, it was invaded by Confederate troops. The invasion brought disaster to the inhabitants generally, and to the wild Indians in particular. Slavery was virtually unknown in New Mexico. Its people, with few exceptions, did not have the slightest conception of the causes for the quarrel between the North and South. But because of its peculiar geographical situation, New Mexico became a battleground of no small national importance.

During the early months of the Civil War, the wild Indians of New Mexico, deceived by outward appearances, took advantage of the fact that Union troops were engaged in fighting a powerful enemy, and ran amuck. When Confederate troops retreated from New Mexico into Texas, Union troops from California, and New Mexico volunteers, commanded by Colonel Kit Carson, engaged in a bloody, devastating war against the Apaches and Navajos. Finally compelled to surrender, the men, women and children of these two tribes were interned for five years in America's first concentration camp near the Texas-New Mexico boundary line. The Indian prisoners were released in 1868 by order of General William T. Sherman.

Any damage inflicted during the Civil War on New Mexico's economy, or visited upon soldiers or civilians, had been repaired within a decade after the end of the war, insofar as it was possible under the circumstances, to alleviate and indemnify. But the disastrous injury sustained by the wild Indians of New Mexico and Arizona as an indirect result of the impact of the Civil War in New Mexico, was of a permanent nature, and was and is irreparable. Ample evidence exists today of the nature, extent and permanency of the injury.

The writer is indebted to many people for kind assistance in the preparation of this volume, so many in fact that it might be advisable not to name any of them for fear that the names of some, who have been exceptionally kind and helpful, might be overlooked. Three close friends of the writer, who gave encouragement and assistance in time of need, have passed away since this work was undertaken: Hon. Colin Neblett, of Santa Fe, former United States District Judge in New Mexico; Monsignor Jules N. Stoffel, of Albuquerque, an authority on the history of the American Occuption; and Charles A. Scheurich, of Clovis, New Mexico, grandson and namesake of Charles Bent, New Mexico's first provisional governor, who made available a copy of a letter written by Kit Carson to his father, Aloysius Scheurich, probably Carson's last letter, and perhaps acceptable as his last will and testament. The writer is indebted to Evelyn Bauer and Marjorie Tichy Lambert of the New Mexico Museum in Santa Fe, Miss Russell of the University of New Mexico Library, A. M. McAnally, former Librarian of the University of New Mexico, presently Librarian of the University of Oklahoma, Geo. P. Hammond, Director of the Bancroft Library at the University of California, and to William A. Brophy, former Commissioner of Indian Affairs, for much assistance and many courtesies. Thanks and appreciation are extended to Mrs. Olive S. Arnold, of Atlanta, Ga., for recollections of her great grandfather, James S. Calhoun, New Mexico's first civil governor; to Pascual Martinez, of Taos, grandnephew of Padre Martinez, and to Gilbert Espinosa, of Albuquerque, for permission to copy a letter written to Pascual's grand-father by Governor Manuel Armijo; to Hon. Carl A. Hatch, United States District Judge in New Mexico, (formerly United States Senator,) for assistance in obtaining photostat copies of the James W. Magoffin letters and correspondence, and to his son, Stewart Hatch, and Wilfred H. McMains, his then able secretaries, for many courtesies; to Dr. Paul D. Hawley, then of Washington, D. C., for information concerning Dr. Jonathan Letterman; to Jubal Early Craig, of Tucson, Arizona, for assistance on Sylvester Mowry; to George D. Chapman, and K. L. Felix Ramlett, Librarian of Bangor Public Library, of Bangor, Maine, for help in tracing the history of James H. Carleton; to Mrs. Betty V. Griffith, Librarian of the Wallace Library, Fredericksburg, Va., for help on the history of Henry Hopkins Sibley; to Dr. T. Kenneth Wood, M.D., of Williamsport, Pa., and to James P. Reardon, of Winchester, Va., for help in tracing the ancestry of Dr. Michael Steck, early day New Mexico Indian Agent; and to Benton H. Willcox, Librarian of the State Historical Society of Wisconsin, of Madison, Wis., for help in tracing the history of Judge Joseph G. Knapp, early day jurist of New Mexico. Finally, I wish to express my thanks and appreciation to Mrs. Ellis Neel, for skill and patience in typing and retyping the manuscript, to Ilda B. Sganzini and Mrs. Maselle L. Deason, for indexing, and to George Fitzpatrick, editor of the New Mexico Magazine, and to my sister, Julia M. Keleher, of the University of New Mexico, for reading the manuscript, fully absolving them however from all responsibility for any of its defects; and to Ernest L. Blumenschein, of Taos, for doing the frontispiece, to Oscar E. Berninghaus, of Taos, for doing the title decorations, and to Thomas H. Tutt, for making the map for the end covers.

> Respectfully submitted,
> WILLIAM A. KELEHER,
> *Albuquerque, N. M.*
> *August 15, 1951.*

TURMOIL IN NEW MEXICO
1846 - 1868

BOOK ONE

General Kearny Comes to Santa Fe

"The undersigned enters New Mexico with a great military force with the object of seeking union and to ameliorate the condition of its inhabitants. . . . All those who shall take arms, and encourage and recommend resistance to the government of the United States will be looked upon as enemies and treated accordingly."

STEPHEN WATTS KEARNY
Bent's Fort on the Arkansas.
July 31, 1846.

CHAPTER ONE

On To The Arkansas

 RESIDENT JAMES K. POLK sent a message to the Congress of the United States on May 11, 1846, formally announcing that a state of war existed between the United States and Mexico. The President blamed Mexico for the war, saying: "War exists, and notwithstanding all our efforts to avoid it, exists by the act of Mexico herself." The Congress formally declared war on Mexico two days later, on May 13.[1] Having assumed that war with Mexico was inevitable, the United States had prepared to fight. With war actually declared, American troops were sent to Mexico by land and sea. In the area west of the Mississippi river, regulars and volunteers were mobilized at Fort Leavenworth, Kansas. These troops, organized into a unit known as "The Army of the West," were placed under the command of Colonel Stephen Watts Kearny,[2] and given the important task of invading and conquering New Mexico and California.

When organized and ready to start from Fort Leavenworth on June 21, 1846, the "Army of the West" was made up of 1,648 men, including the First Regiment of Missouri Cavalry, commanded by Colonel Alexander William Doniphan,[3] two batteries of artillery, equipped with six pounders, commanded by Major Meriwether Lewis Clark, three squadrons of the First Dragoons, commanded by Major E. V. Sumner,[4] and two companies of infantry, commanded by Captain William Z. Angney.[5] The last detachment of Kearny's army left the Missouri river for the Rio Grande on June 27. The cavalry rode and the dragoons marched over a route mapped by the army engineers, which followed roughly the trails blazed by Indian, trapper,[6] trader, and improved as the result of the efforts of Senator Thomas Hart Benton, of Missouri.

Spanish viceroy and captains general had governed New Mexico until Sept. 27, 1821. Spain, while governing Mexico, consistently followed a policy of refusing to issue passports from the United States into New Mexico unless for exceptionally good reasons. New Mexico became a Mexican Territory on July 6, 1824, and a Department on Dec. 3, 1836. Having achieved independence from Spain in 1821, Mexico adopted a "good neighbor policy" of that day, under which Americans were permitted to enter New Mexico without undue restrictions. Ostensibly to promote business and commerce between the United States and Mexico, Senator Benton, of Missouri, introduced a bill in the Senate during the Session of 1824-1825, providing for the establishment of a highway from Missouri to Santa Fe. According to Benton's speech in support of the measure, the highway was to "pass through tribes of our own territory until it reached the Arkansas river," and "with the assent of Mexico," was to continue "from this boundary to Santa Fe, on the Upper del Norte." The highway was to be well marked; security was to be extended to those traveling over it; assurance of good behavior was to be exacted from Indians along the route; and consular service was to be established for the extension and protection of trade and commerce. Urging passage of the bill, Senator Benton referred to the recent adventure of one of his Missouri constituents, "Mr. Augustus Storrs, late of New Hampshire," who had made a trip over the proposed route in May and June of 1822. "This gentleman," Senator Benton said, "had been one of a caravan of eighty persons, one hundred and fifty-six horses, and twenty-three wagons and carriages, which had made the expedition from Missouri to Santa Fe. His account was full of interest and novelty. It sounded more like romance to hear of caravans of men, horses, and wagons, traversing with their merchandise the vast plain which lies between the Mississippi and the Rio del Norte. The story seemed better adapted to Asia than to North America. But, romantic as it might seem, the reality had already exceeded the visions of the wildest imagination. The journey to New Mexico, but lately deemed a chimerical project, had become an affair of ordinary occurrence." [7] Benton's bill, carrying an initial appropriation of $125,000, passed the senate by a vote of 30 to 12. President James Monroe signed it as one of the last acts of his official life. The highway was improved, as provided by the Act, during the administration of Monroe's successor, President John Quincy Adams.

Subsequent events demonstrated that Spain, from its standpoint, had acted wisely in discouraging emigration from the United States to New Mexico. Within two decades after the enactment of the Benton bill, Stephen Watts Kearny, with an American army, bent on conquest, marched over the road built as the result of the reciprocity between the United States and Mexico.

From daylight until twilight of long summer evenings, Kearny's army pushed on toward New Mexico in June and July, 1846, traveling over the seemingly horizonless high rolling prairies between Fort Leavenworth and Pawnee Fork; and across the long stretches of desolate country between Bent's Fort and the Arkansas river. The monotony of the march was relieved from time to time by strange and interesting sights in the prairie country. The troops saw thousands of deer, antelope and buffalo grazing, and stampeding occasion-

ally, frightened at the approach of horses, men and panoply
of war. On the entire journey of hundreds of miles from Fort
Leavenworth to the Arkansas river, the soldiers did not pass
through a settlement or see a single habitation. Bands of
Pawnees, Osages and Comanches, encountered on the prairies,
looked respectfully from a distance as the troops marched
through Indian country.

Colonel Kearny suffered a rather severe illness as his army
traveled toward the Arkansas. Confined to his tent for several
days, and unable, when partly recovered, to mount his horse,
he rode for many hours in a supply train wagon. The jolting
of the wagon fatigued Kearny so greatly that he was transferred, on July 20, 1846, and rode thereafter in Lieutenant
W. H. Emory's spring wagon.[8]

The main body of Kearny's troops reached the Arkansas
(Napeste) river in the "big timber" country (so called because of the large groves of cottonwood trees) on July 24,
1846. Passing near Bent's Fort, the advance guard of the army
was in camp on New Mexico soil on Aug. 1, nine miles west
of the Arkansas. Colonel Kearny and staff reached Bent's
Fort on July 26. Here James W. Magoffin[9] presented to him a
letter from Secretary of War W. L. Marcy, which read:

> I am requested by the President to commend the bearer hereof,
> Colonel James W. Magoffin, to your favorable consideration. He
> has been presented to the President as a gentleman of high char-
> acter and intelligence. He is now and has been for several years
> past a resident of Chihuahua, extensively engaged in trade in
> that and several other Departments of Mexico, and is well ac-
> quainted with the people and the country. His knowledge in
> this respect, his credit with the inhabitants, his means, together
> with his disposition to be useful to the United States, may be of
> eminent service in your expedition against Chihuahua, and the
> President desires that you should avail yourself of his assistance
> to the extent you may need it. As it will be important to derive
> your supplies, as far as practicable, from that country, it is be-
> lieved he will, in this respect, be very useful to you and the public
> service.

After reading the Secretary's letter, and discussing its contents with Magoffin, Kearny called a staff meeting, at which it was decided to send Magoffin to Santa Fe, accompanied by Captain Philip St. George Cooke,[10] escorted by twelve dragoons, carrying a flag, to confer with Manuel Armijo, Governor of New Mexico.

Colonel Kearny issued a proclamation at Bent's Fort on July 31, 1846, in which he told the citizens of New Mexico the objects of his mission. He declared that he was entering New Mexico "seeking union and to ameliorate the condition of its inhabitants." He urged the people to "remain tranquil." The text of the proclamation:

The undersigned enters New Mexico with a great military force with the object of seeking union and to ameliorate the condition of its inhabitants; he does all this by instructions of his government by which he will be efficaciously sustained in order to carry into effect its views. He therefore, recommends the inhabitants of New Mexico to remain tranquil in their peaceable avocations and labors, with the assurance that they will not be molested by the American army, but on the contrary, they will be respected and protected in all their rights, both civil and religious. All those who shall take arms, and encourage and recommend resistance to the government of the United States will be looked upon as enemies and treated accordingly.

When Captain Cooke left for Santa Fe, he took with him a letter from Colonel Kearny, addressed to Governor Armijo, dated Aug. 1, 1846, in which Kearny advised that he intended to take possession of the country "over a part of which you are presiding as governor." He warned Armijo that "the blood which may be shed, the sufferings and miseries that may follow" would, in event of resistance, be on his head. Kearny's letter to the governor:

Headquarters of the Army of the West.
In Camp Upon the Arkansas, at Fort Bent, August 1, 1849.

To His Excellency, Governor and Commanding General,
Don Manuel Armijo, Santa Fe.

Sir: By the annexation of Texas to the United States, the Rio Grande from its delta to its source, forms now the boundary line between them (the United States and Mexico) and I am coming by order of my government to take possession of the country over a part of which you are presiding as governor. I come as a friend and with the disposition and intention to consider all the Mexicans and other inhabitants as friends if they should remain quietly and peaceably in their homes attending to their own affairs. All such persons shall not be molested by any of those who are coming under my orders in their person nor in their property nor in their religion. I pledge myself to the fulfilment of these promises.

I come to this part of the United States with a strong military force, and a still stronger one is following us as a reinforcement. I have more troops than I need to overcome any opposition which you may be able to make against us, and for that reason and for the sake of humanity I advise you to submit to fate, and to consider me with the same sentiments of peace and friendship which I have and protest for you and those under your government. Should your Excellency do this it would be eminently favorable to your interest and that of all your countrymen, and you will receive their blessings and prayers. If, on the contrary, you should decide otherwise, if you should make up your mind to make resistance and oppose us, with such troops as you may be able to raise against us, in that event, I notify you that the blood which may be shed, the sufferings and miseries that may follow, shall fall upon your head, and, instead of the blessings of your countrymen you will receive their curses, as I shall consider all of those your Excellency may present against us armed, as enemies, and they shall be treated accordingly.

I am sending you this communication with Captain Cooke of my regiment, and I recommend him as well as the small party of twelve dragoons, to your kindness and attention.

> With much respect I am
> Your Obedient Servant,
> S. W. KEARNY, *Colonel First Dragoons.*[11]

Now that Kearny had issued a proclamation and had written an important letter to Armijo; now that Captain Cooke, James W. Magoffin, and the twelve dragoons had started on their mission to Santa Fe, the "Army of the West" resumed its march. The last detachment of troops left the Bent's Fort camp on Aug. 4. Crossing the Purgatory river, the soldiers marched over Raton Pass, forded the Vermejo and Little Cimarron, and reached the village of Ocáte on Aug. 11. By Aug. 13, the advance guard watered their horses in the Mora river.[12]

Governor Manuel Armijo had definite information in the first days of July that American troops were on the way to invade New Mexico. On July 11, 1846, the Governor sent an important letter to Colonel Pascual Martinez, of Taos, brother of Padre Antonio Jose Martinez, instructing him to cooperate in arranging for a meeting to discuss the crisis that had developed. The Governor's letter read:

> It is positively known that the forces of the United States which it is announced are coming to take over this Department, are on the march and in order to consult with the most influential sons of the country as to the means we should take for our defense, I instruct you within three days after receipt of this message to present yourself before me bringing with you those citizens named in the list attached who under no pretext will be excused for we are to discuss the welfare of the Department or of its lost cause which should interest all of us. God and Liberty!

A slip of paper attached to the letter was headed: "List of prominent men who should come to this capital with Colonel Pascual Martinez." The names on the list were: The Curate D. Antonio Jose Martinez, Don Blas Trujillo, Don Juan Vigil, Don Cornelio Vigil, Don Buenventura Martinez, Don Carlos Bobian, The Curate Don Jose Maria Valdez, The Curate D. Mariano Lucero, The Curate D. Eulogio Valdez.[13] Six of the men invited met with Governor Armijo in Santa Fe. For a reason not known, Padre Martinez did not attend the meeting. There was little, if anything, that could be done by Armijo's supporters, however influential, to remedy a situation that was already desperate. New Mexico's position became more critical with each passing day. Governor Armijo faced a crisis of national significance. Should he take a bold stand and fight, or should he abandon New Mexico to the invader? Colonel Diego Archuleta, able soldier and influential politician, urged Armijo to defend against the invasion to the last man, with dragoons then in Santa Fe and Taos, and vol-

unteers recruited in the Rio Arriba and Rio Abajo Counties.
On Aug. 8, 1846, Armijo issued a proclamation asking the
people to display the "highest and best devotion to home and
country." Urging them to draw upon their "reserves of patriotism," he assured the New Mexicans that he was "ready to
sacrifice his life and interests for his beloved country."
Armijo signed the proclamation, "your chief, fellow patriot
and friend," but even as he signed he must have known that
his situation was hopeless. The proclamation, probably written by one Iñigo, a lawyer recently arrived from the national
capital, was in part as follows:

The Governor and Commandant General of New Mexico: To
Its Inhabitants: Fellow Patriots: The moment has come at last
when the country requires from her sons, the unlimited decision
and reserveless sacrifices, which circumstances, extreme under
any point of view, claim for its salvation. The troubles with the
United States of America, managed with dignity and decorum by
the Supreme Magistrate of our Republic, have not been satisfactorily concluded as demanded by the unquestionable rights of
Mexico over the usurped territory of Texas. For that reason, it
has been indispensably necessary to suspend the diplomatic relations with the rejected minister and envoy extraordinary from
the North American government. The forces of that government
are now advancing on the department. They have already crossed
the line, and at this date are very near Colorado. Behold, fellow
citizens, the invasion is the sign of alarm that must prepare us
for the combat. The eagle that summoned you at Iguala under the
national standard forming a single family out of us all, with one
single will, calls on you today to gather round the supreme government, and the superior of this department, to defend the most
just and holiest of causes. You then could conquer without external help, led only by your noble efforts and heroic patriotism,
the independence of our nation, which is worthy of better fate.
Today that sacred boon, the fruit of so many and so costly sacri-
fies, is threatened; for, if we are not able to preserve the integrity
of our territory, all that country would very soon be the prey of
the greed and enterprising spirit of our neighbors of the north,
and nothing would remain save a sad remembrance of our political existence. . . . Let us be ready for war since we are provoked
to it. Let us not look at the strength of our enemies, nor at the
size of the obstacles we have to overcome. . . . With respect to the

General Manuel Armijo
Last Governor of New Mexico under Mexican rule

defense of the department in the actual invasion, your governor is dependent upon your pecuniary resources, upon your decision, and upon your convictions, founded on reason, on justice, equity and public convenience.[14]

On Aug. 10, 1846, two days after he issued the proclamation, Armijo asked the Departmental Assembly to appropriate a sum of money then equivalent to $1,000 in American money, to maintain the dragoons. The Assembly appropriated the money, and at the same time authorized the government to borrow a like amount on the public credit. The very next day, however, the Assembly cancelled the appropriation, and revoked Armijo's authority to make a loan.

Upon reaching Santa Fe, Captain Cooke and James W. Magoffin were received by the governor. Cooke described the historic meeting of Aug. 12, 1846:

We made our way with some difficulty toward the Palace.... I entered from the hall, a large and lofty apartment, with a carpeted earth floor, and discovered the Governor seated at a table, with six or eight military and civic officials standing. There was no mistaking the governor, a large fine looking man ... he wore a blue frock coat, with a rolling collar and a general's shoulder straps, blue striped trousers with gold lace, and a red sash.[15]

While Governor Armijo discussed New Mexico's plight with his associates, and conferred secretly with Cooke and Magoffin, the people of Santa Fe became increasingly alarmed and apprehensive. The Governor knew the background and sentiment of his people. He realized that it would be madness to engage the American army in pitched battle. He was familiar with New Mexico's deplorable financial condition. The Departmental budgets had never balanced during the decade between 1836 and 1846. To justify the condition of the treasury, officials pointed to the extraordinary expenditures required to suppress the 1837 insurrection, and to repel the Texas invasion in 1841. For twenty years between 1825 and 1845, New Mexico's administrative expenses were paid almost entirely from import duties collected at ports of entry in Taos and Santa Fe from Americans engaged in the Santa

Fe-Chihuahua trade. Traditionally, customs receipts were used primarily to pay the salaries of the higher officials. Regardless of the cause, there was no doubt but that New Mexico was financially bankrupt in 1845.

In a desperate move to produce revenue, the Departmental Assembly enacted a law on Feb. 14, 1845, at the request of Governor Mariano Martinz de Lejanza (Governor Armijo's immediate predecessor), authorizing "taxation of property in proportion to wealth." Large property owners looked upon this law with distrust, fearing that it might result in burdensome taxes and forced loans, affording officials a legal avenue for confiscation of land and livestock. Governor Armijo was entirely familiar with the "forced loan" method of financing. While a private citizen in 1845, he had been obliged to "advance" five hundred pesos to the Department for administrative expenses. Enactment of the 1845 capital levy law was in large measure responsible for the growth of sentiment that it might not be altogether disastrous if New Mexico became a part of the United States. New Mexicans generally believed that taxation of property to the extent of confiscation would not be tolerated under the American flag.[16]

Possessing an adequate understanding of New Mexico's financial affairs, and available military resources, Governor Armijo decided not to stand and fight the American invaders, nor would he remain in Santa Fe to be captured and humiliated. He determined to seek refuge in flight. On Aug. 4, 1846, expecting that he would leave the capital city at any moment, Governor Armijo signed a power of attorney, by which he appointed Don Gaspar Ortiz to act for him in all legal affairs, and authorized him to carry out the instructions he had given him as to the distribution of his property. The instrument was witnessed by Donaciano Vigil.[17] A few days later the governor left Santa Fe for Albuquerque. Tradition has it that a threatening crowd gathered about the Governor as he started to mount his horse and leave the capital city. But the Governor was always a resourceful man. He had prepared for such an emergency by filling his coat pockets with gold and silver coins of various denominations. When hotheads in the crowd attempted to prevent him from leaving, he tossed coins at their feet. While the crowd scrambled and fought for the coins Armijo spurred his horse, and galloped away toward Albuquerque and Chihuahua.

The people of Santa Fe became a bit panicky when it became publicly known that their governor had deserted them. Don Juan Bautista Vigil y Alarid, a long time political leader, assumed the initiative in a time of crisis. He assumed the title of "Political and Military Governor ad interim of the Department of New Mexico," and tacked up in public places in Santa Fe on Aug. 17 copies of Kearny's proclamation of Aug. 1, 1846. Beneath the posted proclamation Don Juan added a message of his own:

Notwithstanding the means I have set in motion, it has not been possible for me to calm the fears which the flight of General Armijo has infused in its inhabitants, the desertion of his soldiers, or, that which is more, the dread that has been caused because of the approach of the military forces of the United States of North America to this capital; and Whereas, many families are leaving their homes in order to hide in the deserts, as if said forces were composed of cruel and sanguinary savages, believing that they will have no security, no protection of their lives and interest on the part of the chief who commands that army, and in order to quiet these fears down, I have been pleased to command that the proclamation of the said chief of said forces be fixed on the public places.

Late on the night of Aug. 17, Acting Governor Vigil y Alarid sent Nicolas Quintana, acting Secretary, with a letter to General Kearny, in which he advised him of the fears and excitement of the people in Santa Fe, and asked him to order his troops to show the people special consideration in order to "allay the feeling of apprehension." General Kearny had anticipated such a request. Days before, near Raton Pass, he had issued an order telling the men of his command not to disturb "a blade of grass nor an ear of corn" in New Mexico.

The "Army of the West" reached Santa Fe about sundown on Aug. 18, 1846. In fewer than sixty days it had traveled from the Missouri river to the Rio Grande, a distance of 821 miles. The conquest of New Mexico had been accomplished, as Kearny would soon report, "without firing a shot, or spilling a drop of blood." [18]

Lieutenant Emory of Kearny's staff, in his report of Aug. 18, graphically described the events of occupation day:

We were this morning 29 miles from Santa Fe. Reliable information, from several sources, had reached camp yesterday and the day before, that dissensions had arisen in Armijo's camp, which had dispersed his army, and that he had fled to the south, carrying all his artillery and 100 dragoons with him. Not a hostile rifle or arrow was now between the army and Santa Fe, the capital of New Mexico, and the general determined to make the march in one day, and raise the United States flag over the palace before sundown. New horses or mules were ordered for the artillery, and every thing was braced up for a forced march. The distance was not great, but the road bad, and the horses on their last legs.

A small detachment was sent forward at daybreak, and at six the army followed. Four or five miles from old Pecos the road leads into a canon, with hills on each side from 1,000 to 2,000 feet above the road, in all cases within cannon shot, and in many within point blank musket shot; and this continues to a point but 12 or 15 miles from Santa Fe.... Fifteen miles from Santa Fe we reached the position deserted by Armijo.... It is a gateway which, in the hands of a skilful engineer and one hundred resolute men, would have been perfectly impregnable. Had the position been defended with any resolution, the general would have been obliged to turn it by a road which branches to the south, six miles from Pecos, by the way of Galisteo. Armijo's arrangements for defence were very stupid. His abattis was placed behind the gorge some 100 yards, by which he evidently intended that the gorge should be passed before his fire was opened. This done, and his batteries would have been carried without difficulty. ... Another officer and myself were sent down to explore the byroad by which Armijo fled. On our return to the main road, we saw two Mexicans; one the acting secretary of state, in search of the general. They had passed him without knowing him. When we pointed in the direction of the general, they broke into a full run; their hands and feet keeping time to the pace of their nags. ... The acting secretary brought a letter from Vigil, the lieutenant governor, informing the general of Armijo's flight, and of his readiness to receive him in Santa Fe, and extend to him the hospitalities of the city. . . . The head of the column arrived in sight of the town about three o'clock; it was six before the rear came up. Vigil and twenty or thirty of the people of the town received us at the palace and asked us to partake of some wine and brandy of domestic manufacture. It was from the Paso del Norte; we were too thirsty to judge of its merits; any thing liquid and cool was palatable. During the repast, and as the sun was setting, the United States flag was hoisted over the palace, and a salute of thirteen guns fired from the artillery planted on the eminence overlooking the town.[19]

In an address delivered in the plaza in Santa Fe on Aug. 19, General Kearny endeavored to calm the fears of the people, and to assure them that they would have religious freedom; told them that they were no longer subjects of Mexico, but "American citizens, subject only to the laws of the United States." The text of Kearny's address is as follows:

New Mexicans: We have come amongst you to take possession of New Mexico, which we do in the name of the government of the United States. We have come with peaceable intentions and kind feelings toward you all. We come as friends, to better your condition and make you a part of the republic of the United States. We mean not to murder you or rob you of your property. Your families shall be free from molestation; your women secure from violence. My soldiers shall take nothing from you but what they pay for. In taking possession of New Mexico, we do not mean to take away from you your religion. Religion and government have no connection in our country. There, all religions are equal; one has no preference over the other; the Catholic and the Protestant are esteemed alike. Every man has a right to serve God according to his heart. When a man dies he must render to God an account of his acts here on earth, whether they be good or bad. In our government, all men are equal. We esteem the most peaceable man, the best man. I advise you to attend to your domestic pursuits, cultivate industry, be peaceable and obedient to the laws. Do not resort to violent means to correct abuses. I do hereby proclaim that being in possession of Santa Fe, I am therefore virtually in possession of all New Mexico. Armijo is no longer your governor. His power is departed; but he will

return and be as one of you. When he shall return you are not
to molest him. You are no longer Mexican subjects; you are now
become American citizens, subject only to the laws of the United
States. A change of government has taken place in New Mexico
and you no longer owe allegiance to the Mexican government.
I do hereby proclaim my intention to establish in this department a civil government, on a republican basis, similar to those
of our own states. It is my intention, also, to continue in office
those by whom you have been governed, except the governor, and
such other persons as I shall appoint to office by virtue of the
authority vested in me. I am your governor—henceforth look
to me for protection.

Juan Bautista Vigil y Alarid, who had asserted leadership
and assumed the title of "acting governor" when Governor
Armijo fled to Chihuahua, delivered the reply to General
Kearny's address, in the course of which he referred to "the
unfortunate condition of the Poles." The text of the Vigil
address:

General: The address which you have just delivered, in which
you announce that you have taken possession of this great country in the name of the United States of America, gives us some
idea of the wonderful future that awaits us. It is not for us to determine the boundaries of nations. The cabinets of Mexico and
Washington will arrange these differences. It is for us to obey
and respect the established authorities, no matter what may be
our private opinions. The inhabitants of this department humbly
and honorably present their loyalty and allegiance to the government of North America. No one in this world can successfully
resist the power of him who is stronger.

Do not find it strange if there has been no manifestation of
joy and enthusiasm in seeing this city occupied by your military
forces. To us the power of the Mexican republic is dead. No
matter what her condition, she was our mother. What child will
not shed abundant tears at the tomb of his parents? I might indicate some of the causes for her misfortunes, but domestic troubles should not be made public. It is sufficient to say that civil
war is the cursed source of that deadly poison which has spread
over one of the grandest and greatest countries that has ever been
created. Today we belong to a great and powerful nation. Its
flag, with its stars and stripes, covers the horizon of New Mexico,
and its brilliant light shall grow like good seed well cultivated.

We are cognizant of your kindness, of your courtesy and that of your accommodating officers and of the strict discipline of your troops; we know that we belong to the republic that owes its origin to the immortal Washington, whom all civilized nations admire and respect. How different would be our situation had we been invaded by European nations! We are aware of the unfortunate condition of the Poles.

In the name then, of the entire Department, I swear obedience to the Northern Republic and I render my respect to its laws and authority.[20]

On Aug. 22, 1846, three days after reaching Santa Fe, General Kearny issued a proclamation addressed to the inhabitants of New Mexico, in which he advised them of the intentions of his government:

As, by the act of the republic of Mexico, a state of war exists between that government and the United States; and as the undersigned, at the head of his troops, on the 18th instant, took possession of Santa Fe, the capital of the department of New Mexico, he now announces his intention to hold the department, with its original boundaries (on both sides of the Del Norte), as a part of the United States, and under the name of "the Territory of New Mexico."

The undersigned has come to New Mexico with a strong military force, and an equally strong one is following close in his rear. He has more troops than necessary to put down any opposition that can possibly be brought against him, and therefore it would be folly or madness for any dissatisfied or discontented persons to think of resisting him.

Kearny gave assurance of religious freedom, and protection of property:

The undersigned has instructions from his government to respect the religious institutions of New Mexico—to protect the property of the church—to cause the worship of those belonging to it to be undisturbed, and their religious rights in the amplest manner preserved to them—also to protect the persons and property of all quiet and peaceable inhabitants within its boundaries against their enemies, the Eutaws, the Navajoes, and others; and when he assures all that it will be his pleasure, as well as his duty, to comply with these instructions, he calls upon them to exert themselves in preserving order, in promoting concord, and in maintaining the authority and efficiency of the laws. And he requires of those who have left their homes and taken up arms against the troops of the United States to return *forthwith* to them, or else they will be considered as enemies and traitors, subjecting their persons to punishment and their property to seizure and confiscation for the benefit of the public treasury.

It is the wish and intention of the United States to provide for New Mexico a free government, with the least possible delay, similar to those in the United States; and the people of New Mexico will then be called on to exercise the rights of freemen in electing their own representatives to the Territorial legislature. But until this can be done, the laws hitherto in existence will be continued until changed or modified by competent authority; and those persons holding office will continue in the same for the present, provided they will consider themselves good citizens and are willing to take the oath of allegiance to the United States.

The people of New Mexico were released from their allegiance to Mexico:

The United States hereby absolves all persons residing within the boundaries of New Mexico from any further allegiance to the republic of Mexico, and hereby claims them as citizens of the United States. Those who remain quiet and peaceable will be considered good citizens and receive protection—those who are found in arms, or instigating others against the United States, will be considered as traitors, and treated accordingly.

Don Manuel Armijo, the late governor of this department, has fled from it; the undersigned has taken possession of it without firing a gun, or spilling a single drop of blood, in which he most truly rejoices, and for the present will be considered as governor of the Territory.

James Magoffin, "of the Santa Fe-Chihuahua trade," who had cooperated with General Kearny and Captain Cooke in undertaking to achieve the peaceful occupation of New Mexico, wrote a detailed report to Secretary Marcy on August 26, giving the background of an exciting three weeks:

I arrived at Bent's fort on 26 July, where I found Gen'l. Kearny, presented the letter I rec'd from your hand, and was well rec'd. The Gen'l. on the 1st of August, dispatched Capt. Cooke with 12 dragoons, accompanied by myself, with a letter to Gov. Armijo, which was delivered on 12th inst. 10 o'clock P.M. We were well rec'd and dined with his Excellency. Had a long conversation with him & proved to him from Gen'l. K's. letter that the troops then entering the Department were only to give peace and protection to the inhabitants, and assured him that I had been dispatched by the President of the U. S. in order to inform him & the rest of the good people of N. Mexico with whom I was acquainted that this was the only object of our government. I found many of the rich of the Department here, also military officers, with whom I had ample intercourse. I assured them the only object of our government was to take possession of N. M., as being a part of the Territory annexed to the U. S. by Texas and to give peace and quietude to the good people of the country, which gave them entire satisfaction.

That Magoffin's talk was persuasive is indicated by the fact that he won over Colonel Diego Archuleta, second in command to Governor Armijo in the military department:

Was then assured by Colonel Archuleta, 2d in command, that he would not oppose Gen'l. K.'s entrance. Gen'l Armijo on the 15th ordered his troops, say 3,000 in number, to be placed between two mountains, with 4 pcs. of artillery on the road by which our army had to pass. Having promised Gen'l. K. to have an interview with him in his note borne by Capt. Cook 14th inst., say some 50 miles distant at a place called the Vegas, Armijo left this place early on the 16th with 150 dragoons & joined his army, called his officers together & wished to know if they were prepared to defend the Territory. They answered they were not, that they were convinced by the proclamation that they had seen from Gen'l. K. that the U. S. had no intention to wage war with New Mexico, on the contrary promised them all protection in their property, persons and religion. Armijo, *apparently* appeared very much exasperated, gave orders for the troops to be dispersed & in 48 hours they were all at their homes, he himself leaving for the state of Chihuahua, with say 100 dragoons, maltreating all good citizens on his route and pressing their animals.

The American troops, according to Magoffin's report, were graciously welcomed to Santa Fe:

Gen'l. Kearny entered this city on 18th 5 o'c P.M., the authorities & people of the place being ready to give him a hearty welcome. Marched up to the Palace, entered the apartment prepared for him & his suit. Made a handsome & appropriate speech to the

authorities, after which they all swore allegiance to the U. States.
The Palace was crowded & many bottles of generous wine was
drank, being prepared for the occasion by the acting governor.
The next day by request of the Gen'l. the people were assembled
in the publick square where he addressed them in a very handsome manner, after which the people shouted "Long Live our
General & the United States."

That New Mexicans had bowed to the inevitable and had
accepted the occupation philosophically, even with gracious-
ness and courtliness, was indicated by Magoffin's report:

The clergy of the province have all called on the Gen'l. since
his arrival & have returned to their homes perfectly satisfied.
I had the honor of accompanying the Gen'l & his staff to high
mass last Sunday. The church was filled with natural & adopted
sons of the U. S. and all past off in the most perfect order.[21] The
Gen'l. gave on yesterday a splendid ball at the Palace, which was
universally attended by all the reputable citizens of the city &
passed off in handsome style.

The American Occupation, as Magoffin observed it, had
been an unqualified success:

The fact is, to make a long story short, Gen'l. Kearny by his
mild & persuasive manner has induced the good people of New
Mexico to believe that they now belong to the greatest nation
on earth, & that the stars and stripes, which are now so gallantly
waving over the capitol of this city, will allways give them ample
protection from foreign foes. The Gen'l. will leave this week
on a visit to some of the principal towns on the Rio Grand, & I
will leave with him, & proceed to Chihuahua with all possible
speed. Will give you all the news from there as soon as practicable after the arrival of Gen'l. Wool.[22]

CHAPTER TWO

Doniphan's Expedition

GENERAL KEARNY DEVOTED many hours each day, following his arrival in Santa Fe, to conferences with officials who had lost their positions as a result of the Occupation, and with prominent men from all parts of New Mexico. Kearny listened patiently to advice and complaints. He promised fair and just treatment to every law abiding person. He assured the *ricos* that their property would not be confiscated. All callers were told that the American government would not ask for indemnity, or impose taxes to help pay the costs of the Occupation.[23] Roman Catholic clergymen were assured that the American government would not interfere with religious worship, or undertake to establish or support any particular religion. A number of Mexican political and business leaders, in discussing affairs with Kearny, assured him that the people of New Mexico would become reconciled within a reasonable time and would accept the Occupation without resentment or attempt at retaliation. These leaders expressed the opinion that the somewhat disturbing threats of rebellion and revolution, heard from time to time in the capital city, would not result in overt acts.[24]

By Sept. 22, 1846, less than a month after his arrival in Santa Fe, General Kearny made public the names of the men he had chosen to serve as New Mexico's provisional government officials. Among them were Charles Bent (brother-in-law of Kit Carson), of Taos, as governor, and Donaciano Vigil, of Santa Fe, as secretary. On the same day he reported the

21

completion of a code of laws under which the people of New
Mexico were to be governed until the status of New Mexico
could be determined by the Congress of the United States.[25]

Recognizing the possibility that Santa Fe might be attacked,
either by disgruntled New Mexicans, or Indians, General
Kearny, soon after his arrival in Santa Fe, assigned to the Engineers the task of building a fort, work on which had progressed satisfactorily as he prepared to leave for California.[26]

Now that he had been in Santa Fe for a few days, and had
listened to the complaints and grievances of the people, General Kearny became somewhat acquainted with the prevailing
political atmosphere in New Mexico. He was convinced, for
one thing, that the New Mexicans, worn out with waiting for
the Mexican government to protect New Mexico against the
wild Indians, expected the American government to immediately assume that obligation. Mexican and American residents alike, regardless of how they might differ on other New
Mexico problems, told Kearny the same story about Indian
depredations. The Apaches and Navajos, they related, had
defied Spanish and Mexican authority for decade after decade.
They had scourged New Mexico and its people. They had
raided the settlements and ranches, driving away cattle, horses
and sheep. They had stolen harvest time crops of fruit and
grain from Mexican and Pueblo Indian settlers. They had
captured women and children and reduced them to slavery.
They had killed people, wantonly and wilfully.

Impressed by the recital of crimes against the people of
New Mexico, Kearny decided to act without delay, to redress
the wrongs and grievances of which they complained. Recalling the promise he had made to the New Mexicans at Las
Vegas, on Aug. 15, that he would protect their lives and property, Kearny sent messengers into the Navajo country, sum-
moning tribal chiefs to a council in Santa Fe. Only a few
chiefs responded. Kearny told those who attended the council
that New Mexico had become American territory; that fighting between Indians and Mexicans would be tolerated no

longer. He told the chiefs to go back to their own country and tell their people of the new order of things.

Despite the conference in Santa Fe, the Navajos continued to rob and steal from the settlements in the Rio Grande valley. The people appealed to Kearny for help, with the result that he started a campaign against the Navajos on Sept. 18, 1846 (one month from the day after his arrival in Santa Fe) by sending two detachments in different directions, one under the command of Major William Gilpin,[27] the other under the command of Colonel Congreve Jackson. With 185 men Gilpin started for northwest New Mexico. He traveled along the Chama river and reached Abiquiu on Sept. 25. Sixty-five Mexican and Pueblo Indian volunteers, anxious to fight the Navajos, joined Gilpin's forces at Abiquiu. Gilpin remained at Abiquiu until Nov. 25, on which date he started for the San Juan river. Colonel Jackson, with three companies, left Santa Fe on Sept. 18, traveled south to Albuquerque, crossed the Rio Grande at nearby Pajarito, and went west to Cubero, a then important Mexican settlement on the edge of the Navajo country, reaching there Sept. 30.

Confident that Gilpin and Jackson could manage the Navajos, General Kearny left Santa Fe for California on Sept. 25, 1846. Traveling over a fairly good road, Kearny's advance guard was in Tome, some twenty-five miles south of Albuquerque, within a week.[28] The Navajo Indians interpreted General Kearny's departure from Santa Fe as a sign of weakness. They trailed his beef herd and stole several head from it at Algodones, 23 miles north of Albuquerque. They raided settlements at various places between Albuquerque and Polvadera; killed seven or eight settlers, and stole thousands of cattle, sheep and horses. Kearny learned of the raids at La Joya.[29]

Exasperated by the conduct of the Navajos, Kearny sent a message on Oct. 2, 1846, from La Joya, to Colonel Alexander William Doniphan, in Santa Fe, ordering him to march his regiment into the Navajo country, and to demand upon reaching there, that the Navajos surrender all prisoners and all stolen property in their possession. Doniphan was instructed to compel the Navajos to give "such security for their future conduct as he might think ample and sufficient, by taking hostages or otherwise."

Complying with General Kearny's instructions, Colonel Doniphan with 300 men left Santa Fe for the Navajo country on Oct. 26, 1846.[30] Doniphan sent word to Gilpin, who had gone into the Navajo country by way of the Chama and San Juan rivers, and Jackson, who had gone there by way of Albuquerque and Cubero, to meet him at Ojo del Oso (Bear Spring), some miles from present day Gallup, New Mexico.

Doniphan's troops marched from Santa Fe to Galisteo the first day, and to Santo Domingo pueblo, 25 miles from Santa Fe, the second day. Although it was late fall, the soldiers wore summer uniforms. Clothing for the winter, which should have reached Santa Fe by Sept. 1, failed to arrive before the troops left there. Many soldiers abandoned their tents to lighten their load, and as a result suffered intensely while sleeping in the open air at night. By Oct. 30, Doniphan was at Sandia, an Indian pueblo thirteen miles north of Albuquerque, where the troops, because of the high wind and drizzling rain, spent a miserable night. Two days later the troops were in Albuquerque. Fording the Rio Grande, they marched due west, and reached Cubero in ten days.

Doniphan, Gilpin and Jackson joined forces at Ojo del Oso. Five hundred Navajos, and a number of chiefs, had been rounded up and forced, at the point of the bayonet, to attend a council at the rendezvous. Through an interpreter, Colonel Doniphan told the Navajos the things General Kearny had already told them in Santa Fe, and of the General's insistence that lawlessness among the Navajos should be stopped at once. Death by bayonet and bullet, Doniphan told the Navajos, would be the penalty for continued misconduct. In answering Donaphin, the Navajos told him that they were unable to understand the attitude of the Americans. The Navajos, one chief contended, had made war against the Mexicans for years before the Americans started their war. How could the Americans say that the American war against the Mexicans had been justified, and argue at the same time that the Navajos were not justified in continuing their own private war against the Mexicans?

Doniphan patiently explained that the American government had taken New Mexico by conquest; "that when the Navajos now stole property from the New Mexicans, they were stealing from the Americans; and when they killed the New Mexicans, they were killing American people; that this would not be tolerated any longer; that it would be to the advantage of the Navajos to permit the Americans to settle in New Mexico; that a valuable trade would be opened to them, by means of which they could obtain everything they needed to eat and wear in exchange for their furs and pelts." [31] Realizing that argument and oratory would accomplish little, if anything, the Navajos consented to sign a treaty of "permanent peace, mutual trust and friendship" on Nov. 22, 1846. The treaty, containing five short paragraphs, was interpreted, insofar as interpretation was possible, by means of "sign" language, from English into Spanish and then into Navajo. Doniphan signed the treaty on behalf of the United States. Fourteen Navajo chiefs, not one of whom could read or write one word in any language, signed for the Indians, by touching with the forefinger of the right hand a pen held for them, while a cross (X) was made opposite each place designated for signature.

After the treaty had been signed, Doniphan distributed gifts to the Navajos, and they gave blankets to him and his officers. Doniphan bought several hundred sheep and cattle from the Navajos (probably stolen from the settlers), which were driven and herded along toward Chihuahua, grazed and watered by day, watched at night, and butchered as needed.[32]

Believing that the trouble between the settlers and the Navajos had been adjusted, Doniphan left for Zuni Pueblo, with Jackson, Gilpin and a detachment of soldiers to undertake settlement of a bitter war between the Zunis and the

Navajos. The Zunis and Navajos, with Doniphan acting as arbitrator, argued and wrangled almost continuously for three days and nights. A treaty of "peace and amity" between the two tribes was signed on Nov. 26, 1846. Doniphan signed the treaty as the principal witness to the signatures (by mark) of the chiefs. Hopeful that "permanent peace" had been achieved with the Navajo tribe, and that the quarrel between the Navajos and Zunis was at an end, Doniphan, Jackson and Gilpin, and their troops, left the Indian country, and started south and east for the Rio Grande. Officers and men alike were impatient to be on their way to Chihuahua. The troops were barely out of sight when the Navajos and Zunis, despite the recently signed treaty, resumed hostilities. Within a matter of days, the Navajos resumed their raids on the settlements.[33]

CHAPTER THREE

Magoffin Imprisoned

WHEN GENERAL KEARNY left Santa Fe for California on Sept. 25, 1846, James W. Magoffin accompanied him as far as Valverde,[34] on the Rio Grande, a few miles south of Socorro. At the time of Kearny's arrival there, Valverde was a place of great activity. A train of forty Conestoga wagons, carrying merchandise, enroute from the States to Chihuahua, valued at more than $100,000, was being held at Valverde, subject to military orders. James Magoffin and his brother Samuel owned a number of the wagons in the train.

General Kearny reported his movements after leaving Santa Fe, and referred to the historic meeting with Kit Carson near Valverde in a letter written from San Diego on Dec. 12, 1846, addressed to Adjutant General R. Jones, in Washington:

I left Santa Fe, New Mexico, for this country on the 25th of September, with three hundred of the first dragoons under Major Sumner. We crossed to the bank of the Del Norte at Albuquerque (sixty-five miles below Santa Fe), continued down on that bank until the 5th of October, when we met Mr. Kit Carson with a party of sixteen men on his way to Washington City with a mail and papers—an express from Commodore Stockton and Lieutenant Colonel Fremont, reporting that the Californias were already in possession of the Americans under their command; that the American flag was flying from every important position in the territory, and that the country was free from Mexican control, the war ended, and peace and harmony established among the people. In consequence of this information, I directed that two hundred dragoons under Major Sumner should remain in New Mexico, and that the other one hundred with two mountain howitzers under Captain Moore, should accompany me as a guard to upper California.[35]

Captain A. R. Johnson, Kearny's aide-de-camp, killed at daybreak on Dec. 6, 1846, in a fight with Californians at San Pasqual, some forty miles east of San Diego, told in detail about the meeting between Carson and Kearny:

Marched at 9, after having great trouble in getting some ox carts from the Mexicans; after marching about three miles we met Kit Carson, direct on express from California, with a mail of public letters for Washington; he informs us that Colonel Fremont is probably civil and military governor of California, and that about forty days since, Commodore Stockton, with a naval force, and Colonel Fremont, acting in concert, commenced to revolutionize the country, and place it under the American flag; that, in about ten days their work was done, and Carson, having received the rank of lieutenant, was dispatched across the country by the Gila, with a party to carry the mail; the general told him that he had just passed over the country which we were to traverse, and he wanted him to go back with him as a guide; he replied that he had pledged himself to go to Washington, and he could not think of not fulfilling his promise. The general told him he

would relieve him of all responsibility, and place the mail in the
hands of a safe person to carry it on; he finally consented, and
turned his face to the west again, just as he was on the eve of
entering the settlements, after his arduous trip, and when he had
set his hopes on seeing his family. It requires a brave man to
give up his private feelings thus for the public good; but Carson
is one such! Honor to him for it! Carson left California with
15 men, among them, six Delaware Indians—faithful fellows.
They had fifty animals, most of which they left on the road, or
traded with the Apaches, giving two for one; they were not
aware of the presence of the American troops in New Mexico;
they counted on feeling their way along, and in case the Mexicans were hostile, they meant to start a new outfit, and run across
their country. When they came to the Copper mine Apaches,
they first learned that an American general had possession of the
Territory of New Mexico. The Apaches were very anxious to be
friendly with the Americans, and received them very cordially,
much to their surprise.[36]

James W. Magoffin left Valverde with the intention of undertaking for General Wool, in Chihuahua, the same type of
mission he had accomplished for General Kearny in Santa Fe.
He traveled to El Paso del Norte (now Juarez, Mexico), and
started on the journey of more than two hundred thirty miles
across the vast grassy plains of Chihuahua. Going to Chihuahua, for Magoffin, was almost like going to his former home
in Kentucky. He had lived in Chihuahua for some fifteen
years, during all of which time he had served as American
Consul in Chihuahua and in Saltillo, and had engaged in
many important business transactions in various parts of
Mexico. He spoke Spanish fluently; he had married into the
prominent and influential Valdez family; he knew personally
almost every important man and government official in the
entire area.

Fate was not kind to Magoffin in Chihuahua. He was not
permitted to play there a repeat performance of the drama in
which he had been a leading actor in Santa Fe. Instead of
being entertained at dinner by the governor, as in Santa Fe,
Magoffin was arrested upon reaching Chihuahua, and placed
in jail, charged with being a spy. When it seemed as if Chi-

huahua would be forced to surrender to American troops, Magoffin was taken to Durango, four hundred thirty odd miles further south, and imprisoned there. Mexican officials had ample proof of Magoffin's guilt. The evidence was a letter, signed by General Kearny, addressed to the Secretary of War, describing the services James W. Magoffin had rendered for the American government in connection with the occupation of New Mexico. General Kearny had given the letter to Samuel Magoffin (a brother and business associate of James W. Magoffin), who in turn had given it to Henry Connelly, a close friend, for delivery to James W. Magoffin. The letter was intended to furnish Magoffin with proof of the things he had accomplished for the United States, and to enable him to obtain reimbursement for money spent in the service of the government. Unfortunately, Henry Connelly was arrested at El Paso del Norte. The incriminating letter was found on his person, and forwarded first to Chihuahua, and later to Durango. With the positive evidence in their possession that James W. Magoffin had been a spy, the Mexican authorities ordered him to be shot. Former Governor Manuel Armijo (related to Magoffin's deceased wife), then in Durango, intervened and saved his life, contending that Magoffin was an American citizen and that executing him would result in retaliation.

Released from the Durango penitentiary after many months, Magoffin returned to the United States. He went to Washington, and on April 1, 1849, filed a claim asking the government to pay him for his time and expenses while engaged on his mission.

Officials in Washington were not particularly interested in Magoffin's claim. The Mexican War was a thing of the past. Many claims of a more or less similar nature had been filed. Magoffin was not in a favorable position to press his claim. The term of President Polk, who, through Secretary Marcy, had recommended him to General Kearny, was about to expire. General Kearny had died on Oct. 31, 1848. W. L. Marcy was no longer Secretary of War. Fortunately for Magoffin, however, Senator Benton was still in Washington. Benton discussed the claim with President-elect Zachary Taylor, with the result that its merits were considered by the Senate in secret session. Magoffin, asking reimbursement in the amount of $37,780.96, had carefully itemized his claim, omitting any item that might be considered extravagant, or that might prove embarrassing to him, or to the government. In support of his claim, Magoffin submitted facts of interest after the lapse of more than a hundred years:

The above is submitted, not as an account against the United States, but as data to assist in forming an opinion of the amount that ought to be paid me for my services by showing what they cost me. As far as the services themselves, they cannot be valued in money. The bloodless conquest of the Province and the conciliation of the feelings of an invaded people, are services above money value, and these I rendered at great cost, loss & danger to myself. I had peculiar means to be serviceable, & that was known to the government. I had been Consul at Saltillo & Chihuahua fifteen years; I was a merchant in large business; I spoke the language of the country; was married to a Mexican lady; had a general acquaintance with the inhabitants; & had the influence which attaches to such a position in such a country. I went ahead of Gen'l. Kearny and secured the unopposed march into Santa Fe. I went down the country & conciliated the people. The bloodless conquest of N. Mexico & the easy advance of our troops was the fruit; & these are services which cannot be estimated in money. I only show what they cost me. General Kearny gave to my brother, Sam'l. Magoffin at Santa Fe, a written statement of my services, addressed to the Secretary of War, a letter all in his own handwriting, to be forwarded to me at Chihuahua by the first safe opportunity. My brother forwarded it by Doct'r Connelly; he was taken prisoner at El Paso, & all his papers seized & forwarded to the military judge at Chihuahua, where I was then prisoner & the authorities on the search for testimony against me. The military judge brought the letter to me (Gen'l. Kearny's was inclosed in one from my brother) without having shown it to the Governor or General. We understood one another. He told me to tare it up, which I did in his presence; for I was a prisoner & it was not safe for either of us that I should keep it. That affair cost me $3,800 & deprived me of General Kearny's statement to lay before the government. He wrote it, as a matter of precaution & justice to me just before he left for California & his death has prevented me from ever seeing him again.[37]

On September 29, 1848, in Chihuahua, Henry Connelly,[38] long time resident of Mexico, signed a supporting statement, probably prepared by Magoffin, giving his version of the happenings at Santa Fe in mid-August, 1846:

I do hereby certify that being in Santa Fe, N. Mexico, in August, 1846, before the arrival of Gen'l Kearny, & being intimately acquainted with Col. Diego Archuleta & having an opportunity of conversing with him particularly on the subject of impeding the entrance of the U. S. forces into that city, I am in a position to make this statement. On the arrival of Capt. Cook & J. W. Magoffin August 13th, was requested by Mr. M. to give him my opinion respecting the intentions of Gen'l. Armijo, & particularly that of Col. Archuleta, which I did, informing him that the Gen'l. was not determined, but the Col. was decided in making a defense. . . . I then left Santa Fe with many other Americans by permit of Gen'l Armijo, believing it would be unsafe to remain in the city, leaving behind Magoffin. He remained for what purpose I know not, believing a strong resistance would be made a few miles from the city. Must say that I was much astonished as well as gratified to find that Gen'l. K. met with no opposition on his entry into Santa Fe. On the contrary was received with much courtesy by the Acting Governor of the city & the rest of the authorities, Mr. Magoffin being one of the number on his reception at the Palace. The day before Gen'l. K.'s entrance, some five leagues distant, Gen'l. Armijo called his officers, and inquired what would be the best measure to adopt. Col. Archuleta, being second in command, gave as his opinion, that it was unnecessary to make a defence, this was adopted by all. The troops were then disbanded & Gen'l. A. returned with a company of dragoons to Chih'a. Col. Archuleta retired to his country residence. . . . The determination was entirely contrary to all *Munos* & *Palacios*-Mexicans of the best standing in this city being in New Mexico before & on the arrival of Gen'l. K. & knowing the positive intention of Gen'l Armijo & particularly of Col. Archuleta was to defend the place, retired immediately to this city, and reported to the Governor that J. W. Magoffin had been the cause of nonresistance and that he had bought over Gen'l. Armijo & Col. Archuleta. This information with others led to the imprisonment of Magoffin on his arrival here.

While James W. Magoffin was a prisoner in Mexico, his Kentucky relatives became apprehensive, and urged Washington officials to obtain his release. On June 22, 1847, Robert B. McAfee (in the consular service in Bogota from 1833 to 1837,) wrote on behalf of Magoffin's people to Secretary of War Marcy, from Harrodsburg, Ky., seeking his good offices. McAfee's letter told Secretary Marcy, among other things, that Manuel Armijo, New Mexico's former governor, had saved Magoffin's life when he was about to be shot as a traitor, and that Magoffin had been removed from Chihuahua to a Durango prison when it appeared that the Americans would occupy Chihuahua:

Permit me to call to your attention, and that of the President, the situation of Mr. James W. Magoffin, whose widowed mother, and numerous relatives of whom I am one, all reside in this place, and vicinity, consisting of half this county (Mercer, Ky.). He was taken prisoner near Chihuahua last fall and condemned to be shot as a Mexican traitor, having lived in that place as a merchant, and was returning to Chihuahua to look after his affairs from Santa Fe, having been of essential service to Gen'l Kearny, was in advance of him on his march to California, his sentence was suspended at the request of Gen'l. Armijo, his wife being his relation. Mr. Magoffin never became a citizen of Mexico, although authorized to be so, always declined, his wife is dead and his children are at school in this state and Missouri. When Col. Doniphan approached Chihuahua, he was sent off a prisoner to Durango, where I understand he is now detained, still subject to his original sentence. Will you be so good as to request Gen'l. Taylor to take immediate steps for his safety & release. Mr. Magoffin was born in this place and his friends take a deep interest in his release.

Magoffin's claim for reimbursement encountered unexpected resistance in Washington. Secretary of War George W. Crawford contended there had never been any "contract" between former Secretary Marcy and Magoffin. On April 4, 1849, Magoffin answered Crawford's contention by admitting that there had never been any "contract" as such, and in the same letter told of the things he had accomplished in helping to achieve the "bloodless conquest" of New Mexico. Of particular interest is Magoffin's assertion that the Taos revolution could have been avoided if Col. Archuleta had been given a political post:

The remark which you made that Mr. Marcy said there was no "contract" with me for my services in Mexico & the time that has elapsed since, without hearing anything, naturally makes me uneasy, & I write this brief statement for the purpose of showing my views of my case. I certainly made no contract with the Government nor did such an idea enter into my head. I engaged, at the request of President Polk, to go to Mexico, where I had been for many years, to be of service to our troops; & I took what they gave me, to wit, letters to accredit me to the General; they did accredit me and imploy me. I went into Santa Fe ahead of Gen'l. Kearny & smoothed the way for his bloodless conquest of New Mexico. Col. Archuleta would have fought. I quieted him. It was he who afterwards made the revolt which was put down with much bloodshed by Gen'l. Price. Fight was in him, and it would have come out at first, carrying Armijo with him if it had not been for my exertions. I recommended to Gen'l. Kearny to give him some place, which would compromise him, which the General intended to do, but was prevented by some cause to me unknown, and the consequence was the revolt at Taos, the death of Governor Bent, & all the bloodshed that took place. Archuleta fled to the South and did not return till after the peace. He was second in command & had about a thousand of the best troops in New Mexico, and if he had held out for resistance, Armijo would have been obliged to have done the same, and a bloody resistance would have been made in the defiles through which Gen'l. Kearny had to pass.

Magoffin was confident that he could have achieved for Gen. Wool in Chihuahua the same results he had obtained for General Kearny in Santa Fe if Wool had arrived there as had been expected. Magoffin was obviously worried by the political maneuvering:

Bloodless possession of New Mexico was what President Polk wished; it was obtained through my means. I could state exactly how I drew off Archuleta from his intention to fight. The papers which I filed, Dr. Connelly's letter, Major Cooke's and Capt. Turner's, all allude to it, and Gen'l. Kearny's was explicit. After this service, I went forward under the directions of Gen'l. Kearny to render the same service to Gen'l. Wool. I entered Chihuahua.

He did not arrive; & that led to my imprisonment, to the great loss of my property, & the vast expenses which I had to incur. It was to smooth the way for Gen'l. Wool that I went to Chihuahua. If he had come I should probably have done as much for him as I did for Gen'l. Kearny. I have neglected my business for near three years, have not been with my family during that time, have made great expenses, and suffered great losses; and the statement of items which I presented is not an account, but a statement to give some idea of what it would take to remunerate me. The service I rendered is above payment. I was engaged in June 1846, by the President & Secretary of War, in the presence & with the knowledge of Senator Benton; the service and the engagement was acknowledged by President Polk, after I got back, in presence of Senator Atchison, and the only reason for not paying me was the want of money.... Senator Atchison has gone away; Senator Benton is going & I begin to feel uneasy about my compensation.

In the days immediately preceding the occupation of Santa Fe on August 18, 1846, Captain P. St. George Cooke and James W. Magoffin had conspired and cooperated to accomplish a "bloodless invasion." P. St. George Cooke, then a major, wrote a letter from Philadelphia on Feb. 21, 1849, praising Magoffin's services, which was filed in support of his claim:

If the following statement of your important services as came to my personal knowledge during the invasion of New Mexico can serve to elucidate your sacrifices & risks during the war, it gives me pleasure to make it. I shall not easily forget the pleasure which your company gave me when I preceded the Army with a flag, from Bent's fort to Santa Fe, nor the advantages of your knowledge of the country & its language. I am strongly impressed with the skill you exhibited not to compromise your old influence over the Mexican General, by an *appearance* of your real connexion with myself, even furnishing an interpreter, rather than appear on the official occasion; at *night*, however, you accompanied Gen'l. Armijo to my quarters, where, by your aid, we had a secret conference. I then understood the Mexican Governor's real disinclination to actual resistance, to which, I believe, according to our instructions, you gave important encouragement; particularly in neutralizing the contrary influence of the young Colonel Archuleta, by suggesting to his ambition the part in bringing about a pronunciamento of western New Mexico in favor of annexation; Gen'l. Kearny's first proclamation claiming only to the Rio Grande. I had personal knowledge of the high opinion which that General entertained for your discretion & services; and, that it may well be considered a piece of good fortune, that at the expense of a large bribe, you were suffered to destroy the Gneral's own written statement of them—only shows how narrowly you escaped with your life, in your further efforts to serve our government in Chihuahua.[39]

Magoffin's efforts to compel recognition of his claim finally brought results. The Congress appropriated fifty thousand dollars "for the use of the army," with the understanding that all, or a substantial part of the money, would be used to pay Magoffin's claim. Magoffin had hoped that the government would be generous enough to pay him something over and above $37,780.96, the actual amount of his claim, to compensate him to some extent for the suffering and humiliation he had suffered in Mexican prisons. The government, however, not only refused to be generous — it quibbled and haggled about being just. Worn out explaining, defending himself, and answering arguments about the claim, Magoffin feared that government red tape might involve him in endless delay. Although he believed that he should receive all of the fifty thousand dollars appropriated by Congress, Magoffin finally agreed to accept $40,000 in full settlement. Secretary Crawford, evidently a hard trader, made a counter offer of $30,000 "in full of all demands against the United States." Magoffin reluctantly accepted.[40]

More than ever impressed by the fact that republics are ungrateful, Magoffin left Washington. He visited relatives in Kentucky and Missouri, gathered up his children, and began to make plans to resume life some place near where he had interrupted it on the fatal and fateful day in 1846 on which Senator Benton had taken him to the White House for a friendly visit with President Polk.

CHAPTER FOUR

Boundary and Indian Troubles

A PEACE TREATY between the United States and Mexico, known in history as the "Treaty of Guadalupe Hidalgo," which defined the rights, duties and obligations of the respective parties, was signed at Guadalupe Hidalgo (the place of Mexico's most famous religious shrine, then a suburb of the Mexican capital, but now a part of Mexico City), on Feb. 2, 1848. The treaty was ratified for the Mexican government at Queretoro on May 30, 1848. The Senate of the United States ratified the treaty, and it was proclaimed in Washington on July 4, 1848. Under the treaty, the United States achieved the principal objective of the war. In consideration of a promise to pay fifteen million dollars as indemnity, Mexico agreed to relinquish to the United States all claim of right to California and New Mexico. In the negotiations conducted prior to the treaty, it was considered that ten of the fifteen millions of dollars would be paid for California, with its immensely valuable ports of San Francisco, Monterey and San Diego, its hundreds of miles of coast line, and millions of acres of potentially valuable land; and that five million dollars would be considered as payment for relatively unimportant New Mexico, an area north of the Rio Grande and east of the Colorado river, with boundaries that were vague, indefinite and uncertain.

With the treaty of peace effective, all American soldiers in Mexican territory were ordered to return to the United States. Colonel John Macrae Washington,[41] then in Monterey, was

36

appointed military commander and Provisional Governor for New Mexico. Colonel Washington left Monterey on July 28, with 500 troops. Following rough roads and trails that took him through Saltillo, Patos, Mapimi, Chihuahua and Paso del Norte, Washington reached Santa Fe on Oct. 10, 1848. Some weeks after his arrival in Santa Fe, Colonel Washington received a letter, written by Secretary Marcy, which instructed him generally in his duties. Marcy told Washington, among other things, to discontinue customs duty collections, and to refund all duties collected from and after May 30, 1848, the date on which the treaty of peace had been signed at Queretoro. The Secretary referred to New Mexico's peculiar governmental status:

It was expected that Congress would have provided for a territorial government for New Mexico at its last session, but it did not. Its attention at the approaching session will be directed to the subject, and a proper civil government provided. Until this is done, things must remain as they are. It will be the duty of the military authority there to defend the Territory from invasion; to repress and repel Indian incursions, and preserve internal tranquility. The important duty of the military force will be to protect the inhabitants of the Territory of New Mexico in the full enjoyment of life, liberty and property.

Washington was to be discreet and diplomatic in matters relating to the claim made by Texas to a part of New Mexico:

In regard to that part of what the Mexicans called New Mexico lying east of the Rio Grande, the civil authority which Texas has established there is to be respected, and in no manner whatever interfered with by the military force in that department otherwise than to lend aid on proper occasion in sustaining it. In other parts of New Mexico, whatever civil government is found to exist is to be regarded as a government *de facto* and is also to be respected. Texas claims as a part of that state all the territory lying east of the Rio Grande, and the government here has not contested that claim. Whether it is or not a part of Texas, since the peace it is essentially part of the United States.[42]

Restless as a result of the apparent indifference of the Congress concerning New Mexico's welfare, political leaders held a three-day convention in Santa Fe on Sept. 24, 25 and 26, 1849, some two weeks before Colonel Washington's arrival, at which ways and means were considered of lifting New Mexico from political oblivion and economic stagnation.[43]

The convention, without any legal authority to do so, elected Hugh N. Smith, described by Indian Agent James S. Calhoun as "an immensely clever man," to represent New Mexico in the Congress of the United States. Although it was recognized that Smith would have no vote or official standing of any kind in Congress, the convention was determined to have him represent New Mexico in Washington in whatever capacity he might be acceptable there. Anticipating that Texas would press its claim of ownership of New Mexico to the Rio Grande, the convention instructed Smith to assert on behalf of New Mexico a claim to all that territory bounded on the north by the "Indian Territory, on the west by California, on the south by Mexico, and on the east by Texas." The convention adopted resolutions reflecting conditions existing in the New Mexico of 1849:

For the last three years New Mexico has suffered under the paralyzing effects of a government undefined and doubtful in its character, inefficient to protect the rights of the people, or to discharge the high and absolute duty of every government, the enforcement and regular administration of its own laws, in consequence of which, industry and enterprise are paralyzed, and discontent and confusion prevail throughout the land; the want of proper protection against the various barbarous tribes of Indians that surround us on every side, has prevented the extension of settlements upon our valuable public domain, and rendered utterly futile every attempt to explore or develop the great resources of the territory; surrounded by the Eutaws, Comanches, and Apaches, on the north, east and south, by the Navajos on the west, with Jicarillas within our limits, and without any adequate protection against their hostile inroads; our flocks and herds are driven off by thousands; our fellow citizens, men, women and children, are murdered or carried into captivity; many of our citizens of all ages and sexes are at this moment suffering all the horrors of barbarian bondage, and it is utterly out of our power to obtain their release from a condition to which death would be preferable; the wealth of our territory is being diminished; we have neither the means nor any adopted plan by government for the education of the rising generation; in fine, with a government temporary, doubtful, uncertain and inefficient in character and operation, surrounded and despoiled by barbarous foes, ruin appears inevitably before us, unless speedy and effectual protection be extended to us by the Congress of the United States.[44]

The Texas claim to a substantial part of New Mexico, resting in part on the so called "Texas Expedition" authorized by President Mirabeau B. Lamar of the Texas Republic (led by General Hugh McLeod, which started from Austin on June 18, 1841), proved to be the stumbling block which prevented New Mexico from promptly becoming a Territory of the United States. Texas representatives in the Congress steadfastly maintained that Texas, by right of invasion prior to the American Occupation, was entitled to all of New Mexico east of the Rio Grande. They contended that the language used to define New Mexico's boundaries in the treaty of Guadalupe Hidalgo of 1848, exactly described territory located in Texas; and that Texas, through enactment of laws asserting jurisdiction over New Mexico territory, had thereby enlarged her dominion and became entitled to all of New Mexico as far west as Santa Fe, and south along the Rio Grande a distance of several hundred miles from Santa Fe. Finally, the weighty and impressive argument was advanced in support of the Texas contention, that the act of Congress of May 13, 1846, providing for the prosecution of the war with Mexico, by necessary implication, admitted the validity of the Texas title to the territory as far west as the Rio Grande.[45]

A bill was introduced in the Senate in 1850 "proposing to the state of Texas the establishment of her northern and western boundaries, the relinquishment by the said State of all territory claimed by her exterior to said boundaries, and of all her claim upon the United States." The bill provided for payment to Texas of ten millions of dollars, in satisfaction of her claim on New Mexico, through stock to be issued by the government, bearing five per cent interest, one-half, or five millions thereof not to be issued until the federal government had received assurance that certain creditors of Texas had been paid in full and were satisfied. There were rumblings in Washington while the bill was pending, that "Texas might draw the sword" if Congress failed to pass it.[46]

Senator Joseph R. Underwood, of Kentucky, spoke in opposition to the bill on August 7 and 8, 1850. Senators Houston and Rusk of Texas, sponsors of the bill, frequently interrupted Underwood in the course of the debate, asking him many questions. The questions and answers developed many interesting facts concerning early day Texas-New Mexico history. In opposing the bill, Senator Underwood argued:

If we have injured Texas, and she draws the sword to resent it and to redress the wrong, do you expect to silence her complaints and stop her action by $10,000,000? Is she a child unjustly cuffed until she cries out with rage; and is she to be silenced by putting sugar plums in her mouth? Mr. President, we ought to approach and deal with Texas and this whole business like men. We ought to be firm, rational, and just ourselves, and take it for granted that Texas intends to act upon the same high principles. These principles must lead to a peaceable, bloodless settlement of the controversy in due time. I am unwilling to act in a hurry, under an apparent threat.... The United States are only holding possession of a Territory conquered by their arms, acknowledged to belong to them by the treaty of Guadalupe Hidalgo, and paid for by their money. Now, I insist, under such circumstances, that the United States is justified in holding possession until the controversy with Texas is settled either by the Supreme Court, or by arbitration, or by mutual agreement. The complaint of Texas grows out of the refusal to acknowledge her right, and·to give her immediate possession and jurisdiction over the country; and the intimidation, if not threat, that she would be justified in redressing herself by force.

If Texas raised troops to march on New Mexico, they would be guilty of treason, in Underwood's opinion:

Should she raise troops and march them into New Mexico for any such purpose, she would be making war against the United States, and all engaged would commit the overt act of treason, and subject themselves to the traitor's doom. In such an event it would be the duty of the government to repel force by force.

If Texas sends no army to New Mexico there will be no collision. Certainly the United States will not march armies into Texas and attack her, merely because she puts up a claim as baseless as the "fabric of a vision," in the opinion of thousands. If a state of war is to exist, it will be by the act of Texas, and upon her must rest the consequences and the responsibility. . . . For myself, I can assure the Texans that, convinced as I am, that no part of the Santa Fe country belongs to Texas, yet, if the Supreme Court, or arbitrators, or Congress should decide in her favor, no one will submit to the decision more readily or cheerfully than myself. . . .

Texas had not attempted formation of counties in New Mexico until 1849, according to Underwood:

Texas never attempted to form counties, and extend her jurisdiction over any part of the Santa Fe country until last winter. She then passed laws to form counties in this country, and since then a "certain Mr. Neighbours" was sent into the Territory to organize these counties. He has not succeeded. Nor did Texas extend her jurisdiction to the lower Rio Grande until aided by the army of the United States. . . . I have already alluded to the threatened civil war, unless we appease the hot bloods of Texas. If the people of Texas are so avaricious for money, that ten millions will arrest their belligerent propensities—if they prefer money to blood, and that sum will induce them to remain at peace—it might possibly cost us less to hand over the money than to defend the nation against the attack. If, therefore, it was a mere question of dollars and cents, it might be good policy to pass the bill, in case war with Texas is to be the inevitable result of its rejection. But, Mr. President, there are higher considerations. . . . I have endeavored to show that Texas has no right to any part of New Mexico east of the Rio Grande. But even if she is the rightful owner of every foot of it, I hold that it would be treason in her citizens, under state organization, to make war against the United States. She has no right to raise an army, to become an arbiter in her own cause, and to undertake to redress herself by violence and bloodshed. . . .[47]

The controversy over the Texas-New Mexico boundary resulted in the passage of a compromise bill establishing the "Territory of New Mexico," upon certain contingencies, and with reservations. The act of establishment, approved by

President Fillmore on Sept. 9, 1850, provided in the eight-
eenth section that it should be suspended "until the boundary
between the United States and the State of Texas shall be adjusted, and when such adjustment shall have been effected,
the president of the United States shall issue his proclamation,
declaring this act to be in full force and operation, and shall
proceed to appoint the officers herein provided to be appointed in and for said territory."

At long last, five years after the American Occupation, and
almost three years after the signing of the treaty of Guadalupe Hidalgo, the boundary line dispute was settled to the
satisfaction of Texas. Ten millions of dollars was the price
of settlement. The United States had paid Mexico only fifteen millions of dollars as indemnity for both New Mexico
and California. Now that the dispute had been settled by
the Congress, the way was clear for New Mexico to become a
territory of the United States. The President issued the necessary proclamation. James S. Calhoun, Indian Agent in New
Mexico since April 7, 1849, was inaugurated the first governor
of the new Territory at Santa Fe, on March 3, 1851.[48]

CHAPTER FIVE

New Mexico's Wild Indians

PRIOR TO HIS INAUGURATION as the first civil governor of the
Territory of New Mexico, James S. Calhoun, of Georgia,
served for twenty-three months in the difficult, thankless and
poor paying position of Indian agent for New Mexico.[49] Calhoun was in Chattanooga, Tenn., when he received notice of
his appointment as Indian agent for New Mexico. In a letter

accepting the appointment, written from Chattanooga to Commissioner of Indian Affairs William Medill, on April 17, 1849, Calhoun said that he had shipped his goods and baggage, and with his wife and family, "four females in all," expected to leave Chattanooga at once for St. Louis. While making arrangements in St. Lous to continue his journey to Fort Leavenworth, Calhoun accepted the offer of "twenty bold and enterprising adventurers, several of whom had served in the war with Mexico," to accompany him across the plains from the Missouri river to New Mexico. Calhoun's party, strengthened by a soldier escort, joined a caravan of a hundred wagons which left Fort Leavenworth on May 16, 1849. The caravan reached Santa Fe on July 22, 1849, after a journey of nine weeks, over a route that took it through Council Grove, Cimarron Springs, Round Mountain, Ocáte Creek, Las Vegas, Tecolote, San Miguel and the Pecos ruins.

Making camp on the outskirts of Santa Fe, Calhoun spent several days hunting for a house which would rent at a price he was willing to pay out of his salary of fifteen hundred dollars a year. Writing from Santa Fe on July 28, 1849, Calhoun told Commissioner Medill of his trip to New Mexico:

You are already advised of my departure from Fort Leavenworth on the 16th of May, and I have now to inform you that we reached Santa Fe on the 22nd of the present month, having been employed in marching forty-nine days—our halting days numbering nineteen, a greater portion of which was six miles west of the Kaw River, in obedience to an order issued by General Brooks to Colonel Alexander, commanding the troops. This, you will perceive, is the eighth day in camp at this place, not having been able to procure quarters elsewhere; I have the promise, however, of an adobe building at the enormous rent of $100 per month, to which an additional expenditure must be made to Americanize it, so that it may be inhabited with any degree of comfort. This excessive rent I was compelled to submit to, or remain in camp. . . . Until our government established a saw mill near this place, sawed lumber could not be had at any price; since then it has been sold as high as eighty dollars a thousand.

Prices were high in Santa Fe in 1849. Wheat was two dollars a bushel. Hay, scarce at any price, brought sixty dollars a ton. Blacksmiths got four to six dollars for shoeing a horse. Beef and mutton sold for from eight to ten cents a pound. Calhoun told the Commissioner about conditions in Santa Fe:

All houses in this city are built up of adobe, with floors of dirt, and covered by spreading dirt three to six inches thick upon rough boards . . . you will readily conclude, and correctly too, that we have dirty and leaky houses. Plank and scantling are selling in Santa Fe at from fifty to eighty dollars a thousand. Nails are twenty-five cents a pound. Mechanics, with a ration a day, receive a minimum of forty dollars per month. Good sound wheat and corn bring two dollars a bushel, and they are not plentiful at that. Hay and fodder sell for sixty dollars a ton, and very scarce even at such a price. It costs from four to six dollars to have a horse shod. Beef and mutton sell for from eight to ten cents per pound, sugar, twenty-five cents, coffee, at the same price. Tea sells for $1.25. Freight from Fort Independence to Santa Fe costs from 10 to 12 cents a pound. Common servants are paid from ten to fifteen dollars per month, and rations. We are so far from water, we are obliged to have it hauled to us in a wagon.[50]

Calhoun's mission to New Mexico was to undertake the task, single handed, of governing some forty thousand Indians, including the peace loving Pueblos, and the wild Apaches, Navajos and Utes. Although Calhoun must have realized the enormity, perhaps the futility, of the task, nevertheless he courageously shouldered the burden that had been entrusted to him. After discussing the problems involved with Chief Justice Joab Houghton and Colonel Washington he gave an outline of the situation to the Commissioner of Indian Affairs. Under Mexican law, the Pueblo Indians had been recognized as citizens, Calhoun wrote, and they could be counted upon not to cause trouble for the American government:

The obstacles to be overcome in adjusting our Indian relations in New Mexico, and its borders, are of a much more formidable character than has been anticipated. . . . The Pueblo Indians, it is believed, are entitled to the early and special consideration of the government of the United States. They are the only tribe in perfect amity with the government, and are an industrious, agricultural and pastoral people, living principally in villages, ranging north and west of Taos, on both sides of the Rio Grande, more than 250 miles. By a Mexican statute these people, as I am informed by Judge Houghton of Santa Fe, to whom I am greatly indebted for much valuable information, were constituted citizens of the republic of Mexico, granting to all of mature age, who could read and write, the privilege of voting.... These Indians are anxious to have schools established amongst them and to receive agricultural information, which, if granted on a liberal scale, could not fail to produce marked and beneficial results, not only upon them, but upon all the tribes of the Territory....

It would be necessary, in Calhoun's opinion, for the government to feed the wandering tribes to prevent them from committing robberies and murders:

At present, it is the opinion of Colonel Washington, the military commander of this division, that any attempt to conciliate the tribes who have caused the recent and present troubles in this Territory, would have a very injurious tendency. The Indians, presuming upon their knowledge of safe retreats in the mountains, and our entire ignorance of all avenues, except established military roads and well known trails, are not to be subjected to just restraints until they are properly chastised. When they shall feel themselves so chastised, they will sue for peace.... The very gravest subject connected with our Indian affairs in New Mexico relates to the wandering tribes, who have never cultivated the soil, and have supported themselves by depredations alone. This is the only labor known to them. The thought of annihilating these Indians cannot be entertained by an American public—nor can the Indians abandon their predatory incursions, and live and learn to support themselves by the sweat of their own brows, unsustained by a liberal philanthropy ... for no earthly power can prevent robberies and murders, unless the hungry wants of these people are provided for, both physically and mentally.

For months before Calhoun's arrival, the wild Indians had been particularly hostile and aggressive. They had raided the settlements, stolen livestock, and wantonly murdered settlers. The military seemed powerless to prevent the raids, or to capture the perpetrators of the crimes. The settlers were critical of the military, claiming that the soldiers were incapable of defending the settlements; that they lacked the spirit to pursue the Indians on hot trails, and were afraid to follow them to their hideouts. Indian Agent Calhoun wrote to the Commissioner on Aug. 16, 1849, some three weeks after his arrival in New Mexico, to advise him of the situation:

The Indians generally, are in a bad temper. The number of troops are not sufficient here to keep upon them a proper check; and infantry are useful only to protect posts, stations, and property. Mounted troops are the only arm of this country that can be effectively used against the Indian tribes of this remote region.

From all that Calhoun could learn, and from all information available to Colonel Washington, New Mexico's military governor, most of the robberies and murders had been committed by Navajo Indians. As a result, Calhoun and Washington decided to invade the home country of the Navajo tribe. The "Washington Expedition of 1849," as it is known in New Mexico history, was the most pretentious since the Doniphan expedition of three years before. Calhoun and Washington, in advance of the invasion, had the advice of James L. Collins, a long time resident of New Mexico, who spoke some Navajo, was acquainted with some of the Navajo chiefs, and was familiar to some extent with the ways of the tribe.

The expedition, well organized and presenting an impressive appearance, marched out of Santa Fe on Aug. 16, 1849. The organization included 120 regular infantry, 55 regular artillery, 50 New Mexico volunteer infantry, 80 New Mexico mounted militia, and 55 Indians from the Pueblos of Santo Domingo, Santa Ana, Zia and Jemez. The troops were equipped with one six pounder and three mountain howitzers for use in event of major hostilities. The commissary carried rations for five hundred men for thirty days. Lieutenant James H. Simpson, of the Topographical Engineers, was the expedition's official reporter, and two brothers—R. H. Kern (killed by Indians in Utah in 1853) and E. M. Kern—were the official artists.

Following a route that led from Santa Fe over rough roads and rougher trails, the expedition traveled by way of Agua

Fria, Cieneguilla, Santa Domingo and Jemez Pueblo, averaging twelve miles a day. There being no road west of Jemez Pueblo into the Navajo country, the baggage wagons were abandoned there, and pack mules substituted. Striking out north and west from the Jemez river, the expedition passed by the ruins of Pueblo Bonito (even then recognized for their pre historic interest), passed through mile after mile of tediously barren and desert like country; traveled now and then through valleys thick with grass; ascended and descended high mountains; saw a few great forests of yellow pine and blue spruce.

By August 31, two weeks after leaving Santa Fe, Washington's expedition was in the heart of the Navajo country, which from all outward appearances, was anything but a land of bandits or banditry. As proof of their toil and industry, the Navajo men could point to thriving crops of corn and wheat, cultivated on patches of ground that reluctantly yielded the fruits of the earth, in a country where there was little rain.

As evidence of the industry, the Navajo women could exhibit blankets woven with consummate skill and a fine appreciation of native art. Poverty, as it was known in some American communities of the day, apparently did not exist in the Navajo country. Fairly good cattle grazed on the ranges; bands of fat sheep were to be seen in the draws and *canyons*. The whole country seemed to be alive with horses, the prized possession of the Navajos, some of them of fairly good breeds, others mongrel-like. There was every indication that all the people in the Navajo country were getting enough to eat, and everybody seemed to be fairly well clothed, consistent with the Navajo idea of raiment.

Washington and Calhoun speculated on the motives that prompted the Navajos, or at least some of them, to raid the settlements, and to steal livestock, and kill people. They were convinced from their observations in the Navajo country, that overwhelming necessity was not one of the factors contributing to their delinquencies.

Each day, with the approach of sundown, the expedition

went into camp. Seemingly out of nowhere, curious Navajos gathered, sometimes in great numbers, to witness a strange spectacle, wondering, and a bit mystified as to the purpose of such an extraordinary event. At each stopping place, Washington and Calhoun told the Navajos, through interpreter Collins, that the American government was grievously offended because the Navajos had robbed and killed settlers; that the Americans did not propose to tolerate such misconduct; that in times past the Navajos had made promises to the Americans which had been broken; that the time had now come when the Americans would not allow the Navajos to talk of treaties, but would punish them for their misdeeds.

Talk at one meeting, about misconduct and broken peace treaties, was quickly discontinued as the result of a commotion, following the discovery by a soldier, that a Navajo had a horse which had been stolen from him in one of the settlements. In the argument that ensued, a soldier shot and killed Chief Narbona, eighty years old, an innocent bystander. The Navajos stampeded when Narbona was shot.

By September 5, the expedition was at the mouth of Canon de Chelly, a place the Navajos had always considered impregnable to an enemy. Within two days, several detachments of Washington's soldiers had marched through its supposedly impenetrable portals and barriers. Here, in the center of the most thickly populated Navajo country, Washington and Calhoun were surprised to see thriving fields of wheat and well cared for peach orchards.[51]

In the Canon de Chelly, the Navajos gathered about the soldiers and listened to Colonel Washington, who patiently explained the object of the expedition. Accusing the Navajos of having stolen livestock from the settlements, he demanded that they make prompt restitution. Washington described the numbers of sheep, cattle, horses and mules, and their brands, claimed by the settlers to have been stolen by the Navajos. In reply to Washington's accusations, the Navajo chiefs claimed they did not have in their possession any of the animals Washington had described. They stoutly denied that the Navajos had stolen any livestock or had committed any crimes in the settlements. The Apaches might possibly have raided the settlements, the Navajos suggested, and the people of the settlements might have mistaken Apaches for Navajos.

Talking to Navajo chiefs, separately and in council, Washington attempted to impress upon them that it was necessary for them to reform their people. To the proposed reformation the chiefs assented. On Sept. 9, 1849, after days of talking and haggling, Washington and the Navajos entered into a treaty of peace and friendship, signed in an apparently optimistic atmosphere, attended by considerable pomp and ceremony. Army officers and chiefs exchanged gifts, and shook hands in pledge of mutual trust and eternal friendship.[52]

Believing that he had accomplished his mission to the Navajo country, Colonel Washington and a detachment of troops went to Zuni, on the edge of the Navajo country, to investigate a report that the Apaches had attacked the Zuni Indians (a report which proved to be without foundation). The Zunis welcomed Washington and Calhoun to Zuni Pueblo and entertained them with courtesy and hospitality. Leaving Zuni, the expedition turned eastward toward Albuquerque, passing near a high mountain peak, an important landmark to this day for a vast area of country, which Lieutenant Simpson described in his report:

"We found ourselves on the summit of a pass, from which, bearing north of east, some thirty miles off, we caught sight, for the first time, of one of the finest mountain peaks I have seen in this country. This peak I have, in honor of the President of the United States, called *Mount Taylor*. Erecting itself high above the plain below, an object of vision at a remote distance, standing within the domain which has been so recently the theatre of his sagacity and prowess, it exists, not inappropriately, an ever-enduring monument to his patriotism and integrity.[53]

By September 21, the expedition had crossed the Rio Puerco and was traveling on the down slope to the Rio Grande toward Albuquerque. Lieutenant Simpson described the descent to the floor of the valley:

Proceeding a few hundred yards further, we reached the summit of a swell of land, whence could be seen the broad valley of the Rio Grande, the mountains just back of Albuquerque now showing themselves in all the magnificence of their proportions. Shortly after, much to our relief, we met a wagon loaded with barrels of water which had been sent out by Major Howe, from Albuquerque, agreeably to the instructions of the colonel commanding, forwarded by express. The men were exceedingly thirsty, and drank correspondingly. When within seven miles of the Rio Grande, we caught much to our delight, the first sight of its glimmering waters. A mile further, we fell in with a couple more of wagons from Albuquerque, loaded with water and forage for the troops. The river, however, being but five or six miles ahead, the order was given to continue forward. Two miles more brought us to where we could see the town of Albuquerque quartering on our left; houses could also be seen lying scattered for miles up and down the river, the cottonwood very sparsely dotting its banks. Just at dusk, we were winding our way through the little village of *Atrisco,* situated on the Rio Grande, opposite Albuquerque—our camp for the night being to the north of the town, in the midst of a fine plot of pasturage, convenient to the river.

The presidio of Albuquerque had a population in 1849 of about 1,000. The military post, garrisoned by two companies of dragoons, made it the most important place in the entire lower valley. Albuquerque, according to Simpson, had several buildings somewhat impressive in size, with pretentious fronts and porches:

Albuquerque, for a Mexican town, is tolerably well built. Its buildings, like all I have seen inhabited by Mexicans, are of a right parallel—opipedon shape, constructed of adobes (blocks of sun-dried mud), and arranged generally on the four sides of a rectangle, thus creating an interior court (patio) upon which nearly every one of the apartments opens. There is generally but one exterior or street entrance; and this is generally quite wide and high, the usual width being about six feet, and the height seven. They appear to be made thus wide, at least as far as I have been able to discover, to enable the burros (asses) and other animals to go through with their packs. They are generally secured by double doors. There are two or three buildings in the town with extensive fronts and portales (porches), which look, for this country, very well—one of them being the house formerly occupied by Governor Armijo. There is a military post at this place, garrisoned by a couple of companies of dragoons, the commanding officer being Major M. S. Howe, of the 2d dragoons. The population of the town and its immediate suburbs is probably about one thousand. Wood for fuel has to be drawn a distance of twenty-five miles.[54]

Traveling north and east from Albuquerque, Washington's troops passed through Alameda, Sandia, Bernalillo[55] and Algodones, and reached Santa Fe on September 26, 1849. Lieutenant Simpson's most lasting impression of the journey was the "nakedness' of the country through which he had traveled.[56]

Washington, soldier-like, had little to say about the journey into the Navajo country, either informally or in official reports. His companion, Indian Agent James S. Calhoun, however, described it in detail in reports to the Commissioner of Indian Affairs, saying among other things that he had seen the Pueblos of Santo Domingo, Santa Ana, Zia, Jemez, Zuni, Laguna and Sandia, and had talked to the chiefs and inhabitants in each place. Calhoun's journey had provided him with the background for study of one of his most important problems in New Mexico. Besides getting a glimpse of the Pueblo Indians, he had seen the Navajo Indian country, and had talked to the Navajo in his homeland. He had observed his way of life, and appraised the possibilities for "civilizing" him. Calhoun was not interested, as Lieutenant Simpson had been, in the flora and fauna of the country; he was not concerned in speculating about the fate that might have overtaken people who had once lived at Pueblo Bonito. He was quite interested, however, in things that immediately concerned the welfare of the Indians. He was particularly anxious to prevent emigrants, passing through New Mexico on their way to the California gold fields, from molesting and mistreating Pueblo Indians.

Agent Calhoun wrote to the Commissioner on October 1, 1849, reporting generally on the Washington Expedition, in

the course of which he had traveled a distance of 284 miles
from Santa Fe to the Canon de Chelly, a place "rich in its valleys, rich in its fields of grain, and rich in its vegetables and
peach orchards." He told the Commissioner that the Navajos,
in his opinion, were desperadoes and brigands from choice,
rather than from necessity:

The Navajos commit their wrongs from a pure love of rapine
and plunder. They have extensive fields of corn and wheat, fine
peach orchards, and grow quantities of melons, squashes, beans
and peas, and have immense flocks of sheep, and a great number
of mules and horses of a superior breed. They have nothing of
the cow kind. I report to you from personal knowledge, obtained
during Governor Washington's expedition against the Navajos.
... The Navajos derive their title to the country over which they
roam, from mere possession, not knowing from whence they
came or how they were planted upon its soil; and its soil is easy
of cultivation, and capable of sustaining nearly as many millions
of inhabitants as they have thousands. I respectfully suggest,
these people should have their limits circumscribed and distinctly marked out, and their departure from such limits should
be under prescribed rules, at least, for some time to come. Even
this arrangement would be utterly ineffective unless enforced by
the military arm of the country.

The wild Indians of New Mexico needed "just restraints,"
enforced at "the point of a bayonet":

Numerous bands of thieving Indians, principally Navajos,
Apaches and Comanches, are straggling in every direction, busily
employed in gathering their winter supplies where they have not
sown. Not a day passes without hearing of some fresh outrage,
and the utmost vigilance of the military force in this country is
not sufficient to prevent murders and depredations; and there
are but few so bold as to travel alone ten miles from Santa Fe.
How are these wrongs to be remedied? I answer, by compulsory
enlightenment, and the imposition of just restraints, both to be
enforced at the point of a bayonet. ... A vast majority of the
Apaches and Comanches live chiefly by depredation; they look
upon the cultivators of the soil with contempt, as inferior beings,
the products of whose labor legitimately belongs to power—the
strongest arm; and believe that labor, except in war and in love,
and in the chase, is degradation; and the man who has not stolen

a horse or scalped an enemy is not worthy of association with these lords of the woods.

Wild Indians were on the loose in every direction, according to Calhoun's letter to the Commissioner:

The wild Indians of this country have been so much more successful in their robberies since General Kearny took possession of the country, that they do not believe we have the power to chastise them. Is it not time to enlighten them upon this subject, and put an end to their ceaseless depredations? At this moment, above our established Indian country on the Arkansas, these people are committing every depredation within their power, as far as Bent's Fort. These, with the Navajos and Kiowas, are known to be in every section of the Territory.

Calhoun described Zuni, and the outrageous conduct of the emigrants passing through Laguna and Zuni on their way to California:

The Pueblo of Zuni contains more than five hundred Indians, a hardy, well fed and well clothed race, and their location being more than two hundred miles from Santa Fe, and one hundred and thirty miles from Albuquerque, on a good road in every respect, now growing into favor as the best route to California, are subjected to serious annoyances from Navajos north and northwest, and the Apaches south and southeast. But, what is shockingly discreditable to the American name, emigrants commit the grossest wrongs against these excellent Indians by taking, in the name of the United States, such horses, mules and sheep, and grain, as they desire, carefully concealing their true names, but assuming official authority and bearing. A wrong of this kind had been perpetrated a few days previous to our arrival there. . . . Outrages committed against the Laguna Indians are as frequent and flagrant as those mentioned of Zuni. Indeed, the last outrage was of an infinitely more aggravated character. Near the hour of noon recently, the Laguna valley was entered, and sheep and other things demanded; to which the governor of the village replied, no sheep could be furnished at that hour, as their flocks were regularly, every morning, sent off, that they might graze during the day. The emigrants assuming official importance, in their anger, threatened to lynch the alcalde, tied the governor, and in that condition carried him from his home, Laguna, to Zuni, the next Pueblo west.[57]

Calhoun warned the Commissioner of the seriousness of
the Indian situation generally:

To establish a proper state of affairs in this country, with the
economy which the government of the United States should and
will ever observe, requires a strong arm, and a prompt arm,
guided by an enlightened patriotism. Expend your million now,
if necessary, that you may avoid the expenditure of millions
hereafter. . . . The Comanches and Apaches, with all their fragments of other tribes, must be penned up, and this should be done
at the earliest possible day. . . . If the Navajos and Utahs continue
to withhold their submission to our authority and to war upon
our interests, it will be absolutely necessary to remove and concentrate them. . . . The powers in New Mexico have neither the authority nor the means to reduce to order the chaotic mess in this
Territory, and the government at Washington has not thoroughly
comprehended the diversity and the magnitude of the difficulties
to be overcome.[58].

"The whole country," every "hole and corner in it," needed
a purging, according to Calhoun:

I regret to say rumors of Indian troubles have increased, and received some confirmation by the murder of a Mexican within
three miles of Santa Fe. The surgeon who examined a wounded
man on yesterday, says he was shot with sixteen arrows in the
back and two in the front; and that he found arrows upon the
ground. . . . Several Indians came from San Ildefonso to me yesterday also, saying the Navajos were impudent, troublesome, and
dangerous, and that they were in every nook and corner of the
country. . . . The governor and others of Santo Domingo, thirty-
one miles west of Santa Fe, gave me similar intelligence. One of
the owners of Bent's fort, has removed all property from it, and
caused the fort to be burned. Mr. St. Vrain, long a citizen here,
every way reliable and intelligent, says a worse state of things has
not existed in this country since he has been an inhabitant of it.
The number of discontented Indians in this Territory is not
small; and I regret to add, they are not the only evil people in it.
This whole country requires a thorough purging, which can be
accomplished only by a thorough exploration of every hole and
corner of it.

On October 15, 1849, Calhoun wrote to the Commissioner,
complaining about irresponsible traders operating in the Indian country:

So long as these wandering merchants are permitted a free and unrestrained access to the wild and roving Indians of this country, just so long are we to be harrassed by them and their allies, the various bands of robbers and other disturbers of the peace, to be found east, west, north and south, and whose agents these merchants may be. It is through the medium of these traders that arms and ammunition are supplied the Indians who refuse submission to our authority. These traders go where they please without being subject to the slightest risk. . . . Why is it that these traders have no fears, no apprehensions, and pass in every direction through the country roamed over by the Comanches, Apaches, Navajos and Utahs, unharmed in person and property, when these same Indians show by their conduct a determined and eternal hostility to all Mexicans and others who remain quietly at home, and whose wives and children, and property of every kind, are unsafe beyond the shadow of their own homes?

Colonel John Macrae Washington's expedition into the Navajo country terminated his official service in New Mexico. On October 27, 1849, Colonel John Munroe[59] reached Santa Fe, and succeeded Washington as military governor and commander of the military in New Mexico. Disappointed that Munroe, the new military governor, had not brought him a letter or one word of advice or instruction from Washington, Calhoun wrote to the Commissioner reminding him rather sharply that he had been in New Mexico since July 22, "still without the slightest intelligence from the states." Calhoun was critical of many things, particularly the mail service:

The mail facilities are not such as we are entitled to; and that is of infinitely more importance to the government at Washington than to us. The controlling powers should be advised more promptly in reference to the various sinuosities daily perpetrated in this far off region. The truth in relation to governmental affairs here is not understood at Washington; and until we are brought more immediately under the proper supervisory eye, nothing of a highly reputable character may be expected to transpire in this Territory; and how can a proper supervision be had without certain means of receiving early intelligence and promptly transmitting orders?[60]

Government officials in Washington, finally heeding the re-

peated requests of James S. Calhoun (by now serving in the
dual capacity of Governor of the Territory of New Mexico,
and Superintendent of Indian Affairs), sent additional troops
to police the wild Indians of New Mexico, under the command of Colonel Edwin Vose Sumner, a splendid soldier,
who believed in firm discipline. During the American Occupation of 1846, Sumner had served on General Kearny's staff
in New Mexico, and had achieved distinction subsequently in
the battles of Cerro Gordo and Molino del Rey in the Mexican War. Sumner's command, a detachment of dragoons and
infantry recruits, left Fort Leavenworth for Santa Fe on May
26, 1851. Sumner's wagon trains, commanded by Major
Daniel H. Rucker, brought provisions and supplies, horses,
mules and beef cattle for New Mexico and Arizona army
posts.[61]

Colonel Sumner reached Santa Fe on July 19, 1851. Some
days later he wrote to Adjutant General H. Jones at Fort
Leavenworth, advising him of disposition of troops:

I reached Santa Fe on the 19th of July and assumed command
of the Department. My first step was to break up the post at
Santa Fe, that sink of vice and extravagance, and to remove the
troops and public property at Fort Union. I left one company of
artillery in Santa Fe, and shall have a cavalry station within striking distance of that place during the coming winter. I understand many applications have been made to the government, by
the people of Santa Fe, to have the troops ordered back there.
I have no hesitation in saying that I believe most of these applications proceed directly or indirectly from those who have hitherto managed to live, in some way, from the extravagant expenditures of the government. I trust their petitions will not be heeded.

Sumner proposed to establish forts at many places on the
frontier:

I have also withdrawn the troops from the towns of Las Vegas,
Rayado, Albuquerque, Ciboleta, Socorro, Dona Ana, San Elizerio,
and El Paso, and I have established a post, Fort Union, near the
Mora River, and on the line of communications with the Missouri
frontier. This will be the Department Headquarters and general
depot. I have also established a post on the Rio Grande, near
El Paso (Fort Fillmore), one at Valverde on the same river (Fort

Conrad), and one at Canon Bonito (Fort Defiance). These posts have all been selected with a view to cultivation as well as the defense of the frontier, and they are now being built by the troops and the expense will be very small. I propose to establish a post in the Utah country this fall.

The troops in New Mexico were "in a high degree demoralized," in Sumner's opinion, and required discipline:

I consider the withdrawal of the troops from the towns a matter of vital importance, both as it regards discipline and economy. It is unquestionably true, that most of the troops in this territory have become in a high degree demoralized, and it can only be accounted for, by the vicious associations in these towns. These evils are so great, that I do not expect to eradicate them entirely, until I can bring the troops together in considerable bodies, for discipline and instruction.

The Navajo Indians, instead of heeding the warning of the Doniphan expedition in 1846, and of the Washington expedition in 1849, continued to plunder the settlements, to kill people, and in general to defy the American government. Within a month after his arrival in Santa Fe, Colonel Sumner decided to march against the Navajos. He left Santa Fe for the Navajo country on August 17, 1851, with four companies of horse, one company of artillery and two companies of infantry. Sumner followed Washington's route into the Navajo country. He returned by way of Zuni and Laguna. Back in Santa Fe, Sumner reported to Washington:

We saw no Navajos till we passed Canon Bonito, when one of them then came to my camp, and I sent a message by him to the two chiefs who were in that vicinity, that if they would come to me with three of their head men, that I would talk with them. They, however, refused, and in pursuance of the instructions of the War Department, I ordered all Navajos to be fired upon, whenever they were seen hovering about. We killed and wounded a number of them, but I cannot say how many. They never faced us, or gave us an opportunity to inflict upon them any signal chastisement. . . . My object was to attack the Indians, if I found them in Canon Chelle, and destroy their crops. In this I was disappointed, there being no Indians in the Canon, and but very little cultivation there. . . . This Canon is from 100 to 200 yards

wide, and with perpendicular sides of rocks, from 200 to 600 feet
high. After we proceeded about four miles, a party of Indians
on top of the rocks on the left bank, commenced an attack on our
column with a few muskets, and arrows, and by rolling down
stones. Attempts were made to scale the rocks to attack them . . .
but it was found utterly impracticable. . . .[62]

Like Doniphan's expedition of 1846, and Washington's expedition of 1849, Sumner's expedition of 1851 failed to bring
about any important change of attitude or conduct on the
part of the Navajos in their relationship toward the American government. In an attempt to learn why the Navajos persistently refused to cooperate, the Indian Service arranged for
a tribal council at Jemez Springs, on January 27, 1852. The
place chosen for the meeting was a hundred miles away from
the interior of the Navajo country, and as a result the attendance at the council was small. Those attending had no authority to represent anyone but themselves and possibly their
immediate relations. Reporting on the council and the results accomplished, Indian Agent J. Greiner wrote to Governor Calhoun on January 31, 1852:

The names of the chiefs present were Armijo, Rafael Chavez,
Luke Lea, Black Eagle Barbon and Jose Miguel. One of the
young chiefs had not yet received a name—and as he was over six
feet high and of a fine commanding figure, he was christened
Winfield Scott with which name he appeared to be delighted.
Armijo was the principal speaker and the big chief of the Navajos.
After all were seated in Council he said, "I have been a Captain
ever since I was a young man. I have come to tell my Great
Father that my people wish to live in peace and quiet. We wish
to cultivate the soil as our fathers did before us—to have the
water run through our acequia so that we may irrigate our lands
—we do not wish to be molested—we have to depend upon our
finger nails and our toe nails for support.

Chief Armijo told a woeful story of poor crops and of Mexican depredations:

By the labor of our own hands we wish to raise our own crops
—and like the Sun we wish to follow the course of nature. The
bows and arrows we carry are to shoot game with, the deer, the
antelope and the rabbit. But little rain fell from the clouds

last year—our crops failed—and our young men have to support our families by hunting. I have lost my grandfather and two other members of my family who were all killed by Mexicans. I have never sought revenge—my hair is beginning to get gray—I wish to live in peace with everyone—I want to see my cattle and horses to be well grazed and my sheep to be herded safely—and to get fat—which can never be done while my people are at war. We like the Americans—we have eaten their bread and meat and smoked their tobacco—the clothing they have given us has kept us warm in the cold winter and the snow—with the hoes they have given us we will cultivate our land. We are struck dead with gratitude. I am now before you—you can all see me. My name is well known everywhere—my people are better dressed than I am myself—and I am ashamed to appear before you so poorly clad—I wished you to see me just as I am—to tell you I can plant corn and wheat—and raise food for my people to eat. If the Lord will supply us with plenty of clouds—we shall walk about our lands and feel satisfied. . . .

Agent Greiner told Chief Armijo at the Jemez Springs Council that the people living in the Rio Abajo complained that the Navajos had captured their children and taken them away, and stolen their stock; that they could not work their fields for fear of the Navajos. Chief Armijo defended his people against the charges:

My people are all crying in the same way. Three of our chiefs now sitting before you mourn for their children—who have been taken from their homes by the Mexicans. More than two hundred of our children have been carried off and we know not where they are. The Mexicans have lost but few children in comparison with what they have stolen from us. Three years ago they took from my people nearly all their horses. Two years ago my brother lost seven hundred animals. How shall we get them again? My people are yet crying for the children they have lost.[63]

The Council at Jemez Springs, as had been the case with many meetings held previously with Navajos, failed to produce any significant results. Bad men of the tribe, refusing to heed the warnings, went their way as before, robbing and pillaging at every favorable opportunity. On April 9, 1852, Governor Calhoun sent to Colonel Sumner, then in Albuquerque the latest information he had about Indian troubles and told him of his own illness which had confined him to bed in Santa Fe for weeks. The Governor told Sumner in his letter that he was so weak he could sign official papers only with the greatest difficulty, with "head and back propped up by pillows." Although desperately ill, Calhoun was anxious to carry on his official duties.

You are perhaps previously advised of my weak, feeble, and almost hopeless condition. I feel that I am speaking almost as a dying man. Yet I feel desirous of doing all in my power to promote the public weal. But for my utter inability, I should mount my horse and visit you at your quarters. For the past four weeks I have been unable to stand alone without assistance, and for the same period have been confined to my bed.

Three days after he had written to Colonel Sumner, scouts awakened Governor Calhoun at midnight (on April 12, 1852), to tell him of a whispered rumor in Santa Fe that Mexicans and Indians, seeking revenge, had determined to start a "revolution" against the Americans. Mindful of the Taos rebellion of 1847, in which his predecessor, Provisional Governor Charles Bent, had lost his life, Calhoun visualized the possibility of a like fate for himself and family. Arising from his sick bed, Calhoun posted armed guards about the house, and then wrote a message to Senator William C. Dawson,[64] a personal friend, in Washington, informing him of the rumor of a plot, which was sent by stage from Santa Fe to Independence, Mo., and telegraphed from there to Washington.

Reconciled to the inevitable fact that death was shadowing him, Governor Calhoun left Santa Fe for Washington on May 29, 1852, hoping to report to his superiors in Washington, and to then continue on to Georgia to die among relatives and friends. Accompanied by his daughters, Martha Anne and Caroline Louise Calhoun Love, and her husband, William E. Love, Calhoun traveled east in an army ambulance, drawn by four mules. The party was escorted from Santa Fe by a detachment of soldiers. Always a forehanded man, Calhoun anticipated that death might overtake him on the way, and carried a coffin with him as baggage. The Post Surgeon at Fort Union tried to persuade Calhoun to abandon his journey, and remain there for treatment. But the governor, shaking his head feebly, ordered the driver to whip up his mules and be off. The army, in every way possible, helped to accelerate Calhoun's journey over mountain and plain. Fresh mules and drivers were quickly provided at each relay station. Soldiers escorted the ambulance from military post to military post to protect the ailing governor and his family from possible attack by marauding Indians. Death won the race against time. James S. Calhoun, first governor of the Territory of New Mexico, died near Independence, Missouri, either in the last days of June or the first days of July in 1852. His body was laid out in his coffin, "painted inside and out, overlaid with layers of charcoal," and buried on the prairie. Like that of Moses, Governor Calhoun's burial place, far from his Georgia home, is not known to any man.[65]

CHAPTER SIX

The Outlook Was Bleak in '52

DURING THE BRIEF INTERVAL between Governor Calhoun's departure from New Mexico, and the arrival of William Carr Lane, his successor, Colonel E. V. Sumner administered both civil and military affairs.[66] On May 27, 1852, two days before Calhoun left Santa Fe for the east, Colonel Sumner wrote a long letter to Secretary of War C. M. Conrad, recommending that the government turn New Mexico back to the Mexicans and Indians. Sumner's pessimistic, Jeremiah-like letter held out no hope for New Mexico, either at the time or in the fore-seeable future:

Believing that at some leisure moment you would like to see an exact picture of New Mexico, I have drawn up this paper. The facts cannot be controverted; some of the inferences may be questioned, but I think every one of them can be maintained. It may be well to premise that I consider it certain that some radical change must and will be made, in the government of this territory, sooner or later; that the people of the United States will not consent to bear this burden, endlessly, without receiving the slightest return, and without even the possibility of bettering the condition of this people.

Sumner made definite recommendations:

I would submit the following project: Place the territory in the same relation to the government of the United States that it held towards the Mexican government before the war. Withdraw all the troops and civil officers, and let the people elect their own civil officers, and conduct their government in their own way, under the general supervision of the government. It would probably assume a similar form to the one we found here in 1846, viz: a civil government, but under the entire control of the governor. This change would be highly gratifying to this people and I believe they would cheerfully pledge themselves never to ask for any further aid from the United States than the same appropriations that were granted to the other Territories. There would be a pronunciamento every month or two, but these would be of no consequence, as they are very harmless when confined to Mexicans alone.

The government was spending money in New Mexico without hope of return, as Sumner saw it:

With all the economy that can be used, and exertions in agriculture and the like, so long as we hold this country, as we do now, it must be a very heavy burden to us; and there never can be the slightest return for all this outlay—not even in meliorating the condition of the people; for this distribution of public money makes them more idle and worthless. There is no possibility of any change for the better. Twenty—fifty years hence—this Territory will be precisely the same as it is now. There can never be an inducement for any class of our people to come here whose example would improve this people. Speculators, adventurers, and the like, are all that will come, and their example is pernicious rather than beneficial.

Civil government had failed, felons of all kinds were running at large, according to Sumner:

No civil government, emanating from the government of the United States, can be maintained here without the aid of a military force; in fact, without it being virtually a military government. I do not believe there is an intelligent man in the Territory who is not, at the present time, fully sensible of this truth. All branches of this civil government have equally failed—the executive, for want of power; the judiciary, from the total incapacity and want of principle in the juries; and the legislative, from want of knowledge—a want of identity with our institutions, and an extreme reluctance to impose taxes; so much so, that they have never even provided the means to subsist prisoners, and, consequently, felons of all kinds are running at large.

Government money was New Mexico's mainstay in the early fifties, according to Sumner:

The truth is, the only resource of this country is the government money. All classes depend upon it, from the professional man and trader down to the beggar. Before we took the country, a considerable part of the population earned a scanty livelihood at the mines; but this work was abandoned directly when the government money was scattered broadcast among them. These mines are not productive, and never can be made so, in comparison to the inexhaustible mines of California; but a part of this people managed to earn at them a few shillings a day, and that supported them. They will be obliged to return to this work again, as the only means of living, while the rest must get from the soil the few articles that are necessary for their subsistence. There can never be any profitable agriculture in this country. There is but a very small part of it that is arable land; the valleys of the few streams comprise the whole of it; and much of this cannot be cultivated, owing to the efflorescence of salt; and the residue requiring such labor kind of irrigation and cultivation that corn cannot be raised here for less than a dollar a bushel. But, even if it could be raised as cheap as it is in Missouri, there would be no market for it beyond the wants of the government; and no agricultural product would ever pay transportation from this remote country.

Regarding the relationship between the New Mexicans and the Indian tribes, Sumner wanted the government to adopt a neutral, if not an entirely indifferent attitude:

With regard to the protection of these people from the Indians, they would have the same that was extended to them by the Mexican government—that is to say, permission to defend themselves. Besides, they would be much better armed than they have ever been before, and the Indians would have more respect and fear for them. There is, too, a growing disposition on the part of the Indians to remain at peace and support themselves by cultivation. The Navajos and Utahs are perfectly quiet, and the Apaches, the only hostile bands now in the Territory, have committed no depredations within the last month, and have sent in word that they wish to make peace.[67]

Arms and ammunition would be given to the New Mexicans for use against the Indians, according to the Sumner plan:

If the Mexicans should act justly by the Indians, I think there would be no difficulty; but if they did not, and war should ensue, the Mexicans would always steal from the Indians quite as much as the Indians would steal from them, and thus they would be no losers in the end. On this point, too, I would remark that if this Territory was erected into a state, it would be expected that the people would take care of themselves, and they would be no better able to do it than they are now. Again, why are we bound to give any more protection to this Territory than we give to Oregon and Utah? These people are obliged to defend themselves against the Indians. Why not this people do the same? I should think it would be well to give the Mexicans a liberal allowance of arms and ammunition, especially as there is a large supply here that is not worth transporting back.

Few Americans, exclusive of adventurers, would remain in New Mexico, in Sumner's opinion:

It would be impossible for our troops to remain here with Mexican civil officers, for we should have to interpose in their squabbles, which would make them serious matters. There would be no danger of any attempt to throw off our sovereignty; the authorities (and they would soon be absolute) would be too much interested in getting appropriations; besides this, they would know that we could annihilate them at any time. There would be very few Americans remain in the Territory; the number has already diminished very much. They are nearly all adventurers, not intending to reside here permanently; and, when they can no longer make money, they will soon leave. At all events, the few that would remain could take care of themselves quite as well as those did who were here before the war. It may be thought that the abandonment of the new posts so recently established would be a great sacrifice; but it would not be so. They were built entirely by the troops, and cost but little, and labor was beneficial to the command. If there are any obligations upon us, either by treaty or promise, to give more protection to this Territory than to the others (of which I am not aware) I have no doubt but that this people would gladly absolve us from all such obligations to have the government placed in their hands. With regard to the execution of the eleventh article of the treaty of Guadalupe Hidalgo, the advance of two posts to the western limits of Texas (on the Rio Grande) would give all the protection to the inhabitants of Mexico that can be given by troops stationed in this Territory.[68]

Sumner's report to the War Department expressed the viewpoint of many military men of the day who had seen service in New Mexico. The report was pigeonholed in Washington, as Sumner perhaps believed it might be, and he was transferred to duties in other parts of the country where he would be free from concern about Mexicans and Indians. Important men in government in Washington were well aware, without being told by Sumner, that conditions in New Mexico, particularly concerning Indians, were midway between chaotic and appalling.

When the United States acquired New Mexico from Mexico, it inherited as one of the by-products of acquisition a "wild Indian" problem of major proportions. Spain had grappled with it intermittently during the long night of Spanish rule, and Mexico, Spain's successor in government of New Mexico, tried unsuccessfully to solve the problem at various times from 1821 to 1846. Spanish and Mexican administrations had tried in many ways to subjugate the Indians. Attempts to Christianize them had ended in failure. Resort to sword and gun had not accomplished satisfactory results. The Mexican government, as a last resort, agreed to pay the Apaches a subsidy, or bounty, if they would agree to keep the peace. All of the attempts to control the wild Indians met with eventual defeat. Missionaries, energetic and fearless in attempting to save souls for the Heavenly Kingdom, never accomplished much, either under Spanish or Mexican regimes, toward converting either Apache or Navajo. The missionaries finally abandoned any hope of Christianizing either tribe, and left them to their fate.[69]

The wild tribes believed, and their belief had substantial support under moral law, that they owned vast areas of territory in New Mexico. The fact that New Mexico might be governed as of any particular time, by Spain, Mexico, or the United States, did not lessen or impair, in the opinion of the Indians, the validity of their rights. The wild Indians generally looked upon the white settlers as squatters and usurpers. Some of them believed they were justified in raiding the settlements, and in carrying away any booty that might be procurable, whether grain, livestock or human beings. The Navajo Indians looked upon the settlements and Pueblos in the Rio Grande valley as a particularly happy hunting ground. Although sparsely settled, the valley, for a distance of a hundred and fifty miles north and south of Albuquerque, contained hundreds of farms and a number of large ranches. The Navajos raided the defenseless settlers almost at will. They were particularly active and wicked in the spring of 1843, during which they killed several settlers, carried a number of women and children into slavery, and drove hundreds of cattle and sheep to their own country. The victims of the raids complained to the Mexican authorities, asking for help and protection. The Mexican officials gave assurance of prompt punishment of the raiders, but failed to accomplish anything of importance in the way of reprisal. Padre Antonio Jose Martinez, the Curate of Taos, decided to come to the aid of the settlers by publicizing their grievances. He wrote a report to General Antonio Lopez de Santa Anna, President of Mexico, on Nov. 28, 1843, entitled "An Exposition of Things in New Mexico." [70] Copies were distributed to men of influence throughout the Department. Martinez pointed out in the "exposition" that the Mexican government (reversing the policy that had been pursued by Spain), had permitted foreigners to build forts on the Napeste (the Arkansas) and Chato rivers, to the detriment of the "wild Indian tribes of the Department of New Mexico." As Padre Martinez observed the situation, the Indians, as the result of the Mexican government's ineptitude, "had fallen into a miserable condition," and had become thieves and robbers. Not only had the Indians robbed the settlers, Martinez complained, but Indian tribe had resorted to stealing from Indian tribe. Buffalo hunting, which had furnished a plentiful supply of meat for the Indians for generations, was now almost a thing of the past.

The Indians had deteriorated morally, in the Padre's opinion, because avaricious traders in the plains country to the east of New Mexico, had taken advantage of their craving for intoxicating liquor, and had encouraged them to commit crimes of theft and murder. The entire problem, complex and of great detriment to the Indian, was explored and analyzed by Martinez, undoubtedly the best informed man of his day in New Mexico:

At the time of the Spanish rule the foreigners from North America were not allowed to erect forts and establish commercial relations with the North American Indians, as the Spaniards were jealous that, under this pretext, they might cause some troubles with the Indians; but the liberality of our government allowed them to build such forts since the year 1832, near the shores of the Rio del Napeste, del Rio Chato, and near other intermediate places between the plains inhabited by the Indians. But besides the useful and necessary articles, the traders sold the Indians also liquors and ardent spirits, which were prohibited. The result was that these Indian nations became extremely demoralized, and were prompted to greater destruction of buffaloes, in order to satisfy their appetite for strong drinks, which they obtained in exchange. They also made raids in our Department of New Mexico, in order to steal cattle which were bought of them by the proprietors of these forts, thus encouraging and inducing the idle and ill intentioned ones among us to follow their example, and become cattle robbers; selling their booty to the inhabitants or proprietors of the forts.

Giving Santa Anna the background of the New Mexico Indians, Martinez suggested methods for their advancement:

Although the vast uncultivated fields of New Mexico are deserted, they were once occupied by these wild nations, and it was formerly observed that, at a time anterior to the Mexican empire, they were inhabited by an intelligent, numerous and industrious people, the aborigines of our republic. It is well known that, from time immemorial, these tribes subsisted and maintained themselves by hunting the buffalo, the deer and other animals, in the same manner now followed by the Indians of the north and east; also by pillage, committing depredations sometimes against each other, and often uniting against us. It is a true and notorious fact that the wild tribes dwelling in the vicinity, as well as in the different parts of this department of New Mexico, live by the produce of the chase and robberies, since they neither cultivate the lands nor raise cattle, which is done only by the Navajos, unfortunately the most ferocious and the most faithless in their treaties of peace, whenever they happen to make any. This tribe is the only laborious one in raising stock, in agriculture and in various other industries. Regularly, however, they wander to make invasions in the country and wage war against our people. The time employed in these raids is necessarily lost to labor; the fields left uncultivated do not produce enough for their maintenance, and the result is that, unable to live on the production of the soil alone, they have recourse to pillage also.

Buffalo hunting in 1843 was a hazardous occupation:

It is a fact that the various species of deer and other game which formerly roamed the plains in great quantity, throughout the entire country north, crossing the east to the south, have diminished to some extent. In different parts of the semi-circle which runs across the south, passing through the west, the buffalo seem to have almost disappeared in those localities, where, at first they were thought to be inexhaustible, and multiplying under the special dispensation of the Almighty. But the present state of things shows this to be true, and is corroborated by travelers, and also by Indians, who are compelled to go further than heretofore, and remain sometimes two months without bringing any dry meat, which formerly was obtained in large quantities.

Millions of buffalo calves were lost each year, in the Padre's opinion, because the cows were slaughtered in the breeding season:

Now they encounter the same difficulties, but stay away four or five months, and not only return exhausted, after traveling over vast extent of ground, but even without their horses, and frequently without anything at all. This is further affirmed by the settlers residing in the different parts of the north, who bring with them a great quantity of all sorts of articles to exchange for buffaloes, and thus form a traffic very beneficial in various ways to the Indians, obliging them to extend the hunt for the animals for a greater return, in order to sustain themselves, and to obtain the articles sold by the traders. Urged by this necessity, there is no such limitation to the destruction of the buffaloes as is observed by the economy of the different nations, which at certain periods forbid and limit the hunting season; in this manner protecting these animals, and the most precious, which are breeding in the spring, though the latter are not even spared, and thus causes the loss of millions of calves. It is easily imagined that an attack made upon a herd of buffalo cows, amounting to three or four thousand, the most part of them with calves, running away to a distance of fifty or sixty leagues, must naturally cause a great loss, if not of the totality, at least of the greatest part of the young ones, as it is proved by experience. It is certain that the buffaloes must greatly diminish in consequence and that this constant slaughter will finally result in the extinction of the species in a very short time . . . and the Indians will be all the more obliged to resort to pillage and robbery . . . not only to the detriment of the people of the Department of New Mexico . . . but to others of the Mexican Republic.

The Navajos, the Apaches, the Comanches, had committed crimes in many places, over a vast area of territory, according to Padre Martinez, and had even terrorized the people of distant villages in Sonora and Chihuahua. Martinez taunted the people of Chihuahua, claiming they had been timid in the face of demands by the savages:

Should this step be taken by our government, perhaps the evils will fall back on us; for these tribes would seize the opportunity to unite together, enter into a conspiracy against us, would then become powerful by their large number and warlike tactics, and carry their depredations and invasions even into our villages. . . . The Navajos only recently have killed men and women, brought some of the two sexes into captivity, as they did in the valleys of Lobato, Rio Colorado, and in other vicinities of Santa Fe, the capital, and on the outskirts and parts of Rio Abajo. The same thing was done by the Comanches in different departments from Paso del Norte, Carussal, and the intermediate places, Chihuahua, along the coast as far as the boundaries of Durango, and even passing there, turning round Texas, and in Texas itself. Did not the Apaches attack, rob and destroy some villages near Sonora, and commit depredations among the people in the interior of Chihuahua? The inhabitants were so frightened that they brought a proportion of the payment of certain annual pensions to obtain peace. Ah! There our arms have lost their honor, and our valiant fellow citizens have been degraded; our worthy citizens of Chihuahua, who so often desired to gather laurels in New Mexico, and perhaps retake those that fell from the hands of the defenders of its streets and houses, killed by that most vile mob, the Apaches. . . .

Padre Martinez pointed the way by which the savages might be induced to live in a civilized world:

There is no other way, in my opinion, except to induce these Indian tribes to live in civilized society, to cultivate lands, to exercise various arts or industries, to raise cattle and to adhere to the rest of the institutions belonging to the system of government adopted by our republic for this multitude of barbarous nations. . . . I do not desire to intrude, but simply to propose the idea that the deference and gratitude due to the high privilege which directs free speech, and as it becomes a country-loving citizen. . . . It is evident that the Indians of New Mexico, with their nature, although belonging to the same human species, but with all the want of education, dragging a vagrant and uncertain life, urgently require the creation among them of a feeling of self respect, a love of order, and a desire to have their actions governed by ideas other than that of cruelty, since they have neither honor, decency nor conscience, and only consider as superior those that are the bravest and most skillful to kill—their enemies as well as others.[71]

The Padre Martinez report of 1843 addressed to Santa Anna, was destined to be of only temporary importance. Within three years after it had been published, responsibility for behavior of the wild Indians of New Mexico had been transferred from Mexico to the United States.

Provisional Governor Charles Bent, long time resident of New Mexico under Mexican rule, wrote a report on the wild Indians to Commissioner William Medill on Nov. 10, 1846, some two months after being designated as governor by General Kearny, and a few weeks before he was murdered by the Indians in Taos.[72] Governor Bent told Commissioner Medill that some 40,000 Apaches, Navajos, Utes and Comanches roamed about New Mexico. He recommended, among other things, the building of stockade forts in the country where the Utes and Navajos roamed, to hold those tribes in check, and urged the building of a fort on the Arkansas river to protect Missouri-New Mexico commerce. Bent told Medill, as Padre Martinez had told Santa Anna, that the State of Chihuahua paid a bounty to the Apaches to minimize raiding:

The Apaches or Jicarillas, a band of about 100 lodges, or 500 souls, have no permanent residence, but roam through the northern settlements of New Mexico. They are an indolent and cowardly people, living principally by thefts committed on the Mexicans, there being but little game in the country through which they range, and their fear of other Indians not permitting them to venture on the plains for buffalo. Their only attempt at manufacture is a species of potter's ware, capable of tolerable resistance to fire, and much used by them and the Mexicans for culinary purposes. This they barter with the Mexicans for the necessaries of life, but in such small quantities as scarcely to deserve the name of traffic. The predatory habits of these Indians render them a great annoyance to the New Mexicans. The Apaches proper range through the southern portion of this Territory, through the country of the Rio del Norte, and its tributaries, and westward about the head waters of the river Gila. They are a warlike people, numbering about 900 lodges and from 5,000 to 6,000 souls; know nothing of agriculture manufactures of any description, but live almost entirely by plundering the Mexican settlements. For many years past they have been in the habit of committing constant depredations upon the lives and property of the inhabitants of this and the adjoining provinces, from which they have carried off an incredible amount of stock of all kinds. The only article of food that grows in their general range is the maguey plant, and that spontaneously and in very small quantities. Several bands of the Apaches have for some years past received a bounty of so much per head per diem from the government of the State of Chihuahua, with the object of inducing the Indians to cease their depredations, but without having the desired effect.

The Navajo Indians, according to Bent, had large herds of sheep and cattle, acquired in their raids on the settlements:

The Navajos are an industrious, intelligent and warlike tribe, who cultivate the soil and raise sufficient grain and fruits of various kinds for their own consumption. They are the owners of large flocks and herds of cattle, sheep, horses, mules and asses. It is estimated that the tribe possesses 30,000 head of horned cattle, 500,000 head of sheep, and 10,000 head of horses, mules and asses, it being not a rare instance for one individual to possess 5,000 to 10,000 sheep and 400 to 600 head of other stock. Their horses and sheep are said to be greatly superior to those raised by the New Mexicans. A large portion of their stock has been acquired by marauding expeditions against the settlements of this Territory. They manufacture excellent coarse blankets and coarse woolen goods for wearing apparel. They have no permanent villages or places of residence, but roam over the country between the river San Juan on the north and the Gila on the south. The country between these two rivers is about 150 miles wide, consisting of high table mountains, difficult of access, and affording them as yet effectual protection against their enemies. Water is scarce and difficult to be found by those not acquainted with their country, affording another natural safeguard against invasion. Their numbers are variously estimated from 1,000 to 2,000 families, or from 7,000 to 14,000 souls. The Navajos, so I am informed, are the only Indians on the continent having intercourse with white men, that are increasing in numbers. They have in their possession many prisoners, men, women, and children, taken from the settlements of this Territory, whom they hold and treat as slaves.

The Utes were a hardy, warlike people, fond of hunting, but not averse to stealing and killing:

The Utahs inhabit the country north of the Navajos, and west of the northern settlements of the Territory. They number 800 lodges, and about 4,000 to 5,000 souls. Their range of country extends from the Navajo country in about latitude 35 deg. to 40 deg. north. Their range of country is very mountainous and broken, abounding in deer, elk, bear, and other wild game, which serve them for food and raiment. They are a hardy, war-like people, subsisting by the chase. Several bands of them have been carrying on a predatory war with the New Mexicans for the last two years, and have killed and taken prisoners many of the people, and driven off large amounts of stock. Since General Kearny's arrival, these Indians have sued for peace, and measures are now being taken to effect a permanent treaty.

Plains Indians, friendly to New Mexicans, wandered in and out of New Mexico, according to Bent. For years the Comanches, ranging east of the New Mexico mountains, were at peace with New Mexicans, but carried their hostilities far to the south in Mexico:

The Cheyennes and Arapahoes range through the country of the Arkansas and its tributaries, to the north of this Territory. They live almost entirely on the buffalo, and carry on a considerable trade with the Americans and Mexicans in buffalo robes, for which they obtain all the necessaries not derived from the buffalo. They are a roving people, and have for many years been on friendly terms with the New Mexicans. The Arapahoes have about 400 lodges, or 2,000 souls; the Cheyennes, 300 lodges, or 1,500 souls.... The Comanches range east of the mountains of New Mexico—a numerous and warlike people, subsisting entirely by the chase. The different bands number in all about 2,500 lodges, or 12,000 souls. They have been at peace for many years with the New Mexicans, but have carried on an incessant and destructive war with the states of Chihuahua, Durango and Coahuila, from which they have carried off and still holds as slaves a large number of women and children, and immense herds of horses, mules and asses.

Concerning the construction of forts to fight off Indians, Bent said:

I deem it highly necessary to establish stockade forts in the Utah and Navajo countries, with sufficient troops to keep these Indians in check, and from continuing their long accustomed inroads in this Territory. One should also be established at some suitable point on the Arkansas River, for the purpose of protecting travelers between this Territory and Missouri and the settlements that may be extended in that direction from the Indians of that vicinity. Another establishment of that kind will be required in the southern part of this territory, to serve as a safeguard against both the Apaches and Mexicans on the frontiers of the adjoining Mexican states, who it may be confidently expected, will continue to make inroads on this Territory from that quarter for many years to come.[73]

Hugh N. Smith, New Mexico's intelligent and energetic unrecognized Delegate to Congress, then in Washington, wrote a letter on March 9, 1850, to Commissioner of Indian Affairs, Orlando Brown, explaining the differences between Pueblo Indians, and Comanches, Apaches, Utes and Navajos. Apparently a born promoter, Smith suggested that tribal delegations be sent to Washington for the purpose of impressing them with the nation's might and power:

A very desirable effect might be produced upon some of the wild tribes of Indians by sending a delegation from each tribe to Washington City. By allowing the tribes themselves to select some of their principal chief men for this visit, you would secure to those distant savages some idea of the strength and power of the government, a correct knowledge of which would induce a greater disposition to enter into formal stimpulations, and secure a better faith in the execution and observance of their treaties.

Hugh Smith believed, however, that only military might would curb the Indians:

Allow me to remark that neither superintendents, agents, nor formal contractors, nor commissioners, can be effective without the presence and cooperation, for some time, of a strong and active military force; it should be well mounted, and composed of those hardy and adventurous pioneers and mountain men who are to be found upon our frontier, and should always be commanded by an officer well acquainted with Indian character and warfare. The officer commanding against these Indians should be vigilant, prompt, and energetic; undaunted by difficulties or obstacles; he should pursue them through their mountain haunts and wild retreats, and never desist until he has visited their first infractions of their treaty with severe and speedy punishment. Every day we hear of fresh acts of outrages being committed by those Indians, and our government has so long delayed its punishment that they now believe they can commit any depredations with impunity, and will hardly go through with the formality of making a treaty. A timely interference and check, imposed now by our government, might prevent, at comparatively small cost, those massacres and terrible scenes of bloodshed which will undoubtedly ensue if these Indians are permitted to go on and add to their strength by combinations of the different tribes, and which would entail upon our government a succession of military operations more protracted and more expensive than the famous Florida War.[74]

By the fall of 1850, official Washington was abundantly aware that the government, in acquiring New Mexico, had acquired at the same time a vexatious and burdensome Indian problem. Commissioner of Indian Affairs Luke Lea, gave evidence in a report dated Nov. 27, 1850, of a partial realization of the extent of the problem, and of the necessity for formulating a policy to cope with it:

The ruinous condition of our Indian affairs in New Mexico demands the immediate attention of Congress. In no section of the country are prompt and efficient measures for restraining the Indians more periously required than in this territory, where an extraordinary state of things exists, which, so long as it continues, will be a reproach to the government. There are over thirty thousand Indians within its limits, the greater portion of which, having never been subjected to any salutary restraint, are extremely wild and intractable. For many years they have been in the constant habit of making extensive forays, not only within the territory itself, but in the adjoining provinces of Mexico— plundering and murdering the inhabitants, and carrying off large quantities of stock, besides numerous captives whom they have subjected to slavery and treated with great barbarity and cruelty.

The wild Indians attacked not only the white people, but also the peace loving Pueblo Indians:

The atrocities and aggressions are committed, not only upon our own citizens, but upon the Pueblo Indians, an interesting semi-civilized people, living in towns or villages called *Pueblos;* whence they derive their name. Before the country came into our possession, they were in the habit of repairing the injuries they sustained, by retaliation and reprisals upon their enemies, but from this they are now required to desist; and thus, the duty is more strongly imposed upon us of affording them adequate protection.

Unprincipled white men, determined to grab choice lands, were already causing trouble for the Pueblo Indians:

The interference of the government is required, also, to secure them against violations of their rights of person and property by

unprincipled white men, from whose cupidity and lawlessness
they are continually subject to grievous annoyances and oppression. To prevent serious disputes between the Pueblo Indians
and the white inhabitants, it is essentially necessary that commissioners be appointed to ascertain and define the boundaries of
their lands, which they claim to hold under grants from Spain
and Mexico; and to negotiate treaties with them for the purpose
of establishing proper relations between them and the government and citizens of the United States. It is believed that by
pursuing a wise and liberal policy towards them—which their
peculiar situation indicates and invites—they will, in a few years
be fitted to become citizens, and being industrious, moral and
exemplary in their habits, will constitute a valuable portion of
the population of the territory. For a brief period, however,
they will require agents to regulate their intercourse and manage
their relations with the other Indians, and the whites.[75]

That the United States "to some extent," had driven the
Indians of New Mexico from their "cherished resting places
and destroyed the game, their only means of support," was
conceded by Commissioner of Indian Affairs, George W.
Manypenny, in his annual report for 1854. Manypenny believed that it was the duty and obligation of the government
to aid and educate the Indians:

Conventional arrangements are necessary with all the Indians
in New Mexico and Utah, except the Pueblos, for the purpose of
fixing them in proper locations, and of giving to the department
such influence and control over them as will enable it, as far as
possible, to confine them thereon, and to induce them to resort
to agriculture and kindred pursuits, instead of relying as they do
now, for support upon the uncertain and precarious supplies of
the chase; and when that fails, upon the more hazardous and injurious practice of theft and plunder. Our citizens ought to have
protection from Indian depredations, but in the present state
of things in these two Territories, this is impossible. All the military force that could be sent there could not prevent such depredations otherwise than by extermination of the Indians. Without
implements or stock, and untaught and unassisted in the art of
husbandry, they cannot support themselves other than they do.

The Indians, as Manypenny viewed it, were forced to steal
or starve:

When, as is often the case, the chase does not supply their necessities, they must steal or starve. They must either subsist to a considerable extent by plundering the white inhabitants, or they will have to be exterminated; or else they must be colonized in suitable locations, and, to some extent at least, be subsisted by the government, until they can be trained to such habits of thrift and industry as will enable them to sustain themselves. . . . That the obligations of Christian duty, as well as the dictates of humanity, demand the efficient action of the government, must be too obvious to require discussion. We have to some extent taken possession of the lands of these Indians, driven them from their only means of support. We should now aid and teach them to live without this resource, or their destruction is inevitable.[76]

David Meriwether, a widely experienced administrator and politician, succeeded William Carr Lane (who resigned to become an unsuccessful candidate for Delegate-in-Congress) as Governor of New Mexico, and Superintendent of Indian Affairs. He was appointed on May 6, 1853, and took the oath of office Aug. 8, 1853. He served until Oct. 31, 1857, at an annual salary of $1500 as governor and $1000 as Superintendent of Indian Affairs.[77]

In the last days of his administration, Governor Calhoun, in his capacity as Indian Agent, contracted to furnish the Jicarilla Apaches in 1854 with brood mares, corn, beef, salt, and other supplies. The agreement provided that it would not be binding unless approved in Washington. Assuming that the agreement was effective immediately, the Jicarillas went into camp near Abiquiu and waited patiently for the delivery of the promised supplies. The army fed the Jicarillas for weeks while awaiting advice from Washington concerning the agreement. Governor Meriwether was finally notified that the agreement had not been approved in Washington because no funds were available for the purpose. Meriwether went to Abiquiu and attempted to explain the situation to the Jicarillas. The Indians were unable to understand the government's failure to comply with the agreement. The army stopped feeding the Indians. Hungry, cold and restless, the Jicarillas faced a winter of starvation. Fearing the Indians,

the settlers asked the military for protection. Accused of stealing livestock from ranches near Abiquiu, the Indians defended themselves with the usual plea—that they were forced
to steal or die of hunger. Attempts to adjust the grievances
of Indian and settler failed. Dragoons fired promiscuously
into a group of Jicarillas, killed women and children. The
Jicarillas, armed with bows and arrows and a few rifles, retaliated by killing twenty-four dragoons, and wounding twenty-
three, several fatally.[78]

Governor Meriwether told of the difficulties with the Jicarilla Indians in a letter written to the Commissioner from
Santa Fe on Sept. 1, 1854, describing the agreement with Calhoun, and the things that had happened when the government
failed to perform under it:

Open war is the final result, and how long it may continue it is
difficult to say; but as the commanding general has a respectable
force in the field, both in the country of the Jicarillas and Mescaleros, and as the Indians have already sent a delegation in to sue
for peace, I am in daily expectation of such an arrangement, but
should peace be made, it will be impossible for the Indians to
refrain from stealing and subsisting themselves, without material
assistance in provisions, such as corn and beef, on the part of the
United States, until next year.

In his letter to the Commissioner, Meriwether told of a reported alliance between the Utes and Jicarilla Apaches. He
gave the background of the Ute tribe, and described the rela-
tionships with Plains Indians:

The Utahs of New Mexico are a portion of the tribe of the
same name inhabiting the Territory of Utah. They speak the
same language and have frequent intercourse with each other.
From the best information which I have been able to obtain, that
portion of this tribe properly under the superintendency of this
agency, numbers between five and six thousand souls; and they
inhabit and claim all that region of country embracing the
sources of the northwestern tributaries of the Arkansas River,
above Bent's Fort, up to the southern boundary of Utah Territory, and all the northern tributaries of the Rio Grande which lie
within New Mexico, and north of the 37th latitude. This country
is estimated to cover a space equal to twenty thousand square

miles, which would give about five square miles to each soul; but they often extend their wanderings beyond these limits. This is a highly warlike tribe of Indians, are well armed with firearms, and have committed many depredations upon the unoffending inhabitants of New Mexico. They do not cultivate the soil, but depend upon the chase and robbery for subsistence.

The Utes were constantly at war with the Arapahoes and Cheyennes:

A continued feud has existed between the Utahs on one side and the Arapahoes and Cheyennes of the Arkansas, on the other, for many years past; and latterly, the latter Indians, having been supplied with arms and ammunition by our Indian agents and traders, have proved more than a match for the former, and consequently, the Utahs dare not visit the buffalo regions in search of food. This, together with the fact that game is becoming comparatively scarce in this country, has induced if not constrained the Utahs to keep up their ancient custom of theft and robbery. The Utahs are probably the most difficult Indians to manage within the Territory. They are subdivided into several small bands under petty chiefs, who acknowledge no superior, and roam over a vast extent of country, having no permanent place of residence, and hence are often difficult to find. Occasionally, parties will come into the settlements and labor for the citizens for a short time, particularly in threshing out grain, which they are enabled to do with their own horses and mules; then they leave, and nothing is heard of them for months. They have a number of good horses and mules, and frequently, when hard pressed, kill them for food, but they have no other stock of any description, and are always ready for mischief, and hard to overtake in a retreat. Many of this tribe are understood to have made common cause with the Jicarillas in their recent difficulties.

The Jicarilla Apaches, Governor Meriwether reported, numbered about 500 souls, and were troublesome:

The Jicarilla Apaches formerly occupied the eastern part of this Territory, extending from the Rio Grande eastward beyond the Red River, between the thirty-fourth and thirty-seventh parallels of north latitude, but were removed, and located west of the Rio Grande, by my predecessor. A part of this band, under their chief, Chacon, were assembled and fed around a farm in the vicinity of Abiquiu, during the spring and summer of 1853, under an uncompleted compact, which when repudiated by the government, resulted in the Indians going in for robbery and theft for subsistence. These depredations have resulted in open warfare, and the Jicarillas now claim a region of country of indefinite space, west of the Rio Grande, and on the head of the Chama and Puerco Rivers, but they roam over a good many portions of the Territory. It is confidently believed that no other single band of Indians have committed an equal amount of depredations upon, and caused so much trouble and annoyance to the people of the Territory, as the Jicarillas. They are supposed to number about one hundred fifty warriors, and probably five hundred souls; they own a large number of horses and mules, and whenever there is any mischief brewing, invariably have a hand in it. It is this band of Indians, assisted by a party of Utahs, to whom we are indebted for the murder of the party of Americans having charge of the United States mail in 1851, by which eleven valuable lives were lost, and the horrible murders of Mr. White, his wife, child and servant, in 1850, as well as many other murders committed since that time. They rely on the chase for subsistence, and when this fails, resort to depredations upon the flocks and herds of the inhabitants.[79]

The government's failure to approve the Calhoun agreement with the Jicarilla Apaches proved costly to Indian and government alike. The Ute Indians, ranging in adjacent country, allied with the Jicarillas, became ugly and unruly. The army found it necessary to take the field, against both tribes, in the spring and summer of 1855. Detachments under Colonel T. J. Fauntleroy and Colonel Ceran St. Vrain pursued remnants of the two tribes, shot and killed many of them. At a joint council of Utes, Jicarillas and government agents, held August 18, 1855, a treaty of peace was signed. Like most treaties, the effect soon wore off and hostilities were resumed within a short time. Major James H. Carleton, with a detachment of the First Dragoons, was ordered from Albuquerque to Fort Massachusetts, and instructed to subdue the Jicarillas. Guided by Indian Agent Kit Carson, Carleton and his dragoons trailed the Jicarillas for six days. Surprising them at their camp near the summit of Fisher's Peak, in the Raton mountain range, the dragoons shot at the Jicarillas, scattered them, hungry and almost naked, to the four winds. Kit Carson escorted the dragoons back to Fort Massachusetts, and then returned to his home in Taos. After remaining in Taos for a few days, Carson went on a scouting trip of his own. He found the Jicarillas in camp near the headwaters of the Canadian river. He visited with them two days, on September 10 and 11, and heard their grievances. Carson reported to Governor Meriwether on September 26, 1855, that he was convinced that the conduct of the Jicarillas was chargeable directly to the trouble near Abiquiu in 1854, saying, among other things:

They consider that they have nothing further to live for than revenge for the death of their families that were killed by the whites; they have become desperate.[80]

The Mescalero Apaches, probably blood relatives of the Jicarilla Apaches, claimed ownership, both before and after the American Occupation, of a vast region of country on both sides of the Pecos river in southeastern New Mexico, and in West Texas. In the 50's the Mescaleros raided settlements in Texas and as far away as Chihuahua in northern Mexico. Southeastern New Mexico, marked "Indian country" on the maps, was to remain uninhabited by white people for many years. In his report of August 8, 1853, Governor Meriwether told the Commissioner about the Mescaleros:

The Mescalero band of Apaches roam over a vast space of country, embracing portions of the State of Texas, the province of Chihuahua and the Territory of New Mexico, though their residence is about the White Mountains, situated in the southern portion of this Territory. The country claimed by these Indians, as peculiarly their own, lies on the east side of the Rio Grande, and on both sides of the Pecos, extending up the latter river from the northern boundary of Texas, to about the thirty-fourth parallel of latitude. This will cover a space of about fifteen thousand square miles; and as they number about seven hundred and fifty souls, the country occupied by them will average, say twenty square miles to each Indian. This band of Apaches have committed many depredations upon the citizens of this Territory during the last and present years, notwithstanding the energetic

operations of the military to prevent them; but having a portion
of Texas and the Mexican province of Chihuahua to forage upon,
also, their depredations within this Territory have been less
serious than might otherwise have been expected.

The soil in the Mescalero country in the Pecos valley was
suitable for agriculture, but little of it was cultivated by the
Indians. Instead of working the land, the Mescaleros and
Jicarillas engaged in a cooperative horse stealing enterprise:

Although that portion of the Pecos Valley occupied by the
Mescaleros contains some of the most desirable land for agricultural purposes within New Mexico, still they cultivate the soil
to a very limited extent. Game is comparatively scarce in their
country; and hence these Indians subsist in a great measure by
plundering the people of Texas, of Chihuahua, and New Mexico,
by which means they manage to supply themselves with horses
and mules. It is a well established fact that there is, and for a
long time has been, a brisk trade in stolen property between the
Mescaleros and Jicarillas. One band will steal horses and mules
in its own vicinity, which are driven some four hundred miles
to the country of the other, to be exchanged for similar property,
procured in like manner. The character of the country, and the
remote distance of these two bands from each other, enables them
to carry on this traffic in most instances without detection, since
it is very practicable for the one to visit the other without passing through any portion of the settled country, or through the
country of any other tribe of Indians.

The Gila Apaches, ranging in southwestern New Mexico,
roamed for hundreds of miles in every direction. They raided
Mexican settlements in Chihuahua and Sonora. They claimed
ownership of all the land in New Mexico watered by the Gila
River and its tributaries:

The Gila Apaches consist of several bands of the same great
tribe, and derive their name from that of the river upon which,
and its tributaries, they mostly reside. They claim all that region
lying within New Mexico which is watered by the Gila and its
tributaries, but roam over a much larger extent of country, and
commit great depredations in the Mexican provinces of Sonora
and Chihuahua. The facility and impunity with which these two
provinces are plundered and robbed, has measurably saved our
own people from like visitations during the last and present

years. The country claimed by the several bands known by the general name of Gila Apaches will probably embrace an area of twenty-five thousand square miles; and these bands will probably number, in the aggregate, from three thousand five hundred, to four thousand souls, which will give from six to seven square miles of land to each Indian. . . . The whole of the Apache tribes of Indians residing within the limits of New Mexico are supposed to number from seven to ten thousand souls.

Reporting on the Navajos, Governor Meriwether told the Commissioner that they produced an abundance of corn and wheat; that they were successful livestock growers; that they wove woolen blankets which sold for from twenty-five to fifty dollars:

The Navajos are a powerful tribe of Indians, residing on the tributaries of the San Juan River, west of the Rio Grande, and east of the Colorado River, and between the thirty-fifth and thirty-seventh parallels of north latitude. They probably number eight thousand people and occupy and claim a country equal to twenty-five thousand square miles, about three square miles to each Indian. The Navajo country is represented to be one of the finest agricultural regions within New Mexico; and they certainly are very far in advance of any other wild tribe of Indians in this Territory in agriculture and manufactures. With very crude and primitive implements of their own construction, the Navajos manage to raise an abundance of corn and wheat for their own subsistence. They have numerous herds of horses and sheep, and some horned cattle and mules, and on the whole, live in a degree of comfort and plenty unknown to the other wild Indians in this section of the Union. They manufacture their own clothes, principally from the wool of their sheep, and it is a rare thing to see a Navajo uncomfortably clothed. In the manufacturing of blankets they are believed to surpass any other Indians of this continent, and these blankets will compare favorably with any other manufactured by a civilized people. Those made for ordinary use are warm, strong and durable; but occasionally fine ones are made with brilliant and durable colors handsomely blended, which will readily command in this market from twenty-five to fifty dollars each. When it is recollected that these articles are manufactured, and their farms are cultivated, by the hands of the Indians, with implements of their own construction, this people can but challenge our admiration.

The Navajos had a good many bad men among them:

Favorable as this picture is, it also has its dark side; and I am sorry that truth compels me to say, that the people of this Territory have many wrongs to charge to the account of the Navajos. The bright side of the picture which I have drawn does not equally apply to all of this tribe; they have bad men among them, who cannot and will not be restrained. Such men pay but little regard to the Eighth Commandment, which enjoins upon us not to steal; on the contrary, they have heretofore stolen the stock and cattle of their more civilized neighbors. But, under the judicious management of agent Dodge, who has taken up his abode among these Indians, we have had but little cause to complain of them during the present year. There is one band of Navajos who have separated themselves from the remainder of the tribe, and removed eastward to the neighborhood of the Utahs and Jicarillas; and there is reason to fear that this association has been productive of no good to the first named party. Around this band are collected most of the bad men of the whole tribe, and many of the depredations committed in that vicinity have been traced to them; but, on the whole, the Navajos during the present year conducted themselves with great propriety when compared with the Apaches.

Supplementing the Meriwether report of 1853, Indian Agent E. A. Graves, from Dona Ana, New Mexico, reported on the Indians of New Mexico generally, on June 8, 1854. Graves said that the Jicarilla Apaches were a branch of the "great southern Apache tribe, dwelling principally in the northeastern part of this Territory, roaming principally between Abiquiu, west of the Rio Grande, and east of the Rio Puerco, and northeast as far as the Arkansas and the plains." Describing the Jicarillas, and their way of life, Graves reported:

These Indians seem to have little or no connection with their brethren of the south, and may, for all practical purposes, be regarded as a separate and distinct tribe. They live contiguous to the settlements of the New Mexicans in this section of the country. They are, unquestionably, the most indigent Indians in the Territory, which is the result of their lazy and indolent habits. They are occasionally engaged, however, in the manufacture of a species of crockery ware, which they barter to the New Mexicans for corn and other articles. With this exception they live mainly by hunting and committing petty thefts on the New Mexicans. They have been the cause of much annoyance to the citizens of the Territory, and are now in a state of open war with them and the United States government. While they are a cowardly band, they are nevertheless cruel and revengeful, never forgetting an injury, nor letting an opportunity of retaliation escape them if the chances of success are greatly in their favor.

Roaming about in six bands, each with a head chief, the Utes of northwestern New Mexico, according to Agent Graves, were a hardy and muscular tribe, expert horsemen, good shots, well supplied with rifles. The men wore their hair in long braided queues reaching to the ground. The women clipped their hair short:

The Utes speak the same language, and are characterized substantially by the same habits and manners, but occupy different localities in their country, which is west of the Rio Grande, and north of the Navajo country. The Utah is a hardy and athletic Indian, accustomed to endure much hardship and fatigue. They are brave, impudent, and warlike, and are reputed to be the best fighters in the Territory, both as regards skill and courage. They are of a revengeful disposition, and believe in the doctrine of retaliation in all its length and breadth, and never forget an injury. They are well skilled in the use of firearms, and are generally well supplied with rifles, which they handle with great dexterity, and shoot with accuracy. While these Indians use the rifle principally in both peace and war, the other wild tribes in New Mexico rely mainly upon the bow and arrow. The male Utahs wear long braided queues reaching to the ground, while the females wear short hair. The Utahs have no idea of labor, especially of agricultural pursuits, and regard it as beneath the dignity of a warrior.

The Utes raised good horses, and excelled in horsemanship:

They raise good horses, but scarcely any beyond their own wants. They are expert in horsemanship, being excelled by no Indians in New Mexico. They carry on a limited traffic with the New Mexicans in the barter of skins of various kinds, both manufactured and unmanufactured. Beyond this they depend exclusively upon the chase and the hunt for a subsistence. When this fails them, they have no scruples in plundering the New Mexicans in order to make up any deficiency, or any others who may be journeying in their vicinity. I am induced to believe that they are well disposed towards the government and the people of New Mexico. They profess pacific intentions towards both. This tribe of Indians are not wealthy, though they are well supplied with arms, and have a sufficiency of horses. This tribe numbers from six to seven thousand, and from eight hundred to a thousand lodges. It is supposed that there are upwards of five hundred warriors belonging to the different bands. These Indians dwell in a rugged and mountainous country, generally well supplied, however, with wild game, consisting in part of deer, elk and bear. All species of game, however, are gradually diminishing, and at the same time growing wilder and more difficult to obtain, as the Indians say.

The Utah Indians claimed large areas of land along the San Juan river and its tributaries. Graves raised important questions concerning title to the land, some of which remain unanswered to this day:

Some of the best land in this Territory, I am authorized to say, lies within what is known as the Utah country, on that portion of the San Juan River claimed by the Utahs, and along the rivers Rio Puerco, Pinos, Animas, Florida, La Plata and San Jose. All these rivers take their rise in the La Platte or San Juan mountains, running parallel to each other, and emptying into the San Juan, the Las Animas alone furnishing nearly one-half of the waters of the San Juan, which is second only to the Rio del Norte. The Utahs claim to be the rightful owners of this country by virtue of a continued occupancy and possessory title, extending back so far that the "memory of man runneth not to the contrary." The Mexican government, however, never recognized any title in any of the Indian tribes in and to any of the lands occupied and held by her Indians within her boundaries. But this did not, however, discommode the Indians, as they not only held all the land they claimed, but often invaded the Mexican settlements and drove back the inhabitants. It is a principle of national, as well as international law, flowing from the rights of successful war and conquest, that all the rights of the inhabitants of a conquered country, remain as they existed previous to the occupancy and conquest of the country, except the right of sovereignty, until the municipal law is changed or modified by the new sovereign or sovereign power. Congress not having legislated on this subject, consequently the right of these Indians to their territory remains as it did at the time of the conquest. But whether their title be a valid one or not, I apprehend the government of the United States will deal with them, in all of her intercourse, as though their title was good, valid, and legal, and will at no time seek to gain their lands without their consent, and without giving a fair compensation for the same.[83]

According to the Graves report, the Navajos occupied the country in the southwest, "extending from the San Juan River to the Gila, and thence east to where you meet the western settlements of New Mexico.[84]

Graves described the Navajos:

The Navajos are a fierce, intelligent and warlike tribe of Indians. They possess more wealth than all the other wild tribes in New Mexico combined. They are rich in horses, mules, asses, goats and sheep. They raise, by cultivation of the soil, a sufficiency of grain for all purposes of consumption. They are the manufacturers of a superb quality of blankets that are water proof, as well as of coarser woolens. These Indians have an excellent country, on the waters of the San Juan, and in and beyond the *canon* de Chelle, though much of the country between the Gila and San Juan is mountainous or high table land, sweeping off into sandy plains. These Indians have long been the terror of the New Mexicans, carrying on robberies on an extensive scale, and often carrying away many captives, and committing murders; occasionally extending their predatory excursions into the states of Chihuahua and Durango, in the Mexican republic.

Graves believed the Navajos could be induced to give up their migratory life and settle down to farming and livestock raising:

The Navajos are gradually perceiving, however, that peace, and not war, is their policy. Hence their predatory excursions have been growing less for the last two years, and they now profess amicable relations towards the people of New Mexico. They do not live in permanent villages, as do the Pueblo Indians, but migrate from one locality to another, as do all wild tribes of New Mexico. It is believed that these Indians could easily be induced to look mainly to agricultural and stockraising pursuits as their great source of maintenance and subsistence, and to form pueblos or permanent locations. They also claim the country held and

occupied by them by virtue of the same long uninterrupted possessory title as that set up by the Utahs.

"The great Apache tribe proper," according to Graves, had
little or no idea of work, were daring and warlike, cruel and
revengeful. Having served as Indian Agent for many months
at the Southern Apache Agency, Graves was quite familiar
with the Apaches and their characteristics. The Apaches,
with no ideas about work, and little knowledge of farming,
were almost the exact opposites of the Navajos:

The great Apache tribe proper occupy the south and southeastern part of this Territory. They traverse the whole southern
section of this Territory, including the tributaries of the Rio
Grande in that part of the country. These Indians have little
or no idea of manual labor, or manufactures of any description.
An effort was made last year to induce these Indians to commence
tilling the soil, on a farm opened on the Rio Mimbres near the
Copper mines, under their chief, Panc. This enterprise was attended with some little success, and it is believed, if this policy
were persisted in, a change might be wrought in the condition
of these degraded Indians.

Graves said the Apaches were cruel; that they plundered
far and wide. In his opinion, a stern and decisive policy
would be necessary to control their activities:

The Apaches perhaps excel all Indians in this Territory in
savage cruelty and hostile feeling towards the citizens of New
Mexico and our government. They live mainly by plundering
and robbing both Old and New Mexicans, often committing
frightful murders in their predatory excursions. They take many
captives, whom they treat with greatest barbarity, and often sell
their captives to the Comanches, where they fare better, and thus
carry on a traffic in white human flesh with that savage tribe of
Indians. They generally extend their peregrinations into the
Mexican states of Coahuila, Chihuahua and Durango, from which
states they drive off much stock, and take their captives. This
tribe is divided into several bands, numbering altogether seven
or eight thousand people. The Apaches are brave, daring, and
warlike, cruel and revengeful. There is not much game in the
country generally occupied by them. A firm, stern, and decisive
policy should be meted out by the government to these Indians,
as well as to others, when their actions make it necessary.

Graves estimated there were from twenty-four to twenty-eight thousand uncivilized Indians in New Mexico, to say nothing of the Comanches ranging along the borders:

According to latest estimates there are from twenty-four to twenty-eight thousand uncivilized or hostile Indians in this Territory, to say nothing of the Comanches all along the south and eastern borders, who are fierce, powerful and warlike. They number from ten to fifteen thousand, and have done great damage to the northern states of Mexico, driving off their herds and flocks, and forcibly carrying away their women and children into captivity and bondage. On the northern frontier of this Territory, along the Arkansas and its tributaries, considerable tribes, such as the Arapahoes and Cheyennes are to be found. These tribes, as well as the Comanches, subsist mainly on the buffalo. These noble animals of the plains are evidently diminishing in numbers, according to information received, which is believed to be reliable and authentic. These Indians carry on a considerable barter and sale in the disposition of buffalo robes. There are many traders who visit the plains for this purpose. It will thus be seen that there are fifty thousand wild and hostile Indians in, and contiguous to New Mexico.

What policy should the government of the United States adopt in dealing with the New Mexico Indian tribes? Graves asked this question and attempted to answer it:

It is a question not easily answered, but is pregnant with embarrassment and fraught with difficulty. Nevertheless, the government will have to meet it. The sooner the better. It is daily advancing in importance. The means of subsistence of the Indians are gradually growing less each year; while the aggregate number of Indians are not diminishing, yet they seem not to be much on the increase, if any. The circle of country upon which they have been accustomed to conduct the hunt and chase is rapidly contracting. The white man is advancing with a rapid step towards their accustomed haunts, and they and the buffalo are alike driven back.... To exterminate the aborigines of the forest and the mountains is a policy that no enlightened citizen or statesman will propose or advocate. That this race, the aborigines of America, are destined to a speedy and final extinction, according to the laws now in force, either civil or divine, or both, seems to admit of no doubt, and is equally beyond the control or management of any human agency. All that can be expected from an

enlightened and Christian government, such as ours, is to graduate and smooth the passway for their final exit from the stage of
human existence. How is this to be done?

The system of making gifts to the Indians was not accomplishing much, in Graves' opinion:

The government of the United States had adopted a munificent
system of distributing annual and semi-annual presents to her
indigenous Indians, and has attempted to induce them to abandon their wandering pursuits of the hunt and chase, and to
induce them to engage in agricultural avocations as a means of
subsistence; but this humane and benevolent policy has not met
with that success which the facts and circumstances seem to have
warranted. Still, this system should not be abandoned; but, on
the contrary, it should be vigilantly and with energy pressed forward. And if nothing substantial comes out of this policy all hope
of bettering the condition of the Indian seems to be lost. The
Indians of New Mexico, when under the management of the
Mexican government, were accustomed to set her authority at
defiance, and to roam and pillage at pleasure. This we have attempted to check and stop, and I regret to say that we have been
only tolerably successful. These Indians must live; and when
the mountains and forest cease to supply them with food, they
will doubtless seek it from those who have it and if not to be had
peaceably, they will attempt to obtain it by force. No animal
creature, whether civilized or not, will perish for the want of food
when the means of subsistence is within his reach; and if not to
be had without force, it will be had with it. All history, and
man's own instinct confirm this view of the subject, and it is
justified by all the great writers on the law of nature and of
nations. To feed and clothe these Indians, either wholly or par-
tially, is an expensive operation, or to distribute annual or occasional presents among them. It is a policy that promises no
results beyond the simple fact of keeping them quiet for the time
being. As long as this policy is continued, their peace can doubtless be purchased, and they will be kept quiet, but it only post-
pones the evil day.

The Indians of New Mexico, as Graves saw it, should be induced to cultivate the soil, and their territorial limits should
be diminished:

The country now occupied by these Indians is an extensive one,
embracing several hundred miles from north to south, as well as

from east to west, with the Mexican settlements strung along somewhat in the center from Dona Ana to Taos, which makes our dealings with these Indians very expensive and difficult, and affords them ample opportunity to carry on their predatory excursions with comparative impunity. Our chances for detecting and punishing them are greatly lessened by reason of their sparse settlements and great scope of country over which they roam, which is generally rugged and mountainous, and which is a great advantage to them and disadvantage to us. This is so manifest that it only requires an inspection of the map of New Mexico to verify it. Hence I suggest the policy of concentrating and collecting together these Indians, that is, each tribe to itself, into a smaller circle. To do this involves the further policy of establishing farms and ranches in that part of their country adapted to agricultural pursuits, where the effort should be made to induce them to cultivate the soil. This should be done by degrees, and will require time to consummate it. Inducements should be held out to those who lay down the bow and arrow to take up the axe and the hoe.... It is believed that with proper care and attention, and management, the transfer of the Indians to agricultural life would be eminently successful, and would be crowned with gratifying results, and at the end of five or ten years it would prove to be most economical.... Should the military arm of the government be required to give this policy a fair trial, it should be given as far as practicable, and so much force used as might be necessary, and no more.... That the mountains and the plains will at no distant time fail to supply the Indians with necessary food is as certain as that the sun gives light at noonday. This being the case, what is to be done? That the Indians will steal, plunder, rob and murder, in order to get food admits of no doubt. If you make war upon and conquer them the same question arises, what to do with them? You will either have to take care of them or destroy them. The latter the government will not do, but will be forced to do the former.... The Pueblo Indians of New Mexico were evidently once wild, savage and warlike, as are the Utahs, Apaches and Navajos; yet the old Spanish government induced them to abandon their wild roving ways and to cultivate the soil, and to live in villages and pueblos, and they now are, and have been for many years, peaceable and quiet, and live comfortably on the fruits of their labor. May not the wild tribes of today be ultimately induced to form into pueblos, and to cultivate the soil in like manner, and thus gradually relieve the government from the charge of their maintenance?[85]

Indian agents, anxious to arrange a truce between and among warring tribes of Ute and Mescalero Indians on the one side, and Navajo, Kiowa and Cheyenne Indians on the other, held a council at the Archuleta Agency in northern New Mexico in the late summer of 1858. The agents distributed gifts to the Utes and Mescaleros, hunting knives to the men, frying pans, bright calico, red ribbons, and hand mirrors to the women, candy and knicknacks to the children. The Indians helped themselves at all hours of the day and night to beef and coffee, and listened with respect and attention to the request the agents made of them to discontinue the practice of Indian tribe fighting Indian tribe. The Utes were asked the direct question: "Would they give up fighting the Navajos?" The answer was a quick and decisive "No." The next question was: "Would the Utes and Mescaleros give up fighting the Kiowas and Cheyennes?" The answer, a bit reluctantly, was "Yes." This commitment had barely been made, when a messenger rode into the Archuleta Agency with information from Captain Duncan, of Fort Garland, that Kiowas and Cheyennes in large numbers were passing the fort on their way west to attack the Utes. The agency council broke up instantly. Without waiting for details, Ute and Mescalero Apache alike, yelled for their squaws and children, ran for their horses, started for hideouts in the mountains of their own country.

CHAPTER SEVEN

The Navajo and the Soldier

ON SEPTEMBER 27, 1858, Superintendent James L. Collins advised the Commissioner of Indian Affairs of the abortive council at the Archuleta Agency, and gave him the background of events in the Indian country, beginning with the American Occupation. A resident of New Mexico since 1825, Collins was perhaps the best posted man of his day on its Indian affairs. He had accompanied the Washington expedition into the Navajo country in 1849, and had personal knowledge of some of the incidents related in his letter. General Kearny had been inept, as Collins viewed it, at the commencement of the government's negotiations with the Navajos:

When Governor Kearny took possession of New Mexico, he found a war existing, and which had existed for many years, between the Mexicans and Navajos, and, judging from the General's promises to the Mexicans, which were often repeated, he must have considered it an easy matter to relieve them from the war, and to protect them against all further depredations from this formidable foe. He did not remain long enough in the Territory, however, to discover his mistake, for mistake it certainly was. When on a visit to the settlements below Santa Fe, with a large detachment of troops, the Navajos made a descent upon the valley of the Rio Grande, and in sight of the General's command, drove off some of his own stock and a considerable number belonging to citizens. This, together with several other robberies about the same time, caused General Kearny to order out a detachment of men under Colonel Doniphan to move against the Navajos. This movement was made in two divisions, one under Major Gilpin, which took the route to Abiquiu, and entered the

93

country to the north; and the other under Colonel Doniphan himself, which went in far south. They made an ineffectual march through the country, and finally met the Indians at Bear Spring, where they concluded a treaty of peace, the conditions of which, however, were never observed by the Indians, as they continued to murder and steal as before.

Kearny, Doniphan, Walker, Newby, Washington, all failed in trying to guide the Navajos into paths of peace:

Early in the following year, 1847, Major Walker, with a detachment of volunteers, made another campaign against them, and penetrated their country as far as the *Canon* de Chelle. This expedition also proved a failure, only serving to increase the contempt which the Indians had acquired for the American troops. The next year, 1848, Colonel Newby, with a much larger force of volunteers, made a third campaign against the troublesome foe, which like the two former, effected nothing but the enactment of a second treaty of peace, to which the Indians paid no attention, but continued their depredations at an increased rate. These raids became so alarming in 1849 as to induce Colonel Washington, who was then Governor of New Mexico, and military commandant, to take the field himself, which he did with a considerable force of regular troops and volunteers. The Colonel like his predecessors was unsuccessful. He marched through the Indian country, however, and finally met a part of them at the *Canon* de Chelle, and concluded a third treaty of peace, which like those which had preceded it, was not worth the paper upon which it was written; indeed, a part of the same Indians who were present when the treaty was signed, reached the settlements in advance of the Colonel's command and stole a large number of mules that were grazing near Santa Fe, almost in sight of the flagstaff which stands in the Plaza.

Collins described the Jemez Springs Council, and the Sumner expedition:

After this, in the winter of 1851-52, Colonel Sumner of the Army and Governor Calhoun met a large party of warriors and several of the principal chiefs at Jemez and proposed another treaty of peace, to the great amusement of the Indians. Many of them refused to consider the proposition, but finally, after an exciting council among themselves, agreed to sign and make binding the treaty made with Colonel Washington, alleging that it was previously made with Indians who had no authority to treat for the nation. But the effect was the same, murders and robberies continued to increase, until Colonel Sumner was compelled, in defense of the suffering interests of the citizens, to move against them, which he did, early in 1852, at the head of a considerable force of regular troops. They also penetrated as far as the famous *Canon* de Chelle; but the Colonel believing his force insufficient to meet the enemy, concluded to retreat, which it was thought by some he did rather hurriedly. About this time Fort Defiance was built and which for a time produced more effect upon the Indians than all the expeditions that had been made against them. Early in the spring of 1853, the late agent H. L. Dodge, received the appointment of agent for the Navajos. This was a good appointment; Mr. Dodge was well acquainted with the Indians and was able to exercise great influence over them. Depredations were for a short time considerably lessened but never entirely ceased. . . . In the summer of 1853 Colonel Sumner commenced preparations, at the request of Governor Lane, for a formidable campaign against the Navajos, but was relieved of his command by General Garland. . . . Governor Lane was succeeded by Governor Meriwether, who in council with the principal Navajos of the nation, agreed to extend his pardon for all past offenses, creating a very unfortunate influence upon the Indians, who had been told in positive terms by the agents of the government, backed by the presence of troops that they would be punished. . . . By this act, Governor Meriwether gave the Indians a feeling of want of confidence in our own ability to inflict the punishment we had promised. The Indians continued to rob as they had always done. . . . The last and final treaty was made by Governor Meriwether in 1855; but it was not ratified by the Senate, which was not important to the Indians, for they would not have observed its conditions if it had been. . . .

The Navajos held the American government in contempt, and looked upon leniency as a confession of weakness:

The Navajos, at no time since they have been under the control of the United States, have ceased their murders and depredations; and the Mexicans inform us that it has been the same for the last forty years. Their conduct has always exhibited the most palpable contempt for authority and our government, and it is time that respect and obedience were enforced. The liberal and humane policy of the department is neither understood nor appreciated by them; and the presents which they receive are

regarded as mere bribes to purchase their friendship. Their notorious bad faith has made them odious to all other Indians. The
Utahs and southern Apaches are at war with them, and the people
are ready to commence hostilities upon them, whenever permission is granted. It is no doubt true that many of the principal
men of the nation are anxious to live at peace with us, but they
have not the power to control the masses of their people, amongst
whom are those who keep up this system of plunder and murder. . . . When I met the Utahs on the occasion of distributing
their annual presents, they were anxious to make a campaign
against the Navajos, to cooperate with the troops that are now
in the field. I refused to give my consent. I am opposed to the
principle of encouraging one tribe to make war against another,
and especially to their being used as an auxiliary force by the
American troops to fight against other tribes. . . . A war already
exists with the Utahs and Navajos, but I had rather encourage a
spirit of peace than to be instrumental in adding other causes to
those which already exist, for the continuance of hostilities among
them. . . . The Comanches and Kiowas still continue to pay occasional visits to the settlements east of Santa Fe. Colonel Bonneville has ordered the troops at Fort Union to turn them back
whenever notified of their approach.[86]

Although the government was meeting with little success
in its attempts to get the Utes and Navajos to see life the
white man's way, it was meeting with a fair measure of cooperation in its campaign to improve conditions among the Mescalero Apaches. Indian Agent Michael Steck, writing from
near Fort Stanton, New Mexico, on August 10, 1858, advised
Collins of the first attempt to colonize the Mescaleros on the
Pecos River. Agent Steck's report reflected a condition of
affairs that was indeed discouraging. Drunkenness caused
much trouble. Wandering Mescaleros, under the jurisdiction
of a Texas agency, committed depredations on the San Antonio road near El Paso:

The Mescalero band of Apaches are still living in the White
and Sacramento mountains, in the immediate vicinity of Fort
Stanton, and the most friendly relations have been maintained
between those Indians and the military authorities at that
post. . . . Arrangements have been completed to start the Mesca-

leros on a farming operation. A farm has been started at the Alamo Gordo, seventy miles away. . . . During the year quarrels have arisen among the Indians from that fruitful source of evil, drunkenness, that has led to jealousies and ill feeling among different members of the Mescalero band. A part of the Mescaleros living in the southern portion of the Guadalupe mountains, belonging properly to the department of Texas, are giving us constant trouble . . . roaming over the country near Fort Davis, frequently committing depredations on the San Antonio road and in the settlement near El Paso.

The Gila river Apaches, running wild in southwestern New Mexico, were "bad Indians," according to Special Agent G. Bailey. In a letter to the Commissioner of Indian Affairs on November 4, 1858, Bailey reported that over a four-year period the Apaches had stolen thousands of horses, cattle and sheep. Although Bailey's figures seemed fantastic, he claimed that he had obtained them from United States marshals:

The testimony of all who have any knowledge of the Apache concurs in pronouncing him the most rascally Indian on the continent. Treacherous, bloodthirsty, brutal, with an irresistible propensity to steal, he has been for years the scourge of Mexico, as the depopulated villages and abandoned fields of Chihuahua and Sonora too faithfully attest, and grave doubts are expressed whether any process short of extermination will suffice to quiet him. They are not a purely nomadic race. They have for the most part, permanent villages in the mountain valleys north of the Gila, where they cultivate the soil to a limited extent, and where their women and children are beyond the reach of attacking parties. From these fastnesses they descend at pleasure into New Mexico, Arizona and northern Mexico and carry off with impunity whatever is worth stealing. A part of the Mimbres Apaches recently passed Steck's Peak with several hundred head of cattle which they had stolen in Mexico. . . . The amount of property stolen annually by these Indians is incalculable. According to the returns of the United States marshals there were stolen in New Mexico alone, between August 1, 1846 and October 1, 1850, twelve thousand eight hundred and eighty-seven mules, seven thousand and fifty horses, thirty-one thousand five hundred and eighty-one horned cattle, and four hundred and fifty three thousand two hundred and ninety-three head of sheep.[87]

Fairly well behaved during 1857, the Indians in north and northwestern New Mexico resumed their transgressions in the spring of 1858 on such a scale that Governor Abram Rencher, Governor Meriwether's successor, became genuinely alarmed. Rencher wrote to Secretary of State Lewis Cass from Santa Fe on March 13, 1858, to tell him of an impending war between Utes and Navajos:

There is a strong probability that we shall have an Indian war in this Territory and upon its borders. There has been existing for some time past unfriendly feelings between the Navajo Indians and the Utahs, two very powerful tribes of warlike Indians. This spring has been looked to as the commencement of open war. As this would greatly aggravate the sufferings of our Indian tribes, especially the Navajos, who have suffered much during the past winter from famine, an effort has been made by the agents having charge of these Indians to bring about a reconciliation. Santa Fe was fixed upon as the place of the meeting, March 10th the date. A respectable delegation of chiefs from both tribes met here on the 11th, and were in council for a day and a night, but without being able to come to any agreement. The Utah's left early on the morning of the 12th, declaring they would make no treaty of peace with the Navajos, who would not observe it in good faith. I was not present at the talk, not having been invited to do so by those having charge of the conference, but I was told there was much ill feeling exhibited, which those present were not able to appease. The Navajos are the most numerable, but the Utahs are said to be the most warlike and formidable of any of our Indian tribes. Their weapons are rifles, which they use with great skill and success. A war between these tribes would greatly increase their present ills and multiply our Indian difficulties, which in this Territory, are already very great and difficult of adjustment. I can see no bright future for this Territory without some favorable change in our Indian relations.[88]

Governor Rencher wrote to Secretary Cass from Santa Fe on Oct. 16, 1858, complaining of the manner in which the government had been "precipitated" into the latest Navajo war. Rencher reviewed two "incidents" which he contended had alienated the Navajos and caused them to be suspicious of any gesture of American friendship. One incident revolved around the shooting of an Indian boy. The other was the result of differences over grazing rights. Rencher was critical of the hot headed conduct of the army officers involved:

There is seldom anything occurring in this Territory which makes it my duty to communicate to the State Department. Except upon our western borders, the Territory has been generally very quiet. Of the origin of our difficulties with the Navajo Indians, and of the progress of the war in that quarter, the government is more properly advised through other channels. I did not approve of the manner in which we have been precipitated into this war by the independent action of the commander of the post at Fort Defiance. It seemed to me that Major Brooks should have referred the matter to the head of the department before taking such steps as were likely to result in hostilities. If the commanders of separate posts, acting under local or personal excitement, are allowed thus to involve us in war, there would be no end to Indian wars. It does not yet appear what provocation caused the Indian to shoot the negro boy belonging to Major Brooks. That some existed other than the two which have been assigned as the cause of it, I have no doubt. The attack made upon the Indians at Bear Springs was hasty and impolitic, to say the least of it. Captain McLean had been absent from the fort only for a short time, and did not know whether any adjustment had taken place during his absence, or was likely to take place; and yet Mr. Yost, the Indian Agent, tells us in his published letter that the attack was determined on as soon as they saw the trail of the Indians, and, before they came up with them. The Indian agent was present, and instead of protesting against so hasty and unauthorized movement, seems to have approved it. I fear, therefore, there has been at Fort Defiance, too ready a disposition to engage in active hostilities with the Navajos.

Rencher described the Navajo characteristics and his way of life:

Except the Pueblo Indians, the Navajos are more advanced in civilization than any of our Indian tribes. They cultivate the soil, and have large flocks of horses, cattle and sheep. The desire of gain, and often, perhaps the spirit of retaliation, make them very troublesome to our frontier settlements. They make frequent incursions, and steal and carry off the stock belonging to the Mexicans. This has been a constant subject of complaint since my arrival in the Territory, and if these repeated wrongs had been made more prominent as cause of the present war, the castigation which awaits them would have been more proper and salutary.

As subsequent developments demonstrated, Rencher predicted with accuracy the eventual outcome of the troubles with the Navajo tribe:

If the war continues, the inevitable result must be that, their flocks destroyed and their cornfields laid waste, they will become more dependent on us for support and more reckless in their marauding incursions upon our people. Col. Bonneville is preparing to push the war with all the means in his power, but yet disposed to embrace any favorable offers for peace. He thinks he will be able to bring the war to a successful termination, without calling on me for volunteers, but which he will call for in case they should be needed. In these views I heartily concur, and shall cooperate with him to the extent of the power conferred upon me.[89]

On November 29, 1858, Rencher wrote to Secretary Cass again submitting the contention that the trouble with the Navajos might have been avoided if the Indian Agent and the military had resorted to other methods:

It is probable that the Navajo war will be terminated at an early day. The Navajos have sued for peace, and a truce for thirty days has been agreed upon. Captain McLean arrived here last night with the terms of the armistice. They are not satisfactory to Colonel Bonneville nor to the superintendent of Indian Affairs. They have, therefore, added others, which I should think the Indians would agree to if they are as much humbled as it is represented by Colonel Miles, and the Indian agent, Yost. It is certain that no great advantage has as yet been obtained over the Indians. Their knowledge of the country enables them to keep out of the way of our troops, who at times capture and destroy some of their stock, of which they have a large quantity. The war, in my opinion, was unwisely precipitated upon the Indians, and might have been avoided by prudence and fairness on the part of the Indian agent. The rendition of the murderer of the negro boy was improperly made as *sine qua non*. In the armistice that is waived, the Indians alleged that the band to which he belonged has left their country and been outlawed by them. The great object now should be to obtain such an arrangement as will secure the settlements against future depredations by the Indians, and to secure the faithful observance of such an arrangement by the Navajos. Whether they have been sufficiently chastised to bring them to these conditions, remains to be seen. Colonel Bonneville desires no other terms than such as will be mutually beneficial both to the Indians and the settlements upon their borders.[90]

Provoked because of the lack of information in regard to the so-called "Bonneville war," both houses of the New Mexico legislature of 1858 joined in asking Governor Rencher for an accounting on the subject. Rencher sent a special message to the Legislature on Dec. 17 which undertook to advise the legislators of the current status of Indian troubles:

I have the honor to state to the Legislative Assembly of New Mexico that since the separation of the duties of superintendent of Indian affairs from those of the executive department, the governor of the Territory has had nothing to do, officially, with our Indian relations, either in peace or in war. When complaints have been made to him of murders, committed by the Indians, or depredations upon the property of our citizens, all he could do was to refer them to the superintendent of Indian affairs, or to the officer commanding the military department of New Mexico, that the property destroyed by the Indians might be paid for under the laws of the United States, or the Indians punished by the military force sent here for our protection. . . . Having, therefore, no official connection with the war, and no official information on the subject, I did not think it my duty to say anything to you in my annual message upon the Navajo war. Your resolution makes it my duty to submit to you whatever information I may have on the subject. . . . It appears that the war thus far has not been very disasterous on either side. The Indians have not dared in any considerable number to encounter our troops, so as to risk the fate of the war upon a single battle. A few of the Indians have been killed by our troops in small scouting parties, and some of their stock taken or killed; while the Indians have killed a less number of our soldiers, but have shown their well known character of stealing and carrying off stock belonging to the United States and to the people of the Territory. If the Indians have been castigated and humbled, as our Indian agent says they have, we ought to be glad of it, because it is what ought to be done, and, if true, has certainly been done without the effusion of much blood, and shows an humble and submissive spirit on the part of the Navajos, which has not been thought heretofore a part of their character.

Rencher indicated that the Navajos might be induced to sign still another peace treaty:

The superintendent of Indian affairs and the commander of the military department left Santa Fe a few days ago for the seat of war. . . . They will require the surrender of private as well as public property taken by the Indians during the war, and a meridian line shall be established east of which the Navajos shall neither plant nor graze their stock. A peace less favorable to us would be unjust—a mere delusion—and could not last. If the Navajos are humbled, as it is said they are, they must give some better proof of it than empty words.[91]

The relations between the government and the Indians of New Mexico deteriorated rapidly in 1858 and 1859. By 1860 the situation appeared to be almost hopeless. Writing to Washington from Santa Fe on February 4, 1860, Governor Rencher told of trouble with the Kiowas to the east, and with Navajos to the west:

The Indian depredations in this country have become so frequent and so aggravated that public excitement is very great. The mail route to the States has been in the hands of the Kiowas for the last six months; while the Navajos, having failed to comply with their treaty stipulations, are adding to the list of old wrongs other depredations and murders, almost every day. This has resulted in an angry session of the Legislature, and has produced an unfortunate conflict of opinion as to the duty and extent of the powers of some of the departments of the Territory.[92]

In attempting to get something done about the Indian situation Rencher clashed with the army:

I beg to call your attention to a difference existing between the governor of the Territory and the department commander, relative to the power of the former to authorize and direct a military campaign against Indian tribes *at war with the United States,* independent of the commander of the military.

The people of New Mexico, according to Rencher, were impatient and anxious to make war against the Navajos in their own way:

These people prefer to carry on Indian wars in their own way, as they were accustomed to under their former government. One of the first laws, therefore, passed by the Legislative Assembly, was a law to authorize independent campaigns against Indian tribes at war with the United States, under the authority and direction of the governor of the Territory. I am not aware that any former department commander ever objected to it. It appeared to me that the people of this Territory had too little disposition to protect themselves, and were too much disposed to rely upon the federal government for everything. In my last annual message, therefore, I took occasion, at the close of it, to impress upon them the duty and necessity of providing means to protect themselves. Greatly exasperated by recent Indian depredations and murders, they somewhat modified the law relative to Indian campaigns, so as to make them more practical, and to make it less difficult to get them up.

Fauntleroy, for the army, refused to furnish the home guards with arms and ammunition, and threatened to withdraw federal troops from the Navajo war:

Under this law, two companies were soon raised, and they applied to me to arm them, which I did, and applied to Colonel Fauntleroy for the necessary amount of ammunition. This had uniformly been allowed by other department commanders, but which he refused. He declared that he would not furnish ammunition to carry into execution any such law; and that, in case of a war with the Navajos, if I authorized a campaign under the law, he would withdraw the troops from the Indian country. As such an event might be disastrous to the Territory, I shall suspend any action until I can receive your positive instructions on the subject. If the President shall be of such opinion, with the governor and the territorial legislature, that such a law in a country like this is proper and ought to be executed, I wish an order for ammunition to enable me to do it; but if otherwise, I wish the President's prohibition, as nothing else would excuse me with these people for its non-execution.... With the military force in the Territory, aided by these independent campaigns, if they should be allowed, the Navajo Indians could be wiped from existence, if desired, in three months....[93]

Colonel Fauntleroy had opposed passage of the measure referred to in Rencher's letter, claiming it was a slap at the military. Fauntleroy's refusal to honor Rencher's requisition

aggravated an already tense situation. Fauntleroy addressed
the New Mexico Legislature on Jan. 10, 1856. The Legislature reciprocated by adopting a resolution praising "Thomas
T. Fauntleroy, Colonel of the First Regiment of Dragoons
of the United States Army, the gallant commander of the
present expedition against the different tribes of the Jicarilla
Apaches and Utah Indians." The resolution conveyed the
thanks of the assembly to Fauntleroy, and through him to
"the brave and gallant officers and soldiers which he had the
honor to command, for their gallant and soldierly deportment during the campaign." The resolution, commending
Fauntleroy and his men a bit extravagantly, read in part:

By Col. Fauntleroy's gallantry, brave deportment, and soldier.y
daring while traversing the snow clad heights, and breasting with
unshrinking courage the wintry storms and tempests of the north,
he succeeded not only in overtaking those savage and inhuman
forces, but in forcing them to meet his brave command in mortal
combat face to face upon the field of deadly strife, there to decide,
not only the fate of battle, but also the fate of our beloved Territory, there to show those lawless hordes that New Mexico has
her defenders, that she is not so inert and so effeminate as to permit her citizens to be robbed and murdered without visiting upon
the aggressors a just though bloody vengeance . . . through the
perseverance and gallant bravery of that officer and his resolute
command, the said savage bands of Indians have been forced to
acknowledge the superiority of our arms and sue for peace.[94]

Despite Col. Fauntleroy's refusal to furnish the ammunition requested by Governor Rencher, many influential citizens of New Mexico insisted that Territorial troops be sent
out to fight the Navajos. Rencher told his troubles to Secretary Cass in a letter written from Santa Fe on Sept. 4, 1860:

We are likely to have very serious difficulties in this Territory
by the Mexicans moving in armed bodies upon the Navajo Indians, without any authority, either under the laws of the United
States, or of this Territory. After the arrival of the Utah troops,
and after Colonel Fauntleroy had given the Governor and the
people assurances both of his ability and his determination to
chastise the Navajo Indians, the people of this country held a
meeting in Santa Fe, and passed resolutions. . . . Urged on by a

few ambitious or interested leaders, the people held a convention at this place on August 27th, and resolved to "take the matter into their own hands." They appointed officers and agreed to raise a regiment of mounted volunteers, to enter the Navajo country on September 20 in open disregard both of the laws of the United States, and of the Territory. If this movement for mounted volunteers had been made one or two months ago, when the Territory was destitute of troops, and the military commander under orders not to make war upon the Navajos, I might have assumed the responsibility of calling them out, with the hope of being approved. But now, when the Territory is full of troops, and the military commander, under orders from the Secretary of War, is organizing a vigorous campaign against the Indians, I cannot see the necessity of volunteers. I have, therefore, been compelled, under a painful sense of public duty, to resist this movement, and I feel the more embarrassed in the performance of this duty, in consequence of the favor shown it by a few federal officers, especially by the chief justice, whose high position on the bench must give him influence.

Blaming Miguel A. Otero, Delegate in Congress, for the predicament in which New Mexico found itself, Governor Rencher published a statement on Aug. 20, 1860, declaring his position on the question of participation by New Mexico volunteers in the war against the Navajos:

The delegate from this Territory made a specific proposition to raise a regiment of mounted volunteers for this Territory, which was voted down without a division. The silly speech of the delegate no doubt contributed much to the defeat of the measure, as a similar proposition, in favor of Texas, passed the same committee at the same time, but even that did not finally become a law. The delegate travelled out of his way to assail the Governor, and charged him with the responsibility of protecting the Territory by means of the militia, which he said the legislature had enabled him to do, although he must have known the statement was untrue. . . . He contended that the Governor was bound to protect the Territory with his unpaid and unfed militia, because he was opposed to the treaty of peace, and the non-fulfillment of which had brought upon the Territory all those disasters.

The Governor, having had nothing to do with making the treaty, should not be blamed for the results that followed:

Now, to a plain mind, it would seem that those who made the treaty of peace, and who provided that the military should enforce its execution, were much more responsible for the evils which flowed from it than the governor, who had nothing to do with the treaty, and who was opposed to the armistice, but not the treaty, because it was granted at the moment when the Indians could have been crushed at a single blow, under the mistaken confidence in their white crosses and professions of humility, which the Governor then believed a "humbug," and which we know now, from sad experience, was one. . . . The Delegate knew by whose orders, "the late impending and most necessary war against the aggressive and powerful Navajos was suspended, and most efficient troops transferred to Texas and the plains, leaving this territory," in his own language, "almost entirely unprotected. . . ." I leave it to the people to decide whether such a sycophant as the Delegate is worthy to represent a free and suffering people. . . . It is the second time that our Delegate has gone out of his way to assail the Governor of the Territory for the quiet but independent discharge of his public duty. . . . It was the saying of a distinguished ancient writer, that the true test of eloquence was an orator's success. But it seems to be the peculiar characteristic of Mr. Otero's eloquence that it destroys every measure he advocates, and carries every one that he opposes. How long the interest and character of this Territory are to be sacrificed at Washington by such eloquence, it is for the people who suffer from it to determine. . . .

On Oct. 15, 1860, Rencher told Secretary Cass that the Navajos were becoming bolder in their outlawry, that regular troops seemed unable to protect the situation:

Our Indian troubles continue without abatement; indeed the Navajos are more daring in their robberies than at any previous time. Not long since, they seized and carried off at 2 o'clock in the day, upwards of two hundred mules from within eight miles of this city. A company of mounted troops were sent in pursuit of them, but as usual were unsuccessful in overtaking the Indians. The volunteer forces raised in August, of which I informed you, have gone, without authority of law, into the Navajo country, leaving their own homes unprotected, while the regular army certainly does not afford the protection which is expected of it, and which it could and would do under a different direction of its powers.

The New Mexico volunteers, without authority from Rencher, and contrary to his advice, had gone out to punish the Navajos. Writing to Secretary Cass on Nov. 10, 1860, Rencher said:

I have the honor to herewith enclose a copy of the *Santa Fe Gazette* telling of the unauthorized invasion of the Indian country by the volunteer force now in the field against the Navajos. . . . These volunteers went out without my authority, and against my advice. . . . It was one of the conditions of their organization that they should not be subjected to the control of the department commander, or of the governor of the Territory, or have any communication with either of them. . . . The volunteers have penetrated, with some difficulty, into the heart of the Navajo country, taken possession of their corn fields, captured a large amount of stock belonging to the Indians, with some hundred captives, chiefly women and children . . . and are waiting a favorable opportunity to return. This information was brought back by some Pueblo Indians, who were a part of the expedition, and who brought back some five thousand sheep and horses as their portion of the spoils. It is known that Mr. Phifer, a sub-agent for the Utah Indians, made an expedition into the Navajo country, with a force consisting of Mexicans and Utah Indians, and captured and brought away a large amount of stock, and some Indian captives. These unauthorized expeditions into the Navajo country by other Indian tribes are known to the superintendent of Indian affairs, and I presume are approved by him. The *Gazette* is owned by him, and edited by the agent for the Navajo Indians. . . . It would be difficult, if not impossible, for the Governor to successfully prosecute these violations of the law of the United States, as has been suggested by you, while those who are appointed the special guardians of the Indians, encourage such violations. But for a few interested speculators, backed by some federal officers, these unauthorized expeditions would never, in my opinion, have been organized.[95]

Major E. R. S. Canby, stationed at Fort Garland (then in New Mexico), with the Tenth Infantry, was sent to Fort Defiance in August, 1860, to cooperate with Colonel Fauntleroy in fighting a campaign against the Navajos. Canby spent months in the field, trailing Navajos, negotiating with tribal chiefs, attempting to reach a satisfactory solution of the complex problems confronting the army and the Indians. Of more than passing interest is the fact that Major Henry H. Sibley was Canby's second in command. Although Canby acted patiently and persistently, and eventually signed a treaty with the Navajos, he failed to accomplish any permanent reform in their conduct.[96] In a word, Canby failed as Kearny, Doniphan, Washington and Sumner had failed before him.

The Civil War intervened and forever deferred a definite decision on the quarrel between Governor Rencher and Colonel Fauntleroy. There was little hope that the army in time of war could discipline Navajo Indians. Fauntleroy and Sibley resigned from the Union Army and fought on the side of the Confederacy. Canby was soon called from Fort Defiance to Santa Fe to become commander of the military district of New Mexico. In a matter of months, Navajos and Apaches, to name only two tribes, were to be entirely independent of military surveillance, free to commit crimes, and to escape immediate punishment, but the Indians of New Mexico were living in the proverbial fool's paradise. The time was to come, months hence, when the Civil War would be over, affording the military an opportunity to wage a campaign of retribution against them, the like of which New Mexico Indians had never witnessed. Innocent Indians, and guilty Indians, were to experience a long night of suffering, which would bring in its wake starvation, disease and death; which would mean punishment for them and their children's children to the fourth generation.

NOTES AND PROFILES

[1] No attempt will be made here to discuss the Mexican war. Hundreds of books and documents have been published in English and Spanish covering every conceivable phase of the war. In the writer's judgment the works of two men have stood the test of time — "The War with Mexico," by Justin Harvey Smith, New York, 1919, and "The United States and Mexico, 1821-1848," by George Lockhart Rives, of New York, although Rives, at times, is inaccurate in writing on New Mexico's participation in the war. For a study of the Mexican War from the viewpoint of a New Mexican of Spanish-American ancestry, see "Guerra Mexico Americana," by Benjamin M. Read, Santa Fe, 1910. For an interesting *ex post facto* exposition on the war, see President Polk's message to Congress Dec. 7, 1847, Ex. Doc. 1, 3th Cong., 1st Sess., in which he contended

that Mexico "had wantonly violated the rights of persons and property; had disregarded her solemn treaties; had failed to comply with stipulations for payment of indemnity to injured American citizens; had refused to yield to pacific counsel and the demands of justice; had refused to hear the conciliatory terms which an American minister had been authorized to propose; had involved the two countries in war under wholly unjustifiable pretexts by invading Texas, striking the first blow, and shedding the blood of our citizens on our own soil." On Aug 1, 1950, President Truman signed a resolution adopted by the Congress under which some 66 flags, guidons and other emblems captured in the Mexican War, were returned to Mexico.

2 Stephen Watts Kearny was born in Newark, N. J., Aug. 30, 1794. When the war of 1812 began, Kearny was a student at Columbia University. He entered the army as a lieutenant in the 13th Infantry, and distinguished himself for bravery at the assault on Queenstown Heights on Oct. 13, 1812. Remaining in the army after the war of 1812, Kearny served in many important capacities. In 1845 he led an expedition to South Pass, in the southwest Indian country. Fifty-two years old in 1846, a veteran with thirty-four years of army service, the then Colonel Kearny (promoted to be a brigadier general on June 30, 1846) was given command of the "Army of the West," and instructed to conquer New Mexico and California. After the peaceful occupation of New Mexico in August, 1846, Kearny went to California. On Dec. 6, 1846, he was twice wounded in action in the battle of San Pasqual. Leaving California after a bitter controversy with John C. Fremont, Kearny served as civil governor of Vera Cruz and Mexico City in 1848. He died in St. Louis, Mo., on Oct. 31, 1848, from an illness contracted in Mexico.

3 Alexander William Doniphan was born in Mason county, Kentucky, July 8, 1808, died in Richmond, Missouri, Aug. 8, 1887. Doniphan was graduated from Augusta College, Ky., in 1826, began the practice of law in Lexington, Mo., in 1830. In 1833, Doniphan moved to Liberty, Clay County, Mo., where he became prominent at the bar. Doniphan studied military tactics under Col. Albert Sidney Johnston at Fort Leavenworth, and subsequently became a brigadier general in the Missouri militia. At the head of Missouri troops, Doniphan imposed terms on Joseph Smith, Mormon leader, following which Smith and his people left that state. When the Mexican war began in 1846, Doniphan was commissioned a colonel in the United States Army, and led the 1st Regiment of Missouri Mounted Volunteers into New Mexico. The Atchison, Topeka & Santa Fe railroad reached its namesake town on Feb. 9, 1880, having followed to a considerable extent the route Doniphan had traveled over on horseback in 1846. On Aug. 5, 1880, Doniphan rode into Santa Fe on the railroad. He revisited the scenes of Occupation days and was interviewed for the *Era Southwestern* of Aug. 7, 1880, by Max Frost, later editor and publisher of the Santa Fe *New Mexican*.

4 Edwin Vose Sumner was born in Boston, Mass., June 30, 1797, died with the rank of major general at Syracuse, N. Y., March 21, 1863. Educated at Milton (Mass.) Academy, he entered the army in 1819 as a second lieutenant of infantry. He saw service in the Black Hawk war, was on General Kearny's staff with the Army of the Occupation in 1846, and became a general officer in the Mexican war. Sumner returned to New Mexico in 1851 as commander of dragoons, and led a campaign against the Navajo Indians in 1852. In 1861 Sumner was one of three officers assigned to guard President-elect Abraham Lincoln on the way from Springfield to Washington when it was feared that an attempt might be made to assassinate him. On April 25, 1861, Sumner relieved General Albert Sidney Johnston as commander of the Department of the Pacific in San Francisco. Sumner participated prominently in major battles of the Civil War, particularly at Antietam and Fredericksburg. While in New Mexico in 1852, Sumner submitted an official report in which he strongly urged that the United States return New Mexico to the "Mexicans and Indians."

5 After the Mexican War, Captain Angney remained in New Mexico and became active in politics. He was a delegate from Santa Fe county to the convention held on Sept. 24, 1849, to formulate plans for a territorial form of government.

6 For an account of early day trapping in New Mexico, see "Ewing Young in the Fur Trade of the Far West," by Joseph J. Hill, Oregon Historical Quarterly, Vol. XXIV, No. 1. In 1811 and 1812, Robert McKnight, Benjamin Shrive, James Baird, Alfred Allen, Michael McDonough, William Mines, Samuel Chambers, Peter Baum and Thomas Cook, employed as trappers by Auguste P. Choteau & Co., of St. Louis, were arrested for being in New Mexico without passports. They were held in jail in Santa Fe for many months, despite strong pleas to the Spanish ambassador in Washington for their release. For the official correspondence between the American and Spanish governments concerning the demand for the release of the prisoners, see "Message and Documents Relating to the Imprisonment of Certain American Citizens at Santa Fe by the Spanish Authorities in 1811-1817," in *Old Santa Fe*, Santa Fe, N. M., April, 1914.

7 Thirty Years in the U. S. Senate, Vol. 1, p. 42.

8 William Hensley Emory (cousin of Bishop John Emory of the Methodist Episcopal Church in Maryland, prominent in his day as a clergyman and educator) was born in Queen Anne County, Md., Sept. 9, 1811. He was graduated from the U. S. Military Academy in 1831, retired in 1876 with the rank of brigadier general, died Dec. 1, 1887. Emory was on General Kearny's staff in New Mexico in 1846, served with distinction in the Mexican War and in the Civil War with the Union Army. From 1848 to 1853 Emory was employed as a commissioner and astronomer in working out boundary line problems between the United States and Mexico. His services in 1853 under the Gadsden Treaty were particularly valuable. A prolific writer, Emory published "Notes of a Military Reconnaissance in Missouri and California," New York, 1848 (also printed as an official government report), and "Report of the United States and Mexican Boundary Commission" (Washington).

9 James ("Santiago") Wiley Magoffin, one of the most colorful characters in Southwestern history, was born in Harrodsburg, Kentucky, in 1799, died in San Antonio, Texas, Sept. 28, 1868. Magoffin left Kentucky in 1828, and was engaged for many years in the Santa Fe trade as a merchant and trader. Ordinarily he made one or two trips a year from Chihuahua through Santa Fe to St. Louis. Magoffin married Mary Gertrude Valdez (related by marriage to Governor Manuel Armijo) in Chihuahua in 1830. Wishing to educate his children in the States, Magoffin took his family to Independence, Mo., in 1844, and settled on a farm. Mrs. Magoffin died in Missouri within a year, leaving her husband and six children. As a result of a chance meeting with Senator Thomas Hart Benton, of Missouri, Magoffin became involved in the conquest of New Mexico. After his experience incident to the conquest, Magoffin made his home for many years in Magoffinsville (now El Paso, Texas), at which place he engaged in many mercantile enterprises. Magoffin took a prominent and active part in supporting the South in the Civil War. Magoffin's brother, Beriah Magoffin, was an early day governor of Kentucky.

10 Philip St. George Cooke (first cousin of Philip Pendleton Cooke, Virginia poet), was born near Leesburg, Va., on June 13, 1809, died on March 20, 1895. Cooke was graduated from West Point in 1827. He served for some years at Southwestern frontier army posts. In 1843 he escorted a party of Santa Fe traders to the Arkansas river. In 1846 Cooke accompanied Kearny's "Army of the West" to New Mexico, and represented Kearny in negotiations with Governor Armijo designed to effect a peaceful occupation of Mexican territory. In June, 1861, Cooke published a letter declaring that he owed allegiance to the general government rather than to his native state of Virginia, and fought on the Union side in the Civil War. Cooke wrote "Scenes and Adventures in

the Army" (Philadelphia, 1856), and the classic "Conquest of New Mexico and California" (Putnam's Sons, 182 Fifth Avenue, New York, 1878).

11 On June 18, 1841, General Hugh McLeod, in command of 320 soldiers, traders and adventurers, left Austin, under authority of President Mirabeau B. Lamar, of the Texas Republic, and traveled to New Mexico. The probable object of the expedition was to exercise dominion over New Mexico to the east bank of the Rio Grande. A secondary objective was to extend Texas trade territory into New Mexico. Members of the expedition suffered great hardship on the journey. Its first detachment reached a point near present Tucumcari, Quay County, New Mexico, on Oct. 5, 1841. A few days later a part of the expedition reached San Miguel, on the Pecos river, in present San Miguel County. Through treachery on the part of some of McLeod's men, a number of the members of the expedition were tricked into stacking arms at San Miguel and surrendering to General Manuel Armijo's forces. The prisoners, badly treated enroute, were marched to distant Mexico City, and imprisoned there. Taking pity on the marching prisoners, the women of Algodones, New Mexico, gave

them food and melons as they passed through that then comparatively important settlement. Among those captured and taken into the Mexican interior and held prisoner for seven months, was George Wilkins Kendall, a newspaperman. Born in Amherst (later Mount Vernon), N. H., on Aug. 22, 1809, Kendall died in Bowie, Texas, on Oct. 22, 1867. Learning the printer's trade at Burlington, Vt., Kendall drifted about the country for many months, earning his living setting type. Going to New Orleans in 1835, Kendall and an associate established the *Picayune* on Jan. 27, 1837. Partly for health reasons, but mostly because he sought adventure, Kendall joined the so called "Santa Fe Expedition" in 1841. No newspaperman ever had a better opportunity to write "on the spot" news about an expedition, but the difficulty was that Kendall had no way of getting copy to his paper in New Orleans. After being released from his Mexican prison, and returning to the United States, Kendall wrote "Narrative of the Texas-Santa Fe Expedition," a best seller of its day, published in two volumes in New York in 1844, and in London in 1845. The book went through many editions, and is a classic. Kendall's life was summed up by the inscription on his tombstone at Bowie, Texas: "Poet, Journalist, Author, Farmer—eminent in all; clear head, stout heart, a man of many friends, best beloved by those who knew him best." For a sketch of Kendall's life, see App. Cyc. of Am. Biog., Vol. 3, p. 513. For some comments on the Santa Fe Expedition from the viewpoint of a New Mexican, see Read's "Illustrated History of New Mexico," Santa Fe, 1912, p. 403. For comparative purposes, see "Expedition to Santa Fe, an Account of Its Journey from Texas Through Mexico, with Particulars of Its Capture," by Thomas Falconer, New Orleans, La., 1842, reprinted with letters and notes, and an introduction by F. W. Hodge, New York, 1930. See also "Kendall of the Picayune," by Fayette Copeland, University of Oklahoma Press, 1943. Hugh McLeod, the officer commanding the ill-fated excursion to New Mexico, was born in New York City, Aug. 1, 1814, died in Dumfries, Va., Jan. 2, 1862. He was graduated from West Point in 1835, and commissioned in the U. S. Army, but resigned the same year to fight for Texas against Mexico. After being imprisoned in Mexico for almost a year because of his participation in the New Mexico expedition, McLeod was released through intercession by the United States government. He served as a member of the Texas Congress in 1842-43, fought in the Mexican War in 1846, and became an officer in the Confederate Army in 1861.

12 Mora, "the first settlement we had seen in 775 miles," according to Emory, was a settlement of some 200 houses in 1846. Emory reported: "The first object I saw was a pretty Mexican woman, with clean white stockings, who very cordially shook hands with us and asked for tobacco. In the next house lived Mr. Boney, an American, who has been some time in this country, and is the owner of a large number of horses and cattle, which he manages to keep in defiance of wolves, Indians and Mexicans. He is a perfect specimen of a gen-

erous open hearted adventurer, and in appearance what, I have pictured to myself, Daniel Boone, of Kentucky, must have been in his day. He drove his herd into camp and picked out the largest and fattest, which he presented to the army. Two miles below, at the junction of the Mora and Sapello, is another American, Mr. Wells, of North Carolina; he has been here but six months, and barring his broad brimmed sombrero, might have been taken for a sergeant of dragoons, with his blue pantaloons with broad gold stripes on the sides and his jacket trimmed with lace. I bought butter from him at four bits the pound." For the day by day narrative of the Kearny expedition from Fort Leavenworth to Santa Fe, see Ex. Doc. 41, 30th Cong. 1st Sess., ordered printed Feb. 9, 1848.

13 The original letter from Governor Armijo to Colonel Pascual Martinez, written in very legible handwriting, with the well known flourish following the Governor's signature, is presently owned by Pascual Martinez, of Taos, grandson of Colonel Pascual Martinez. I am indebted to Pascual Martinez, and to Gilberto Espinosa, of Albuquerque, for permission to copy the letter, and for the English translation. It is interesting to note that four out of the ten names on the Governor's list (counting Pascual Martinez as being listed) were priests. Padre Martinez, top man on the list, became involved in a jurisdictional quarrel, after the American Occupation, with Bishop J. B. Lamy (fictionized in Willa Cather's immortal "Death Comes for the Archbishop"). Padre Mariano Lucero, pastor of the Catholic Church at Arroya Hondo in 1846, seventh on the list, sided with his friend, Padre Martinez, in the controversy with Bishop Lamy, and suffered severe ecclesiastical penalties. Don Juan Vigil, third name on the list, assumed the title of "Acting Governor of New Mexico," after Governor Armijo fled from Santa Fe. Don Cornelio Vigil, fourth on the list, was a Justice of the Peace at Taos. On Feb. 22, 1843, Vigil placed Guadalupe Miranda and Carlos Beaubien in possession of a tract of land, later famous as the Maxwell Land Grant, which Governor Armijo granted on Jan. 11, 1841, to Beaubien, the sixth name on Armijo's list (spelled Bobian), and to Guadalupe Miranda, his associate.

14 Read Collection, Santa Fe.

15 Cooke's "Conquest of New Mexico and California," 1878.

16 A province of Mexico until Dec. 30, 1836, New Mexico became a "department" on that date, and was entitled thereafter to vote for candidates to the Departmental legislature in Santa Fe, and to elect representatives to the Departmental Congress in Durango. On June, 17, 1844, when the population was 67,736 (including Pueblo Indians), Governor Mariano Martinez de Lejanza proclaimed an act of the assembly dividing the Department into three districts, designated as Central, North and Southeast, the districts in turn being subdivided into seven counties, Santa Fe, Santa Ana, San Miguel del Bado, Rio Arriba, Taos, Bernalillo and Valencia.

For a study of conditions in New Mexico between the years 1821 to 1846, see the series of articles, "New Mexico under Mexican Administration," by Rev. Lansing Bartlett Bloom, in *Old Santa Fe*, beginning with Vol. 1, No. 1, July 1, 1913, and ending with Vol. 2, No. 4, April 1, 1915. Rev. Mr. Bloom's views concerning the value of the work of the Roman Catholic Church in New Mexico under Spanish and Mexican rule were challenged by *Revista Catolica*, then published in Las Vegas, N. M., now published in El Paso. See *Revista Catolica*, Oct. 26, 1913, and *Old Santa Fe*, Jan., 1914, for a review of the work of the Society of Jesus in Mexican Provinces, and for a reference to bible reading in New Mexico under the Franciscans. For Rev. Mr. Bloom's reply to his critics, see *Old Santa Fe*, April, 1914.

For a description of men and events of the Pre-Occupation period, see "Santa Fe in 1837 and 1838," and "Santa Fe in 1846," by W. H. H. Allison in *Old Santa Fe*, Oct., 1914, and April, 1915.

For a report dated Sept. 26, 1846, signed by scores of citizens of Santa Fe, addressed to the President of Mexico, purporting to give the background of Governor Armijo's conduct during the days and weeks preceding Aug. 18, 1846, see "Notes and Documents," by Prof. Max L. Moorhead, New Mexico Hist. Rev., Jan., 1951. Included in the same article are the report of Gov. Armijo, written in Chihuahua, Sept. 8, 1846, addressed to the Minister of Foreign Relations, Interior and Police, and letters of Gen. Kearny and Henry Connelly to Armijo, and Armijo's reply to Kearny of Aug. 12, 1846.

[17] Vigil papers.

[18] Santa Fe, in 1846, as today, more than a century later, was an important capital city. The population of 1846 was variously estimated at from 2000 to 4000. Santa Fe's public square, then as now, was in the center of the town. The government administration building, called the Palace (still in use), occupied the entire north side of the plaza. Merchants and traders occupied the remaining three sides. Burro trains, carrying Taos whiskey, foodstuffs and stove wood, entered the plaza in a seemingly never ending procession. In late summer the burro trains brought fruit and vegetables to the plaza market — onions, red and green peppers, apples, peaches and melons. Eggs, cheese, corn husks (neatly tied in bundles, used as cigarette wrappers), tobacco, piñons (pine nuts), bread and meat, were the year round staples. New Mexicans loved gay music. The waltz was the most popular dance. Women of means in Santa Fe dressed quite fashionably. They wore skirts of great width and fullness, shawls instead of hats. El Paso del Norte wine, although more expensive, was preferred over wines of the Rio Abajo. Gambling, for high stakes and low, was an accepted and popular pastime. Numerous bands of sheep grazed in the hills and valleys outside of Santa Fe, furnishing an ample supply of lamb and mutton, but there was little demand for wool. A single fleece from the sheep's back in 1846 brought four cents. The equivalent of one dollar in American money was the prevailing price for the privilege of shearing the wool from one hundred sheep.

Santa Fe and its people were described in Emory's report of August, 1846, Ex. Doc. 41, 30th Congress, 1st Sess., 1848: "The population of Santa Fe is from two to four thousand, and the inhabitants, it is said, the poorest people of any town in the province. The houses are of mud bricks, in the Spanish style, generally of one story, and built on a square. The interior of the square is an open court, and the principal rooms open into it. They are forbidding from the outside, but nothing can exceed the comfort and convenience of the interior. The thick walls make them cool in summer and warm in winter. The better class of people are provided with excellent beds, but the lower class sleep on untanned skins. The women here, as in many other parts of the world, appear to be much before the men in refinement, intelligence, and knowledge of the useful arts. The higher class dress like the American women, except, instead of the bonnet, they wear a scarf over the head. This they wear, asleep or awake, in the house or abroad. The dress of the lower class of women is a simple petticoat, with arms and shoulders bare, except what may chance to be covered by the reboso. The men who have means to do so, dress after our fashion; but by far the greater number, when they dress at all, wear leather breeches, tight around the hips and open from the knee down; shirt and blanket take the place of coat and vest. The city is dependent on the distant hills for wood, and at all hours of the day may be seen jackasses laden with wood, which is sold at two bits (twenty-five cents) the load. These are the most diminutive animals, and usually mounted from behind, after the fashion of leap frog. The jackass is the only animal that can be subsisted in this barren neighborhood without great expense; our horses are all sent to a distance of twelve, fifteen, and thirty miles, for grass."

[19] Ex. Doc. 7, 30th Cong., 1st Sess. p. 30.

[20] Vigil Papers.

[21] Emory described the occasion of Kearny's attendance at high mass in Santa Fe on Aug. 30, 1846: "Today we went to church in great state. The

governor's seat, a large, well stuffed chair, covered with crimson, was occupied by the commanding officer. The church was crowded with an attentive audience of men and women, but not a word was uttered from the pulpit by the priest, who kept his back to the congregation the whole time, repeating prayers and incantations. . . . Except the governor's seat and one row of benches, there were no seats in the church. Each woman dropped on her knees on the bare floor as she entered, and only exchanged this position for a seat on the ground at long intervals, announced by the tinkle of a small bell. The interior of the church was decorated with fifty crosses, a great number of the most miserable paintings, and wax figures, and looking glasses trimmed with pieces of tinsel. The priest, a very grave, respectable looking person, of fair complexion, commenced the service by sprinkling holy water over the congregation; when abreast of any high official person he extended his silver water spout and gave him a handful. . . ." Ex Doc. 41, 30th Cong., 1st Sess. 1848. Although he attended Roman Catholic services in Santa Fe, General Kearny was not of that faith. He attended services in his official capacity as a mark of respect, and for the purpose of demonstrating in public that he meant what he had said in Las Vegas on Aug. 15, 1846, when promising religious freedom on behalf of his government. New Mexico, at the time of the occupation in 1846, was preponderantly Roman Catholic. In Las Vegas, on Aug. 15, touching on the religious question, Kearny said, among other things: "I am not a Catholic myself — I was not brought up in that faith; but at least one-third of my army are Catholics, and I respect a good Catholic as much as a good Protestant." Ibid.

22 Original Magoffin papers, Washington. For more than a hundred years writers, historical and otherwise, have intimated in their writings that Manuel Armijo, New Mexico's last governor under Mexican rule, was bribed by or through James W. Magoffin to offer only a feigned resistance to the entry of Kearny's troops into New Mexico. There is no evidence of a satisfactory nature known to this writer to support the contention. Magoffin and Capt. P. St. George Cooke chilled Armijo's enthusiasm, if any existed, to challenge the invading army, but it is extremely doubtful if they resorted to bribery of any sort. Armijo doubtless had accurate information, easily available from spies sent out from Santa Fe, of the size of Kearny's army, and its equipment, and might have decided without any suggestions from Magoffin or Cooke that resistance against the invaders under the circumstances would result in the wholesale slaughter of his soldiers, and the storming of Santa Fe, with death and injury for the inhabitants.

Of more than passing interest is Governor Armijo's last will and testament, a copy of which, made by Severo A. Baca, clerk of the Probate Court of Socorro County, on Jan. 25, 1873, was given in 1885 to W. G. Ritch, Secretary of New Mexico. Armijo died on Dec. 9, 1853, seven years and a few months after the American Occupation. A free translation from the Spanish language records in San Miguel Church, Socorro, N. M., is as follows: "Socorro, on the 20th of January, 1854, I Father Don Nicolas Valencia, hereby record in the death register the burial of the corpse of Manuel Armijo. . . . I buried him in the church. . . . He received, before his death, the Sacraments of Penance, Extreme Unction, Holy Eucharist." The date of Armijo's will is unknown, but its contents would indicate that he was not a wealthy man at the time it was executed. Carefully worded in Spanish, executed at Limitar, New Mexico, Armijo's residence, the will was quite specific in its provisions, which was a custom and legal requirement of the time. The witnesses were Pedro Baca, "Judge of Probate," and seven other "attendants," Manuel Vigil, Lupe Perea, Jose Maria Gonzales, Vicente Pino, Eusebio Romero, Juan Albino Gonzales and Vicente Silva. The testator declared that he had been "married according to the customs of our holy mother church, with Maria Trinidad Gabaldon, now deceased, from which marriage I had no succession." Some clauses in the will, taken at random: "I direct that when God shall be pleased to take me from this to the eternal life, my body be buried in my parish church, San Miguel del Socorro;" "I declare that I leave one thousand dollars for primary education for a public school at this town of Limitar;" "I declare that I leave 104 cattle, 98 mules, 4 mares, 3 horses, 3 burros, 25 hogs, a small share of sheep, I do not know the number existing;" "I declare I leave a store in Las Cruces, another store of goods at Limitar;" "I declare I own the sixth part of the Las Animas grant, and the sixth part of the Rayado grant;" "I declare that I own 10 wagons furnished for running, with eight harnesses each . . . a coach and a carryall, furnished, and five carts and 10 plows with their appurtenances;" "I declare that I own in the possession of Cristobal Armijo, one thousand and seventy dollars, which he has to pay in goods of the commerce of Mexico, also a string of fine pearls, valued at $1,000;" "I declare that after all my debts and bequests are paid, I leave as my universal heir, my daughter Ramona Armijo, & to her all my property and effects recognized in my estate;" "I declare that I appoint as full executor, Gaspar Ortiz, second Hilario Gonzales, third, Domingo Castillo, whom I pray and request for the love of God, that after fulfilling and executing this, my last will, to deliver to my heir all the amount remaining of my estate without any distinction in any emergency, that she may enjoy the same in peace during the time God shall permit her."

Of peculiar interest is the legend, told and retold for many years in and about Limitar, that General Armijo's well-to-do father sold his sheep, cattle and most of his possessions, receiving gold coins in payment. Fearful of robbers, and believing that officials might take his gold through a capital levy or forced loan, the senior Armijo, on a pitch dark night, took an aged and beloved Indian servant with him to do the digging, and buried his treasure on his ranch near Limitar. Then, old man Armijo, according to the legend, sorrowfully killed the trusted Indian servant, and buried him near the treasure. Armijo then carefully shovelled and tamped the earth to remove all evidence of a recent excavation. Still fearful that the hiding place might be discovered, Armijo caused hundreds of sheep to stampede over the treasure mound, so that all traces of its existence might be obliterated. The sheep trampled the ground in all directions to such an extent that Armijo himself was never able thereafter to locate the place where he and the Indian had buried the treasure. As a result, Armijo's son, Manuel, was obliged to begin life in very modest circumstances. To this day in Limitar, there are those who do a little digging occasionally, on the nearby *ranchitos,* hopeful of stumbling on the Armijo fortune of gold coins.

Manuel Armijo was undoubtedly a man of outstanding military and administrative ability. Having previously served two terms as governor, during which he demonstrated ability to put down revolutions and rule with the proverbial "iron hand," Armijo was appointed for a third term of five years on July 24, 1845, but did not take over the office in Santa Fe until November 16 of that year.

Dr. Henry Connelly, one of the principals in the negotiations between and among Lieutenant P. St. Geo. Cooke, James W. Magoffin, Governor Manuel Armijo, and Colonel Diego Archuleta, in pre-invasion days in Santa Fe, offered a resolution in the New Mexico legislature of 1853, adopted without a dissenting vote, expressing regret because of General Armijo's death, which read in part: "Resolved, that this Council has heard with profound regret of the death of our distinguished citizen, General Armijo, who expired on the 9th of this month. Resolved, that this Council offer the most sincere condolence to the family and friends of General Armijo and to the Territory for the loss of one of its greatest benefactors. Resolved, that in respect to the memory and distinguished services of General Armijo this Council now adjourn until 10 o'clock tomorrow morning." See Session Laws, N. M., 1853.

[23] Among those who called on General Kearny in Santa Fe, to inquire about probable policy under the American government was Jose Leandro Perea, of Bernalillo, one of the most influential men in the New Mexico of his day. He was accompanied to Santa Fe by Francisco Perea, a nephew, grandson of Fran-

cisco Xavier Chaves, one time governor of New Mexico under Mexican rule. Educated at St. Louis University, Francisco Perea spoke English fluently and served as interpreter for the conversations between Kearny and Jose Leandro Perea. In the summer of 1853 and again in 1860, Francisco Perea, joined by other owners, drove some 50,000 sheep in each year from New Mexico to California along the Gila river and across the Mojave desert. Francisco Perea was elected Delegate in Congress from New Mexico in 1863. See "Colonel Francisco Perea" by W. H. H. Allison, in "Old Santa Fe," Santa Fe, N. M., Oct., 1913.

24 Despite this assurance, the so-called "Taos Rebellion," or "insurrection," took place within ninety days after Kearny had left Santa Fe for California. For official report of Colonel Sterling Price on the Taos rebellion, written from Santa Fe on Feb. 15, 1847, see Ex. Doc. No. 1, 30th Cong., 1st Sess., p. 520. The Price report contains the contemporaneous account of the murder of Governor Charles Bent, Sheriff James W. Leal, and other officials at Taos, Arroya Hondo and Rio Colorado; and details of the resultant punitive expedition. One paragraph from Price's report: "On the 14th of January, Governor Bent left this city for Taos. On the 19th of the same month, this valuable officer, together with five other persons, were seized at Don Fernando de Taos by the Pueblos and Mexicans, and were murdered in the most inhuman manner the savages could devise. On the same day, seven Americans were murdered in the Arroya Hondo, and two others on the Rio Colorado." For a description of the fighting at Mora, on Jan. 25, 1847, see supra 530-534. Governor Charles Bent wrote a letter from Santa Fe to Secretary of State James Buchanan, on Dec. 26, 1846, advising that Colonel Doniphan had made a treaty of peace with the Navajo Indians, but that he, Bent, had "but little ground to hope that it would be permanent." In the same letter, Bent told Buchanan that he had learned of a conspiracy against the American government:

"On the 17th instant I received information from a Mexican friendly to our Government that a conspiracy was on foot among the native Mexicans, having for its object the expulsion of the United States troops and the civil authorities from this Territory. I immediately brought into requisition every means in my power to ascertain who were the movers in the rebellion . . . but as several days have elapsed, I am apprehensive that they will have made their escape from the Territory. So far as I am informed, this conspiracy is confined to the four northern counties of the Territory." On Jan. 13, 1847, Bent left Santa Fe for his home in Taos. On the night of Jan. 19, Governor Bent, Sheriff Stephen Lee, Circuit Attorney James W. Leal, Prefect Cornelio Vigil, and others, citizens and officials of the United States, and Mexican supporters of American authority, were assassinated in the town of San Fernando de Taos. On the same night, and as part of the same conspiracy, seven Americans were killed at Arroya Hondo, and two at Rio Colorado. An Indian runner reached Santa Fe on Jan. 20 with news of the Taos massacre. Donaciano Vigil took over as temporary provisional governor in Santa Fe, and issued fiery worded proclamations, declaring that the government would pursue energetic measures toword "all the refractory until they are reduced to order," as well as to "take care of and protect honest and discreet men." Colonel Sterling Price and his forces in Santa Fe went into action. The battles of Canada, Embudo, Taos and Mora followed. Provisional Governor Vigil reported in a circular from the "Supreme Government of the Territory," on Feb. 12, 1847: "The government troops triumphed over the rebels successively at La Canada, Embudo and Taos, where the victory was decisive. There were killed in the field and town of Taos about 200 rebels; the remainder begged their lives and a pardon, which was granted them; and they were left at liberty to pursue their occupations in the security and peace which they themselves had disturbed." For a comprehensive narrative of the Bent murder and Taos insurrection, with accompanying documents and letters, see "Letter from the Secretary of War, Elihu Root, Transmitting, in Response to Resolution of the Senate of June 5, 1900, a Report on the Insurrection Against the Military Government in New Mexico and California in the years 1847 and 1848," Senate Doc. No. 442, 56th Cong.,

1st Session. Root's letter contained important information taken from the files and records of the War Department. The report cites the case of Leitensdorfer v. Webb, 20 How. 176, as authority that the conquest of New Mexico by the military forces of the United States had been accomplished by the campaign of 1846.

Colonel Sterling Price, who led the American troops in the storming of Taos, was born in Prince Edward County, Va., Sept. 11, 1809, and died in St. Louis, Mo., Sept. 29, 1867. Price studied at Hampden Sidney College in Virginia, read law and moved to Charlton County, Mo., in 1831. Elected to the Missouri legislature, he served as speaker of the House in 1840-44. Elected to the Congress in 1844, Price resigned in 1846 and organized the Second Missouri Cavalry Regiment for the Mexican War. Price followed Kearny and Doniphan into New Mexico in 1846. After the Taos insurrection, Price left New Mexico and served for a time as military governor of Chihuahua. At the end of the Mexican War he returned to Missouri, where he held various political offices. On May 18, 1861, he was appointed Major General of the Missouri State Guard and subsequently fought for the Confederacy in many important engagements in the Civil War, among them Lexington, Pea Ridge and Corinth. When the Confederates surrendered, Price went to Mexico, but returned to Missouri in 1866.

Lieutenant Abert described the situation in Santa Fe shortly before the Taos rebellion. As of Dec. 23, 1846, he reported: "About midday I reached Santa Fe and found all the Americans there talking about an intended insurrection which had fortunately been discovered. Sentinels had been placed in every direction, all the field pieces and heavy guns had been parked in the plaza, everything was in a state of preparation and everybody in a state of vigilance. The chief conspirator had arranged the organization of the several detachments and the plan of attack; one company was to assemble in the church called the 'parroquia,' another in the valley of the Tesuque, north of Santa Fe. In the dead of night, at a signal from the bells of the church towers, the conspirators were to rush into the streets, seize the guns and massacre the whole body of troops. The persons of the governor, Charles Bent, and the commanding officer, Colonel Price, were to be seized by parties appointed for that purpose." The next day Abert wrote: "The artillery are busy making preparations to march, in order to reinforce Colonel Doniphan; the clanking of the anvil is incessant; caissons and gun carriages are strewed around the forges. At this juncture it is almost doubtful whether the safety of our citizens does not require that the artillery should remain. It is expected that the wagons loaded with money for the troops will be attacked; a company has been sent to warn and escort them. We hear that San Miguel is in a state of insurrection, and the whole country seemed rife and ready to tear down the glorious stars and stripes. . . . I had a long talk with Mr. St. Vrain about the practicability of going to the United States by way of the Canadian. . . . He cautioned me not to attempt it, as he had been warned by the Kiowas of a settled determination of the Comanches to kill all the whites who should attempt to go through their country. . . . This hostile feeling on the part of the Indians has been produced by the great mortality which has this year prevailed among their children, which the Indians attribute to sorcery, saying the whites have a great medicine, and have blown an evil breath upon the children, and they have made a vow to wreak vengeance upon the white man." See Ex. Doc. No. 41, p. 512.

Ceran St. Vrain, New Mexican resident for many years prior to the American Occupation of 1846, in order to help suppress the Taos rebellion, raised a company of mounted volunteers, composed of 11 officers and 68 privates, which was sworn into federal service by General Sterling Price in Santa Fe on Jan. 23, 1847. St. Vrain's company was made up of American and French-Canadian mountain men, fur traders, trappers, teamsters and miners. The muster roll of St. Vrain's company is a valuable and authentic source of information on New Mexico's "first families" of a hundred years ago. St. Vrain's men saw service in skirmishes at La Canada on Jan. 24, at Embudo on Jan. 29, at Taos

Pueblo on Feb. 4. They were discharged on Feb. 20, 1847. Fifteen years later St. Vrain helped recruit and organize the First Regiment of New Mexico Volunteers, which was sworn into the federal service at Santa Fe on Jan. 29, 1862. St. Vrain served briefly as colonel of the regiment. His successor was Christopher ("Kit") Carson. For an interesting summary of the troubles in Taos in 1847, see "The Taos Rebellion," by E. Bennett Burton, Old Santa Fe, Vol. 1, No. 2, Oct. 1913.

25 General Kearny wrote to the Adjutant General in Washington from Santa Fe on Sept. 22, 1846, enclosing a copy of the laws prepared for the government of New Mexico, and a complete list of appointments to civil office in New Mexico. Concerning the laws, known as "The Kearny Code" for a hundred years, General Kearny wrote: "I take great pleasure in stating that I am entirely indebted for these laws to Colonel A. W. Doniphan, of the first regiment of Missouri mounted volunteers, who received much assistance from Private Willard P. Hall, of his regiment. These laws are taken, part from the laws of Mexico — retained as in the original — a part with such modifications as our laws and constitution made necessary; a part are from the laws of the Missouri territory; a part from the laws of Texas; and also of Texas and Coahuila; a part from the statutes of Missouri and the remainder from the Livingston Code. The organic law is taken from the organic law of Missouri Territory." See Act of Congress, June 4, 1842; and Compiled Laws of New Mexico, 1897, p. 9, for full text of the Kearny letter, furnished to the compilers by Hon. Thomas Benton Catron, of Santa Fe.

Both Doniphan and Hall, while working on the code in Santa Fe, were congressional candidates in Missouri, Doniphan on the Whig, and Hall on the Democratic ticket. Doniphan notified Hall that he had been elected, congratulated him, and offered him a discharge from the army so he could take his seat in the Congress. Declining the offer, Hall went to California with Captain P. St. George Cooke, who praised him for his cooperation on the march from Santa Fe to San Diego "in the most active and venturesome duties." See Ex. Doc. 41, p. 562. Returning to Missouri Hall became active in politics after the war, being elected governor, and to other high offices. He died November 14, 1882. See *Las Vegas Gazette*, Nov. 21, 1882.

An original copy of the "Kearny Code" is a valuable collector's item. Five hundred copies were printed in Santa Fe by "General" Oliver P. Hovey, on type and press belonging to the United States Quartermaster's department. Like many printers, who fail to get "cash with order" on political jobs, Hovey experienced difficulty in collecting the money for printing the laws. The background of the printing of the code was given in a report of the Committee on Territories, No. 60, House of Representatives, 34th Congress, 3d Sess., submitted on Jan. 10, 1857, which recommended payment: "The Committee on Territories have examined the memorial and affidavit of Oliver P. Hovey . . . from which it appears that on the 7th of October, 1846, the said Hovey was employed by Charles Bent (then acting governor of New Mexico) to print the code of laws for New Mexico which was promulgated by General Kearny, who, under instructions from the War Department, had established a civil government in New Mexico in that year. It appears that said Hovey executed said printing, and delivered five hundred copies of the laws for the use of the government, according to contract, for which it had been agreed that he should be paid a reasonable compensation. That his bill of charges for the work amounted to $1,705, but that Governor Bent having died before he (Hovey) had delivered but one hundred copies of the work, he had received but one hundred fifty dollars of the amount, and has not since then been able to prevail upon the government of New Mexico to pay him the balance, though he has repeatedly applied for the same." Hovey eventually received payment in full for printing the code, eleven or twelve years after he had done the work.

26 The fort (named Fort Marcy) was built under the direction of Captain Randolph Barnes Marcy, of Massachusetts, Kearny's regimental quartermaster.

Lieutenant Emory, of Kearny's staff, selected the site and drew the plans and specifications. Lieutenant J. W. Abert, of the Topographical Engineers, during a courtesy call on Colonel Doniphan in Santa Fe, on Oct. 3, 1846, inspected the fort and described it in an official report of that day: "Fort Marcy is situated on a prominent point of the bluffs commanding the city. The distance of the centre of this work, from the flagstaff in the plaza, is but 665 yards. The whole of the interior is defiladed from all the surrounding heights within range; 10 guns may be brought to bear upon the city. The slopes are revetted with adobes. The blockhouse and magazine are constructed of pine logs one foot square. The only approachable point is guarded by the blockhouse, which also assists to protect the entrance of the fort." See Ex. Doc. 41, 30th Cong., 1st Sess. Although named for Secretary of War W. L. Marcy, many people assumed that it had been named for Captain Marcy, the builder. In the early stages of construction, Marcy used laborers and mechanics drawn from Kearny's army. When Kearny left Santa Fe for the west, Marcy employed civilians until the arrival of General Sterling Price. Men recruited from Price's troops finished the fort in 1847. Captain Marcy, father-in-law of General George B. McClellan, of Civil War fame, was brevetted brigadier general on March 13, 1865, for gallant and meritorious services on the battlefield. Marcy was retired at his own request on Jan. 2, 1881, after having served in the army for 40 years. He died in Orange, N. J., Nov. 1, 1887, at the age of 76 years. In 1867 the original Fort Marcy was abandoned, and a new Fort Marcy was built a short distance to the west, on a site north of the Palace of the Governors, now occupied by business and residence properties, in the vicinity of Washington and Lincoln Streets. The second Fort Marcy was located on the site where the Spaniards had built a fort in 1791. James A. Donovan, millwright under Captain Marcy while the original Fort Marcy was being built, remained in Santa Fe after the Mexican War and built a grist mill near the mouth of Santa Fe canyon. "Donovan's Mill," as it was known for many years, was still in operation as late as 1887. The War Department, over the vigorous objection of the citizens of Santa Fe, abandoned historic Fort Marcy on October 10, 1894. Men and equipment were loaded on Santa Fe railroad cars, and moved to Fort Sill, Oklahoma. In 1896 Santa Fe's governing body proposed that the War Department grant the Fort Marcy property to the American Invalid Society of New England, or convert it into an Indian reservation. Both proposals were rejected. The government finally conveyed the Fort Marcy reservation to the city of Santa Fe in trust for public purposes.

[27] William Gilpin, born in Delaware County, Penn., on Oct. 4, 1822, was appointed first governor of Colorado Territory by Abraham Lincoln on March 22, 1864. Tutored for entrance to the University of Pennsylvania by Nathaniel Hawthorne, Gilpin was graduated from that institution. He attended West Point for a time, and was a newspaper editor in St. Louis before enlisting in the army at the beginning of the Mexican War in 1846.

[28] Lieut. Emory left Santa Fe on Sept. 25, 1846, a few hours after Kearny, with instructions to follow the road "over the ground heretofore travelled and chronicled as far as Tome." In his report, Emory described a call upon Senora Maria Trinidad Gabaldon Armijo, wife of General Manuel Armijo, late governor of New Mexico: "At Albuquerque I was directed to call and see Madame Armijo, and ask her for the map of New Mexico, belonging to her husband, which she had in her possession. I found her ladyship sitting on the ottoman smoking, after the fashion of her countrywomen, within reach of a small silver vase filled with coal. She said she had searched for the map without success; If not in Santa Fe, her husband must have taken it with him to Chihuahua." Ex. Doc. No. 41, 30th Cong., 1st Sess., p. 46.

[29] Emory's reports of Oct. 2 and 3, 1846, described the raids. On Oct. 2: "We received a message at La Joya from the *major domo* of the neighboring rancheria, cautioning us to be watchful of our animals, that forty Navajos had passed the river last night. The incursions of these Indians have prevented the

settlement and cultivation of this part of the country." On Oct. 4, Emory noted that he "longed to cross the mountains and explore the haunts of the Apaches . . . but we are not on an exploring expedition; war is the object; yet we have now marched one thousand miles without flashing a sabre." Emory believed that Apaches, and not Navajos, had attacked Polvadera: "Arrived at the town of Polvadera, which we found, as its name implies, covered with dust; we received full accounts of the attack made on the town by the Apaches the day before. The dragoons arrived too late to render assistance. About one hundred Indians, well mounted, charged upon the town and drove off all the horses and cattle of the place. The terrified inhabitants fled to their mud houses, which they barricaded. The people of Limitar, a town below, came to the rescue and seized the pass between Polvadera and Socorro. The Indians seeing their retreat with the cattle and goats cut off, fell to work, like savages as they were, killing as many of these as they could, and scampered off over the mountains and cliffs with the horses and mules, which they could more easily secure." Ex. Doc. 41, p. 50.

30 Colonel Sterling Price reached Santa Fe on Oct. 3, 1846, relieving Doniphan. On Oct. 26, 1846, the very day Doniphan left Santa Fe for the Navajo country, the Navajos staged a spectacular raid south of Albuquerque, killing a number of people and driving off 5,000 sheep within 20 miles of the town. Livestock owners in the Rio Grande valley drove their herds to the mountains. The valley was in a stage of siege and alarm. "Voluntarios" from the settlements hurried to an appointed rendezvous, and started for the Navajo country ahead of Doniphan, armed with muskets and *escopetas* (a firelock, a gun), with cartridge boxes buckled around their waists.

31 John Taylor Hughes, a Missouri school teacher, told the story of the first journey into the Navajo country under the American flag, in "Doniphan's Expedition," for more than 100 years the outstanding work of its kind. Hughes was born near Versailles, Woodford County, Kentucky, July 25, 1817. The Hughes family moved to Howard County, Missouri, in 1820. John Taylor Hughes taught school in Missouri, enlisted in the army at the outbreak of the Mexican War, accompanied Doniphan to New Mexico, and went with him into the Mexican interior in 1846. He fought in the Confederate Army during the Civil War, became a brigadier general, and was killed at the battle of Independence, Mo., on Aug. 11, 1862. Hughes finished writing "Doniphan's Expedition" at Liberty, Mo., on Sept. 25, 1847, less than a year after the actual happening of events he described. The first edition of the book was printed in 1847 by J.A. and U.P. James, printers and publishers, Walnut Street, between Fourth and Fifth Streets, Cincinnati, Ohio. Only a few copies of the 1847 edition are known. U.P. James, 167 Walnut, Cincinnati, published an edition of the book in 1848, and in the same year published a paper back edition which sold for twenty-five cents a copy. Some authorities are of the opinion that the paper backs were published before the bound volume of 1848. See also "Doniphan's Expedition," a reprint of Hughes, edited, with notes, by William Elsey Connelly, Topeka, Kansas, May 7, 1907. On motion of U. S. Senator W. J. Stone, of Missouri, "Doniphan's Expedition" was printed as a Senate Document on October 21, 1914. For comparative purposes, see "A Journal of the Santa Fe Expedition under Colonel Doniphan," by Jacob D. Robinson, Portsmouth Journal Press, Portsmouth, N. H., 1848, and reprint with notes by Carl L. Cannon, Princeton University Press, 1932; see also "Campaign in New Mexico," by Frank S. Edwards, published by James S. Hodson, London, 1848, in which a passing reference is made to the Navajo Indian difficulties of the period.

32 The commissary estimated that one sheep furnished fresh meat for seven soldiers for one day.

33 For Doniphan's preliminary report on the Navajo expedition, see Ex. Doc. No. 1, p. 496, 30th Cong, 1st Session, Dec. 7, 1847. Returning from the Navajo country, Doniphan's troops reached the Rio Grande near Socorro, on

Dec. 12, 1846. Doniphan reported: "We proceeded from Socorro to Valverde, where we found the large caravan of American merchants awaiting our arrival; and we proceeded to prepare our train to obey the order of General Kearny, requiring me to report to General Wool." Doniphan had a total of 856 effective men, armed with rifles—no artillery. The troops reached Doña Ana, a troop concentration point near present day Las Cruces, New Mexico, on Dec. 22, and started the next day for El Paso, some forty-five miles to the south. On Dec. 25, 1846, Mexican troops, estimated to number 1220, offered resistance. Writing from Chihuahua on March 4, 1847, Doniphan described the fighting north of El Paso, known as the battle of Brazito (sometimes called Bracito): "The enemy halted at a half a mile and formed in line of battle— the Vera-Cruz dragoons on the left, the Actevo battalion of Chihuahua on the right, and their infantry, with the militia from El Paso in the center. Before we had fully formed, they sent a lieutenant near our lines with a black flag, with a demand that the commander of our forces should go to their lines and confer with their commander; declaring at the same time, unless it was complied with they would charge and take him, and neither ask nor give quarter. The reply was more abrupt than decorous—to charge and be d——d. With my permission a hundred balls would have pierced the insolent bearer of the pirate flag; but I deemed it most proper for the honor of our country to restrain them. . . . At the return of the black flag, the enemy commenced his charge and opened fire on us. . . . Our forces were ordered to receive their fire, without returning it, until it could prove effective. . . . The loss of the enemy was 43 ascertained to be killed, about 150 reported at El Paso to have been wounded, of whom a large number died. Our loss was none killed—7 wounded, all since recovered. Thus ended the battle of Brazito." Supra, p. 498. Doniphan entered El Paso without opposition on Dec. 27, 1846. Here he learned that General Wool had not advanced to El Paso, as had been anticipated. Doniphan reported: "We were, therefore, compelled to await the arrival of our artillery at that point (El Paso) until the 1st day of February, 1847, their baggage and provision train until the 5th. On the 8th we commenced our march to Chihuahua." Doniphan reported from Chihuahua on March 4, 1847: "On the evening of the 8th of February, 1847, we left the town of El Paso del Norte, escorting the merchant train or caravan of about 315 wagons for the city of Chihuahua. Our force consisted of 924 effective men; 117 officers and privates of the artillery; 93 of Lieut. Col. Mitchell's escort, and the remainder, the 1st regiment of Missouri mounted volunteers." The battle of Sacramento, north of Chihuahua, was fought on Feb. 28. Doniphan reported: "On the 1st day of March we took formal possession of the capital of Chihuahua in the name of our government. We were ordered by General Kearny to report to General Wool at this place. Since our arrival, we hear he is at Saltillo, surrounded by the enemy. Our present purpose is either to force our way to him, or return by Bexar, as our term of service expires on the last day of May next." Supra, pp. 409-502.

34 Valverde was a settlement of some importance between 1820 and 1825. The inhabitants abandoned it in 1825, discouraged by repeated raids by Apaches and Navajos. When Kearny camped at Valverde in 1846 nothing remained of the settlement but a few adobe walls. Although only a name place today, Valverde retains important historical significance. It was at Valverde that Kearny camped on his way to California in 1846. Kit Carson reached the vicinity of Valverde on Oct. 5, 1846, with the news, perhaps a bit premature, that "California had surrendered without a blow, and that the American flag floated in every port." Valverde was truly a "soldier's farewell" in 1846. "Many friends here parted that were never to meet again. Some fell in California, some in New Mexico, and some at Cerro Gordo." On Feb. 21, 1862, some sixteen years after Kearny's and Carson's paths crossed near Valverde, Union troops under Canby, and Confederate troops under Sibley, fought "The Battle of Valverde," an important battle of the Civil War in New Mexico.

35 Ex. Doc. No. 1, 30th Cong., 1st Sess., p. 513. An interesting aside on Kearny's journey from New Mexico to California in 1846, was furnished by General E. V. Sumner, Commander of the Department of the Pacific, in a letter written from San Francisco to Asst. Adjt. Gen. Townsend, in Washington, on Sept. 7, 1861: "I fitted out General Kearny's command of 100 men on the Rio Grande in 1846. I gave him the best of everything in the regiment, and yet when he arrived on this coast, this small force was completely broken down and unable to contend successfully with the Californians who attacked him. OR Series I, Vol. 1, part 1, p. 610.

36 Ex. Doc. No. 41, p. 572. Antone Robideaux, of St. Louis and Taos, Kearny's interpreter, accompanied Kearny from Santa Fe to California. At San Pascual, on Dec. 6, 1846, he was wounded in battle with the Mexicans, receiving a lance in the spine which blinded him. Robideaux was discharged in California without traveling expenses, and made his way home via Peru, Jamaica and New Orleans. He was finally recommended for a pension by a reluctant congress. H. R. Rep. 226, 34th Cong., July 19, 1856. In his report for Dec. 7, Lieutenant Emory made an interesting reference to Robideaux: "Don Antonio Robideaux, a thin man of fifty-five years, slept next to me. The loss of blood from his wounds, added to the coldness of the night, 28° Fahrenheit, made me think he would never see daylight, but I was mistaken. He woke me to ask if I did not smell coffee, and expressed the belief that a cup of that beverage would save his life, and that nothing else would. Not knowing there had been any coffee in camp for many days, I supposed a dream had carried him back to the cafes of St. Louis and New Orleans, and it was with some surprise I found my cook heating a cup of coffee over a small fire made of wild sage. One of the most agreeable little offices performed in my life, and I believe in the cook's, to whom the coffee belonged, was, to pour this precious draught into the waning body of our friend Robideaux. His warmth returned, and with it hopes of life." Ex. Doc. 41, p. 111.

37 Magoffin's itemized account included the following: "My time, a merchant in business, which I had to neglect for two years & eight months @ $300 per mo. $9,000; my expenditures, to wit, from Washington to Independence, $50.00 for a small waggon with springs, $150.00 for 1 pair horses, $160.00 for 1 pair mules, $160.00 for an escort of 6 Mexicans to El Paso, after leaving Gen'l Kearny, $150.00; of money rec'd. in Chihuahua as per certificate of U. Commercial Agent of the U. States, which was expended in bribes in that city in order to extricate from the military judge, Gen'l. Kearny's written statement of my services in Santa Fe, New Mexico directed to the Secretary of War, Washington, $3,800; losses sustained at Chihuahua, during my imprisonment . . . being a suffering in purse, as well as in body, for that imprisonment, $15,968.96, total $37,780.96." To substantiate a part of his claim, Magoffin attached to it a certificate signed on October 1, 1848, by John Potts, a British subject, who had acted as American Commercial Agent at Chihuahua. The Potts certificate declared that in April, 1847, Samuel Magoffin had sold 311 bales of merchandise in Chihuahua, the property of James W. Magoffin, a brother, at half value, upon which the purchaser was obliged later to pay duties amounting to $15,968.96, which James W. Magoffin refunded to the purchaser in 1848.

38 Henry Connelly, New Mexico's Civil War governor, was born in Fairfax County, Virginia, on Sept. 1, 1800. He died in Santa Fe on Aug. 12, 1866. Bishop J. B. Lamy celebrated the requiem funeral mass. Burial was in San Rosario cemetery. Appointed governor of the Territory by President Lincoln, Connelly was inaugurated on Sept. 4, 1861, and served until July 16, 1866, when he was succeeded by Robert B. Mitchell. When a small boy, Connelly was taken by his parents from Virginia to Kentucky, where he was reared, educated liberally, and studied medicine. In 1820, he left Kentucky and settled in Clay County, Missouri, where he practiced medicine until 1824, in which year he joined a party of merchants starting across the plains from Independence for Santa Fe. Except in emergencies, Dr. Connelly did not prac-

tice medicine in New Mexico. In and out of New Mexico for several years, Connelly went to Chihuahua in 1828, and was a merchant in that place from 1828 to 1848. During that period, he made a number of trips across the plains from Mexico to Missouri and return. He was one of the first persons to make the trip from Chihuahua to New Orleans over the "Staked Plains" country through eastern New Mexico and northern Texas. When James Wiley Magoffin and Gov. Manuel Armijo were negotiating in 1846, looking toward a bloodless invasion of New Mexico by General Stephen Watts Kearny, Henry Connelly was in Santa Fe, and took an important part in the conferences between the two men. In 1849 Connelly was married to the widow of Don Mariano Chavez, and maintained a pretentious ranch home at Los Pinos, near Peralta, Valencia County. He rented this property to the federal government on May 15, 1862, for a term of five years at an annual rental of $5,000, with no privilege of cancellation prior to expiration date. A Union fort, called *Los Pinos*, was established on the Connelly place. When the Texans invaded New Mexico in the spring of 1862, Connelly helped to maintain the supremacy of the federal government. He was at Fort Craig during the battle of Valverde in February, 1862. When Confederate troops occupied Santa Fe on March 22, 1862, Connelly moved the territorial capital to Las Vegas. He planned to move the capital to Fort Union in event the Texans were successful in the battle of Glorieta. Santa Fe *Gazette*, Aug. 18, 1866. OR Series I, Vol. XLVIII, p. 1234.

39 In reviewing the Magoffin claim, Secretary of War Crawford made specific reference to three bribes: "For $3,800, the amount expended in bribes in Chihuahua, in order to obtain possession of Gen'l. Kearny's statement of his services in Santa Fe, then in the hands of the military judge, & which, if not destroyed, would have placed his life in jeopardy," and "for $1,000 paid by Magoffin to the authorities in Durango for his release from imprisonment, and $500 for money given to a Mexican friend for making arrangements for that release."

40 Senator Thomas Hart Benton in "Thirty Years' View," Vol. 2, p. 684, New York, 1860, gave his recollection of Magoffin's part in the invasion of New Mexico, and of the attempts to induce the government to reimburse him: "Returning to the United States after the peace, Magoffin came to Washington in the last days of Mr. Polk's administration, and expected remuneration. He had made no terms, asked nothing, and received nothing, and had expended his own money, and that freely, for the public service. The administration had no money applicable to the object. Mr. Benton stated his case in secret session in the Senate, and obtained an appropriation, couched in general terms, of fifty thousand dollars for secret services rendered during the war. The appropriation, granted in the last night of the expiring administration, remained to be applied by the new one—to which the business was unknown, and had to be presented unsupported by a line of writing. Mr. Benton went with Magoffin to President Taylor, who ... gave orders to the Secretary of War to attend to the case if there had been no change in administration. The Secretary (Mr. Crawford, of Georgia), higgled, required statements to be filed, almost in the nature of an account; and, finally, proposed thirty thousand dollars. It barely covered expenses and losses; but, having undertaken the service patriotically, Magoffin would not lower its character by standing out for more. The paper which he filed in the war office may furnish some material for history—some insight into the way of making conquests—if ever examined."

41 John Macrae Washington was born in Virginia in October, 1797. Graduated from the U. S. Military Academy in 1814, he saw service on many fronts, engaging in operations in the Creek nation, in the Florida war against the Seminoles, and on the northern border during the Canada troubles in 1839-40, distinguishing himself in the Mexican War. With his regiment, the 3rd Artillery, Washington was on board the steamer San Francisco when she was

wrecked off the Cape of Delaware in Pacific waters on Dec. 24, 1853. Washington, a number of other officers, and 180 soldiers, were drowned.

42 Ex. Doc. No. 18, 31st Cong., 1st Sess., p. 202.

43 Delegates attended the convention from New Mexico's seven districts, Rio Arriba, Taos, San Miguel, Santa Fe, Santa Anna, Bernalillo and Valencia. Delegates to the convention: Manuel Armijo y Mestas and Ambrosio Armijo y Ortiz, from Bernalillo County; Joseph Nangle and Salbador Lucero from Rio Arriba; Gregorio Vigil and Manuel Antonio Baca from San Miguel; Miguel Montoya and Francisco Tomas Baca from Santa Ana; Manuel Alvarez, E. Vaudry Deroin and W. Z. Angney, from Santa Fe; Ceran St. Vrain, Antonio Jose Martinez and Antonio Leroux, from Taos; Juan Jose Sanchez, William Curtis Skinner, Mariano Sylba, Antonio Jose Otero and Manuel Antonio Otero, from Valencia. Padre Antonio Jose Martinez, of Taos, was elected president of the convention without opposition. Ex. Doc. No. 18, 31st Cong. 1st Sess.

44 Ex. Doc. No. 18, 31st Cong., 1st Sess., p. 103. When New Mexico failed to achieve a Territorial form of government, New Mexico politicians attempted to force the powers in Washington to accept New Mexico as a state of the Union. Hugh N. Smith, rejected as a "Delegate" in Congress, managed to collect $2,000 mileage and $5.00 a day from the time of his arrival in Washington until his claim to a seat was rejected by a vote in the House of Representatives. See Appropriation Act, Sept. 20, 1850. The Congress likewise paid W. S. Messervy, chosen as representative from New Mexico, when it "assumed" statehood in 1850, but refused to compensate his companion, "United States Senator" Richard H. Weightman. A bill for Weightman's relief was introduced in Congress, H.R. No. 467, and favorably reported out by a committee on July 19, 1856. In making its report the committee referred to a particularly interesting incident in New Mexico's political history: "At the close of the Mexican war, the military government which had been established by the President of the United States in New Mexico was temporarily continued, in the absence of other forms of government, with the *presumed* consent of the inhabitants of that Territory. The people of the Territory, however, soon memorialized Congress for the usual form of Territorial government, and sent an agent, Hugh N. Smith, to Washington, for that purpose, with the style of Territorial delegate. Congress did not at that time grant the Territorial government asked for. Abandoning hope of obtaining such government, and viewing the *de facto* government as anti republican and obnoxious; the people of New Mexico, following the example of Tennessee, Vermont and other states, formed, in 1850, a State constitution, in the absence of all sanction of the general government, and presented it to Congress, asking admission into the Union. Mr. W. S. Messervy, who had been chosen a representative, and Mr. Richard H. Weightman, who had been chosen a senator in Congress, came to Washington as the agents of New Mexico, the latter as early as August, or September, 1850, bringing with him a copy of the new constitution, and placing it in the hands of the President of the United States, who transmitted it to Congress on the 9th of September, 1850. Mr. Messervy arrived at Washington at a later date, and attended the second session of the 31st Congress; they both remaining until the 4th of March, 1851. Congress refused to admit New Mexico as a State, but at the same time organized the present Territorial government for the Territory." Citing the case of Thomas Hart Benton, who received per diem and mileage as a Senator from Missouri, beginning Nov. 14, 1820, although Missouri was not admitted into the Union until Aug. 10, 1821, and similar cases involving "agents," from California and Michigan, the committee recommended that Weightman be paid for services rendered, as a "senator" from New Mexico. Reports, No. 228, 1st Session, 34th Cong., and No. 3, 1st Sess 35th Cong., Jan. 6, 1856, and July 8, 1856.

Richard Hanson Weightman was born in Maryland in 1818, died while commanding a brigade at Wilson's Creek, Mo., on Aug. 10, 1861. Weightman entered West Point in 1837, but was expelled in the same year for cutting a cadet in the face with a knife. In August, 1854, Weightman, using the same knife, fatally stabbed famed Francis X. Aubrey, following a sensational bar room fight in La Fonda in Santa Fe. Aubrey had just returned from a route-finding trip from California. Weightman had recently returned from Washington, where he had represented New Mexico as Delegate in Congress. The men became involved in an altercation over an article recently published in Weightman's newspaper in Santa Fe. Aubrey claimed that the newspaper article had reflected on his honor and integrity. Weightman claimed after the stabbing that he had not read the article and had not inspired it. According to Demetrio Perez, an eye witness, Aubrey in the heat of the argument threw a glass of whiskey in Weightman's face and instantly drew his pistol. Weightman stabbed Aubrey through the heart. After a sensational trial, Weightman was acquitted of murder. Weightman's close friends claimed that he suffered terribly from remorse after killing Aubrey; that he "could ever see the dead man's face before his eyes," and expressed the belief that he died gladly at Wilson's Creek.

45 President James K. Polk referred to the boundary dispute in his message to the Congress on Dec. 7, 1847: "New Mexico is a frontier province, and has never been of any considerable value to Mexico. From its locality, it is naturally connected with our western settlements. The territorial limits of the State of Texas, too, as defined by her laws, before her admission into our Union, embrace all that portion of New Mexico lying east of the Rio Grande, while Mexico still claims to hold this territory as a part of her dominions. The adjustment of this question of boundary is important." Ex. Doc. 1, 30th Cong. 1st Sess. In his message to the House on Jan. 21, 1850, President Zachary Taylor referred to the claim made by Texas to a part of New Mexico: "A claim has been advanced by the State of Texas to a very large portion of the most populous district of the Territory commonly designated by the name of New Mexico. If the people of New Mexico had formed a plan of a State government for that Territory as ceded by the treaty of Guadalupe Hidalgo, and had been admitted by Congress as a State, our constitution would have afforded the means of obtaining an adjustment of the question of boundary with Texas by a judicial decision. At present, however, no judicial tribunal has the power of deciding that question, and it remains for Congress to devise some mode for its adjustment. Meanwhile, I submit to Congress the question whether it would be expedient, before such adjustment, to establish a territorial government, which, by including the district so claimed, would practically decide it in her favor. In my opinion such a course would not be expedient, especially as the people of this Territory still enjoy the benefit and protection of their municipal laws, originally derived from Mexico, and have a military force stationed there to protect them against the Indians. It is undoubtedly true that the property, lives, liberties and religion of the people of New Mexico are better protected than they ever were before the treaty of cession." Ex Doc. 17, H.R. 31st Cong. 1st Sess. p. 3.

46 Senator William H. Seward, of New York, later Secretary of State, delivered an interesting speech in the United States Senate on July 26, 1850, in support of a proposed amendment to the bill providing for settlement of the New Mexico-Texas boundary dispute. Seward contended that the President should be authorized to issue a proclamation declaring New Mexico admitted as a state on presentation of her constitution, and that New Mexico should be authorized to appoint three commissioners to be associated with the commissioners to be appointed by the United States and by Texas, in settling the boundary question. . . . Among other things, Seward said: "Sir, New Mexico is obliterated from the memory of the Senate and of the Congress of the United States. It is a name no longer to be spoken here. What was the territory of New Mexico, as a distinct territory, has ceased to be spoken of here, otherwise than as an unoccupied, an unappropriated, an undefined part of the domain of the United States. But New Mexico had just exactly the same

individuality and the same rights in coming into this Union that Texas had. New Mexico was annexed by conquest, and Texas by treaty. But Texas was admitted into the Union by treaty as a state; and New Mexico was admitted into the Union, after conquest, by treaty, with the agreement that it should be a state. Now, there is a question in dispute between New Mexico and Texas—a boundary dispute. That question is vital to New Mexico, because the boundary claimed by Texas would include the capital, and all the most valuable and most densely settled portions of New Mexico. Congress is engaged in settling that boundary question, and proposes to settle it by a commission. Congress appoints commissioners to treat with Texas, and invites Texas to appoint commissioners with equal authority with those of the United States. So far, so well. But here is New Mexico, the other party in interest, the equal of Texas in rights, in justice, in position, in everything except what you withhold from her—the sovereignty of a state. She is unrepresented here. She has no voice here. And while she has no representative, no voice here, you deny her a share in the commission. I ask you now to fulfil your treaty obligations. Bring New Mexico in here as a state, that she may meet Texas as a state. Let her take part in this debate. Let us hear her present her wrongs and her rights. I have no doubt that she will speak as eloquently as the state of Texas on her side. Bring New Mexico in here. Before you decide upon her fate, give her a hearing. She appeals to you. Strike, if you will, but hear." See "The Works of William H. Seward," Baker, Vol. 1, p. 119 et seq.

[47] See "Speech by Mr. Underwood, of Kentucky, on the bill defining the boundary between Texas and New Mexico, and to pay $10,000,000 to Texas, delivered in the Senate of the United States, August 7 and 8, 1850." Printed at the Congressional Globe Office, 1850. Texas was heavily in debt in 1850. Its revenues were comparatively small and entirely inadequate to liquidate the public debt in the foreseeable future. Financial rather than legal reasons prompted the settlement of the boundary question. Texas needed ten millions of dollars more than she needed more territory.

[48] The act of Congress of September 9, 1850, establishing New Mexico as a Territory, on condition subsequent, fixed the boundary between Texas and New Mexico as the 103 degree meridian of longitude west of Greenwich. To quote from a report prepared by Guy P. Harrington, former U. S. Cadastral Engineer: "In accordance with the description in the Act of September 9, 1850, an area of approximately 70 miles north and south and 150 miles east and west in the present state of Colorado was included in the Territory of New Mexico. This area extended approximately from the present town of Chama to the northeast corner of New Mexico and was intended to cover the basin of the Rio Grande. The western boundary extended to the boundaries of the present state of California and embraced all of the present state of Arizona and a sizeable area in the present state of Nevada. The boundary between the United States and Mexico was considerably north of its present position. It followed the Gila River to approximately 110 degrees west longitude from which point it followed the meridian to approximately 32 degrees north latitude thence east to the Rio Grande. In 1853 the Gadsden purchase was effected which brought the boundary between the two Republics to its present position. The next change in the boundary of New Mexico occurred in 1861 when Colorado was established as a territory by act of Congress. In this act the boundary between Colorado and New Mexico was established as the 37th parallel of latitude where it remains substantially today. This act eliminated the area contained in the present confines of Colorado. Arizona was organized as a territory in the Act of Congress dated February 24, 1863. The area was carved entirely from the western portion of the Territory of New Mexico. The boundary between the two territories was fixed as the 32nd Meridian of longitude west of Washington which is the present boundary between the states. The boundaries of New Mexico have remained substantially fixed since 1863. . . ."

That portion of the then Territory of New Mexico known as Los Conejos, being the extreme northern portion of New Mexico, was severed from New

Mexico and annexed to the Territory of Colorado by act of congress approved February 28, 1861. The sole purpose of the severance, affecting 3,000 native born New Mexicans, was to give evenness and symmetry to the southern boundary of Colorado at the expense of New Mexico. Hon. Francisco Perea, Delegate in Congress, belatedly protested against the severance, in a letter written to James M. Ashley, chairman of the Committee on Territories in the House, on January 1, 1865, and attempted to reclaim the lost territory for New Mexico, contending the act of severance had been passed without consultation or warning. Santa Fe *Gazette*, February 18, 1865.

The boundary disputes between Texas and New Mexico, and between Colorado and New Mexico, offer an inviting field of study. Much of the litigation between Texas and New Mexico revolved around questions concerning the location of the Rio Grande in 1850. The controversy with Colorado dealt to a considerable extent with the accuracy of the Ehud N. Darling survey of 1868, and the lines extended by John J. Major and Levi S. Preston in 1874 and 1900. For the background of the disputes and information on basic documents see State of New Mexico v. Texas, 275 U.S. 280, 276 U.S. 698; State of New Mexico v. State of Colorado, 267 U.S. 498. The boundary controversy between New Mexico and Colorado has not yet been finally settled. A Colorado-New Mexico boundary commission has been supervising surveys since 1925. With 308 miles of the survey finished, the prospects are that the remaining 27 miles will be resurveyed during 1951 or 1952. See Santa Fe *New Mexican,* Jan. 5, 1950.

49 On April 30, 1929, Eugene Manlove Rhodes, famed New Mexico writer, wrote from Three Rivers to Governor R. C. Dillon in Santa Fe, describing a book he was then preparing to write on the history of New Mexico, in which he said: "I grind away at that book. But it is hard work and comes slowly. I find that I covered too much territory. The miners have a story of their own, the freighters, the railroaders, the sheepmen, the soldiers; the farmers have their own tragedy. The story of the surveyors; the forest service, a hundred others. The Butterfield stage line alone would need a better book than I can write. Or Eddy's adventures in railroad building. Do you know, my mind is of such a low and grovelling order that this same Eddy seems to me as romantic a figure as any of the old Spanish explorers? Or Kit Carson? To build a railroad—two of 'em—from nothing—and to build them with no money, or in one case with no water? Some adventure; and he made it stick. So I had to draw in my horns. At the rate I began, it would have required 150,000 pages. Did I say Eddy? I retract. The most interesting figure I have found in New Mexico history—the most interesting figure I have found in all history—bar Camille Desmoulins and Marco Polo—is your predecessor Calhoun, first American civil governor of New Mexico. If ever a man was sent to make ropes of sand Calhoun was the man."

50 Report of the Com. of Ind. Affairs, 1850.

51 An old timer told the writer that his grandfather had told him many years ago about the peach trees in the Navajo country, by saying: "By Gad, Sir, those Navajos out there had fruit trees that bore fruit."

52 The treaty of Sept. 9, 1849 (9 U.S. Statutes at Large, 974), was between John M. Washington, "Governor of New Mexico, and Lieutenant Colonel Commanding the Troops of the United States in New Mexico, and James S. Calhoun, Indian Agent, representing the United States of America," and Mariano Martinez, Head Chief, and Chapitone, second Chief, "on the part of the Navajo Tribe of Indians." The Indians signing "by mark," acknowledged sovereignty of the United States, and conceded it had the exclusive right to regulate the trade and intercourse of the Navajos. Hostilities were to cease; the Navajos were to deliver up all American and Mexican captives, and all stolen property. The people of the United States were to have free and safe passage "through the Territory of the said Indians." The United States was to have the right to establish military posts, agencies and trading houses at such places as it might elect, and pledged itelf to "designate, settle

and adjust" the boundaries of the Indian country, and to grant the Indians "such donations, presents and implements, and adopt such other liberal and human gestures, as said government may deem meet and proper." In form, content and execution the treaty was as formal as if the government of the United States had negotiated a treaty with England, France, Germany, or some other great world power, instead of a group of wild Indians.

53 After returning to Santa Fe, Simpson added a footnote to his journal: "Since my return to Santa Fe, I find 'Mount Taylor' can be seen from Fort Marcy and other surrounding heights, the airline distance being as great as one hundred miles."

54 On September 12, 1849, Navajo Indians stole 134 mules and horses, valued at $75.00 each, from Bent & Beck, merchants at Santa Fe, in a raid about twelve miles outside town. The Bent and Beck depredation claim was considered in the 37th Congress, 3rd Session, Rep. Com. No. 76, in the 39th Congress, 1st Session, Report No. 74; and in the 43rd Congress, 1st Session, Report No. 95. The Beck part of the claim was pressed by James Preston Beck, Administrator of the estate of Preston Beck, Jr., deceased. A copy of the last will and testament of Preston Beck, Jr., made on April 1, 1854, was attached to the claim papers, declaring that the testator had business interests in the firm of "S. and P. Beck, lately conducted at Boonville, Missouri, and Lexington, Missouri," and that certain business interests were owned solely by the testator and his brother, Simpson Beck, deceased. Congress authorized payment of the claim after a long investigation. The Navajos stole, it was finally determined, "eighty mules, sixteen mares, and a few horses, jackasses and colts." Preston Beck, Jr., died in Santa Fe in 1858 as the result of knife wounds received in a duel to the death with one Gorman, a clerk in the store of Richard Owens. Gorman died in the thick of the fighting. Beck staggered out of the duelling ring alive, but died a week later.

Washington's treaty with the Navajos was signed on Sept. 9, 1849. The raid near Santa Fe occurred on or about Sept. 12 of that year. Undoubtedly the Navajos implicated in the raid of Sept. 12 did not know that a treaty had been signed three days before in the Canon de Chelly country, more than two hundred miles away.

55 Bernalillo (Little Bernard) was described by Simpson as "presenting some respectable looking *rancho* residences, surrounded by well cultivated grounds, which are fenced by adobe walls, some of them twelve feet high, and crowned with cactus, to prevent their being scaled." The Perea family entertained Lieut. W. H. Emory at dinner at Bernalillo, in September, 1846, as he was on his way from Santa Fe to San Diego. According to Emory, the plates, forks and spoons of the Perea tableware were "of solid New Mexican silver, clumsily worked in the country." Emory described the dinner at the Pereas: "The middle of the table was strewed with the finest white bread, cut in pieces, and within the reach of every cover. At close intervals were glass decanters filled with wine made on the plantation. The dishes were served separately. The first was soupe maigre; then followed roast chicken, stuffed with onions; then mutton, boiled with onions; then followed various other dishes, all dressed with the everlasting onion; and the whole terminated by chili, the glory of New Mexico, and then *frijoles*. Chili, the Mexicans consider the chef-d-ouevre of the cuisine, and seem really to revel in it; but the first mouthful brought the tears trickling down my cheeks, very much to the amusement of the spectators with their leather lined throats. Chili was nothing more nor less than red pepper, stuffed with mince meat." See Emory's report, Ex. Doc. 41, 30th Cong., 1st Sess., 1848. As the members of the Perea family died, the silverware was divided among many descendants. Mary Lester Field, of Albuquerque, devoted more than forty years to locating and acquiring the scattered Perea silverware. Mrs. Field donated the collection to the University of New Mexico in 1943, almost a hundred years after Emory had seen it at Bernalillo.

56 Lieut. Simpson finished his scholarly, well written report in Santa Fe, and forwarded it to Washington on April 11, 1850. The report was entitled "Journal of a Military Reconnaissance under the command of Brevet Lieutenant Colonel John M. Washington, Chief of the Military Department, and Governor of New Mexico, in 1849, by James H. Simpson, A.M., First Lieutenant, Corps of Topographical Engineers." Printed as Executive Document, numbered 64, Simpson's Narrative, as it became generally known, is of great present day historical value. Simpson's report, beautifully illustrated, under the name "Journal of a Military Reconnaissance from Santa Fe to the Navajo Country," was published as a book in Philadelphia in 1852 by Lippincott, Grambau & Co. (successors to Grigg, Elliott & Co.), a copy of which is in the Ayer collection, Newberry Library, Chicago. While preparing his report in Santa Fe, Simpson consulted Chief Justice Joab Houghton, Provisional Secretary Donaciano Vigil, Translator; Samuel Ellison, James L. Collins, Capt. Henry L. Dodge, U. S. Army, and Lieut. Lorenzo Torres, of the Mexican volunteers. Simpson made a study of Spanish Colonial history while in New Mexico, and wrote an article, "Coronado's March in Search of the Seven Cities of Cibola and Their Probable Location," for the Smithsonian Institution Report for 1869, which was published also as a government document in 1871.

James Hervey Simpson was born in New Brunswick, N. J., on March 9, 1813. He died of pneumonia at 2 Monroe Street, St. Paul, Minn., on March 1, 1883. Appointed as a cadet to West Point on Sept. 1, 1828, Simpson was graduated on July 1, 1832. For the next forty-seven years, until retirement in 1879, Simpson served the army in many important capacities, principally with the topographical engineers. After a brief artillery experience in the Seminole Indian War in Florida, he worked on river and harbor improvements in various parts of the country until 1849, in which year he undertook the exploration and mapping of a route from Fort Smith, Arkansas, to Santa Fe, New Mexico. Simpson explored and reported upon a new route from Salt Lake to the Pacific Coast in 1859-1861, over which the Union Pacific Railroad was later constructed. Simpson served in many important capacities during the Civil War, helping, among other things, to plan the defense of the City of Washington. He was made a brigadier general on March 13, 1865. See St. Paul *Daily Globe,* March 2, 1883, St. Paul *Dispatch,* March 2, 1883, and St. Paul and Minneapolis *Pioneer Press,* March 3, 1883. The *Press* said in its obituary notice that Princeton University conferred the degree of Master of Arts on Simpson in 1848. Princeton has no record, however, of having conferred any degree on Simpson.

57 Ex. Doc. 17, p. 207, 31st Cong., 1st Sess.

58 Supra, p. 207.

59 Col. John Munroe, Washington's successor, was born in Scotland about 1796, was graduated from West Point in 1814, died in New Brunswick, N.J., on April 26, 1861. Munroe served in Indian wars in Florida, and in the Mexican War. Unable to understand New Mexico's politics, Munroe became involved in serious administrative difficulties during the brief time he served as provisional governor.

60 Ex. Doc. No. 17, p. 226.

61 While enroute to New Mexico, cholera broke out among Sumner's troops, killing Surgeon Kennedy and thirty-four soldiers. Daniel Henry Rucker, born in Belleville, N. J., April 28, 1812, spent his boyhood in Grasse Isle, Mich., enlisted in the U. S. Army on Oct. 13, 1837, died in Washington, D. C., in 1910. Rucker served as an officer in New Mexico for some years in the 50's, living part of the time in Albuquerque in a house owned and at one time occupied by Governor Manuel Armijo, later owned by his nephew, Juan Cristobal Armijo. The Armijo residence, then immediately west of the Bernalillo County courthouse of 1886, was razed in 1912 and a two-story house was built on the site for Charles Boettger. Ann Rucker, daughter of Major Rucker,

born in the Armijo house in Albuquerque, was married to General Phil H. Sheridan in Chicago, on June 3, 1873.

62 See "The Official Correspondence of James S. Calhoun while Indian Agent at Santa Fe and Superintendent of Indian Affairs in New Mexico," edited by Annie Heloise Abel, Government Prtg. Office, 1915, containing many reports and letters previously filed in several offices in Washington. Collected in one volume through Compiler Abel's foresight and diligence, the letters and reports are important sources of New Mexicana.

63 Calhoun's Correspondence, Abel. See also "The Journal of John Greiner," by Dr. Annie Heloise Abel, *Old Santa Fe*, July, 1916.

64 William C. Dawson, United States Senator from Georgia, from 1849 to 1855, was born in Greene Co., Georgia, Jan. 4, 1798, died in Greensborough, Georgia, May 5, 1856. Dawson was prominent in Georgia politics for a generation.

65 David B. Whiting, of Santa Fe, in Independence, Mo., at the time, wrote a letter from there on July 1, 1852, to Manuel Alvarez, in Santa Fe, which is helpful in fixing the approximate date of Calhoun's death. Whiting wrote: "The Governor (Calhoun) will arrive here tomorrow or the day after." The Legislature of New Mexico adopted a resolution on Jan. 10, 1853, expressing regret because of the death of "the late Governor James S. Calhoun," and appropriated three hundred dollars to be "expended in erecting a slab of marble at his tomb with a suitable inscription," and providing that the members of the legislature should "wear the accustomed badge of mourning for thirty days in honor of his memory." (See Laws, 3rd Sess., p. 119.)

While serving as Governor of New Mexico, Calhoun was subjected to much criticism and frequent newspaper attacks. The *St. Louis Republican* was particularly aggressive and vindictive. The *Republican* charged that Calhoun was the "representative of the mercantile interests in New Mexico," that he had "licensed hordes of traders who went into Utah to despoil the Indians," and that he had "failed to cooperate with the military." No doubt but that Calhoun had frequent brushes with the army. He contended that army officers believed "the military was independent of and superior to the civil power." Calhoun and Colonel Sumner failed to see eye to eye on New Mexico affairs. Regardless of attacks in hostile newspapers, and grumblings from the military, there is substantial evidence that James S. Calhoun was competent, alert and intelligent in handling affairs relating to New Mexico and particularly diligent in attending to Indian affairs. The truth of the matter is that Calhoun had a task that was too big, too overwhelming for any one man, or group of men, to grapple with successfully. The "Indian problem," which Calhoun was expected to solve in a matter of months, is a momentous, unsolved problem in New Mexico, more than a hundred years after Calhoun's arrival in New Mexico.

Details of the life of James S. Calhoun, New Mexico's first civil governor, are not readily available. The writer is indebted to Calhoun's great granddaughter, Mrs. Olive S. Arnold, of Atlanta, Ga., for some hitherto unavailable information. James S. Calhoun was born in South Carolina at a date unknown, but probably between 1800 and 1806. When a young man, he settled in Baldwin County, Georgia, and soon became prominent in political affairs when the Georgia state capital was in Milledgeville. Calhoun served as judge of the Inferior Court of Baldwin County from 1828 to 1829, in the Georgia House of Representatives from Baldwin County from 1830 to 1832; and represented Muscogee County in either the House or State Senate from 1835 to 1840. Beginning in 1846 Calhoun served as a captain in a regiment of Georgia volunteers, and was a Lieutenant Colonel when the regiment was mustered out in 1848. While in Muscogee County, Calhoun engaged in the shipping business in Georgia under the name of Calhoun & Bass. During one of the intermittent Indian wars, the "Annie Calhoun," one of the firm's ships, was seized and destroyed by the government. The government paid $15,000 as indemnity. Calhoun was considered a man of substantial wealth for some years before he left Georgia for New Mexico. Among other things he owned vast land holdings along the entire length of the Chattahoochee river through Georgia and Florida to the Gulf of Mexico. For a time Calhoun was in the Consular service in Havana, Cuba. While in Cuba, Calhoun studied Spanish. Knowledge of that language was helpful to him in New Mexico. During the years of his residence in Georgia, Calhoun was considered somewhat of a "grandee." Coming to New Mexico where dried apples were considered a luxury in 1849, Calhoun experienced difficulty in adjusting himself to the crude frontier conditions. Nevertheless he remained at his post, and served in important capacities in New Mexico until he was forced to leave by what proved to be mortal illness.

66 William Carr Lane, Calhoun's successor as governor of New Mexico, a native of Virginia, one time post surgeon in the United States Army, took the oath of office in Santa Fe on Sept. 13, 1852. Major James Henry Carleton, post commander at Fort Union, with a detachment of dragoons, met Lane on the east bank of the Arkansas river on Aug. 16, 1852, and escorted him to Santa Fe. Soon after being inaugurated, Governor Lane made an extensive tour of the lower Rio Grande valley in New Mexico. Manuel Armijo, last governor of New Mexico under Mexican rule, met Gov. Lane on the outskirts of Limitar, near Socorro, on Oct. 13, 1852. Governor Lane rode in Armijo's carriage, escorted by a cavalcade of citizens on horseback. While Lane was Armijo's guest in Limitar, he was treated by his host with "much kindness and ceremony," according to Carr's official report of the trip. On March 19, 1853, Governor Lane wrote a sharply worded letter to Colonel D. S. Miles, commanding officer at Fort Fillmore, concerning New Mexico's right to a strip of land, then in dispute, which later became American territory under the Gadsden purchase of 1854. Lane reminded Miles that the "army was subordinate and auxiliary to, the civil authorities of the U. S. in all the states and territories," that he had taken a stand on the disputed strip "under the best legal advice in the Territory," that he was not afraid that his action would be "disapproved either by the President or the People." Ready to fight both the U. S. Army and the Mexican government, Governor Lane declared: "The Gov't and the people of the U. S. have disapproved and repudiated Mr. Bartlett's line: The Board of Commissioners have been dissolved, and we know not when another Board will assemble; the authorities of the state of Chihuahua have usurped authority, in the acknowledged Territory of New Mexico, and trampled upon the rights of the citizens of the U. S. The Exve. Department of New Mexico (in the exercise of an undoubted Right and plain Duty), has asserted the Rights of the U. S. and of the Citizens, and some 350 U. S. troops who are unemployed, and are within 5 miles of the scene of action; fold their arms, in frigid tranquility and thereby sustain the enemies of their country!"

Governor David Meriwether, Lane's successor as governor of New Mexico, escorted by U. S. troops, took possession of the disputed territory (a strip on the west side of the Rio Grande 34 miles wide by 170 miles long) late in 1854, following an order of the day issued by General John Garland, commanding the military District of New Mexico, on Nov. 15, 1854.

The Gadsden Treaty between the United States and Mexico, negotiated in part by James Gadsden, Envoy Extraordinary and Minister for the United States, signed on Dec. 30, 1853, was proclaimed in Washington on June 30, 1854. For details of the petty bickering that was one of the obstacles incident to the boundary line project see "Report of the Secretary of War on Col. J. D. Graham," Aug. 25, 1852, Ex. Doc. No. 121, 32d Cong., 1st Sess. James Gadsden, principal negotiator in the "Gadsden Purchase," was born in Charleston, S. C., May 15, 1788, died in that city on Dec. 25, 1858. Gadsden was graduated from Yale in 1806; served in the war of 1812 against Great Britain; served as aide-de-camp to Gen. Andrew Jackson in 1818. and as adjutant under John C. Calhoun in 1822. Resigning, he became a planter in Florida and aided in removing the Seminoles from northern to southern Florida. Returning to South Carolina, Gadsden became president of the South Carolina railroad. President Pierce made him minister to Mexico in 1853. On Dec. 30 of that year he negotiated the treaty which bears his name by which a new boundary line was agreed upon between the United States and Mexico, modifying to a considerable extent the treaty of Guadalupe Hidalgo of 1848. Under the treaty the United States acquired territory now forming a part of Arizona and New Mexico, for which the United States agreed to pay $10,000,000. The treaty was confirmed by the senate, but with such changes that Gadsden was obliged to renew his negotiations with Mexico. He was superseded as minister before the final provisions of the treaty were agreed upon.

67 Writing from Albuquerque to the Adjutant General in Washington, on September 24, 1852, Sumner, perhaps cheered up a bit since his letter of May 27, advised: "I have the pleasure to report that all things continue quiet in this department. The only hostile Indians in the territory are a small band of Apaches, headed by Chief Delgadito, who continues sour and suspicious, but he has committed no depredations of late and I think he will soon come into the treaty. The new posts in the Indian country have had the happiest effect; indeed it is plain that this is the only certain way of controlling Indians." See S. Doc. 1, Records of U. S. Senate, 32nd Cong., 2d Sess.

68 Senate Doc. 1, Records of U. S. Senate, 32nd Cong., 2nd "Sess., pp. 24-27.

69 Official Washington, to some extent, was aware of the "wild Indian" problem. In his message to the Congress on Dec. 7, 1847, in discussing reasons to justify the conquest of New Mexico, President James K. Polk said: "There is another consideration which induced the belief that the Mexican government might even desire to place the province of New Mexico under the protection of the government of the United States. Numerous bands of fierce and warlike savages wander over it, and upon its borders. Mexico has been and must continue to be, too feeble to restrain them from committing depredations, robberies and murders, not only upon the inhabitants of New Mexico itself, but upon those of the other northern States of Mexico. It would be a blessing to all these northern States to have their citizens protected against them by the power of the United States." Ex. Doc. 1, 30th Cong., 1st Sess., pp. 10, 11.

70 The "exposition" was printed by "J.M.B." (Jesus Maria Baca) on the Padre Martinez Press in Taos. District Judge Luis Armijo, of Las Vegas, N. M., was the owner of a copy of this interesting and valuable item of New Mexicana. For the background of the Martinez Press and publishing between the years 1834-1860, see "The History of Early Printing in New Mexico," by Douglas C. McMurtrie, N. M. Hist. Rev., Oct., 1929.

71 Rep. Com. Indian Affairs, 1867. Antonio Joseph Martinez, "priest of Taos," as he was widely known, loomed large in the history of New Mexico in the ten-year transition period between 1845 and 1855. Born in Abiquiu, Rio Arriba County, New Mexico, on Jan. 7, 1793, Martinez died in Taos, on July 27, 1867, "surrounded by his many brothers, and a large circle of friends and relatives." In 1812, when 19 years old, Martinez was married to Maria de la luz Martinez (no kin), who died in 1813, leaving a daughter, Luz, who died in 1825. After his wife's death, Martinez went to Durango, Mexico, and studied for the Roman Catholic priesthood. Ordained in Durango on Feb. 12, 1822, he remained there for a short time, and then served for some months in 1823 and 1824 as an assistant pastor at Tome, in Valencia County, and at Abiquiu, Rio Arriba County, New Mexico. In May, 1824, Martinez was appointed parish priest in Taos, where, two years later he established a college in his own residence, primarily for the education of young men for the priesthood, but lay students were admitted to some courses of study. The seminary faculty consisted of several teachers. Martinez managed the seminary and taught grammar, rhetoric and theology; and devoted considerable time also to the study of Spanish and Mexican law. He used his knowledge of law years

later, as a member of the New Mexico legislature under the American flag, when he drafted the statute on testaments. Martinez served as a member of the Departmental Assembly of New Mexico from 1830 to 1836. Compelled to leave Taos over night because he had become involved in a minor political revolution in northern New Mexico, Martinez went to Santa Fe and sought the protection of Governor Manuel Armijo, who appointed him as chaplain of dragoons. On Aug. 10, 1838, on an expedition to suppress the revolution, Armijo and his dragoons camped at the foothills of Puertocito de Pojoaque, a few miles north of Santa Fe. Jose Gonzales, revolutionary chieftain, learning of Armijo's presence in the neighborhood, sought for and was granted an interview with him. At the interview, Gonzales said to Armijo: "Comrade, how are you? I have come before you to ask a guarantee for my pueblo, that no tax be imposed upon it, and I will then abide by law and order." To this Armijo replied: "What you ask is out of the question and cannot be considered. My object is to establish peace and order, and this I shall do by the shortest route." Turning to Padre Martinez, standing nearby, Armijo ordered: "Father Martinez, hear this man's confession, so that he may be executed by firing five shots into him." Padre Martinez obeyed the General's order. Gonzales was executed. In 1835 Martinez acquired a printing plant (probably brought to Santa Fe from Mexico in 1833 or 1834 by Antonio Barreiro, and transferred by Barriero to Ramon Abreu), and for a short time published in Taos *El Crepusculo* (The Dawn), the first newspaper to be established west of the Missouri river. On the same press Martinez printed alphabet and syllable cards, and books on Christian Doctrine, spelling, logic, physics and arithmetic. Among the students at Martinez' school were Antonio Joseph and Francisco Manzanares, both of whom later became prominent in New Mexico affairs. Twenty students from the Martinez school became Roman Catholic clergymen, among them Jose Manuel Gallegos, who was deprived of his clerical faculties, by order of Bishop John B. Lamy, in 1852, while serving as curate of the church of San Felipe de Neri in Albuquerque, after which Gallegos became a political leader and was elected Delegate in Congress. In September, 1846, within 30 days after the American Occupation, Padre Martinez called his pupils together at Taos for a serious talk: "Boys, you entered this college to study for the priesthood, and in this matter I have done all that I possibly can to aid you in obtaining your wishes. But since the form of government has changed, it may also be proper to change ideas. The genius of the American government is in perfect harmony with the toleration of cults, and the complete separation of church and state. By this time you see that the clergy has been deprived of many of its privileges." Innocenia Martinez, a student, asked a question: "What is the American form of government?" Martinez replied: "Republican." Then, to illustrate the difference between the governments of Mexico and the United States, Martinez added: "Let us pretend that the American government is a burro, but in this instance it is not the clergy riding the burro, but the lawyers." Following the American Occupation, Martinez served as a member of the New Mexico legislature during the years 1851 to 1853. He was elected president of the assembly in 1851 by unanimous vote, and made an excellent presiding officer. Martinez died a poor man. He had served as a clergyman for forty years, the latter years of his life marred by the controversy carried on with Bishop Lamy over clerical jurisdiction. A rebel and reformer at heart, Martinez was obviously a combination priest and politician, something that was not considered out of the way in his day and time. He fought church and state alike, under the Mexican government, whenever he believed either institution to be in the wrong, the church because of what he claimed to be its policy of allowing the clergy to exact excessive and oppressive tithes and fees for marriages, funerals, and like services; and the state because of its opposition to the reforms contended for by Benito Juarez. See "Memorias Sobre La Vida del Presbitero Antonio Jose Martinez," the eulogy delivered by Pedro Sanchez (who had been a student under Padre Martinez at the Taos Seminary), at Taos on Feb. 22, 1903, printed in the same year by Santa Fe New Mexican Printing Co.

72 Although neighbors in Taos for years, Charles Bent and Padre Martinez distrusted and disliked each other. Bent believed that Martinez esteemed and exalted himself too greatly, and took advantage of his position in the church and in politics. Martinez liked to preen himself on his superior knowledge of languages and the classics. This irked Bent, and prompted him to write letters to associates criticizing and belittling Martinez. For a photograph of one of Bent's letters indicative of his attitude toward Martinez, written by Bent to Manuel Alvarez from Taos, Jan. 30, 1841, see Read's "Guerra Mexico-Americana," Santa Fe, 1910, appendix, p. 40.

73 Ex. Doc. 18, 31st Congress.

74 Rep. of Com. Ind. Affairs, 1850.

75 Rep. Com. Ind. Affairs, 1850. The Commissioners referred to in Luke Lea's report, C. S. Todd, Robert B. Campbell and Oliver P. Temple, were instructed on October 15, 1850, to cooperate with the Bartlett boundary commission, to proceed "to collect statistics and to make treaties with the Indians residing within the limits of the United States upon the borders of Mexico, to find out everything possible about the several tribes, their manners, customs, mode of living, religion—everything relating to the character and history of the Indians as it may be in your power to collect."

76 Rep. Com. Ind. Affairs, 1854.

77 Meriwether had an important career before and after coming to New Mexico. Born in Louisa County, Va., Oct. 30, 1800, Meriwether was educated in Kentucky country schools, engaged in the fur trade beginning in 1818. He entered politics as a democrat, and was a member of the Kentucky legislature for 13 terms between 1832 and 1883, serving as Speaker of the House in 1859. Meriwether was a member of the Kentucky Constitutional Convention in 1849, and was appointed to the U. S. Senate by the Governor of Kentucky, on the death of Henry Clay, serving from July 15 to Dec. 20, 1852.

78 Rep. Com. Ind. Affairs, 1854.

79 Rep. Com. Ind. Affairs, 1854.

80 Rep. Com. Ind. Affairs, 1856. Christopher (Kit) Carson led a life of story book adventure, much of it in New Mexico. Born in Madison County, Kentucky, on Dec. 24, 1809, Carson was in New Mexico as early as 1826, employed by Ewing Young, in Taos, as a fur trader and trapper in 1829. From 1829 on, with time out for journeys to the Northwest and to California, Carson was continuously a resident of New Mexico. As trapper, guide and companion, Carson ranged from the Missouri river and the Rocky Mountains, to the Pacific ocean. He was employed as a guide by Lieut. J. C. Fremont, quite by accident, in St. Louis, on May 22, 1842, and accompanied him on a number of venturesome expeditions. Carson was in California in 1846, an eye witness to the stirring scenes that culminated in California becoming American territory. Leaving Los Angeles on Sept. 15, 1846, carrying dispatches from Col. Fremont to Washington, Carson made his way through hostile Apache Indian country from the Colorado to the Gila, to the Mimbres, to the Rio Grande. General Stephen Watts Kearny was in camp at Valverde, on the Rio Grande, when Carson reached there. Kearny ordered Carson to guide him back to California. Carson participated in the battle of San Diego, in which he rendered valuable aid. At the conclusion of the Mexican War, Carson returned to New Mexico, and led a comparatively quiet life until 1855, when he was appointed agent for the Ute Indians by President Franklin K. Pierce, a position he held until 1861, not without difficulty because he could not read correspondence sent to him from Washington, and was obliged to rely on others to read it. Unable to write and with no understanding of figures, or of budgets, it was inevitable that Carson's Indian agency accounts became muddled, resulting in a clash with

Governor David Meriwether. Carson was arrested and detained on Meriwether's order until the apparent inconsistencies in the accounts could be reconciled. Carson helped to organize the New Mexico Volunteers at the outbreak of the Civil War, signing the muster roll at Taos on Sept. 20, 1861. Ceran St. Vrain was made Colonel of the Volunteers because of his prestige and prominence in New Mexico, but accepted the commission with the understanding that he would resign as soon as the regiment had been organized. When St. Vrain resigned, Carson became Colonel. Carson was present with his command at the battle of Valverde on Feb. 21, 1862. When orders were given by General Canby for the Union troops to withdraw, he did so, "after having given a good account of himself and his men in action." The Santa Fe Gazette, in describing Carson's participation at Valverde, said: "Carson had the honor of taking his regiment in good order from the field when all else was confusion badly confounded." Carson was mustered out of the United States military service with the rank of brigadier general at Santa Fe on Nov. 20, 1867. Several months before his death, a correspondent for the Washington (D.C.) *Chronicle* visited Carson at Fort Garland, Colorado (once a part of New Mexico). Carson told the news correspondent that he was born near Richmond, Madison County, Kentucky, in 1809; that his father moved the family to Kentucky during his childhood; that when sixteen years old he traveled west with a band of trappers and traders, and lived for eight years among the Indians during which time he did not see a settlement or a white man; that while living with the Indians he dressed as an Indian, adopted the Indian way of life, and spent much time hunting.

The Santa Fe *Gazette*, of November 16, 1867, copied parts of the *Chronicle* article which, among other things, contained an interesting description of Carson's physical build and personality. The correspondent's description of Carson's manner of speech, in groping for a word, was evidence of senescence, a preliminary symptom to a stroke of apoplexy that probably caused his death: "Five feet six in his stockings, deep chested and squarely set, with the slightest stoop of the shoulders, feet and hands small, an oval face, very young looking for its fifty-eight years of care; light blue eyes, gentle as a woman's and clear as a boy's; the mouth well cut, but with straight lines around the corners and the appearance of having been made from harder material than the rest of the face; the nose not remarkable; with thorough Saxon hair falling to the shoulders, and looking a little thin on top and streaked with threads of silver; a mustache of the same light color was the only hair on the face. He wore the brigadier general's uniform in a careless, half Indian way, measured his words as if his life depended on expressing himself in proper shape. Sometimes he would stop in conversation, as if to recall a word, and, naturally, I would suggest one, but with the greatest indifference, he would pass my aid unnoticed, and using some strong Saxon phrase of his own, finish the subject, oblivious to any remarks, questions or conversation around him."

On June 12, 1868, the Santa Fe *Gazette* published the news of Carson's death: "From Fort Lyon, Colo., under date of May 24, we have by letter the details of the death of Kit Carson. He expired at that post on the 23rd, at 4:35 p.m., in consequence of the rupture of an artery in his throat. A few weeks previous his condition became dangerous, and he was removed from his house to the quarters of Major Tilton, the post surgeon who was attending him. The body was laid in state in the office of the Adjutant. He was temporarily buried on the evening of that day, it being understood that the remains would subsequently be removed to Taos, New Mexico, to be interred with those of Carson's wife, who there died only a few weeks before his demise. Carson's last words indicated the full possession of his mental faculties, the consciousness of his situation, and the strong social feeling which characterized him throughout life. The words were a simple 'good bye'."

Charles A. Scheurich, long time resident of Clovis, New Mexico (who died on Oct. 12, 1949, in his eighty-second year), grandson of Governor Charles Bent, was the owner of the last letter signed by Kit Carson. Written to Charles Scheurich's father, Aloysius Scheurich, of Taos, the letter was probably dictated by Carson, word for word, and was in effect a codicil to his will: "Mouth of Purgatoire River, May 5th, 1868 — Dear Compadre: I have received your letter and it has been a satisfaction to me to hear that you are all well. I arrived here on the 11th of last month, sick and worn out, but began to improve from that time and would be comparatively healthy if the misfortune, losing my wife, hadn't happened. Those were trying days for me. My health is improving now and I am very apt to be on the other side of the mountains by the end of this month; it is almost necessary for me to go, as much on account of business as for the sake of my health, to avoid the heat during the summer months. You have had before this the particulars of my wife's death and I need not repeat them here. My children are all well. We are farming as much as can be done without going to any great expense. I had a ditch taken out and everything works well in that respect. I intended to build me a house, but as I apprehend some trouble about our land, I decided to wait until matters are settled. Now I have told you of my own intentions and prospects, I expect you will appreciate the interest I am taking in you and yours and let me know what your calculations are for the future. It is my intention to send my wife's corpse to Taos, as soon as the weather is cool enough to do so and have taken the necessary steps to have this done, even if I myself should be called away, she shall rest as close to her family as possible. I have given the necessary orders to have my own body, if I should die, and that of my wife's sent together to Taos, to be buried in our graveyard near Elfego. I want neither her nor myself to be buried in the church. My best regards to the old lady,[81] Terresina and your boy,[82] who I am told is a fine child. Please tell the old lady that there is nobody in the world who can take care of my children but her, and she must knew that it would be the greatest of favors to me, if she would come and stay until I am healthier and may make such arrangements as would suit her. She has two children here and is among those nearest to her. The country has changed much since she was here last, no danger of Indians now. A greater number of people are living here, than then. If she should determine to come, let me know immediately, and I will send a carriage for her. Chipita Gorda is nursing the baby, which is doing very well, but still I am anxious to get another nurse. Remember me to all my friends, more particularly Miller, and don't delay to give an answer.

Yours truly —   C. Carson.

[81] Governor Bent's widow.

[82] Charles A. Scheurich.

[83] As a result of a decision handed down in 1950 by the Indian Claims Commission, the Ute Indians will receive $33,000,000 as compensation for the lands taken from them by the federal government in 1846 and subsequent years.

[84] Graves described a vast sweep of country, roughly embracing the present day New Mexico counties of Grant, Luna, Sierra, Catron, western Socorro, western Valencia, western Bernalillo, McKinley, part of Sandoval, and all of San Juan. The Navajo Indians filed a claim against the federal government in 1950 for some $25,000,000 as compensation for lands alleged to have been taken from them subsequent to the American Occupation.

[85] Rep. Com. Ind. Affairs, 1854. In the mid 50's, Indians from the plains country traveled in and out of New Mexico, seemingly curious, spying out the land almost like tourists of a later day. The Kiowas, Arapahoes and Cheyennes from the Arkansas river country, made several excursions into New Mexico, stealing livestock indiscriminately as they went along, killing Utes at every opportunity, and occasionally shooting a Jicarilla Apache. A party of Cheyennes, claiming they owned hunting rights in New Mexico, traveled in 1854 to the edge of the white settlements in San Miguel County, stole a large number of livestock, compelled eleven captive herders to return with them to the

Indian country to look after the stolen animals. Comanches from Texas, who came to New Mexico on a hunting trip in the fall of 1855, were driven off by the Jicarilla Apaches. In the summer of 1855 a party of Comanches from Texas called on Governor David Meriwether in Santa Fe, to complain that they had been driven from their own country by the Osage Indians. They asked Meriwether's permission to remain in New Mexico, but he advised them to go back to Texas and tell their grievances to their own Indian agent. For many years the Comanches and Kiowas committed depredations on the eastern frontier of New Mexico, and in northern Texas. In 1856, the Comanches became more than ordinarily daring, and conducted raids through the settlements of New Mexico, penetrating as far west as the Rio Grande. Coming and going, they robbed and pillaged, stole cattle and horses at will. They stole fifty mules near Las Vegas, and terrorized the settlers along a wide strip of territory in that vicinity. The Comanches staged other large scale raids in New Mexico in 1857 and 1858, defied Indian agents and soldiers, galloped on stolen horses up and down the Pecos river, dared rival tribesmen to stand still long enough to fight. Although state and territorial boundary lines meant nothing to the Indians, the federal government, through its officers and agents, was anxious to have them recognized and respected, and attempted in the mid 50's to discourage aimless tribal wanderings. Col. Albert Sidney Johnston, later a major general in the Confederate army in the Civil War, took command of the Second Cavalry on the Texas frontier, beginning on January 1, 1856, and attempted to stop Comanche and Kiowa depredations on Texas settlements in Young County. Johnston was convinced that whiskey, sold to the Indians by unscrupulous white men, was largely responsible for the Indians' behavior. The Texas legislature of 1855, seeking a remedy for the evil, passed a law prohibiting the introduction of liquor within ten miles of an Indian reserve. Rep. Com. Ind. Affairs, 1856. Sale of intoxicating liquor to Indians was not yet prohibited by federal law. John R. Baylor, in the Indian country since boyhood (who distinguished himself five years later by leading Texas troops in the invasion of New Mexico in the early months of the Civil War), appointed a special agent for "Texas Indians" in 1856, cooperated with Albert Sidney Johnston in a campaign to tame the Indians. Comanches, ranging in and about Fort Belknap, proved to be Baylor's most troublesome charges. The Texas legislature of 1855 passed an act granting additional reservation in the Pecos river country, in the western part of the state, for the settlement of the Indians, but the provisions for resettlement were vague and confusing, and resettlement was never accomplished. Rep. Com. Ind. Affairs, 1856.

86 Rep. Com. Ind. Affairs, 1858, pp. 188-191.

87 Rep. Com. Ind. Affairs, 1858.

88 See Correspondence with the Governor of New Mexico relating to Indian disturbances in that Territory, January 7, 1861, 36th Congress, 2d Session, Ex. Doc. No. 24. Governor Rencher was a North Carolina lawyer. Before coming to New Mexico he had served in the U. S. Congress and as U. S. minister to Portugal.

89 Ibid.

90 Ibid.

91 Ibid. Judging from available information, the "Bonneville War" of 1857 against the Indians of New Mexico was conceived in stupidity and executed in iniquity. There is reason to believe that Col. B. L. E. Bonneville, for a time in command of troops in New Mexico, was an old granny, a fussbudget and cruel to the Indians. Born in France in 1795, Bonneville was graduated from West Point in 1815, died in Fort Smith, Ark., June 12, 1878. He planned the so called Gila Expedition of 1857 in the expectation that the army would virtually exterminate the Gila Apaches in southwestern New Mexico. Troops were con-

centrated from three directions to carry the fight against the Gilas. Col. W. W. Loring, with 300 men, left Albuquerque for the Apache country on May 1, 1857. With Loring's troops on the march, Col. D. S. Miles left Fort Thorn, and Major E. Steen left Tucson, each at the head of strong detachments. For weeks Loring, Miles and Steen, under Bonneville's command, hunted Indians up and down the Gila and Mimbres rivers, and in the Mogollon mountains. Troops under Bonneville and Miles had a skirmish with the Apaches on the Gila on June 27, 1857, killing twenty-four, capturing a number of women and children, an engagement which seems a bit ghastly considered in retrospect. For important material on the Gila Expedition of 1857 see the Journal and Letters of John Van Deusen Du Bois in "Campaigns in the West," edited by Dr. George P. Hammond, Arizona Historical Society, Tucson, 1949.

Bonneville engaged in explorations in the Rocky Mountains and in California from 1831 to 1836. Washington Irving edited and amplified Bonneville's records of his journeys, published in Philadelphia in 1837, as "Adventures of Captain Bonneville in the Rocky Mountains and the Far West."

92 Troops stationed at Fort Defiance in the Navajo country in 1859 failed to subdue the Indians. The Navajos, or Indians disgused as Navajos, ranged far and wide in 1858, '59 and '60. Navajos were blamed for a raid near Fort Craig in February, 1860. Troops stationed there were ordered to pursue the raiders, but the order was countermanded when word reached the fort to be on the lookout for raiding Comanches and Kiowas. On Oct. 15, 1860, Indians, believed to be Comanches or Kiowas, stole 500 of the army's beef herd near Hatch's ranch at Tecolote in northeastern New Mexico. Soldiers from Fort Union killed between 10 and 15 Kiowas in a surprise attack on their camp 50 miles to the east.

93 Governor Rencher issued a requisition upon Col. Fauntleroy, Department Commander for New Mexico, on Jan. 30, 1860, for ammunition for 200 men, 30 rounds to the man, 160 muskets and 40 rifles, to be used in fighting Indians in Socorro County. The requisition had been authorized by an amendment to the "military law" of New Mexico, passed on Jan. 28, 1857, providing that property recovered from Indians was to be appraised and delivered to the true owner, less one-third of its value, which would belong to the volunteers as a bonus. Under the law the volunteers were to operate under the instructions of the Governor and "independent of all other military authority."

94 See Joint Resolution IX of N. M. Session Laws for 1855-56. Thomas Turner Fauntleroy was a native of Richmond County, Virginia, a veteran of the second war with Britain, and of the Mexican war. He fought Indians in New Mexico off and on for ten years before the Civil War. Fort Fauntleroy, on the edge of the Navajo country, in western New Mexico, was named in his honor. Although he was 65 years old at the time, Col. Fauntleroy, writing from Santa Fe on March 25, 1861, offered his services to Virginia in event of war. The offer was accepted, Fauntleroy reported for service in Richmond, on May 12, 1861, and was commissioned a brigadier general in the Confederate Army. While fighting Indians in New Mexico, Col. Fauntleroy wrote a letter to Gen. Winfield Scott, in which he said: "The greatest embarrassment arises from the fact that many of the claims set up against the Indians of New Mexico for plundering, stealing stock and the like, are either fabricated, or to a considerable degree exaggerated, and if war is to be commenced upon the simple presentation of these claims, the cause for war becomes interminable, or the Indians must be extirpated." See H.R. Mis. Doc. No. 85, 36th Cong., 1st Sess., May 21, 1860.

95 Ex. Doc. 24, H. R. 36th Cong., 2d Sess.

96 See "On the Navajo Trail—The Campaign of 1860-61" by Max L. Heyman, Jr., N. M. Hist. Review, January, 1951. See also "The Federal Indian Policy in New Mexico," and "The Government and the Navajo, 1846-1858," by Dr. Frank D. Reeve, New Mex. Hist. Rev., July, 1937, Jan., 1939.

SOURCES

Act of Congress, Sept. 9, 1850.
Benton's "Thirty Years in the U.S. Senate," Vol. 1, p. 42.
Cooke's "Conquest of New Mexico and California," 1878.
"Doniphan's Expedition," by John Taylor Hughes, 1847.
Doniphan's "Report on the Navajo Expedition," Ex. Doc. No. 1, 30th Cong., 1st Sess.
Emory's Report, Ex. Doc. 41, 30th Cong., 1st Sess.
Ex. Doc. 7, 30th Cong., 1st Sess., p. 30.
Ex. Doc. 17, H.R., 31st Cong., 1st Sess.
Ex. Doc. 18, 31st Cong., 1st Sess.
Kearny's letters and proclamations.
Las Vegas Gazette, Nov. 21, 1882.
James W. Magoffin's Correspondence and Papers, Bureau of the Budget, Washington.
"The Official Correspondence of James S. Calhoun while Indian Agent at Santa Fe and Superintendent of Indian Affairs in New Mexico," edited by Annie Heloise Abel, Washington, 1915.
Read Papers, Santa Fe.
Rep. Com. Ind. Affairs, 1850, 1854, 1856, 1858, 1867.
Santa Fe Gazette, Feb. 18, 1865; Aug. 18, 1866; Nov. 16, 1867; June 12, 1868.
Simpson's "Journal of a Military Reconnaissance Under the Command of Brevet Lieutenant Colonel John M. Washington, Chief of the Military Department and Governor of New Mexico in 1849," Ex. Doc. 64 (also published in 1852 under the title, "Journal of a Military Reconnaissance from Santa Fe to the Navajo Country.")
Treaty of Guadalupe Hidalgo, 1848.
Treaty with Navajos, Sept. 9, 1849.
Vigil Papers, Santa Fe.
"The Works of William H. Seward," Baker, Vol. 1.

REFERENCES

Act of Congress, June 4, 1842.
"Campaign in New Mexico," by Frank S. Edwards, 1848.
Copeland's "Kendall of the Picayune," 1943.
Era Southwestern, Santa Fe, Aug. 7, 1880.
Ex. Doc. 24, Jan. 7, 1861, 36th Cong., 2d Sess.
Ex. Doc. 34, 36th Cong., 2d Sess.
Ex. Doc. 121, 32nd Cong., 1st Sess.
Falconer's "Expedition to Santa Fe," 1842.
"The Federal Indian Policy in New Mexico," and "The Government and the Navajo," 1846-1858, by Dr. Frank D. Reeve, N.M. Hist. Rev., July 1937, Jan., 1939.

"Guerra Mexico Americana," by Benjamin M. Read, 1910.

H.R. Mis. Doc. No. 85, 36th Cong., 1st Sess., May 21, 1860.

H.R. Rep. 60, 34th Cong., 3d Sess.

H.R. Rep. 226, 34th Cong.

"The History of Early Printing in New Mexico," by Douglas C. McMurtrie, N.M. Hist. Rev., Oct. 1929.

"The Journal of John Greiner," by Dr. Annie Heloise Abel, Old Santa Fe, July, 1916.

Kendall's "Narrative of the Texas-Santa Fe Expedition," 1844.

Letters of John Van Deusen DuBois in "Campaigns in the West," Tucson, 1949.

"Memorias Sobre La Vida del Presbitero Don Antonio Jose Martinez," Santa Fe, 1903.

N.M. Laws, 3rd Sess., 1853.

N.M. Laws, 1855-56, Joint Resolution IX.

N.M. Laws, Compiled, 1897, p. 9.

Official Reports, Series I —
    Vol. 1, Part 1, p. 610.
    Vol. XLVIII, p. 1234.

Old Santa Fe, July, 1913, thru April 1, 1915.

"On the Navajo Trail — The Campaign of 1860-61," by Max L. Heyman, N.M. Hist. Rev., Jan., 1951.

Oregon Historical Quarterly, Vol. XXIV, No. 1.

President Polk's Messages, Ex. Doc. 1, 30th Cong., 1st Sess.

Read's "Illustrated History of New Mexico," 1912.

Reports, 228, 34th Cong., 1st Sess., and 3, 35th Cong., 1st Sess.
        76, 37th Cong., 3rd Sess., 74, 39th Cong., 1st Sess.
        95, 43rd Cong., 1st Sess.

Revista Catolica, Oct. 26, 1913.

Robinson's "A Journal of the Santa Fe Expedition Under Doipan," 1848, (Carl L. Cannon reprint, Princeon, 1932.)

Senate Doc. 1, 32nd Cong., 2nd Sess.

Senate Doc. No. 442, 56th Cong., 1st Sess.

"The United States and Mexico, 1821-1848," by George Lockhart Rives.

"The War With Mexico," by Justin Harvey Smith, 1919.

BOOK TWO

The Confederates Invade
New Mexico

"So far Mr. Lincoln is not making much headway in suppressing the rebellion. He has got himself thrashed at every fight from Manassas to Mesilla, and today we dare them to attack us at any point."

JOHN ROBERT BAYLOR,
Mesilla, New Mexico.
Feb. 1, 1862.

CHAPTER ONE

Baylor, Sibley and Canby

 ENSING THE EXISTENCE of internal dissention reflected at military posts, Apache, Navajo and Ute Indians became unusually bold and troublesome in 1860. Comanches and Kiowas, from the remote Plains country, added to the difficulties of the situation, riding in and out of New Mexico, looting supply trains, stealing livestock, and murdering those who opposed them. Because of the Indian scares, stagecoach travel and mail runs were abandoned for weeks at a time. The military, half heartedly, so it seemed, attempted to drive the Indians back to their own country, and to keep them there, but without success. Regardless of the acuteness of the Indian situation, it became of secondary importance to the threat of conflict between the North and South. As a result, the army deferred, or abandoned entirely, any attempt to pacify or control the Indians. Officers and enlisted men at military posts in the Territory talked and argued much about such things as slavery, the right of a state to secede from the Union; about allegiance to the state where one was born; about a man's duty when the time came to make a choice between North and South. Higher ranking officers in New Mexico, as elsewhere (all of whom had been graduated from West Point Military Academy), were obliged to consider seriously questions of vast importance to themselves, their careers, their families and their country. What course should they pursue under the circumstances? Remain loyal to the Union, or go with the Confederacy?[1] Captain Richard Stoddert Ewell (grandson of Benjamin Stoddert, first Secretary of the U. S. Navy), resigned his commission in New Mexico on May 7, 1861, to eventually become a Lieutenant General in the Confederate Army before the end of the war. Three major officers — Thomas Turner Fauntleroy, of Virginia, Henry Hopkins Sibley, of Louisiana, and William Wing Loring, of North Carolina, all stationed in New Mexico at the time, resigned their commissions on the same day, May 13, 1861. Colonel William James ("Old Pete") Longstreet, of South Carolina, and Lieutenant Colonel George Bibb Crittenden, of Kentucky, both then in New Mexico, resigned on June 1 and June 10, 1861, respectively. Ewell, Fauntleroy, Sibley, Loring, Longstreet, Crittenden! Their names were well known, and highly respected in every army post in the southwest. Their resignations, body blows to the Union cause, proved a source of great encouragement to the Confederate leadership in New Mexico and Arizona.

Colonel Loring, of the Mounted Rifles, having assumed command of the District of New Mexico, on March 22, 1861, resigned in less than sixty days.[2] The Comanche Indians doubtless tried Loring's patience during the few weeks he served as military commander in New Mexico, but he refused to be drawn into actual combat with them. Doubtless aware that war between the States was imminent, Loring sent the Comanches a message on April 22, urging them to attend a peace council. The Comanches sent word back to Loring that they had no time to talk about peace. As to the raids Loring had complained about, the Comanches, as usual, placed the blame on the young men of the tribe.[3]

Colonel Henry Hopkins Sibley, who resigned from the United States Army on May 13, 1861, was perhaps the best known, and most vocal of the Union officers in New Mexico who went over to the Confederacy. Although trained for the army, Sibley was more of a mechanical engineer than a fighting man. Fame of a kind, and fortune to some extent, already belonged to him through his invention of the Sibley tent, later supplemented by the Sibley stove. The handful of officers, who had elected to remain in New Mexico and continue loyal to the Union, bade Sibley a regretful good-by, as he left Fort Marcy in Santa Fe, and stopped at Fort Craig on his way to Fort Bliss, at El Paso, already in the hands of the Confederacy.

While waiting in El Paso for the San Antonio stagecoach, Sibley wrote a letter on June 12, 1861, to Colonel Loring in Santa Fe, telling him how glad he was to be in Confederate territory:

We are at last under the glorious banner of the Confederate States of America. It was indeed a glorious sensation of protection, hope and peace. Though its folds were modest and unpretending, the emblem was still there. The very Southern verdure and familiar foliage, as we progressed on our journey, filled us with enthusiasm and home feeling. We shall have no trouble from here down to San Antonio. The stage runs regularly semi-weekly, carrying five passengers and a reasonable amount of baggage, reaching San Antonio in six days; thence to Berwick Bay in stages, and to New Orleans by mail.

Sibley brought Loring up to date on the military situation in El Paso, suggesting that it would be important to the cause if he could arrange to retain his place as Department Commander for a week or two:

Van Dorn is in command at San Antonio. He has ordered four companies of Texas troops to garrison this post. They cannot be expected here before July 1. Meanwhile, Colonel Magoffin, Judge Hart, and Crosby are very much exercised and concerned on account of the public stores here in their present unguarded condition. There are full supplies of subsistence and ammunition here for two or more companies for twelve months. The loss of these supplies by capture or destruction would occasion serious embar-

rassment to the cause . . . you may, by delaying your own departure a week or two, add much to the security of this property.

Apparently Sibley had contemplated leading his Union
command into the Confederate camp, and now reproached
himself for his failure to do so:

> I regret now more than ever the sickly sentimentality (I can
> call it by no other name) by which I was overruled in my desire to
> bring my whole command with me. I am satisfied now of the dis-
> affection of the best of the rank and file in New Mexico, and that
> we are regarded as having betrayed and deserted them. I wish
> I had my part to play over again; no such peace scruples should
> deter me from doing what I considered a bounden duty to my
> friends and my cause. I do not advocate the meeting of duplicity
> and dishonesty by the like weapons, but if I capture the treasury
> buildings I shall certainly not send back to my enemy the golden
> bricks. . . . My love to those who love me.[4]

Major Edward Richard Sprigg Canby, widely experienced
soldier, a man of integrity, absolutely loyal to the Union, was
ordered to Santa Fe from Fort Defiance, New Mexico, and on
June 23, 1861, took over the command made vacant by Loring's resignation. Finding his troops confused as to loyalties,
and thoroughly disorganized, Canby's first work was to up-
grade their morale.[5]

As early as May 20, 1861, Secretary of War Simon Cameron
was convinced that New Mexico was in danger of being invaded from Texas.[6] District Commander Canby believed
that the enemy would attack Union forces in New Mexico
as quickly as troops and supplies could be concentrated. As
Canby saw it, New Mexico had little or nothing in the way of
supplies and commodities to attract an enemy, but he was
convinced that the Confederates were anxious to gain possession of the territory as part of an ambitious over-all plan.

New Mexico suffered severely from a succession of drouths
in 1859 and 1860. Prospects for crops seemed poor in 1861.
Union troops in New Mexico were not equipped or prepared
to fight. Draft animals and cavalry mounts at every post were
in poor condition. Remounts from across the plains, promised

for months, had not been delivered. New Mexico's poorly bred range horses were of little value for military use. A minimum of sixty days was required to get supplies from Fort Leavenworth, on the Missouri river, by mule or oxen train, to Fort Union, a distance roughly of 700 miles.

By June 1, 1861, within two weeks after assuming command of the military in Santa Fe, Colonel Canby had information that Confederate forces would attempt to invade New Mexico at a point in the vicinity of El Paso. It soon became common knowledge in Santa Fe and elsewhere in New Mexico, that Captain John Robert Baylor, of the Second Texas Mounted Rifles, Confederate States of America, a fast stepping and energetic Texan if there ever was one, was on the road from San Antonio to El Paso, at the head of several hundred fighting men. When it appeared that war was inevitable, Baylor mounted his horse and rode almost from daylight to dark, recruiting men in the villages, and on the farms and ranches, ostensibly to "hunt buffalo on the plains," but actually to invade New Mexico. Baylor spared neither whip nor spur on his recruiting mission. By May 1, 1861, his muster rolls had been signed by one thousand men. The recruits were required to furnish their own horses, saddles, guns and ammunition. In the early days of the "buffalo hunt," the recruits were enthusiastic, but as the first excitement wore off many dropped out of line on the seven hundred-mile journey, and returned home. Baylor, and some four hundred rough, tough and determined Texas riflemen, reached Fort Bliss on July 1, 1861. Baylor's forces were welcomed to El Paso by a committee headed by Judge Josiah F. Crosby, Judge Simeon Hart, and Colonel James Magoffin, three of the wealthiest men in the southwest, and zealous supporters of the Confederacy.[7]

On June 16, 1861, Colonel Canby ordered Major Isaac Lynde,[8] commanding officer at Fort McLane (near the Santa Rita copper mines), to abandon that fort, and remove his command, and all public property, to Fort Fillmore. Marching from Fort McLane at the head of Companies A, B, E and

G of the 2nd Infantry, Major Lynde reached Fort Fillmore on July 5, 1861, relieving Major Gilbert Rene Paul. Companies D, I and K, already at Fort Fillmore, became part of Lynde's command. Upon reaching Fort Fillmore, Lynde complained that it could not be successfully defended. He wrote to Colonel Canby on July 7 and again on July 9, asking authority to abandon the fort as indefensible, because "it was located in a depression, commanded on three sides by the hills, within six pounder range," and "water for men and animals, had to be taken from the Rio Grande, a mile and a half away."[9]

Assuming the offensive in the first major skirmish of the Civil War on New Mexico soil, Colonel John R. Baylor left Fort Bliss on July 23, 1861, with 250 troops. Marching north along the Rio Grande, Baylor crossed the river near San Tomas, and in less than 24 hours was in camp some 600 yards from Fort Fillmore, planning to attack the fort at daylight. Union scouts reported Baylor's position, and the plan for a surprise attack was abandoned. Baylor moved his troops the next day, July 25, to Mesilla, four and one-half miles to the northwest. Confederate sympathizers in and about Mesilla hailed the arrival of Baylor's troops with joy and enthusiasm.

Presumably the Union troops at Fort Fillmore were ready to fight Baylor to a finish. As of July 23, the day on which Baylor moved northward from Fort Bliss, Lynde at Fort Fillmore had about 700 effective troops, and adequate equipment. Out of an abundance of caution, Canby had sent him 300 additional rifles and muskets and 12,000 cartridges from Fort Craig, and twenty thousand additional rations of subsistence from Albuquerque. Canby was confident that Lynde was strong enough not only to defeat Baylor, but to recapture Fort Bliss.

On the afternoon of July 25, 1861, at 4 p.m., Lynde left Fort Fillmore and advanced toward Mesilla, with one howitzer and six companies of the Seventh Infantry, a total of 380 men. Halting his troops at a point two miles south of Mesilla, Lynde sent Post Adjutant Edward J. Brooks, and Post Sur-

geon James Cooper McKee, toward the town with a flag of
truce. They were greeted at the outskirts of Mesilla by two
Texans on horseback, Major E. Waller and Colonel Herbert,
"carrying double barreled shotguns on the front of their saddles." Brooks and McKee delivered Lynde's demand for "an
unconditional surrender of the forces and the town." Waller
and Herbert delivered Baylor's answer: "If Lynde wished
the town—come and take it." After firing two howitzer shots
toward Baylor's forces at long range, both of which fell short,
Major Lynde ordered an attack. The Union troops advanced
slowly, laboriously hauling the howitzer by hand through the
deep sand. As Lynde's forces approached Mesilla, Baylor's
troops fired at them from the houses and fields by the roadside, killing three Union soldiers, and wounding six, including two officers. Major Lynde at once ordered a retreat to
Fort Fillmore. Baylor's men returned to camp near Mesilla.[10]

Upon returning to Fort Fillmore, Major Lynde took counsel with his fears. He was convinced that the fort could not
be defended against Baylor's artillery. He feared that Baylor
would lie in wait for him at Mesilla and prevent him from
reaching Fort Craig, more than a hundred miles to the north.
In what he conceived to be a desperate situation, Lynde decided, in a moment of panic, to abandon Fort Fillmore and
attempt to reach Fort Stanton, 154 miles to the northeast.
Lynde apparently failed to consult the staff before reaching
his decision to abandon the fort, the order for which was
given within an hour after the troops had returned from the
skirmish with Baylor at Mesilla.

For several hours before abandonment, the garrison at
Fort Fillmore slept fitfully, with arms in hand. The wagons
were loaded with ammunition and supplies; ambulances were
made ready for the women and children. Horses and mules
were fed and watered. Everything was made ready for the
quick dash from the fort to San Augustine Springs, seventeen
miles away to the east, in the Organ mountains, the first objective. In and about the loading of supplies it was all too
evident that some of the supplies were to be left at the fort.

Word was whispered about the barracks that boxes of hospital brandy, and kegs of medicinal whiskey, in goodly number, were to be abandoned. As the soldiers appraised the situation, abandonment of a military post under orders was one thing, but abandonment of high class liquor was a much more serious matter, one that required consideration and reflection. The soldiers met the situation sensibly, and in the beginning, with discretion. First one trooper, then another, and then many, took a moderate swig of the-soon-to-be-abandoned liquor, then each helped himself to a drink that seemed more appropriate to the occasion. One sergeant of the "old army" decided that a drop of brandy, or perhaps two or more, on the road to Fort Stanton might be eminently fitting under the circumstances. Pouring the water out of his canteen, he replaced it with liquor. Others, recognizing the sergeant's commendable conduct, substituted liquor for water in their canteens. But, on the cross country march from Fort Fillmore to San Augustine Springs, soldiers with liquor in their canteens instead of water suffered severely from thirst. Long stretches of rough, sandy road, without a drop of water to touch hot lips and burning throat, proved the undoing of many a good fighting man. Soldier after soldier collapsed and fell by the wayside, begging for water.[11]

The evacuation of Fort Fillmore was accomplished during the night of July 26, 1861. By daylight of July 27, Lynde's entire command of some seven hundred men, together with the women and children of the post, traveling on horseback, walking, riding in buggies, wagons and ambulances, were on the road which led to Fort Stanton.

Baylor's scouts, up and about by sunrise, saw heavy clouds of dust in the air in the direction of the Organ mountains. Sensing the significance of the dust, Baylor sent a detachment to take possession of Fort Fillmore. In a matter of moments Baylor was in the saddle, in hot pursuit of the fugitives. Baylor quickly overtook the stragglers of Lynde's army. There was no need to ask them to surrender. All they wanted was water—cool water—any kind of water. Baylor's men handed their canteens from one to the other of the stricken soldiers, and quickly made them prisoners. Baylor hurried on to a pass in the Organ mountains, four miles south of San Augustine Pass, from that day to this known as Baylor's Gap. Galloping through the gap, Baylor and his troopers rode north until they reached San Augustine Pass, where they suddenly and dramatically confronted the Union troops.[12]

It was not until Sept. 21, 1861, that Baylor found time to make a complete report on the happenings of an eventful day:

On July 27, a little after daylight, my spies reported a column of dust seen in the direction of the Organ mountains distant 15 miles on the Fort Stanton road. I could from the top of a house with a glass see the movements of the enemy. I immediately ordered the command to saddle and mount, for the purpose of intercepting them at San Augustine Pass. I reached the river, one mile distant, when I received intelligence that a messenger had arrived from the fort, and stated that the enemy had fired the buildings; that the fire had been extinguished, and that but little had been destroyed. . . . After getting water for my men I started in pursuit of the enemy, who had passed along San Augustin Pass. I charged . . . upon gaining the summit of the Pass, a plain view of the road to the San Augustin Pass was presented. The road for 5 miles was lined with the fainting, famished soldiers, who threw down their arms as we passed and begged for water. . . . I was in a few moments sent for by Major Lynde, who asked upon what terms I would allow him to surrender. I replied that the surrender must be unconditional. To this, Major Lynde assented, asking that private property should be respected. The articles of capitulation were signed, and the order given for the enemy to stack arms. Major Lynde's command was composed of . . . nearly 700 men. My own forces at the surrender was less than 200.[13]

Federal troops set fire to government stores, according to Baylor, and abandoned Fort Stanton, as a result of Lynde's surrender:

. . . The news of the capture of Major Lynde's command created a stampede among the United States troops, who hastily abandoned Fort Stanton, after having destroyed a considerable portion of their supplies, and government property of all kinds, and all would have been destroyed except for a storm of rain, which extinguished the fire intended by the enemy to destroy the fort. The few citizens living near the fort took possession of it, and saved a valuable lot of the stores. The Mexicans and Indians in large numbers demanded the right to pillage the fort, which was granted. The citizens, being weak to resist, not knowing that they would get aid from me or not, were forced to abandon the fort to the Mexicans and Indians.[14]

Post Surgeon James Cooper McKee, an eyewitness to Lynde's surrender at San Augustine Springs, described the events of the day:

Everything was in unutterable and indescribable confusion. Ruin was on every side of us. The enemy was steadily advancing. On or about noon I drove my two horse buggy into camp at San Augustine Springs, found the companies in camp, and Lynde comfortably enjoying a lunch, as if nothing were going on, his command safe, instead of a wreck and scattered along the road for miles. It was the sublimity of indifference. In a short time the Texans were seen advancing in line of battle to the number of some three hundred. Our men, numbering at least five hundred infantry and cavalry, trained, disciplined, and well drilled soldiers, were drawn up in an opposite line, forming a striking contrast to the badly armed and irregular command of Texans. The enemy advanced to within three hundred yards of us, when Lynde raised and sent out a flag of truce, which was met and negotiations commenced with a view to surrender. They demanded an unconditional surrender, the same that Lynde had demanded of them at Mesilla. Lynde sought to modify this, but his request was refused, and to do the Texans full credit for humane conduct, they stated that two hours would be granted to remove the women and children to a place of safety, a most marked contrast to the cowardly conduct of Lynde at Mesilla, when he ordered the artillery to open fire on the town full of them.

Staff officers protested, but their protests were of no avail:

At this time all the officers assembled, and proposed waiting on Lynde and protesting against the surrender on any terms. One by one, from the senior down to the junior, we gave in our protest. It was farcial and ludicrous in the extreme. . . . It was too late, even had any one of the senior line officers been bold enough to seize the command by displacing Lynde, and putting him in arrest. . . . Blind, unreasonable obedience to orders was the ruin of our command. An unconditional surrender was at last agreed upon. Eleven companies of cavalry and infantry, between five and six hundred veterans, well disciplined and drilled troops, with two pieces of artillery, abandoned on the road, arms, and equipment, some two hundred cavalry horses, with mules and wagons and two or three hundred head of beef cattle, were unconditionally surrendered.[15]

Major Lynde's version of the happenings of the day of surrender was given in a report subsequently written for the Bureau of Military Justice, of the War Department:

I had never been over that route myself, but it was represented to me by officers acquainted with the road that it was about 22 miles to San Augustine Springs, the first water on the road, and that at that point there was plenty of water. We proceeded very well on our way until the sun arose, when it became excessively hot, and soon afterwards the men and animals began to show signs of fatigue and suffering from want of water. When within about five miles of the springs, I determined to push forward with the mounted force and procure as much water as they could carry and bring it back to the Infantry in the rear. At this time there was no indication of pursuit. On reaching the springs I found that the water was in limited quantity and not sufficient for my whole command. After filling all the vessels, I started back. . . . I had not proceeded far . . ., when I became so much exhausted from the fatigue and the excessive heat that I could sit on my horse no longer, and I had to stop and dismount, sending on the mounted force. After sitting by the roadside for some time, I was enabled to return slowly to the springs, but suffering from such intense pain in my head as to be almost blind. Reports came in repeatedly that the men were giving out and every effort was made to send out water to them. . . . A body of mounted Texans soon made their appearance in our vicinity. When I found that three out of four of our howitzers had been captured with more than half of our train, and all our men who were in our rear, amounting to from 150 to 200, and that I could not bring more than 250 men, all told, on parade, and most of them nearly worn out . . . it was hopeless to resist longer. A parley was held and terms of surrender agreed upon.[16]

Now that he had outmaneuvered Major Isaac Lynde, had captured hundreds of his soldiers; now that he held Fort Fillmore, and had frightened the North into abandoning Fort

Stanton, Colonel Baylor was ready to issue an important proclamation. Confident of staff approval, Baylor, on Aug. 2,
1861, declared that part of New Mexico lying south of the
thirty-fourth parallel, to be the Confederate Territory of Arizona, designated Mesilla as its capital, and proclaimed himself governor of the new territory. Although Baylor had
achieved an important victory over Major Lynde, his days and
nights were not free from concern. He learned in Dona Ana,
New Mexico, on Oct. 24, 1861, that General E. V. Sumner,
then commander of the Department of the Pacific in San
Francisco, had been ordered to land troops at Mazatlan, or
Guaymas, and march them through northern Mexico into
Texas (an expedition which was abandoned before it was
undertaken). Baylor promptly wrote to Judge Simeon Hart,
in El Paso:

No sign of the enemy thus far. I will have them watched and
let you know in time all the news. Cannot you send pony[17] to
Chihuahua to ascertain if Sumner is coming across? I learn he is
coming, and think it should be seen to by all means. Keep cool,
for we have time. They will get no reinforcements from Kansas,
and if Sumner does not come we will bag the whole party before
spring.

Baylor told Hart in another letter written on the same day:

Tell Crosby and Magoffin to be calm, and do not create a panic.
All will turn out all right. A little time is all we want. You will
hear of some tall guerilla work before long. Canby is at Craig
with 2,500 men, and expects to move against me by Nov. 1. With
three more companies I would fight them, but don't think it prudent now.[18]

Asking for reinforcements, Baylor wrote to the Commander of the Department of Texas on Oct. 25, 1861, saying:

I have petitioned time and again for reinforcements, to prevent
disaster, but a deaf ear has been turned to my request. I shall be
compelled to fall back, as my force is too weak to meet Canby.
Abandonment of the country will necessarily be attended with a
great sacrifice of property, and subject the friends of our cause
to persecution and ruin. . . . If it is the wish of the colonel commanding the department that Arizona should be abandoned, and

I presume it is, he can congratulate himself upon the consummation of that event.[19]

On Aug. 8, 1861, a few days after Baylor had captured Fort Fillmore, General Canby issued an order suspending the writ of habeas corpus throughout New Mexico:

The writ of habeas corpus has been suspended in order to enable every commander to guard against the treasonable designs of persons disloyal to the government of the United States, particularly agents and spies, persons engaged in furnishing information to, or in other treasonable correspondence with, the enemy, or in inciting insurrection or rebellion.

Canby warned that care should be taken to guard against any abuse of the power by unauthorized arrests or by annoyances to peaceable and well disposed citizens. Except in case of overt acts, arrests were to be made only by the superior commander of any district, post or body of troops in the service of the United States, and only upon probable cause of suspicion of being dangerous to the public safety.

Canby fully realized his predicament. Hampered by lack of money to pay his troops, and facing other serious obstacles, Canby wrote to the Paymaster General in Washington on Nov. 18, 1861, describing the situation:

The military operations in this department have for several months past been greatly embarrassed and are now almost entirely paralyzed by the want of funds in the pay department. Many of the regular troops have not been paid for more than twelve months, and the volunteers not at all. This has occasioned a great deal of suffering. . . . An unsuccessful attempt was made some time since to borrow money for the Government, and the chief quartermaster and chief commissary have united with me in promising that this money shall be repaid in Treasury notes, bearing 7.3 per cent interest from the date of the loan; or failing in this arrangement, I have personally pledged myself for the interest.[20]

Canby was not only harassed by lack of funds to insure the necessary preparations for turning back the Confederates. He was faced with Indian trouble which might develop into serious proportions at any time and divert him from defending the Territory against the invaders. Governor Connelly told Washington about the attitude and conduct of the Navajos in a letter written from Santa Fe on Oct. 26, 1861, in which he proposed the sword and starvation as remedies:

The Navajo Indians are still very troublesome. Although in a state of armistice, granted to them to test their professions of a desire for peace, and the truth of their promises to abstain from further depredations upon our property, I am sorry to say that such depredations are of daily occurrence. Even those who profess to be of the peace party, and are in daily intercourse with the troops about Fort Lyon and among our citizens, receiving presents of corn and flour, upon their departure from the settlements have driven off large flocks of sheep, mules and horses. Extermination by the sword or by starvation is our only remedy for the evils which they have caused and will continue to cause our people so long as there is one in existence. Something might perhaps be done by the Government in the way of their colonization, placing each tribe upon a reservation, with farming implements for their use, and a steady, practical farmer to instruct and assist them, together with a blacksmith and a carpenter. Agency buildings in their midst, and these surrounded by the lands and property of their most influential chiefs, together with a respectable military force in the neighborhood, but off of their reservation, are means which seem to present the most probable advantage to the Indians, and a hope of their earlier pursuit of their habits of civilized life. These, with the entire prohibition of all intercourse with the citizens, except their authorized agents, might lead to some amelioration of their condition, and in time produce a change in their disposition to lead a predatory life.[21]

It was not only the Navajos who were misbehaving. The Mescalero Apaches, the Utes, the Kiowas and Comanches, were all restless and milling about, according to Colonel Canby's report of Dec. 1, 1861, to the Assistant Adjutant General of the western department of the army of St. Louis:

Our relations with the Indians in New Mexico are daily becoming more unsatisfactory. The depredations of the Navajos are constant. The Mescalero Apaches are becoming more daring in their inroads, and incursions have been made by the Kiowas and Comanches, ostensibly in pursuit of the Utes, but their depredations have not been confined to them. Between the Navajos and the people of New Mexico a state of hostilities, with occasional intervals of peace, has existed almost since the first settlement of the country. Each party claims that the treaty of peace has been broken by the other, and it is impossible now, even if it were profitable, to inquire into which is in the right. Each successive war has reduced the Navajos in strength and wealth, and has, by reducing them to poverty, added to the strength of the *ladrones,* or war party. There is no doubt but that many of these difficulties, if not caused, have at least been greatly aggravated by the illegal acts of a portion of the Mexican people, and in some cases have been the direct cause of the difficulties that immediately followed them. The consequences of these acts have almost invariably fallen upon that portion of the Navajos known as the peace party, and upon those of the inhabitants who have property to lose, while the aggressors profit by the sale of their booty and captives. These acts are not restrained by the moral sense of the community, and so long as these marauders find a ready sale for their plunder and for their captives, it will be impossible to prevent these depredations, and the consequent retaliations by the Indians.

Extermination of the Navajos or their removal and colonization were the alternatives:

These remarks apply more particularly to the Navajos, but they are pertinent to our relations with all the surrounding Indians; and unless measures can be adopted by which this system, encouraged by the sympathies of the people, and fostered to some extent by the Territorial laws, can be broken up, the country will be involved in interminable evils. Recent occurrences in the Navajo country have so demoralized and broken up that nation, that there is no choice now between their absolute extermination or their removal and colonization at points so remote from the inhabitants of the settlements as to isolate them entirely from the inhabitants of the Territory. . . . Aside from all considerations of humanity, the extermination of such a people will be a work of the greatest difficulty. The country they inhabit is practically destitute of resources for military operations to a degree that can only be realized from personal observation. The Navajos are too cowardly to fight in number, but are adroit robbers, and any operations that may be carried on against them will ultimately resolve itself into a chase of individual thieves, and will be procrastinated indefinitely.

Canby proposed to settle some Navajos in communities under government protection:

As a question of economy and expediency, I have determined, in concert with the superintendent of Indian Affairs for this Territory, to establish such of the Navajos as have heretofore acted in good faith in communities, where they can be isolated and protected until some permanent arrangement can be made by the Government. The policy of settling them on reserves, removed from the Mexican population, protecting them, assisting them until they are able to sustain themselves as heretofore—repeatedly recommended by the superintendent of Indian Affairs and the commander of this department—is in my judgment, the only policy that gives any assurance of success.[22]

Regardless of how acute the Indian situation might be, Canby recognized that its solution was secondary in importance to the immediately pressing problem of defending against Confederate troops from Texas, now concentrated in southern New Mexico. The settlement of difficulties with the Indians must be deferred until another day. Canby's direct and pressing problem was to prepare to fight an enemy which would ask no quarter and give none.

Summing up the situation in New Mexico, Canby wrote a newsy letter from Santa Fe on Dec. 8, 1861, to the Adjutant General of the Army in Washington, informing him about down to earth things, men, horses and mules, money, artillery and beef:

The Confederate force in the Mesilla Valley is about 800 men of their regular troops and from 200 to 400 men organized from the floating population of the Mesilla. These troops are indifferently clothed and subsisted. They have fifteen pieces of artillery. . . . The resources for supplying an army in this country are limited almost exclusively to articles of forage and subsistence. . . . The horses and mules of the Territory are generally too light for cavalry or draught, and those purchased here for the use of the army are generally brought from the east. The articles that can be procured here are beef, flour, beans, and an inferior quality of salt. The cost of the beef will be greater than if the cattle are purchased in the western states and driven out. The quantity of flour that can be procured will not exceed three or three and a half million pounds in ordinary seasons. All the beans and salt that may be needed can be procured. Very great embarrassments have frequently been experienced in this department from the want of coin to meet the necessities of disbursing officers, and to obviate this difficulty, I have heretofore suggested that arrangements be made to send it out at frequent intervals and in small amounts by the express companies, instead of, as heretofore, but once in each year, and in larger amounts. In this last case, it falls into the hands of the Mexican capitalists and is exported.[23]

While Canby was involved in Santa Fe with troubles incident to financing his troops, holding off wild Indians and adopting means to repel a Confederate invasion from various possible directions, Henry Hopkins Sibley, now a brigadier general (with the title "Commander of the Army of the Confederate States of America in the Southwest"), was riding at the head of a brigade of a thousand men, enroute from San Antonio to El Paso. After leaving New Mexico, following his resignation from the Union Army, Sibley had gone to Montgomery and then to Richmond, where he succeeded in persuading President Jefferson Davis that New Mexico was the natural gateway for an expedition that would result in the acquisition of New Mexico, Colorado, Arizona, and probably California. Jefferson Davis gave Sibley a free hand to manage the proposed campaign. Adjutant and Inspector General S. Cooper wrote a letter to Sibley in Richmond on July 8, 1861, reading in part as follows:

In view of your recent service in New Mexico and knowledge of that country and the people, the President has entrusted you with the important duty of driving the federal troops from that department, and at the same time securing all the arms, supplies and materials of war. You are authorized to take into the Confederate States service all disaffected officers and soldiers on the original commissions of the officers and enlistment of the latter.

Cooper's letter directed that Sibley proceed without delay to Texas, "and in concert with Brig. Gen. Van Dorn, in the speediest manner possible, organize from the Texas troops two full regiments of cavalry and one battery of howitzers." The details of the campaign in New Mexico were left to Sibley's discretion. He was to be guided by circumstances and his "own good judgment." Secretary of War L. P. Walker gave Sibley a letter to Governor Edward Clark, at Austin, Texas, directing him to make available to Sibley such facilities "as would best insure his early success in raising the troops." Official orders were forwarded from Richmond to Brigadier General Earl Van Dorn, at San Antonio, notifying him that President Davis had directed Sibley to proceed to Texas, and "carry out certain measures, of which Sibley would inform him upon his arrival."

Returning to Texas, Sibley established his headquarters in San Antonio, and began the work of organizing the brigade. "Camp Sibley" was established on the Salado, five miles from San Antonio on the Austin road, and a second camp was established on the Leone. Sibley had his trials and tribulations in organizing and equipping his expedition. Obviously exasperated, he complained about many things, among them that he had been delayed in raising and organizing his brigade because of lack of cooperation on the part of Governor Clark, a charge Clark resented and vigorously denied.

There was justification for Sibley's anxiety. Baylor wrote to him from Dona Ana, "Arizona," on Oct. 25, advising that Canby, with 2,500 men, eleven companies of U. S. regulars, and 13 companies of New Mexico volunteers, were on the march for Dona Ana, with a battery of artillery; that he proposed to fall back to Fort Quitman, and to Fort Davis, if necessary, as he was too weak to meet the enemy, and asked for reinforcements to be sent to him at once. Baylor told Sibley of the rumor that General E. V. Sumner would land California troops at Guaymas and was expected to meet Canby at Mesilla. From El Paso on Oct. 27, 1861, Simeon Hart wrote Sibley advising that he had $40,000 to $50,000 available, and was using 30 to 40 wagons furnished by Baylor to haul supplies from Sonora. Among other things, Hart said: "Baylor's command is in peril. I hope God in His goodness will so order things as not to make his retreat necessary from Arizona." By Nov. 10, 1861, Baylor was more optimistic.

On that date he wrote to Colonel H. E. McCulloch, Commanding the Department of Texas at San Antonio: "I shall, with my mounted force, push for Santa Fe, and hold the country until the arrival of General Sibley." [24]

Sibley's name was magic throughout the Southwest. When word reached the interior of Texas that he was organizing a brigade, men began to arrive at his headquarters, eager to sign the muster role. On Aug. 27, 1861, Captain William P. Hardeman reached camp with his company from Caldwell and Guadalupe Counties followed soon by Colonel James Riely, Captain William R. Scurry and Captain H. Raguet (of Nacodoches), and their companies. By Sept. 20, 1861, the full compliment of companies had been mustered into the service and the organization of the First Regiment had been completed. Colonel Tom Green, Texas "hero of heroes," organized the Second Regiment at Camp Manassas on the Salado, two miles above the First Regiment camp. By Oct. 4, the Third Regiment, under Colonel William Steele (late captain in the U. S. Cavalry, who had served with Sibley in New Mexico), had been organized and was ready for service. The brigade was drilled, disciplined, and whipped into shape for the days of fighting to come.

The troops of the brigade were equipped with almost every known type of weapon. Many soldiers brought their own guns with them, and required no instruction on how to load or fire them. Some of the volunteers had squirrel guns, others had bear and sportsmen's guns, still others had single and double barreled shotguns, an innovation in warfare, which took a terrible toll of Union lives a few weeks later at the battle of Valverde, in New Mexico. In addition to the smaller weapons, the brigade was equipped with 6 mountain howitzers. By late fall in 1861, the brigade was ready to march for New Mexico. "Boots and Saddles" was sounded at daylight on Oct. 22, and the men of the First Regiment under Colonel Riely mounted their horses, and descended from the hills into San Antonio. The regiment had no band, so the men sang "The Texas Ranger." The ladies of San Antonio presented the regiment with a flag in the plaza at San Antonio, and General Sibley delivered a patriotic address. Sibley spoke eloquently from a prancing horse, but only a few men in the front ranks heard his words because of the noise and commotion.

With Riely's Regiment gone from San Antonio, company after company of the Second and Third Regiments followed according to schedule. Because of the scarcity of water between San Antonio and El Paso it was necessary to follow a rigid program of arrival and departure of troops from each camp and watering place. Colonel Thomas Green's regiment left for New Mexico on Nov. 2, and Colonel William Steele's regiment left on Nov. 20. The journey of some 700 miles to El Paso was one of hardship for men and horses. Measles and other contagious diseases dogged the footsteps of the troops. Many members of the brigade never reached New Mexico. Fifteen men in one company died enroute of the measles.

General Sibley left San Antonio on Nov. 18, 1861, "to assume in person the command of our forces in the Territory of New Mexico, and to conduct the military operations there and in Arizona." Sibley was accompanied by his staff officers, Major A. M. Jackson, who had been Secretary of the Territory of New Mexico until just before the war, I. Ochiltree, Captain Dwyer and Judge J. F. Crosby, Assistant Quartermaster and receiver of property to be confiscated in New Mexico. Arriving in El Paso on Dec. 12, Sibley established his headquarters at Fort Bliss.

Realizing the importance of establishing favorable relations, if at all possible, with adjacent states in Mexico, Sibley wrote a letter from Fort Bliss on Dec. 16, 1861, to the governor of Sonora, Mexico, telling him that he had entire possession of Arizona "including and comprising the towns and settlements of the Mesilla Valley," and asking for concessions in the State of Sonora, the right to procure and trade in supplies, for permission to march troops through the state if necessary.[25]

General Stephen Watts Kearny

General Edward Richard Sprigg Canby

General Henry Hopkins Sibley

In memory of the Confederates
who died at Glorieta Pass in New Mexico

Courtesy John Gaw Meem, Santa Fe

General James Henry Carleton

Ruins of officers' quarters, Fort Bliss, Texas, 1863

Navajo Indian captives at Bosque Redondo

Navajo Indian captives near Cañon de Chelle

Sallyport at Fort Bliss, Texas at end of Civil War

Dr. Michael Steck

On December 20, 1861, Sibley issued a proclamation addressed to the people of New Mexico, in which he declared federal taxes abolished forthwith, gave assurance of friendship, promised utopian like government for everybody:

An army under my command enters New Mexico, to take possession of it in the name and for the benefit of the Confederate States. By geographical position, by similarity of institutions, by commercial interests, and by future destinies, New Mexico pertains to the Confederacy. Upon the peaceful people of New Mexico the Confederate States wage no war. To them we come as friends, to reestablish a governmental connection agreeable and advantageous both to them and to us; to liberate them from the yoke of a military despotism erected by usurpers upon the ruins of the former free institutions of the United States; to relieve them from the iniquitous taxes and exactions imposed upon them by that usurpation; to insure and to revere their religion, and to restore their civil and political liberties.

The Northern cause had already failed, according to General Sibley:

The existing war is one most wickedly waged by the United States against the Confederate States for the subjugation and oppression of the latter by force of arms. It has already failed. Victory has crowned the arms of the Confederate States wherever an encounter worthy of being called a battle has been joined. Witness the battles of Bull Run, of Manassas, of Springfield, of Lexington, of Leesburg, of Columbus, and the capture in the Mesilla valley of the whole force of the enemy by scarcely half their number.

Assured of protection of life and property, the people were told to go quietly about their business:

The army under my command is ample to seize and to maintain possession of New Mexico against any force which the enemy now has or is able to place within its limits. It is my purpose to accomplish this object without injury to the peaceful people of the country. Follow, then, quietly your peaceful avocations, and from my forces you have nothing to fear. Your persons, your families, and your property shall be secure and safe. Such forage and supplies as my army shall require will be purchased in open market and paid for at fair prices. If destroyed or removed to prevent me from availing myself of them, those who so cooperate with our enemies shall be treated accordingly, and must prepare to share their fate.

To those New Mexicans who had joined the Union forces, General Sibley issued a solemn warning:

It is well known to me that many among you have already been forced by intimidation or inveigled by fraud into the ranks of our foes. The day will soon arrive when you can safely abjure their service. When it comes, throw down your arms and disperse to your homes, and you are safe. But persist in the service, and you are lost.

Federal taxes were abolished, and Sibley assured New Mexicans a strong and lenient government under the Confederacy:

When the authority of the Confederate States shall be established in New Mexico, a government of your best men, to be conducted upon principles with which you are familiar and to which you are attached, will be inaugurated. Your religious, civil, and political rights and liberties will be reestablished and maintained sacred and intact. In the meantime, by virtue of the powers vested in me by the President and Government of the Confederate States, I abrogate and abolish the law of the United States levying taxes upon the people of New Mexico.

Sibley appealed to his old comrades in arms to join him in his crusade for the Southland:

To my old comrades in arms, still in the ranks of the usurpers of their government and liberties, I appeal in the name of former friendship: Drop at once the arms which degrade you into the tools of tyrants, renounce their service, and array yourselves under the colors of justice and freedom! I am empowered to receive you into the service of the Confederate States; the officers upon their commissions, the men upon their enlistments. By every principle of law and morality you are exonerated from service in the ranks of our enemies. You never engaged in the service of one portion of the old Union to fight against another portion, who, so far from being your enemies, have ever been your best friends. In the sight of God and man, you are justified in renouncing a service iniquitous in itself and in which you never engaged....[26]

CHAPTER TWO

From Valverde to Apache Cañon

UNION FORCES faced a discouraging prospect in New Mexico in the fall of 1861. Fort Fillmore had been captured; Fort Stanton had been abandoned. Colonel Baylor's Texas Riflemen had outwitted and outgeneralled Union troops at San Augustine Springs. It was high time for the federal government to take the situation seriously. On Sept. 4, 1861, President Lincoln nominated Dr. Henry Connelly, a long time resident of New Mexico, to be governor of the Territory as successor to Gov. Abraham Rencher, of North Carolina, suspected of being sympathetic to the Southern cause. With Connelly as governor, and Colonel Canby as Commander of the Department of New Mexico, the Territory was safely in the hands of loyal and patriotic administrators. The Territorial Legislature convened in Santa Fe on Jan. 1, 1862, in an atmosphere of intense political excitement. Although Confederate sympathizers had tried desperately, they had been unable to elect their legislative candidates. Lines were sharply drawn in House and Council on slavery and anti-slavery questions. Governor Connelly's message to the Legislature was anti-slavery. It was soon apparent that "Union men" had the majority in the Legislature. One of its first acts in the Session of 1862 was to repeal "An Act Entitled 'An Act Providing for the Protection of Slave Property in this Territory'," which had been passed by the Legislature on Feb. 3, 1859. Repeal of the 1859 law demonstrated that New Mexico had reversed itself on the slavery question, and

165

gave notice to the world that New Mexico had officially identified itself with the Union cause.

On Jan. 25, 1862, the Legislature passed a wartime measure conferring broad general powers upon the Governor. This act made the Governor commander in chief of the militia, and authorized him to take the steps necessary "to repulse and drive from the soil, the now invading army." The bill, carrying the emergency clause, authorized the Governor, among other things, to suspend the writ of habeas corpus:

The Territory now being invaded by armed troops, rebels against the government of the United States and enemies of the Territory and its people; the Governor as commander in chief of the militia, is hereby authorized and required to organize and call into service the entire force of the Territory, whether it be in horses, arms, ammunition or other property, or means, and direct the same jointly with the forces of the United States, to repulse and drive from the soil, the now invading army. He shall have the power, whenever the security of the country and people may require, to suspend the writ of habeas corpus by proclamation in such districts as he may deem necessary. The powers herein specified shall cease as soon as the enemy shall be subjugated and the integrity of the Territory secured.

The words used by the Legislature in the war powers act, "to repulse and drive from the soil, the now invading army," were not idly used. By Feb. 5, 1862, the First, Second and Third Regiments of Sibley's brigade were in camp on the east bank of the Rio Grande, opposite Fort Thorn, New Mexico. Here General Sibley established temporary headquarters. He had by-passed Fort Fillmore because smallpox was reported to be prevalent there. On Feb. 14, Sibley issued the command of "forward march!" Two days later, Feb. 16, the "Army of New Mexico" was in battle formation, within sight of Fort Craig, and in plain view of the Union forces.

That a crisis existed in New Mexico, from the military standpoint, was recognized by the Secretary of War in Washington. Company B of the Second Colorado Regiment sent to reinforce Canby, by means of forced marches, reached New Mexico in a matter of days.[27] On Jan. 31, 1862, General Geo.

C. Wright, commanding the Department of the Pacific in San Francisco, ordered Colonel James H. Carleton to organize an expedition of California troops to march to the relief of Arizona and New Mexico, but Canby did not learn of such a contemplated troop movement until months later.

Canby had planned originally to move south along the Rio Grande, and attempt to recapture Fort Bliss. He abandoned this idea upon learning that Sibley had left Fort Bliss, and was traveling northward along the Rio Grande. Canby then decided to concentrate his troops at Fort Craig, on the Rio Grande, 176 miles from Santa Fe, and about 140 miles north of Fort Bliss. Governor Henry Connelly, who accompanied the Territorial militia from Santa Fe to Fort Craig, wrote to Secretary of State Seward from Fort Craig on Feb. 5, 1862, advising him that Texas troops, advancing along the Rio Grande, were reported to be at Fort Thorn, 80 miles away, "without a doubt marching forward to determine by a decisive battle the fate of the Territory." Connelly was optimistic: "I have no fears of the result here. We will conquer the Texan forces. If not in the first battle, it will be done in the second or subsequent battles. We will overcome them. The spirit of our people is good, and I have here and enroute 1000 and more of the *elite* of the yeomanry of the country to aid in defending their homes and friends." [28]

On Feb. 11, 1862, Governor Connelly advised Seward that the enemy, "exceeding an estimated 3,000 men," was within 20 miles of Fort Craig. Fully 4,000 men were under arms at Fort Craig, including 1,200 of regulars. Connelly told Seward: "Today our forces march out to meet them. The battle will most likely take place on the 13th, about 10 miles below. We have no fears of the result. Enthusiasm prevails throughout our lines."

The fighting between the Confederate and Union troops at Valverde[29] began soon after daylight on Feb. 21, 1862, and continued throughout that day and the next. The battle of Valverde was a spectacular and dramatic engagement. As early as Feb. 8, General Canby sent detachments of regulars

and volunteers on reconnaissance marches from Fort Craig
south along the Rio Grande to learn whether troops camped
on the edges of the *Jornada del Muerto* were isolated detachments, or General Sibley's main body of Confederates. Canby's detachments marched to Adobe Walls, a few miles to
the south, and returned to Fort Craig without having obtained any definite information. Spirits were high at Fort
Craig. Apparently everybody inside the walls of the fort,
from Canby on down to the lance corporal's bunkey, felt
supremely confident of victory. The atmosphere at the fort
changed a bit at daylight on Feb. 19, when a Confederate
column marched northward in plain view of every observer.
Confederate scouts on horseback boldly crossed to the west
side of the Rio Grande, rode along a ravine toward the center
of the plain opposite Fort Craig. Union troops, concentrated
on the southeastern corner of the fortifications, watched their
movements. The Confederate scouts took a leisurely look
at Fort Craig, apparently estimated the number of troops
within the fortifications, seemingly considered its points of
strength and weakness. Major Duncan, and a detachment
of Federal Mounted Rifles, started toward the Confederate
scouting party. The scouts discharged a volley as Duncan's
men approached them. Duncan and his men discreetly returned to the protection of the fort. Captain James ("Patty")
Grayton, volunteering to do a bit of independent recon-
noitering, rode into the ravine alone on his gray pony, reaching a point within the enemy's musket range. Grayton galloped and wheeled his horse about, like a circus performer,
in order not to expose himself too greatly to Texas sharpshooters, but soon decided to retire to a position of safety.
The Confederate scouts recrossed the river and went into
camp, joining their comrades arriving from the south in apparently ever increasing numbers. Federal scouts, standing
on parapet walls at Fort Craig, were able to count the number
of enemy campfires. The voices of the Confederates from
the opposite side of the river could be heard distinctly at

Fort Craig during the night when the wind blew from the east.

On Monday, Feb. 20, 1862, scouts at Fort Craig saw quite plainly a long line of transport supply wagons a mile and a half away, traveling northward on the east side of the river, definite evidence that Sibley had decided not to attack Canby. Buglers at Fort Craig quickly sounded the call to arms. Troops were given one day's cooked rations in a haversack and an extra supply of ammunition for every cartridge box. One company after another marched down the steep bank leading from the fort, crossed the Rio Grande, and started for the bluffs on the opposite side. When the advance guard of Union troops reached the tableland several hundred yards east of the fort, the Confederates fired at them from cannon mounted on a commanding ridge. No doubt but that Sibley, from the standpoint of military strategy, occupied an advantageous position. The adobe walls of Fort Craig were well within range of his cannon. Unable to form a satisfactory line, the Union soldiers dispersed and sought refuge wherever they might find it to save their lives in the face of a hail of bullets from the carbines of Confederate sharpshooters. In crossing the river, the federals had seen their company commanders wade into the chilling water in full dress and accoutrements. Few privates dared to refuse to follow the example of their officers. As a result most of the men plunging into the river reached the opposite side wet up to the hips. Many of them spent a miserable night, suffering from the cold, their teeth chattering, longing for a cup of hot coffee. The Union troops returned from the plain to Fort Craig at daylight on Feb. 21. They were given another day's rations and ordered to march north along the Rio Grande a distance of four miles to a place known as the "hay camp." Colonel Ben S. Roberts, in command of most of the regular troops, and a light battery, was ordered to reconnoitre in the same direction. Reaching a point on the west bank of the Rio Grande (known nineteen years later as San Marcial), Roberts observed Confederate detachments on the east bank of the river. Precipitately, Roberts gave the order to fire, something Canby had not authorized. Learning of the firing and impending conflict, Canby hurried from Fort Craig to support Roberts.[30]

Thus began the famous battle of Valverde. The weather at noon time on Feb. 21, the date of the sanguinary battle, was warm, almost hot, and the wind blew a gale. As the engagement got well under way, Canby had many effective soldiers in the field, but more who were ineffective, as the subsequent fighting demonstrated. He had at his command six companies of the crack 5th U. S. Infantry (which since the Mexican War had seen service in Texas, Florida and Utah), led by Captain Selden as regimental commander, and Lieutenant Anderson as regimental adjutant. He had a light battery, composed of the Second Dragoons and Mounted Riflemen, which Lieutenant Anderson had organized and drilled, but which at the time of the battle was commanded by Captain McRae, of the Rifles.

Colonel Christopher (Kit) Carson, with a full regiment of New Mexico Volunteers, was in the fighting, supported by two companies of Colorado troops, called Pike's Peakers, commanded by Captain Theo. H. Dodd. Rations had been issued at Fort Craig on the previous day for 4,200 men, rank and file, indicating that the Federals had at least 3,000 troops ready for service. Now that the battle was under way, the Union forces fired their field pieces and muskets, and the balls and bullets rattled against the cottonwood trees on the opposite bank of the Rio Grande, where the Confederate column was in position. To shield his men from unnecessary exposure, Colonel Roberts ordered an advance. Horse and footmen sprang forward into the waters of the Rio Grande. This was the signal for the Confederates to open fire. Scores of Union men were shot and killed as they attempted to cross the river. Others, badly wounded, were drowned. Company K, with two 24 pounders, successful in crossing the river, directed a steady fire at the Confederate position. Texas lanc ers, charging in column to take Company K's battery, were repulsed with serious losses. The Colorado "Pike's Peakers," conspicuous because they wore gray blouses, with a red stripe in front, proved a ready target, but fought valiantly. The Texas batteries, manned by excellent gunners, killed scores of Canby's men. Within a matter of hours it was all too apparent that the Union forces were being routed. Realizing that their situation was already desperate, Union artillerymen cut the traces of their horses and escaped as best they could. Sibley's lancers, charging murderously, captured the Union's heavy artillery. Within six hours after the fighting had begun, there was no doubt but that the Confederates had won the day at Valverde. An hour before sundown, when the battle, for the Union side, had turned into a rout, Canby's adjutants and aides-de-camp brought the orders to the field: "Retreat to the fort! Let every man escape the best he can." [31]

Theo. Noel, of the 4th Texas Cavalry, an eyewitness, described the first day's fighting at Valverde from the Confederate viewpoint:

Up to this time (Feb. 20, 1862, when six miles south of Fort Craig) our journey had been performed with but little trouble, but now comes the tug of war . . . deep ravines to cross, mountains to climb, our teams were fast giving out, both for the want of food and water . . . daylight found the advance portion of the brigade within two miles of the river, Fort Craig being in the valley below. . . . No courier was necessary to bring back the news that the enemy was coming; like wild fire it flew, many were wont to leave the train and go meet them. The battle of Valverde commenced at 9 am (Feb. 21, 1862). The enemy having taken their position in the valley between us and the river, and it being impossible for us to either dislodge or flank them, an open field fight was the order of the day. The enemy evinced no disposition to attack us in our position. Knowing that we were suffering from want of water, and that we were either compelled to fight them on their own ground or perish, they were content to allow us to make the first "pass," which we did by opening on them with Teel's, Riely's and Fulerod's batteries. After dancing to our music for a short time they commenced to move on to our right wing. Being repulsed in this they determined to dislodge us by their artillery, which they brought from the opposite side of the river

and placed in position some 600 yards in our advance, quite out
of range of our small pieces and squirrel guns. For a time they
piped a lively air for us. A cavalry charge was ordered on our
right; two companies of the Second Regiment were the ones
picked on. "The Lancers" were drawn up in battle; a charge was
sounded, with shouts they bounded forward. Scarcely had they
advanced to within one hundred yards of the enemy's infantry
column ere twenty nine horses lost their riders, and back the
squadron came. In a few moments afterwards a charge on the
battery was ordered. Seeing the column advancing on the battery,
Colonel Green ordered the whole line to charge. For a few moments the strife was terrific beyond description. The battery was
taken but not until every man belonging to it was killed. Such
desperate fighting on the part of the enemy has never since been
witnessed. Captain McRae, who commanded the enemy's battery,
fell pierced with many bullets while vainly trying to urge the
infantry support forward to his rescue. In this charge we carried
everything before us, routing the enemy, we drove them to the
river, where they "took water," on short notice, more like a herd
of frightened mustangs than like men. Many of them were killed
in crossing the river. In the charge upon the battery we lost the
most of our killed and wounded. The enemy formed on the opposite side of the river. Colonel Scurry collected all the cavalry together in order to make the victory a complete one. On his reaching the river, and as he was just in the act of crossing, the enemy
sent a flag of truce to our Commander, asking to be allowed to
bury their dead. Under cover of the truce which was granted
them they saved themselves by sudden flight to Fort Craig. . . . Besides the battery, we captured large quantities of provisions, and
small arms and accoutrements. Every Yank had one or more canteens and (bread basket) haversacks. Many of their canteens were
filled with whiskey, and it is said that those of the battery were
tinctured with ether. Our half starved boys "gormanized sumptu-
ously," on Yankee light bread and other most delicious eatables.
That night we bivouaced on the field.[32]

Union officers were put to task to defend the results of the
fighting at Valverde. Captain Gurden Chapin, of the Seventh Infantry, writing from Santa Fe on Feb. 28, 1862, to
Major General H. W. Halleck, in St. Louis, blamed the defeat on the instability of New Mexico's volunteer troops.
Chapin praised Canby's leadership, saying among other

things: "Colonel Canby did everything which man could do to retake his battery and save the day. He beseeched and begged, ordered and imperatively commanded, troops to save his guns, and a deaf ear met alike his supplications and commands."

Some great blunders, no doubt, were committed on each side at the battle of Valverde. Seemingly, the Union forces had the upper hand on the battlefield until 5 o'clock in the afternoon of Feb. 21. At that hour, according to Canby's report of Feb. 22, to the Adjutant General of the Army, "in a desperate charge of the Confederates, McRae's battery was taken, the supporting party repulsed and thrown into confusion and driven from the field at the moment when success seemed certain." "With deep sorrow," Canby reported that three officers and 65 men had been killed, three officers and 157 enlisted men had been wounded; one officer and 34 enlisted men were missing.[33] On the Confederate side, thirty-six men were reported dead, 150 wounded, and one missing. The dead on both sides were buried, under flags of truce, on the battlefield, not far from the muddy waters of the Rio Grande. Colonel William Steele, carrying a flag of truce for the Confederacy, went to Fort Craig personally to request medical and hospital supplies for his wounded men. These were furnished at once by Canby's order. Union soldiers wounded at Valverde were taken to Fort Craig. The Confederate wounded were taken to Socorro and Albuquerque.

General Sibley reported briefly on the results at Valverde. Writing from the battleground on Feb. 22 to General S. Cooper, Adjutant and Inspector General at Richmond, he said that the Confederates never had more than 1,500 men engaged in the battle, while the enemy had 3,500 men on the field, of whom 1,200 were "old regulars." In their respective reports, both Canby and Sibley were in agreement on the statement that the Confederates had used double barreled shotguns at a most critical period of the fighting.[34] In his report, Canby said: "Armed with double barreled fowling pieces and revolvers, and converging as they approached, the

Confederates poured a rapid and destructive fire into Mc-Rae's battery, only to be met with a terrible fire of grape and double canister. McRae's gallant band was driven from the field, but not until it had lost in killed and wounded and prisoners, nearly one-half of its effective force." Reporting on the same phase of the battle, Sibley said: "Batteries were charged and taken at the muzzle of double barreled shotguns, thus illustrating the spirit, valor, and invincible determination of Texas troops; nobly have they emulated the fame of their San Jacinto ancestors." [35]

Having defeated Canby decisively at Valverde, Sibley by-passed Fort Craig, and started for Albuquerque.[36] On Feb. 21, 1862, General Canby issued an order from Fort Craig to the commanding officers at Albuquerque, Santa Fe and Fort Lyon, which read:

After a severe battle today, the enemy has succeeded in effecting a lodgment on the river above this place, and will probably succeed in cutting off your communications with the upper country. You will hold yourself prepared to remove or destroy all public property, and particularly provisions, so that nothing that is useful may fall into the hands of the enemy. All trains and detachments now on the way should be turned back.

As they advanced on Albuquerque, the Confederates were aware that Union forces were evacuating the town because of the clouds of smoke plainly visible for many miles. Theo. Noel, of the Fourth Texas Cavalry, later described the situation:

As we came in sight of Albuquerque we beheld three large columns of smoke ascending, as it were, to the very heavens. This told the tale for us. Our advance had been made known. On our approach, instead of giving us a fight, the garrison, which consisted only of cavalry, applied the torch to all the government houses and property in the place. If it could have been possible for us to have hindered this, the Confederate Army of New Mexico would never have experienced any inconvenience for the want of clothing or commissaries.[37]

Reaching Albuquerque at daylight on March 2, 1862, the Confederates raised their flag in the plaza and took possession of the town in the name of the Confederate States of America. The Confederates quickly sent a detachment of troops to Cubero, some 65 miles west of Albuquerque, which returned in a few days with twenty-one wagon loads of supplies stored there for the use of Union troops.[38] How Union troops evacuated Albuquerque in advance of the arrival of the Confederates was told by Captain Herbert M. Enos in a letter from Fort Union on March 11, 1862, to Quartermaster James L. Donaldson advising him of the burning of the public property in Albuquerque:

The night of March 1 passed without the appearance of the enemy, but believing that he would soon be upon me, and not hearing of any troops being on the way from Santa Fe to hold the town, I gave the order to fire the public property at about 6:30 on the morning of the 2nd. The destruction would have been complete had it not been for the great rush of Mexican men, women and children, who had been up the whole night, waiting anxiously for an opportunity to gratify their insatiable desire for plunder. The only property that was not burned consisted of molasses, vinegar, soap and candles, and a few saddles, carpenter's tools, and office furniture. Most of these articles were carried off by the Mexicans. The destruction of the stores involved the destruction of the buildings containing them, as it would have been impossible with the force and the short time at my disposal to have removed the property from the buildings in order that it might be burned. Had I attempted to carry out this plan I am of the opinion that the native population would have overpowered me and saved the property for the enemy.[39]

Sibley's troops apparently "lived off the country," as they marched from Valverde through Socorro, Peralta and other towns on the way to Albuquerque. Writing on March 23, 1862, from Las Vegas, to which place he transferred the official business of the territorial capital, Governor Henry Connelly told Secretary of State Seward his understanding of the situation:

The enemy in force are now occupying a pass in the mountains east of Albuquerque, some 15 miles, called Carnuel. . . . I am sorry to say that the Texans have not behaved with the moderation that was expected, and that desolation has marked their progress on the Rio Grande from Fort Craig to Bernalillo. Exactions and confiscations are of daily occurrence, and the larger portion of those who have anything to give or lose are here on this frontier, seeking a refuge from their rapacity, and have left their houses and contents a prey to the invaders. My own house, 90 miles from Santa Fe, was despoiled of its entire contents, including a valuable stock of goods, together with everything in the way of subsistence. On yesterday there arrived at this place some 20 of our most prosperous and respectable citizens from the neighborhood of Albuquerque and Bernalillo, who fled from the exactions of Sibley; among the number a gentleman of eighty years of age, Don Pedro Jose Perea, and his three sons, upon whom a demand had been made for a large sum of money, which they had not in their houses, having advanced all their available means to the disbursing officers of the government but a short time before. The threat of personal violence in case of refusal so alarmed them, that they left their houses and entire contents at the mercy of the enemy.[40]

Sibley's brigade, with the exception of some companies left in Albuquerque to hold that town, left for Santa Fe on March 3, 1861. A detachment was sent to Carnuel, fifteen miles east of Albuquerque, to guard against the possibility that Union troops might attempt to enter Albuquerque by way of Tijeras Canyon. The brigade advance guard, under Major Pyron, was at Algodones, 22 miles north of Albuquerque, on March 5. Word was passed along in the ranks that plenty of fighting might be expected before April 1.[41]

Reconciled to the inevitable fact that the Confederates would take Santa Fe, the people of the capital city learned of the enemy's approach without undue alarm. Santa Fe had managed, sixteen years before, to live through a somewhat similar crisis, when Kearny's troops had occupied the city. In the face of another like emergency the inhabitants were calm and confident of their ability to cope with the situation.

Major Donaldson, commander of Union troops in Santa Fe, conceding that the town could not be successfully defended "because it was commanded on all sides by hills," complied with Canby's instructions to evacuate. He burned all government owned non-movable property. A train of 120 wagons, carrying movable supplies from Albuquerque and Santa Fe was started from Santa Fe for Fort Union on March 4, 1862. The last wagon of the train "arrived under the guns of Fort Union," six days later.[42] By noon of March 5, 1862, the last of the Union forces in Santa Fe had left for Fort Union, leaving the Territorial capital without protection, and assuring the oncoming Confederates of a victory without a single shot being fired by way of token defense.

Although Santa Fe was exposed to the oncoming Confederates, help was on the way. Colonel John P. Slough, in command of a regiment of the First Colorado Volunteers, some 1,300 regulars and volunteers, left Denver City, Colorado, for New Mexico, on Feb. 22, 1862. Slough learned enroute of the Confederate victory at Valverde, and that Fort Union and Santa Fe were in danger of falling into the hands of the enemy. Upon receiving this information, Slough marched his troops, as "infantry had never marched before," 172 miles in 5 days "through snows and wintry winds." Slough's troops rested brifly at Fort Union, leaving there on March 22 for Santa Fe.[43]

The Confederates took possession of Santa Fe on March 23, 1862. Copies of Sibley's proclamation issued at Albuquerque on March 13, calling upon the people of New Mexico to support the Southern cause, were distributed throughout the capital. Two days after their arrival in Santa Fe, the Confederates marched eastward, intending to attack Fort Union.[44]

Some thirteen hundred Union troops left Las Vegas for Santa Fe at daylight on March 24. The troops included several companies of the 5th U. S. Infantry, a troop or two of the old Rifle Regiment, subsequently the Third Cavalry, and troops from Colorado known as Pike's Peakers, all in command of John P. Slough, a lawyer, and Major John M. Chivington, a minister of the gospel.[45] It was inevitable that a battle would take place. The Colorado troops, under Slough and Chivington, reached Pigeon's Ranch[46] on March 26, 1862. Colonel W. R. Scurry, of the Confederates, reached Pigeon's Ranch sometime before the Colorado troops, to reinforce

Major Pyron. There has been some doubt as to just what occurred at Pigeon's Ranch on the fateful day of March 27,
1862, when Union and Confederate forces came to bush-
whacking grips with each other.

Twelve years after the war was over, Louis Hommel wrote
the story of the fighting at Pigeon's Ranch, after having
walked over the battlefield many times, and obtaining information from participants or eyewitnesses.[47] As Hommel
heard the story, the Union troops were marching toward
Santa Fe from Las Vegas. They had ascended and descended
the mountain ranges, confident of reaching the capital before
many hours. To quote Hommel's version:

> The men were now resting at the watering place of Pigeon's
> Ranch; the cavalry had gone on as an advance guard and every-
> thing being serene in the neighborhood, men and beasts were tak-
> ing it as comfortably as could be expected under the circum-
> stances, little dreaming that those clusters of trees and felled pine
> in the vicinity contained masked batteries and a foe, waiting only
> to spring, tigerlike, upon his prey, when least thinking of danger,
> but so it happened. Hardly had the guard mounted the bluff to
> the rear of Pigeon's Hotel, to keep a lookout over the troops here
> and to watch the road, when from the mouth of a dozen pieces
> of artillery, in the shape of grape and canister, deadly missiles
> were hurled into the crowd of soldiers around the water tank,
> trying to moisten their parched lips.
> A spell of confusion followed, officers shouting for their men
> to "fall in," soldiers running hither and thither, hunting their
> arms and places in the ranks. By the time the Union forces were
> in fighting trim, the Texans had also left their ambush, seeking
> now a face to face battle. The ground on each side was bravely
> contested; but after awhile, when the Confederates silenced their
> guns and somewhat abandoned the contest, the federal troops
> beat a hasty retreat toward Fort Union. But why did the Texans
> retire from the field, having the advantage of the day? At Rock
> Corral, about eight miles further west, toward Santa Fe, the Tex-
> ans had their large supply train corralled; and the advance guard
> of the federal troops, upon finding that the battle was raging
> behind them, and this train was almost unprotected, made a flank
> movement into the hills, emerging below Rock Corral, and now
> attacked the train from the rear. The Texans, knowing that they
> were fighting ahead, and thinking this to be the Canby column,

abandoned their trust. With the speed of almost lightning itself, on panting steeds and with sweating brow, the Texans announced to the column ahead, that Canby had taken the train, and thinking themselves thus between two fires, abandoned the field and took to the mountains. In this manner, both parties, thinking themselves badly whipped, retired from the scene of slaughter, as quick as horses and their own legs could carry them. Only the day after did they both find out their mistake, but each with different result. Col. Slough marched triumphantly back to Fort Union, and the Texans, finding themselves without supplies, their train having been burned, retired to Santa Fe. The graves of the dead in the field on Pigeon's Ranch have been made to deliver up their contents for burial in the cemetery at Santa Fe; but not a single corpse could be recognized or identified to show whether it belonged to Texan or Federal soldier; all bear the following description on their headboards: "Unknown, Removed from Pigeon's Ranch." [48]

The skirmish at Pigeon's Ranch, although important, was not a deciding factor in the attempt of the Confederates to get through the Union lines to Fort Union. Through a strange twist of fortune, "Preacher" Chivington contributed in greatest measure to the Confederate setback. Peering down in the early morning of March 28, from a mountain top, Chivington's scouts, through a spy glass, saw "corraled almost in one place 80 wagons and one field piece, all in charge of 200 men." Believing that it might be possible to execute a surprise movement, and cripple the enemy's supply and ammunition train, Chivington hurried down the mountain side, maneuvered into the rear of the train, and attacked. Because the attack came from their rear, a rumor quickly gained credence in Confederate ranks that it had been made by Canby, their opponent at the battle of Valverde. Actually Canby was at Socorro, 140 miles to the south. The rumor gained momentum among the rank and file, resulting in great confusion and finally consternation in Confederate lines. Beginning his attack on the enemy's rear at 10 o'clock in the morning, of March 28, Preacher Chivington was enabled to write a report by nightfall, saying that his men had captured the Confederate wagon trains, "all loaded with ammunition, clothing, subsistence, and forage," and that "all of them were burned upon the spot, or rendered entirely useless."

Recovering from their initial surprise and confusion, the Confederates "planted their battery and began to throw grape and shell" at the "Preacher's" soldiers. The fighting continued until sundown. In the late afternoon, riding jaded horses, Chivington's men spurred on in one final effort of the day, "made a flying charge on the enemy, running over them and trampling them under the horses' feet." When the Apache Cañon skirmish ended on the evening of March 27, the Union side reported 5 killed and 14 wounded, the Confederates 32 killed, 43 wounded, and 71 taken prisoner.[49]

There were other skirmishes on March 26, and on following days, but Preacher Chivington's surprise attack on the Confederates, his extraordinary success in destroying their train of supplies and ammunition, was the most important action in the entire series of engagements in the Glorieta mountains.

Colonel W. P. Scurry, of the Fourth Texas Cavalry, reported on the fighting in Apache Cañon, from Santa Fe, on March 30, 1862, saying that "another victory had been added to the long list of Confederate triumphs." He listed 33 Texans killed, 35 wounded, against 38 Federals killed, 58 wounded. Scurry described the circumstances which had prompted a Confederate retreat:

Our train was burned by a party who succeeded in passing undiscovered around the mountains to our rear . . . they fired upon and severely wounded Rev. H. L. Jones, our chaplain, of the Fourth Regiment. He was holding in his hand a white flag when fired upon. . . . The loss of my supplies so crippled me that after burying my dead I was unable to follow up the victory. My men for two days went unfed and blanketless unmurmuringly. I was compelled to come to Santa Fe for something to eat. At last accounts the Federalists were still retiring toward Fort Union. . . . I do not know if I write intelligently. I have not slept for three nights, and can scarcely hold my eyes open.

There were those in Santa Fe, and elsewhere in New Mexico, who hotly contested "Preacher" Chivington's right to the honor and glory that came to him as the result of burning the Confederate train in Apache Cañon. The squabble continued off and on for several years. In Santa Fe it was contended that James L. Collins, long time United States Indian Affairs official, was the man who conceived the idea and suggested it to the military, and who should have received the major share of the credit.

The controversy about Apache Cañon honors was taken to the Legislature, which adopted a resolution on Jan. 23, 1864, which did not mention Chivington, but asked the President of the United States to promote two regular army officers for "distinguished service" in Apache Cañon.[50]

The Rio Abajo *Press,* published at Albuquerque, took up the cudgels for Captain Lewis, without mentioning his fellow officer, Asa B. Carey, in its issue of March 8, 1864, saying:

The people of the Territory are very grateful to the Colorado Volunteers for largely contributing to the rescue of New Mexico from rebel invaders, and will hand down their just praises to the remotest generation. At the same time we object to Col. Chivington's strutting about in plumage stolen from Captain William H. Lewis, 5th U. S. Infantry. The 28th of March, 1862, was the memorable day on which Sibley's invading expedition was knocked on the head. While Slough was engaging the enemy in front, Companies A and G 5th Infantry, and some three hundred Colorado Volunteers, under Colonel (then Major) Chivington, made a detour, in order to reconnoitre from a mountain. Some one of the party suggested the practicability of attacking the Texans' rear guard and destroying their supply trains and baggage. Major Chivington, after two hours persuasion, consented to let the party go and make the attack. Lewis was the senior officer present, led the party, made the attack, destroyed the train and supplies, while Chivington, doubtless in imitation of the daddy of Edward the Black Prince, at Agincourt, remained on the mountain, viewing the scene from afar. Colonel Chivington made *his* report, and was made a Colonel thereupon; and there is no calculating the altitude he expects to attain by virtue of the report aforesaid; but we opine he will be no more successful than he was in a certain transaction in horseflesh we wot of.... Captain William H. Lewis is as modest as he is gallant, and therefore, did not urge his claims for reward of his meritorious conduct on that occasion; but his friends are determined that the truth of history shall be vindicated, even if Lewis does not receive the promotion he is entitled to. From what we can ascertain, the Union Army, at Apache Cañon, on that occasion, would have been a "used up congregation," had not Lewis, by that exploit, demoralized the rebel forces through their "bread baskets." Major Chivington should have been sent home to follow his profession of a preacher rather than promoted to a Colonelcy, while Lewis should have been made a General. Had Lewis been unsuccessful, he would have caught it like sixty, and Chivington would have said: "I told him so; but he was very rash and imprudent." Justly, the man who would be blamed for the miscarriage of that achievement, should be the recipient of reward for its triumphant accomplishment, and especially when it is one upon which defeat was probably changed into victory.

On March 31, 1862, several days after the fighting in the Glorieta Mountains, Col. Scurry sent a detailed report of the skirmish, addressed to Major A. M. Jackson, Assistant Adjutant General of the Army of New Mexico. Replete with descriptions of the fighting, and of individual acts of bravery and heroism, Scurry reported that he was encamped at Galisteo on March 26, when he received an express from Major Pyron in late afternoon saying that he was in a sharp conflict with the enemy, about 16 miles distant, and urging him to hasten to his relief. According to Scurry's report, Pyron's critical situation was "made known to the command, and in ten minutes the column was formed and the order to march was given." The road being almost impassable, Scurry's men had great difficulty in getting across the mountains to the scene of the conflict. Scurry reported later: "It is due to the brave men making this cold night march to state that where the road over the mountain was too steep for the horses to drag the artillery, they were unharnessed, and the men cheerfully pulled it over the difficulties by way of hand." Scurry reached Pyron's camp at Johnson's ranch at 3 o'clock the next morning. Describing the fighting that followed, Scurry reported:

When we ready to advance, the enemy had taken cover, and

it was impossible to tell whether their main body was stationed behind a long adobe wall that ran nearly across the canon or had taken position behind a large ledge of rocks in the rear. . . . I took command of the right and immediately attacked the enemy who were at the ranch. Majors Ragnet and Pyron opened a galling fire upon their left from the rock on the mountain side, and the center charging down the road, the foe were driven from the ranch to the ledge of rocks alluded to where they made their final and most desperate stand. At this point three batteries of eight guns opened up a furious fire of grape, canister, and shell upon our advancing troops. Our brave soldiers, heedless of the storm, pressed on, determined if possible to take their battery. A heavy body of infantry, twice our number, interposed to save their guns. Here the conflict was terrible. Our men and officers, alike inspired with the unalterable determination to overcome every obstacle to the attainment of their object, dashed among them. The right and center had united to the left. The intrepid Ragnet and the cool, calm, courageous Pyron had pushed forward among the rocks until the muzzles of the guns of the opposing forces passed each other. Inch by inch was the ground disputed, until the artillery of the enemy had time to escape with a number of their wagons. The infantry also broke ranks and fled from the field. So precipitate was their flight that they cut loose their teams and set fire to two of their wagons. The pursuit was kept up until forced to halt from the extreme exhaustion of the men, who had been engaged for six hours in the hardest contested fight it had ever been my lot to witness. The enemy is now known to have numbered 1,400 men, Pike's Peak miners and regulars, the flower of the U. S. Army.

Scurry remained on the battlefield during March 29th to superintend the burial of the dead and provide comfort for the wounded, and then marched his men to Santa Fe, to procure supplies and transportation to replace the equipment that had been destroyed by the enemy.[51] Retreating toward Santa Fe, Scurry perhaps had in mind that he would be back in the Glorieta Mountains before many days, ready to fight again. Such was not to be, however. The Union forces, through a freak maneuver by Chivington's command, had dealt a death blow to the hopes of the Confederacy. Within a few days the high command of the now beaten army decreed that there was no alternative but to go back to Albuquerque. That movement had its danger too, because there was always the possibility that Canby, defeated at Valverde on Feb. 22, might be lurking about, seeking retaliation and vindication.

In his report of March 31, Colonel Scurry mourned the loss of fellow officers, praised those officers who had survived the gory conflict:

The country has to mourn the loss of four as brave and chivalrous officers as ever graced the ranks of any army. The gallant Major Shropshire fell early, pressing upon the foe and cheering his men on. The brave and chivalrous Major Ragnet fell mortally wounded while engaged in the last and most desperate conflict of the day. He survived long enough to know and rejoice at our victory, and then died with loving messages upon his expiring lips. The brave, gallant Captain Buckholts and Lieutenant Mills conducted themselves with distinguished gallantry throughout the fight and fell near its close. Of the living it is only necessary to say that all behaved with distinguished courage and daring. This battle proves conclusively that few mistakes were made in the selection of the officers of this command. They were ever in the front, leading their men into the hottest of the fray.[52]

General Canby remained at Fort Craig until March 31, 1862, some five weeks after the battle of Valverde of Feb. 22, waiting and hoping for some word from Fort Union. When the commissary at Fort Craig showed signs of depletion, the troops were placed on short rations. Canby occupied a rather helpless and vulnerable position. Sibley held Santa Fe and Albuquerque to the north. Fort Bliss, to the south was likewise in enemy hands. No help could be expected from California for months. As a result no supply trains could get to Fort Craig from any direction and its garrison faced possibilities of slow starvation. No word came from Fort Union. Rations being at a danger point, Canby decided to risk going northward along the Rio Grande. Leaving Col. B. S. Roberts with a skeleton force to offer token resistance in protecting Fort Craig, Canby marched out of the gate of the fort with about 1,000 troop remnants, among them Infantry and Cavalry regulars; Captain Grayton's company of scouts, odds and ends of volunteer companies under Captain Eaton, and Captain Sena of Santa Fe, and the artillery, made up of two 24-pounders which Captain Brotherton had managed to salvage out of the debacle at Valverde. At Socorro, seventy-five miles from Albuquerque, Canby heard for the first time that the enemy had been turned back at Apache Cañon.[53]

Encouraged by the good news and compensated somewhat for the disappointment resulting from the defeat at Valverde, Canby's troops marched along the Rio Grande through the ancient villages of Limitar, Polvadera, Casa Colorado, Los Lunas, Isleta, Los Padillas, and Atrisco, reaching Los Barelas, on the outskirts of Albuquerque, on April 9, 1862. Canby's scouts reported that a large force of Texans were in town. Pickets were thrown out, rifle pits dug and the two 24-pounders were placed in position. The bombardment of Albuquerque began shortly after daylight on April 10. Confederate batteries answered the fire from a position near Huning's Mill at Rancho Seco. Several of the six-pound round shot came dangerously near Canby's gunners, at times throwing sand in their eyes.[54] Louis Hommel, in the Las Vegas *Gazette* of Sept. 15, 1867, described some of the events of the day:

After the cannon duel had lasted for awhile, some of the Union citizens of Albuquerque came to report that the Texans would not allow either women or children in town to seek refuge, and it was ordered to "cease firing." The command went back into camp, and soon thereafter a council of war was held. The results of this were that at sundown large campfires were built; but soon after dark the wagons were packed, and nearly the whole force, except buglers, drummers, fifers, took the road towards Tijeras Canon. The musicians, at about 8 o'clock played off tattoo, then jumped on horses, and under a small escort soon caught up to the silently retreating column. The march up in the canon was continued as far as the village of San Antonio, some twenty miles east of Albuquerque. There, after laying over one day an express reached the command from Las Vegas. The next morning Canby ordered a "march about" back towards the Rio Grande. On the 15th of April, 1862, after having made supper near the mouth of the canon, at Tijeras, 18 miles east of Albuquerque, the wagons were loaded again and on went the column, silently, without the cracking of a whip, or the lighting of a pipe, during most of the night, marching to Peralta. Coming within range of that town, the wagons were corraled, and everybody slept, or rather watched, in the ranks, for daylight to appear.[55]

Hommel described the fighting at Peralta, some sixteen miles south of Albuquerque:

The 16th of April, 1862, commenced to dawn beautifully upon the belligerents at Peralta. At the first break of day General Canby ordered the federal battery to open fire upon the town; but he surely was mistaken if he had thought the retreating Texans wouldn't respond. Hardly had the first 24 pound shell burst over a group of the enemy when there appeared the white smoke from the muzzle of the Confederate six pound field pieces; perhaps the very ones captured at Valverde, and soon the course of the solid shot could be traced coming down upon Canby's men. The first ball fell short, bounced over the troops and buried itself in the loose ground of the mesa close to the rear; the second was better. After making the circle high up in the air, it came on whizzing and everyone in the federal camp could hear the crash it caused among a pair of wheel mules in the battery, tearing away the whole face of the saddle mule and knocking the off wheeler on the head just under and behind the ear. Both animals came to the ground, perhaps not even knowing what struck them. As the train with ammunition and provisions was only a few paces off, the general ordered it further to the rear, as also the cavalry and infantry to "deploy" towards the main road from Albuquerque to Peralta. Canby kept on advancing towards Peralta, after having sent a few companies of New Mexico Volunteers up the country to garrison Albuquerque and Santa Fe. The Texans retreated across the Rio Grande, between Peralta and Los Lunas; but were harrassed in their march at every available opportunity, until a few days after, while trying to cross the sand hills above Socorro, Canby cut them off from reaching water and nearly the whole column abandoned the march as an army. What little stores had been spared them in former reverses, or nearly all, were destroyed, or buried in the sandhills, and detached parties struck out, on their own responsibility, for their home in Texas.[56]

That the Confederates, now homeward bound, were anything but downhearted, was indicated in a letter written by Governor Connelly from Santa Fe on April 20, 1862, to Secretary of State Seward. Having taken over the Governor's residence at Peralta, a spacious home, built of adobe bricks, flanked by two rows of tall poplar trees along an entrance driveway, the Texans made the most of their stay as his Excellency's uninvited guests:

The fugitive forces of the Texans reached Albuquerque from Santa Fe on the 13th inst., and uniting with the small force there, took up their line of march down the river on the east side, not being able to cross the stream at Albuquerque. They had progressed only twenty miles, when they were overtaken by General Canby at and in full possession of my residence. It being late at night when General Canby arrived within hearing of their position, his ears were saluted with the "sound of revelry by night." The violin was in full blast, accompanied by other and more noisy instruments. The enemy seemed to be entirely unconscious of Canby's approach, nor was his presence known to them until next morning. My residence is surrounded by quite a dense forest of trees, extending in every direction for at least a half mile, and the only approach for vehicles is on the main road. The *acequias* for the purpose of irrigation, running across and parallel with the road, offer no small impediment to the operation of artillery. ... The position of the enemy was a strong one and General Canby did not think it prudent to make any demonstration. During the day after he arrived a cannonading was carried on by both sides without any serious results. ... During the next night the enemy silently left their position, and passed below a mile or two to a ford in the river, where they attempted to cross, but their teams, being weak, and the river swollen by the spring floods, the whole of their train, consisting of sixty wagons, was left in the river and on the banks, the mules alone having crossed over to the opposite shore.[57]

General Sibley sent preliminary reports to General S. Cooper, in Richmond, from Albuquerque, on March 31, and a complete summary of the entire New Mexico situation from Fort Bliss, on May 4, 1862. In the report of May 4, Sibley detailed the operations of his army for February, March and April, 1862. He emphasized the difficulties that had confronted the Confederacy in New Mexico:

It is due to the brave soldiers I have had the honor to command to premise that from its first inception the "Sibley brigade" has encountered difficulties in its organization and opposition and distaste to the service required at its hands which no other troops have met with. From misunderstandings, accidents, deficiency of arms, and the like, instead of reaching the field of its operations early in September as was anticipated, I found myself at this point as late as the middle of January, 1862, with only two regiments and a half, poorly armed, thinly clad and almost destitute of blankets. The ranks were becoming daily thinned by those two terrible scourges to an army, smallpox and pneumonia.

In his report to Cooper, Sibley gave his reasons for leaving Santa Fe after the debacle in the Glorieta mountains, saying, among other things, that forage and supplies were unobtainable there. Sibley explained that he had started his troops from Santa Fe for Manzano, in the Sandia mountains, "intermediate between Fort Union, Albuquerque and Fort Craig, and securing as a line of communication the road to Fort Stanton," but had changed his plans upon receiving news from Albuquerque by fast express that Colonel Canby was on his way north from Fort Craig. "The entire force was accordingly moved by forced marches in the direction of Albuquerque," Sibley wrote, arriving there too late to encounter the enemy, "but in time to secure our limited supplies from the contingency of capture." Having studied his predicament from every standpoint, Sibley decided against turning east from Albuquerque in order to make another attempt to take Fort Union, and started for Texas, traveling south along the Rio Grande. Sibley's report of May 4, 1862, was in striking contrast to the optimistic tenor of his letter of Dec. 20, 1861, addressed to the people of New Mexico:

My chief regret in making this retrograde movement was the necessity of leaving hospitals at Santa Fe, Albuquerque and Socorro. Everything, however, was provided for the comfort of the sick; and sufficient funds, in Confederate paper, provided them to meet every want, if it be negotiated. It has been almost impossible to procure specie upon any terms. One thousand dollars is all I have been able to procure for the use of hospitals and for the secret service. The *ricos,* or wealthy citizens of New Mexico, had been so completely drained by the Federal powers, and adhering to them, had become absolute followers of their army for dear life and their invested dollars. Politically they have no distinct sentiment or opinion on the vital question at issue. Power and interest alone control the expression of their sympathies. Two noble and notable exceptions to this rule were found in the brothers Rafael and Manuel Armijo, the wealthiest and most respectable native merchants of New Mexico. The latter had been pressed into the militia, and was compulsorily present in the action at Valverde. On our arrival at Albuquerque they came forward boldly and protested their sympathy with our cause, placing their stores, containing goods amounting to $200,000 at the disposal of my troops. When the necessity for evacuating the country became inevitable, these two gentlemen abandoned luxurious homes and well filled storehouses to join their fate to the Southern Confederacy. I trust they will not be forgotten in the final settlement.

That General Sibley was discouraged over possibilities in New Mexico was obvious from the final paragraph of his report:

It is proper that I should express the conviction, determined by some experience, that, except for its political geographical position, the Territory of New Mexico is not worth a quarter of the blood and treasure expended in its conquest. As a field of military operations it possesses not a single element, except in the multiplicity of its defensible positions. The indispensable element, food, cannot be relied on. During the last year, and pending recent operations, hundreds of thousands of sheep have been driven off by the Navajo Indians. Indeed, such were the complaints of the people in this respect that I had determined, as good policy, to encourage private enterprises against that tribe and the Apaches, and to legalize the enslaving of them.

The Confederates had "beaten the enemy in every encounter and against large odds"; Sibley reported, and the entire campaign was "prosecuted without a dollar in the Quartermaster's Department":

We have beaten the enemy in every encounter and against large odds; from being the worst armed, my forces are now the best armed in the country. We reached Fort Bliss last winter in rags and blanketless. The army is now well clad and well equipped in other respects. The entire campaign has been prosecuted without a dollar in the quartermaster's department. But, sir, I cannot speak encouragingly for the future, my troops, having manifested a dogged, irreconcilable detestation of the country and the people. They have endured much, suffered much, and cheerfully; but the prevailing discontent, backed up by the distinguished valor displayed on every field, entitles them to marked consideration and indulgence. These considerations, in connection with the scant supply of provisions and the disposition of our own citizens in this section to depreciate our currency, may determine me, without waiting for instructions, to move by slow marches down the country, both for the purpose of remounting and recruiting our thinned ranks.[58]

Sibley's valedictory to the soldiers of the Army of New Mexico was delivered on May 14, 1862, at the James Magoffin residence, at "Magoffinsville" (near Fort Bliss), El Paso, Texas, in which he had established his headquarters after the retreat from New Mexico. Pitched on a plane of language that approached the heights of eloquence, Sibley's message to his comrades-in-arms was a bit pathetic. He carefully avoided any reference to the defeats and disasters the Army had experienced in the preceding sixty days:

It is with unfeigned pride and pleasure that I find myself occupying a position which devolves upon me the duty of congratulating the Army of New Mexico upon the successes which have crowned their arms in the many encounters with the enemy during the short but brilliant campaign which has just terminated.

Called from your homes almost at a moment's warning, cheerfully leaving friends, families and private affairs, in many cases solely dependent upon your presence and personal attention, scarcely prepared for a month's campaign, in the immediate defence of your own firesides, you have made a march, many of you over a thousand miles, before ever reaching the field of active operations.

The boasted valor of Texans has been fully vindicated, Valverde, Glorieta, Albuquerque, Peralta, and last, though not least your successful and almost unprecedented evacuation, through mountain passes and over a trackless waste of a hundred miles through a famishing country, will be duly chronicled, and form one of the brightest pages in the history of the Second American Revolution.

That I should be proud of you—that every participant in the campaign should be proud of himself—who can doubt?

God and an indulgent Providence have guided us in our councils and watched our ways: Let us be thankful to Him for our successes, and to Him let us not forget to offer a prayer for our noble dead.[59]

NOTES AND PROFILES

[1] Second Lieut. John V. Dubois, stationed at Fort Union, New Mexico, noted in his diary on Feb. 12, 1861: "Nothing but secession talked of at this post. Of all the officers here only Lt. McRae of North Carolina, Capt. Shoemaker and myself are thoroughly loyal." A month later, March 10, 1861, Dubois wrote: "I became involved in several very bitter political discussions here and threatened, if an effort were made to seduce my regiment from its allegiance, I would assume command myself and fight it out. Propositions were made to me to go in the Southern army and high positions were offered me, but of course declined, although it is hard to fight as a 2nd Lieutenant when I might have a much higher rank. . . . The soldiers are loyal, most of the officers going South themselves, and all the West Pointers except Longstreet urge their soldiers to remain true." On March 17, 1861, Dubois wrote: "All the officers of the Rifles have as yet resisted all inducements but I do not think they will do so long. Tremendous efforts are being made to coax them South. and the pretense is that this matter will be settled without a war, and after a peaceable separation. Very few officers would not prefer to serve the South, who have always treated us well, to the North who have always abused us." See "Campaigns in the West," p. 110, Ariz. Pioneer *Press*, Tucson, 1849.

[2] William Wing Loring, born in Wilmington, N. C., Dec. 4, 1818, died in New York City on Dec. 30, 1896. Loring had an interesting career from the day he joined a company of volunteers, at the age of 13, to fight Seminole Indians in Florida, until he retired after serving as a pasha commanding a brigade in the Khedive's army in Egypt, following the Civil War. Loring participated in a number of battles and skirmishes in the Mexican War of 1846. He was prominent in military affairs in New Mexico and Utah in the 50's. He fought in Navajo skirmishes, led troops in Bonneville's Gila Expedition in New Mexico in 1857, and accompanied an expedition from Fort Union to Salt Lake City, leaving March 10, and returning Sept. 13, 1858. Leaving New Mexico in 1858, Loring toured Europe and the Holy Land. Lieut. John V. DuBois talked to Loring when he stopped at Fort Union enroute to Santa Fe to assume command of the Department of New Mexico, in March, 1861. DuBois confided to his diary: "I doubt Loring's loyalty, but he says he is sound. He brought with him the 1st copy I had seen of Mr. Lincoln's inaugural address. Five states have seceded, hoisted a southern flag & are in open arms to resist what they call invasion. This will be a long and bloody war. It will last five years at least and may not be a success. If we could only keep the West Pointers true there would be very little fighting in the South, for they could not organize and equip an army. But Jeff Davis will take with him many of our best men." See "Campaigns in the West," Ariz. Pioneers Historical Soc., Tucson, 1949, p. 111. Union officers accused Loring of conspiring with Crittenden and others to convert to the Confederate cause the entire unit of Mounted Rifles then on duty in New Mexico. Crittenden was born in Russellville, Ky., March 20, 1812, died in Danville, Ky., Nov. 27, 1880. Crittenden, like Loring, led an adventurous life, in and out of the army. A volunteer in the Texas revolution of 1835, he was taken prisoner in Mexico. While Crittenden and other Americans were Mexican prisoners, their captors gave them an opportunity to gamble for their lives. Each prisoner was allowed to draw a bean from a box. Most of the beans were white, but there were two or

three black beans in the lot. By the rules of the game, the man who drew a black bean would not be shot. Every man who drew a white bean knew that he had in effect signed his own death warrant. In the raffle, Crittenden drew a black bean. He quickly traded it with a fellow prisoner with a wife and children in the States, who had drawn a white bean. Learning of Crittenden's generous and courageous act, the prison Commandant deferred the time of Crittenden's execution, and he was later released through the efforts of Daniel Webster.

3 OR Series I, Vol. 1, p. 602. On Feb. 25, 1861, a month before Loring assumed command of the military in New Mexico, Apache Indians attacked a public oxen train of 15 wagons, transporting army supplies from Fort Craig to Fort Buchanan, Arizona. A soldier escort succeeded in beating off the attackers, and the train reached Fort McLane safely. Some days later the same train left Fort McLane for Fort Buchanan. Wagonmaster William D. Kirk piloted the wagons to Janos, Chihuahua, Mexico. OR Series I, Vol. 1, p. 600. On June 23, 1861, Colonel Canby sent Lieut. Donald C. Stith on a mission to the governor of Chihuahua, with a letter requesting the return of the property. Canby wrote the governor: "This flagrant robbery and breach of faith will be fully reprobated by your excellency, and I have the fullest confidence that you will at once, in the exercise of your powers, direct the restoration of the public property, and the delivery of the robber. . . ." OR Series I, Vol. 4, p. 43. Confederate soldiers arrested Stith at Guadalupe, Mexico, and took him to Fort Bliss as a prisoner of war. When arraigned before Col. John R. Baylor, Stith was ordered paroled. Baylor explained that his soldiers had exceeded their authority in making the arrest on Mexican soil. By Nov. 11, 1861, Captain Stith was in San Antonio, Texas, holding a commission as Assistant Adjutant General, C.S.A. Ibid, pp. 43, 136.

4 Henry Hopkins Sibley was born in Louisiana, July, 1816, died in Fredericksburg, Virginia, Aug. 23, 1886. Graduated from the U. S. Military Academy on July 1, 1838, Sibley was at once appointed 2nd Lieutenant of the 2nd Dragoons; promoted to 1st Lieutenant, and then to a captaincy in 1847, and was made Major of the 1st Dragoons in 1861. He served in the Florida war in 1838-1840, and during the Mexican War participated in the siege of Vera Cruz, in the battles of Cerro Gordo, Contreras, Cherubusco, Molino del Rey, and in the capture of the City of Mexico. After the Mexican War, Sibley served on frontier duty, in the Utah expedition, 1857-59, superintended construction of Fort Union, New Mexico, and took part in an expedition against the Navajos in New Mexico in 1860. He resigned from the United States Army on May 13, 1861, and on July 7, 1861, was commissioned a Brigadier General in the Confederate Army, with instructions to drive federal troops out of New Mexico. He assumed command of all the forces of the Confederate States on the Rio Grande, at and above Fort Quitman, Texas, as of Dec. 14, 1861, with iurisdiction extending specifically "to all southern forces in the Territory of New Mexico, and Arizona," under the designation of "Army of New Mexico," an area which was modified subsequently. During the war, in New Mexico, Sibley's forces defeated Union troops under Canby at Valverde, captured Albuquerque and Santa Fe, almost succeeded in reaching Fort Union. After the Civil War, Sibley entered the service of the Khedive of Egypt. See OR Series I, Vol. 4, p. 157, and *Free Lance,* Fredericksburg, Va., Aug. 24, 1886. While in the Union Army, Sibley invented a tent, modelled after the wigwams of the Sioux and Comanche Indians. He obtained Letters Patent on the invention, and the United States government contracted for its use. At the close of the Civil War the United States officials refused to carry out the terms of the contract. After his death a claim was brought before Congress in the interest of the family, but was disallowed. At the time of Sibley's death, the *Free Lance* said: "General Sibley was an active, intelligent and enterprising officer. His social qualities being of a high order, were ever appreciated by his fellow officers. He was the inventor of the celebrated

Sibley tent, for the use of which he contracted with the government previous to the late war. Had the government kept its part of the contract with the old soldier, he would have been spared many anxious moments, and his latter days deprived of much embarrassment."

Colonel Longstreet, who resigned from the Union Army in New Mexico on June 1, 1861, "borrowed" an army ambulance and team of mules and went to Fort Bliss. Before his resignation was accepted Longstreet made an accounting of funds in his custody as Paymaster in New Mexico and Arizona. At the time of making the accounting, Longstreet was reported to have said: "Although circumstances have forced me to be henceforth a foe, the government of the United States shall have no cause to say that I am not a gentleman." Citing his age and long experience in accounting, Longstreet applied to President Jefferson Davis for the post of Paymaster General in the Confederate Army. Davis replied, saying that the services of an officer with his experience should not be wasted as Paymaster General; that he needed generals in the line. First commissioned as a brigadier general, Longstreet was later promoted to Lieutenant General. After the war he led an exciting life as a civilian. Canby, who succeeded Loring as commander of Union forces in New Mexico, was displeased by Longstreet's conduct after resigning from the army. He complained that Longstreet wrote letters from El Paso to Canby's officers, urging them to join the Confederacy, assuring them of commissions "rank for rank," and payment in gold for all Union Army arrearages. Longstreet also hinted, according to Canby, that there was a ready market, with payment in gold, for all army horses and mules that Union soldiers might find it convenient to deliver in El Paso. Canby was particularly irritated when Union soldiers in New Mexico and Arizona were handed copies of a so-called government decree rendered by a judge in El Paso holding that the United States had been dissolved; and that neither officers nor soldiers were bound to that government by their oath of allegiance. Simeon Hart, of El Paso, according to Canby, was extremely active during the early months of 1861, holding out inducements to Union officers and privates to desert their posts.

Captain John P. Hatch, of the Mounted Rifles, then in Santa Fe, was instructed by the War Department on May 11, 1861, not to pay any monies due from the United States to Simeon Hart, claiming that he had "sympathized with and actively engaged in aiding those who were in favor of the cause represented and advocated by the Confederate States." The order of May 11, 1861, stopped payment on substantial sums of money due Hart for grain and supplies delivered at Fort Bliss, Texas, which fell into the hands of the Confederates. "Subsequent to the suppression of the rebellion," as the official records described it, Simeon Hart was pardoned by the President for having identified himself with the Confederacy. Hart subsequently presented various claims to the War Department, some of which were allowed, and others contested and not paid as the result of litigation terminating in 1885. See Hart vs. United States, 118 U.S. 62. Juan S. Hart, administrator of the estate of Simeon Hart, deceased, filed one claim before the Court of Claims, which was allowed in part. A bill for relief on that claim was introduced in the Congress, and considered by a committee on Aug. 10, 1894. Contingent upon amending the claim in some particulars, the committee recommended payment, saying "that previous to the 11th day of May, 1861, Simeon Hart was a citizen of the United States and a resident of El Paso, Texas, and carried on at that place a large and profitable business; and as a part of the business in which he was engaged he furnished, under contracts, various kinds of army supplies, consisting of quartermaster and commissary stores, to the different U. S. military posts in Texas and New Mexico." See Claim of Juan S. Hart, H.R. 53rd Cong., Report No. 1407.

5 Canby was reluctant to believe that there was any truth in rumors that his predecessor, Loring, had gone over to the Confederacy. But on July 24, 1861, Canby expressed doubt about Loring's loyalty in a letter to Major Isaac Lynde, Commanding Officer at Fort Fillmore: "When Col. Loring left this

place, every officer here had implicit confidence in his integrity, but I am sorry to say that some information received since he left has shaken that confidence. It is a long step from confidence to absolute distrust, but it is necessary that you should be on your guard against any betrayal of the honor or interests of the United States."

Edward Richard Sprigg Canby, 44 years old in 1861, "tall, soldierly in appearance, inclined to be reserved and silent, kind and courteous in manner," was appointed Commander of the District, later Department, of New Mexico, effective as of May 14, 1861, with the rank of colonel. Stationed at Fort Defiance, New Mexico, in the Navajo country, at the time of his promotion, with the rank of major, with the 10th U. S. Infantry, Canby could already look back on many years of military experience in the south and west. He assumed command of Union troops in New Mexico, at a most critical time. Sibley, Longstreet, Loring, Ewell, and other major officers in New Mexico, had resigned their United States Army commissions at the outbreak of the war, or soon thereafter, and accepted commissions in the Confederate army, impairing to a great extent the morals of the troops in the Territory. Major Lynde's abandonment of Fort Fillmore, New Mexico, and subsequent surrender of some 700 Union troops to Col. John Robert Baylor, of the Texas forces, on July 27, 1861, less than three months after Canby assumed command of the District of New Mexico, was a staggering blow. Canby, however, worked patiently to get his forces in readiness for future fighting. Some six months later, on Feb. 21 and 22, 1862, Canby personally led Union troops in battle against Sibley, and his Confederate forces, at Valverde, New Mexico. Here Canby experienced a disastrous and discouraging defeat. Canby remained at his post as Commander in New Mexico until the last Confederate soldier had returned to Texas. In dealing with Sibley's forces, Canby held to the theory that hunger, thirst, and disease would hurt Sibley to a far greater extent than bullets. Canby predicted that Sibley would eventually have great difficulty in feeding his troops and getting forage for his horses in sparsely settled New Mexico. Canby's predictions proved uncannily accurate.

Born in Kentucky, Aug. 1, 1817, son of Israel T. Canby, one-time candidate for governor of Indiana, Edward Richard Sprigg Canby was appointed as a cadet to West Point from Indiana in 1835, and was graduated and commissioned a second lieutenant in 1839. Canby saw service in the Florida war, in Gen. Scott's army in Mexico, and was assistant Adjutant General of the Tenth Military Department headquarters at Monterey, Cal., in 1849, serving with W. T. Sherman, then a first lieutenant in the 3rd Artillery. Ex. Doc. 17, p. 890. Promoted to be a brigadier general, and later a major general of volunteers, Canby was relieved as commander of the Department of New Mexico by Gen. James H. Carleton, and served thereafter in various important capacities in the east and south. He was commander of troops in New York City during the draft riots; and on May 4 and May 26, 1865, then in command of the military division of West Mississippi, received the surrender of the armies of Taylor and Kirby Smith, the last of the Confederate Armies in the field. According to Gen. G. W. Cullum's appraisal, in *Dictionary of American Biography*, Vol. 3, p. 469, Canby's superiors and subordinates "knew him as a great commander—too modest and reserved to win the popular recognition that he merited—wherever he went, order, good feeling and tranquility followed his footsteps." General Canby was a first cousin of Edward T. Canby, father of Henry Seidel Canby, chairman of the editorial board of the *Saturday Review of Literature*, who wrote to the author in response to an inquiry: "After I had begun to go to Charleston, S.C., rather frequently, I learned to my horror that General Canby had been Military Governor there after the war, and feared my name would be anathema. But I was told that my friends there had looked up his record, which was excellent even at that terrible moment." Several years after the war, Canby became commander of the Department of the Columbia in the Northwest. For thirty years off and on, he had dealt with the Indians in many parts of the south and west, and was known as "the Indian's friend." He was murdered by a fanatical Modoc

Indian at Lava Beds, in northern California, on or about April 10, 1872. The Santa Fe *New Mexican* published a brief account of General Canby's death: "Our dispatches today bring the sad news of the death of Gen. E. R. S. Canby. He was killed, murdered, assassinated by treachery at a moment when he was in the execution of his official duties, and at a time when it was least expected. The Modoc Indians who have been causing so much trouble lately are his murderers. They got up a 'peace council,' and invited General Canby to be present. In all good faith and confidence, he went, hoping that this turn of affairs indicated a settlement of the Modoc question forever. He never left the council alive. The treacherous savages fell upon him while the smoke of the calumet was still ascending, and in cold blood butchered him. There is no doubt but that the council was a sham—a cunning trap laid to get General Canby in their hands. . . . General Canby was well known in New Mexico as commander of the forces during the war; and won the enviable reputation of a competent general and popular administrator. He made hosts of warm friends among our people, who will mourn his loss only less than the kind wife he leaves, whose memory is held sacred in the hearts of many a soldier who received visits from her in the hospitals during the war."

It was unfortunate for the Apache and Navajo Indians that Gen. Canby did not continue as commander of the Department of New Mexico throughout the Civil War years. Undoubtedly he would have looked upon the Indian troubles from a different viewpoint than his successor, General James H. Carleton. Coming from a family of Quakers, with a heritage of mercy, compassion and understanding of, and for fellow human beings, it is quite certain that Canby would have worked the Navajos out of their difficulties without a Bosque Redondo.

6 OR Series I, Vol. 1, p. 605. Major J. C. Fremont wrote to Secretary Cameron, from St. Louis, on Aug. 1, 1861, proposing that 3,000 men be recruited on the Pacific coast, moved by steamer to Guaymas, Mexico, and marched overland to El Paso, Texas, "from which to threaten Arkansas and Texas." OR Series I, Vol. 3, p. 428. In all probability, Fremont had not yet heard that Baylor had invaded New Mexico, and captured Fort Fillmore, on July 27, 1861.

7 Barely forty years old when he reached New Mexico in 1861, John Robert Baylor had already achieved fame in Texas as a man of action, fearless, resourceful, impetuous, perhaps impudent and imprudent on occasions. Few men in Texas of his day and time lived a more colorful or spectacular life. Although born in Kentucky in 1822, Baylor lived most of his life in Texas. He was related to Judge Robert K. Baylor, founder of Baylor College. Descended from prominent Virginians, some of whom were famed in the Revolutionary War, and the War of 1812, Baylor was the son of John Walker Baylor, an army surgeon with the Seventh Infantry, stationed for several years at Fort Gibson, in the Indian Territory. Reared in Indian Territory and Texas, it was said of John Robert Baylor, even in young manhood, that "he became thoroughly proficient in all the accomplishments of the western frontier and the backwoodsman, besides possessing those of the well educated gentleman;" that he was a man of "exemplary moral character and domestic virtues, good sense, quick decision, frank, pleasant manners, and fearless courage," that he had "served Texas faithfully in trying times, when Mexican and Indian invasions continually threatened her settlements." For a short time in 1855 and 1856, Baylor served as a special Indian agent at Fort Belknap, in the Comanche country, but resigned to engage in farming. While farming, he studied law and was elected to the legislature. Defying Indian officials and army authorities alike, he raised a force of 350 men, and led them in a brush with the Indians and United States troops near the Brazos Agency, on May 23, 1859. In Civil War years Baylor's capture of Major Isaac Lynde and several hundred Union troops from Fort Fillmore, New Mexico, on July 27, 1861, caused a sensation throughout the nation. Baylor was promoted to become a brigadier general, served for a time as military governor of the Confederate Territory of Arizona, and later served for a time as a member of the Confed-

erate Congress from a Texas district. After the war, Baylor lived in San Antonio, where he was active in local politics. Later he moved to Uvalde, Texas, and died on his ranch near there on February 8, 1894. Baylor had several encounters with desperate characters while living near Uvalde, but always managed to more than hold his own. In one altercation at Uvalde on May 1, 1881, between Baylor and "old man Gilcrease," the latter was killed, which prompted the Fort Clark *News* to comment: "We do not know much about General Baylor, but he is represented to us as a man who does not seek a fight, but who is always ready to defend himself whenever occasion requires." But few Texans made more or better "copy" for newspapers in his day and time than John Robert Baylor. See "Captain John R. Baylor and the Frontier Trouble," with Baylor genealogy, The Charleston (S.C.) *Daily Courier,* June 16, 1859; *Daily Delta* (La.), June 10, 1859; "Gen. John R. Baylor at Uvalde," *The Comanche Chief,* Uvalde, Tex., May 7, 1881; "Baylor Whips Federals at Mesilla," *The Countryman,* Aug. 28, 1861; "Origin of Distinguished Baylor Family in Texas," San Antonio *Express,* May 28, 1911; "Death of John R. Baylor," Dallas *Morning News,* Feb. 9, 1894, Austin *Daily Statesman,* Feb. 9, 1894.

8 Isaac Lynde, born in Vermont, was graduated from West Point on July 1, 1827; died April 10, 1886.

9 Fort Fillmore today is little more than a name place. The one-time adobe walls of the fort have crumbled to dust; the grounds are thickly covered with cacti and mesquite brush. Approximately 4 miles south of Las Cruces, New Mexico, about the same distance from Mesilla, New Mexico, and some 36 miles north of El Paso, Texas, Fort Fillmore was located on a site of previous historic significance, variously known as Brazito, Bracito and Brasit, where Col. Alexander William Doniphan defeated Mexican troops on Dec. 24, 1846. Established on Sept. 23, 1851, Fort Fillmore was named after President Millard Fillmore. It was built to take the place of military posts abandoned at Dona Ana, five miles north of Las Cruces, and Franklin, later El Paso, Texas. The buildings at Fort Fillmore were made of adobe, with flat, dirt covered roofs. The walls extended upright on all sides, forming a parapet. Officers' quarters and quarters for enlisted men were at opposite ends of the fort. In between were the administration buildings and the hospital; and a mile to the east, toward the Organ mountains, was the cemetery. A grove of cottonwood trees between the post and the Rio Grande provided a welcome touch of greenery in spring and summer. In the days that are gone forever, Fort Fillmor was an important military post.

Mesilla, which had a population of 2,420 in 1860, sleeps lazily in the sun today, dreaming of its one-time grandeur and significance in the life of the Southwest. The plaza, or village square, is probably much the same today as it was in the 50's and 60's, when Mesilla was an important crossroads town on the hub of the highways between San Antonio and Los Angeles, between Independence, Mo., and Chihuahua; when it was the capital of the Confederate Territory of Arizona; when Colonel John Robert Baylor (Governor of Arizona) was its leading citizen, and when Roy Bean, years later the "last law west of the Pecos," lived there. Both Baylor and Bean owned real estate in Mesilla, which was confiscated by the federal government and sold at public auction. For a time it was uncertain whether Mesilla was in Mexico or the United States. The question became moot as a result of the Gadsden Purchase. Located some 700 miles from San Antonio and about 800 miles from Los Angeles, Mesilla was widely known as the only stage stop between those terminals where a traveler might be assured of good meals and a bed with sheets, blankets and pillow cases.

10 For sidelights on the Fort Fillmore surrender, see "Narrative of the Surrender of a Command of U. S. Forces at Fort Fillmore, New Mexico, in July A.D. 1861, by Major James Cooper McKee," Whipple Barracks, Prescott, Arizona, 1878, second edition, 1881, third edition, John A. Lowell & Co., Boston, 1886. Surgeon McKee wrote of Brooks: "This man Brooks, born in and ap-

pointed from Michigan, was a secessionist and a traitor, and used his position to assist the old imbecile Lynde in carrying out his infamous and cowardly schemes. As Adjutant, he was the confidential adviser of the commanding officer. No doubt he urged nonresistance and surrender. . . ." Describing the exchange of shots on the outskirts of Mesilla on July 25, McKee wrote: "Major Lynde and Lieutenant Brooks rode up to me from somewhere on our right front, where they had been fired on. Brooks had a slight scratch from a bullet on one of his forearms, and his sword had been struck. They were the worst scared men I ever saw. The grey beard and hair of Lynde were a fitting frame for that pale face and cowardly soul."

11 Las Vegas *Gazette,* Aug. 25, 1877.

12 Four years after the surrender of San Augustine Springs, Lynde wrote: "We evacuated Fort Fillmore at 1 o'clock a.m. on July 27th, 1861, and took up the line of march to Fort Stanton. Until daylight the command advanced without difficulty, but when the sun arose the day became intensely hot, and soon after, the men began to show signs of fatigue . . . men and teams began to suffer and fall by the wayside. . . . Under the circumstances I considered our case hopeless; it was worse than useless to resist; honor did not demand the sacrifice of blood after the terrible suffering our troops had already undergone, when that sacrifice would be totally useless. . . . I surrendered my command to Lieut. Col. Baylor." Lynde and Baylor agreed on terms of surrender, which were written down and signed. See Records in re Isaac Lynde, Bureau of Military Justice, of the War Department, National Archives. For the official reports and communications on the Lynde surrender, see OR Series I, Vol. 4, pp. 1 to 45.

13 OR Series I, Vol. 4, p. 18.

14 When word of the Fort Fillmore evacuation and San Augustine Springs debacle reached Department Commander Canby in Santa Fe, he wrote to Washington on Aug. 4, 1861: "I hope to be able to restore the Territory to its normal condition. This news about Lynde has roused the people of New Mexico from their apathetic condition, and I have no doubt but that the organization of an efficient home guard and the completion of the volunteer troops that have been called for will be speedily effected." OR Series I, Vol. 4, p. 19.

Colonel B. S. Roberts abandoned Fort Stanton on Aug. 2, 1861, set fire to public stores for which transportation was not available, and marched to Albuquerque with two companies of infantry. Fort Stanton, New Mexico (now a government merchant marine hospital), on the right bank of the Bonita river, 9 miles from Placitas (the present town of Lincoln), was established on May 4, 1855, in memory of Captain Henry Whiting Stanton, of the First Dragoons. Stanton was shot through the head by Apache Indians in the Sacramento mountains on January 19, 1855. The site of the fort was made a military reservation on May 12, 1859. On Aug. 17, 1872, the reservation, excluding a tract 16 miles square, was relinquished to the Interior Department.

The Mescalero Apaches ambushed a spy party of four Confederates in the vicinity of Fort Stanton, on Sept. 1, 1861. The Confederates were out looking for Union soldiers who might still be in that country. While cooking breakfast in a grove of pine trees, not far from a spring, in the mountains, the Confederates were greeted by a shower of Apache arrows. Three of the scouts, Joseph Emmanacker, T. G. Pemberton, and Joseph V. Mosse, were killed. The fourth man of the party, Floyd A. Sanders, mounted his horse, spurred him down a mountain side and got away, followed by a shower of arrows and shouting Indians. Sanders made his way back to Fort Stanton, and guided reinforcements to the scene of the fighting. The bodies of Pemberton and Emmanacker were found and buried. A salute was fired over their graves, and a cross was cut in a tree to mark the place of burial. Mosse's body could not be found, although Sanders was positive he had seen him shot through the head, and **fall to the ground.**

On the night of Sept. 1, 1861, the Mescaleros raided the Mexican settlement of Placitas (now Lincoln). Lieutenant John R. Pulliam took fifteen men from Fort Stanton and hurried to Placitas, killing five Indians before the shooting was over.

From all appearances, all Union soldiers had escaped from the Fort Stanton country. The whole countryside seemed to be infested with Indians. The Confederates loaded their wagons and marched away from Fort Stanton, going to Dona Ana, on the Rio Grande. OR Series I, Vol. 4, pp. 24-25.

15 See "Narrative of the Surrender of a Command of U. S. Forces at Fort Fillmore, New Mexico," by Major James Cooper McKee, Whipple Barracks, Prescott, Arizona, 1878.

16 Baylor paroled Major Isaac Lynde, and all troops captured at San Augustine Springs. Lynde went to Albuquerque, and then to his home in Vermont. On Nov. 25, 1861, the Adjutant General's office in Washington issued General Orders No. 102: "Major Isaac Lynde, 8th Infantry, for abandoning his post—Fort Fillmore—on the 27th of July, 1861, and subsequently surrendering his command to an inferior force of insurgents, is, by direction of the President of the United States, dropped from the army as of this date." H. R. Ex. Doc. No. 11, 37th Cong., 2nd Sess.

On Dec. 4, 1861, the House of Representatives adopted a resolution asking "what measures had been, or ought to be taken, to expose and punish such of the officers now on parole as were guilty of treason or cowardice in surrendering Fort Fillmore, in New Mexico, to an inferior force of Texas troops. . . ." In response to this resolution, General Thomas reported: "It is believed that no other officer in command was in any way involved in the suspicion of complicity in the offense, and the commanding officer, Major Lynde, was the only person on whom the responsibility could rest." Ibid.

After being "dropped from the Army," because of his conduct at Fort Fillmore, Isaac Lynde worked diligently for more than five years to regain his rank and standing. His case was investigated by the Bureau of Military Justice of the War Department. Finally, on Sept. 18, 1866, Gen. U. S. Grant wrote a letter to Secretary of War Stanton saying that Lynde was over 62 years old; that he had been dismissed from the army without trial or investigation; and ordered his reinstatement and immediate retirement. This was accomplished on order of President Andrew Johnson on Nov. 27, 1866.

17 Probably a code word.

18 OR Series I, Vol. 4, p. 128.

19 OR Series I, Vol. L, part I, p. 765.

20 OR Series I, Vol. 4, p. 75.

21 OR Series III, Vol. 1, p. 601.

22 OR Series I, Vol. 4, p. 77.

23 Ibid, p. 477.

24 OR Series I, Vol. L, part 1, p. 683.

25 There is temptation to follow a side path and tell of the efforts of Sibley and his officers to get concessions in the states of Chihuahua and Sonora, Mexico, but such a narrative would be too far afield. Colonel James Riely went as Sibley's representative to Gov. Luis Terrazas, of the state of Chihuahua. He left Fort Bliss on Dec. 21, 1861, and was in Chihuahua on Jan. 8, 1862. Riely had letters of introduction to Terrazas and others from Don Simeon Hart, which opened many doors for him. Writing from Fort Bliss, on Jan. 26, 1862, Riely told Postmaster General John H. Reagan, of the Confederate cabinet, of the success that had attended his mission: "I know you feel a deep concern in whatever concerns Texas, hence I trouble you with a short note. The mail after this will no doubt carry to Richmond the dispatch of

General H. H. Sibley in relation to my mission to the Governor of Chihuahua. My mission was entirely successful. There is no doubt but there had been some understanding about marching troops through Chihuahua from California. It will not now be permitted. The command now leaves no enemy on its flank. General Sibley has the honor through me of having obtained the first official recognition of the Confederate States of America by any foreign power. I was received, accredited, and treated with as a colonel in the Army of the Confederate States of America. Uniformed as such, and wearing my sword, I was received by the Governor at all our official interviews. As such he wrote me, and as Brig. Gen. H. H. Sibley of the Army of the Confederate States of America was his communication addressed, and as such was I accredited to General Sibley. So you see we are fully recognized. General Sibley has ordered me to Sonora upon a similar mission.... We must have Sonora and Chihuahua. I will write you of my progress in Sonora. I made the trip of (going and coming) 600 miles to Chihuahua through the Apache country with only an escort of six Mexicans, and finished my negotiations in twenty-one days. Don't you think this does quite well.... With Sonora and Chihuahua we gain southern California, and by a railroad to Guaymas render our state of Texas the great highway of nations. You are at liberty to lay this note, if you see fit, before President Davis. He may not recollect me, but once knew me as aide-de-camp and partner to our lamented friend General Rusk...." OR Series I, Vol. L, part 1, p. 825.

An El Paso informant wrote to Canby on Jan. 25, 1862, advising him of the arrival of General Sibley and his staff and that "S. Hart has done more to aid and assist Sibley than the balance of the capitalists have, and had gone so far as to give a list of the principal capitalists in New Mexico, to confiscate their property, which is their aim."

[26] See Correspondence, Operations in Tex., N. Mex., and Ariz. OR Series I, Vol. 4, p. 90. A tense situation developed between Sibley and Baylor over jurisdictional matters and extent of authority in New Mexico, which threatened for a time to seriously interfere with Confederate operations in the Southwest. On Dec. 14, 1861, General Orders No. 10 were issued from Fort Bliss declaring that Brig. Gen. Sibley assumed from that date the command of all Confederate forts on the Rio Grande at and above Fort Quitman, and all in the Territory of New Mexico and Arizona, to be known as the "Army of New Mexico," with temporary headquarters at Fort Bliss. The orders of Dec. 14 left Baylor in a quandary as to his position. However, on Dec. 20, six days later, general orders No. 12 were issued, signed by A. M. Jackson, Asst. Adjt. General, Army of New Mexico, by order of Brig. Gen. H. H. Sibley, providing as follows: "The general command of the forces of the Confederate states, assumed by Brig. Gen. H. H. Sibley, in General Orders No. 10, and the proclamation of martial law promulgated by him, not being intended to abrogate or supersede the powers of Col. John R. Baylor, as civil and military governor of Arizona, he will continue the full exercise of that office."

[27] Companies A and B of the Second Colorado Regiment, recruited in Colorado mining camps in the fall of 1861, were mustered into federal service at Fort Garland (then in New Mexico), on or about Dec. 1, 1861. Both companies saw active service in New Mexico. For interesting sidelights on the activities of Colorado troops in New Mexico during the war, see "Three Years and a Half in the Army, or History of the Second Colorados," by Mrs. Ellen Williams, Allerton, Iowa (wife of a bugler in the campaign against Sibley), Fowler & Wells Company, 753 Broadway, New York, 1885. For more accurate information, see "Colorado Volunteers in the Civil War—The New Mexico Campaign in 1862," by Dr. William Clarke Whitford, State Historical Society, Denver, 1906, and "History of the First Regiment of Colorado Volunteers," by Ovando J. Hollister, 1863, reprinted under the title, "Boldly They Rode," Golden Press, Lakewood, Colo., 1949.

[28] OR Series I, Vol. IX, p. 644.

29 *Val* for vale or valley, and *verde* for green, actually a green valley, Val-verde was appropriately named. How Valverde derived its name was told by Fray Angelico Chavez in *El Palacio*, December, 1949: "Don Antonio de Val-verde y Cosio was a soldier of the Reconquest who later served as Governor. He moved from Santa Fe to Guadalupe del Paso, and it is very likely this site was named for him or one of his immediate descendants." For many years Valverde was traditionally a "King's axe," sanctuary, with good grazing for animals, abundant water in the nearby Rio Grande, shade trees and firewood. By common consent among Indians and travelers, during the Spanish colonial period, Valverde was acknowledged as a place for rest and recuperation, with immunity from attack or counter attack. Horse stealing and pilfering were frowned upon. Valverde was an ideal place for trade and barter, for mending harness and repairing wagons.

With 22 buildings and structures, Fort Craig in 1862 was one of the most important military posts in New Mexico. For many years Fort Craig, orig-inally established to protect the country against Navajos and Apaches, has been nothing but a pile of ruins of lava rock and adobe. Built on the west side of the Rio Grande, the site of Fort Craig is 111 miles from Albuquerque, about 100 miles north of Fort Fillmore. The battle of Valverde was fought about one and a half to two miles north of Fort Craig, on the west side of the Rio Grande. Commanding a magnificent view of the Fra Cristobal Mountains to the east, and the San Mateos to the west, Fort Craig in its heyday was pre-ferred by many soldiers as a place for doing a hitch in the military service. The fort was built by mistake on the Pedro Armendaris land grant, instead of on public domain. When the mistake was discovered, Gen. John Garland leased 22,895 acres of the grant land on May 28, 1854, from the Armendaris heirs, at a yearly rental of $2,000 in gold. The lease was renewed and ex-tended by Brevet Captain John P. Hatch, commanding officer at Fort Craig, on May 25, 1859, and by Col. John C. McFerran, by command of General J. H. Carleton, on Jan. 27, 1865. A controversy arose in later years over the va-lidity of the lease and there was criticism of the "enormous rent" that was being paid by the government, with the result that the premises were in-spected in 1867 by Brevet Colonel A. I. Alexander, who reported, among other things, that "the warehouses at Fort Craig are the best built I have seen in the district, well ventilated, fire proof and very commodious.... The land is of no earthly value." A claim for back rent was finally allowed by the com-mittee on military affairs in Washington in 1870. For an interesting discus-sion of the question as to why the government built a fort on privately owned land, when it owned millions of acres of public domain in the vicinity, see report on claim of the heirs of Pedro Armendaris, H. of R. 41st Cong., 2d Sess., Ex. Doc. 73. The report gives the history and genealogy of the Armen-daris family, and discusses the validity of the grant. The report says, among other things, that Fort Conrad, not far from Fort Craig, was abandoned in 1853. Fort Craig was relinquished and the improvements sold by the govern-ment on March 3, 1885. See Rep. Com. Gen. Land Office 1901, p. 280. Collateral descendants of Pedro Armendaris, the original grantee of the Armendaris Grant, live in Mexico City.

30 Benjamin Stone Roberts, born in Manchester, Vt., in 1811, was gradu-ated from West Point in 1835, died in Washington, D. C., on Jan. 29, 1875. He resigned from the Army on Jan. 28, 1939, and served as chief engineer in building the Champlain and Ogdensburg railroad in New York. In 1842 Roberts went to Russia to assist in railroad construction. Returning to the United States he studied law, was admitted to the bar, and in 1843 began to practice in Iowa. He served with distinction in the Mexican War, and was in the army in New Mexico at the beginning of the Civil War. He was in command of Fort Stanton when it was evacuated by federal troops on Aug. 2, 1861. Roberts fought in the battle of Valverde, in New Mexico, on Feb. 21 and 22, 1862, and in later combats between Union and Confederate troops in Albuquerque and Peralta. Promoted to Colonel and then to Brigadier Gen-

eral, Roberts saw service outside of New Mexico at Cedar Mountain, the second battle of Bull Run, and other major engagements. After the war Roberts was a professor of military science at Yale University until Dec. 15, 1870. Inventor of a breech loading rifle, Roberts spent many years perfecting and developing it. For gallant and distinguished services during the Mexican War, the legislature of Iowa presented Roberts a sword of honor on Jan. 15, 1849.

31 Adapted from an eye witness account of the battle of Valverde by Louis Hommel, itinerant printer, published in Las Vegas *Gazette*, Sept. 1, 1877. See reports of Colonel Canby, Colonel Benjamin S. Roberts, Major Thomas Duncan, Colonel C. Carson, Colonel Miguel E. Pino, Lieutenant Colonel Jose M. Valdez, Captain B. C. Cutler, for details of the battle of Valverde, written from the Union viewpoint; and reports of Brig. Gen. Sibley, Major C. L. Pyron, of the Second Texas Mounted Rangers, Lieut. Col. William R. Scurry, and Major Henry W. Raguet, of the Fourth Texas Cavalry. Col. Thomas Green, of the Fifth Texas Cavalry, Col. William Steele and Captain Powhatan Jordan, of the Seventh Texas Cavalry, and Captain Trevanion T. Teel, of the Texas Light Artillery, written from the Confederate viewpoint, all in OR Series I, Vol. IX, pp. 486-525. Sibley was incapacitated for many hours during the battle of Valverde. Col. Green was the Confederate marshal of the day. Union soldiers circulated reports at Valverde that Sibley's "illness" was the result of excessive use of intoxicating liquor. One extremist referred to him as "a walking whiskey keg."

32 Noel's Campaign, Shreveport, 1865.

33 "The battle of Valverde was a fierce and desperate fight. Much blood was shed on both sides; it left many wounded, dying and dead. In that battle General Canby showed himself the brave, considerate commander and after it was over, as he went through the ranks of the wounded, he wept as only a comrade would who loved his fellow soldier." From "Three Years and a Half in the Army," by Mrs. Ellen Williams, supra, p. 8.

34 A correspondent sent a description of the fighting at Valverde from Albuquerque on Feb. 23, 1862, to the St. Louis *Republican,* saying that "the Texans charged desperately and furiously from time to time, with hundreds of picked men, armed with carbines, revolvers and seven-pound bowie knives." That the fighting was desperate was borne out by statements contained in the report of Col. Thomas Green, Fifth Texas Cavalry, written from "Camp Valverde," on Feb. 22, addressed to Major A. M. Jackson, Assistant Adjutant General, Army of New Mexico: "At the command to charge, our men leaped over the sand bank, which had served as a good covering to them, and dashed over the open plain, thinly interspersed with cottonwood trees, upon the battery and infantry of the enemy in front, composed of United States Regulars and Denver City Volunteers, and in a most desperate charge and hand to hand conflict completely overwhelmed them, killing most of their gunners around their cannon and driving the infantry into the river. Never were double barreled shotguns and rifles used to better effect. A large number of the enemy were killed in the river with shotguns and six shooters in their flight." Green reported 36 Texans killed, 150 wounded, 1 missing, and estimated the enemy's loss in killed and wounded "at least 350 or 400." OR Series I, Vol. IX, p. 519.

35 Several New Mexico forts were named in memory of Union officers who lost their lives as a result of the fighting at Valverde, among them Forts McRae, Selden and Wingate. General Canby seemed deeply impressed by McRae's valor on the battlefield, saying in his report from the field that he was "a man whose memory deserves notice from a higher authority than mine; pure in character, upright in conduct, devoted to his profession, and of a loyalty that was deaf to the seductions of family and friends, a man who died, as he had lived, an example of the best and highest qualities that man can possess." McRae's body was buried at Fort Craig, but five years after the

battle of Valverde, it was disinterred, taken east, and buried at West Point. The body was met by a committee at Huning's mill in Albuquerque on April 20, 1867, and escorted through the town by a procession, led by a cavalry horse, draped in mourning "with boot in stirrup," a detachment of U. S. Infantry and 300 citizens. The body was taken from Albuquerque to Fort Marcy, on the outskirts of Santa Fe, where a similar tribute was paid. From Santa Fe the body was escorted to Fort Union, and conveyed on east from military post to military post until it reached its final destination. Born in North Carolina, Alexander McRae was a member of a prominent family of that state. He was graduated with honors from the U. S. Military Academy in June, 1861. His family and kinsmen are said to have disowned and disinherited him when he remained loyal to the North at the outbreak of the war. The Santa Fe *Gazette* of Aug. 22, 1868, published an article reciting the saga of young McRae, copied from the *Cincinnati Times,* which said in part: "For five years no relative visited his grave at Fort Craig. The bodies of his brother officers sleeping beside him had all been removed by the loved ones of the dead. And it was only a year ago that his simple grave was opened and his remains conveyed to West Point. It seems fitting that the nation for which he died should enshrine his grave within the grounds of his alma mater, as a living monument for the admiration and imitation of the cadets whose lives should be like his. Over his grave no parent, no brother or sister, no relative brings the chaplet of laurel, and without a mourner bearing his name, the memory of the gallant McRae belongs to his countrymen, one and all. The most heroic death in the national army was his. Let his grateful countrymen and countrywomen hallow his memory, who has none of his blood to mourn his death and adore his fame."

McRae's bravery was referred to in a description of the battle of Valverde, written from Albuquerque on Feb. 23, 1862, published in the St. Louis *Republican* of March 23, and summarized in the Daily Alta California of April 21: "With his artillerymen cut down, his support either killed, wounded or flying from the field, Captain McRae sat down, calmly and quietly, on one of his guns, and with revolver in hand, refusing to fly or desert his post, he fought to the last, and gloriously died the death of a hero, the last man by his guns."

Benjamin Wingate, another hero of Valverde, brevetted a major before his death, was born in Indiana, enlisted in the army in 1846, served throughout the Mexican War in forces commanded by Gen. Winfield Scott, participated in the attack on Chatupeltepec Heights. Wingate advanced through the ranks from private to captain. He was shot in the leg at Valverde on Feb. 21, and died from shock and blood poisoning after two leg amputations. His body was eventually removed from Fort Craig to the national cemetery in Santa Fe, and buried in grave 287. Wingate's grandnephew, Riley M. Edwards, resided until recently in Socorro, N. M. Other relatives live in Darlington, Mo. In the fall of 1860, Benjamin Wingate supervised the construction of the fort which was later to be named in his memory. This fort was originally named Fort Fauntleroy, in honor of Col. Thomas Fauntleroy, of Virginia. When Fauntleroy resigned his commission in the U. S. Army, and joined the Confederacy, the fort for a time was known as Fort Lyon, but following Benjamin Wingate's death was renamed Fort Wingate.

Fort Selden, 14 miles north of Las Cruces, New Mexico, was named after Major Henry R. Selden, another Union officer who participated prominently in the battle of Valverde. Leading "the old Fifth Regiment" at Valverde, Selden was killed in action on Feb. 21.

36 General Sibley made a somewhat detailed report on the battle of Valverde from Fort Bliss, Texas, on May 4, 1862, addressed to General S. Cooper in Richmond. Among other things, Sibley said in his report that he had been confined to an ambulance for several days before Feb. 21, the day on which the fighting began, but that "on the 21st, considering that the impending battle must decide the question at issue, although very weak, I took the saddle

at early dawn to direct in person the movement ... but at 1:30 p.m. having become completely exhausted, and finding myself no longer able to keep the saddle I sent my aides and other staff officers to report to Colonel Thomas Green, of the Fifth Regiment, who conducted the operations." In his report of May 4, 1862, Sibley complained that Canby's forces violated the code in the use of flags of truce: "A flag of truce was opportunely dispatched by the Federal Commander before he reached the gates of his fort, and which was for two hours supposed by our troops to be a proposition to surrender. This flag had for its object the burying of the dead and removal of their wounded; and I regret to state here, for the sake of old associations, that, under this flag, and another sent next day, the enemy, availing himself of our generosity and confidence in his honor, not only loaded his wagons with arms picked up on the field of battle, but sent a force up and actually succeeded in recovering from the river one 24 pounder which had been left in our hands. Even a guidon and a flag, taken in the same way, under the cover of night, and a white flag, were boastingly pointed to, in an interview under a flag of truce between one of my aides and the Federal commander at the fort, as trophies of the fight." OR Series I, Vol. IX, p. 507-512.

Thomas Green, Texas "hero of heroes," emigrated from Tennessee to Texas when a boy, participated in the battle of San Jacinto, which resulted in the establishment of the Texas Republic; fought in Indian skirmishes in Texas, and in the Mexican War. Tom Green was killed at Blair's Landing, near the Texas-Louisiana border, on April 12, 1864, when struck in the forehead by a shell from the Black Hawk, a Union gunboat.

37 Noel's "Campaign," Shreveport, 1865.

38 Upon arriving in Albuquerque, Confederates commandeered what they could find in the way of beef cattle, sheep, horses, mules and forage. The big livestock owners had taken the precaution to drive their herds as far away from Albuquerque as possible. Some Albuquerque merchants were ruined financially because of loyalty to the Confederate cause. Prominent among them were the brothers, Manuel and Rafael Armijo. Drafts given to them "redeemable in gold" to the total amount of $200,000, in payment for merchandise delivered to the Confederates at Mesilla and Albuquerque, were not honored on presentation. The Union government struck out at "southern sympathizers," under an Act of Congress permitting confiscation and sale of real and personal property of those declared guilty of disloyalty. Besides losing some $200,000 to the Confederates, the Armijo Brothers lost the remaining part of their fortune to the Union government through confiscation. Their store, flour mill, ranches, $38,964.40 in United States money, and other properties in Albuquerque and Mesilla, were condemned and ordered sold by decree of the United States court in Albuquerque on June 14, 1864. The Rio Abajo *Press* published the legal notices preliminary to public sale. In addition to the sale of the Armijo properties, the court ordered the sale of real estate in Mesilla belonging to Col. John R. Baylor, one time governor of the Confederate Territory of Arizona, of Roy Bean (later of "Law West of the Pecos" fame), and of his brother, Samuel G. Bean. In Albuquerque the government also confiscated the property of Spruce M. Baird, a lawyer, (Texas representative when Texas was claiming New Mexico to the Rio Grande), and that of Julian Tenorio, a poet, who composed and recited verses in praise of "Los Confederados del Sur," and Jose Maria Chavez, a minister of the gospel. The Rio Abajo *Press* of June 7, 1864, summed up the predicament of "those persons who did everything in their power to bring the people of New Mexico under the galling yoke of rebeldom," by referring to legal notices then being published ordering the sale of confiscated property: "The owners of portions of the property advertised, exerted themselves to induce the rebels to invade this Territory, and they all made themselves so conspicuous in operation against their country that remaining in it, while loyalists were in power, was too perilous for them. Some of these cases were in court for over one year, and none of them less than eight months, before

the decree of confiscation was entered. Due proclamation was made for the claimants to appear and show cause why the property should not be condemned and sold; but none appeared in person, and outlaws cannot appear by attorney; so the infernal faultfinding of attorneys and shirking judges, and the exceptional cavilling of newspaper organs cannot make the decree void. When these cases were on the docket, they frightened away every judge from our district except Judge Knapp. This assertion may seem strange to persons unacquainted with New Mexico, but a few words will make its truthfulness apparent. Rafael Armijo (now in San Antonio, Texas), and Manuel Armijo (at last advices in Richmond, presenting a claim to the rebel government) have large and influential family connections. Relatives generally in this Territory stand by each other, right or wrong; and the judge who might do his duty against one of them, does it at the risk of having powerful influence against him."

39 OR Series I, Vol. IX, p. 526.

40 OR Series I, Vol. IX, p. 651.

41 OR Series I, Vol. IX, p. 656.

42 OR Series I, Vol. IX, p. 527.

43 Troops concentrated at Fort Riley, Kansas, held in readiness to march to New Mexico's relief, were released for other service when the Colorado troops left Fort Union for Santa Fe.

John P. Slough had a stormy career. Born in Cincinnati, Ohio, he studied law and was admitted to the Ohio bar. Moving to Kansas, he was an unsuccessful candidate on the Democratic ticket for governor in 1857. Slough went to Colorado in 1860, practiced law, and was elected judge of a miner's court. He was one of the first to help raise a regiment following the outbreak of the Civil War, for which he was commissioned a colonel. After the war, Slough went to Washington, was commissioned a brigadier general, and appointed military governor for Alexandria, Virginia. Returning to Santa Fe, he became chief justice of the Territorial Supreme Court. Slough was shot and instantly killed in Santa Fe on Sunday, Dec. 17, 1867, by W. L. Rynerson, a member of the House of Representatives of the Territorial Legislature from Dona Ana County. Rynerson, who came to New Mexico as a sergeant in the California Column, had unwisely introduced a resolution in the legislature undertaking to censure Slough for alleged unprofessional conduct. It later developed that Rynerson scarcely knew Slough, and had been imposed upon in the matter of the resolution. The two men met in the billiard room of La Fonda in Santa Fe, several days after the resolution had been introduced. In the course of the argument that ensued, Rynerson shot and killed Slough with bullets fired from a Colt's revolver. Arrested, placed in custody of the United States Marshal, confined in the guardhouse, Rynerson was acquitted on a plea of self defense. Prominent in Lincoln County politics, during the days of "Billy the Kid," Rynerson died in Las Cruces on July 4, 1893. For detailed reports on the Rynerson preliminary hearing, which resulted in his acquittal, see Santa Fe *Gazette*, Dec. 21, 1867, and Jan. 11, 1868. Attorney Merrill Ashurst prosecuted the case for the Territory. Rynerson was defended by Kirby Benedict, former Chief Justice of the Supreme Court of New Mexico, and by Stephen B. Elkins, who later became United States Senator from West Virginia. On Aug. 10, 1867, a few months before he was killed, John P. Slough, according to the Santa Fe *Gazette* of Aug. 17, 1867, "went to Pigeon's Ranch to select suitable cemetery grounds for the proper interment of the brave soldiers who fell in the battle near that place during the last war, selecting a beautiful spot one hundred feet square, and sloping toward the road, about a quarter of a mile this side of the ranch." The bodies of both Union and Confederate soldiers killed in the various skirmishes in the Glorieta mountains were eventually buried in the National Cemetery in Santa Fe. Brigadier General Latham Anderson, U. S. V., blamed Slough for the near Union disaster at Glorieta: "After the reverse at Valverde nothing remained for Canby but to strive for a junction with the troops at Fort Union. In this he was thwarted for a time by the fact that Col. J. P. Slough, against his instructions, brought on a decisive engagement with the enemy at Canon Glorieta, on the 28th of March. Slough's main force was driven from the field, and the defeat would have been disastrous had not the flanking party, under Major Chivington, of the 1st Colorado Volunteers, and Captain W. H. Lewis, 5th U. S. Infantry, succeeded in destroying the Texas train. The rumor is said to have spread among the Texans that they were being attacked in the rear by Canby's column. This caused a panic among part of their force, and prevented an effective pursuit of Slough's defeated troops." See "Canby's Service in the New Mexico Campaign," by Latham Anderson, Battles and Leaders of the Civil War, Vol. 2, p. 697.

44 The Confederates were anxious to capture Fort Union, at the time the principal military supply depot in the Southwest. It is probable, however, that if Union troops had been forced to abandon Fort Union they would have burned the warehouses and their contents. If Sibley had succeeded in capturing Fort Union and its supplies, he would probably have reached the mines in Colorado without difficulty.

As of Aug. 15, 1861, an inventory of government supplies at Fort Union showed an eastern cost value of $271,147.55. Ceran St. Vrain and Kit Carson signed a joint letter to Canby in Santa Fe calling his attention to the fact that Fort Union was open to attack "from Arkansas and Upper Texas." The letter was written at a time when it appeared that volunteers were to be sent to Fort Union to relieve regular troops. St. Vrain and Carson told Canby that such a move would be a mistake.

45 John Milton Chivington, who left his pulpit to take up the sword during the Civil War, was born near Lebanon, Ohio, on January 27, 1821. He died in Denver, Colorado, Oct. 4, 1894. Chivington joined the conference of the Methodist Episcopal Church at Pleasant Green, Cooper County, Missouri, and was ordained a preacher in 1848. A powerful and persuasive personality in camp meetings in Illinois, Missouri and Nebraska, Rev. Mr. Chivington moved to Denver in 1860 and became presiding elder of the Rocky Mountain conference. Opposed to slavery on principle, Chivington joined the army at the outbreak of the Civil War. Dr. William Clarke Whitford, author of "Colorado Volunteers in the Civil War, the New Mexico Campaign in 1862," Colorado Historical Society, Denver, 1906, described "Preacher" Chivington as follows: "Chivington developed extraordinary military ability, although he had no military training before he abandoned the pulpit for the battlefield. In action he became the incarnation of war. The bravest of the brave, a giant in stature, and a whirlwind in strife, he had, also the rather unusual qualities that go to make soldiers personally love such a leader, and eager to follow him into the jaws of death." After Sibley's retreat toward Texas, Chivington and his Colorado Volunteers served some months at Fort Craig, in southern New Mexico. Chivington returned to Colorado late in 1862, where he became involved, unfortunately, in the celebrated so-called "Chivington Massacre" on Big Bend of Sandy Creek, on Nov. 29, 1864, in which hundreds of Cheyenne Indians were killed. Chivington, then colonel commanding the expedition against the Indians, sent two reports on the day of the fighting. One of them, sent to the Commanding Officer in Denver, said: "I have not the time to give you a detailed history of our engagement today; or to mention those officers and men who distinguished themselves in one of the most bloody Indian battles ever fought on these plains. . . . We made a forced march of forty miles and surprised, at break of day, one of the most powerful villages of the Cheyenne nation, and captured over five hundred animals; killing the celebrated chiefs One Eye, White Antelope, Knock-Knee, Black Kettle and Little Robe, with about five hundred of their people, destroying all their lodges and equipage, making almost an annihilation of the entire tribe. . . . I will state for the consideration of gentlemen who are opposed to fighting these red scoundrels, that I was shown by my chief surgeon the scalp of a white man, taken from the lodge of one of the chiefs, which

could not have been more than two or three days taken; and I could mention many more things to show how these Indians, who have been drawing government rations at Fort Lyon, are and have been acting." For the statements, affidavits and testimony in the Chivington investigation by the Doolittle congressional committee, beginning March 7, 1865, see pp. 26-95, Rep. on Cond. of Ind. Tribes, 1867.

46 The property of Encher Pigeon, a French Canadian, early day settler in the Upper Pecos river country. See Las Vegas *Gazette,* Jan. 9, 1875.

47 Published in the Las Vegas *Gazette,* May 23, 1874.

48 The fighting in the mountains east of Santa Fe on and about March 27, 1862, extended over considerable country. There were several skirmishes, including those at Pigeon's Ranch, Apache Canon, Johnson's Ranch and Kozlowski's Ranch, this latter place being owned by Martin Kozlowski, a veteran of five years' service in the Union Army, a resident of New Mexico since 1857. For narratives of the fighting, see reports of Col. John P. Slough, Lieut. Col. Samuel F. Tappan and Major John M. Chivington, of the First Colorado Infantry, for the Union version; and reports to Brig. Gen. Henry H. Sibley, and Col. William R. Scurry, Fourth Texas Cavalry, for the Confederate version. OR Series I, Vol. IX, pp. 530-545. The skirmishes were fought in beautiful mountain country, studded with towering pine trees, grassy meadows and foliage. Although the skirmishes took place more than 85 years ago, there have been but few changes in the countryside.

49 OR Series I, Vol. IX, p. 539.

50 The resolution read as follows: "Be it Resolved: That the President of the United States be, and he is hereby respectfully solicited, to confer upon Captain William H. Lewis of the 5th Regiment of United States Infantry, the rank of Major, for his meritorious and distinguished services in attacking the rear guard of the rebel army, in Apache Cañon, and in destroying the entire train and commissary stores of the said army, on the 28th day of March, 1862; Resolved further: That the President be and is hereby respectfully solicited to confer upon Asa B. Carey of the 13th Regiment of the United States Infantry, the rank of major, for his meritorious and distinguished services in attacking the rear guard of the rebel army, in the Apache Cañon, and in destroying the entire train and commissary stores of said army, on the 28th day of March, 1862." Laws N. M., 1864, p. 124.

51 Union and Confederate dead at Apache Canon and Pigeon's Ranch were buried at Kozlowski's Ranch. Santa Fe *Gazette,* Dec. 15, 1866.

52 OR Series I, Vol. IX, p. 545. For Sibley's report on the fighting in the Glorieta Mountains, see OR Series I, Vol. IX, p. 540. The skirmishes fought in Apache Cañon, at Pigeon's Ranch, and elsewhere in the mountains east of Santa Fe, afforded little opportunity for the Confederates to use the hand to hand fighting, and double barreled shotgun technique used so effectively at Valverde on Feb. 22, 1862. The Confederate troops were at a distinct disadvantage also, because they were obliged to travel up hill most of the way from Santa Fe to the battlefields. The Federal troops found it possible in many instances to look down on the enemy from mountain tops. That General Sibley had hoped to "make a strong demonstration on Fort Union," was revealed in his report of May 4, 1862, from Fort Bliss. Although he was not present in person at the fighting in the Glorieta mountains, Sibley reported on some of the more important phases of the battles. Sibley was apparently in Santa Fe, either at the time of the fighting or shortly after. He reported optimistically that "after the fighting near Glorieta, the whole exultant army assembled." He found "the sick and wounded comfortably quartered and attended; the loss of clothing and transportation made up from the enemy's stores and confiscations, and indeed, everything done which should have been done." While in Santa Fe, Sibley met many friends, "who had been in durance," among

them "General William Pelham, who had been but recently released from a dungeon in Fort Union." OR Series I, Vol. IX, p. 506.

Some confusion and conflict are inevitable in comparing the reports of Union and Confederate officers, not only because of the difference in viewpoints, but because the reporting officers used different names to describe the places of battle. For example, the Confederates identified the fighting in Apache Cañon as "the Battle of Glorieta," while Union reports referred to it as "the Battle of Apache Cañon."

53 In the Las Vegas *Gazette* of Sept. 15, 1877, Louis Hommel told the circumstances under which Canby heard the news of the Confederate disaster at Pigeon's Ranch: " 'Doc' Strachan, a resident of Albuquerque, joined the command just south of Socorro, with important dispatches from the commanding officer of the northern district. In the meadow, below Socorro the column formed a hollow square and the dispatch was read aloud. It notified General Canby that General Sibley's column had a fight with the Federal troops of the northern district, in which the Texans lost their whole train of supplies, and considered themselves routed so badly that they commenced their retreat toward Texas. The whole Federal column, from the commanding officer down to the lowest private in the rear ranks, gave three rousing cheers. The Texans, in charge of the hospital at Socorro, seeing the column in line and hearing the cheers, perhaps thought General Canby intended to storm the town, quickly hoisted the hospital flag and sent a delegation to advise him that but a few well Confederate troops were in town, as guards and nurses of sick and disabled Texans."

On April 17, 1862, more than two weeks after the fighting in the Glorieta mountains, Col. James H. Carleton, then on the march from California to the Rio Grande, wrote a note to the Department of the Pacific in San Francisco asking for information: "I beg you will learn by telegraph the result of Sibley's operations in New Mexico. From the reports of the fight at Pigeon's, near Santa Fe, it would seem the Texans had already been masters of Santa Fe, the capital, and were on their way through Apache Cañon east of that city toward Fort Union. It is important that I be kept informed by express of all intelligence received by telegraph or through the papers, of the operations of the enemy, and his fortune, whether good or bad, in that country, which you may receive." OR Series I, Vol. L, part 1, p. 1009.

54 When the Confederates were ready to evacuate Albuquerque on April 20, 1862, they buried six cannon under the direction of Major Trevanion T. Teel. Twenty-seven years later, on Aug. 18, 1889, Major Teel, then a resident of El Paso, Texas, was in Albuquerque, and told the story of the burying of the cannon to Captain Jack Crawford, the Poet Scout, then living at Fort Craig, New Mexico. Teel offered to point out the place where the cannon had been buried, in the darkness of the night, so many years before. Teel and Crawford, and a hundred curious citizens, repaired to a place about five hundred feet northeast of the San Felipe Church. As Teel remembered it, the cannon had been buried in a plot of ground surrounded by a high adobe wall. After stepping off ground here and there, and becoming oriented, Teel said: "Dig here, and you ought to find them." The next day, shortly after daylight, half of Albuquerque turned out as witnesses to the excavation. Harry S. Whiting, Post Commander of G. K. Warren Post No. 1, Grand Army of the Republic, headed a delegation of Union veterans, while a sprinkling of Confederate veterans were in the crowd. Armed with pickaxes and shovels a "digging committee" began to explore. A complication arose when diminutive Sofre Alexander, owner of the land, objected to the digging, claiming that it would ruin his chile plants and destroy his field of alfalfa. George Lail, a mining man, offered Alexander $100 for permission to go ahead with the digging. Alexander refused, and hurried away to employ a lawyer to ask for a court injunction to prevent trespass on his land. Determined to dig for the cannon, Lail wrote out a mining location notice which he posted on Alexander's property, and staked out a claim, which was permissible under the law, and told the diggers to go ahead with their mineral prospecting. Alexander and his lawyer went

to the courthouse and asked for a preliminary injunction from Judge William D. Lee, a veteran of the Union Army, which was refused on the ground that Alexander would not suffer irreparable damages. Announcing his decision on the law, the court added: "Besides, Sofre, I'm curious myself about those cannon. I'd like to see if those rebels really buried them there. I don't believe they ever captured any of our cannon at Valverde." The cannon were there, sure enough, after the workmen had dug here and there for many hours. All six were stamped "U.S." and bore the name of the manufacturers, C. A. & Co., Boston. At first it was believed the cannon had been brought to New Mexico from Texas, but Louis Hommel, of Las Vegas, who had been a bugler in Company B of the 5th New Mexico Volunteers, said definitely that they were part of McRae's battery, captured by the Confederates at Valverde on Feb. 22, 1862. After the cannon had been recovered, there remained the question of custody and ownership. A committee of the Grand Army of the Republic attended a town council meeting and requested permission to retain custody. The Confederate veterans about town objected strenuously. The *Morning Democrat* said: "It would puzzle any one to give a reason why the G.A.R. should have charge of the guns. They neither captured them nor recovered them, and their effort to appropriate them at the expense of the city, is one which a large majority of the people of Albuquerque will most certainly condemn." The cannon were taken to Judge L. S. Trimble's corral, now the site of the Hilton Hotel in Albuquerque. After much bickering and quarreling, they were divided between Albuquerque's town government and the Colorado Historical Society.

55 Canby went from Albuquerque to Tijeras Canon for the purpose of effecting, if possible, a junction with the Colorado Volunteers who had fought the Confederates in the Glorieta mountains, retreated to Fort Union, and then, under Canby's orders, started for Santa Fe and Albuquerque.

56 As of April 18, 1862, Ovando J. Hollister, a soldier with Colorado Volunteers, described Gen. Canby's physical appearance and personality, as Union troops pursued the Confederates south of Peralta: "Gen. Canby is usually seen near the head of the column attended by his staff and a few mounted troopers as an escort. Tall and straight, coarsely dressed in citizens' clothes, his countenance hard and weather beaten, his chin covered with a heavy grizzly beard of two weeks' growth, a cigar in his mouth which he never lights—using a pipe when he wishes to smoke—he certainly has the air of superiority, largely the gift of nature, though undoubtedly strengthened by long habits of command. His person is portly and commanding, his manner dignified and self possessed, his whole appearance such as to inspire confidence and respect from his fellows. I think him a man of foresight and judgment, patient, prudent and cautious—of great courage, both moral and physical, and as true to the Government as any man in existence. I know that many with as good opportunities of observing him as mine have come to precisely an opposite opinion, but I do not think his history, closely examined, will sustain them." See "History of the First Regiment of Colorado Volunteers," by Ovando J. Hollister, 1863, reprinted as "Boldly They Rode," by The Golden *Press*, Lakewood, Colorado, 1949.

57 OR Series I, Vol. IX, p. 665.

58 OR Series I, Vol. IX, pp. 507-512. For the complete day by day correspondence on the operations of the Federal and Confederate Armies in New Mexico during the period of June 11, 1861, to Feb. 1, 1862, see OR Series I, Vol. IV, pp. 1-89. The results in New Mexico might have been different if Baylor, instead of Sibley, had conducted the campaign. This is the view expressed by Major Trevanion T. Teel several years after the Civil War. Teel recalled that Sibley, while at Fort Bliss, had discussed with him the contemplated New Mexico campaign. Teel recalled his talk with Sibley: "Upon the arrival of his brigade at Mesilla, Sibley was to open negotiations with the governors of Chihuahua, Sonora and Lower California, for supplies. The ob-

jective aim and design of the campaign was the conquest of California, and as soon as the Confederate Army should occupy the Territory of New Mexico, an army of advance would be organized, and 'On to San Francisco,' would be the watchword; California had to be conquered so there would be an outlet for slavery.... If the Confederates succeeded in occupying California, New Mexico and Arizona, negotiations to secure Chihuahua, Sonora and Lower California, either by purchase or conquest, would be opened; the state of affairs in Mexico made it an easy thing to take those states.... The direct cause of our discomfiture and the failure of our campaign in New Mexico was the want of supplies of all kinds for the use of our army. The territory which we occupied was no storehouse. Canby's order to destroy everything that would be of any use to the Confederates had been fully enforced. Thus we were situated in the very heart of the enemy's country, with well equipped forces on our front and rear. General Sibley was not a good administrative officer. He did not husband his resources, and was too prone to let the morrow take care of itself.... Had Colonel John R. Baylor continued to command, the result might have been different." See "Battles and Leaders of the Civil War," Vol. 2, p. 700

⁵⁹ See Noel's "A Campaign from Santa Fe to the Mississippi," Shreveport, La., 1865. The remnant of Sibley's brigade left Fort Bliss for the interior of Texas on June 5, 1862. Reorganized, and with renewed determination to "fight another day," Sibley's Brigade subsequently participated in the battles of Galveston, Franklin, Brashear City, Morgan's Ferry, Mansfield, Pleasant Hill, in Texas and Louisiana. By Dec. 10, 1864, all that was left of the Brigade was at Fulton, Ark., enroute to Texas. The Civil War, for Sibley's Brigade, was at an end.

Noel's appraisal of Sibley: "By nature he is a very sanguine man, too much disposed to confide in and ask advice of those under him, and it is but seldom that a man of that disposition is found who is possessed of a sufficient amount of precaution. Gen. Sibley had all confidence in his ability to move with his Brigade upon New Mexico, and without resistance take possession of all its garrisons, forts and country. Of this I am confident he was sanguine, and had not things changed quickly after he left there (after resigning from the Union Army), garrisons being fortified, forts being strengthened, and the general aspect of affairs changed while he was organizing his Brigade and marching from Texas—the result of the campaign might have been vastly different."

El Paso, Texas, the place where Sibley delivered the salutatory and valedictory of his New Mexico campaign, was isolated from the north and east for some five years during the Civil War. On May 6, 1866, a coach arrived in Franklin (El Paso), Texas, from San Antonio, carrying the first official United States mail between those two places since the beginning of the war. James W. Magoffin, one of the coach passengers, brought with him to Franklin written authority from Provisional Gov. Andrew Jackson Hamilton, of Texas, to organize "El Paso County," by filling in the names of appointees in commissions he had previously signed in blank. Captain David Hammett Brotherton, in command at Fort Bliss, refused to recognize Magoffin's authority and forbade the incumbents in office to surrender any records or papers to Magoffin's appointees. Magoffin's unexpected return, with powers plenipotentiary from the anti-secessionist governor of Texas, caused considerable excitement in El Paso. See Santa Fe *Gazette*, May 19, 1866.

SOURCES

H.R. Ex. Doc. No. 11, 37th Cong., 2nd Sess.

H.R. Ex. Doc. No. 73, 41st Cong., 2nd Sess.

"Narrative of the Surrender of a Command of U.S. Forces at Fort Fillmore, New Mexico, in July, A.D. 1861," by Major James Cooper McKee, Boston, 1886.

N.M. Laws, 1864, p. 124.

Theo. Noel's "A Campaign from Santa Fe to the Mississippi," Shreveport, 1865.

Official Correspondence — Parole of Major Isaac Lynde, National Archives, Washington.

Official Reports —
    Series I,
        Vol. 1, pp. 600-605.
            3, p. 428.
            4, pp. 1 to 477, at random.
        IX, pp. 485 to 665, at random.
        L, Part 1, p. 683 to 1009, at random.
    Series III, Vol. I, p. 601.

Report on Condition of Indian Tribes, Washington, 1867.

REFERENCES

"Battles and Leaders of the Civil War," Vol. 2, pp. 697, 700.

"Campaigns in the West," Ariz. Hist. Soc., Tucson, 1949.

Claim of Juan S. Hart, El Paso, H.R. 53rd Cong., Rep. 1407.

"Colorado Volunteers in the Civil War — the New Mexico Campaign in 1862," by Dr. William Clarke Whitford, Denver, 1906.

Hollister's "History of the First Regiment of Colorado Volunteers," 1863 (reprinted under the title, "Boldly They Rode," Lakewood, Colo., 1949).

"Three Years and a Half in the Army, or History of the Second Colorados," Ellen Williams, New York, 1885.

NEWSPAPERS AND PERIODICALS

Albuquerque Morning Democrat, Aug. 19, 1889.

Las Vegas Gazette, May 23, 1874; Jan. 9, 1875; Aug. 25, 1877, Sept. 1, 15, 1877.

Rep. Com. Gen. Land Office, 1901, p. 280.

Rio Abajo Press, Albuquerque, Mar. 8, June 7, 1864.

Santa Fe Gazette, May 19, Dec. 15, 1866; Aug. 17, Dec. 21, 1867; Jan. 11, Aug. 22, 1868.

Santa Fe New Mexican, April 10, 1872.

In re Baylor:
    Austin Daily Statesman, Feb. 9, 1894;
    Charleston (S.C.) Daily Courier, June 16, 1859;
    The Comanche Chief, Uvalde (Tex.), May 7, 1881;
    The Countryman, Aug. 28, 1861;
    Daily Delta (La.), June 10, 1859;
    Dallas Morning News, Feb. 9, 1894;

In re Sibley:
    Free Lance, Fredericksburg, Va., Aug. 24, 1886.

BOOK THREE

Carleton's California Column

"Have your sabers very sharp, that they may readily cut through clothing. Cavalry recently mounted on California horses cannot use any kind of firearms with success. The men should practice dismounting to fight on foot a good deal. If a rush is made by Texans on horseback with revolvers upon your cavalry while mounted, if the sabers are sharp I would recommend closing in with them as quick as thought. The cold steel will win against the pistol. If they fly, follow with the pistol."

JAMES H. CARLETON,
Fort Yuma, Arizona.
May 2, 1862.

CHAPTER ONE

Soldiers, Wagons and Mules

FFECTIVE SEPT. 13, 1858, that part of New Mexico lying west of the one hundred tenth meridian of west longitude (present day Arizona), was transferred from the Department of Missouri to the Department of California, with headquarters in San Francisco. The designation "Department of California" was changed to "Department of the Pacific" on Jan. 15, 1861. The transfer gave the Department of California (later Pacific) command over military affairs in Arizona, which had at the time three pretentious forts: Fort Breckenridge, near the San Pedro river, on the Overland Mail route to California; Fort Buchanan, half way between Tucson and Los Nogales; and Fort Mojave, on the Colorado river, on

213

Beale's wagon road from Albuquerque to Los Angeles. The Department of the Pacific, as of Jan. 17, 1861, was commanded by Brigadier General Albert Sidney Johnston. Fifty-eight years old at the time, Johnston could look back upon a long and enviable record of service in both the army of the United States and the army of the Republic of Texas.

On Feb. 23, 1861, within less than five weeks after assuming command of the Department, Johnston's adopted State of Texas "severed relations" with the Union. Texas, having "seceded," for all practical intents and purposes, many persons in authority in Washington, Richmond, San Francisco, and elsewhere, speculated upon the course Johnston might pursue. Would he remain "loyal" to the Union, or would he align himself with the Confederate cause? General Johnston alone held the answer to the question. It was said that during his few weeks of residence in San Francisco, Johnston "never spoke one word on the great question which at the time occupied the public mind, one way or the other; that the impression was general up to the time of the sudden and unexpected arrival of General Sumner, that he was a loyal and true officer".[1] On April 9, 1861, having served less than ninety days, Johnston resigned as commander of the Department of the Pacific. His letter to the Secretary of War said: "I have the honor to tender the resignation of my command in the Army of the United States, and to request that it may be submitted to the President for his action; and I have also respectfully to ask that my successor may be appointed and ordered to relieve me as soon as practicable." Some three thousand miles away in Washington, Secretary of War Simon Cameron wrote the word "Accepted" across the face of the letter. Powerful friends in Washington had hoped that Johnston would remain loyal to the Union. Postmaster General Montgomery Blair discussed Johnston's status with President Lincoln, and the President, on Blair's recommendation, signed a commission which would have made him a major general. The commission was mailed to Johnston in San Francisco. When Blair learned that Johnston had resigned, he ordered the San Francisco postmaster to return the letter to Washington.

Although friends and well wishers might speculate on Johnston's future conduct, the War Department could not afford to do so. On April 1, 1861, eight days before Johnston resigned, Secretary Cameron, on recommendation of General Winfield Scott, appointed Brigadier General Edwin Vose Sumner as commander of the Department of the Pacific. Well known throughout the southwest, Sumner had served as a member of General Kearny's staff in 1846 when American troops invaded and conquered New Mexico. Decorated for "gallant and meritorious conduct" at Cerro Gordo and Molino del Rey, in the Mexican War, Sumner returned to New Mexico in 1851, established Fort Union, and led an expedition into the Navajo country.

Traveling incognito, Sumner sailed from New York on April 1, 1861, crossed by rail from the Atlantic to the Pacific side of the Isthmus of Panama, and arrived in San Francisco on April 24. The following day he presented his credentials to General Johnston and assumed command of the Department. Four days later Sumner wrote to Colonel E. D. Townsend, Assistant Adjutant General in Washington, describing the military and political situation in California:

I have the honor to report that I arrived here (San Francisco) on the 24th instant, and on the 25th relieved General Johnston in the command of this department. My departure from New York was not known here till the night before my arrival. It gives me pleasure to state that the command was turned over to me in good order. General Johnston had forwarded his resignation before I arrived, but he continued to hold the command, and was carrying out the orders of the government. . . . There is a strong Union feeling with the majority of the people of this state, but the secessionists are much the most active and zealous party, which gives them more influence than they ought to have with their numbers. I have no doubt but there is some deep scheming to draw California into the secession movement; in the first place as the "Republic of the Pacific," expecting afterward to induce her to join the Southern Confederacy. There are a

number of influential men in Los Angeles who are decided secessionists, and if we should have any difficulty it will commence
there.

As Johnston left the command, and Sumner took over,
there was talk in San Francisco of the things the South might
attempt to do on the Pacific coast. There were rumors that
the South intended to seize the peninsula of Lower California
and annex it to the Confederacy; that the Confederates
planned to seize Guaymas and Mazatlan, two important Mexican seaports; that large forces of Confederates were maneuvering in Arizona, and would soon cross the Colorado river
and attack California; that Confederate gunboats were going
to attempt to capture steamships on the run between San
Francisco and Acapulco. Sumner made moves, here and there,
on the chess board of war, which demonstrated that he was
no novice in military affairs. On April 29, 1861, he ordered
abandonment of Fort Mojave, on the Colorado river, previously maintained to protect the Albuquerque-Los Angeles
mail route, because, as he wrote, "it was an entirely useless
post, with no hostile Indians near it, and no traveling whatever on the road it was intended to protect".[2] Five days later,
on May 3, 1861, Sumner ordered Major James H. Carleton,
a former comrade in arms, to abandon Fort Tejon, and take
Company K of the First Dragoons, to Los Angeles. Carleton's
dragoons reached Los Angeles on May 15, 1861, in time to
prevent Southern sympathizers from carrying out a "secessionist program," which included hoisting the Bear flag in
the public square. Ten days later, the dragoons stood at attention and fired a volley as "loyal citizens" raised the Union flag
over the Los Angeles county courthouse, a ceremony which
had been planned for some weeks, but which had been deferred because of threatened "secessionist" interference.[3]

Albert Sidney Johnston left San Francisco for Los Angeles
on April 28, 1861. He remained in Los Angeles with his
brother-in-law, Dr. John S. Griffin, a resident there, from
May 3 to June 16. Soon after arrival in Los Angeles, Johnston noticed that he was being followed, day and night, pre-

sumably by Secret Service men of the Union army. Johnston
interpreted the constant surveillance to mean that his former
associates in the Union army did not trust him. Friends impressed upon him that he might be arrested at any moment.
Although there was reason to believe that he wished to remain neutral as between the North and South, the constant
surveillance helped Johnston to make up his mind. He decided to offer his services, and as subsequent events proved,
his life, to the Confederacy. He knew that it would be fool-
hardy to attempt to reach a southern port by steamer. Los
Angeles had no railroad connection with the outside world.
Johnston decided to travel overland by horse and buggy.
He talked about his plans with intimate friends, and then
confided in Randolph, once his slave, whom he had manu-
mitted in 1860, and thereafter employed at prevailing wages.
Randolph, who had been Johnston's devoted servant, body-
guard and confidante for years, and who was to be with him
when dying at Shiloh a few months later, made all arrangements for the cross country journey. He bought a good team
of mules, a buggy, and a Mexican pack mule. Randolph balanced a load nicely on the pack mule, tied the rope with the
diamond hitch he had learned in Texas. The shortest and
safest way "south" from Los Angeles would be by way of
Fort Yuma, on the California side of the Colorado river,
thence through Tucson, to Mesilla on the Rio Grande. Randolph knew all the secret plans for the expedition. He knew
that a party of former United States army officers, recently
resigned, and a number of California citizens, anxious to return to the South, would join the General's party at the house
of John Rains, on the Warner ranch, in San Diego county.
Later Randolph learned the names of the army officers, Major
Armistead, Captain Alonso Ridley (elected as leader of the
expedition), Lieutenants Hardcastle, Brewer, Riley, Shaaf,
Mallory and Wickliffe. Still later, Randolph was to hear that
four of the nine army officers—Johnston, Armistead, Mallory
and Brewer—had been killed in battle. With Randolph driving the mule team, and the pack mule trailing along, General

Johnston left Los Angeles (population 4,385) on June 16, 1861. Following Captain Ridley's instructions, and using the road map he had furnished, the distinguished traveler and his driver were soon in the open country, headed toward the Colorado river. By June 22, 1861, the entire party had assembled at John Rains' place. Traveling each day from 4 o'clock in the afternoon until late at night or early morning, to avoid the heat of the desert, the expedition reached the Colorado river at a point near Fort Yuma on July 5, and camped within hailing distance of the fort for three days. Officers and men at Fort Yuma, probably aware of the identity of the travelers and their destination, made no effort to interfere with them. At Blue Water, some miles east of the Colorado river, Johnston learned that Union forces were evacuating Arizona; that they had abandoned and burned supplies and buildings at Fort Breckenridge, and had burned Tucson's only grist mill. On July 22, Johnston's party reached Tucson. Distant columns of smoke gave credibility to the rumor that Union troops were abandoning Fort Buchanan, and burning everything that might be used by the enemy. Six days later, on July 28, General Johnston arrived in Mesilla, New Mexico, on the Rio Grande. He had traveled nearly 850 miles since June 16. Colonel John Robert Baylor met Johnston at Pichacho (Spanish for heel), a small settlement on the Rio Grande, 55 miles east of Cooke's Peak, and 6 miles above Mesilla. Only 20 hours before, Baylor had captured Fort Fillmore and compelled the surrender of 700 Union troops. Upon meeting General Johnston, Colonel Baylor at once offered him the command of his troops. Johnston accepted Baylor's tender of command a bit reluctantly, remarking to Captain Ridley that "it was like being asked to dance by a lady—he could not refuse." Johnston remained in Mesilla for several days as Colonel Baylor's guest, and then went to Fort Bliss, some thirty-five miles south. Two weeks after arriving at the Rio Grande, Johnston left for San Antonio and continued on to Richmond, arriving there about Sept. 1,

1861. On April 6, 1862, less than six months later, Johnston was killed at Shiloh.[4]

The first battle of Bull Run, which, from the Northern viewpoint, converted "rebellion" into "civil war," was fought in northeastern Virginia on July 21, 1861, on which date General Albert Sidney Johnston was approaching Tucson, Arizona. The Department of the Pacific was notified of the battle by dispatches sent by telegraph to the end of the line at the Missouri river, and carried thence to San Francisco by pony express and telegraph. The New York *Herald* of July 22, with details of the battle, reached San Francisco on Aug. 28. On July 22, 1861, the day following First Bull Run, the Congress of the United States passed an act providing for "the raising of troops to protect life and property." Pursuant to the provisions of this law, Secretary of War Cameron on Aug. 14, 1861, sent a message to Governor John G. Downey, of California, "by telegraph to Fort Kearny, and thence by pony express and telegraph," asking him to "please organize, equip, and have mustered into service at the earliest date possible four regiments of infantry and one regiment of cavalry, to be placed at the disposal of General Sumner." Downey wrote Secretary Cameron on Aug. 25 that "no time was being lost" in meeting the requisition for troops; that "men were being enlisted rapidly," and that "the fife and drum were being heard in every village." On Sept. 2, 1861, Downey advised President Lincoln that California had raised its quota of 1,500 volunteers; that they would be organized as the First California Infantry and First California Cavalry, and would be under the command of Colonel James H. Carleton, "an officer of experience, patriotism and gallantry, who deserved to be promoted to the rank of brigadier general."[5] Most of the men recruited under Governor Downey's call for volunteers were miners. Nearly all of them gave Calaveras and Amador county addresses when signing the muster rolls. But few native born Californians responded to the first call for soldiers.

Volunteers for the infantry were quartered at Camp Downey (named after the governor) in Oakland, at a place where in later years "the railroad left the mainland," and the cavalrymen were quartered at Camp Merchant, near Lake Meritt, in Oakland. It was intended originally that the California Volunteers would be sent to Fort Bridger, on Block's Fork of the Green river, in Utah, to protect the overland mail.

General Sumner, in San Francisco, sifted the many rumors regarding possible Confederate moves. A report reached him on July 10, 1861, which later proved incorrect, that "Earl Van Dorn had been seen at the head of 1,300 men on the road between San Antonio and El Paso." Staffbound officers in Washington, poring over maps, and attempting to anticipate Confederate strategy, added to the confusion prevailing at headquarters in San Francisco, as the result of issuing and countermanding orders. In one important instance, General Winfield Scott ordered General Sumner on Aug. 16, 1861, to ship California troops by sea from San Francisco to Mazatlan, Mexico, and march them overland from there through Sonora and Chihuahua to western Texas "to regain the public property in Texas and draw off insurgent troops from Arkansas and Missouri." Although certain in his own mind that Scott's plan was visionary and impractical, Sumner nevertheless set in motion the machinery required to execute the order. Before going too far with his arrangements, however, Sumner wrote on Aug. 30, 1861, to General Townsend in Washington, offering an alternative plan:

In marching to Texas I would respectfully represent that Guaymas will be a much better point of departure than Mazatlan. The roads and country from the former are much better than the latter. I suppose, however, that the route must depend on the one taken by the secessionists, if they should move in this direction. I would suggest whether it would not be a more feasible plan to take my command by sea to some point in Texas, there to meet such an additional force from the north as the commanding general might think necessary. This plan would give me the necessary munitions, which it would be impossible for me to carry across the continent; besides this, a march at the usual rate across those deserts would inevitably unfit volunteers for some time for efficient service in the field.[6]

As the result of Sumner's diplomatic suggestion, Scott's plan was discussed in Washington by the military, and California's United States Senator Milton S. Latham. The War Department decided to abandon the plan on Sept. 10, 1861, and so notified Sumner. Senator Latham wrote a note to General Sumner from Washington on Sept. 17, 1861, in which he said: "I will tell you, when we meet, who it was that secretly got the expedition to Texas countermanded." [7]

The plan to get troops to Texas by way of Mexico having been abandoned, Sumner was relieved as Commander of the Department of the Pacific, and assigned to important duties in Washington. His successor was General George G. Wright, a veteran of nine years service on the Pacific coast, recognized as a loyal Union man.[8] Now that he was in command of the Department, Wright decided to divert to southern California the troops that had been raised to protect the Overland Mail Route. He notified Washington of his plan on Sept. 17, 1861:

I am compelled to assume the high responsibility of changing the destination of the troops ordered to the plains. The disaffection in the southern part of this state is increasing and becoming dangerous, and it is indispensably necessary to throw reinforcements into that section immediately. The rebels are organizing, collecting supplies, and evidently preparing to receive a force from Texas, and the worst feature of the affair is this: They have managed to seduce the native Californians by telling them that they will be ruined by taxes to maintain the war. I shall establish a strong camp at Warner's ranch on the road to Fort Yuma, which will support that post, prevent the gathering of rebels in that vicinity, and be prepared to repel any force advancing through Arizona. The only available troops I have at this moment are those raised for the Overland Mail Route.[9]

General Wright assumed that Washington would approve the plan contemplated in his letter of Sept. 17. On Sept. 16, the day before he wrote his letter, Company "A" of the First Regiment of California Infantry Volunteers, sailed from San

Francisco. Disembarked at San Pedro on Sept. 19, Company
"A" marched that day some twenty miles to Camp Latham,[10]
at Santa Monica. Wright continued to send troops to south-
ern California as rapidly as three ships, the Shubrick, the
Active, and the Senator, could shuttle between San Francisco
and San Pedro. By Oct. 7, 1861, the entire First Regiment of
Infantry, was at Camp Latham. Thirty days later five companies of the First Regiment of California Cavalry were at
Camp Carleton, near San Bernardino.[11] On Oct. 10, 1861,
Major Edwin A. Rigg, with four companies of First Infantry
California Volunteers, left Camp Latham for Camp Wright,
recently established at Warner's Ranch, 137 miles to the east,
on the Fort Yuma road; named for Colonel Geo. G. Wright,
the new department commander. Rigg marched the infantrymen from Camp Latham to Camp Wright in seven days.
They stood the march remarkably well after the first two or
three days, "their feet blistered somewhat, but by frequent
bathing soon got well." Rigg described the camp and prevailing conditions in a letter written to Colonel Carleton on
Oct. 25. The camp was "beautifully located" at the intersec-
tion of the San Diego road with the Yuma road. Water was
plentiful and wood could be easily procured, but the climate
was objectionable: "It blows terribly the greater portion of
the time, and Dr. Prentiss thinks it unhealthy." Supplies
were freighted by mule team from San Diego in seven days.
The mules were in bad shape from "the fact that a number
of them are without shoes and cannot be shod either here or
at San Diego; there are no shoes or nails at either place."
Rigg reported the usual story of military organization difficulties—shortage of pants, blankets, woolen socks and drawers.
Because of the lack of blankets, the men complained of the
cold nights. Stoves for the Sibley tents would have been very
acceptable.[12]

Sixth U. S. Infantry regulars, commanded by Lieutenant
Colonel George Andrews, stationed at Fort Yuma, were ordered on Oct. 1, 1861, to proceed to San Diego, and embark
for New York, for service on the Atlantic seaboard. On Oct.

16, Colonel Carleton (promoted a few days later to the command of the Los Angeles military district) ordered Lieutenant Colonel Joseph R. West, whom he described as "a most excellent officer and gentleman," to leave Camp Latham with Companies E, G and H of the First California Infantry, and to relieve the garrison at Fort Yuma.[13] Carleton's instructions to West were specific:

It is important to the interest of the service that you reach Fort Yuma with the least possible delay. Besides, promptness in executing orders must be the cardinal point in all movements of the First Infantry. You must know that Fort Yuma in a strategic point of view, is an outpost to all of southern California. It is on the line whence must come the only troops which can possibly menace the state from Texas to Arizona overland. If you are not surprised, your force, properly managed, with the desert as an auxiliary, will never be whipped, to say the least.

West was to control traffic on the Colorado river:

You will seize all the ferryboats, large and small, upon the Colorado River. All the crossing of the river must be done at one point under the guns of the fort. All persons passing into Sonora or to Arizona from California, must take the oath of allegiance before they pass; so must all coming into California by the route overland via Yuma. Do not hesitate to hold in confinement any person or persons in that vicinity, or who may attempt to pass to or from California, who are avowed enemies of the government, or who will not subscribe to the oath of allegiance. Keep an exact record of name, place of residence, age, occupation, and whence he came and whither he is to go, of each person passing the river to or from California.... Should you be menaced by an enemy force, you will make any, and if necessary every, sacrifice to destroy that enemy before he reaches the edge of the desert.[14]

Leaving Camp Latham on the day Carleton's order was issued, the three companies of infantry marched eighteen miles the first day, to Lagunita, thence on succeeding days to Reed's Ranch, Chino Ranch, Temescal, Laguna Grande, Temecula, Gifalter's Place and Camp Wright, on Warner's Ranch, in San Diego county. The distance, 140 miles, was accomplished in eight days.[15]

Hadji Ali, a Turk, Carleton's express messenger, reached

Camp Wright at 9 o'clock on the night of West's arrival with a letter in which Carleton expressed concern over many things. He was particularly anxious over the water situation in the desert country:

It will be important that you at once send forward a party, even if they make forced marches, to clean out the wells. To be certain that you have not too many men and animals at a watering place at one time, you had better cross the desert by companies, each one day behind the other. You had better go with the advance company, that you may send back words of advice to those in the rear. All this is to be done only in the event that the waters on the desert have disappeared and the wells become filled. Should this not be so, of course your troops can be kept together. I feel great anxiety that your men make the march without suffering. Better march mostly by night from Vallecito on. Great forecast and care must be exercised by yourself in this matter. Have the men drink heartily before setting out on a march and husband their canteens of water. I desire you will report to me all the details of how you managed this matter and give me your views as to the best methods for troops to cross the Yuma desert. Hadji Ali, the Turk who takes this letter to you, can give you much information. . . . I have ordered Captain Andrews to send a company of infantry to help clean out the wells, commencing on the east side of the desert. So let Hadji Ali, the expressman, go on without delay.[16]

West wrote a "friendly note" to Carleton on Oct. 25, "in preference to any official communication," telling him of his plans for the march across the desert wastes from Camp Wright to Fort Yuma. He proposed to feed his men, most of whom were "green troops," on jerked beef and beans. West arrived at Camp Wright with Companies E, G and H. Having exchanged two companies at Camp Wright with Major Rigg, West left for Fort Yuma with Companies B, H and I, on Oct. 25, 26 and 27, starting one company each day. Seven men left Camp Wright on Oct. 24 in advance of the troops to clean out the wells. The command was divided to accommodate the troops at the watering places. In order to avoid the excessive heat of the day, most of the marches were made at night. Enroute to Fort Yuma, the troops marched through

San Felipe, "an old overland mail station," through Vallecito, thirty miles away, where there was "an old mail station
in a narrow pass between two ranges of hills," thence over a
heavy sandy road to Palm Springs ("water in limited supply,
and requires to be prepared for a command; the locality
could be used for a camp"), and on Carriso Creek; thence
over a level plain with desert brush, "to Sackett's Well, and
on to Indian Well, where there is an old mail station entirely
deserted," about fifteen miles from Signal Mountain, a prominent landmark. From Indian Well on to New River Station,
"over a barren, alkali plain, with a few patches of mesquite;
dusty and heavy for wagons; at New River, an old mail station, deserted." From New River to Alamo, over a "heavy
road on a barren flat," where there was "another old deserted mail station." From Alamo Station, through Gard-
ner's Wells to Salt or Seven Wells, "an old mail station,
water plenty, but brackish, wood abundant." The infantrymen left Salt Wells on Nov. 2, at 4 p.m., traveling nine miles
to Cook's Wells, where water and wood were "good and
abundant," thence fifteen miles to Pilot Knob, where they
camped "on the bank of the Colorado at the foot of the mountain." Leaving Pilot Knob at 1:30 p.m., on Nov. 3, West's
command reached Fort Yuma, a distance of ten miles, at 4:30
p.m.[17] Built at a strategic point on a high bluff on the west
bank of the Colorado river, Fort Yuma commanded a superb
view of California, Mexico and Arizona. With its vast store
of supplies, Fort Yuma represented an investment by the
government of more than one million dollars. After reaching
Fort Yuma, West began to comply with Colonel Carleton's
instructions of Oct. 16. He seized the boats at Gonzales' Ferry,
twenty-six miles below, on the Colorado river, despite the
fact that it was in Mexican territory. While interviewing
chiefs of the Yuma tribe of Indians, West learned that the
Yumas were at war with the Maricopas and Pimas. River men
pointed out to him that it was practicable to ship supplies by
salt water from San Francisco to the mouth of the Colorado,
and thence upstream to Fort Yuma in small steamers. Anx-

ious to protect Fort Yuma from attack by the enemy, West built one work 350 feet in length on a low hill to the west, and three small works at different points. West assured Carleton that if the enemy attacked him, he would "fight him to the bitter end sure, standing or running." To further strengthen the defenses of Fort Yuma, West urged Carleton to furnish him with two 12 or 18-pounder pieces with the required ammunition. On Nov. 13, 1861, he wrote Carleton: "I shall soon have matters all snug in my grasp and hold them so." [18]

On Dec. 7, 1861, Department Commander Wright took action which resulted many months later in important and significant events in New Mexico and Arizona. He telegraphed the Adjutant General in Washington, proposing to send Colonel Carleton "with his own regiment and the First Battalion of Cavalry, with a battery of artillery, to reopen the Southern Mail route—recapture Forts Buchanan, Thorn, Fillmore and Bliss." The expedition was to move as soon as practicable, through Fort Yuma. Closing the telegram, Wright said: "The troops are ready and anxious. I have the force to hold the whole country this side of the Rio Grande." [19] Two days later, on Dec. 9, Wright wrote to the Adjutant General giving details of the proposed expedition, and advising him of the number of troops available, and their probable disposition:

I have now in southern California the First California Volunteer Infantry, Colonel Carleton; the First California Volunteer Cavalry, a battalion of five companies, under Colonel Eyre. I estimate that this force, with the battery which I propose to send, will amount to about 1500 men. They are fine troops and well officered, and under the command of Colonel Carleton, an officer of great experience, indefatigable and active, the expedition must be successful. I have never seen a finer body of volunteer troops than those raised in this state. They are anxious for active service, and feeling, as we all do, that we are able to retake all the forts this side of the Rio Grande, I may be pardoned for urging the movement. The difficulties and delays experienced on the present route of the overland mail show us the absolute necessity for opening the southern route; and why should we continue to act on the defensive, with Fort Yuma as our advanced post, when we have the power and will to drive every rebel beyond the Rio Grande? [20]

Wright's telegram of Dec. 7 to the Adjutant General, supplemented by his letter of Dec. 9, suggested one of the important reasons behind the plan to try to recapture the country between the Colorado river and the Rio Grande. That was the possibility of resumption of mail service over the southern route, much to be preferred in the winter months to the route through northern California, Nevada and Utah, occasionally blocked for weeks at a time by snow and ice.[21] The southern mail route, which carried mail and passengers from Independence, Mo., through Albuquerque, to Los Angeles, abandoned the line between Mesilla and Tucson on Aug. 23, 1861. The route agent at Tucson told of the abandonment in a note to Ammi White, at Pima Villages: "The mail between Tucson and Mesilla will stop for the present, as the country is under martial law." White relayed the information to Colonel George Andrews, commanding officer at Fort Yuma: "Enclosed please find Mesilla papers, containing full accounts of the proceedings of the rebels in eastern Arizona. You will see that they have possession of the entire country. Twenty of their troops are at Tucson now and 100 are expected in a very few days." [22] The Adjutant General submitted Wright's plan to Major General Geo. B. McClellan, who in turn gave it his approval on Dec. 18, setting in motion a train of events which resulted in the creation of Carleton's California Column, destined to play a tragic part in the months to come in the lives of Apache and Navajo Indians in New Mexico and Arizona.

General Wright named Colonel James H. Carleton as commander of the expedition to the Rio Grande. A veteran of many years service in the army, Carleton quickly recognized the dramatic possibilities inherent in the venture. He visualized spectacular marches by his troops over desert country in California and Arizona. He saw an opportunity to "strike a blow for the old flag." At his headquarters in Los Angeles,

Carleton began the prodigious task of organizing the expedition. It would be necessary to arrange to transport and sustain some sixteen hundred troops, infantry, artillery and
cavalry, a distance of eight hundred fifty-nine miles. In addition to the troops, there would be hundreds of civilian employes—teamsters, wagon bosses, blacksmiths, horseshoers,
cooks, waiters and roustabouts. It would be necessary to
locate and buy horses, mules, wagons, equipment and supplies of all kinds for man and beast. Shuttling between Los
Angeles, San Pedro and San Francisco, arranging for the start
of the great adventure, Carleton bought supplies in a wartime market. Prices advanced daily, almost hourly. Carleton
paid from $80 to $90 a head for second grade horses and
mules in Los Angeles, many of which were rejected later as
unfit for service. In San Francisco, to the dismay of fellow
officers, Carleton was allowed to commandeer a number of
fine horses recently trained for use by the Second California
Cavalry, "because the exigencies of the service required it,"
and was also allowed to wangle three Concord ambulances
recently received at the Presidio from the east. Hay cost
$60.00 a ton, and the price of barley soared in Los Angeles to
the fantastic price of $9.96 a bushel, causing Carleton to send
a frantic message to cavalry officers: "Have the horses and
mules eat more hay and less barley." Beef on the hoof, delivered at any place between Los Angeles and Fort Yuma, was
contracted for at 9⅜¢ per pound. By dint of diligent effort,
working almost day and night, Carlson managed to acquire
most of the things needed for the expedition. From army
warehouses, and market place, from private traders and speculators, he got together and shipped, either by land or sea,
countless items: saddles, bridles, harness, carbines, sabres,
revolvers, ammunition, knapsacks, haversacks, horseshoes,
horseshoe nails, and tools for setting them; charcoal for blacksmiths' fires; nosebags and hobbles, rope, water kegs, bedding and cooking utensils. He accumulated and shipped
great quantities of staples: Compressed potatoes, dessicated
vegetables, pork, bacon, ham, flour, beans, rice, tea, coffee,

sugar, molasses, vinegar, pickles, candles, soap, salt, lime juice, whiskey, hospital stores, dried apples, black pepper, pemmican.[23] Having had wide experience in the Indian country, and believing it desirable to establish friendly relations with Indians in Arizona and New Mexico, Carleton bought 5,000 pounds of odds and ends for use in the Indian country. He personally made out the list of things needed for Indians:

Tobacco, knives, small looking glasses, vermillion paint, beads, needles and linen thread, awls, arrow points, fish hooks and lines, hoes, a few scarlet blankets for the chiefs, 10,000 yards of manta, i.e., shirting, calico, etc., to purchase wheat.

The apparent objects and purposes of the expedition were stated in an article, probably written by Captain J. C. Cremony, in the *Daily Alta California,* of Jan. 18, 1862:

Col. Carleton is indefatigable in his exertions to prepare for his march to the eastern frontier. He spends all of his time in camp, except occasional visits to San Pedro, arranging for the movement. The expedition under the command of Col. Carleton is the most important to California, of any which has taken place on this coast since the timely arrival of General Sumner. It contemplates the holding in perfect check the Indians of our own eastern frontier, those of southern Utah and central and western New Mexico. This alone is no small object, but it appears easy of accomplishment by an officer of the ability and energy of the commander of this expedition, and one so conversant with the country and Indians. Although these objects are of great importance, the securing of which by a force of fifteen hundred men, will be no small feat, yet there is beyond this a measure of still greater importance, and for the success of which the Colonel is bending all the energies of his mind. This measure looks beyond the subjugation of Indians, or the guarding of our frontier against secessionists within or without the state. It is the opening of a mail route upon a line over which the overland mail can be transported with punctuality and expedition at any and all seasons of the year. The country from Los Angeles to Mojave and thence to Albuquerque, in New Mexico, presents no obstacle and is never obstructed by snow.

Extraordinarily heavy rains in southern California in the early months of 1862 prevented Carleton from getting the expedition under way on schedule time. The entire country seemed to be inundated. It became impossible to keep the wagons rolling on the road to the Colorado river. The *Daily Alta, California,* of Feb. 17, 1862, described the situation in western Arizona:

The Gila river has not, within the past 30 years, been so swollen as it was by the late storm. The Gila's banks overflowed, and the Colorado river was unable to carry the flood waters between its banks. Fort Yuma was surrounded by water. The waters of the Colorado washed away nearly all the houses at Colorado City.

Troops at Camp Wright, impatiently waiting for the rains to subside so they could move on to Fort Yuma, became obstreperous. Colonel West reported the situation to Carleton on Feb. 19:

I regret to have to inform you that all of Company A, First Infantry California Volunteers, with the exception of the non commissioned officers and one private, refused to obey the order this morning to "drill with knapsacks on." There are twelve men in the guard house now for the same offense, and with over one half the command in a state of mutiny I have not deemed it judicious to endeavor to enforce authority, being fearful that little reliance can be placed upon the remainder to that end. In fact, this refusal to do duty amounts to a demoralization of the whole command; the scepter of authority being once cast down, no dependence can be placed upon any order being obeyed. Drills must be suspended because orders to "drill with knapsacks on," cannot be carried into effect, and I have no discretion in the premises.

Company A's argument to West was that the men were already bogged down carrying a rifle, bayonet, ammunition and other accessories; that to require them to carry a knapsack in addition would make pack horses out of them. That the infantry had right and justice on their side was evident. The regulations required that knapsacks contain the following items: one great coat, blanket, forage cap, woolen shirt, drawers, stockings, towel, two handkerchiefs, two combs, one fine and one coarse, sewing kit, soap, toothbrush, canteen, haversack, tin cup, fork, spoon, plate and sheath knife.

Shocked by news of the mutiny of Company A, Carleton wrote to West at once:

I have always regarded Company A as one of the finest I have ever seen in service—one of the first I should have chosen to follow me into any battle where the integrity of the country or the glory of the flag was to be maintained.... We are about to commence a movement with limited means of transportation over a desert country. Unless the soldiers carry their knapsacks at the commencement of the march it will be impossible to transport a sufficiency of food, of ammunition, of clothing, of hospital stores. So the purpose of the expedition will have to be abandoned, or the men, like good soldiers, must be willing to sacrifice personal convenience for a short time to attain an important object. Read all this to those men. Read the Articles of War to them. Remind them of their oaths. Give them one hour to reflect on the unhappy consequences of such conduct. Let them see how unworthy it is of them as soldiers, how degrading to themselves as men, how much it reflects upon their company and regiment, how disgraceful it is to California, to the flag, to the country. If, then, any one man amongst them does not feel ashamed of such conduct, and feel willing to obey orders promptly and cheerfully, the only alternative left is to have that man at once mustered out of the service without pay. The country has plenty of soldiers, and California has enough of them even here, who stand ready to take his place and obey orders. Depend on that.... There is one thing those men can count upon: The colors of the First Infantry of California will go forward, even though every man in the regiment but one refuses to go with them.[24]

Carleton's rhetoric won the day. Company A succumbed to his eloquence, and grumblingly agreed to obey the "knapsack order." [25]

Bit by bit, Carleton tied together the loose ends of the expedition schedule, and made ready to start his troops eastward. On Feb. 24, 1862, he received the news that the brig, W. D. Rice, had sailed from San Francisco with government stores for Fort Yuma. On Feb. 25 Carleton ordered Major David Fergusson, First California Volunteers, to move his command from Camp Carleton near San Bernardino to Fort Yuma. On March 7, Carleton ordered four companies of the First and Fifth Regiments of Infantry of California Volunteers, to take up the line of march at noon from Los Angeles to Camp Wright. On March 15, he ordered Captain N. J. Pishon and his company of First Cavalry California Volunteers to proceed without delay to Fort Yuma, and to see that every man fit to take the field was furnished with "a good horse, a good Sharp's carbine, a good revolver, Navy size, and a good sabre, ground sharp." Pishon's cavalrymen were to travel light: "The men need have but the clothes they wear, and food, powder and ball. Let there be not one moment lost."

While Colonel Carleton was completing arrangements in Los Angeles for the expedition to the Rio Grande, the Confederate army was engaging in actual combat in New Mexico. However, Carleton did not learn until March 22, 1862, a full month after the event had taken place, that Sibley's Brigade had soundly whipped Canby's forces at Valverde, near Fort Craig, New Mexico. Alarmed by the news and sensing its implications, Carleton wrote at once to the Department in San Francisco:

Sibley's appearance on the Rio Grande make the recapture of Fillmore, Bliss and Thorn not so easy a task as when those places were held by Baylor and his 900 men. Therefore, as it is your purpose to have the force under my command make a demonstration in that direction, I submit if it would not be well to have Bowie's regiment ready to assist me in case it should be necessary for it to do so.[26]

Responding to Carleton's appeal, the Department added to his command the Fifth Infantry, California Volunteers, commanded by Colonel George W. Bowie, Company A, Third U. S. Light Artillery, commanded by First Lieutenant John B. Shinn, then at Camp Drum, and Captain John C. Cremony's company, Second California Cavalry. These additions to Carleton's command gave him 2,000 men instead of 1,500 as originally planned.

With definite information that Sibley was on the march in New Mexico, and that he had defeated the Union troops in his first major encounter, Carleton decided it was time to accelerate the movement of the troops at his command. On March 31, he issued three important marching orders. He ordered Colonel Bowie to leave Camp Latham for Camp Wright with his Fifth Cavalrymen, and ordered Colonel West to leave Camp Wright for the Pima Villages on the Gila river, east of Fort Yuma, with Companies C and K, First Infantry, and Companies B and G, Fifth Infantry, and Companies B and D, First Cavalry. He ordered Lieutenant Colonel E. E. Eyre to "mount the rank and file of Company B, First Cavalry, 90 men in all," and to report to Colonel J. R. West. On April 9, Captain E. D. Shirland was ordered to "take up his line of march from Camp Drum, near San Pedro," with Company C, First Cavalry California Volunteers. General Wright notified the Adjutant General in Washington on April 19 that "Colonel Carleton was on the march," adding:

Carleton's command has been supplied with everything deemed necessary for a successful campaign. He has a wagon train (200 wagons), his own regiment (First Infantry), First Cavalry (five companies), and Shinn's battery. The Fifth Infantry California Volunteers is being concentrated at Fort Yuma as a reserve and support for Carleton's command.[27]

No doubt but that Carleton's expedition was an impressive one, in striking contrast to Sibley's poorly equipped brigade that had marched from San Antonio to El Paso, and thence into New Mexico only a few short weeks before. In addition to the two hundred wagons mentioned in General Wright's dispatch to Washington of April 19, Carleton's expedition with its 2,000 men had an abundance of accessories of war, including nine hundred draft mules, twenty-five pack mules, 425 cavalry horses, 125 horses for artillery and cavalry horses, and tons of supplies of almost every kind.

CHAPTER TWO

On to the Rio Grande

WHILE COLONEL CARLETON in Los Angeles was preparing, during January, 1862, to move Union troops toward New Mexico, General Sibley was in Fort Bliss, El Paso, Texas, more than eight hundred miles to the east, preparing to move his brigade into New Mexico north along the Rio Grande. On Jan. 27, 1862, General Sibley ordered Captain S. Hunter, of Company A, C.S.A., then of Colonel John Robert Baylor's command, to "take post at Tucson to protect western Arizona and to open communications to southern California." Sibley's order to Hunter was a large one, but he undertook to carry it out to the best of his considerable ability. By Feb. 28, 1862, Captain Hunter, with 100 Confederate Cavalry, was in Tucson. According to his official report Hunter was received there "with open arms and great enthusiasm." Resourceful, and on the move early and late, Hunter maneuvered his small detachment in Arizona skilfully and intelligently. His ability to strike at one place, and to move on quickly and strike in another place many miles away, soon produced in the minds of Union officers the impression that Hunter's command was made up of hundreds of men.

Upon learning in Los Angeles of Captain Hunter's activities in Arizona, Carleton wrote to Major E. A. Rigg, then at Fort Yuma, on March 15, 1862, advising him that he was anxious to "lay hands on Hunter and his band of renegades and traitors," and urged him to try to capture both Hunter and Tucson in the same operation. "There must be trails and

234

bypaths of the great traveled road known to the Indians,"
Carleton said in his letter to Rigg, "through which a force
could be piloted so as to fall upon Tucson unawares of a
single person in it." Carleton outlined a plan by which
Captain William McCleave, of the First Cavalry, using the
pretext that he was going out to fight Tonto Indians, would
take forty men, and "kill or capture Hunter."

Carleton warned Rigg of the danger involved: "Hunter
and his men are not to be underrated. They will fight well.
They are armed with the cavalry musketoon and one or two
revolvers per man. They are mounted on American horses,
but have no sabres. They have three wagons for transportation." Carleton was also anxious, incidentally, to have Mc-
Cleave capture "one Elias Brevoort of Santa Fe, a spy and a
traitor." If captured, McCleave was to make short shrift of
Brevoort, according to Carleton's instructions: "Let him be
where he may, in the vicinity of Tucson; when caught, let
him be tried by a military commission; and if he be found
guilty of playing the spy or traitor, let him be hung as speedily as possible." [28]

Determined to have Hunter taken prisoner if at all possible, Carleton wrote not only to Rigg, but also direct to
Capt. McCleave:

If by forced marches you can follow trails, and unawares fall
on Hunter at Tucson with his 100 mounted Texans, you having
your company of infantry, it would be a coup that would last you
all your life. It will require great resolution, great labor, great
privations and first rate dash and pluck—every man determined
never to give up from the word go, and success is yours. You
should have spies ahead to keep you warned of danger from am-
bushes enroute, and to let you know all about the enemy. What
you do must be done at once. If the men take only the clothes
they stand in, no great coat, one blanket, and only provisions
and ammunition, you can haul some forage until you come within
striking distance.... If Hunter has been reinforced... all of
which you will learn at the Pima villages ... then you must re-
consider your plans.... Infantry are much better than your un-
instructed cavalry on horseback. Once they get Hunter's men
under fire they will make them howl. If I were you I should de-

pend on all my men on foot. Hunter's men are mounted on strong American horses and can ride you down; but if you can get at them in the night, I doubt if even a man gets into the saddle. I am anxious for you to have this duty, but you are not to leave anything to chance, not to go to Tucson unless you are certain you can succeed.[29]

Two days later, on March 17, 1862, Lieut. Ben C. Cutler wrote to Major Rigg again, at Carleton's direction, urging quick action in undertaking to capture Hunter and take Tucson:

Work quick, night and day, and you are bound, all of you, to get immense credit. If you can, destroy or capture Hunter and his men, and send me their flag. . . . If McCleave's party is not successful and they cannot purchase beef, they will not starve as long as they have horses and mules. . . . If our force is shrewd, and knows the strength of the enemy in advance of them, which they ought, and doubtless will know from the Indians, it would seem impossible for them to fail in taking Tucson. In case of success, every secession man in that town must be brought to Fort Yuma. The party, besides, must endeavor to catch Colonel Reily, if possible. He has gone down to Hermosillo, with twenty men. . . . There must be no surrender. If McCleave's party is obliged to retreat, from falling in with an overwhelming force, they must fall back, fighting inch by inch, until they get back.[30]

Captain McCleave and eight picked men left Fort Yuma, ostensibly to fight Tonto Indians. Their real mission was to attempt to bag Captain Hunter. Major Rigg, then in Fort Yuma, told the outcome of McCleave's strategy in a letter written to Carleton, then in Los Angeles, on March 30. McCleave had gone to Ammi White's house, at the Pima Villages, arriving there at daylight on March 20:

Knocking at the door, he found a person who answered and of him, McCleave inquired if Mr. White lived there. Receiving an answer in the affirmative, he said he desired to see Mr. White personally. He was told that he should be called, and Captain Hunter, who was asleep in the house at the time, was awakened and informed of an officer and two men of the U. S. troops being there. He came out and represented himself as Mr. White, asking Captain McCleave if those were all the men he had with him, to which the Captain replied, "No; I have six more at the next station." In the meantime more of Hunter's men had collected, and Hunter suddenly drew his pistol and announced his being a captain in the Confederate army, at the same time informing McCleave that he was his prisoner. McCleave had, however, thinking that he was amongst friends (seeing no uniforms), taken off his arms, and his men were putting up their horses.[31]

Hunter had arrested White, a widely known Union sympathizer, shortly before McCleave's arrival at the Pima Villages, had tied his hands and feet, and threatened to hang him. Hunter's men helped themselves to White's chickens and hogs, wrecked his flour mill and confiscated 300,000 pounds of flour. Hunter gave most of the flour to the Pima Indians, after obtaining a promise from them that they would not allow it to fall into the hands of Union troops.[32]

Lines were tightened in California and elsewhere in the southwest, as the Civil War moved into its second year. The tenseness was indicated when the Los Angeles *Star* was barred from the mails as of Feb. 17, 1862, because it was being used "for the purpose of overthrowing the government of the United States." [33]

Union troops commanded by Gen. Edward Richard Sprigg Canby, and Confederate troops commanded by Gen. Henry Hopkins Sibley, fought a bloody battle at Valverde, on the Rio Grande, Feb. 21, 1862. Ten days before the battle of Valverde, the *Daily Alta California* published a vigorously worded editorial, stating its viewpoint and reflecting purported dominant sentiment in California:

It is stated that a rebel force of 3,900 is on its way to Fort Yuma, 3,000 at Mesilla, under command of Gen. Sibley, and 900 at Tucson, under command of Colonel Baylor, with the intention of attacking Fort Yuma. The statement, we think, must be exaggerated; but assuming that it is correct, we have quite a strong force in that quarter already, and it is understood that more are ready to march. It is difficult to determine whether any demonstration on California is intended or not. Arizona is certainly of not sufficient importance for the concentration of so large a body of troops. It may be that the foolish idea of invading California is entertained by the rebel junta at Richmond, based on the past political history of our state. It is undoubtedly true that for many years southern men have held the reins of government on the Pacific coast, not because they were in the majority, but for the most part being men not brought up to any industrial pursuit, the field of politics was the only one left to them, while the energies of the mass of the people were directed to other channels. The result of the late election demonstrated what close observers had long before ascertained, that they constituted a very small minority of our population, and that whenever lines were drawn, they were found to be forced into the background. . . .

California had no connection whatever with the "rebel states," as the *Daily Alta* saw it:

We have no connection whatsoever with the rebel states. We never had and never will have any trade with them, for they produce nothing save sugar that we require. All our interests lie northwards, and it is from that section of the Union that we have received everything for which we are indebted to the general government. The southern politicians have always been our enemies. It was they who threatened to dissolve the Union if California was admitted; and it was they who defeated every project, the Pacific Railroad included, calculated to promote our happiness and prosperity. If the disaffected among us, and there are some, should for a moment think of joining the invaders, if invasion be meditated, it would be well for them to ponder beforehand upon the perils of the path before them. To think of attaching this state to the skirts of rebeldom is simply absurd, and to attempt to force her into an independent position, nothing but the dream of madmen. It will be their duty to lend neither countenance nor support to the invaders of the soil of their adopted state. If a contrary policy should be pursued, there will be martial law and provost marshals in earnest. Disaffection will have to be suppressed by the military authorities, and there are men and arms enough to do it, no one not entirely blinded by prejudice, can for a moment doubt.

Colonel Carleton left his Los Angeles headquarters and started for Fort Yuma on April 13, 1862. As of April 19, 1862, all California troops were on the march, strung out for hundreds of miles between Camp Latham and the Gila river, a total of 2,000 soldiers, fifteen companies of infantry, five companies of cavalry, and Shinn's light battery of artillery. Two hundred wagons, drawn by six and eight mule teams, each wagon loaded up to 3,000 pounds, carried the supplies necessary to support the troops in the field. Each mule team had one wagon master and three assistant wagon masters. The teamsters, employed in San Francisco, carried revolvers and "riflemen's knives."

The march across the desert from Camp Wright to Fort Yuma was as spectacular and dramatic as Carleton had expected it would be. Traveling in early morning and late afternoon, company after company of cavalry and infantry crossed the desert with little confusion, without a glimpse of the enemy, or suffering a single fatality. Because of the scarcity of water on the desert, detachments and companies traveled on schedules timed to the capacity of wells and watering places. The infantrymen, armed with Sharp's carbines, army revolvers and sabres, were told by their officers that the "rebels" were armed with revolvers, knives, Mississippi rifles and shotguns, but had no sabres.[34]

The California infantrymen found conditions none too inviting in the desert country. Writing from Cariso Creek, near Palm Springs, on April 27, 1862, the correspondent of the *Daily Alta California* described the effect of the climate on man and beast:

I arrived at this place on the 25th instant enroute for Fort Yuma, and thence to meet the foe in Arizona, or wherever he is to be found. Cariso Creek is located on the western edge of the Colorado desert, 122 miles from Yuma, the whole distance being one unbroken waste of blinding white sand, which reflects the rays of the sun with terrible lustre and withering effect. Men, mules and horses sink under its power, as if suddenly blighted, losing all energy, and relaxing every fibre to absolute flaccidness.[35]

Colonel Joseph Rodney West, with four companies of infantry, and two companies of cavalry, California Volunteers, left Camp Wright for Fort Yuma on April 5, 1862. West's command remained for a brief time at Fort Yuma, and continued eastward to the Pima Villages, reaching there on April 30. Carleton reached Fort Yuma on May 2. The next day he wrote West a long letter of advice and encouragement:

I do not believe that Sibley can spare troops enough from the Rio Grande to make a respectable stand against us in Arizona, nor do I believe that he would come 300 miles away from his magazines to fight us, when if he waits we will doubtless attempt to go to him; so, admitting that Hunter still lingers there to watch our movements and to count our force up to the last moment, then to go, I have thought it would be well to entrap him, if possible. This duty, if practicable, from intelligence in your possession, I leave with you. I have fancied it would be agreeable to you to put up the Stars and Stripes in Arizona; but we can afford to wait until all is ready, in case the enemy is too strong for you.[36]

Assuming that West would encounter Confederates either in or near Tucson, Carleton instructed him on the tactics to be employed in the fighting:

Have your sabers very sharp, that they may readily cut through clothing. Cavalry recently mounted on California horses cannot use any kind of firearms with success. The men should practice dismounting to fight on foot a good deal. If a rush is made by Texans on horseback with revolvers upon your cavalry while mounted, if the sabers are sharp I would recommend closing in with them as quick as thought. The cold steel will win against the pistol. If they fly, follow with the pistol, but have our men well kept together, and well in hand, or they will not succeed. In closing against cavalry with cavalry, and in hand to hand encounters on horseback, it is well to get your enemy in your power by cutting off his reins, killing his horse, etc. If your cavalry happen to be on foot and the Texans happen to be on foot and attempt to make a rush upon your men with revolvers, as is their custom, teach your men not to use their fire arms until the enemy is about to close, then to draw the saber and rush upon him with the speed of lightning. If he run, use the pistol until the shots are exhausted and then the carbine. It is my opinion that a judicious use of the saber on foot or on horseback will tell very much in your favor.

Carleton advised West not to allow his men to underrate the enemy:

Pray teach your men not to despise their enemy. Those men whom they go to encounter are determined men and will fight with desperation. You must be sure to take or send enough men to overpower them without a doubt. The Texans are fond of getting into an adobe town and of loop holing the houses and there make a stand. In this event, by seizing some prominent row of buildings and by cutting your way from room to room until you get into the heart of the town, you gain all the advantages they themselves possessed. At Taos, New Mexico, in February, 1847, our people cut holes through walls and threw, by hand, 12 pounder shells with fuses lighted in among the enemy. These cleared the place they occupied in a few moments.... I fully rely on your prudence and vigilance and resolution.... Should you succeed you will hold the town and have your wounded cared for at that point. If the enemy is in force at Tucson then you are not to move against it until further orders, and not even then unless in your judgment the chances of success are nearly all in your favor.[37]

Carleton left Fort Yuma on May 16, 1862, and was at Fort Barrett,[38] Pima Villages, a distance of 180 miles, by May 24. From Fort Barrett Carleton wrote to Major Drum, in San Francisco, saying that the weather had been "intolerably hot," but that the troops "had marched admirably notwithstanding." Hunter and his rebels, according to Carleton, had left Arizona for the Rio Grande. Apaches had attacked Hunter near Dragoon Springs, so Carleton heard, had killed four of his men, and stolen thirty mules and twenty-five horses. Praising the Pimas and Maricopas, Carleton told Drum that they were "the finest Indians I have ever seen, and will be of great service to us and to the Overland Mail Company, which will eventually run over this route." Carleton requested Drum to supply the Pimas with "100 stand of the old percussion muskets, 10,000 rounds of buck and ball cartridges, and a supply of bullet molds for the muskets," to protect themselves and punish the Apaches, "their hereditary enemies." Carleton predicted "that as soon as the rebels are brushed away from Mesilla, the Overland stage from Independence, Missouri, via Santa Fe, Fort Thorn, Tucson, Los Angeles, to San Francisco, can commence its trips before the snows of winter set in again." [39]

The advance guard of the Californians reached Tucson on

May 20, 1862.[40] Captain Hunter and his rebel forces left Tucson a week before the advance guard of the California troops reached there. Hunter had done his utmost, with a hundred men, to accomplish the task that Sibley had given him on Jan. 27, 1862. Carleton notified the Department in San Francisco from the Pima Villages on May 25, of the occupation of Tucson:

The advance guard of this column, under Lieut. Joseph R. West, First California Volunteer Cavalry, took possession of Tucson, in this Territory, on the 20th inst., without firing a shot. All the secession troops who were in the Territory, and all of the secessionists, have fled—the troops to the Rio Grande, the citizens to Sonora. Our arrival is hailed with great joy by all the people who remain.[41]

Tucson, of major importance, territory previously held by the Confederates, was almost a ghost town when the advance guard of the California Cavalry reached there on May 20. Gradually, however, the people returned. Some of them had left months before, at the time Captain Hunter and his Confederates had moved in. Others had left when Hunter evacuated Tucson, fearing reprisal upon the arrival of the Union troops. General Carleton reached Tucson on June 2, 1862. His arrival was greeted by a salute fired by every gun in Shinn's battery. Carleton had maneuvered quite a bit to achieve the salute. According to schedule, Carleton was due to reach Tucson several hours ahead of the artillery. Carleton was resourceful enough, however, to rearrange the schedule so as to allow the artillery to reach Tucson in time to salute him.

No doubt but that Tucson was a shambles between the time Hunter and his Confederates abandoned the town, and the arrival of the advance guard of the California Column. There was no law, and little order. Carleton's immediate task following his arrival, as he viewed it, was to establish some semblance of order as quickly as possible. Declaring on June 8, 1862, that an emergency existed, he designated himself military governor of Arizona, and proclaimed martial law.

He explained his purpose in an elaborately worded proclamation, addressed to "whom it may concern," which was read at tattoo call on June 8, and to the entire command at dress parade the next day. The proclamation, in part, was as follows:

The Congress of the United States has set apart a portion of New Mexico and organized it into a Territory complete in itself. This is known as the Territory of Arizona. It comprises within its limits all the country eastward from the Colorado River, which is now occupied by the forces of the United States known as the Column from California; and as the flag of the United States shall be carried by this column still farther eastward, these limits will extend in that direction until they reach the farthest geographical boundary of this Territory. Now, in the present chaotic state in which Arizona is found to be, with no civil officers to administer the laws—indeed, with an utter absence of all civil authority—and with no security of life or property within its borders, it becomes the duty of the undersigned to represent the authority of the United States over the people of Arizona as well as over all who compose or are connected with the Column from California. Thus, by virtue of his office as military commander of the U. S. forces now here, and to meet the fact that wherever within our boundaries our colors fly there the sovereign power of our country must at once be acknowledged and law and order at once prevail, the undersigned, a military governor, assumes control of this Territory until such time as the President of the United States shall otherwise direct.[42]

In an explanatory note to the Department at San Francisco, Carleton told of the various steps he had taken to maintain order in Tucson:

I shall try to straighten up matters here so that when a man does have his throat cut, his house robbed, or his fields ravaged, he may at least have the consolation of knowing there is some law that will reach him who does the injury. I inclose herewith a paper which seems to touch that point. I have not called it a proclamation, because, nowadays, every military commander makes one, and I had hoped to shun, in this respect, their example. Whatever the name the instrument may go by, I hope you will see nothing in it that is not just and called for by the necessities of the case. It already seems to have gratifying results. I shall send to Fort Yuma for confinement, starting them today, nine of the cutthroats, gamblers, and loafers, who have infested this town to the great bodily fear of all good citizens. Nearly every one, I believe, has either killed his man, or been engaged in helping kill him. I shall send on a detailed account of the causes which justify their arrest and removal from this Territory. They should be held prisoners at Alcatraz until the end of the war. If discharged at Fort Yuma, they will all get back here again and give trouble.[43]

Carleton's proclamation, intended to put the fear of the Lord into craven hearts, was followed up by the promulgation of rules and regulations for the government of a people living in a community reconciled to the whims of fortune. No man of lawful age would be allowed to live in Arizona, according to the regulations, who did not forthwith swear allegiance to the United States of America. No words or acts would be tolerated which might "impair the veneration which all good patriots should feel for our country and government." Trials for capital offenses were to be conducted by a military commission, composed of army officers. "Unless public safety absolutely required immediate action," no executions were to be carried out until the President of the United States would have an opportunity to review the proceedings. Common law rules of evidence were to prevail at the trial of all civil actions. Suits involving title to land were to be tried before a military tribunal, subject to appeals to be taken to the civil courts when established.[44] Carleton gave fair warning to gamblers, drifters and adventurers: "No man who does not pursue some lawful calling or have some legitimate means of support shall be permitted to remain in the Territory." [45]

Three days after he had proclaimed himself military governor of Arizona, by executive order Carleton appointed Lieut. Benjamin Clarke Cutler[46] as "Secretary of State of the Territory," authorized him to administer oaths, and required him to "preserve all acts and proceedings of the Governor in his executive department." Carleton directed Cutler to forward an authentic copy of all executive proceedings, through the General Commanding the Department of the Pacific, to the President of the United States. By executive order dated June 12, Cutler levied a license tax on all business establishments in Arizona, excepting only those selling forage, subsistence stores, fruits and vegetables. Gambling houses were taxed $100 a month for each and "every table in said house wherein any banking game" was played. Every "keeper of a bar" was obliged to obtain a license at $100 a month. All money collected from licenses was to be deposited in a hospital fund established for the benefit of the California Column's sick and wounded. Violation of the provisions of the executive order subjected the violator to a fine, and seizure of all gambling paraphernalia and stocks of merchandise and liquors.[47]

Now that he was in the saddle in Tucson, absolute ruler of everybody and everything in Arizona, General Carleton left nothing undone to impress the inhabitants with the scope of his power and authority. He rather relished working out the niceties of ridding Tucson of the "gamblers, cut throats and murderers," who "loitered about in the wake of Captain Hunter's departure." These "vermin," as Carleton described them in one communication, were stranded in Tucson, with no place to go, and no way to get there. Carleton packed them off to Fort Yuma where they were confined in a dungeonlike prison which afforded a splendid view of the Colorado river country, and where they remained indefinitely, with plenty of time to consider their plight, with no possible chance for release through civil channels. The writ of habeas corpus had been suspended, and not only that, but there was no civil court of competent jurisdiction within hundreds of miles of Fort Yuma.

That Carleton did not pick on the tin-horn gambler in Tucson, and let the big fellow go free, was demonstrated when he caused the arrest of Sylvester Mowry, formerly of Rhode Island, a retired United States army officer, and later a mining promoter and operator, who had been in Arizona off and on since 1855.[48] Obsessed with the idea that Mowry was in some way identified with the Secessionist movement, Carleton issued an order for his arrest on June 8, 1862. At the time of his arrest Mowry was operating an important silver mine and smelter at Patagonia, seven miles north of the Sonora, Mexico, line.

The Mowry mine had produced ore in paying quantities, and supported for some time the liveliest mining camp in Arizona. The adobe camp buildings were dominated by the smelter's high brick chimney, on the top of which, in iron grill work, were the words, "Mowry Silver Mine." The Mowry camp had four hundred inhabitants in 1862, and furnished employment to a large number of Mexicans from across the border in nearby Sonora. The property had been financed and made a successful operation by the untiring labors and unceasing efforts of Sylvester Mowry. He was looked upon in the years before the Civil War by most people in and about Tucson as a "true friend of Arizona."

When Carleton reached Tucson on June 1, 1862, he received a letter, dated "Mowry Silver Mine," which had been written on May 11, 1862, signed by "T. Scheuner, Metallurgist, M.S.M.", probably a Mowry employee. Carleton considered the contents of the letter sufficient justification for Mowry's arrest. Scheuner's letter to Carleton was as follows:

Dear Sir: Seeing that you and your army have advanced to Arizona Territory and have gloriously taken possession of that Territory from those impudent Rebels, I take pains to post you and your army up so you may know what is going about and around you.

Mr. Sylvester Mowry is one of the officers of the Southern Rebellion, and has all the time furnished ammunition to the rebellion party and keep a good many in his place (at the mine) for to attack your troops. Nothing but a few weeks ago he has sent by Sergeant Fort three thousand caps, powder, etc. His blacksmith and carpenter are raising a six-pounder brass piece for to receive Northerners, as he says himself, and has offered to bet $100 that he would be Governor of the Territory in less than six months. That was last March when he offered that bet, and that he, with his twenty Americans (all Southerners) could whip a hundred of your troops, etc.; and he has made port holes all through his corral for that purpose.

If you are going up there I advise you not to go during day-time, as he has two men constantly on the hill looking out for any of your men coming.

It has to be during the night, after sundown or early in the morning, and corral him in his house, and a guide to enter the corral through the big gateway, as he leaves inside the corral plenty of Mexicans there to be had, to show you where he lives, and tell you all about him, and there is less than half a mile another town where there is a lot of Southerners also, but you can easily cut them off if you choose, unless they don't take the trail to Santa Cruz, Mexico, as they very probably will, as good many have already left. Any other news that you may wish, I shall be very happy to serve you and your people.[49]

From Tucson, on June 10, 1862, Carleton wrote to the Department of the Pacific in San Francisco advising of Mowry's impending arrest:

I have sent to arrest Mr. Sylvester Mowry and all the people at his mine. It is possible I shall be obliged to hold Mr. Mowry as a prisoner. That he has been guilty of overt as well as covert acts of treason there is hardly a doubt. I consider his presence in this Territory as dangerous to its peace and prosperity.[50]

Details of Mowry's arrest were given in a report written from Tucson by Lieutenant Colonel Eyre, of the First Cavalry, on June 16, 1862. Eyre reported to Acting Adjutant General Cutler that he had left Tucson on June 8, with thirty soldiers, reached the Patagonia mines at midnight on the 12th, and at 3 o'clock the next morning awakened Mowry and arrested him. That Mowry received slight consideration at the time of his arrest was indicated by Eyre's report:

On being arrested, Mr. Mowry asked for himself, together with the others, to be paroled and left at the mine. This I declined doing, my orders being peremptory to bring them all with me back to Tucson. Soon after daylight, Captain Willis and Mr. Mills, private secretary to Lieutenant Mowry, made an inventory in duplicate of all the movable property at the mine ... and on the 14th I left the mine with Lieutenant Mowry and twenty-one other prisoners for Tucson, where I arrived on the 16th, and turned over the prisoners to Lieut. Col. West, by order of the colonel commanding.[51]

Following Carleton's instruction, Acting Adjutant General Cutler summoned a board of officers to convene in Tucson on June 16, to "investigate certain charges and facts tending to show that Mr. Sylvester Mowry, of the Patagonia Mines, is an enemy of the United States, and that he has been in treasonable correspondence with well known secessionists." Upon considering the evidence, the board found that "said Mowry is an enemy of the United States, and that he has been in treasonable correspondence and collusion with well known secessionists, and has afforded them aid and comfort when they were known publicly to be enemies to the legally constituted authority and government of the United States." Finding that there were "sufficient grounds to restrain the said Sylvester Mowry of his liberty," the board of officers ordered him to trial before a military court.

On July 2, Carleton confirmed the findings of the board and directed that Mowry be confined at Fort Yuma "until orders should be given by competent authority." [52] Mowry was taken to Fort Yuma, and imprisoned there until Nov. 4, 1862, when he was unconditionally released without apology or explanation. Following Mowry's arrest and imprisonment, Carleton appointed Colonel West, of the California Column, to be "receiver" of the mining property. West posted a guard at the property to prevent theft, but with Mowry in jail mining and smelting ceased entirely, and the property disintegrated rapidly.

Cutler sent the papers in Sylvester Mowry's case to Secretary Seward in Washington. Seward passed them on to Secretary of War Stanton on Aug. 16, 1862, with a memorandum:

I have the honor to enclose a letter of the 6th ultimo and the accompanying papers, addressed to this department by Benjamin C. Cutler who styles himself, "Military Secretary of the Territory of Arizona." As that Territory has not been organized by Act of Congress, and consequently no civil officers have been appointed therein, it is presumed that the communication of Mr. Assistant Adjutant General Cutler would have been more properly addressed to the War Department.[53]

Insofar as known, Carleton and Mowry were not personally acquainted with each other. But, beginning in the summer of 1862, they engaged for years in combat, conducted on Carleton's part by military arrest, court martial, and imprisonment, and on Mowry's part by personal solicitation of assistance from influential people, by writing letters, publication of newspaper articles, and by means of litigation. Mowry appealed to many sources for help, but in time of war there were few inclined to heed his complaints. Seeking redress in the courts, Mowry filed suit against Carleton on Dec. 12, 1863, in the Fourth District Court of California. Alleging unlawful seizure of his mining property, he claimed damages in the sum of $1,029,000. Carleton employed Attorney Hall McAllister, of San Francisco, to defend the action. Senator William Conners, of California, at Mowry's request, introduced a resolution in the United States Senate, on June 24, 1864, asking the War Department for "information touching the course of Gen. Carleton toward Mr. Sylvester Mowry."[54] The resolution, a formal gesture, received scant attention.

Having learned in the summer of 1864 that Mowry might return to Arizona, Carleton wrote a letter from Santa Fe on August 11 of that year, requesting Colonel George W. Bowie, Commanding the District of Arizona, at Franklin, Texas, to order his arrest:

Colonel: I have heard unofficially that one Sylvester Mowry, a traitor to his country, is about to come to Arizona within the limits of this department. You will at once give orders to the commanders of your different posts to have this Mowry arrested and kept securely confined in the guard house, until such time as an opportunity may present for so doing, when he will be sent to Fort Yuma, Calif., and there turned loose, with orders not again to come within the boundaries of this department. He will be arrested the moment he arrives in Arizona. Let this be done effectually. I will not tolerate this villain's presence within my command.[55]

Apparently doubtful of the strength of his position in Mowry's case, Carleton reconsidered and wrote to Colonel Bowie on the next day, August 12, modifying his instruction:

Since writing to you the letter stating that, in case Mowry came to Arizona, to arrest and send him under guard beyond the limits of the department, I have thought better that you send word to Colonel Coult first to notify Mowry that unless he leaves the department he will be sent away, as he is regarded as an enemy of the United States. In case, then, he does not go, he will be placed beyond the limits of this department, unless he has permission to remain in it from higher authority than myself. I regard his presence in Arizona as dangerous to the peace and security of the people. He was once in correspondence with rebel authorities, and may again be guilty of treasonable practices.[56]

Back in Arizona, from trips to Washington and New York, still fighting Carleton, Mowry sought vindication through a resolution he caused to be introduced in the Arizona Legislature of 1865. Upon learning of the resolution, Carleton, on Feb. 4, 1865, wrote a personal letter to Governor John N. Goodwin, at Prescott, the then territorial capital, explaining the Mowry case in detail, telling him, among other things:

Mowry's conduct, conversation, associates, and principles, placed him with the enemies of the government when the war broke out. He held treasonable correspondence with Jefferson Davis and other rebel leaders; and that he aided and abetted the enemies of the government is conclusively shown by the proceedings of the Board of Officers, a copy of which has for a long time been on file in the War Department.

Governor Goodwin vetoed the resolution, but Mowry's friends in the Legislature introduced a substitute, which was adopted, primarily because the legislators were anxious to hasten the development of Arizona's mineral wealth, and believed that Mowry had the ability and industry to accomplish much in that direction.[57]

Although the advance guard of the California Column, under Colonel West, reached Tucson on May 20, it was not until a full month later that an advance guard of the Column left Tucson for the Rio Grande, some 300 miles to the east.

This time the honor of commanding the advance guard went to Lieut. Col. E. E. Eyre, of the First California Cavalry. Eyre's command of 140 men, which had been held for day after day in Tucson, on Carleton's orders, hopeful for the beginning of the summer rains, left Tucson at 3 o'clock in the morning of June 21, 1862. Traveling through a country known to be infested by Apaches, the advance guard was on the alert, day and night, to protect against possible sudden attacks by either Indians or "secessionists."

According to Eyre's official report, the cavalrymen marched "under a broiling sun and over a country utterly destitute of water for distances ranging from 35 to 60 miles," following the route used by Overland Mail stages before the war. Eyre's command passed through Cienega de Los Pinos, the San Pedro Valley, Dragoon Spring, Ewell's Station, Apache Pass, San Simon Station, Lightendorffer's Well, Round Mountain Canon, Densmore's Station (Soldier's Farewell), Cow Springs, the Mimbres River, and Cooke's Canon. The road forked in two directions at Cooke's Spring, near Cooke's Canon. One fork led southeast to Mesilla, the other northeast to Fort Thorn. Near Cooke's Spring, "on the hill, about a half mile distant," the cavalrymen could see the ruins of a now abandoned mail station.

After being on the way from Tucson for almost two weeks, Eyre's detachment reached Fort Thorn,[58] on the Rio Grande, on July 4, 1862, "where the national colors were raised amid the loud and continued cheers of the assembled command; this was the first time the stars and stripes floated on the Rio Grande below Fort Craig since the occupation of the country by the Confederate troops." [59]

As Union troops under Eyre were marching to the Rio Grande from the West, Confederate troops were preparing to abandon the Confederate "Territory of Arizona," and return to Texas. Writing from El Paso on July 12, 1862, to General S. Cooper, Adjutant and Inspector General in Richmond, Colonel William Steele [60] reviewed the situation confronting him, and gave the reasons for the abandonment. He had no money; he had been compelled to take food and forage away from the Mexicans, which they resented and resisted; his troops were homesick and in many instances almost naked:

Of the strength of the force with which I was expected to hold the Territory—about 400 men, you will be able to form a just estimate from the detailed report also submitted herewith. After General Sibley had withdrawn from the country the greater portion of his command, the Mexican population, justly thinking our tenure very frail and uncertain, showed great unwillingness to sell property of any kind for Confederate paper, which would of course be valueless to them should I be compelled to retire, which was at any time probable; and as I was without specie with which to make purchases, I was obliged to seize upon such supplies as were required for the subsistence of the troops and such means of transportation as would enable me to move my command whenever the necessity might arise for so doing. This occasioned so much ill feeling on the part of the Mexicans that in many instances armed resistance was offered to foraging parties acting under my orders, and in the various skirmishes which took place one captain and several men of my regiment were killed by them. Besides this, the troops with me were so disgusted with the campaign and so anxious to return to Texas that in one or two instances they were on the point of open mutiny and threatened to take the matter in their own hands unless they were speedily marched back to San Antonio.

The enemy was being reinforced by troops from California, Colorado and Kansas:

In the meantime the forces from California, about 1,500 strong, were steadily approaching, and on the 6th of July their advance was seen at Fort Thorn, on the Rio Grande. Troops from Fort Craig had been seen the day previous, moving toward the same point. Knowing this, and that the enemy, after leaving garrisons behind, would be able to bring 3,000 troops against me, independent of a recent reinforcement which they had received—of 500 men—from Pike's Peak, and 250 more with six rifle cannon, who escorted the paymaster from Kansas, the necessity of moving my force became imperative. I was then at Fort Fillmore, with but little ammunition, and notwithstanding the efforts I had made, with very inadequate means of transportation. I abandoned the Territory on the 8th of July and marched for Fort Bliss, at which point I am now.

Steele sold all surplus public property at Fort Bliss and gave the specie for general hospital purposes:

As soon as this move had been determined on, the sale was ordered of all public property at Fort Bliss which was too bulky or not worth transportation. This sale was held for specie and breadstuffs. The specie was turned over to the general hospital which I am compelled to leave at Franklin. There was besides a considerable quantity of stores that could not be sold and which were too weighty for transportation, such as horse and mule shoes, cannon, ammunition, tents, etc. ... I am now about to start for San Antonio with very limited means of transportation, and insufficient supply of breadstuff and beef, depending on the contingency of meeting provisions forwarded from San Antonio, and with troops in many instances almost naked.[61]

With bands playing and company colors flying, the first ten companies of infantry of the California Column, five companies of cavalry, and one field battery of four pieces, a total of fifteen hundred effective troops, left Tucson for the Rio Grande on July 17, 1862.[62] Lieutenant Cutler scheduled the departure of the troops, one company starting each day, an arrangement deemed necessary because of scarcity of water enroute. Cutler's order sounded the keynote for the march:

This is the time when every soldier in this Column looks forward with a confident hope that he, too, will have the distinguished honor of striking a blow for the old Stars and Stripes; when he, too, feels in his heart that he is the champion of the holiest cause that has ever yet served the arm of a patriot.[63]

General Carleton left Tucson for the Rio Grande on July 23, 1862, after having been in Tucson about two months, confident, as he started toward the Rio Grande, that he had established law and order in Arizona. On the way to New Mexico he sent scouts with dispatches for General Canby at Santa Fe, but they were ambushed and murdered, probably by Apache Indians, before reaching the Mimbres river.[64]

Ten days out of Tucson, Carleton reached Ojo de la Vaca (Cow Spring), Arizona, 60 miles west of the Rio Grande. From here Carleton sent a scout with a letter to General Canby in Santa Fe, notifying him that he was on the way to

New Mexico, and suggesting the possibility of a campaign into West Texas:

I beg to be fully instructed by you in all the measures wherein myself or the California Column can be of the most service. We have not crossed the continent thus far to split hairs, but with an earnest resolution to do our duty whatever be our geographical position; and so the marches of this column tend always toward the heart of the rebellion; the men will forget their toils and sufferings on the Great Desert in their hope ultimately to reach the enemy. As the gallantry of the troops under your command has left us nothing to do on the Rio Grande, it would be a sad disappointment to those from California if they should be obliged to retrace their steps without feeling out the enemy. I hope I do not ask too much when I inquire whether a force could not profitably be thrown into West Texas, where it is reported the Union men are only waiting for a little help to run up the old flag.[65]

Marching from Cooke's Spring to Santa Barbara, three miles above Fort Thorn, Carleton's detachment of cavalry, consisting of 240 horses and mules, was ferried across the Rio Grande in flat bottomed boats, and reached the fort on Aug. 7, 1862.

Booming guns greeted Carleton's arrival at Fort Thorn. The American flag was flying once again at Fort Thorn, where, for many months, the Confederate colors had flown. Carleton received at Fort Thorn a cordial message from General Canby, in which he acknowledged Carleton's dispatch of Aug. 2, and told him to use his own judgment "in regard to disposition of troops in Arizona and southern New Mexico." Every able bodied Confederate soldier, Carleton was told at Fort Thorn, had crossed over the New Mexico line into Texas. On Aug. 8, Carleton wrote to Colonel Marshall S. Howe, Third U. S. Cavalry at Fort Craig, acknowledging information he had furnished, and added: "I shall be happy to see you. Pray, who are the army officers serving in this country? We know no more of the condition of affairs here than we would have had we just dropped from the moon." [66]

On Aug. 10, 1862, Carleton started for Las Cruces, about 45 miles south of Fort Thorn, with three troops of cavalry.

While in Las Cruces, where he remained several days, Carleton issued an order on Aug. 14, addressed to "Commanders of Towns living along the Rio Grande between the Jornada del Muerto and Fort Bliss, Texas," directing them to require the people to clean up the streets and repair their dwellings, to forthwith establish sanitary regulations; to police the streets; and to adopt rules and regulations for the health of citizens and soldiers alike. Carleton's order assured the people that a new day had arrived:

> The people may now rest assured that the era of anarchy and misrule—when there was no protection to life or property, when the wealthy were plundered, when the poor were robbed and oppressed, when all were insulted and maltreated, and when there was no respect for age or sex—has passed away; that now, under the sacred banner of our country, all may claim and shall receive their just rights. Therefore let the burden of anxiety be lifted from their hearts, and once more let them pursue their avocations with cheerfulness, and with the full confidence that the protection which now shelters them from injustice will always be stronger in proportion as they shall be powerless to protect themselves.[67]

Carleton went from Las Cruces to Fort Bliss,[68] Texas, forty miles to the south, and reported from there: "At the town of Franklin, opposite El Paso, I found a surgeon of the Confederate Army and 25 sick and disabled soldiers whom I made prisoners of war by order of General Canby." Making the Confederates "prisoners of war," however, was merely a technical procedure. Actually Carleton furnished the Confederates with medicine, tobacco and badly needed provisions.

Leaving Fort Bliss, Carleton followed the Rio Grande into Texas for 10 miles. He advised Lieut. Col. Drum in San Francisco of his motive:

> The object of my march was to restore confidence to the people. They had been taught by the Texans that we were coming among them as marauders and robbers. When they found we treated them kindly and paid them a fair price for all the supplies we required they rejoiced to find, as they came under the

old flag once more, that they could now have protection and will be treated justly. The abhorrence they expressed for the Confederate troops and of the Rebellion convinced me that their loyalty to the United States is now beyond question.[69]

A troop of California Cavalry, under command of Capt. John C. Cremony, marched one hundred miles from El Paso, and "hoisted the Stars and Stripes over Fort Quitman," Texas, on Aug. 22, 1862. On the same day, Capt. E. D. Shirland started a march from Fort Quitman to Fort Davis (between present day Alpine and Marfa), 140 miles to the east, by way of Eagle Springs, Van Horn's Wells, Dead Man's Hole, and Barrel Springs. Shirland "hoisted the flag" at Fort Davis, and reported on conditions there:

The place was entirely deserted, but in one of the buildings of the Overland Mail Company I found the dead body of a man lying on the floor, shot through the body with a bullet, and arrow wounds on the head and arm.[70]

It had taken Carleton ten long months to move his troops from the Pacific to the Rio Grande. That the California Column was on its way to New Mexico had been widely heralded for months. Arrival of California troops in New Mexico days after the Confederates had left for Texas proved to be an anti climax. The debacle at Fort Fillmore, and resultant surrender of a large number of Union troops to Baylor at San Augustine Springs, had lost their initial galling aspects. The shock resulting from the battle of Valverde, in which Sibley had defeated Canby, had become less humiliating after the retreat of Sibley's brigade, following the skirmishes at Pigeon's Ranch and Apache Canon, in the Glorieta mountains. New Mexico and its people were no longer in jeopardy.

With New Mexico safe from further Confederate attack at least for the present, General Canby was relieved as Commander of the Department of New Mexico. His successor was General James H. Carleton. By Sept. 20, 1862, Carleton was in Santa Fe, busily engaged at his favorite occupation,

writing letters, reports and proclamations. He wrote a long
letter to Colonel Drum in San Francisco, detailing the things
of importance in connection with the California troop movement since July 22, the date of his last general report. Praising a number of his officers generously, Carleton urged promotion for several. Carleton expressed gratification that
"thus far the instructions of the General Commanding the
Department of the Pacific have been carried out . . . the Southern Overland Mail route has been opened, and the military
posts in Arizona, southern New Mexico, and northwestern
Texas have been reoccupied by troops composing the Column from California." Carleton was modest in telling Drum
about the march of the California Column into New Mexico:

It was no fault of the troops from California that the Confederate forces fled before them. It is but just to say that their having
thus fled is mainly attributed to the gallantry of the troops under
General Canby's command. That they were harried in their
flight, by the timely arrival of the advance guard of the Column
under Lieutenant Colonel Eyre, there cannot be a doubt. The
march from the Pacific to the Rio Grande by the Column from
California was not accomplished without immense toil and great
hardships or without many privations and much suffering from
heat and want of water. . . . The march of the Column from California in the summer months across the great Desert, in the driest
season that has been known for thirty years, is a military achievement creditable to the soldiers of the American Army, but it
would not be just to attribute the success of this march to ability
on my part. The success was gained only by the high physical and
moral energies of that peculiar class of officers and men who composed the Column from California. With any other troops, I am
sure I would have failed.[71]

From Santa Fe on Sept. 21, 1862, Carleton published an
order eulogizing the California Column, in which he said
that California "had reason to be proud of the sons she had
sent across the continent to assist in the great struggle in
which our country is now engaged." The order read in part:

In entering upon the duties that remove him from immediate
association with the troops constituting the Column from Cali-

fornia, the commanding general desires to express his grateful acknowledgment of the conduct and services of the officers and men of that command.

Traversing a desert country, that has heretofore been regarded as impracticable for the operations of large bodies of troops, they have reached their destination and accomplished the object assigned them, not only without loss of any kind, but improved in discipline, in morale, and in every other element of efficiency. That patient and cheerful endurance of hardships, the zeal and alacrity with which they have grappled with and overcome obstacles that would have been insurmountable to any but troops of the highest physical and moral energy, the complete abnegation of self, the subordination of every personal consideration to the grand object of our hopes and efforts, give the most absolute assurance of success in any field or against any enemy. California has reason to be proud of the sons she has sent across the continent to assist in the great struggle in which our country is now engaged.

In the final paragraph of his order, Carleton took note of the fact that Colorado troops too, had played a part in the great drama:

The commanding general is requested by the officer who preceded him in the command of this department to express for him the gratification felt by every officer and soldier of his command at the fact that troops from the Atlantic and Pacific slope—from the mountains of California and Colorado, acting in the same cause, impelled by the same duties, and animated by the same hopes—have met and shaken hands in the center of this great continent.[72]

That Carleton was quite proud of the march across the desert, and confident that it would have its place in history, was evident from the contents of a letter he wrote from Santa Fe on Nov. 15, 1862, to Senator Latham of California, then in Washington:

I worked hard with our California boys, and got them safely through the desert. When time wears away and people begin to think again, the passage of 2,000 men over the great desert in the heart of summer will be thought to be not a contemptible achievement. I could not have done it with any other troops. The men were devoted to me, and never murmured in all their hardships and sufferings. When all their toils and privations are thought of by myself, and when I look back and see that a single mistake would have been a horrible disaster, I shudder at my responsibility even with that small force. It is a matter that will never be properly appreciated, but if one can fancy a desert with its hot sands, its brassy sky, its utter desolation, and its want of everything which would go to sustain life, and then imagine a caravan of 2,000 men and 1,800 animals passing over it, one could fancy what would be his feelings of responsibility as he saw them on their weary journey and saw them gathering around the scanty supplies of water with famished looks, and absolutely holding him responsible all the time that the supply should meet their wants. What if one of his calculations failed? You can imagine the result. I felt a great burden fall from my shoulders when I saw the Rio Grande. I assure you that I would not encounter the same anxiety again for ten major-generals' commissions.[73]

NOTES AND PROFILES

[1] *Daily Alta California*, San Francisco, April 14, 1862. In his own mind, Johnston had considered for some years the possibility of inevitable conflict. On Sept. 12, 1856, from San Antonio, Texas, he had written to his son, William Preston Johnston: "I notice with sorrow the progress of fanaticism in the North. What do they want? We want the Union with the Constitution. We want a share in its glorious, benevolent, civilizing mission, and its high and magnificent destiny. Our whole hearts are devoted to its support and perpetuity. We want the rights and independence of the States and the security to individuals guaranteed by its Constitution; we claim immunity from interference and intervention."

Born in Washington, Mason County, Kentucky, Feb. 3, 1803, Albert Sidney Johnston was graduated from the United States Military Academy at West Point, eighth in his class, on June 1, 1826. While at West Point Johnston formed a lifelong friendship with Jefferson Davis. Lieutenant Johnston served in the Black Hawk War in 1832, and participated in a few minor skirmishes against Indians. He resigned from the army on April 24, 1834. When Texas declared its independence from Mexico Johnston "offered his sword" on July 15, 1836, to General Sam Houston, and he soon became a senior brigadier general in the Texas army. As a result of the rapid promotion, Colonel Felix Huston challenged Johnston to a duel. In the exchange of shots, Johnston was wounded. On Dec. 22, 1838, President Mirabeau B. Lamar appointed Johnston as Secretary of War of the Texas Republic. In 1846 Johnston reentered the United States Army and rendered distinguished service in the Mexican War. In 1856 and 1857 he commanded troops in the Comanche Indian country in Texas. When difficulties arose between the Federal government and people of the Mormon faith, Johnston was assigned to service in Utah. While there Johnston was named a defendant in litigation in Texas involving title to a tract of land he had acquired, and had occupied and cultivated between military assignments. Lawyers in Texas advised Johnston that it might be possible to have the lawsuit removed to the United States District Court on the ground that he was a resident of a state or territory other than Texas. Johnston's answer to the suggestion, written on Aug. 27, 1859, indicated the

value he placed on his Texas citizenship: "My citizenship in Texas was obtained at the cost of the bloom of health, and the prime of life spent in the
service of the state, and of property, which, if I had it now, would constitute
a princely estate. I will not give it up now, though I should lose in consequence every foot of land I have in the State. This I would regard as a mere
mess of pottage in comparison with my citizenship." William Preston Johnston's "Life of Albert Sidney Johnston," 1878.

2 Peter R. Brady, post interpreter at Fort Mojave, New Mexico (Arizona),
from April 19, 1859, until May 27, 1861, when the post was abandoned, described conditions on the route of the thirty-fifth parallel, in a statement made
to Major Edwin A. Rigg, First Infantry California Volunteers, Commanding
Officer at Fort Yuma, Cal., on March 4, 1862: "The road from Los Angeles to
Fort Mojave as far as Lane's ranch, on the Mojave river, is tolerably good for
wagons, being over a rolling country, hard and gravelly. There is plenty of
water and tolerable grazing. From Lane's on to Fort Mojave it is over a sandy
desert, very scarce of water and destitute of grass. The price of freight paid
by the sutler at Fort Mojave was never less than 15 cents per pound, and Government paid Banning, of Los Angeles, as high as 53 cents per pound for
freight delivered at the post; distance 285 miles. This fact speaks for itself.
From Fort Mojave to Albuquerque, 550 miles, the route was pronounced
impracticable by every one who has ever traveled over it, except Mr. Beale.
Lieut. C. J. Ives, astronomer to the boundary survey, told me that the route
was impracticable for various reasons. First, on account of the very high
mountains that you are compelled to cross, and second, on account of the
scarcity of water, and that he did not consider it practicable for pack trains
more than three months in the year, March, April and May. Then there
was plenty of grass and water. The mail party who were carrying the mail
from St. Joseph, Missouri, to Stockton, Cal., over this route in the winter and
spring of 1859 pronounced it impracticable for wagons. They never made a
single trip during the time they were running within schedule time." OR
Series I, Vol. L, part 1, p. 911.

3 OR Series I, Vol. L, part 1, pp. 480-487. For reports on 1861 "secessionist"
activities in Los Angeles, San Bernardino and San Francisco, see OR Series I,
Vol. L, part 1, pp. 496, 548, 550, 554, 559, 563, 564, 568, 589, 664. For "secessionist" activities during the same period in Carson City and Nevada City,
Nev., Ibid, 499, 500, 506.

4 See William Preston Johnston's "Life of Albert Sidney Johnston," 1878;
letter of Aug. 11, 1861, from F. W. Pickens, Columbia, S. C., to President Davis,
OR Series I, Vol. L, part 1, p. 566. For an interesting appraisal of General
Johnston's conduct and demeanor while in command of the Department of
the Pacific, see sketch by Captain George F. Price, 2nd Cal. Cav. Rec. Cal. Men
in War of Rebellion, Sacramento, 1890, p. 7. Baylor described Johnston's arrival in New Mexico in a report written from Dona Ana, "Arizona," on Sept.
21, 1861: "After getting rid of the prisoners captured in the Isaac Lynde surrender at San Augustine Springs on July 27, I immediately selected a strong
position near the village of Pichacho to await the arrival of Captain Moore's
command. Here I was joined by Brig. Gen. A. S. Johnston, with a party of
officers of the U. S. Army, who had resigned and were enroute to Richmond,
Va., also a party of Californians under command of Capt. Alonzo Ridley.
I tendered to Brigadier General Johnston the command of my forces, believing that the best interest of the service required that I should relinquish the
command to an officer of his rank and distinguished ability, which he did
me the honor to accept, and remained in command until there was no further need for his services." OR Series I, Vol. 4, p. 19.

5 OR Series I, Vol. L, part 1, p. 601.

6 OR Series I, Vol. L, part 1, p. 594.

7 OR Series I, Vol. L, part 1, p. 624.

8 Born in Vermont in 1803, Gen. Geo. G. Wright was graduated from West Point on July 1, 1822. He served in the Mexican War, and in 1858 commanded an expedition against the Spokanes. Wright was drowned on July 30, 1865, in the wreck of the "Brother Jonathan."

9 OR Series I, Vol. L, part 1, p. 623.

10 Camp Latham was named for U. S. Senator Milton Scott Latham, who was born in Columbus, Ohio, May 23, 1827, went to California in 1850, died in New York City on March 4, 1882.

11 The 1860 census gave San Bernardino a population of 557, San Bernardino County, 2,504. There was considerable excitement on election day in San Bernardino in 1861, according to the report of Capt. John W. Davidson, of the First Dragoons: "On September 5, election day at San Bernardino, I was directed to keep my squadron in hand near town to repress disorder, and not to leave until after the polls were closed. At sundown I drove up to the polls alone in a buggy, and asked the inspector if they were closed. He replied that in a few minutes he would announce it. Meantime many persons gathered around my buggy (there were 200 or 300 people still near the polls) having sticks in their hands, and commenced shouting: 'Hurrah for Jeff Davis! Hurrah for The Southern Confederacy!' Most of the persons had revolvers. One of them said that if the Union men felt themselves stronger there that day, he could beat them robbing and burning any day. I rose up in my buggy and called the attention of the people that there were men in their midst who openly avowed themselves robbers and house burners, and gave comfort and heart to the enemy by their shouts, and then turning through the crowd, I drove over one man, went down to my camp about 300 yards off, where the squadron was standing to horse, and brought up a platoon of dragoons, and riding into the crowd, stated that I would seize anyone who hurrahed for Jeff Davis. I told them that free discussion was one thing, and the utterance of treasonable language another; that these men had expressed their opinions in the ballot box that day, but that openly hurrahing for the southern Confederacy was seditious, and I, as a Federal officer, was bound to put it down. The Union men, who up to this time had not opened their mouths, then cheered the Federal government, the Jeff Davis men slunk away from the crowd, and I marched my men away. It was a novel position. I felt I must submit to the defiance and dishearten the Union men, or take the bull by the horns and show them that such conduct will not be tolerated in this state." OR Series I, Vol. L, part 1, p. 615.

12 OR Series I, Vol. L, part 1, p. 680. Assistant Surgeon Randle described Camp Wright in a letter to Surgeon J. M. McNulty, of the First California Volunteers, parts of which McNulty quoted to Col. Carleton in a letter of Nov. 5, 1861: "The wind blows here a perfect gale more than half the time, driving the dust in clouds, and blinding the eyes of every one, and infiltrating into every coffee pot, camp kettle and water bucket. The wind blows so hard that a fire cannot be made on some days. The camp is located four miles from fire wood, which is cottonwood. The water here is strongly impregnated with alkali. The weather is very cold, and growing colder. Snow falls here a foot deep frequently in winter, and some times remains a week on the ground." OR Series I, Vol. L, part 1, p. 704.

13 Joseph Rodman ("Dandy") West, born in New Orleans, Sept. 19, 1822, attended the University of Pennsylvania; served as a captain of volunteers in the Mexican War; emigrated to California in 1849, engaged in commercial pursuits there until the outbreak of the Civil War. For a time West published the San Francisco "Prices Current." In Civil War years, West served as lieutenant colonel of the 1st Calif. Infantry in California, Arizona and New Mexico. Mustered out of the army as a brevet major general on Jan. 4, 1863, West lived in Texas and Louisiana. He was elected U. S. Senator from Louisiana, as a Republican, and served from March 4, 1871 to March 3, 1877.

14 OR Series I, Vol. L, part 1, p. 662.

15 Warner's Ranch was a place of historic interest in Mexican War days. Stephen Watts Kearny, guided by Kit Carson, according to Emory's report, Ex. Doc. No. 41, p. 105, reached Warner's Ranch on Dec. 2, 1846: "Emerging from a narrow valley covered with evergreen oak trees, we saw in the distance the beautiful valley of the Agua Caliente, waving with yellow grass, where we expected to find the rancheria owned by an American named Warner. Our progress was slow and painful; we thought Warner's rancheria never would open on our eager sight, when suddenly it burst upon our view at the foot of the hill. We were mistaken for Indians, and soon were seen horsemen at full speed leading off cattle and horses to the mountains. We quickened our pace to arrest this proceeding. The rancheria was in charge of a young fellow from New Hampshire, named Marshall. We ascertained from him, that his employer was a prisoner to the Americans in San Diego, that the Mexicans were still in possession of the whole country except that port, San Francisco, and Monterey; that we were near the heart of the enemy's stronghold, whence he drew his supplies of men, cattle and horses, and that we were now in possession of the great pass to Sonora, by which he expected to retreat, if defeated, to send his prisoners if successful, and to communicate with Mexico. . . . To the south, down the valley of the Agua Caliente, lay the road to San Diego. Above us was Mr. Warner's backwoods, American looking house, built of adobe and covered with a thatched roof. Around, were the thatched huts of the more than half naked Indians, who are held in a sort of serfdom by the master of the rancheria. I visited one or two of these huts, and found the inmates in great poverty. The thermometer was 30 deg., they had no fires, and no coverings but sheepskins. They told me, that when they were under the charge of the missions they were all comfortable and happy, but since the good priests had been removed, and the missions placed in the hands of the people of the country, they had been ill treated." Emory Report, Ex. Doc. 41, p. 105.

Capt. A. R. Johnson (soon to be killed in battle) described Warner's Ranch in a journal entry of Dec. 2, 1846: "Arrived at Warner's Ranch very unxpectedly to them. This point is about 60 miles from San Diego, and perhaps 80 from the Pueblo. It is occupied by an American, from Connecticut, who settled in this country, and became naturalized, married, &c. He is now on the main route leading to Sonora, and of course is very much exposed to both parties. He is now said to be a prisoner in the hands of the Americans. . . . We found Warner's a place which would be considered a poor location in the United States, with a hot spring and a cold one on his place; a good place for stock, but bad for grain, one would think. We are told wheat yields thirty fold. The labor is performed by California Indians, who are stimulated to work by three dollars per month and repeated floggings." Ex. Doc. 41, p. 613.

16 OR Series I, Vol. L, part 1, p. 672.

17 For the day by day travel log of West's march from Camp Latham, near Los Angeles, beginning on Oct. 16, 1861, and ending at Fort Yuma, on Nov. 3, a distance of 301½ miles, see OR Series I, Vol. L, part 1, pp. 710-714.

18 OR Series I, Vol. L, part 1, pp. 678, 721. Rec. Cal. Men in War of Rebellion, p. 21.

19 OR Series, Vol. L, part 1, p. 751. The Pacific Telegraph line was completed to Salt Lake City, Utah, from the east on Oct. 18, 1861. Brigham Young sent a telegram on that date from Salt Lake to J. H. Wade, President of the Pacific Telegraph Co. at Cleveland, Ohio, congratulating him and his associates upon the success of the enterprise, and expressing his devotion to the constitutional government of the United States. The telegraph line from San Francisco to Salt Lake City was completed and in operation on Nov. 1, 1861. Ibid, 666.

20 OR Series I, Vol. L, part 1, p. 752.

21 On Oct. 18, 1862, nearly ten months after Wright's letter of Dec. 9, 1861, Gen. Carleton wrote from Santa Fe to Postmaster General Montgomery Blair advising him that the Southern Overland Mail Route had been opened: "Our troops now occupy Mesilla and Tucson. Besides I have established a post at Apache Pass, and have now in successful operation a chain of vedettes from Tucson to Los Angeles. One great purpose had in view by this movement was to give your department an opportunity to remove the overland mail from its present route, where, in the Sierra Nevada and eastward from the range of mountains to Salt Lake, for months in the year the mail is obstructed by snows. Tons of mail matter it is said the company was obliged to leave along the road on this account last winter. The Bannock and Shoshone Indians west of Salt Lake, and the Sioux Indians between Salt Lake and Kansas, are more hostile and offer greater risks to the safe transit of the mails by that route than are offered by any Indians on the southern mail route. If the mail should run from Independence, Mo., or Fort Leavenworth, Kans., via Santa Fe, thence down the Rio Grande to Mesilla, and thence over the Southern Overland Mail Route to Los Angeles, it would have little or no obstructions by Indians; would absorb the present mail to New Mexico; would afford to this Territory a daily mail; would absorb the present mail from Los Angeles to San Francisco, and afford that portion of California with a daily mail. It would run through a country where in winter there are no obstructions by snows, and over which it ran in other years almost invariably on schedule time. On the southern route from Mesilla to Los Angeles the road is good; the stations are nearly all built, and many are yet in tolerable repair; the wells are dug, and I have been informed by the agent of the company in San Francisco, Mr. Louis McLane, that if the southern mail route should again be opened the road could be restocked and the mail set running in sixty days from the time the order to the effect should be given. Time has proved and will always prove that the Northern Overland Mail Route in winter is not a sure, safe, practicable route. No sophistries can stop the snow from blocking the road west of Salt Lake and through the Sierra Nevada, and none can prove that the southern mail route is not now entirely practicable. Should the people on the Pacific Coast be granted a daily overland mail by your Department, your Department will be sure to find that it must be by the southern route." OR Series I, Vol. L, part 2, p. 181.

22 OR Series I, Vol. L, part 1, p. 588. Carrying United States mail in the southwest was a hazardous undertaking in the fifties and sixties. Elias Brevoort and Joab Houghton, of Santa Fe, entered into a contract under bond on July 2, 1854, to carry a monthly mail between Santa Fe, Albuquerque, Socorro, Doña Ana, Fort Fillmore, New Mexico, and Frontero, El Paso, San Elisario, Magoffinsville, Leona and San Antonio, Texas, for an annual compensation of $16,750.00. The provisions in the Brevoort-Houghton contract were exacting. The mail was to be carried between Santa Fe and San Antonio once a month, on a fixed schedule of arrivals and departures, which allowed not to exceed seven minutes time at each mail station for "opening and closing the mails." The contractors agreed to carry the mail "in a safe and secure manner, free from wet or other injury, in a boot under the driver's seat, and in preference to passengers, and to their entire exclusion if its weight and bulk require it." Some details of the Brevoort-Houghton contract: "To take the mail and every part of it from, and deliver it, and every part of it at, each post office on the route, and into the postoffice at each end of the route, and into the postoffice at the place at which the carrier stops at night, if one is there kept; and if no office is there kept, to lock it up in some secure place at the risk of the contractor . . . The contractor agrees that he will not transmit by himself or agent, or be concerned in transmitting commercial intelligence more rapidly than by mail, and that he will not carry, out of the mail, letters or newspapers which should go by post." The mail, carried in two horse coaches, left Santa Fe on the first day of each month, arrived at San Antonio in twenty-

five days, left San Antonio on the first day of each month, arrived at Santa Fe in twenty-five days. Brevoort and Houghton became involved in a dispute with the government over their contract, considered first in the Court of Claims, and later in the House of Representatives, with the result that the amount claimed by the mail contractors was considerably reduced. See Report C. C. No. 266, H. of R. 36th Cong., 2d Sess., Dec. 1, 1860.

23 OR Series I, Vol. L, part 2, p. 48. Pemmican making was probably the first industrial enterprise established in Los Angeles. The *Daily Alta* of Feb. 2, 1862, told of its establishment: "Col. Carleton has prevailed upon the people of Los Angeles to prepare a pemmican for his expedition. Pemmican is the name of a food prepared by the Indians of the missions, and adopted also by the inhabitants of New Mexico. It is made by cutting meat into thin sheets, or small strips, then drying it until the moisture is driven off. It is then pounded and seasoned, and as much hot fat or lard as it will absorb, incorporated with it. Then it is pressed into bags or bales." Carleton's pemmican was a failure as an article of diet. A soldier told of its unpopularity in a letter to the *Daily Alta* written from near Tucson, published Aug. 10, 1862: "Pemmican for the men has proved a most unpalatable and unhealthy diet. It appears to have been made of rotten old dried beef and the refuse of a soap factory—the meanest food ever served to a hungry man. Fresh mule meat would be a luxury in comparison."

24 OR Series I, Vol. L, part 1, p. 887.

25 On July 17, 1862, in Tucson, Carleton relented and reversed himself on the knapsack regulations. He issued an order which provided: "That every soldier may move forward with a light, free step; now that we approach the enemy, he will no longer be required to carry his knapsack." OR Series I, Vol. L, part 1, p. 9.

26 OR Series I, Vol. L, part 1, p. 945.

27 OR Series I, Vol. L, part 1, p. 1014.

28 OR Series I, Vol. L, part 1, p. 930.

29 OR Series I, Vol. L, part 1, p. 932.

30 OR Series I, Vol. L, part 1, p. 938.

31 OR Series I, Vol. L, part 1, pp. 939 and 966. When Hunter abandoned Tucson he sent Capt. McCleave and Ammi White to Mesilla as prisoners of war. They were paroled to the limits of the town until July 7, 1862, when McCleave was exchanged for two Confederate lieutenants who had been held prisoner at Fort Craig. White was released by Capt. William Steele as he prepared to abandon Mesilla and leave for Fort Bliss on July 8, 1862. OR Series I, Vol. L, part 1, p. 125. Capt. Hunter "traveled light" in Arizona, according to an affidavit made in Tucson on Oct. 3, 1862, by H. S. Stevens. Stevens declared in his affidavit that he had accompanied a detachment of Confederate troops which left Mesilla in January and arrived in Tucson in February, 1862; that the whole number of Hunter's detachment did not exceed 75 men from the time of arrival in Tucson until it left for the Rio Grande in May, 1862. Among other things, Stevens declared: "That Hunter's company was not drilled nor disciplined during its stay in Tucson; that the horses of the company were kept in the corral of the Overland Mail Company; and that the men of Hunter's company slept each where he liked, in any part of town he chose, as a general thing, while the company occupied Tucson." OR Series I, Vol. L, part 2, p. 151.

That McCleave was a splendid soldier and a fine man is indicated in a letter written by Carleton from Santa Fe on Nov. 14, 1862, to Maj. Gen. Henry W. Halleck in Washington, urging his promotion: "Captain William Mc-

Cleave, of Company A, First Cavalry California Volunteers, served ten years under my command, nearly all the time as a first sergeant in Company K, First Dragoons. When the California Volunteers were organized he became the ranking captain in the First Cavalry. While on a scout last spring he was taken prisoner by the secessionists, and was not exchanged for four months. When he came to draw his pay he presented to the United States $582.50, stating in his letter of transmittal, 'I am not here for pecuniary purposes, and respectfully ask that the amount revert to the Federal Government, whose servant I am.' This was the pay which accrued while he was a prisoner. In a letter to myself Captain McCleave says: 'I prefer a clear conscience rather than possess anything the ownership of which is doubtful, and especially in times like these, when the Government is engaged in such a desperate struggle, I can but render my humble assistance in the noble work.' The devotion of this noble Irishman to the country of his adoption should be known. If you can give him a helping hand you may rest assured you cannot assist a finer soldier or one whose heart is in all respects without fear and without reproach. He should belong to the regular service. He possesses all the elements of which heroes and patriots are made." OR Series I, Vol. L, part 2, p. 223.

32 Captain Hunter told of his movements in Arizona, of the arrest of Ammi White, and the capture of Captain McCleave, in a letter written to Col. John R. Baylor from Tucson on April 5, 1862: "After a march, made as rapidly as practicable from the Rio Grande, attended by some violently stormy weather, I have the honor of reporting to you my arrival at this place on February twenty eighth. My timely arrival with my command was hailed by a majority, I may say the entire population, of the town of Tucson. I found rumors here to the effect that the town was about being attacked by a large body of infantry....I started with the rest of my command for the Pimos Villages, where ...I arrested A. M. White, who was trading with them, purchasing wheat, etc. for the Northern troops, and confiscated the property found in his possession ... among which were one thousand five hundred sacks of wheat ... which I distributed among the Indians, as I had no means of transportation and deemed this a better policy of disposing of it than to destroy or leave it for the benefit of the enemy. While delaying at the Pimos Villages, awaiting the arrival of a train of fifty wagons, which was reported to be enroute for that place (which report, however, turned out to be untrue), my pickets discovered the approach of a detachment of cavalry, which detachment, I am happy to say to you, we succeeded in capturing without firing a gun. This detachment consisted of Captain McCleave and nine of his men, First California Cavalry. The Captain and Mr. White I sent in charge of Lieut. Swilling to the Rio Grande." "Record of California Men in the War of the Rebellion," p. 45, Sacramento, 1890. Captain Hunter and "eighty rebels" were reported to have evacuated Tucson on May 14, and to have reached Dragoon Spring, on the way to Mesilla on May 18. Hunter was reported back in Mesilla on May 27, 1862. Col. J. R. West wrote to Lieut. Col. E. E. Eyre from Cottonwood Spring, on May 17, 1862: "So Hunter staid at Tucson until the 14th. He was playing bopeep in the neighborhood. I suspect he is doing so yet. If he flickers around the candle a little longer he will get his wings singed." OR Series I, Vol. L, part 1, p. 1048.

33 *Daily Alta California*, April 15, 1862.

34 Carleton was a stickler for discipline. He wrote to his cavalry officers: "If the days are hot, you must travel at night. Your men (cavalry) must walk half the time by watch. Practice as you march along, one hour each day, the sabre exercises." Carleton operated a line of military couriers and dispatch riders between Los Angeles and Fort Yuma. Ordinarily the ride, with usual change of horses, required six days. Col. Carleton was described in the newspapers of the day as a great commander. The *Daily Alta California* correspondent praised him highly: "The more I see of Col. Carleton, the more I

am confident of his entire fitness and ability to command the forces now under him, and conduct the important campaign entrusted to his charge. His vigilance is sleepless, and his energy untiring. With all the attention to detail, even minutiae, which characterizes the thorough disciplinarian, he possesses the ability to elaborate and carry out operations on a large scale, and with remarkable accuracy and timeliness." *Daily Alta,* May 15, 1862. Two wagons were assigned to each company to carry mess furniture, camp and garrison equipage, ten days rations, and other essential property of the company. To prevent overloading, every article was weighed at the commencement of the expedition. Officers, from Carleton on down, were limited to eighty pounds of baggage, including bedding and mess kit. Some wells on the Yuma desert furnished only a trickle of water, so small in quantity that it was dipped out in a pint cup. At one place on the desert it took nearly all night to water 100 horses and mules.

[35] The California troops followed a route, 859 miles in distance, from the Pacific ocean to the Rio Grande, taken in three "strides" as Carleton called them: From Los Angeles to Fort Yuma, on the Colorado river; from Fort Yuma to Tucson; from Tucson to the Rio Grande. The route: Los Angeles, Monte, San Jose, Chino Ranch, Temescal, Laguna, Temecula, Dutchman's, Oak Grove, Warner's Ranch, San Felipe, Vallecito, Palm Springs, Carriso Creek, Sackett's Wells, Indian Wells, New River, Norton's Wells, Gardiner's Well, Cooke's Wells, Algodones, Fort Yuma, Gila City, Mission Camp, Antelope Peak, Mohawk, Texas Hill, Stanwix's Ranch, Burke's Station, Oatman's Flat, Kenyon's Station, Gila Bend, Maricopa Wells, Casa Blanca, Pima Villages, Oneida Station, Blue Water Station, Pichacho, Point of Mountain, Tucson, Cienaga, San Pedro, Dragoon Springs, Apache Pass, San Simon, Stein's Peak, Soldier's Farewell, Cow Springs, Mimbres River, Cooke's Spring, Pichacho (on the Rio Grande), Mesilla. OR Series I, Vol. L, part 1, p. 1017. Cooke's Spring, located at the foot of Cooke's Peak in New Mexico, directly on the road from Mesilla to Tucson, 60 miles west of Mesilla, was named after Col. P. St. Geo. Cooke, on the staff of Gen. Stephen Watts Kearny at the time of the American Occupation of Santa Fe on Aug. 18, 1846. Cooke led the Mormon Battalion through New Mexico to California in the fall of 1846.

Cooke's Spring was an important stage stop before and after the Civil War. It was at Cooke's Spring that General Carleton established Fort Cummings in 1864 in memory of Dr. Joseph Cummings, killed by Navajo Indians in the Canon de Chelle country on Aug. 17, 1863. Long since abandoned, today a place of crumbling ruins, the Fort Cummings that was may be reached by turning off the highway at Florida (pronounced flohr-ree-dah by the initiated), on the Hatch to Deming highway, and traveling 6 miles to the west. Of historic Fort Cummings, General Carleton wrote in 1865: "Fort Cummings is built at Cooke's Springs, at the eastern end of Cooke's Canon, directly on the road from Mesilla to Tucson, and completely controls the old resort of the Apaches. In this canon, until Fort Cummings was established, the Apaches made frequent and fatal attacks on small parties of travelers, and once killed the driver and every passenger upon the stage, some nine in all. Except Apache Pass, in Arizona, it was by far the most dangerous point on the southern route to California. It was established by myself over a year ago, is calculated for a company of infantry, and say, half a company of cavalry, and should in my opinion, be kept up as long as the Apache Indians infest the country about the head of the Mimbres and Gila rivers, in the Burro and Florida mountains." See OR Series I, Vol. XLVIII, p. 1234.

[36] OR Series I, Vol. L, part 1, p. 1048.

[37] Ibid, p. 1045. From Fort Yuma on May 3, 1862, Carleton sent couriers through the Apache country with a message to General Canby at Santa Fe, advising him, among other things, that he could move on from Tucson, or Fort Breckenridge, as soon as instructed, adding: "It will afford me pleasure to enter into any plan you may suggest, so my force can be of service to you

aₙd to the cause. Let me know your strength, your situation, your purposes; the strength, situation, and probable purposes of Sibley and his troops." The message did not get through to Canby. On May 15, 1862, at Fort Yuma, Col. Carleton issued an order of the day declaring "that the forces belonging to the United States, which are now moving from the Department of the Pacific toward Arizona and New Mexico will hereafter be known as the Column from California." OR Series I, Vol. L, part 1, p. 1075. On May 24, 1862, Carleton ordered the name of Fort Breckenridge, on the San Pedro river, changed to Fort Stanford, in honor of the Governor of California, and ordered Col. E. E. Eyre, First Cavalry, California Volunteers, to reoccupy the fort, which he did for a brief time. But for the war, Fort Breckenridge would have been a six company post, according to Carleton. He described it as "commanding a site near the junction of the Aravaypa and San Pedro rivers, the best point for a post in Arizona." "Aside from being one of the posts on the chain of communication from California to the Rio Grande," Carleton wrote, "it was a fine place for weak and broken down horses to recruit, the grazing in the San Pedro valley the year round being reported as very fine." After capturing Tucson, Col. West was ordered to reoccupy Fort Buchanan. West, together with Capt. Emil Fritz, and a detachment from the First Infantry, went to Fort Buchanan, but found on arrival there that all buildings had been destroyed. The site being of no importance, Carleton withdrew the garrison from there to Tucson. Carleton reported: "The colors were put up at Fort Buchanan, thus consecrating the ground anew to the country." OR Series I, Vol. L, part 1, p. 1129.

38 Named in memory of Lieut. James Barrett, of the First Cavalry, California Volunteers, killed in a skirmish with rebels near Pichacho Station, April 15, 1862.

39 OR Series I, Vol. L, part 1, p. 1095.

40 "The Presidio of Tucson," as it was known under Spanish and Mexican rule, had a population of between 400 and 500 people, "mostly Mexicans," according to Carleton's official report, "among them a few Americans and foreigners, principally gamblers and ruffians, traitors to their country—secessionists." OR Series I, Vol. L, part 1, p. 142. The United States census for 1860, however, gave Tucson a population of 1820.

41 OR Series I, Vol. 9, p. 553. Commissioned a brigadier general of volunteers April 28, 1862, Carleton received the commission and assumed his new rank and title while in Tucson, on or about June 15. In marching from Fort Yuma to the Pima Villages, Carleton's troops followed a route which took them to Gila City, Mission Station, Filibuster Camp, Antelope Peak, Mohawk Station, Lagoon Camp, Texas Hill, Grinnel's Ranch, Grassy Camp, Berk's Station, Oatman Flat, Kenyon Station, Shady Camp, Gila Bend, Desert Station the Tank, and Maricopa Wells. Gila City was described as "a collection of deserted huts, seventeen and a half miles from Fort Yuma." The mines in the immediate vicinity of Gila City "had been abandoned in consequence of better diggings being found on the Colorado, about one hundred miles above." The Gila water was reported palatable. The banks of the Gila were "fringed with green willows and cottonwood, a striking contrast to the desert country to the east." At Antelope Peak, Carleton was received by a salute of eleven guns from Shinn's battery. Soldiers at Antelope Peak built green bowers to protect them against the sun's heat, "running in regular rows and looking like the booths of a fair." The camp at Antelope Peak was "alive with military life." The mountain produced a fine echo, "the result of the sound of a bugle or the report of a gun." Passing through Oatman Flat, "which derived its name from the Oatman family, murdered there in 1851," the soldiers saw "a solitary grave, nicely enclosed, with the simple inscription, 'The Oatman Family, 1851'." *Daily Alta,* June 23, 1862. Carleton's command reached Maricopa Wells on June 3, 1862, having marched 80 miles in 48 hours. Mari-

copa Wells was described as being "located on an extensive alkaline plain, covered with short, horny, saltish grass, with a few mesquite trees here and there, just enough to furnish a scant shade from the scorching heat of midday." Ibid, June 28, 1862. Great heat prevailed in the Maricopa Wells country in the summer time. The *Daily Alta California* correspondent used the plural, "heats," in describing the climate as of June 19, 1862: "The heats are so intense that animate and inanimate creation give evidence of being deeply effected; the very rocks seem to be disintegrating. There is no lack of breeze, which comes laden with caloric as if from the blast of a furnace, parching the skin and dessicating the whole frame. The advent of night is scarcely a relief to this intolerable withering of everything; the thermometer standing at 104 at 10 o'clock in the morning for several days in succession." Ibid, July 12, 1862. During June and July, 1862, at 2 o'clock in the afternoon, at Fort Yuma, on the California side of the Colorado river, the thermometer usually registered 108. OR Series I, Vol. L, part 1, pp. 496-536.

42 Carleton was mistaken in saying as of June 9, 1862, that Arizona had been established as a Territory. The act making Arizona a Territory was not signed until Feb. 24, 1863.

43 OR Series I, Vol. L, part 1, p. 1129. The *Daily Alta California* correspondent, writing from Tucson on June 16, 1862, told about the town: "Tucson may be properly described in these few words; a little old, Mexican town, built of adobe, and capable of containing about fifteen hundred souls. The Santa Cruz river runs within a mile of the town, and feeds the numerous ditches that irrigate the beautiful little valley that extends to the hills to the westward, and which was, a week since, one vast field of fine grain, harvesting having commenced. The climate of Tucson is dry and healthy, and the soil will produce almost anything planted. The peach, quince, fig and pomegranate grow to perfection." *Daily Alta*, July 10, 1862. Tucson's civic atmosphere in the summer of 1862 was described by the *Daily Alta's* correspondent in an article published in that paper on July 12: "This territory has been the refuge and paradise of rascals of every type, who have made it unsafe for them to dwell elsewhere. Escaped convicts from California and desperadoes from Texas and New Mexico, comprise the majority of its population, who scruple not at the commission of the most hideous crimes and excesses of iniquity. Dreading each other, for they are ranged in cliques, they make common cause against the native inhabitant, whom they murder without ceremony. General Carleton has already commenced a vigorous course against these noxious vermin, and seems determined to make a clean sweep. . . . All civil law has been suspended and crimes and misdemeanors are brought before a board of army officers, who try the cases and pronounce sentences, which, together with a complete written statement of the cases, is laid before the General for his approval, disapproval, or modification. The arrests made up to this time, have been of the vilest wretches, and have had a most salutary effect, and have given the vicious to understand that they are under rigid and unbending surveillance. The avenger is on their track, and they will yet feel the weight of his heel on their traitor necks."

44 OR Series I, Vol. L, part 1, p. 96. Major David Ferguson, of the California Column, wrote to Gov. Ignacio Pesquiera, of the State of Sonora, Mexico, on Sept. 15, 1862, enlisting his aid in straightening out property titles in and about Tucson: "It appears that when the troops of the Republic of Mexico were withdrawn from the Presidio of Tucson that the military commandant took the records of the town to Sonora with him. Many of the people here, being simple minded persons, have not the proper titles to prove their right to property really belonging to them, having either failed to get written grants or having lost the evidences necessary to establish their claims. Many of the citizens of Sonora also have equitable claims difficult to establish. Without the records it will be impracticable to settle questions of title to land, thus giving unprincipled men an advantage over honest men, who cannot

establish their rights. Your excellency would confer a great favor and further the ends of justice by ordering the return of the records referred to if they are not necessary for the archives of your state." OR Series I, Vol. L, part 2, p. 121.

45 OR Series I, Vol. 9, pp. 561-562.

46 Benjamin Clarke Cutler (who died in Santa Fe on Oct. 18, 1867, at the age of 34 years) was the son of Rev. Benjamin Clarke Cutler, who was born in Roxburg, Mass., on Feb. 6, 1798, died Feb. 10, 1863 in Brooklyn, N. Y., where he served as pastor of St. Anne's Episcopal Church for 30 years.

47 OR Series I, Vol. 9, pp. 692-693. Traveling over the Gila desert from the Colorado river to Tucson severely taxed the endurance of men and animals alike. Waiting in Tucson for "the seasonal rains to fill up the water holes," so he could proceed toward the Rio Grande, Carleton wrote on June 10, 1862, to Major Drum in San Francisco, saying: "It would surprise you to see how the great heat and dry air of the desert have affected our wagons. The tires have to be cut and reset and a large amount of other repairs have to be made to keep them from going to pieces.... The intolerable heat and the alkali dust of the Gila desert makes the transportation of supplies from Fort Yuma to Tucson a matter of great difficulty. The teamsters suffer greatly with inflamed eyes and with coughs. You can judge how thick this dust is when I assure you that through the extensive mesquite thickets through which the road leads, it is impossible for a teamster to see his own lead mules. The dust is impalpable and spreads out over the country on either hand like a lake, and there it remains for some time after the wagons have passed along. By these lakes of dust I have seen the exact position of a train more than ten miles distant. The tires of the wagons get loose, and the sand working in the joints of the wheels soon grinds them into an utterly unserviceable condition. I have two shops in operation in Tucson, but not over two wagons a day can be put in running order with all the force I can bring to work upon them." OR Series I, Vol. L, part 1, p. 1147.

48 Sylvester Mowry, colorful early day resident of Arizona, was born in Providence, R. I., in 1830, died in London, England, on Oct. 16, 1871. Mowry was graduated from the U. S. Military Academy in 1852. After a year of frontier duty in California, he was assigned to exploring work for the Pacific Railroad in 1853 and 1854. He served at Fort Yuma from 1854 until 1857. Becoming interested in mining in Arizona, then a first lieutenant, he resigned from the army on July 31, 1858. Mowry was elected as a delegate from Arizona to the 35th Congress, but the bill establishing Arizona as a Territory did not become a law, and he was not seated. President Buchanan appointed Mowry on the commission to establish the Nevada-California boundary line in 1860, but he was removed in 1861 as the result of a political squabble. Like many early day army officers, with much spare time, Mowry turned to writing. He wrote "Memoir of the Proposed Territory of Arizona," Henry Polkinhorn, Printer, Washington, 1857, "The Geography and Resources of Arizona and Sonora," a third and enlarged edition of which was printed in New York in 1864, and numerous articles for newspapers and magazines, many of them defending his own mining property rights and protesting the rough treatment he received from the U. S. Army during the Civil War.

49 History of California Men in the War of the Rebellion, State Office, Sacramento, 1890, p. 53.

50 OR Series I, Vol. L, part 1, p. 1147. For an early day description of the Mowry mine, see *The Apache Country, a Tour Through Arizona and Sonora*, by J. Ross Browne, Harper & Brothers, N. Y., 1869.

51 OR Series I, Vol. L, part 1, p. 1143.

52 OR Series I, Vol. IX, p. 694. Sylvester Mowry's attitude while a prisoner at Fort Yuma, was described in *The Daily Alta California* of Nov. 13, 1862:

"Mowry is a prisoner here at Fort Yuma, swearing furiously about General Carleton; boasts of his ability to have cut up the Californians if he had been so disposed, and says he will be released in a few days, and intends to make Uncle Sam pay dear for imprisoning him."

53 Ibid, p. 690.

54 Santa Fe *Gazette,* July 23, 1864.

55 OR Series I, Vol. XLI, part 2, page 662.

56 Ibid, p. 674. The New York *World* published an article on Feb. 1, 1865, which, among other things, contained the charge that: "Mr. Mowry was deprived of his property for more than two years, and its proceeds, amounting to hundreds of thousands of dollars, were stolen, and divided between Carleton and his agents. Mr. Mowry was imprisoned for months, and finally, when discharged after trial by a military commission, was fully acquitted of all charges preferred against him. General Carleton thereupon, by sheer military force, banished him from the Territory, and so prevented him from obtaining his rights through the civil authorities, on the pretense that his presence was dangerous to the peace and security of the Territory. After more than two years of this persecution, Mr. Mowry has been restored to his rights of property by the courts of law, and the Legislature of Arizona has thoroughly endorsed him and as thoroughly condemned General Carleton." Taking notice of the *World* article, Carleton said in the Santa Fe *Gazette*: "I have had all kinds of abuse, and the rhetoric of Billingsgate heaped upon me through the *World* newspaper, for having done my duty in this matter."

Mowry's mining property was confiscated and ordered sold by the United States District Court of the Second Judicial District, in Albuquerque, on April 1, 1864. Strangely enough, the decree ordering the sale was signed by Judge Joseph G. Knapp, of Mesilla, who had himself engaged in a running battle for months with General Carleton over passport requirements. Knapp, like Mowry, knew what it was to incur Carleton's wrath. The notice of confiscation of Mowry's property was published in the Rio Abajo *Press* at Albuquerque. The property was sold at public auction for $2,000, leaving the lawyers to fight out the legal question as to whether or not, the New Mexico courts, having acquired jurisdiction of the cause prior to the organization of Arizona as a Territory, continued to retain jurisdiction thereafter. The public sale of the Sylvester Mowry "silver mining property, known as the Patagonia, or Mowry silver mine, with the buildings, machinery and lands, situate in Dona Ana County, New Mexico, in the Santa Cruz mountains, 23 miles from Fort Buchanan, together with a large stock of merchandise, and a printing press, type and outfit," was advertised for July 18, 1864. The properties of W. T. and G. H. Oury, of Arizona, were confiscated, as Mowry's had been, and ordered sold at Mesilla, Dona Ana County, on the same date that was set for the Mowry sale. See Rio Abajo *Press,* Albuquerque, June 14, 1864.

57 At its January session in 1865, the Arizona legislature passed the following resolution: "Whereas, on or about the 24th day of August last, Lieut. Sylvester Mowry, claiming to be a resident of this Territory, and largely interested in the mines thereof, having returned thereto for the purpose of looking after his interests therein, was placed out of said Territory in pursuance of an order issued by Gen. James H. Carleton, the Commander of the Department of New Mexico, by the military forces under his command; wheretofore be it Resolved by the Council, the House of Representatives concurring; that such action on the part of General Carleton was unnecessary, and that in our opinion the presence of the said Mowry in this Territory was not dangerous to the peace thereof. That the courts of this Territory are competent judges of all violations of the laws of the United States, and of the Territory of Arizona committed in their jurisdiction, and have all necessary power to punish all violations thereof." The resolution had been introduced on October 24, 1864, by Coles Bashford, president of the Council. The joint

committee on judiciary, to which the resolution was referred reported it back to the Council with a "do not pass" recommendation, but despite this, the resolution was adopted in Council, and after being amended by the House, was adopted by a vote of 11 to 5. Although the democrats in the legislature claimed a victory, the republicans contended adoption of the resolution was only a "political vindication." The feud between Carleton and Mowry ended on October 17, 1871, when Mowry died in London, England, where he had gone for medical treatment, and to raise money to refinance and rehabilitate his Arizona mining properties. In a city of millions of people, it was only natural that Mowry's death would receive less than three lines of type. The London Evening *Standard* of Saturday, Oct. 21, 1871, published the following notice: "Mowry, 17, at 12 Park Place, St. James' Street, London, the Hon. Sylvester Mowry, aged 38."

58 Established on or about Dec. 1, 1853, Fort Thorn was named after Captain Herman Thorn, who was drowned in the Colorado River in Arizona on Oct. 16, 1849, while leading troops enroute to California. Fort Thorn was located at the upper end of the Mesilla Valley, on the west side of the Rio Grande, with a splendid view of the Caballo and Fra Cristobal mountains to the east, near the settlement of Santa Barbara, 85 miles south of Fort Craig, 51 miles north of Fort Fillmore.

Born in New York, N. Y., Herman Thorn sought an appointment to West Point, but, failing to receive it, accepted an appointment in the Austrian army, with rank equivalent to that of corporal in the United States army. Serving with a hussar regiment under the Austrian flag for five years, mostly near Turkish territory, Thorn resigned at the beginning of the war with Mexico, offering his services to the regular army of the United States. Although he had reached the grade of first lieutenant in the Austrian army, and had been in severe actual fighting abroad, Thorn's application for a commission was rejected on the ground that he had not been graduated from West Point. Senator Thomas Hart Benton protested, and appealed to President Polk. The President, overruling his army advisers, sent Thorn's name to the Senate for a commission, and through Benton's efforts the nomination was confirmed. Thorn rendered distinguished service in some of the more important battles in Mexico, particularly in the battle of Molino del Rey. The name of Kit Carson of New Mexico was rejected for a commission in the regular army by the army hierarchy at about the same time that Thorn's name was rejected, "because he did not come through the West Point gate," according to Senator Benton's contentions. For Senator Benton's views on the Thorn and Carson cases see "Thirty Years in the United States Senate" by Benton, Vol. 1, p. 183.

59 OR Series I, Vol. L, part 1, p. 122.

60 Born in Albany, N. Y., in 1819, Col. William Steele died in San Antonio, Texas, on Jan. 12, 1885. Graduated from West Point in 1840, Steele served in the Florida war, the military occupation of Texas, and the war with Mexico. He was stationed in Texas from 1849 to 1852, and in New Mexico from 1852 to 1854; and fought Indians in Kansas, Dakota and Nebraska from 1854 until he resigned his commission in the Union army on May 30, 1861, to accept a commission as Colonel of the 7th Texas Cavalry. Steele fought with Sibley's brigade in New Mexico, and commanded troops in the Confederate Territory of Arizona. He left Fort Fillmore, near Mesilla, for San Antonio, on July 8, 1862. Steele was made a brigadier general in San Antonio on Sept. 12, 1862, and assigned to the command of the Department of Western Arkansas and the Indian Territory. He commanded troops in Galveston in December, 1863, and a cavalry division in Louisiana in 1864, opposing Gen. Nathaniel P. Banks. Beginning in 1874 Steele served as adjutant general of the state of Texas for a number of years, during which time he painstakingly compiled lists of escaped prisoners and fugitives from justice, which he published and furnished at considerable expense to the sheriffs of the various counties in Texas. A

check in 1878 disclosed that many men who were on Steele's honor roll had left Texas for the more salubrious climate of the neighboring Territory of New Mexico.

61 OR Series I, Vol. L, part 2, p. 21.

62 OR Series I, Vol. IX, p. 682.

63 OR Series I, Vol. L, part 1, p. 91.

64 Some days out of Tucson, two miles east of Apache Pass, Carleton encountered the gruesome remains of "nine white men murdered by the Indians." Describing the massacre, Carleton reported: "They were a party traveling from the Pinos Altos mines to California. One of them had been burned at the stake. We saw the charred bones and the burnt ends of the rope by which he had been tied. The remains of seven of these men were buried on the spot." Carleton established Fort Bowie at the scene of the massacre, equipping it with 113 soldiers from the California Column. The newly established fort "commanded the water in Apache Pass, around which the Indians have been in the habit of lying in ambush and shooting troops and travelers as they came to drink."

65 OR Series I, Vol. IX, p. 559. Leaving Ojo de Vaca, Carleton's detachment marched to Pichacho de los Mimbres, 22 miles south-southwest from the copper mines of Santa Rita, 12 miles east of the Pinos Altos gold mines. At this place some miners called on Carleton and told him that from 90 to 100 American, German, French and Mexican miners, with their wives and children, had been hemmed in at Pinos Altos by the Apaches, and were slowly starving to death. Carleton sent two wagons loaded with provisions, escorted by soldiers, for their relief.

66 OR Series I, Vol. L, part 2, p. 56.

67 OR Series I, Vol. L, part 1, p. 144. Carleton stopped for a brief time at Dona Ana, near Las Cruces, which was described by the *Alta Daily California* correspondent as being "built of adobe, with a woebegone appearance, and altogether the wreck of what it was ten years ago." The *Daily Alta* correspondent estimated populations as follows: Dona Ana, 500; Las Cruces, 700; Mesilla, 1,000.

68 Named after Lieut. Col. John Bliss, of New Hampshire, who died Nov. 22, 1854, after serving in the army since 1812.

69 The *Daily Alta California* of Oct. 17, 1862, published a correspondent's description of the situation in and about Franklin (now El Paso), Texas: "Much the largest and finest building in this portion of the country, is Hart's Mills, located on the northern bank of the Rio Grande, within one mile of Franklin, which is immediately opposite El Paso, Mexico. This place was built by one Simeon Hart, who made every dollar he earned by effecting flour and other contracts with the United States government. He is an American and formerly dwelt near Chihuahua, in the state of Chihuahua, Mexico. When Forts Thorn, Fillmore, Bliss, Quitman and Davis were built, Hart got the contracts to supply the troops of these several forts with flour, whereupon he ground money from good natured, easy going Uncle Sam, while he ground the wheat, bolting the eagle as fast as he bolted the flour. Simeon Hart and James Magoffin have for years past been ravening upon the vitals of the government. . . . Magoffin had the hay and wood contracts, as well as other small pickings, while Hart battened upon the U. S. for flour and grain. . . . It was Hart who induced Jeff Davis to send a column of Secessionists under Sibley to New Mexico, promising Davis to furnish all the subsistence . . . When Fort Bliss and all its contents were delivered over to the rebels, Magoffin was appointed receiver for the State of Texas.

70 Shirland's Report to Carleton, Sept. 2, 1862, OR Series I, Vol. 9, pp. 577-588. According to the *Daily Alta California* of Nov. 13, 1862, all Texans not in the hospital at Franklin had gone to San Antonio, by the middle of August, 1862. Upon Carleton's arrival at the Rio Grande, according to the *Daily Alta* "Carleton relieved Col. E. E. Eyre as Commander and took charge with a vim which soon straightened things out." Praised for "fine administrative power and quick perception of the wants of the country," Carleton accomplished much, according to the correspondent: "The lurking disloyalists were caged —troops distributed up and down the river—the people were assured of protection, encouraged to forget past troubles and return to their business vocations." Upon Carleton's return from Fort Bliss, he received orders to relieve Gen. E. R. S. Canby as Department Commander in New Mexico. The *Daily Alta* said he "hurried to Santa Fe without a day's rest." As to the California Column, the correspondent reported: "The troops reached the Rio Grande in fine health and fighting trim, and certainly they are the best, most cheerful, temperate, brave, patriotic body of men in the world, and grieve over the prospect ahead of them, cooped up in garrisons along the Rio Grande, without the hope of meeting the rebels or participating in the struggle for the Union."

71 OR Series I, Vol. 9, p. 570. Eulogizing the California Column, at the laying of the cornerstone of the monument dedicated to the Union soldiers who lost their lives at Valverde and Apache Canon in 1862, in the plaza at Santa Fe on Oct. 24, 1867, Governor R. B. Mitchell said: "The Column of California's brave sons, that arrived in New Mexico, while disappointed in not being able to have joined in the work of expelling the invader from New Mexico, were enabled to turn their swords against the hostile savages within our borders, and the rich valleys of the Territory instead of being the scenes of conflict and devastation by contending armies, were filled with peaceful happy laborers." Santa Fe *Gazette*, Oct. 26, 1867.

72 OR Series I, Vol. XV, p. 575.

73 OR Series I, Vol. L, part 2, p. 225.

SOURCES

"History of California Men in War of the Rebellion," Sacramento, 1890, pp. 7, 21, 53.

H.R. Rep. 1083, 51st Cong., 1st Sess.

William Preston Johnston's "Life of Albert Sidney Johnston," 1878.

New Mexico Session Laws, 1860-61, p. 16.

Official Reports —
    Series I,
       Vol. 4, p. 19.
          IX, pp. 553 to 694, at random.
          XV, pp. 575 to 918, at random.
        XLI, Part 2, pp. 662, 674.
      XLVIII, p. 1234.
          L, Part 1, pp. 9 to 1147, at random.
          L, Part 2, pp. 21 to 434, at random.

    Series III, Vol. III, p. 798.
         4, Vol. 2, pp. 960, 1036.
         X, Vol. XV, p. 599.

Rep. Com. on Claims, No. 23, Senate, 40th Cong., 2nd Sess., Jan. 30, 1868.
Rep. Com. Ind. Affairs, 1867.
Rep. Cond. Ind. Tribes, 1867.
U.S. v. Simeon Hart, 73 U.S. Rep. 914.

REFERENCES

"The Apache Country, a Tour Through Arizona and Sonora," by J. Ross Browne, 1869.
"The California Column," by Capt. Geo. H. Pettis, Hist. Soc. of N.M., 1908.
Ex. Doc. 41, pp. 105, 613.
"Peace With the Apaches of New Mexico and Arizona," by Vincent Colyer, Washington, 1872.
Rept. Court of Claims, No. 266, H.R. 36th Cong., 2d Sess., Dec. 1, 1860.
"Thirty Years in the United States Senate," by Thomas H. Benton.

NEWSPAPERS AND PERIODICALS

Daily Alta California, San Francisco, Jan. 18, Feb. 2, 11, 17, April 14, 15, 27, May 15, 20, June 16, 19, 23, 28, July 10, 12, Aug. 10, Oct. 17, Nov. 14, 1862.
London Evening Standard, Oct. 21, 1871.
New York World, Feb. 1, 1865.
Rio Abajo Press, Albuquerque, Mar. 23, April 21, Nov. 3, Dec. 1, 1863; June 14, July 18, 1864.
Santa Fe Gazette, July 23, 1864; Jan. 13, Sept. 2, 1865; July 27, Oct. 26, 1867.
Santa Fe New Mexican, Nov. 21, 1863.

BOOK FOUR

The Long Walk

"The days and nights were long before it came time for us to go to our homes. The day before we were to start we went a little way toward home, because we were so anxious to start. We told the drivers to whip up the mules, we were in such a hurry. When we saw the top of the mountain from Albuquerque we wondered if it was our mountain, and we felt like talking to the ground, we loved it so, and some of the old men and women cried with joy when they reached their homes."

MANUELITO, *the Last Navajo Chief to Surrender to Carleton's Soldiers, Nov. 7, 1866.*

CHAPTER ONE

First the Apaches

Y EARLY FALL OF 1862, New Mexico had been freed entirely from the threat of the Confederate invader. Insofar as New Mexico might be concerned, the Civil War now belonged to history. Sibley, Baylor, Green, Scurry and Pyron, (to name only a few of the gallant Confederate officers who had fought bravely on New Mexico soil,) had returned to Texas, with the remnants of a defeated, but still proud and valiant army. Misfortune had dogged the footsteps of the Confederates in their campaign to win New Mexico for the Southland. Disease had taken a heavy toll. Measles in Texas, and smallpox and pneumonia in New Mexico, had caused the death of almost as many Confederate soldiers as had been killed in

277

battle. General Sibley's valedictory, delivered on the eve of his departure from the Rio Grande, reflected the sentiment of his troops. Worn out and discouraged, most of them were glad to leave a country in which they had endured great hardship, that was in many respects a foreign land, in which Spanish was spoken almost exclusively by the inhabitants, a country which had never known the fragrance of the honeysuckle or the beauty of the magnolia in Springtime.

The Confederates, to use a word from General Carleton's official report, had "fled" from New Mexico in advance of the coming of the California troops. With the enemy back in Texas, and no immediate prospects for participation in the war, Carleton's California troops were soon at loose ends, with nothing of importance to occupy their time, or test their metal.

After the invaders had left the Territory, the inhabitants gradually resumed the routine of their lives. Natives of the Mesilla Valley, through which soldiers of both armies had marched and counter-marched during the early months of the war, demonstrated sufficient confidence in the turn of events to shovel here and there in fields and orchards, retrieving family plate and other valuables buried at the first sign of approaching trouble. Saloon keepers brought from hiding places the bottles of whiskey, wine and champagne that had been concealed to prevent sales to soldiers for Confederate money.

For a time General Carleton found it possible to keep his troops busy repairing streets and roads and rehabilitating army posts. But the soldiers soon grew tired of such employment, grumbling that they had enlisted to fight a war, not work as laborers. Dissatisfaction soon grew into resentment. The men demanded action in the field, or a discharge. In self defense, Carleton looked about for a task that would capture the imagination and challenge the abilities of 1,500 able bodied men. With no Confederates on the horizon, Carleton's active mind fastened on the idea of fighting Indians. He explored the possibilities in that direction with Governor Connelly in Santa Fe, and received his assurance of cooperation. Before many days had passed, Carleton and Connelly agreed on a plan to start a war against the Apache and Navajo Indians. They decided that Colonel Kit Carson, of Taos, would ɔe the ideal man to command the troops in the field. When approached, Carson was not particularly enthusiastic about undertaking the campaign. He believed that the Indians could be brought to terms without a war. Convinced, in their own minds, that there was no alternative but a finish fight with the Indians, Carleton and Connelly prevailed upon a reluctant Kit Carson to accept leadership in the campaign. Governor Connelly's stepson, J. Francisco Chaves, was named second in command.[1]

Theoretically, General Carleton was the ideal officer to carry on the war against the Indians. But few men in the United States Army could match his experience in the west. He had been a witness to the evolutionary period in the life of the American Indian, which he described on one occasion as "the inevitable conflict between culture and civilization — the process of the Indian being pushed back by the white man toward the setting sun."[2]

Those who had been well acquainted with Carleton in the days when he commanded dragoons in New Mexico in the mid-fifties were aware that he was a many-sided man, with puzzling traits of character. While in Albuquerque in 1853, Carleton demonstrated that he was a public spirited citizen. He helped to build streets, planned drainage facilities, and prepared specifications for improving the plaza.[3] That Carleton had no scruples about owning slaves was evidenced by a transaction consummated in Santa Fe on Nov. 18, 1852, when he gave a bill of sale to William Carr Lane, governor of New Mexico, for "one negro man, named Benjamin," identified as "a slave for life," about 21 years old, being "the same slave which James Henry Carleton, the vendor, had bought of George Stille, in Missouri," and for "one negro woman, named Hannah," identified as a slave for life, about 23 years old, and being "the same slave which James Henry Carleton, the vendor, had bought of Matthew Hughes, of Missouri." [4]

Carleton deplored drunkenness in a soldier, whether private or officer, whether on or off duty. For a time, in 1853, Carleton was stationed at Fort Union, New Mexico. The post sutler, in Carleton's opinion, was too ambitious to sell whiskey to the soldiers. On one occasion Carleton ordered the arrest of several intoxicated enlisted men, and had them placed in the guardhouse. Carleton then ordered a squad of soldiers to enter the sutler's quarters, roll out several kegs of whiskey, break the staves with pickaxes, and empty the liquor into the gutter. Every man at Fort Union was profoundly shocked when it became known that the post commander had wantonly ordered the destruction of good liquor — liquor that had been hauled by oxen team a distance of more than seven hundred miles from the Missouri river. Aided and abetted by Carleton's fellow officers, the sutler went to Taos and sued Carleton for damages. When the case was tried the judge was not particularly impressed by Carleton's plea of extenuating circumstances, and rendered judgment against him for $425.60 and costs. Carleton paid the judgment out of his own pocket, but wrote an explanation of the incident to Washington, asking reimbursement. Many months later, the War Department allowed Carleton's claim, a bit mystified, perhaps, at the vagaries of the military in the far west. [5]

In the opinion of those who knew him well, Carleton was a stern, unbending officer, "unsurpassable for energy, intelligence, vigor and integrity." [6] Perhaps the word "rigid" described him most adequately. There was no indication of flexibility in his make up. Seemingly, whenever he made up his mind about a man, or a situation, there was no swerving, no deviation. Soldiers of the California Column discovered this characteristic in Carleton's make up as they marched over mountains and deserts from California to New Mexico. They had discussed him and his proclivities endlessly around camp-fires at night. They had seen the zeal with which he had chased down men accused of disloyalty to the Union in southern California. They had witnessed the energy and vindictiveness with which he had pursued Sylvester Mowry, the Arizona mining operator. They had seen enough of Carleton's conduct and methods to know that he was, at least, a very peculiar man.

Having determined upon a campaign against Apache and Navajo Indians, Carleton wrote to the War Department on Sept. 22, 1862, stating his reasons for undertaking it, and advising of the disposition of troops:

I find that during the raid made into this Territory by some armed men from Texas, under Brigadier General Sibley, of the army of the so-called Confederate States, the Indians, aware that the attention of our troops could not, for the time, be turned toward them, commenced robbing the inhabitants of their stock, and killed in various places, a great number of people; the Navajos on the western side, and the Mescalero Apaches on the eastern side of the settlements, both committing these outrages at the same time, and during the last year that has passed, have left the people greatly impoverished. Many farms and settlements near Fort Stanton have been entirely abandoned.

To punish and control the Mescalero, I have ordered Fort Stanton to be reoccupied. That post is in the heart of their country, and hitherto when troops occupied it those Indians were at peace. I have sent Colonel Christopher Carson (Kit Carson) with five companies of his regiment of New Mexico volunteers, to Fort Stanton. One of these companies, on foot, will hold the post and guard the stores, while four companies under Carson, will operate against the Indians until they have been punished for their recent aggressions. Lieutenant Colonel J. Francisco Chaves with four companies of the same regiment, will move into the Navajo country and establish and garrison a post on the Gallo, which was selected by General Canby; it is called Fort Wingate. I shall endeavor to have this force, assisted by some militia which have been called out by the Governor of the Territory, perform such service among the Navajos as will bring them to feel that they have been doing wrong.[7]

No doubt but that the Mescalero Apaches in southeastern New Mexico, disregarding the advice of officials in the government service, had committed crimes which called for vengeance at the hands of officials of the federal and territorial government. Lorenzo Labadie,[8] a reliable Indian Agent of the Anton Chico agency, wrote a report to Superintendent Collins, at Santa Fe, on Sept. 25, 1862, describing recent Mescalero depredations. Labadie wrote that during the month of August alone, the Mescaleros had killed forty men and six children. Over a period of months, he reported, they had raided settlements and committed numerous other atrocities, and had stolen much livestock:

The Mescalero band of Apaches have been in a continuous state of hostility for the past year, and have committed heavy depredations upon the people, which they have been permitted to do without any movement being made against them by the military. During the latter part of August, they killed some forty men and six children, and carried a number of children into captivity, some of whom, after keeping them in the mountains for several days, were stripped, and turned loose to find their way back to the settlements. The property robbed consisted of horses, mules, donkeys, and cattle, and large numbers of sheep. I visited the country of this marauding band last year, accompanied by an escort of soldiers, but they had secreted themselves in the mountains or moved south into Mexican territory. In July last a party of eighty men, Mexicans, made an expedition into their country in pursuit of stolen property; they returned with four Indian children, captives, and about forty horses and mules, among which were seven of their own previously stolen. The children I took to the military commandant at Fort Union, where they remain.

Labadie reported that the Navajos, coming from hundreds of miles away, had "murdered many persons, and carried off many women and children as captives," and driven off one hundred thousand sheep, forty-five thousand of which had been driven from the grazing grounds of the Canadian River:

The Navajos, I am sorry to say, are still in a hopeless state of hostility; they have committed heavy depredations upon the people during the year, murdered many persons, and carried off many women and children as captives. They have driven off over one hundred thousand sheep, and not less than a thousand head of cattle, besides horses and mules in large numbers. During August they drove off some forty-five thousand sheep from the grazing grounds on the Canadian river. To the east of Anton Chico the citizens collected in force and succeeded in recovering all the sheep, except what had been killed and destroyed by the Indians, and killed some seven or eight Indians. This condition of the tribes is truly disheartening to the citizens. There is no security for life or property, and unless the government takes immediate steps to stop these depredations, the country will be stripped of every species of property it now contains. The only permanent remedy for these evils is the colonization of these Indians. Reservations should be at once located, and the Indians forced to reside upon them. The Mescalero Apaches have the best lands, and with the aid of the government, they can soon be made to raise grain and vegetables enough for their support. The Navajos should also be confined to agricultural districts. They now range over the entire Territory. No part of it is exempt from their marauding incursions.⁹

Basing his letter partly on Labadie's report, and on information from other sources, Collins wrote to the Commissioner of Indian Affairs on October 10, 1862, giving the background of the difficulties with the Indians:

The invasion of our Territory by the Texans has had a most unfortunate effect upon some of the Indian tribes within this agency. For nearly one year that portion of New Mexico known as Arizona, was in the military occupation of the enemy, and all the Indians in that district of country were thus placed beyond the limits of our jurisdiction for the time being. . . . The band of Apaches which is the occasion of the most trouble at the present time is known as the Mescalero. They roam upon our eastern frontiers, from Fort Stanton to the neighborhood of Fort Union, a distance of about two hundred and fifty miles. Since the abandonment of Fort Stanton last year, by our troops, this band has been in a state of hostility, and has committed many depredations upon our citizens. The crimes of which they have been guilty are of the most grave character, among which is included that of murder.

The Gila Apaches roaming the country west of Mesilla, in southwestern New Mexico, had killed a number of people and forced others to flee for their lives, according to Collins:

In the general term, "Gila Apaches," are embraced all the Apaches which live west of Mesilla in the country watered by the Mimbres and Gila Rivers. . . . To a very great extent they have carried on hostilities against the whites, breaking up the settlements in the valley of the Mimbres, and compelling the settlers to fly for protection to more densely settled parts of the Territory.... The mining and agricultural districts in that portion of the Territory west of the Rio Grande have been almost entirely abandoned.... When the California troops were marching to Arizona under General Carleton last summer, they encountered the Gila Apaches at the Apache Pass, some hundred fifty miles west of Mesilla. In a skirmish which one company of the command had with them, and from the stealthy murders in the pass, nine men lost their lives. The command, after it had gone through the pass, found the remains of nine other men who had been murdered by these Indians, one of whom had been burned at the stake. These unfortunate victims had started from the Pino Alto mines, in July, to go to California. This pass is on the great thoroughfare to California and has been the scene of many barbarities, especially about the time of the breaking up of the Butterfield overland mail. A military post has been established in the pass at a point which commands the water in it, and which is garrisoned by a force sufficiently strong to keep the Indians off. This cannot but be attended with the most salutary results to a large region of the country. Deprived of the water from the springs at the pass, the Indians will be compelled to abandon the place of resort for mischief doing, and travelers will be guaranteed immunity from the dangers to which they have heretofore been subject.[10]

On the same day on which General Carleton advised Washington of the contemplated campaign against the Indians, Sept. 22, 1862, Governor Henry Connelly issued a proclamation calling for the reorganization of the Territorial militia by October 15. Connelly's proclamation sounded the keynote for the campaign against the Indians:

For many years past you have been suffering from the hostile inroads of a perfidious tribe of Indians, who notwithstanding the efforts of the government to ameliorate their condition and administer to their wants in every respect, do not cease daily to encroach upon the rights and depredate upon the lives and property of the peaceful citizens of New Mexico.

For a long series of years have we been subjected to the rapacity and desolation of this hostile tribe, which had reduced many wealthy citizens to poverty, and the greater part of our citizens to want and mendacity; which had murdered hundreds of our people, and carried our women and children into captivity. Almost every family in the Territory has to mourn the loss of some loved one who has been made to sacrifice his life to these blood-thirsty Navajos. Our highways are insecure, and the entire country is now invaded and overrun by these rapacious Indians, murdering, robbing and carrying off whatever may come in their way. Such a state of things cannot and must not longer be endured.

For more than a year past we have been menaced by, and finally suffered the invasion of Texas forces; to repel which, and relieve the Territory from the more powerful and not less rapacious foe, required all the energies and exhausted the resources of the Territory. During this period of time the Indians have, with impunity, preyed upon every interest of our people, and reduced them to a state of poverty which has not been felt for the last fifty years.

We are now free from all appearance of a Confederate force upon our frontier, but the attention of the military will be constantly drawn to any new dangers that may threaten from the same, or any other quarter, and will, consequently, not be able to send into the Indian country any large force for the length of time necessary to subjugate the Indians and recapture the immense amount of property of which our people have so recently been despoiled. This duty pertains to the militia of the Territory; for this purpose you are to reorganize, never to be disbanded until we have secured indemnity for the past and security for the future.

It belongs to the people to relieve themselves of the evils they are suffering, and administer such chastisement to these marauders as they deserve. We have the power to do so, and that power must be exercised.[11]

On paper, Carleton's problem seemed simple of solution. First, whip the Mescalero and Gila Apaches. Then subdue the Navajos. By Oct. 12, 1862, Colonel Kit Carson was at Fort Stanton, in the heart of the Mescalero country. Upon his arrival, Carson found Fort Stanton in a dilapidated condition. Only the bare walls remained of a one-time rather imposing group of buildings. Windows, doors and everything that could be moved had been stolen and carried away, the result of the abandonment of the fort by federal troops on Aug. 2, 1861.

Carleton instructed Carson, somewhat in detail, in regard to the methods to be used in the campaign against the Mescaleros. He was to send his mounted companies down to the junction of the Rio Hondo with the Pecos river, "to act as an outpost to this country; to keep scouts well down the river towards Delaware creek to see that no force advances up the Pecos from the direction of Fort Lancaster, in Texas, without your having timely notice of the fact, so that you can send me word." Carleton was confident that Carson's soldiers would locate the Indians: "As your scouts come near the mouth of the Penasco they will, doubtless, find a plenty of Mescaleros." Carleton ordered Carson to kill Indian men without compunction:

All Indian men of the Mescalero tribe are to be killed whenever and wherever you can find them. The women and children will not be harmed, but you will take them prisoners, and feed them at Fort Stanton until you receive other instructions about them.

Mescaleros willing to surrender were to be lectured:

If the Indians send in a flag and desire to treat for peace, say to the bearer that when the people of New Mexico were attacked by the Texans, the Mescaleros broke their treaty of peace, and murdered innocent people, and ran off their stock; that now our hands are untied, and you have been sent to punish them for their treachery and their crimes; that you have no power to make peace; that you are there to kill them wherever you can find them; that if they beg for peace, their chiefs and twenty of their principal men must come to Santa Fe to have a talk here; but tell them fairly and frankly that you will keep after their people and slay them until you receive orders to desist from these headquarters; that this making of treaties for them to break whenever they have an interest in breaking them will not be done any more; that that time has passed by; that we have no faith in their promises; that we believe if we kill some of their men in fair, open war, they will be apt to remember that it will be better for them to remain at peace than to be at war.[12]

Although Carleton's instructions to Carson were specific, he told him in the same letter to use his discretion:

I do not wish to tie your hands by instructions; the whole duty can be summed up in a few words: The Indians are to be soundly whipped, without parleys or councils, except as I have told you.

Considering the possibility that the Texans might invade New Mexico again, this time by way of the Pecos river country, Carleton warned Carson to be on his guard against mistaking soldiers of the California Column for the enemy:

Be careful not to mistake troops from below for Texans. If a force of rebels comes, *you* know how to annoy it; how to stir up their camps and stock by night; how to lay waste the prairies by fire; how to make the country very warm for them, and the road a difficult one.[13]

Carson's troops hunted for Mescaleros in the mountains and valleys within a radius of one hundred miles of Fort Stanton. Carleton ordered two companies of the California Column from Fort Fillmore, under Captain McCleave, and two companies of the Column from Fort Franklin, Texas, under Captain Nathaniel J. Pishon, to "cooperate with Carson; yet to be independent of him." According to Carleton's order, McCleave and Pishon were to proceed "by way of Dog Canon, operate to the eastward and southeastward of that noted haunt of the Mescaleros," and to remain in the field until Dec. 31, 1862. Carleton's instructions to McCleave and Pishon were very specific:

There is to be no council held with the Indians, nor any talks. The men are to be slain whenever and wherever they can be found. The women and children may be taken as prisoners, but of course, they are not to be killed. . . . Much is expected of the California troops. I trust that these demonstrations will give those Indians a wholesome lesson. They have robbed and murdered the people with impunity too long already.[14]

While Carson, McCleave and Pishon hunted Mescalero Apaches in the Sacramento and Guadalupe mountains, and southeastern New Mexico, General John R. West, with headquarters in Mesilla, began a campaign against the Gila Apaches in southwestern New Mexico. Carleton's instructions to West were very definite. He was to ask for no quarter, and to give none. Carleton impressed upon West the importance of opening up country occupied by the Gila Apaches, which Carleton believed to be a vast storehouse of precious minerals. With the opening up of the country in mind, Carleton ordered West to attack the Gilas wherever and whenever he found them:

There must be no peace, or conference, with any Indians living on any of the tributaries of the Mimbres, or the headwaters of the Gila, down as far as Fort Stanford,[15] until they are completely subdued; and not then, until the subject has been duly considered, and decided upon at these headquarters. If possible, the present war against the Apaches, and the one about to be inaugurated against the Navajos, will be continued *without intermission* to that point where a prospect is opened which may disclose that no other war will be necessary. So all instructions, operations, and efforts will look to no other conclusion. The campaign sweeping the Florida mountains, about which I have twice written you, should be borne in mind. Information should be gathered concerning that region, the best guides known, and the work done at the earliest practicable moment. This is a settled purpose, and will, I am sure, meet with a prompt and hearty cooperation on your part. Driven from the Gila, the Apaches will naturally seek asylum in those mountains. There the *maguey* grows, which is their principal food, and in the month of May they will begin to prepare it.[16]

While commanding New Mexico volunteers at Fort Stanton, Kit Carson had much to occupy his time. General Carleton's prolific instructions, sometimes seemingly contradictory, arrived at the post almost daily. Every letter from Carleton urged Carson to hunt out the Mescaleros, to kill all the males who resisted, but to "save the women and children." Then there was the matter of camp discipline. This bothered and annoyed Carson. He had no particular liking for army rules and regulations. In fact, Carson was not familiar with very many of them. As a result, he was willing to tolerate a type of discipline patterned somewhat along the lines of a council of Plains Indians.

The easy going routine at Fort Stanton was disrupted on

Nov. 9, 1862, after the arrival there of Dr. J. M. Whitlock, close friend of Kit Carson. Almost everybody at the fort knew "Doc" Whitlock, either personally or by sight. He had served as a surgeon in Carson's regiment of Territorial Militia prior to its reorganization on Sept. 22, 1862. Whitlock's errand at Fort Stanton was to ask Carson to sign a recommendation for an appointment as surgeon with the reorganized militia. While at the sutler's store at the fort, on the lookout for Carson, Dr. Whitlock came face to face with Captain James ("Paddy") Grayton. Every man who had ever done a hitch in the cavalry in New Mexico or Arizona knew "Paddy" Grayton. Between terms of service, Grayton had run a saloon near Fort Breckenridge. At the outbreak of the Civil War, Grayton quit the liquor business and resumed soldiering. He fought bravely at the battle of Valverde, New Mexico, on Feb. 21, 1862, and seemingly had the respect of every officer and enlisted man in his outfit. Whitlock, however, had no good word for Grayton. In fact, he disliked him to such an extent that he had recently written the editor of a Santa Fe newspaper, accusing Grayton of serious misconduct. Whitlock's story, according to his published communications, was that Grayton, while stationed at Patos, in the Mescalero Indian country, with a detachment of soldiers, had inveigled several Apaches into camp, invited them to drink from a keg of whiskey, and when they had become intoxicated, had ordered his soldiers to shoot them down in cold blood. Meeting each other unexpectedly at Fort Stanton, the two men exchanged fighting words. Grayton demanded that Whitlock "take back" the statements he had written about him to the newspapers, saying they were "libelous slanders," and reflected on his honor. Whitlock, refusing to retract a single word, countered with the proposition that if given time and opportunity, he would be able to prove everything he had said or written. Grayton then challenged Whitlock to a duel. Whitlock accepted the challenge. Grayton went to his tent to get his pistol. Whitlock waited for him at the officers' quarters. When Grayton reappeared, Whitlock fired at him, but missed. Grayton then fired at Whitlock. The bullet from Grayton's gun shattered the stock of Whitlock's pistol, and wounded him in the wrist. Whitlock fired a second shot, which hit Grayton near the heart, inflicting a fatal wound. Whitlock threw away his now useless pistol, with its shattered stock, and entering the sutler's store, took a shotgun from the gun rack and loaded it, and stood by. Comrades carried Grayton to his tent, where he died within a matter of minutes.

Grayton's comrades started for the sutler's store. Whitlock, carrying a shotgun, hurried out by the back door, but was almost immediately shot and killed. Whitlock's body was thrown into an entrenchment ditch. Soldier after soldier of "Paddy's" company passed by the body and shot at it with revolver, rifle or shotgun. The "long roll" was sounded. The garrison was ordered to "fall in under arms." An examination showed that Whitlock's body had been riddled by one hundred thirty gunshot wounds.

Captain Santiago L. Hubbell's Company G, fully armed, was the first company on the parade ground in response to the "long roll." Colonel Kit Carson took command. Ordering Captain Grayton's Company H drawn up in front of Company G, he then ordered Hubbell's Company G to "load" and "ready." He then ordered Company G to disarm every member of Company H from the lieutenant down to the lowest private in the rear rank. No soldier in the regiment had ever seen Kit Carson in such a towering, threatening rage. "I have you scoundrels to swing before sunset!" Carson shouted. When the last man of Company H had been disarmed, Carson walked to his tent.

Allowing for a brief cooling period, Lieutenant Menhard went to Carson's tent, and advised him against any violent act until some way could be found to punish the men actually guilty of the atrocity. Other officers, long time associates of Carson, gathered about him and persuaded him to have the ringleaders in the Whitlock shooting arrested, placed in irons, and held under guard until they could be surrendered to the civil authorities. Padre Damasio Taladrid,[17] the regimental chaplain, preached the sermon at Grayton's funeral the next day, taking for his text "no mataras" (Thou Shalt Not Kill).[18]

Carson's war against the Mescalero Apaches was a pitifully one-sided affair. Most of the Indians were armed with bows and arrows. Only a few had rifles. The Indians with rifles had little or no ammunition. Dragging their squaws and children with them, the Mescaleros wandered from place to place in the mountains and forests, hiding like hunted animals, no match whatsoever for Kit Carson's soldiers, well armed, well fed and well clothed. Within a week after Carson's troops had reached Fort Stanton, they had shot and killed thirty-two Mescaleros, among them Jose Largo and Manuelito, two important chiefs. It was a comparatively easy task for Carson to induce the Mescaleros to surrender. Within a few weeks he had gathered up five hundred men, women and children, and sent them to Bosque Redondo[19] as "prisoners of war." By Jan. 4, 1863, Carson reported to General Carleton that "the Bonito and Pecos valleys might now be cultivated without danger of Indian depredations.[20]

Having made comparatively short work of the Mescalero Apaches in the southeastern part of New Mexico, Carleton was all primed to step up his campaign against the more aggressive, more wily and resourceful Gila Apaches, in the southwestern part of the Territory. On Jan. 3, 1863, he wrote to Washington from Fort Craig, advising of his plans:

Unless I hear beyond a doubt that Baylor's forces are coming, I shall organize and send into the country around the head waters of the Gila an expedition to punish, for their frequent and recent murders and depredations, the band of Apaches which infest that region. The Pinos Altos gold mines can then be worked with security. From all I can learn, that is one of the richest auriferous countries in the world; one whose development will tend greatly to the prosperity of this Territory. Should I be so successful as to whip those Indians, I propose at once to establish a military post near the Pinos Altos mines, not only to furnish protection to the miners already working there, but to have a moral effect in preventing the Indians from further depredations.[21]

Optimistic about the results to be expected in the campaign against the Gila Apaches, Carleton wrote to the War Department advising of the situation, as of Feb. 1, 1863:

By the time the spring opens the Apaches of the Gila will doubtless have been subdued, when I propose to punish the Navajo Indians for their recent murders and wholesale robberies. It is not practicable with my present force and amount of means to make effective demonstrations on more than one tribe at a time. It may be set down as a rule that the Navajo Indians have long since passed that point when talking would be of any avail. They must be whipped and fear us before they will cease killing and robbing the people.[22]

Soldiers of the California Column, commanded by General West, killed many Gila Apaches in the merciless campaign waged against them in the late fall of 1862 and spring and summer of 1863. Although better armed than the Mescaleros, the Gilas were unable to cope with soldiers equipped with late model rifles, an abundance of ammunition, and adequate rations.[23] Scouting parties were sent out to locate Gilas, with particular instructions to be on the lookout for Chief Mangus Colorado.[24] The day came when a detachment of soldiers encountered the Chief, and engaged him in seemingly friendly conversation. Using the pretext that he was wanted at Fort McLane for a consultation, the soldiers enticed Mangus Colorado away from his band. That was the last the Gilas ever saw of their Chief, dead or alive. From Santa Fe on Feb. 1, 1863, Carleton wrote to Washington to tell of the killing of Mangus Colorado, and to outline his plans for further action against the Gilas:

There are no new rumors of an advance of rebels from Texas. ... At this moment I consider the possibility of such an advance so remote that I feel justified in employing the troops under my command in chastising the hostile tribes of Indians by which the settled portions of the Territory are surrounded. The Mescalero Apaches have been completely subdued. I have now 350 of that tribe at Fort Sumner and en route thither. These comprise all that are left of those Indians, except a few who have either run off into Mexico or joined the Gila Apaches. I shall try to settle what have come in on a reservation near Fort Stanton and have them plant fields for their subsistence the coming year. The expedition ordered into the Gila country has already been quite successful. Mangus Colorado,[25] doubtless the worst Indian within our boundaries, and one who has been the cause of more murders and of more torturing and of burning at the stake in this country than all others together, has been killed; and in one battle a few days since over 20 of his followers were killed (the bodies counted) and quite an amount of stock captured. Amongst this stock were found some of the United States mules captured from one of our trains in an attack made on it by these Indians last November on the Jornada del Muerto. Hostilities against the Gila Apaches are now prosecuted with vigor and will be productive of lasting benefits.[26]

The death of Mangus Colorado was mentioned by Carleton in a letter written on April 27, 1863, to Samuel J. Jones, early day resident of Mesilla, but in Kansas City at the time. That Carleton proposed to get the Apaches out of the way, so as to permit mining of precious metals was disclosed by his letter:

Unless I am compelled by Confederate forces to abandon the rich country about Pinos Altos and on the Rio Prieta, it will be held permanently. Our troops have already killed Mangus Colorado, his son, his brother, and some sixty of his braves, and I am still prosecuting hostilities against the Gila Apaches, and propose to do so until people can live in that country, and explore and work the veins of precious metals which we know abound, with safety. The country along the Rio Prieta, and further down the Gila, gives promise of richness in gold and silver. I have two companies surveying a road from Fort Craig to Fort West.[27]

Not long after Mangus Colorado was killed, ugly stories began to bob up here and there in New Mexico, purporting to describe the events leading up to his death. It was freely whispered about that the famous Apache chief had been murdered in cold blood. Two years passed, however, before any man in New Mexico was sufficiently courageous to refer to the Mangus killing publicly because of the possibility of prosecution under martial law. It was left for Judge Joseph G. Knapp, of Mesilla, bitter opponent of Carleton on many questions touching public interest, to sign his name to an open letter addressed to Carleton, criticizing his "black flag" policy in dealing with the Indians. Knapp contended that Carleton's methods not only prevented the Indians from surrendering, but drove them to commit acts of violence and desperation. Published in the Santa Fe *New Mexican* of April 14, 1865, Knapp's letter told of the savagery and brutality of those responsible for Mangus Colorado's death:

But little more than two years have passed since Mangus Colorado, the most powerful of all Apache chiefs, voluntarily came into one of your posts and agreed to deliver himself and band of Apaches to your control. He was confined in the guardhouse; that night he was aroused from his sleep, some say that a soldier threw something and hit him, and others that he was punched with a pole, and because he raised himself up to see what had disturbed his sleep, he was instantly perforated with bullets and killed. Next morning at day dawn his lodge was attacked, and his wife and daughter shared the fate of husband and father. Not content with having killed a prisoner of war, without cause, your soldiers tore the scalp from his head and severed his head from his body, and after boiling the flesh, they exhibited the skull as a badge of honor, while the scalps of himself, his wife and daughter are worn as ornaments. This single violation of all the laws of civilized warfare, has kept from your possession the most powerful of all Apache bands. He may have been as cruel and as wicked as he is reported to have been, but that will not justify such treatment after he had voluntarily placed himself in the possession of your troops. I might cite many other instances in which the prisoners of war in your possession, even women and children, have been brutally murdered. You have taken no steps to call the authors of these crimes to an account. . . . This black flag policy has, as might have been expected, borne its consequent fruit. It has prevented the Indians from surrendering themselves, and led them to revenge.[28]

The death of Chief Mangus Colorado, and of many of his tribesmen, did not stay General Carleton's hand, or prevent him from carrying on the bitter warfare against the Gila Apaches. On March 13, 1863, he wrote a letter to General West, at Mesilla, approving his plan for a springtime expedition of extermination:

Your plan not to stay for one moment hostilities against the Apaches meets with my views and carries out my exact wishes.

I do not look forward to any peace with them, except what we must command. They must have no voice in the matter. Entire subjugation, or destruction, of all the men, are the alternatives.[29]

By March 19, 1863, General Carleton advised Washington of the preliminary results of the campaign against the Mescalero Apaches. Four hundred men, women and children of that tribe, he reported, had been brought in from "their fastnesses in the mountains above Fort Stanton," and taken to Fort Sumner, at the Bosque Redondo, on the Pecos river, leaving about one hundred, the remainder of that tribe, who were believed to have fled to Mexico, or to have joined the Gila Apaches. Referring to the Mescalero Apaches, Carleton ended his letter of March 13 to the War Department on an optimistic note: "You will feel pleased to learn that this long dreaded tribe of murderers and robbers is brought to so promising a condition." Carleton added: "The country around Fort Stanton is fast filling up with settlers."

That Carleton meant exactly what he said in directing his campaign to exterminate the Apaches at any and all cost, was quite evident from the instructions he sent from time to time to staff officers. On July 27, 1863, West, then at Hart's Mills, Texas, requested Carleton to furnish additional troops to cooperate with Major McCleave in southwestern New Mexico. Carleton ordered Colonel Rigg at Fort Craig to send Company K of the First California Volunteers to reinforce McCleave's command. Reminding Rigg "that California troops always find and whip the Indians," Carleton mapped out a program:

Proceed with great caution, without noise of trumpets or drums, or loud talking, or the firing of guns, except in battle; to march silently, mostly by night; to build fires of dry twigs that no smoke may arise from them; to have no fires by night; to kill every Indian man they can find; to be gone thirty days; to have pack mule transportation where wagons cannot go; to remember that California troops always find and whip the Indians.

By midsummer of 1863 the Mescalero Apache tribe, almost in its entirety, had been cowed and subdued, imprisoned at Bosque Redondo. Some few had escaped and were still at large, but the skeletons of many Mescaleros lying in the crevices and canyons of the Sacramento mountains, their bones picked clean of flesh by coyotes and buzzards, told the price paid for refusing to surrender. The Gila Apaches in southwestern New Mexico had been driven back, slowly and relentlessly, from their country, starving and homeless, into the wilds of Arizona and Mexico. The white man's mining of precious metals in the Gila river country could now proceed with reasonable assurance against molestation. With these things triumphantly achieved, Carleton announced his determination to proceed against the Navajos, a tribe, which he said, "still continued to plunder and murder the people."[30]

CHAPTER TWO

Then the Navajos

TAKING ADVANTAGE of a situation in which New Mexico and California troops were employed in fighting Apaches in the southern part of New Mexico, segments of the Navajo tribe conducted frequent and daring raids in 1863 along the Rio Grande, from near Santa Fe on the north to Socorro on the south. With apparent recklessness and utter disregard for consequences, the Navajos ransacked ranches in the vicinity of Bernalillo, Albuquerque, Los Padillas and other river settlements, terrorizing the inhabitants, and driving off many hundreds of head of livestock. Ranging a long distance from their usual haunts, the Navajos, on one foray in 1863, stole 1,600 sheep from grazing grounds almost within sight of the guns at Fort Craig. Troops from the fort trailed the marauders for more than a hundred miles toward the Navajo country. When it appeared as if the soldiers might overtake them, the Navajos abandoned the stolen stock and disappeared on the horizon. The soldiers returned to Fort Craig, with the usual excuses, poor mounts, and lack of field rations, for failing to get the Indians, dead or alive.

Army officers and administrative officials were invariably notified, officially or unofficially, of losses sustained by settlers in Navajo raids. But officers and officials professed to know little or nothing, officially at least, about the conduct of soldiers and settlers in dealing with the Indians. Few New Mexicans cared to recall the bitter feeling that had developed among the Navajos, following an occurrence at Fort Fauntleroy, New Mexico, on Sept. 22, 1861.

The Navajos, in great numbers, visited Fort Fauntleroy on ration day, ordinarily the first Saturday of each month. A custom had grown up at the fort of having the Indians race their horses against soldiers' horses. Among the Navajos, horse racing was more than a sport. It was almost an obsession. They were willing to gamble almost anything they had, money, horses, a wife or two, on the outcome of a match race. Indians and soldiers bet freely on the outcome of the races. Some officers bet horses instead of money. If they won, they could sell the horses to the government for cash. If they lost, they could pay their bets with horses belonging to the government. It was not difficult for them, with the assistance of conniving clerks, to adjust their accounts to cover up their manipulations.

In the early sixties, Fort Fauntleroy was an oasis in remote Indian country, in western New Mexico.[31] The Navajos went to Fort Fauntleroy on a fixed day each month to receive rations of meat, flour and other provisions. The rations were distributed in the hope and with the expectation that the Indians would reciprocate by not raiding the white settlements. For the Navajos, ration days were days of importance and excitement. Men, women and children traveled great distances, on horseback and on foot, to see the fort, watch the soldiers, and get their provisions for the ensuing month.

Ration day at Fort Fauntleroy, Sept. 22, 1861, began like most other ration days. The weather was ideal. The tang of fall was in the air, heavy with the scent of cedar and piñon. The Navajos were in good humor on this particular day, willing to unbend and be quite friendly in their own stolid way. The soldiers, enthusiastic about the horse racing program scheduled for the afternoon, mingled freely with the Indians, trading tobacco for Indian trinkets, and whiskey for Navajo blankets.

The afternoon horse races proved the big attraction of the day. Horses won and horses lost. Indian and white man, in a spirit of true sportsmanship, paid off on their wagers. The final, and most important, race of the day was between Post-Surgeon Kavanaugh's quarter horse, with Lieutenant Ortiz riding, and an Indian pony, owned by Pistol Bullet, a giant Navajo, who stood 6 feet 4 inches in his moccasins. Large sums of money were bet on this race. Both entries were off to a good start, but in a matter of seconds, the Navajo rider and his horse were in serious difficulty. All the spectators, or so it seemed, rushed out at once to learn what had happened. The cause became quickly known when it was seen that the bridle rein of Pistol Bullet's horse had been recently slashed with a knife, which caused the rider to lose control of his mount. In the meantime Kavanaugh's horse had finished the course. Claiming they had been tricked, the Navajos angrily demanded that the race be run again. But the judges of the meet, all soldiers, held that the matter of a defective bridle had been just a bit of hard luck for the Indians. They officially declared Kavanaugh's horse winner of the race. When an interpreter announced the decision of the judges in Navajo, and the Indians realized that they had lost their bets, they made a wild rush for the inside of the fort. The officer of the day ordered the sentries to shut the gates and keep all Navajos on the outside. To celebrate the victory, the Kavanaugh horse was paraded about inside the post grounds. Crowds of soldiers, beating drums and playing on fifes and fiddles, joined in the celebration. An apparently drunken Navajo tried to force his way inside the fort. Sentry Morales fired at him point blank. Hearing the shot, the Navajos still outside the fort, fearing trouble, bolted for the open country, dragging squaws and children with them. Soldiers, with rifle and bayonet, pursued the Navajos. In the mêlee twelve Navajos were killed and forty wounded. The terrified Indians fled for their lives, leaving their dead and wounded behind. One soldier shot and seriously wounded a squaw, and shot to death her two small children. Captain Nicholas Hoydt, of the 1st New Mexico Volunteers, an eyewitness to this wanton outrage, arrested the soldier, disarmed him and started to take him to the guardhouse. Lieutenant Ortiz, rider of the Kavanaugh horse, intervened. Pointing a cocked pistol at Hoydt's head, Ortiz shouted: "Give this soldier back his arms, or else I'll shoot you, damn you!" Hoydt obeyed, but immediately reported the incident to the commanding officer. The commandant coolly told Hoydt that "Lieutenant Ortiz had done perfectly right, and that the soldier had been fully justified, and should be praised for the deed, instead of being punished."

Having made short work of Hoydt, the commanding officer ordered the officer of the day to bring out two mountain howitzers, to fire upon the Indians, and to continue firing at them as long as they were within range. When the sergeant in charge of the howitzers, seeking an excuse to delay firing at the Indians, pretended that he had not understood the order, the officer of the day cursed him, and told him to obey orders or he would be shot. The howitzers were then placed in position, and fired repeatedly in the direction of the fleeing Navajos.[32]

Sept. 22, 1861, marked a day of vast importance in Navajo memory. From that day forward, all Navajo Indians, excepting a few squaws, favorites of officers, remained miles away from Fort Fauntleroy. Ration day at Fort Fauntleroy was discontinued. Horse racing between Navajo and American mounts was abandoned. The Navajos nursed their grievances and waited for a day of retaliation.

The "horse race" incident at Fort Fauntleroy was only one of many similar unfortunate happenings over the years which impressed the Navajos as being unjust, inexcusable, and unforgivable. That the army, or at least a part of it, had been too quick on the trigger, too severe and too impatient in treating with the Navajos, was the seasoned judgment of James L. Collins, perhaps the best informed man on Indian affairs in New Mexico during the critical period of 1858 to 1863. Testifying before the Doolittle Congressional committee at Santa Fe, on July 5, 1865, Collins recited the background of Navajo difficulties:

I came to the territory first in 1827; I came as a merchant and trader. I traded back and forth from 1827 to 1843, making a trip once in three years. In 1843 I came and went into Old Mexico, and since then I have resided most of the time in Old and New Mexico; and since the war with Mexico I have resided in New Mexico all the time. I was superintendent of Indian Affairs from 1857 until 1863, when I turned the office over to Dr. Steck. There has been a state of hostility between the Mexicans and Navajos ever since I have been here. I took charge of the office in 1857, and at the end of the year the conduct of the Indians was better than it had been previous to that time. The pacific disposition of the Indians was occasioned by the large amount of presents they received that fall. Previous to that time the amount of presents had been small; I issued the goods to them myself. That disposition on the part of the Indians continued until June the next year. Although all depredations on their part had not ceased, still it was the most peaceful time we had with the Indians since I had been in the Territory. About the commencement of June in 1858, a difficulty occurred between the Indians and the troops at Fort Defiance, occasioned by the Indians allowing their animals to run on lands which had been set apart by an arrangement with them as meadow lands for cutting hay for the post. Major Brooks was then in command of the post. The Indians were notified to keep their animals off. Finally, after they had been on the ground several times, a company of mounted men, under Captain McLane, of the rifles, was sent out, who ordered about seventy of the animals shot within the limits of the meadow. The result was, a very short time after this, a black boy, servant of Major Brooks, was killed by the Indians. The killing of the boy led to the war, which has continued up to this time. After the killing of the boy a demand was made by Major Brooks of the principal men of the tribe for the delivery of the murderer, who were finally told that unless he was given up in thirty days, war would be made on the tribe.

General Garland authorized an expedition against the Navajos, although Collins believed diplomacy would have accomplished more than bullets:

At this state of the case the facts were reported to General Garland, who was then in command of the department. General Garland, though not approving of the course which had been pursued, still thought proper not to recede from the demand that had been made, but thought proper to exact it. The result was an expedition against the Indians, under Colonel Miles. My opinion was consulted, and I advised more specific means, and not to commence hostilities until every effort had been made to secure the murderer. An agent was sent out, in cooperation with the troops, to try and get the murderer and preserve the peace. He failed, the Indians refusing to deliver him up. The agent went with Captain McLane, with instructions to prevent hostilities until a council could be held with the chiefs, but on the way Captain McLane met some Indians and attacked them, getting wounded himself. Notwithstanding this attack, the Indians were collected and a council was held, but it resulted in nothing, the Indians stating they had no authority to deliver up the murderer, but offered to pay any price for the negro killed. The offer was refused, the troops insisting upon the delivery of his murderer. The consequence was open hostilities. The troops moved against the Indians in every direction, but they were not sufficiently damaged to bring them to terms. General Garland concurred in this opinion, but was relieved about this time by Colonel Bonneville. This war continued until some time in November, when an armistice was concluded for thirty days. Colonel Bonneville and I went out to see the Indians at the expiration of the armistice, which was about December 25, at which time we concluded a peace with them. My opinion was that the war had been improperly commenced, and was improperly concluded by not making the Indians comply with the demand made upon them. The treaty was never carried into effect, and in the summer of 1859 another expedition was sent against the Indians,

under Major Simonson. He went out with instructions to enforce that condition of the treaty which required the Navajos to
surrender all the stock they had taken during the hostilities. He
failed to do so. That expedition was as great a failure as the
other. Hostilities continued. The Indians continued their depredations, committing robberies and murders to a considerable extent, until 1860, when General Canby took command and made
an expedition against them. During this time the Mexicans
turned loose upon them, captured a good many of their women
and children. General Canby was not very successful in his expedition. He went into their country, they asked for peace, and he
made a treaty with them and withdrew the troops. They, however, continued their hostile depredations just about as before.

The war of the rebellion caused a suspension of hostilities
between American troops and the Navajos:

About that time the Rebellion broke out, and the Texans made
their invasion. All the troops were withdrawn from the Navajo
country. The Navajos continued their depredations as usual. . . .
I cannot say I could, but I was encouraged to think, but for the
difficulty about the meadow lands and the killing of the negro
boy of Major Brooks, I would have been able to maintain peace
with the Indians. The impression was that they were becoming
more pacific. The Indians told me in council that they had agreed
to surrender the meadow lands to the post. That year there was
a drought. The Indians told me that they did not intend to vio-
late the arrangement about the grass. I was with the expedition
of 1849 under Colonel Washington and passed over a good deal
of the Navajo country. We passed into the country at the head
of the Chaco *arroya;* went through the valleys; and in one, the
valley of Chella, there were perhaps 400 or 500 acres under cultivation, the crops that year looking well. It was a rainy season,
and grain and crops looked well, Indian corn, pumpkins and
peaches. The valley of the Chella has no running water, it sinks
into the sand, and crops there will grow without irrigation;
think the whole amount of cultivation in all the valleys would
reach 1,500 to 2,000 acres. Such is the character of the Navajo
country that there is rain, say once in four or five years; there is
a good crop, and other years a failure. There is plenty of timber
—pine, some scrub oak. Some of the water brackish, some good.
Water in the valley of Chella is good. Water at Fort Defiance
very good.[33]

Regardless of past history, the time came in the early part of 1863, when American troops began a war against the Navajos, which was to make them pay a frightful toll for their transgressions. New Mexico volunteers, commanded by Lieutenant Colonel J. Francisco Chaves, arrived at Fort Wingate on Feb. 1, 1863, marking the first step in Carleton's campaign to chastise the tribe. Complying with Carleton's instructions, Chaves held a council with Navajo chiefs, at Fort Wingate in early summer of 1863. He urged them to get their people to come to terms. Carleton had told Chaves, in a letter written on June 23, 1863, that July 20 would be the time-limit. After that date there would be no more talking:

Send for Delgadito and Barboncito again and repeat what I before told them, and tell them that I shall feel very sorry if they refuse to come in; that we have no desire to make war upon them and other good Navajos; but the troops cannot tell the good from the bad, and we neither can nor will tolerate their staying as a peace party among those against whom we intend to make war. Tell them they can have until the twentieth day of July of this year to come in—they and all those who belong to what they call the peace party; that after that day every Navajo that is seen will be considered as hostile and treated accordingly; that after that day the door now open will be closed. Tell them to say this to all their people, and that as sure as that the sun shines all this will come true.[34]

By April 14, 1863, the First Regiment, New Mexico Volunteers, under the command of Colonel Kit Carson, was getting ready to move against the Navajos. The Rio Abajo *Press,* in Albuquerque, in an editorial, recalled that "Colonel Bonneville, in 1859, had told the Navajos what would happen to them, if they did not behave themselves," and had warned them that "they would be hunted from mountain to mountain, like wolves." Carleton issued a proclamation in Santa Fe on June 15, giving reasons for going to war against the Navajos:

For a long time past the Navajo Indians have murdered and robbed the people of New Mexico. Last winter, when eighteen of their chiefs came to Santa Fe to have a talk, they were warned, and were told to inform their people, that for these murders and robberies, the tribe must be punished, unless some binding guarantees should be given that in the future these outrages should cease. No guarantees have yet been given; but on the contrary, additional murders and additional robberies have been perpetrated upon the persons and property of our unoffending citizens. It is, therefore, ordered that Colonel Christopher Carson, with a proper military force, proceed without delay to a point in the Navajo country known as Pueblo Colorado, and there establish a depot for his supplies and hospital, and thence to prosecute a vigorous war upon the men of this tribe until it is considered, at these headquarters, that they have been effectually punished for their long continued atrocities. . . . Unless otherwise ordered by competent authority, this new post will be known as Fort Canby, in honor of Gen. E. R. S. Canby, United States Army, the recent commander of the department of New Mexico.

Carson's command consisted of 27 officers, 476 mounted, and 260 dismounted men. Although most of the soldiers were New Mexicans, the command included a number of regulars from Fort Union, and a sprinkling of officers and men from the California Column. On July 10, Carleton went to Los Pinos, the mobilization point for Carson's troops, 20 miles south of Albuquerque, to give last minute instructions for the campaign.[35]

In its inception the campaign against the Navajos appeared to meet with favor on the part of the people of New Mexico. Members of the militia were glad to have an opportunity to serve under a commander widely known as a hunter, trapper and mountain man, and as a soldier and Indian fighter in the years of his maturity. It was generally conceded that Carson had "given a good account of himself," at the battle of Valverde, on Feb. 22, 1862, and had emerged from it "with his reputation for energy and courage untarnished." [36] Relatives and friends said farewell to the troops at Los Pinos on July 7, 1863, as they started for the Navajo country, singing a popular song of the day:

> Get de bones, get de banjo,
> Get de soundin' tambourine;
> When de 'casion calls for moosic,
> You can count dis darkey in.[37]

Carson's troops left Los Pinos on July 7, 1863, reached Fort Wingate on July 14, and were at Fort Defiance, in the heart of the Navajo country, on July 20. A band of Ute scouts joined Carson at Fort Defiance, ready and anxious to fight against the Navajos — their traditional enemy. Carson gave the Utes rations, rifles and ammunition, and told them to go out and find the Navajos. Within a week the Utes reported to Carson that they had killed eight Navajo men and captured four women and seven children.

That Kit Carson had requested permission to use Utes in the campaign against the Navajos was evidenced by a letter General Carleton wrote to the War Department on June 1, 1863:

I beg respectfully to submit, with my approval, Colonel Carson's request, for consideration of the war department, believing the money expended in the employment of these Indians to use against the Navajos will be profitably laid out. The Utes are very brave, and fine shots, fine trailers, and uncommonly energetic in the field. The Navajos have entertained a very great dread of them for many years. I believe one hundred Ute Indians would render more service in this war than more than double their number of troops. They could be mustered as a company, or preferably, could be employed as spies and guides.[38]

Willing enough to track down and kill Navajo men, the Utes asked Carson's permission to keep captured women and children "for their own use and benefit." Carson wrote to Carleton from Fort Defiance on July 24, 1863, asking him to approve such an arrangement, saying there was no other way "to sufficiently recompense these Indians for their invaluable services." Carson was anxious to have the arrangement authorized for the Utes. In his letter Carson told Carleton:

As a general thing, the Utes dispose of their captives to Mexican families, where they are fed and taken care of, and thus cease to require any further attention on the part of the government. Besides this, their being distributed as servants through the Territory causes them to lose that collectiveness of interest as a tribe which they will retain if kept at any one place.... The Utes more than come up to the expectations I had formed of their efficiency as spies, nor can any small straggling parties of Navajos hope to escape them.

The War Department would not permit the Utes to retain captive Navajo women and children, and Carleton instructed Carson on Aug. 18 to send all Navajo captives, without exception, to Santa Fe, where the superintendent of Indian Affairs would "make such disposition as to their future care and destination as might seem humane and proper."

In order to "stimulate the zeal of the troops and employees," Carleton authorized Carson to pay twenty dollars for every serviceable horse and one dollar for every sheep captured from the Navajos and delivered to the quartermaster.

Determined to carry on his campaign in the heart of the Navajo country, Carson established a supply depot named Fort Canby "in a place known as the Pueblo Colorado, near a mountain, about 21 miles westward from old Fort Defiance, and about the best place that could have been selected for such an establishment." On July 24, 1863, Carson reported to Carleton:

The Navajos have planted a large quantity of grain this year. Their wheat is as good as I have ever seen. Corn is rather backward and not so plentiful.

By July 26, 1863, Carson was on a reconnaissance trip to the north and west of Fort Canby, on the lookout for Navajos everywhere.[39]

Needless to say, the Navajos were in no position, in 1863, to defend themselves in a war in which American troops were the aggressors. An inventory of their resources in that year would have disclosed that they had as many as fifty thousand sheep, hundreds of cattle, and thousands of horses. The horses, which they never shod, and never fed grain, had no worth beyond the fictitious value the Indians placed upon them. They had a few hundred Spencer rifles and Colt's revolvers, owned by individuals in scattered parts of the Indian country, and a small supply of lead and gunpowder, acquired from Mexican traders. They had a good many bows and arrows, but the Navajos were never considered expert bowmen. They owned many bridles, saddles, and saddle blankets of their own make. Unlike the Pueblo Indians, the Navajos were not a forehanded people, but lived from season to season with little thought of a tomorrow. As a result, when Carleton started the war against them, the Navajos had no surplus supplies of grain or food. Carleton and Carson calculated that it would be only a question of time until they would be starved into submission. To hasten the day of starvation, Carleton ordered Carson to cut down and destroy all wheat and corn in the Navajo country.

While the Utes ferreted out the Navajos, the Navajos retaliated by striking at Kit Carson at every opportunity. Soon after he had established Fort Canby they made a raid on his camp at nearby Black Rock, in the night time, ran off the sheep and goats in his commissary, butchered and cooked some of them almost within rifle shot range. In the same raid, the Navajos stole Kit Carson's favorite horse. Carson gave a rifle and provisions to Tabesi, his Piute Indian boy, and told him to stay on the trail until he got the horse. When two days had passed, and Tabesi had not returned, Carson felt certain that the Navajos had killed him.

On July 23 and 24, 1863, Carson returned to camp on the *Rio de Pueblo Colorado,* "after having been nearly thirty-six hours continuously in the saddle.[40] On July 25, as part of the plan to starve the Navajos into submission, Carson ordered Major Cummings to "send out a party tomorrow to bring in all the grain on this creek, which will amount to over 75,000 pounds of wheat and a large amount of corn; the latter, when dried, will answer for fodder for the animals in the winter." A detachment under Cummings' command chopped down the grain and carried it to Carson's camp, but the Navajos killed Cummings in retaliation within three weeks.[41] On August 6, Captain Pfeiffer, with an escort of ten men, destroyed 10 acres of corn. Returning from a scouting trip to the Moqui and Orabi valleys, Pfeiffer, on Aug. 19, destroyed 15 acres of wheat and 120 acres of corn in the Canon de Chelle country.

Ute scouts brought word to Carson that Navajos were finding sanctuary in Zuni Pueblo, and that they suspected that

Zunis were helping Navajos to escape from the net that had
been spread out to kill or capture them. Carson forwarded
this information to Carleton, and received a reply, written
from Santa Fe on Sept. 19, 1863, which threatened reprisal:

> I recommend, unless you can produce the same results by more
> gentle measures, that you seize 6 of the principal men of the Zuni
> Indians, and hold them as hostages until all Navajos in and near
> their villages are given up, and all stolen stock surrendered. You
> will assure the Zunis that if I hear that they help or harbor
> Navajos, or steal stock from any white men, or injure the person
> of any white men, I will as certainly destroy their village as that
> the sun shines.[42]

In his letter of Sept. 19, Carleton told Carson that the Navajos were to be given the choice of going to the Bosque or being
destroyed:

> If any Indians desire to give themselves up, they will be re-
> ceived and sent to Fort Wingate, with a request from that post
> that they be sent to Los Pinos. No Navajo Indians of either sex,
> or of any age, will be retained at Fort Canby, as servants, or in
> any capacity whatever; all must go to Bosque Redondo. You are
> right in believing that I do not wish to have those destroyed who
> are willing to come in. Nor will you permit an Indian prisoner
> once fairly in our custody to be killed, unless he be endeavoring
> to make his escape. There is to be no other alternative but this:
> say to them, "Go to the Bosque Redondo, or we will pursue and
> destroy you. We will not make any peace with you on any other
> terms. You have deceived us too often, and robbed and murdered
> our people too long, to trust you again at large in your own coun-
> try. This war shall be pursued against you if it takes years, now
> that we have begun, until you cease to exist or move. There can
> be no other talk on the subject." As winter approaches, you will
> have better luck.[43]

Governor Henry Connelly advised Secretary Seward in a
letter written from Santa Fe on Aug. 23, 1863, of the progress
of the Navajo campaign:

> There is nothing of importance transpiring within the imme-
> diate limits of the Territory, except the Navajo war, that would
> be worthy of your attention. The war is just beginning, and noth-
> ing yet has taken place that would indicate the success that may

attend our arms. There are now in the field against that tribe about twelve hundred men, well equipped and supplied, from whom much good is expected. The force is insufficient for the purpose of subjugation, but it is the most that General Carleton can spare from his scanty means for that part of the Territory. The remainder of the troops this side of the Jornada are stationed at Fort Craig, Pinos, and Albuquerque, on the Rio del Norte, and at Stanton, Union, and Garland, on the more eastern and northern frontiers, all of which are constantly in active service, pursuing small predatory bands of Indians that constantly infest the mountains and adjacent plains in search of property to carry off or lives to take. The depredations daily committed are astonishing, and, although much of the stock is recaptured by the troops, it is seldom that an Indian is killed or captured. They keep near the mountains, and when closely pursued, abandon the stock, and take refuge on foot in the heights and recesses of that safe retreat.

By Sept. 1, 1863, General Carleton had adopted a definite campaign policy. All male Navajo Indians who resisted American troops were to be shot and killed. All captives, and all who surrendered voluntarily, were to be sent to Bosque Redondo, a place Carleton had selected as a "reformatory for Indians," located on the Pecos river, near Fort Sumner, New Mexico, about four hundred miles east of the Little Colorado river. Carleton had inspected the Bosque Redondo country in 1852 and in 1854. On both occasions he had been impressed by the immense sweep of country. It seemed to him that the country offered great possibilities for resettlement of a large tribe of Indians. Carleton went to the Bosque a third time, in the spring of 1863, and decided that "there was not another area of vacant land between the Pecos and Colorado rivers that possessed the favorable inducements it seemed to offer as a rehabilitation center." The Bosque, as Carleton expressed it, "was a country with thousands of acres of rich bottom land on which it would be possible to grow a variety of crops of the kind required to support a great many people." The rolling plains spreading out in every direction seemed to offer ideal grazing for thousands of sheep and cattle, "plains over which the Navajo could not pass, and at the same time elude pursuit and capture." The Pecos river appeared to him "to be a stream that would always furnish sufficient water for irrigating large tracts of agricultural land; and there seemed no reason why excellent drinking water could not be developed at less than fifty feet." [44]

Convinced in his own mind that the Bosque Redondo was the ideal place in which to undertake the great experiment of transplanting the Navajo tribe, Carleton advised the War Department of his program on Sept. 6, 1863. The Navajos, according to the program, were to be captured and sent to the Bosque. The Bosque would serve as a "spacious tribal reformatory, away from the haunts and hills and hiding places of their country." Here the Navajos "would be treated kindly, the children taught to read and write, the old Indians would die off, and the young ones would take their place." Little by little, as Carleton expressed it, "the Navajos would become a happy, contented people." Carleton's preliminary report was optimistic:

I have the honor to report that I have this week sent fifty-one Navajo Indians—men, women and children, to Fort Sumner, at the Bosque Redondo, on the Pecos River, where, as I have informed you, I have four hundred and twenty-five Mescalero Apaches held as prisoners.

The purpose I have in view is to send all captured Navajos and Apaches to that point, and there to feed and take care of them until they have opened farms and become able to support themselves, as the Pueblo Indians of New Mexico are doing. The War Department has already approved of this in the case of the Apaches, and authorized that Fort Sumner should be a chaplain post, so that the chaplain there could educate the Indian children. This year those Indians have been contented and happy. They planted, under the direction of their agent, and with a little help, some large fields of corn; and now that they have their acequia dug, will next year raise quite enough to support themselves. This the Navajos can be persuaded to do as well.

Carleton believed, mistakenly, that the Apaches and Navajos spoke the same language. In his judgment, there was enough land at the Bosque for both tribes. He could see nothing to prevent the success of the project:

At the Bosque Redondo there is arable land enough for all the Indians of this family (the Navajos and Apaches have descended from the same stock and speak the same language), and I would respectfully recommend that now the war be vigorously prosecuted against the Navajos; that the only peace that can ever be made with them must rest on the basis that they move on to these lands, and cease to be nomads. This should be a sine qua non; as soon as the snows of winter admonish them of the suffering to which their families will be exposed, I have hopes of getting most of the tribe. The knowledge of the perfidy of these Navajos, gained after two centuries of experience, is such as to lead us to put no faith in their promises. They have no government to make treaties; they are a patriarchal people. One set of families may make promises, but the other set will not heed them. They understand the direct application of force as a law, if its application be removed that moment they become lawless. This has been tried over and over again, and at great expense.

The Navajos were not to be trusted any more than "the wolves that run through the mountains," as Carleton saw it:

The purpose now is, never to relax the application of force with a people that can no more be trusted than the wolves that run through the mountains. To collect them together, little by little, on to a reservation, away from the haunts, and hills, and hiding places of their country; there be kind to them; there teach their children how to read and write; teach them the arts of peace; teach them the truths of Christianity. Soon they will acquire new habits, new ideas, and new modes of life; and the old Indians will die off; and carry with them all latent belongings for murdering and robbing. The young ones will take their places without these belongings, and thus, little by little, they will become a happy and contented people; and Navajo wars will be remembered only as something that belongs entirely to the past. Even until they can raise enough to be self-sustaining, you can feed them cheaper than you can fight them.

There was no place in the Navajo country suitable for a reservation, in Carleton's opinion:

You will observe that the Bosque Redondo is far down the Pecos, on the open plains, where the Indians can have no lateral contact with settlers. If the government will only set apart a reservation of forty miles square, with Fort Sumner, at the Bosque Redondo, in the center, all the good land will be covered, and keep the settlers a proper distance from the Indians. There is no place in the Navajo country fit for a reservation; and even if there were, it would not be wise to have it there, for in a short time, the Indians would steal away into their mountain fastnesses again, and then, as of old, would come a new war, and so on ad infinitum. I know these views are practical and humane—are just to the suffering people, as well as to the aggressive, perfidious, butchering Navajos. If I can have one more full regiment of cavalry, and authority to raise one independent company in each county of the Territory, they can soon be carried to a final result.[45]

Carleton's orders, as Carson understood them, made it impossible for him to offer the Navajos any choice between bullets and starvation on the one hand, and unconditional surrender on the other. Carleton directed the Navajo campaign from his headquarters with zeal, efficiency, and with every indication of enthusiasm. He wrote letter after letter to his staff officers, spurring them on to greater efforts. Carleton's messages to his officers in the field revealed a fixed determination, amounting almost to an obsession, to get the Indians to Bosque Redondo alive, or to have them killed in the field. On Aug. 3, 1863, he wrote to Captain William H. Lewis, Commanding Officer at Albuquerque, ordering him to begin a thirty-day Indian hunt in the nearby Sandia mountains:

Send a company of infantry from your post to scour the eastern slope of the Sandia mountain country, from Tijeras Canyon northwardly towards the Placer Mountains, with instructions to kill every male Navajo or Apache Indian who is large enough to bear arms, and who may be living in the fastnesses of the region. The company will keep the field for thirty days and start at once.

On the same day, Carleton sent a "shoot to kill" order to Captain Samuel Archer, at Los Pinos, some twenty miles south of Albuquerque. The obvious purpose was to have Archer head off and kill any Indian who might try to escape from the Lewis dragnet:

Send a company of infantry from your post to scour the country thoroughly from Abo Pass northwardly along the eastern slope of the Manzano mountains to Tijeras canyon. The troops will not go into any towns lying east of the Manzano mountains, but

will be busy scouting, and will be instructed to kill every Navajo
or Apache Indian large enough to bear arms. No women or
children shall be killed; these will be captured and held until
further orders. . . . It is believed that in the fastnesses of those
mountains are many of these Indians. They will doubtless be
found well up toward or at the crest of the ridge. There are
points along the western base where there is water which can be
reached by wagons with rations from time to time. The subsistence to be carried in the mountains will be bacon, flour, sugar
and coffee. These will be carried by the men in haversacks, and
by a few pack mules from one point to another, where a wagon
can reach the base of the mountains, as the command progresses
northward.

In a message to Colonel Rigg, at Fort Craig, on August 4,
1863, Carleton suggested "lying in wait" tactics:

I have been informed that there is a spring called Ojo de Cibola
about fifteen miles west of Limitar, where the Navajos drive
their stolen cattle and "jerk" the flesh at their leisure. Cannot
you make arrangements for a party of resolute men from your
command to be stationed there, for, say, thirty days, and kill
every Navajo and Apache they can find? A cautious, wary commander, hiding his men, and moving about at night, might kill
a good many Indians near that point.

Two days later, August 6, 1863, Carleton lectured Rigg in
a letter in which he chided him for lack of results, citing the
things he, Carleton, had accomplished years before, in track-
ing down Apaches, with Kit Carson as a guide:

It is sincerely hoped, and expected, that you will be able to arrange some plan by which the predatory bands of Indians infesting your district may be destroyed. This is a subject that not only
demands your attention, but your action. The troops must be
kept after the Indians, not in big bodies, with military noises and
smokes, and the gleam of arms by day, and fires, and talk, and
comfortable sleep by night; but in small parties moving stealthily
to their haunts and lying patiently in wait for them; or by following their tracks day after day with a fixedness of purpose that
never gives up. In this way, as large a command as that at Craig
ought not to be run over or hooted at by a few naked Indians
armed with bows and arrows. Some flour, bacon, a little coffee
and sugar, thrown on a pack mule, with the men carrying say

two or three days' rations in their haversacks, and it will surprise the country what a few resolute men can do. If a hunter goes after a deer, he tries all sorts of wiles to get within gunshot of it. An Indian is a more watchful and a more wary animal than a deer. He must be hunted with skill; he cannot be blundered upon; nor will he allow his pursuers to come upon him when he knows it, unless he is the stronger.

I have made these few remarks because I desire you to impress upon your officers and men the utter folly of going after Indians unless these rules are observed. I once, in this country, with some good trackers under Kit Carson, followed a trail of Apaches for over a fortnight. I caught them. Others can do as well.

On August 17, 1863, Carleton ordered Lieut. Erastus W. Wood, five non-commissioned officers, and thirty-one privates from Company A, 1st Infantry, California Volunteers, to go to the Valles, near Jemez Springs, forty miles west of Santa Fe, "and there, and in that vicinity, to lie in wait for thirty days, to kill every Navajo or Apache Indian who attempts to go through that noted thoroughfare. No women and children will be harmed; these will be captured." Five weeks later, on Sept. 27, Lieutenant P. A. J. Russell, with 4 mounted men of the California Volunteers, and a party of Pueblo Indians, started from Valle Grande in the Jemez mountains, trailing a band of Navajos, which had recently stolen stock from Pueblo villages, on the Rio Grande. Russell's command surprised the Navajos at Jemez Springs, killed 8 men, captured 20 women and children, recovered 125 sheep and 2 horses.

The ground at Fort Canby and in the Canon de Chelle country was covered with a foot of snow by Nov. 1, 1863, an event which moved the regimental poet laureate to compose "Johnny Navajo," eight verses of which were published in the Rio Abajo *Press* of Dec. 8. The bandmaster at Fort Canby set the words to music. One verse of the eight:

> Come dress your ranks, my gallant souls, a standing in a row,
> Kit Carson he is waiting to march against the foe;
> At night we march to Moqui o'er lofty hills of snow,
> To meet and crush the savage foe, bold Johnny Navajo.
> Johnny Navajo! O Johnny Navajo!
> We'll first chastise, then civilize, bold Johnny Navajo.

When the statistics for 1863 were released at military headquarters in Santa Fe, it was found that the Indian campaign had resulted as follows: Indians killed, 301; wounded, 87; captured, 703. Soldiers killed, 14; wounded, 21; officers killed, 3; wounded, 4. Assistant Adjutant General Cutler issued an order of the day on Feb. 24, 1864, praising the troops for their splendid accomplishments in 1863:

The zeal and energy shown by the officers and soldiers, and the fortitude with which they have encountered hunger, thirst, fatigue and exposure, in their pursuit of hostile Indians within this department during the past year, are deserving of the highest admiration. Not less is this due to those parties who were so unfortunate as not to overtake the Indians than those who came up with them. All toiled and suffered alike. The gallantry which every one has shown when there was an opportunity to close with the enemy, proves that virtue among the troops in New Mexico is common to all.

New Mexico's citizen-soldiers came in for general commendation:

The alacrity with which citizens of New Mexico have taken the field to pursue and encounter the Indians is worthy of all praise. Many of them have been conspicuous for their courage, and all have shown a settled determination to assist the military in their efforts to rid the country of the fierce and brutal robbers and murderers who for nearly two centuries have brought poverty to its inhabitants, and mourning and desolation to nearly every hearth throughout the Territory.

Cutler predicted that the year 1864 would see the end of hostilities that had lasted 180 years:

The department commander congratulates the troops and the people on the auspicious opening of the year 1864. For one hundred eighty years the Navajo Indians have ravaged New Mexico, but it is confidently expected that the year 1864 will witness the end of hostilities with that tribe. Then New Mexico will take a stride towards that great prosperity which has lain within her grasp, but which hitherto she has not been permitted to enjoy.[46]

While the entire area was covered with deep snow, Colonel Kit Carson left Fort Canby on Jan. 6, 1864, with 375 men, and reached the mouth of the renowned Canon de Chelle in six days. Entering the canyon, Carson's troops killed 23 Navajos, wounded many others, took 34 prisoners and 200 sheep. Two hundred Navajos, men, women and children, surrendered at daybreak the next day. They told Carson that their people were "in a complete state of starvation, and that many of their women and children had already died from this cause." Starving women captives, clothed in rags, clung tightly to their children, plainly in a starving condition, fearful that they would be taken from them and killed. The prisoners told Carson that for ten days before surrender they had eaten nothing but cedar berries and piñon nuts, and that all the men would give up if they understood the conditions of surrender, and could be assured of being protected from violence.[47] Carson sent messengers into the canyon to herald far and wide that until 10 o'clock the next morning all Navajos could surrender, and could rely on his promise that they would be fed and would not be punished. On the same day Carson sent Captain Carey, with a detachment of 75 men, into the canyon, with instructions to explore it from east to west and to destroy all the peach orchards, "of which there were many," and to destroy the dwellings of the Indians.[48]

Carson reported the details of the Cañon de Chelle expedition to Carleton, adding a bit of embroidery, probably the work of a diligent staff officer:

We have shown the Indians that in no place, however formidable or inaccessible in their opinion, are they safe from the pursuit of the troops of this command, and have convinced a large portion of them that struggle on their part is a hopeless one. We have demonstrated that the intentions of the government toward them are eminently humane, and dictated by an earnest desire to promote their welfare; that the principle is not to destroy, but to save them, if they are disposed to be saved. When all this is understood by the Navajos generally, as it soon will be, and when they become convinced that destruction will follow on resistance, they will gladly avail themselves of the opportunities offered them of peace and plenty under the fostering care of the government, as do all those now with whom I have had any means of communicating. They are arriving almost hourly, and will, I believe, continue to arrive until the last Indian in this section of the country is enroute to the Bosque Redondo. The benefits to the government and the Territory of this wise policy introduced by the general commanding with regard to these Indians cannot be too highly estimated. It has been repeatedly demonstrated that any treaties heretofore made with those people, so long as they were permitted to remain in their country, were entirely disregarded as soon as the force applied to them was removed, and both by inclination and from want they recommenced to murder and rob the citizens. The policy of placing them on reservations changes all this. The force will still bear upon them, but without oppressing them, and their wants will be supplied until such time as by their industry they are able to supply themselves.

Supplementing Carson's report, Captain A. H. Pfeiffer, of the First Cavalry, New Mexico Volunteers, sent in a report which told of his experiences in the Cañon de Chelle campaign:

Indians on both sides, whooping, yelling and cursing, firing shots and throwing rocks down upon my command. Killed 2 buck Indians in the encounter and 1 squaw, who obstinately persisted in hurling rocks and pieces of wood at the soldiers. Six prisoners were captured on this occasion.... On account of the fighting and necessity of being constantly on the lookout, I was unable to destroy a large orchard of peach trees.... At some places the canon spreads out like a beautiful savanna, where the cornfields of the savages are laid out with farmer-like taste, and supplied with *acequias* for irrigation. At other places the canon is confined to a narrow compass in a zigzag, meandering course, with high projecting rocks, and houses built thereon, perforated with caverns and mountain fastnesses 300 or 400 feet above the ground as hiding places. Here the Navajos sought refuge when pursued by the government, and here they were enabled to jump about on the ledges of the rocks like mountain cats, hallooing at me, swearing and cursing and threatening vengeance on my command in every variety of Spanish they were capable of mastering. A couple of shots from my soldiers with their trusty rifles caused the redskins to instantly disperse, and gave me a safe passage through this celebrated Gibralter of Navajodom. At the place where I encamped the curl of the smoke from my fires ascended to where a large body of Indians were resting over my head, but the height was so great that the Indians did not look larger than crows, and as we were too far apart to injure each other no damage was done, except with the tongue, the articulation of which was scarcely audible.[49]

Writing from Las Cruces, on Feb. 7, 1864, Carleton told General Thomas, in Washington, in rather glowing words, of the success that had attended the expedition into the Canon de Chelle:

It will be seen by these papers that the operations of the troops during the severely cold weather has been of the most praiseworthy character, and been crowned with unparalleled success. This is the first time any troops, whether the country belonged to Mexico or since we acquired it, have been able to pass through the Canon de Chelle, which, for its great depth, its length, its perpendicular walls, and its labyrinthian character, has been regarded by eminent geologists as the most remarkable of any fissure upon the face of the globe. It has been the fortress of the tribe since time out of mind. To this point they have fled when pressed by our troops. Colonel Washington, Colonel Sumner, and many other commanders have made an attempt to go through it, but had to retrace their steps. It was reserved for Colonel Carson to be the first to succeed, and I respectfully request the government will favorably notice that officer and give him a substantial reward for this crowning act in a long life spent in various capacities in the service of his country fighting the savages among the fastnesses of the Rocky Mountains. . . .[50]

By Jan. 25, 1864, Carson was able to report that he had 500 Navajo prisoners at Fort Canby, and that 1,000 more were on their way to the fort to surrender. Carson added to his report:

I do not think I am premature in congratulating the general commanding on the speedy and successful result of his measures to restore permanent peace and security to the people of New Mexico.[51]

No doubt but that Carson was succeeding in his campaign to starve the Navajos into submission. By Feb. 1, 1864, hundreds of them were huddled together at Fort Canby, pending completion of arrangements to move them to Bosque Redondo. Ill, their appearance cadaverlike, their clothing mostly rags, the Navajo prisoners were indeed objects of pity. Hungry, weary, and frightened, they waited at Fort Canby, dreading the future, ready to believe as true the rumor that they were to be marched away "across three rivers," and then poisoned. Some few sympathetic soldiers at Fort Canby looked at the prisoners, and turned away, mumbling "poor creatures." And poor creatures they were indeed. Their wheat fields had been laid waste; their fruit trees had been chopped down and burned; their means of livelihood had been taken away.

The campaign had succeeded to such an extent that by March 1, 1864, Chief Herrera and 2,400 Navajo prisoners had been rounded up and were at Fort Canby waiting to start for the Bosque Redondo. The Bosque had not been officially established as an Apache reservation until that date; and no reservation had as yet been established for the Navajos. However, General Carleton was determined to place the Navajos, as well as the Apaches, at Bosque Redondo. The poet laureate of Carson's regiment had written another poem, expressing the sentiment of the day, which was published in the Abajo *Press* of March 22, 1864:

> They are gatherin' in fast,
> In each valley and plain,
> To remove from the land
> They shall ne'er see again;
> And their cry of deep sorrow will sadly echo,
> When they take a last look at their lov'd Navajo.

Captain Thompson, with a detachment of seven officers and 47 soldiers, started with his Navajo prisoners from Fort Canby for the Bosque at daylight on March 5. The 2,400 men walked in funeral-like procession, in twos and fours, silent, grim and gloomy. Small wonder the Navajos walked along as if on their way to the grave. During two weeks, between Feb. 20 and March 6, 1864, one hundred and twenty-six of their tribesmen had died at Fort Canby from disease, malnutrition, gunshot wounds, and other causes.[52] The Navajo prisoners were permitted to take 3,000 sheep and 473 horses with them to the Bosque. Thirty wagons carried equipment and supplies, eight of them pulled by ten mules each, twenty by six-mule teams.[53]

Following Carleton's orders, Thompson followed a route which took him to Fort Wingate, across the Rio Puerco and Rio Grande to Los Pinos, twenty miles south of Albuquerque, and thence east over the mountains towards the final destination. After many days, the Navajo caravan reached the Pecos river, crossed over to the east bank. Captain Thompson delivered his prisoners, the first large contingent to reach the Bosque, and took a receipt for them. The Navajos were assigned to a miserable camp in the Bosque Redondo. They were certain by this time that dreadful things would happen to them. They had been warned all their lives, from infancy on, against crossing three rivers. Forced to travel to the Bosque, they had violated all admonitions of mothers and medicine men. They had crossed three rivers, the Rio Puerco, the Rio Grande, and the Pecos.

Now in their new environment, even the bravest of the Navajos were dazed and cowed. Ignorant of what the future might hold for them, they dreaded the uncertainty as a frightened child dreads the dark of night. Without tools of any kind, the Navajo men were put to work building mud houses, but their progress was unsatisfactory. Such work was beyond their experience. Officers from Fort Sumner, a mile and a half north of the Bosque, visited the prison camp occasionally, but never remained for any length of time. Sentinels, carrying guns, guarded the Navajo prisoners closely, instructed to shoot any who might try to escape. A stoic and silent people, the Navajos were stunned when at long last they were prisoners, and in an alien land. They had little to eat, and scant protection, night or day, against wind and weather. The Navajos were too cowed to murmur openly. Some of them looked to the sun by day, and to the moon and stars by night, praying for deliverance from bondage. Some of them, homesick and heartsick, listened to the hum of western wind, seeking a mystic whisper of hope and encouragement.[54]

As predicted in Assistant Adjutant General Cutler's pronouncement of Feb. 24, 1864, the Navajo campaign gained momentum in 1864, a year destined to be fateful for the entire tribe. In a detailed recital of activities for 1864, published in Santa Fe on Feb. 18, 1865, Cutler told of the most important events of the year. He stressed the hardships endured by the military, and indicated possibilities for a successful termination of the campaign:

During the year 1864, the few troops serving within the department of New Mexico were obliged to undergo extraordinary labors, privations and hardships in following the line of their duty. Early in the year while the country was still covered with snow, their marches in pursuit of Navajo Indians, in continuation of the campaign begun in the summer of 1863, the frequent combats with bands of that tribe, not only in the Navajo country, but in the open plains to the east of the Rio Grande, and the will to encounter and endure hardships, on the part of both officers and men, which would be creditable to any troops in the army. It was often their lot to be compelled, from the nature of the country, and sometimes from limited means of transportation, to carry their blankets and provisions on their backs, and to struggle for days through deep snows, over mountains, through forests, and down through the deep mazes of the most wonderful canons in the world, in pursuit of a wily and active enemy, who was familiar with every rod of that distant and, in many places, hitherto inaccessible region.

Cutler was lavish in his praise of the soldiers who fought against Navajos:

It was their lot to feel that even though they were successful in their efforts, far beyond the success which had attended the labors of others who had preceded them in campaigns against the Navajos, still they would win none of that *eclat* which those received for, perhaps, no harder service on other fields. It was their lot to show fidelity, and integrity, and earnestness in their labors for the public good—prompted to this course, not by the expectation of applause or advancement, but by a feeling honestly to discharge their duty, though no approving eye witnessed their labors or their sufferings, and they had no credit save that shown in the mirror of a clear conscience, or by the approval of their own hearts. The results which followed such labors will be considered as remarkable in the annals of Indian warfare.

While troops under Kit Carson's direction continued the Navajo round-up in the Canon de Chelle country, Navajos already captured and held at Bosque Redondo, were making desperate attempts to escape. One hundred Navajos made a break and got away from the Bosque on Jan. 5, 1864. A troop of cavalry from Fort Sumner, accompanied by twenty-five Mescalero Apaches as scouts and guides, pursued the Navajos and overtook them twelve miles west of the Pecos river. In the fighting that followed forty Navajos were killed, ten wounded, fifty recaptured and returned to the Bosque in irons.[55]

Although all Mescalero Apaches had presumably been surrendered, and were in detention camp at Bosque Redondo, there were signs from time to time that some Mescaleros were still at large. Carleton was notified in Santa Fe on Aug. 12, 1864, that Mescalero Apaches had stolen fifty mules belonging to A. M. Parker, while Parker was traveling on the Fort Stanton road enroute from Santa Fe to El Paso. It was reported that the Mescaleros had driven the mules into the Dog Canyon country in the Sacramento Mountains. Carleton ordered the commanding officers at Fort Craig and Fort McRae, "to get on the trail, with men and guides, to take twenty days supply of flour, bacon, sugar and coffee, no bedding, to go light and catch the Indians." Carleton's order was quite specific: "Rescue the mules and destroy the Indians. . . . Every man must be a Cossack in going lightly equipped, and a hero when the Indians are come up with, and good luck attend you." [56]

Although Bosque Redondo was within striking distance of the Mescalero Apache country, nevertheless the Mescaleros imprisoned there were dissatisfied and unhappy. Much of the dissatisfaction resulted from the fact that Navajo and Mescalero had never been very friendly, but the principal irritant was that Navajo prisoners greatly outnumbered Mescalero prisoners. As a result of the dissatisfaction with their plight, the entire Mescalero population, men, women and children, left the Bosque for their own country on Nov. 10, 1865. When Carleton learned that the Mescaleros had escaped, he sent a characteristic message to Major Emil Fritz,[57] commanding officer at Fort Stanton:

You have doubtless heard of the escape of the Mescalero Apaches from the Bosque Redondo. Now is not the time for yourself or your command to swap horses. Keep everything in order for fighting—everything on the alert. Help the people with all possible protection. Show in your own person no boy's play now. Those Indians have got to be recaptured or killed, the men, and I want your zealous help at once, and with no relaxation, to do it until it is done. Raise the whole of that part of the country to a determined spirit to get those Indians now, or they will never enjoy quiet or security. Keep a record of all you do. If the people will rise as one man the Indians will soon succumb; but if there is dilly dallying and talk and no energy on the part of the troops and the people that part of the country might as well be given up to the Indians first as last. . . . You can have no drones about your hive now; all must work.[58]

CHAPTER THREE

Baylor, Governor of Arizona

THE CONFEDERATE TERRITORY OF ARIZONA, formed from southern and western portions of New Mexico, was created by an Act of the Confederate Congress on March 10, 1861. A year later, March 13, 1862, President Jefferson Davis nominated John Robert Baylor, "Colonel Commanding of the Second Regiment, Texas Mounted Rifles," to be governor of Arizona. The Senate promptly confirmed Baylor's nomination, as well as nominations of other officials for Arizona: Robert Josselyn, Mississippi, secretary of the Territory; Alexander M. Jackson, New Mexico, chief justice; Columbus Upson, Texas, associate justice; Russell Howard, Arizona, attorney general; Samuel J. Jones, Arizona, marshal.[59] Baylor had been de facto governor of Arizona since his proclamation at Mesilla on Aug. 2, 1861, a few days after his spectacular victory over Union troops near Fort Fillmore. Baylor purchased a home at Mesilla, the capital of the new territory, and conducted official business from there. The Confederate flag flew over many vantage points in New Mexico and Arizona in the spring of 1862. Governor Baylor had many problems to solve, some connected with military affairs, others relating to civil administration. As Baylor saw it, however, the problem demanding immediate attention was that of suppressing hostile Apache Indians. The Apaches had killed Baylor's soldiers, robbed his supply trains, and menaced his operations. No stagecoach, mail carrier or traveler on trail or highway was safe from attack by Indians. Baylor's authority extended over a vast area of Apache country, reaching from the Gila to the Mexican border and the Colorado river. Baylor was not a man to sit idly by and hear about Indian atrocities without attempting to fight back. He had lived in Indian country for many years and believed he knew considerable about Indians and their ways. Annoyed and exasperated beyond endurance, Baylor decided he would give the Apaches of Arizona an object lesson they would never forget. He wrote a letter on March 20, 1862, from Mesilla, to Captain Thomas Helm, commanding the Arizona Guards, at Tucson, ordering him to use a pretext to get the Indians in council, and then massacre the adults. Baylor's letter in part:

I learn from Lieut. J. J. Jackson that the Indians have been into your post for the purpose of making a treaty. The Congress of the Confederate States has passed a law declaring extermination to all hostile Indians.

Baylor told Helm how to proceed:

You will, therefore, use all means to persuade the Apaches or any other tribe to come in for the purpose of making peace, and when you get them together kill all the grown Indians and take the children prisoners and sell them to defray the expenses of killing the Indians. Buy whiskey and such other goods as may be necessary for the Indians and I will order vouchers given to cover the amount expended. Leave nothing undone to insure success, and have a sufficient number of men around to allow no Indian to escape. Say nothing of your orders until the time arrives, and be cautious how you let the Mexicans know it. If you can't trust them, send to Captain Aycock at this place, and he will send thirty men from his company—but use the Mexicans if they can be trusted, as bringing troops from here might excite suspicion with the Indians. To your judgment I instruct this important matter and look to you for success against these cursed pests who have already murdered over 100 men in this Territory.[60]

Sibley's defeat in New Mexico in the spring of 1862 meant the end, or so it seemed, to Baylor's dreams for the Confederate Territory of Arizona. But Baylor was a man of tougher fibre than Sibley. Even as Sibley was delivering his farewell to the remnant of his brigade in El Paso on May 14, 1862, Baylor was in Richmond promoting another plan for recapturing New Mexico and Arizona. In his dual capacity as "Governor of Arizona," and Colonel of Texas Riflemen, Baylor laid his reinvasion plans before his superior officers. Addressed as "Governor of Arizona," "Present," in Richmond, Baylor received written authority from Secretary of War George W. Randolph on May 29, 1862, to raise five battalions of partisan rangers of six companies each, either mounted or on foot, "to be regularly enlisted and mustered into service for war." The rangers were to receive bounty with the pay of other volunteers, but were to be obliged to furnish, so far as possible, their own arms and equipment, and the mounted men their own horses. To quote briefly from Randolph's order:

These troops will be under your command as Governor of Arizona, and will be organized under your direction. Field officers will be appointed to each battalion upon your recommendation; company officers must be elected. One battalion may be enlisted for twelve months, into which no person liable to conscription can be admitted.[61]

Baylor spent the months of June and July furthering his reinvasion plans. Having accomplished as much as possible in the interest of his plans in Richmond, Baylor was in San Antonio on Aug. 1, 1862, where he announced that he had been officially authorized to raise an army of 6,000 men and to "retake and hold New Mexico at all hazards." The reinvasion, according to Baylor's plans, was to be financed with money furnished through French drafts given in exchange for cotton delivered in Mexico.[62]

News of Baylor's newly projected campaign spread quickly throughout New Mexico and Arizona. Secessionist leaders in El Paso were jubilant when they learned that Baylor might fight again, according to a letter written at Hart's Mill, Texas, on Nov. 11, 1862, by Major Rigg, addressed to Colonel West, then in command of Union troops in the District of Arizona, with headquarters at Mesilla. Information available to Rigg had convinced him that Baylor had raised 6,000 men, and that only solution of transportation problems then stood in the way of speedy movement of troops from Texas to New Mexico. Conditions in New Mexico were much different in the fall of 1862, however, than at the time of Baylor's first invasion in the summer of 1861. Now, instead of contending with a frightened and confused Major Isaac Lynde at Fort Fillmore, Baylor's reinvasion forces, if they attempted to march into New Mexico, would be forced to fight troops from California commanded by General Carleton, which had arrived in New Mexico in detachments beginning on July 4, 1862. Anxious to prevent Baylor from getting a foothold in New Mexico, Carleton wrote from Santa Fe to Colonel West, in Mesilla, on Nov. 18, 1862, outlining a comprehensive plan of offense and defense. As Carleton envisaged Baylor's movements, it would be necessary for him, before reaching the Rio Grande in New Mexico, to march his troops more than 600 miles from the point of mobilization in Texas. While Baylor's troops marched toward El Paso, it would be possible for

West, in Carleton's opinion, to adopt effective defense measures. Carleton instructed West to commandeer all the grain in the Rio Grande valley, by purchase if possible, by confiscation if necessary; and to arrest and imprison every person suspected of disloyalty to the Union:

You will at once secure all the corn and grain which you can possibly buy from the people at San Elizario, Socorro, Ysleta, Franklin, La Mesa, La Mesilla, Las Cruces and Dona Ana, commencing at the points lowest down on the Rio Grande, and so on up, and have it all carefully stored and guarded at Mesilla. If the people will not sell it to you it must be seized and receipt given for it. Offer and pay a fair, even a liberal, price for it, and avoid any appearance of coercion until all other means fail. . . . The people living in El Paso County, Texas, as well as those living in the Mesilla Valley, should be be caused to believe that when the Texans come it will be again to fatten upon them without pay; that rather than submit to this it will be better for them to move their families for the time being into El Paso, on the Mexican side, or above the Jornada del Muerto. So far as we are concerned it would be better that they move to El Paso, so as to help exhaust the provisions on that side of the river. . . . When the enemy is near, all good Union men among the Americans will rally around you. All doubtful Americans and foreigners, the moment the enemy appears, are to be seized and sent, strongly guarded, to Fort Craig. There, with a spade at least, they can help defend the flag which has hitherto protected them and which they would now desert. . . .

West was to set fire to the property of known Southern sympathizers, and to lay waste the means of making bread:

The houses and stores owned by secessionists who ran off to Texas, the enemy will expect to repossess when they come back. These, commencing at San Elizario and coming up, including those at Fort Bliss (burn off the roofs), Franklin, Hart's Mill and dwellings, and all of those belonging to this class of men in Mesilla and Las Cruces, will be laid in ashes. Of course the destruction of all the buildings herein enumerated will be the last thing done when you know the enemy is coming, and before you feel compelled to retire. You will also destroy Bull's Mill, at Mesilla, and Grandjean's Mill, at Las Cruces, in case you are compelled to fall back. Thus you must not only take the breadstuffs, but you must destroy as far as possible all means of making bread by the rebels. The Mexican population who prefer to remain behind can grind their corn on *metates* as of old; so that the destruction of these mills will be no serious blow to them. You know that the destruction of these mills and all the fine quarters I have named will embarrass Baylor and his forces to a very great degree. I am aware of just how sharp you will look out and how hard and effectually you will work to cripple him in other ways than these which I have enumerated.[63]

Carleton ordered West to sweep the country clean of live-stock in advance of Baylor's coming, and to destroy all means of river transportation:

As a further injury, when you are sure he is near at hand, buy up or take on receipts all cattle and horses and mules which you can get and have them driven northward well out of the way. The ferry boats on the Rio Grande will all, large and small, be destroyed, as well as all lumber with which others can be made.

Believing that the Mexican population could be incited to undertake guerrilla warfare against the Baylor forces, Carleton suggested that they be encouraged to become active in widespread terrorism:

You will remind the Mexicans of how they were robbed before, and animate them, as you can do, with a settled determination to attack the enemy from every cover; to shoot down his teams; to stampede his stock when grazing; to destroy the bridges over the *acequias;* to hover by night around his camps; to set fire to the grass and all kinds of fodder which his animals might otherwise get; to shoot down his men by night; and then before day scatter singly in all directions, and then to repeat this over and over again until he feels the just vengeance of a people who never did him harm, but whom before he wantonly and ruthlessly insulted, oppressed and robbed. Inspire them with this, and let me know the number of arms you can safely place in their hands, and I will have them nearby, so that you can distribute them at the last moment.

Carleton complimented West highly, urged him to demonstrate for Baylor's benefit the calibre of California troops:

Your duty in general terms is marked out, and I know you will do it well. If I had to choose a man for the place you are now on, I tell you frankly I should choose yourself. Instill into the minds of all your subordinates but half your address, your energy, your forecast, your resolution, and Baylor and his people will have reason to remember the handful of Californians he may find below the Jornada.[64]

Notwithstanding the possibility that Baylor might attempt a second invasion of New Mexico, General Carleton was confident enough of the strength of his position to release the Colorado troops which had helped to defeat Sibley, expressing his views in a letter written from Santa Fe to Governor John Evans, at Denver City, on January 28, 1863:

That the so called southern Confederacy, looking to a permanent separation from the Union, will desire to have a strip of territory extending across the continent to cover the silver and gold fields of Arizona and to have a port on the Pacific there cannot be a doubt; and that there will be a strong effort made to this end sooner or later, unless we are more successful in the East than we have recently been, is more than probable.[65]

The fortunes of war and other untoward circumstances prevented John R. Baylor from carrying out his ambitious plan for a second invasion of New Mexico. There were other and weightier reasons, perhaps, but one of the contributing factors to the decision by Confederate leaders to abandon support of the contemplated expedition, was Baylor's Indian entrapment letter of March 20, 1862. A copy of the letter found its way into unfriendly hands and it was used effectively in many places, in and out of Indian country, as evidence of the existence of a definite Confederate policy to exterminate the Indian tribes. When criticized in Richmond and elsewhere because of his "kill the Indians" order, Baylor pleaded justification. In a long and interesting letter written from Houston, Texas, on Dec. 29, 1862, to Major General J. Bankhead Macgruder, commanding the District of Texas, New Mexico and Arizona, Baylor told Macgruder that the order for wiping out the Apaches had not been intended for publication; that he did not expect it would "be paraded before the country as it has been by the malice of those who entertain no good feeling for me." Writing on "Governor of Arizona" stationery, Baylor refused to recant or apologize for his conduct:

I do not feel it consistent with my opinions and feelings on the subject of Indians and Indian policy to retract or disavow a word of the order referred to. . . . While I sincerely regret that it has been viewed in such an unfavorable light by His Excellency the President, as to induce him to deprive me of the command of the brave men, most of whom are my old frontier comrades whom I was prepared to lead to battle against both abolition and savage foe, yet I cannot alter the convictions and feelings of a life time. I can still do my country some service should my State be invaded, and in that hour Texans, I know, will not refuse me a place in their ranks to meet and exterminate a foe hardly less cruel and remorseless than the Comanche or the Apache.[66]

The intelligence that Baylor's reinvasion plans of 1862 had been countermanded had not reached Union officers as late as May 15, 1863. General West wrote from Mesilla on that date to Carleton in Santa Fe, saying that he was still expecting the Texans to return, and strongly recommended fighting to retain the Mesilla Valley, saying: "To abandon this valley without a struggle to hold it, would demoralize its people and destroy their faith in the protection of the government." In a clear sighted statement, West expressed the belief that the then current campaign against the Apaches should be suspended if it became necessary to fight Baylor: "The Texans are our immediate foes. To punish the Indians will contribute nothing toward suppressing the rebellion. That is the object of this war, I take it, and I cannot bring myself to believe that it is good policy to give up one foot of territory here we now hold. . . . If the troops I have asked for are sent to me, a Texan will never be seen north of the Jornada, except as a prisoner." [67]

Even as late as December 31, 1864, John R. Baylor clung tenaciously to his belief that the Confederacy should look to New Mexico for help in recruiting men for the cause. In Richmond at the time, Baylor wrote to Secretary of War James A. Seddon exploring the possibilities:

In the present emergency, when the resources of the country are so far exhausted, it becomes a question of paramount importance as to where recruits can be had for our armies, and every effort should be made to fill up our decimated ranks.... The only section where men of southern birth can be raised in large numbers, who sympathize with us and who would join us in this struggle, is southern California and New Mexico. A considerable number might be raised on the Rio Grande. The only plan for getting those men from southern California is to send an expedition for the recapture of Arizona. This would open the route into southern California and enable those who are disposed to join us, to do so ... from 15,000 to 20,000 men could be raised in southern California ... and one or two brigades of New Mexicans could be raised.... In order to accomplish this it would be necessary to send an expedition of 2,500 men and retake Arizona, and if possible, New Mexico.... Another field for recruiting would be Mexico.... Should the government conclude to undertake such a move as I have indicated, I would suggest that a formidable alliance might be made with the numerous Indian tribes on the route between Missouri and New Mexico ... to the resources of New Mexico and Arizona and their ability to sustain the forces sent or raised there I have no question. An abundance of wheat, corn and stock is raised in that country to subsist any force the government would send there, except, perhaps, the beef, which can be driven from Texas with great ease.[68]

Willing to serve "in such rank as the President might think proper to confer," Baylor was optimistic over the possibilities of reoccupying Arizona:

In my opinion, the surest and speediest means of recruiting in those Territories would be to organize a force in the spring and make a sudden move upon Arizona, and occupy it, then send into the mines and recruit from among the miners, the greater part of whom are southern men, and at the same time organize the Mexican population, who would join us in considerable force, making, between the two, such a force as to hold the Territories unless a very strong force was sent against us, and in that event we could at any time fall back into Texas.... As to the means for carrying on this expedition, they can be furnished from the cotton which is in Texas in abundance ... and if that cannot be spared ... Texas has another means of raising specie which could be made available, and that is by the sale of beef cattle; thousands can be collected in western Texas and easily driven into Mexico and sold for specie. There are a number of refugees from New Mexico and Arizona who would not hesitate to contribute means for the recovery of their homes; among them are men of wealth who have offered assistance. Once in the Territories, which are now abundantly supplied with goods, enough property could be confiscated for the use of the government to defray the expenses of the troops, and as the United States government is now working numerous silver mines I see no reason why we might not control the same mines and make them yield a revenue for our purpose.[69]

President Jefferson Davis personally may have thought well of Baylor's plan, but passed it on for a final conference between Baylor and Secretary of War Seddon. Apparently, Seddon was not favorably impressed. He rejected Baylor's scheme in its entirety, believing it impractical and visionary. Baylor accepted Seddon's decision as gracefully as possible, but held firmly to the thought until the day he died that he could have enlisted a brigade of volunteers, and could have led them in person, in a grand, spirited, dashing campaign, which would have resulted in the recapture of Arizona, and probably New Mexico, for the flag and Southland he loved more than life itself.

The action of the Confederacy in establishing a "Territory of Arizona" was one of the important factors which prompted the Congress of the United States to divide New Mexico almost in half, north and south, and establish for the Union the "Territory of Arizona." In addition to the fact that the Confederacy was establishing a territory carved out of a part of New Mexico, the Congress perhaps considered, incidentally at least, the highly persuasive argument that Arizona was a potential Golconda, and that its gold deposits, if developed, would vastly increase the wealth of the nation.

The 1859 map of New Mexico compiled "chiefly for military purposes," by Secretary of War J. B. Floyd's Bureau of Topographical Engineers, shows the New Mexico of that time as being bounded on the north by Kansas and Utah, on the south by Texas and Mexico, on the east by Texas, and on the west by California. Although the name "Arizona" did not appear on the map of 1859, it was officially recognized under that name as a part of the Territory of New Mexico. New Mexico's attitude toward Arizona in the fifties was a bit contemptuous, the prevailing opinion being that it was a desert waste, inhabited by wild Indians, and of no importance to New Mexico, politically, economically or otherwise. Missouri, much further in distance from New Mexico, was of greater importance to New Mexico, and more accessible, than Arizona.

Following completion of the Gadsden purchase, the area known as Arizona was designated as a county of New Mexico. The village of Tubac was originally the county seat of the county of Arizona, but the New Mexico legislature on Jan. 8, 1861, changed the county seat to Tucson, and provided that "the district and probate courts of said county of Arizona" would thereafter be held at Tucson.[70] The legislature of 1861 authorized the governor of New Mexico to appoint probate judges and sheriffs for the counties of Dona Ana and Arizona, to hold office until an election to be held on Sept. 25, 1861. On Jan. 30, 1861, the New Mexico legislature formed Dona Ana and Arizona counties into a senatorial district, with the right to elect one member to the Territorial Council. Doubtless the statute of 1861 affecting Dona Ana and Arizona counties was enacted as the result of agitation for the establishment of a Territory of Arizona by some residents of Dona Ana county, long dissatisfied at being a part of New Mexico. Dona Ana county citizens, in 1861, sponsored a short-lived movement for the creation of a Territory of the United States, to be called "Montezuma Territory," to be comprised of Dona Ana County, New Mexico, and a portion of Texas, identified as "Franklin County." At the time Dona Ana county claimed a population of six thousand, and secessionists in Mesilla, the county seat, supporting the "Montezuma Territory" movement claimed the entire population, without exception, wanted to "secede from New Mexico." [71] The New Mexico legislature, on Jan. 28, 1863, authorized the organization of Dona Ana and Arizona counties, but the act was nullified as to Arizona when President Lincoln signed the bill creating the Territory of Arizona on Feb. 24, 1863. New Mexico viewed indifferently the shearing off of the "County of Arizona." The Rio Abajo *Press*, of Albuquerque, referred to the event complacently on March 23, 1863:

A friend who knows, writes to us that the creation of Arizona leaves New Mexico's boundary line 120 miles due west of Santa Fe, of Albuquerque, 94 miles, of Mesilla 65 miles, of the big bend near Fort Thorne, 42 miles. This division of our Territory is decidedly long division; longitudinally, long concocted and requiring a man who can look a long way into the future to see those "ten thousand white inhabitants," we read about. It will have a population as soon as the Governor and others get there, and the sun will continue to rise and set there as usual until its effulgent beams be substituted by the brilliant genius who engineered the project through Congress.

Apparently no one had ever thought much about the derivation of the word "Arizona," before it was established as a Territory. Philologists expounded their theories as to the origin of the name. John N. Goodwin, Arizona's newly appointed governor, suggested that "Arizona" was a corruption of *arrida zona*, signifying arid belt. Sylvester Mowry, an Arizona pioneer, contended that "Arizona" was derived from an Indian word meaning "silver regions." Others argued that the name was a combination of two Spanish words, *oro* and *zona*, meaning gold belt. Regardless of the origin of the name, there was some evidence tending to show that Arizona had been made a territory largely as the result of political maneuvering in Washington, which gained and maintained momentum following rumors of important discoveries of gold east of the Colorado river.

Although the nation was at war the President appointed officers for the new Territory shortly after the passage of the organic act. Escorted by Captain Butcher and a detachment of the 11th Missouri Cavalry, the newly appointed officials for Arizona reached Santa Fe on Nov. 21, 1863. Colonel J. Francisco Chaves, in command of detachments of Missouri and New Mexico troops, escorted the officials from Santa Fe to Albuquerque, and thence to Fort Whipple, Arizona. The Rio Abajo Weekly *Press,* of Albuquerque, on Dec. 1, 1863, published the names of the new Arizona officials: Governor, John N. Goodwin, of Maine; Secretary, Richard C. McCormick, of New York; Assistant Secretary, H. W. Fleury, of New York; Chief Justice, William F. Turner, of Iowa; Associate Justices, Joseph P. Allyn, of Connecticut, and William T. Howell, of Michigan; Attorney General, Almon Gage, of New York; Surveyor General, Levi Bashford, of Wisconsin; Marshal, M. B. Duffield, of California; Assistant Marshal, C. A. Phillips, of Illinois; Superintendent of Indian Affairs, Charles D. Poston, of Kentucky; Postmaster, Rev. H. W. Read, of Washington City; Assistant Postmaster, William Thompson, of Kansas.

The newly appointed officials were guests of honor at receptions in Santa Fe and Albuquerque. Questions asked in Albuquerque developed the information that Marshal M. B. Duffield and Superintendent of Indian Affairs Charles D. Poston, who had been in California at the time of their appointment, were enroute to Arizona from the Pacific coast. Rev. H. W. Read, the newly appointed Postmaster for Arizona, who had been a missionary in New Mexico in 1855, had gone to Washington in 1857 to work as a clerk in the Treasury Department. The Santa Fe *New Mexican* of Nov. 21, 1863, said that Rev. Mr. Read was "a preacher of no mean ability," and that he had taken the place as Postmaster in Arizona, "hopeful that he might be useful there, especially in the evangelical field." The Arizona officials left Albuquerque on Dec. 2, 1863, for Whipple Barracks, Arizona, an estimated distance of 396.8 miles. Traveling by way of Fort Wingate, the party reached Navajo Springs, just west of the New Mexico line on Dec. 29. Governor Goodwin issued a proclamation at Navajo Springs announcing his intention to establish and organize the government of Arizona. The officials reached Fort Whipple on Jan. 22, 1864. Because there was no artillery at the post, the governor and his staff were welcomed by a salute fired from anvils, after which they formally established at Fort Whipple the first capital of Arizona, housed in newly and crudely built barracks.

The people of Tucson were sorely disappointed that Fort Whipple had been chosen as the territorial capital. They had been confident that Tucson was to be the capital city. Residents of La Paz, a settlement on the Colorado River, 120 miles north of Yuma, claiming a larger population than Tucson, wrote to Governor Goodwin, insisting that it was the logical place for the capital. Before many days, Governor Goodwin began to realize that Whipple had its defects. Although the water was good, the supply was inadequate for a town of any considerable size. Timber for logging and lumbering was 20 miles away. It was not long before the governor conceded that Whipple Barracks would be suitable only for a "temporary sojourn." As a result, Prescott, a nearby hamlet, was made the capital. The governor arranged to take a census of the Territory, and politicians discussed setting an early date for an election of Arizona's delegate in Congress. Men who had helped to lobby the bill through Congress to make Arizona a Territory had claimed it had 10,000 inhabitants, exclusive of Indians. Now that Arizona had become a Territory, the promoters were a bit embarrassed, and urged Governor Goodwin to go slow in taking the census, pointing out that many people who had left Arizona during the war years would return at the war's end, and could be counted by the census enumerators.

On Sept. 1, 1864, the government asked for bids on a mail route from Albuquerque to Prescott, a distance of approximately 459 miles, via Atrisco, Cubero, Fort Wingate, Agua Fria, Zuni, Jacob's Wells, Leroux Springs and Woolsey's Rancho. Mail was to be carried each way once a week. The trip one way could be made in six days. A contract was let, but abandoned after a few trial trips. Three years later, Prescott, worn out with miserable round about letter service, was asking that the Albuquerque mail route be reestablished, contending that:

The distance between Albuquerque and Prescott is a little

more than 400 miles, six days travel, plus eight from Fort Riley, Kansas, on the western terminus of the railroad. Prescott would get its mail in 14 days—say 16 from St. Louis. Now our mails are seldom less than 35 and usually 45 days in coming.[72]

It was only natural that miners in the California Column, marching through Arizona and New Mexico, would prospect for precious metals at every opportunity. General Carleton was somewhat gold-minded himself. He had observed several gold rushes in his lifetime, and was not reluctant to have a hand in starting one. Carleton and his miner-soldiers believed, in all seriousness, that great wealth in gold could be produced in Arizona and New Mexico. As Carleton saw it, the golden treasures were there, but mining could not be carried on until the wild Indians were subdued.[73]

Henry Connelly, New Mexico's governor, learned about the Arizona gold discoveries unofficially from desert rats and prospectors, who reported that they had been driven away from their claims by the Indians. Both Connelly and General Carleton, in Santa Fe, became intensely interested in the reported gold strikes, and wrote a number of letters to stimulate interest in development. Connelly wrote to Secretary of State Seward on August 23, 1862, advising him of the discovery of "very rich and extensive gold fields" in Arizona. Connelly indicated the necessity for strengthening of the military forces to hold back the hostile Indians:

The most interesting matter that now occupies the attention of our people, and would create a fear of an almost entire depopulation of the laboring part of our community, is the discovery of very rich and extensive gold fields (placers) in the Territory of Arizona, about 400 miles west and south from Albuquerque. . . . This gold exists in a country entirely unpopulated, and has been for ages the haunt of the different bands of Apache Indians. They will doubtless make resistance to its occupancy by the miners, as they are now doing, and many lives will be lost unless a strong military force should be stationed around the mining district and regularly scour the country of all hostile Indians. At this time General Carleton has not a force sufficient for such purpose, and indeed not for the purpose of chastising the Navajos, with whom we are now at war. A regiment of mounted men in addition to the force already here is of the utmost importance. General Carleton has asked for such regiment, but I fear it will not be granted.[74]

On Jan. 27, 1863, General Carleton returned to Santa Fe from Pinos Altos in the southwestern part of New Mexico, excited about discoveries "in which the gold can be seen distinctly with the naked eye." Carleton believed that the "pathway would be cleared to nature's vast storehouse of mineral wealth," if the Indians could be "pushed back, and flogged into submission." By Feb. 1, 1863, soldiers of the California Column were engaged in a dual enterprise — fighting Apache Indians, and mining for gold. Carleton established Fort West, in the Pinos Altos country, equipping it with four companies, to protect miners, and inaugurated a furlough system to give the soldiers an opportunity to prospect and mine for gold. Carleton referred to the plan in a letter to Gen. Thomas in Washington:

The evidences of rich gold fields and of veins of silver and inexhaustible mines of the richest copper in the country at the head of the Mimbres River and along the country drained by the Upper Gila are of an undoubted character. It seems providential that the practical miners of California should have come here to assist in their discovery and development. I have sent four companies of California Volunteers to garrison Fort West in the Pinos Altos gold region, one fourth of the command at a time to have one month's furlough to work in the gold mines on their own account. In this way the mines and the country will become developed, while the troops will become contented to remain in service where the temptation to leave it is very great.[75]

That General Carleton was influenced by gold mining potentials in reaching decisions on military matters was evidenced in a letter written to Major General Henry W. Halleck, in Washington, on May 10, 1863:

I am aware that every moment of your time is of value to the Country, and I would not presume to ask you to even read this note did I not believe that what is herewith enclosed would be of interest to you as a general, and therefore, as a statesman. Among all my endeavors since my arrival here, there has been an effort to brush back the Indians so that the people could get out of the valley of the Rio Grande, and not only possess themselves of the arable lands in other parts of the Territory, but, if the country contained veins and deposits of the precious metals, that they might be found. So I reestablished Fort Stanton, and at least a hundred families have gone to that vicinity to open farms and they are commencing to find gold there.

The Gila River country, Carleton told Halleck, was a country "evidently teeming with millions on millions of wealth":

I established Fort West, and have driven the Indians away from the head of the Gila, and they are finding gold and silver and cinnabar there. There is no doubt in my mind that one of the richest gold countries in the world is along the affluents of the Gila, which enter it from the north along its whole course. Thus you can see one reason why the rebels want, and why we may not permit them ever to have, a country evidently teeming with millions on millions of wealth.

Carleton urged Halleck not to think of New Mexico as a drain upon the general government:

Last winter I asked for one hundred thousand dollars to make a wagon road from near Fort Craig to the Gila. My request was not listened to, and I endeavored to open the road without help. Strategically, you will see its value. Intrinsically, as I had anticipated, it would be beyond price. My preliminary survey has not been successful, but I do not despair of success. You will see by the enclosed notes what signs of mineral wealth are already discovered. If I only had one more good regiment of California Infantry, composed, as that infantry is, of practical miners, I would place it in the Gila country. While it would exterminate the Indians, who are a scourge to New Mexico, it would protect people who might wish to go there to open up the country, and would virtually be a military colony when the war ended, whose interests would lead the officers and soldiers to remain in the new El Dorado. Pray give this a thought. It is not a chimera, but a subject worthy of the attention of the government *now*. California, you remember, was not considered as valuable an acquisition until its gold startled the whole world. Do not despise New Mexico, as a drain upon the general government. The money will all come back again.[76]

Stories of rich gold strikes were accepted as "gospel truth" in many parts of New Mexico in the early 60's. Chief Justice Kirby Benedict, of the Supreme Court of New Mexico, left the bench and abandoned his official duties to join a party of prospectors bound for the Arizona gold fields. Judge Benedict had succumbed to the gold fever after receiving a nugget from Captain Joseph Walker.[77] Benedict's departure for the gold fields prompted Carleton to write a second letter to General Halleck, dated June 14, 1863:

I have seen the gold that Captain Walker had sent to Judge Benedict. It is coarse and seems to be of the first quality. By taking Whipple's wagon road via Zuni, the Coconino caves, and thence across the head waters of the Rio Verde to a stream marked on the map of New Mexico, published by the War Department of 1859, *Val de Chino,* I believe this gold region would be reached by a fine, practicable road within three hundred fifty miles from Albuquerque. . . . There is evidence that a country as rich, if not richer in mineral wealth than California, extends from the Rio Grande northwesterly, all the way across to Washoe. If I could but have one first class regiment more of infantry, I could brush the Indians away from all that part of the country east of the Colorado River.

General Carleton wrote a letter to Captain Walker at "The Walker Mines, Arizona," on June 22, 1863, advising that he was starting the war against the Navajo Indians, and predicting that people would flock to the gold fields:

I am just commencing active operations against the Navajos. I enclose an order which organizes the expedition. You see the new fort will be about twenty-five miles southwest of old Fort Defiance, and this will be the nearest point for your people to get supplies in case of accident. The sutler there will doubtless have a large stock of goods, and I will tell him about keeping on hand such articles of prime necessity as you all might require. I will send you a map of the country so that you may know about where Fort Canby will be situated. I send you another similar map, on which you can trace your new gold fields. . . . The people will soon flock into the country around the San Francisco mountains, will soon open farms and have stock enough for the mines. All they want is military protection on the road, and in that country, until they have got a good foothold, they then will take care of themselves.... If I can be of any service to yourself or party, it will afford me pleasure to help you. If I can help others to a fortune, it will afford me not quite as much happiness as finding one myself, it is true—but nearly as much. My luck has always been not to be at the right place at the right time for fortunes. I have been a little too far ahead, or else a little too much behind, for that.

On the same day, June 22, 1863, Carleton instructed Captain Nathaniel J. Pishon, First Cavalry, California Volunteers, at Fort Craig, New Mexico, to escort John A. Clark, New Mexico's Surveyor General, to the gold fields. Carleton gave Pishon detailed instructions for the journey:

Have great care taken of your animals. When you arrive at the new diggings I want each of your men to prospect and wash, and I want you to report the exact time they severally work and the amount of gold each one obtains in return for his labor during that time. Much reliance will be placed on these statistics. The people must not be deceived, nor be inveigled into that distant desert country without knowing well what they may expect to find. If the country is as rich as represented—and of this I have no doubt—there will, on your return, be a revolution in matters here which no man now can even dream of.... Have an eye on the best location for a post of California troops in the heart of the gold country, one of infantry and one of cavalry. In returning by the Whipple route to Albuquerque, mark the country well for the whole way from the gold region. Take your best men with you, and things to wash with. Send me a few specimens for the War Department on your return.[78]

Several days later, June 26, 1863, Carleton wrote a long letter to Surveyor General Clark saying that he had talked to "a gentleman named Groom," who apparently convinced the General that he knew considerable of the gold fields:

Since you left, I have seen a gentleman named Groom, who last fall came from the new gold diggings on the Colorado River, ascending William's fork to the San Francisco mountains, and thence in by Zuni to Fort Wingate and Albuquerque. He is very anxious to return to the new gold fields, having always entertained the purpose of so doing as soon as he was able. I have told him to go to Fort Craig and consult with yourself, Colonel Riggs and Captain Pishon on the subject of your journey. He is firmly of the opinion that he can guide the party to the point indicated in Mr. Benedict's letter as the one where most gold was found—by the route from Zuni. ... In case you determine to go from Fort Craig via Zuni, and so on Whipple's route ... with three good wagons and teams you can take flour, bacon, sugar, coffee, salt, etc., enough for the party for seventy odd days, and travel light. ...

Carleton advised Clark to prepare carefully for the journey, and be constantly on the lookout for danger signals. He recommended early morning and evening travel to escape the heat:

Great care and forecast must be exercised to have everything which will be indispensably necessary, and not an ounce more. ... From Fort Craig to Zuni there is a wagon road over which troops have travelled ... there are men living in Socorro, and in the neighborhood of Fort Craig, who know this route. ... In case no guide can be found for the country between Fort Craig and the Whipple route, your party can come up the river to Los Lunas and go out on the road via Fort Wingate. ... In case you go by the Fort West route, Mr. Groom, being an old and experienced packer, can be employed in this capacity. ... Great care and vigilance must be exercised with regard to Indians. *Never* be off your guard; *never* become careless; be sure when your stock is grazing to have men *with arms in their hands* always with them; and always on the alert and awake. I cannot impress this matter too strongly upon your mind. In my experience I have found that to travel mornings and evenings, and to lie by in the heat of the day, keeps the stock in better order than to make the whole march without turning out to graze. I wish you luck.

Having given instructions to Captain Pishon, who would lead the escort taking Surveyor General Clark to the Arizona gold fields, General Carleton sent a last minute letter to Colonel Rigg of the California Column, at Fort Craig, dated Santa Fe, June 26, 1863:

Great care should be taken to fit out this party down to the minutest detail. Some medicines should be taken along, some lint, some bandages, a field tourniquet, and the like. The wagons should be minutely inspected, the boxes locked, and extra linchpins, hame-strings, buckskins for mending harness, rope for packing, two lanterns made secure from breakage (in case a man is wounded at night); axle grease and auger, saw, some wrought nails. If the party goes to the gold fields via the Whipple route, Groom can act as a spy and herder. If they go via Fort West, and Tucson, and the Pima villages, Groom should be employed as a packer, at reasonable compensation.

Apparently convinced that an important gold field had been discovered in Arizona, Carleton wrote to men of high rank in the War Department, and to men prominent in other branches of the government in Washington, suggesting that Providence was about to bestow great favors on the American nation. In two letters written from Santa Fe on September 13, 1863, Carleton indicated that thoughts of gold were uppermost in his mind. One letter was written to General Thomas, his military chief, and the other to Postmaster General Montgomery Blair. In the letter to Thomas, Carleton pleaded for an additional regiment of cavalry for use in New Mexico "to whip the Indians, and to protect the people going to and at the mines":

Pray let serious attention be given to the new discoveries of gold. A new revolution in all that pertains to this country is on the eve of commencing, and the government should provide for approaching emergencies. The people will flock to the mines, and should be protected. Providence has indeed blessed us. Now that we need money to pay the expenses of this terrible war, new mines of untold millions are found, and the gold lies here at our feet, to be had by the mere picking of it up! The country where it is found is no fancied Atlantis; is not seen in golden dreams; but it is a real, tangible El Dorado, that has gold that can be weighed by the steelyards—gold that does not vanish when the finder is awake.[79]

In his letter to Postmaster General Blair, Carleton described with enthusiasm the "new gold fields that had been discovered along the Gila River, and upon the line of the 35th parallel, between the Rio Grande and the Colorado." Eliminating "the insignificant village of Tucson" from serious consideration as a possible site for Arizona's capital city, Carleton urged the building of post roads and establishment of mail routes in anticipation of the rush to the gold fields:

You will at once perceive that the capital as well as the population, of the new territory of Arizona will be near that oasis upon the desert out of which rise the San Francisco Mountains, and in and beside which are found these extraordinary deposits of gold, and not at the insignificant village of Tucson, away in the sterile region toward the southern line of the Territory. This will render absolutely indispensable a new mail route over the Whipple road to the new gold fields, and thence crossing the Colorado at old Fort Mojave, and thence up the Mojave River and through the Cajon Pass to Los Angeles, California. People flocking toward these mines will clamor for, and will deserve to have mail facilities. They will go from the east; they will come from California; therefore liberal appropriations should be made early in the approaching session of Congress to prepare the road; to establish a post near the San Francisco Mountains; to reestablish old Fort Mojave; to have a first class permanent ferry across the Colorado at that point; to provide for an overland mail from Albuquerque to Los Angeles.

With moving eloquence, Carleton directed the Postmaster General's attention to the part the California Column had played in connection with the discovery of the golden treasure:

There is no doubt but the reports of the immense deposits of gold are true. As a statesman you will readily imagine all of the political results which must ensue at once from such startling developments when they obtain publicity. . . . For myself there comes no little satisfaction in the thought that, for all the toil through the desert of the troops composing the Column from California, there will yet result a substantial benefit to the country; that if those brave fellows, who encountered their hardships so cheerfully and patiently, who endured and suffered so much, have not had the good fortune to strike a good, hard, honest blow for the old flag, they have, at least, been instrumental in helping to find gold to pay the gallant men who have had that honor. Somebody had to perform their part in the great drama upon which the curtain is about to fall. The men from California accepted unmurmuringly the *role* that gave them an obscure and distant part upon the stage, where it was known that they could not be seen, and believed they would hardly be heard from; but in the great tragedy so cruelly forced upon us, they tried to perform their duty, however insignificant it might be, and to the best of their ability; and now a finger of that providence who has watched over us in our tribulation, and who blesses us, lifts a veil, and there, for the whole country, lies a great reward.[80]

By-passing military channels, as he had done in writing to Postmaster General Montgomery Blair on Sept. 13, 1863, Carleton wrote on Sept. 20, 1863, to Secretary Salmon P. Chase, of the Treasury, stressing the importance of the newly discovered gold fields:

Knowing the great interest which you feel in all matters that will increase the prosperity of our country—and more particularly, at this time, in all matters that relate to its moneyed resources—I have ventured to write you concerning the new gold fields recently discovered near the San Francisco Mountains, on the 35th Parallel, and between the Rio Grande and the Rio Colorado. Surveyor General Clark, of this Territory, has just returned from these new gold fields, and has written a letter to myself, giving a brief account of what he saw. General Clark is prudent in his expressions ... from what he says ... a large region of country, extending from near the head of the Gila along the southern slope of the Sierra Blanca, Sierra Mogollon, San Francisco Mountains, and thence to the Colorado, is uncommonly rich, even compared with California, in gold, silver, cinnabar and copper. On the Prieta affluent to the Gila, from the north, gold was found by my scouting parties last winter as high as "forty cents to the pan." If I can but have troops to whip away the Apaches, so that prospectors can explore the country and not be in fear all the time of being murdered, you will without a shadow of a doubt, find that our country has mines of the precious metals, unsurpassed in richness, number and extent by any in the world. ... The gold is pure. I send you herewith a specimen of copper from near Fort West, on the Gila, and two specimens of pure gold from the top of Antelope Mountain ... sent to me by Mr. Swilling, the discoverer of the new gold fields near the San Francisco Mountains.

Carleton asked Chase to present a nugget of gold to President Lincoln:

If it be not improper, please give the largest piece of gold to Mr. Lincoln. It will gratify him to know that Providence is blessing our country, even though it chasteneth.

The letter ended with down to earth suggestions for a development program:

Now, would it not be wise for Congress to take early action in legislating for such a region; to open up new roads; to give force to subjugate the Indians; to give mail facilities; to claim rights of seigniorage in the precious metals, which will help pay our debts? To so eminent a statesman as yourself it will be sure to occur that timely steps should be taken for the development and security of so rich a country.[81]

The "vast gold fields" Carleton imagined to exist proved to be a mirage. It was copper — not gold — which brought great wealth to owners and operators in Arizona and New Mexico in the years subsequent to the Civil War. Copper mines, of vast importance in the nation's economy, are producing today in both states on a scale beyond the dreams of Carleton or his soldier-miners of the California Column.

Carleton maintained keen interest in mines and miners even after Arizona's Golconda failed to materialize. This sustained interest was reflected in an article he wrote to the Santa Fe *Gazette* of July 27, 1867, following a trip through country which today has Silver City, Grant County, New Mexico, as the hub. Accompanied by Governor Robert B. Mitchell, Charles P. Clever, a candidate for Delegate in Congress, and Captain John Pratt, U. S. Marshal for New Mexico, Carleton left the Rio Grande at Fort Selden "where there was a fine ferry" (covered now by the waters of Elephant Butte lake), on June 15, 1867. Carleton's party traveled all night, and reached Fort Cummings, 58 miles away, at 8 o'clock the next morning, having stopped three hours during the night to feed the horses "grama grass of fine quality and very abundant." Carleton wrote that "the spring at Fort Cummings yields excellent water and has the capacity for the animals of a regiment of cavalry and those of its train." The party rested at Fort Cummings until 5 o'clock in the evening of June 16, and then started for Fort Bayard, traveling five miles through Cooke's Canon, over a rough road, thence to the Mimbres River over a road "which was very fine indeed, with much of it down a gradually descending grade through pasturage which can hardly be excelled." From Fort Cummings to the

Mimbres, "it was eighteen and three-fourths miles." Describing the country, Carleton reported:

Here the road for Arizona bears off to the left, while that for Fort Bayard and Pinos Altos keeps onward, gradually inclining to the right from a west to nearly a northwest course. About six miles from the Mimbres we came to what is known as the Hot Spring. . . . A mile beyond the hot spring is an abundance of cold water. Thence on to Fort Bayard, say, seventeen miles. The road is somewhat rough in places from loose stones—but as a general thing it is most excellent. The scenery on either hand and in front is of the most charming description, and the air, as you gradually ascend toward the mountains to the northwest becomes cool and invigorating. One could hardly imagine a more delightful drive than this from the Hot Spring to Fort Bayard. . . . Fort Bayard, as yet, is only an assembly of log houses. It has a capacity for some three or four companies. It was intended to build the fort of a more durable material. Some stone foundations for the permanent quarters have already been commenced. A post of four companies of cavalry and two of infantry at this place would be strong enough soon to drive off or destroy the marauding Apaches which are now so great an obstacle to the filling up by farmers, stock growers and miners of this important part of New Mexico. . . . This post is about half way between the Santa Rita copper mines and the town of Pinos Altos by roads you are obliged to travel if you are in a carriage. By an air line the copper mines are nearest. As the crow flies, Pinos Altos is about eight miles west of Fort Bayard, and the Santa Rita mines are about five miles eastward from the post. The Hanover copper mine is about seven miles in an air line in a northerly direction from the post. From the summit of the ridge east of the copper mines, and say, three miles distant to eight or ten miles west of Pinos Altos, there is a belt of country from NE to SW by ten miles broad that is *known to be* filled with rich veins of gold, silver, copper, lead, iron and other metals in combination.

By June 19, Carleton's party was at Pinos Altos. Here they remained until June 22. Carleton quickly absorbed the lore of the camp and described it for the *Gazette*:

In May, 1860, a Col. Snively and a party of California miners came to this region and discovered gold near the present site of the town of Pinos Altos, in what is known as Rich Gulch. In June of that year people commenced to work in placers. In December,

1860, there were, say, fifteen hundred here from Chihuahua, Sonora, Texas and California. They, at that time, averaged fifteen dollars per day. Other gulches were discovered by Thomas Mastin with a party of prospectors, and worked until 1861, when the Apache Indians made raids on the stock of the miners and nearly stripped them of the means to prosecute their labors. A severe battle was fought between the miners and a band of Apaches under Mangus Colorado and Cochise. The Indians numbered about five hundred warriors and came into the town, now known as Pinos Altos, on Sept. 27, 1861. Captain Thomas Mastin, one of the discoverers of the gold in Rich Gulch in 1860, commanding a body of volunteers, was killed in the fight. The Indians were driven off, but the impression that they made on the minds of the inhabitants of the town was so great as to induce most of the latter to go away. The breaking out of the Rebellion also had the effect to induce many to leave, but Virgil Mastin, brother of Thomas Mastin, stayed on, and between 1861 and 1864 opened up new mines, the Atlantic, Adriatic and Bear Creek. The Apaches swooped down again and stopped the work until 1866, when Virgil Mastin, Samuel J. Jones, Joseph Reynolds, J. Edgar Griggs and Jacob Amberg organized the Pinos Altos Mining Company, and installed a steam mill at Pinos Altos which worked day and night crushing twenty tons of ore in twenty-four hours, sank shafts, dug a tunnel which drifted seven hundred fifty feet, and installed air shafts and tramways.

Carleton described the conditions in the camp. The population in October, 1866, did not exceed 60 miners, but in June, 1867, there were between 800 and 1,000 inhabitants. Provisions were cheap. Super-fine flour could be bought at eleven dollars the sack of a hundred pounds. The town was something over five thousand feet above sea level, built exactly on the summit of the "great chain of mountains dividing the waters falling into the Atlantic from those falling into the Pacific." Pinos Altos was eight miles from Fort Bayard, thirty miles from the Mimbres Hot Springs, thirty-six miles from the Mimbres river, thirteen miles from the Santa Rita copper mines, one hundred fifteen miles from Mesilla "on the Rio Grande," one hundred ten miles from Fort Selden, thirty miles from "old Fort West on the Gila river," and one hundred seventy miles from Tucson. Freight could be hauled from Mesilla to Pinos Altos, at two and one-half cents per pound. Carleton predicted:

Before six years shall have passed away, there will be a town at or near Pinos Altos larger than the city of Denver.... It may be doubted if there is on the known surface of the earth an equal number of square miles on which may be found as many as rich and extensive veins of the useful as well as of the precious metals as at and near Pinos Altos, New Mexico.

Carleton's article ended on a note of prophesy:

When the vast mineral, pastoral and even agricultural resources of New Mexico are well understood, it will require a prophet to foresee that she will one day, not far distant, occupy a proud position as one of the states of a great Republic.

Although Carleton's predictions for Pinos Altos did not come true specifically, nevertheless time has vindicated his opinion on the region as an entirety. The Pinos Altos region, it is believed, is the only "six metal" mining belt in the southwest — where gold, silver, lead, zinc, copper and manganese have been produced in commercial quantities.

CHAPTER FOUR

Post War Indian Policy

INDIAN AFFAIRS in the west were at sixes and sevens as the Civil War came to an end in 1865. The federal government soon began the task of picking up fragments of its vague and undefined Indian policy. Cease fire orders between North and South found the Western Indian tribes, almost without exception, in a hostile, threatening mood. The Indians, col-

lectively as tribes, and as individuals, were sullen and resent-
ful, ready to seize any means to rectify grievances, real or
imaginary, suffered at the hands of the white man. The army,
which had appropriated almost exclusive jurisdiction over
Indians during the war years, was well aware of the underly-
ing causes for disturbance in the Indian country. General
U. S. Grant indicated a personal interest in the welfare of the
Indians, and requested Major General John H. Pope to prepare a report to the War Department. Pope submitted his
report from St. Louis on Aug. 1, 1865. As he saw it, the army
was confronted with a huge task, in protecting the country
against the Indians, but he blamed the white man for much
of the trouble:

All of the tribes of Indians east of the mountains, and many
west, are in open hostility. They attack the mail coaches, emi-
grant trains, and small posts continually. The United States is
required to protect the great overland routes passing in several
directions through this great Indian region. Protection is thus
required along 3,500 miles of road, nearly all of which lies in an
uninhabited country, and yet over which are daily passing with
U. S. mails to the Territories and the Pacific, crowds of emigrants,
and great trains of supplies for the mining regions, as well as individuals and small parties of travelers. The threatened difficulties with the Mormons in Utah also demand attention, and the
civil officers appointed for that Territory by the government, as
well as the citizens of the United States now there and going
there, absolutely need military protection to enable them to remain in the Territory at all. This condition of affairs certainly
demands a considerable military force, if the government means
to assure security of life and to property of emigrants across the
plains and to settlers in the newly opened Territories.

A reversal of Indian policy was necessary, as Pope viewed
the situation:

The Indian question is most difficult, and I confess I do not
see how it is to be solved, without an entire change of the Indian
policy which has hitherto been and must, under the laws now
be pursued. The development of the rich mining regions in the
Territories of itself has attracted great throngs of emigrants, and
their number has been ten-fold increased by the necessary results

of the late civil war. Thousands of families who have been disloyal or have been sympathizers with the South have, since the conclusion of the war, found it difficult, if not impossible, to live at their homes, and have left the states of Missouri, Arkansas, southern Illinois, Kentucky, and no doubt other southern states, to make their homes in the new Territories. Many thousands of men who have been discharged from the army are also seeking the mining regions. A surprising emigration has been going forward ever since the opening of spring, and seems still to flow on without cessation. Not alone, or even generally, are the great overland routes pursued by these great throngs of emigrants. Every route supposed to be practicable is explored by them. They make highways in every direction across the great plains. No part of that great region, however inaccessible, escapes the prying eyes of the gold seeker, and no route which promises discoveries of value or in any manner shortens his routes of travel is neglected.

Pope pointed out the white man's inconsistency in dealings with the Indian:

Of course, neither the movements nor the conduct of these parties can be controlled. No man except themselves can say what wrong they do to the Indians by robbing, by violence, or by dispossessing them of districts of country which they have occupied unmolested for centuries, yet the United States government is held responsible if any danger is incurred by them or any loss of life or property sustained anywhere in the vast and remote region they are traversing. What the white man does to the Indian is never known. It is only what the Indian does to the white man (nine times out of ten in the way of retaliation) which reaches the public.

The Indian was in a deplorable predicament, as the result of the engulfing tide of emigration:

The Indian, in truth, has no longer a country. His lands are everywhere pervaded by white men; his means of subsistence destroyed and the homes of his tribe violently taken from him; himself and family reduced to starvation, or to the necessity of warring to the death upon the white man, whose inevitable and destructive progress threatens the total extermination of his race. Such is the condition of affairs on the great plains and in the ranges of the Rocky Mountains. The Indians, driven to desperation and threatened with starvation, have everywhere commenced hostilities against the whites, and are carrying on with a fury and courage unknown to their history hitherto. There is not a tribe of Indians on the great plains or in the mountains east of Nevada and Idaho of any consideration which is not now warring on the whites. Until lately the U. S. troops, small in number and utterly incapable on that account of affording security to the whites or the protection of the Indians, have been strictly on the defensive. ... The difficulty lies in the fact that we can promise the Indian under our present system nothing that he will ask with any hope that we can fulfill our promise.[82]

The Indian and his problem had been before Congress on occasion during the war years, but action had been deferred because of necessity for solving without delay seemingly more pressing problems directly associated with military operations. Now that other problems could be considered, the Indian problem pressed for solution.

Under a joint resolution introduced in the Senate on Jan. 29, 1865, and adopted on March 3, the appointment of a committee was provided "to investigate the condition of the Indian tribes and their treatment by the civil and military authorities." A join committee was appointed under the provisions of the resolution, composed of James R. Doolittle,[88] of Wisconsin, Vice President L. F. Foster, and J. W. Mesmith, from the Senate, and William Windom, A. W. Hubbard, William Higby and Lewis W. Ross, from the House. The committee organized and began work at Fort Leavenworth on May 17, 1865. Doolittle, Foster and Ross were designated as a sub-committee to investigate Indian affairs in Colorado and New Mexico, traveled across the Plains in an army conveyance to Fort Garland, Colorado, and after taking testimony there, proceeded to Taos and Santa Fe. A delegation from Santa Fe met the committeemen at Arroyo Hondo, several miles from Santa Fe and escorted them to the capital, entertained them at a ball and reception on the night of July 3. The committee hearings began in Santa Fe on July 4. Senator Doolittle had a genuine interest in the plight of the New Mexico Indians. On more than one occasion his attention had been directed to the problem in New Mexico by Judge Joseph G. Knapp, a former resident of Wisconsin, Doolittle's home state. Federal and territorial officials, army officers, politicians and prominent citizens from all parts of the Territory, attended the hearings in Santa Fe. The investigation had been too long deferred. The army had dominated Indian affairs in New Mexico throughout the Civil War years almost to the entire exclusion of the Bureau of Indian Affairs. As a result of army domination, the Mescalero and Gila Apaches had been almost exterminated, and the mighty Navajo tribe had been compelled to submit to captivity and had been transplanted at the point of gun and sword from western New Mexico and northern Arizona, to the Bosque Redondo near the Texas line. American soldiers, with rifle and mountain howitzer, had shot and killed hundreds of Indians during the war years. Indians by the score had died from starvation and disease. Indian families had been broken up, never to be reunited, through a system of peonage which had been tolerated in New Mexico for many years.[84]

On the first day of the committee hearings, General James H. Carleton voluntarily removed one important subject from the list of things to be investigated when he announced the abolition of martial law which had been in effect in New Mexico since Aug. 8, 1861.[85]

General Carleton, the principal witness before the committee, attempted to justify the policy he had followed in dealing with the Indians of New Mexico for more than three years. He gave the committee the background of the troubles with the Navajos:

With the exception of one or two intervals of a few years each, there has been a constant state of hostility between the pople of New Mexico and the Navajo Indians. Even in these intervals occasional forays were made into the settlements to capture sheep and cattle. The Mexicans would follow them into their country to recapture the stolen stock, and would kill some of the Indians and capture some of the women and children and make slaves of them. But in times when open hostilities existed these efforts were increased on each side to capture stock and women and children, so that the country was kept in a continual state of commotion. This was the state of things when we acquired the territory from the Republic of Mexico. To the best of my recollection, Colonel Doniphan, who came here with General Kearny, made the first expedition into the Navajo country in 1846. Colonel Washington made an expedition into their country in the year 1849; General Sumner in 1851. From 1851 until 1859, there was a period of comparative quiet, interrupted, as I have stated, by occasional forays, particularly on the part of the Navajos. In 1859, war broke out again and in 1860, the Navajos attacked Fort Defiance. About this time Colonel Miles made an expedition into their country, and also Colonel Bonneville; and finally General Canby made a long campaign against them, leading his troops in person. When the Texan invasion of this country occurred, after General Canby's campaign against the Navajos, and when every soldier was employed to repel that invasion, then the Navajos, as well as the Apaches, rode over the country rough shod. This was in the winter of 1861 and in the spring and summer of 1862. I relieved General Canby in command of the department; and this was the condition of the Navajos and Apaches at that time.

Carleton told of the expense incurred and difficulty experienced in getting horses and mules into New Mexico, and of stampedes and runaways on the way from the States, resulting in the loss of many animals:

The Indian difficulties in New Mexico, since the treaty with Mexico, have obliged the United States to keep in the Territory a force whose average strength has been at least three thousand men, employes and all reckoned in. This covers a period of eighteen years. A large proportion of these troops have been cavalry, the most expensive arm of the military service, especially in New Mexico, where forage is very expensive. The horses required as remounts for this cavalry have to be brought across the plains from the states at great risk and expense. Sometimes large numbers have been stampeded enroute and have never been heard from since. Many die before they reach this country. Those which arrive here it takes at least a year to acclimate; and after this the loss of horses by death, by being broken down, and lost on scouts, and killed in action, and stolen by Indians, is enormous, compared with losses of cavalry in any other country. The same holds true of the mules, more numerous necessarily than the cavalry horses, by reason of the extent of country over which supplies have to be hauled to subsist and clothe the troops.

Troops were not needed in New Mexico, in Carleton's opinion, except for Indian fighting:

With the exception of the troops employed to repel the Texas invasion, there has been but little necessity for troops in this country since we acquired it in 1848, unless to fight the Indians. And if it should happen that the nomadic Indians can be placed on reservations and kept there until they become sufficiently domesticated to be contented in that condition of life, I cannot see any reason why troops would be more necessary in New Mexico, than in Illinois, except, perhaps, a small police force kept along the boundary line of Mexico. While it is difficult to say, exactly, my opinion is that about one-half of the forces employed have been necessary by the difficulties with the Navajos. . . . I feel constrained to say that much of the hostility manifested by many of the people of New Mexico against the reservation system grows out of the fact that when this system goes into successful operation there will be no more tribes from which they can capture servants and the military force being reduced to a very small number, the millions of dollars annually expended here on account of the military establishment will in a great measure, cease.[86]

Supplementing his oral testimony before the committee hearing in Santa Fe on July 3, 1865, Carleton wrote a letter to Senator Doolittle on July 25, 1865, in which he recommended unequivocally that the Navajos and other "wild Indians" be placed on reservations of their own, taught the Christian religion, and given land allotments in severalty. Carleton wrote quite sympathetically of Indian rights:

In my opinion, lands should be held in severalty. Surveys should be carefully made, and each family or head of family should have a part allotted to him. The human being, white or red or black, who plants a tree or a vine, or builds a house, or makes a field or garden, identifies himself with it—loves it; his children are born there, and the associations connected with all these things constitute and give birth to what we call home love and home feeling. We have taken quite enough from the Indian. Let them have and keep really a home. If they have rights at all upon the earth, that is one of the dearest. Let us not rob them of that.

Referring particularly to the Navajos in New Mexico, Carleton said:

The young Indians upon the Navajo reservation, which is just
starting in New Mexico, are the most docile and industrious. The
full grown ones are lazy, and can hardly be reclaimed from their
savage desire to roam about and lead a life of idleness. They
must die off, and the young ones grow up to take their places, before any marked improvement in this people will be observed.

Convinced that the Indian should be managed by the army,
Carleton advocated placing the Bureau of Indian Affairs in
the War Department:

The Indian Bureau should be placed under the War Department, as it was before the Department of the Interior was created
and organized. When under the War Department, which also
controls the forces operating in the Indian countries, there would
be no conflicts of opinion about what should be done in a given
case; for, as the fountain whence might emanate instructions,
whether to commanders, superintendents or agents, would be one,
so the different streams of authority and regulations, descending
through these subordinates would be of the same character.

Carleton advocated the abolishment of the office of Commissioner of Indian Affairs, and the appointment of an army
officer to rule the Indians:

In my opinion, the office of Commissioner of Indian Affairs
should be abolished, if it be incompatible with the law to have
an officer of the army to fill it ex-officio. Contemplating the placing of the Indian Bureau under the direction of the War Department, and organizing it systematically, so that its operations
should harmonize with those of the troops, and the two run together as parts of the same machine, with no cogs mis-matching,
no jarrings, no belts loose, it would be next to impossible to find
a citizen who would understand Indian affairs, Indians, Indian
countries, Indian wants, and at the same time understand military
affairs. But it is easy to find many an officer in the United States
Army, who from long service in Indian countries, understands
all these matters. . . . I would have not only the head of the Indian
Bureau an officer of the Army, but each commander of a military
department should be ex-officio superintendent of Indian Affairs
for all the Indians in that department; and the Commander of
one post nearest any one tribe of Indians in that department,
should be the agent, ex-officio, for that tribe.[87]

It was a waste of time, in Carleton's opinion, to negotiate treaties with the Indians:

I would, especially for all wild tribes of Indians, have reservations set apart by law, and enforce the same by arms. I would not make any treaties at all with such Indians. To go through the forms of making a treaty with a party, when the government is determined to have matters its own way anyhow, is a mockery beneath the dignity of the United States. We can do right without resorting to any theatricals simply for effect.[88]

Kirby Benedict, Chief Justice of the Supreme Court of New Mexico since 1858, a resident of the Territory and judge of the court since 1853, testified before the Doolittle Committee on July 4. Demonstrating that he had been a close observer of conditions in New Mexico during critical years of the Territory's history, Judge Benedict's testimony was intelligent and informative:

A general friendship prevailed between the Navajos and the people until an irritation occurred at Fort Defiance, from a negro having been killed at that place in a quarrel with an Indian who had come to the post. The negro is said to have been claimed as the slave of the commanding officer; satisfaction was required of the Navajos for the killing of the negro . . . they offered to pay a sum of money, but the military exacted the delivery up of the Indian who had done the killing. Excuses were offered, among others, that the Indian had fled beyond the tribe and their reach. The military remained unsatisfied, hostile feelings grew stronger and stronger on the part of the Navajos, and the military, but which finally extended to and included the inhabitants of the Territory. Stealing, robberies and barbarities ensued, and the Indians, as a tribe, became involved, until the depredations upon life, security and property were so frequent and ruinous, a campaign was made against them under the command of Colonel Kit Carson, which was successful in bringing them to subjection, and causing a surrender as captives, of the principal portions of the tribe, men, women and children. The Navajos were in the habit of making forays upon the ranches and settlements, stealing, robbing and killing and carrying away captives; the finding of herds and driving off sheep and other animals was carried on to a very ruinous extent; the killing of persons did not seem so much the object of their warfare as an incidental means of succeeding in other depredations. Sometimes, however, barbarous vengeance was exhibited and a thirst for blood. They carried away captives. . . .

Speaking from personal experience, Benedict told the committee how the custom had been tolerated in New Mexico of capturing, buying and selling Indians and of holding them in peonage:

There are in the Territory a large number of Indians, principally women and children, who have been taken by force, or stealth, or purchased, who have been among the wild tribes of New Mexico or those adjoining. Of these a large proportion are Navajos. It is notorious that natives of this country have sometimes made captives of Navajo women and children . . . the custom had long existed here of buying Indian persons, the tribes themselves have carried on this kind of traffic. Destitute orphans are sometimes sold by their remote relations; poor parents also make traffic of their children. The Indians obtained in any of the modes mentioned are treated by those who claim to own them as their servants and slaves. They are bought and sold by and between the inhabitants at a price much as is a horse or an ox. Those who buy, detain and use them, seem to confide in the long established custom and practice which prevails, and did prevail before this country was a portion of the United States. Those who hold them are exceedingly sensitive of their supposed interest in them, and easily alarmed at any movements in the civil courts to dispossess them of their imagined property. The rich, and those who have some quantities of property, are chiefly those who possess the persons I have mentioned; those usually who have much popular influence in the country, and the extent of this influence is one of the means by which they hope to retain their grasp upon their Indian slaves. The prices have lately ranged very high. A likely girl of not more than eight years old, healthy and intelligent, would be held at the value of four hundred dollars or more. I know of no law of this Territory by which property in a Navajo or other Indian can be recognized in any person whatever, any more than property can be recognized in the freest white man or black man. In 1855, while holding district court in Valencia County, a proceeding in habeas corpus was had before me on the possession and services of a Navajo girl then twelve years old, and who had been held by the petitioner seven years. On the trial I held the girl to be a free person, and adjudged accordingly. In 1862 a proceeding in habeas corpus was instituted before me by an aged man who had held in service many years an Indian woman, who had been, when a small child, bought from the Payweha tribe of Indians. The right of the master to the possession and services of the woman on the one side, and the right of the woman to her personal freedom were put distinctly in issue. Upon the hearing I adjudged the woman to be a free woman; I held the claim of the master to be without foundation in law and against natural rights. In each of the cases the party adjudged against acquiesced in the decision and no appeal was ever taken.

Capturing Indians and selling them into peonage was traditional, according to Judge Benedict, in the days before the American conquest:

In the examination of the cases it appeared that before the United States obtained New Mexico, captive and purchased Indians were held here by custom in the same manner as they have been held since. The courts are open to them, but they are so influenced by the circumstances which surround them they do not seem to think of seeking the aid of the law to establish the enjoyment of their right to freedom. . . . So far as I have learned from history, whether by tradition or otherwise, the Navajo Indians for ages have been at alternate war and pacee with the inhabitants who have resided here. They are reputed to have made themselves quite wealthy by robbing through long years the flocks of the people of New Mexico. The Spanish and Mexican governments administered here had frequent troubles with the tribe, and sometimes brought them to continue for a time at peace. . . . When the Navajos have been at hostilities with the Mexican people, the latter have sometimes, in small parties, made campaigns into the Navajo country, and taken, where they could, captives and stock.[89]

Colonel Kit Carson, field commander of the American troops in the fighting against Mescalero Apaches, Navajos, Kiowas and Comanches, under Carleton's supervision, expressed his views on the Indian situation to the sub-committee in a letter written from Fort Lyons, Colorado, on Aug. 19, 1865. Better informed, perhaps, on most phases of western Indian life, than any other man of his day, Kit Carson agreed generally with General Carleton's testimony before the committee. Carson believed, as did Carleton, that the War Department should have sole authority over the Indians. "Indian agents," according to Carson, were responsible for much of the misbehavior of the Indians. Written in excellent English, Kit Carson's letter may have expressed his views but it was probably prepared by General Carleton:

I have been long convinced that the only rule that can be successfully applied to the government of Indians is one firm, yet just, consistent and unchangeable; for the Indian, judging only by the effect of that which appeals to his senses, as brought directly under his observation, regards with contempt a weak and indecisive policy as the result of fear, hesitation and cowardice, while a changeable and capricious one excites his apprehension and distrust. Both of these courses should be cautiously avoided. The rule for the government of Indians should be strong enough to inspire their respect and fear, yet protecting them from both internal dissension and external aggression. This can only be effected by a military rule, and I am therefore of the opinion that the sole control of the Indians should be vested with the War Department. As at present managed, jealousies among the employes of the different departments naturally exist, and they are too often actuated by the feelings of prejudice, which result in a want of that harmonious cooperation of action in the execution of official duties, so necessary to effect successful results. Indian agents, appointed solely by political influence, are often swayed by personal gain in the transaction of their business, making the government appear to act in bad faith towards the savages; then making promises, impossible to fulfill, to shield themselves from attack, they excite feelings of hostility that can only be quenched in blood. To this cause, and that of repeated acts of aggression on the part of the numerous reckless frontiersmen that swarm upon the borders of the Indian territory, may be attributed many, if not most, of our recent Indian wars, massacres, murders, extending from Minnesota to California.

Carson reminded the committee that one Indian tribe differed from another, and the tribes had feuds of their own to consider:

Allow me to suggest the necessity of extreme caution and circumspection in locating Indians, to prevent internal dissensions, upon reservations. Different tribes, besides being of different

degrees of advancement in civilization, have feuds of long standing to excite them, ambition of chiefs to satisfy, and long cherished traditions of delayed revenge to gratify. There is nothing
inimical in the bold, courageous, marauding Comanche—the wild,
treacherous, agricultural Navajo, or the lazy, degraded, almost
brutalized Digger. These tribes are types of the different North
American Indians, and from these, or a more extensive list carefully prepared, classifications should be made to govern officers
entrusted with their removal . . . for one wild tribe looks down
on another with a contemptuous pride—strange to us, but perfectly natural to their untutored minds, as they possess a less
degree of skill in the barbaric virtues of murder, violence and
theft. . . .

Contending that the Navajo colonization experiment had
been a success, Kit Carson argued for military supervision of
other Indians:

The beneficial results derived from placing the Navajos upon
a reservation in New Mexico is a successful vindication of the
policy of placing Indians on reservations, an example of the
propriety of military rule, and appears to be actuated by feelings
of humanity, charity, and sound political economy. A consideration of the latter question might seem more the province of the
statesman than the soldier; but in deciding a policy that has at
heart the welfare of thousands of human beings, that seeks to
convert them from fierce and reckless murderers to peaceful tillers
of the soil, from a source of continued expense to one of actual
benefit—to remove far from the white settler, and inspire confidence and respect in the savage, I am satisfied that the teachings
of experience will not be overlooked or even lightly regarded.
Time must elapse before really practical results can be derived
from any Indian policy; but if the one so favorably commenced
in New Mexico be carried into effect with other tribes, I am in-
dulging in no chimerical or utopian idea in believing that in
the next generation civilization can advance undisturbed into
the vast interior of our country, while from the reservations the
hum of busy, productive industry will resound, and the prayers
of Christianity be heard from every tribe, and America stand
proudly foremost among the nations as the exemplar of mercy,
humanity, and philanthropy, as she now does of civilization and
progress. . . . Commanding officers of posts on Indian reservations
should be defacto Indian agents; then representing the power of
the government by inflicting punishment for misdeeds and being

also dispenser of its benefits, they will be looked up to with increased respect and fear ... this system would seem to afford greater checks to the accomplishment of frauds, and greater facilities for their detection when perpetrated.[90]

New Mexico-born Padre Antonio Jose Martinez, long-time "curate of Taos," who had contributed much to New Mexico's official life under the Mexican as well as the American flag, submitted his views to the Doolittle Committee by letter dated July 23, 1865. Twenty-two years before, Padre Martinez had written a somewhat similar communication to General Santa Anna in which he described the condition of the Navajo and Apache tribes as of that time. Little, if anything, had happened during the years between 1843 and 1865 to improve the lot of the Indians. Their plight, in fact, seemed worse after the American Occupation than before. In writing to the committee, Padre Martinez was making his last important contribution toward a better understanding of the Indian problem in New Mexico. Padre Martinez advocated a number of reforms for the benefit of the Indians, some of which the Indian Service eventually adopted. Writing particularly of the Navajos, Martinez said:

I have to state, that from the first year of this century, since I was nine years old, I have remarked that the Navajos, who inhabit the land west of the Rio Abajo, in New Mexico, sometimes were at peace, and other times at war. They always observed this alternative, though the first periods were longer, say from four to five years, but seldom more than the second, which were two, three or even five years. Then New Mexico was under the authority of the Spanish government, which maintained one hundred soldiers of the line, with their respective officers, in the city of Santa Fe, the capital. The governor was always the colonel, being the first officer of the troops sent from the State of Chihuahua, and others, but never from New Mexico, though the soldiers and officers were from here, and when Mexico became independent of Spain, sometimes the highest officer was governor; sometimes, also, a native citizen of the country would hold the superintendence of Indian affairs when the soldiers took the field in times of war.

Under Mexican rule, the governor had authority to draft men into the army to fight Indians:

By orders of the governor, the inhabitants were drafted, in order to place the army on a good footing so as to enforce respect, even to conquering the Indians, and thus obtain peace; so it occurred with the Navajos. The men who were to make the campaign amounted from five to six hundred, perhaps one thousand. Only a small number of soldiers went; the largest number stopped in the pasture lands to protect the cattle that remained, and thus maintained themselves during the summer and winter without need of buying provisions. As for the rest of them, until they had completed the number, they made a requisition on the inhabitants in the vicinity in certain proportions. Some furnished provisions at their own expense; others offered riding animals, tents, equipments, subsistence for themselves, arms, powder, shot, and arrows as well as bows; and when they were assembled to start on their enterprise, they were all passed in review; and those who were not mounted were made to purchase their equipments and ammunition, and though the government forces took a great quantity with them, none was distributed until what the others carried was entirely exhausted, and for this were exempt from contributions.

Padre Martinez described frequent clashes between the Utes and Comanches, "a nation of the north," which always "caused the death of a great number on both sides, alternately victorious, pursuing each other when hunting the buffalo, carrying away the children and some of the females captured, selling some in New Mexico, killing others, and ill treating the rest so much that many of them died." The Padre advocated prohibition against the sale of "ardent spirits" to Indians:

I think the remedy would be to induce them to temperance, to live in healthy and permanent places, to build good houses, till the land, plant corn, raise cattle and adapt themselves to industries; and now and then the men will go hunting, using the game for food, and the skins to make shoes—always owning a place to live in with their families; prohibit the sale of ardent spirits, encourage them to peace and good will towards other nations with which they are at war; give them the idea that there is a God, Author, Creator and Preserver of us all, and whom we

acknowledge, worship and thank; who desires that all men be in
good relation to each other, and to whom He has given the ideas
of immortality of the soul, of the end of all earthly joys after our
life, and the punishment of wicked deeds, by Him, the Supreme
Judge of all.[91]

The Doolittle Committee report was submitted to Congress
in 1866, and filed away for future reference. Other matters,
of greater national importance, were before the Congress for
consideration. The committee hearings in Santa Fe had accomplished one thing of major immediate importance for
New Mexico, and that was the abolition of martial law. Men
were free once again to speak and write as they pleased, within
the limitations of the civil law, on all questions affecting public interest.

The Department of the Interior began an independent investigation into Indian difficulties in New Mexico late in
1865, sending Special Agent Julius K. Graves from Washington with instructions to study the public reaction to the facts
developed in the Doolittle Committee hearings. Leaving Fort
Leavenworth on Nov. 6, 1865, Graves crossed the Kansas
plains, traveled by way of Fort Aubrey, Fort Lyon, and Bent's
old fort on the Arkansas, reaching Santa Fe on Dec. 30, 1865.
He attended the opening session of the Territorial Legislature on Jan. 1, 1866. In a report to Washington, Graves said
that "the Indian question was the all absorbing topic of conversation among the entire community." Each individual
"seemed to have peculiar ideas upon the subject, and freely
announced and advocated them." Graves found that the New
Mexico politicians held divergent opinions about the Indians,
and that most of the controversy revolved "around the selection of the Bosque Reservation as a permanent home for the
Navajos." He reported that "while many favored, others opposed this policy as being detrimental to the territory; and
from this standpoint the whole matter seemed to drift off into
a question of political expediency." Graves handed blank
ballots to Governor Henry Connelly and members of the Legislature, requesting answers to two questions about Navajo

Indians: Should they continue to be held as prisoners at Bosque Redondo? If not, what disposition should be made of them? [92] Most of the legislators refused to answer the questions.

Graves was sent to Santa Fe for the specific purpose of undertaking to justify the Department's position on the Navajos, adopted on recommendation of the military. Reporting to Washington, Graves sustained Carleton and his policies without exception or qualification. Recommending that Bosque Redondo be set aside as a permanent home for the Navajos, Graves eulogized Carleton:

I should prove recreant to the duty you have imposed upon me were I to close this communication without bestowing a just tribute upon the wisdom, energy and indomitable perseverance of Major General James H. Carleton, and the manner in which he has conducted the military department of New Mexico, with especial reference to the Indians of the Territory. Under his efficient administration the atrocities which formerly marked the daily routine of life in this section have dwindled into comparative insignificance. He has conquered the greater portion of the powerful Navajo tribe, which for upwards of a century had been a constant terror to the people, and placed these savages upon the broad road to civilization. The selection of the Bosque Redondo as a home for, and the location of these Navajos upon this reservation, was a wise and laudable undertaking, shifting, as it did, the scenes of their former barbarisms for the more elevating tendencies of their present home, surrounded as it is by all the arts of peace, whose victories, as will be acknowledged, in the eventual civilization of this tribe, are more renowned than war.

Graves estimated in 1866 there were 6,447 Navajo Indians confined at Bosque Redondo, with 1,200 more at large; that twenty years before, in 1846, there were 13,500 Navajos in the Territory, a decrease in the figures of 1866 of almost one-half, accounted for, he reported, by the incessant Indian warfare. Referring to peonage Graves said:

A practice, sanctioned by territorial law, has obtained by which the whites are encouraged to make volunteer expeditions or campaigns against the Indians. Theoretically, those participating in these raids are rewarded with the plunder obtained, but should report at the territorial offices all the captives, while practically, in most cases, the captives are either sold, at an average of $75 to $400, or held in possession, in practical slavery. This state of things of course keeps up a state of hostility among the Indians. The intervention of Congress is asked to put a stop to this practice.

Special Agent Graves reported to the Commissioner that slavery, "either in the ordinary Mexican form, that of a state of continual imprisonment or service for debt, or in that of practical enslavement of captive Indians," was the universally recognized mode in New Mexico of securing labor and assistance. No less than 400 Indians "are thus held in Santa Fe, alone," Graves reported. "The arguments to sustain the system are the same as those formerly used in behalf of slavery in the states. The treatment of the Indian slaves varies with the whims and feelings of their holders. Sometimes they are, doubtless, better off then when free. In spite of the stringent orders of the government, the system continues, and nearly every federal officer holds peons in service. The superintendent of Indian Affairs has half a dozen." [93]

Following an inspection trip to Bosque Redondo, Graves described the physical surroundings and conditions there:

This reservation, on the Pecos River, comprises forty square miles, with Fort Sumner as a centre. A principal acequia, or irrigating canal, seven miles long, supplies the lateral canals necessary. There were 2,000 acres under cultivation by the Navajos, who were running 47 ploughs. Vines and fruit trees are coming forward well. Vegetables grow to great size. South of the fort and east of the Pecos River there are 2,000 acres more of arable land, and more in the immediate vicinity. There is a fine growth of young cottonwoods coming forward, which will eventually furnish fuel. Mesquite root is now plentiful for fuel, and other kinds at a distance of twenty-five miles which can be cut and floated down the river. Pasturage of nutritious grass is abundant; water good, though sometimes brackish. The capacity of the reservation is sufficient for both Navajos and Apaches but the latter should not be kept with the former, as they are not friendly. Four hundred soldiers now keep the peace, but if the Navajos were sent back to their own country, an army would be necessary. The land should be surveyed into small lots and divided among the families.[94]

With the findings of the Graves report to sustain him, Commissioner Cooley, of the Bureau of Indian Affairs, submitted a pro-Carleton report to the Secretary of the Interior in 1866. Discussing the Navajo problem at some length, Cooley offered his report "so that when Congress shall take up the subject for the purpose of providing such means as may be necessary to do justice to a Territory whose loyal people have suffered, and are suffering much from Indian depredations, and who are knocking loudly at the door of Congress for relief," it would have facts available upon which to base a policy.

"Mr. Graves is clearly of the opinion that the policy of General Carleton has had an excellent effect," Commissioner Cooley wrote in his report. He added that Graves had reported "that the Navajos are doing well on the reservation; and that it is best that the government should, once for all, put an end to quarrels among the people on this subject, by deciding that the Indians shall be retained at that reservation, and providing the necessary appropriations for taking them into the charge of civil authorities. As it is now, there is a divided jurisdiction, the Indians being prisoners of war, and sustained as to all supplies beyond what they raise themselves, by rations issued by the military authority, while they also have a regularly appointed agent, and an annual distribution of supplies in clothing and the like, of $100,000, appropriated by Congress. Such a state of things should not continue. Either they should be supported and educated in self-supporting industry by the military alone, or they should be turned over to some other authority. The division of jurisdiction makes trouble constantly."

Discussing the Mescalero Apaches of New Mexico, Commissioner Cooley reported that they had left Bosque Redondo when the Navajos, under Carleton's directions, were placed there. The Mescaleros, according to Cooley's report, occupied "a position of peculiar interest, for some five hundred of them were upon the Bosque Redondo reservation, originally set apart for them, and faithfully tilling the soil, with ample success, when the Navajos were removed to that place. Being at feud with the Navajos, and outnumbered by them, they gradually left the reservation, until, at last accounts, not more than a dozen were left, and thus the fruits of two or three years labor in reclaiming them from their savage life has been lost."

CHAPTER   FIVE

At Bosque Redondo

VIEWED THROUGH General Carleton's eyes at Departmental headquarters in Santa Fe in the spring of 1864, the campaign against the Navajos was proving an unqualified success. Within one year after starting the war, Carleton had demonstrated that the Navajos were not invincible, as they had believed, but that they could be ferreted out and driven from their most remote mountain hideouts. He had demonstrated that the Navajos could be starved into submission and compelled to surrender. He had demonstrated that they could be held prisoners on a Pecos River reformatory four hundred miles from their home land. As the campaign progressed, however, and as Navajos by the thousand were confined at Bosque Redondo, Carleton began to realize the magnitude of the project he had undertaken. The truth was, that Carleton had not made adequate preparation in advance, for the second phase of the campaign, which involved the discipline and subsistence of his prisoners. Belatedly realizing the existence of a crisis, Carleton called a meeting in Santa Fe, which was attended by the men who had conceived and executed the campaign — Carleton, the general commanding, Kit Carson, field commander, James L. Collins, long time Indian agent, and Governor Connelly. These men, and others with them, discussed the problems involved. As might be expected, it was decided at the conference that Carleton's campaign had achieved beneficial objectives. The task of making a declaration in writing to this effect was given to Collins, and on March 4, 1864, he wrote the following letter to Carleton:

In response to your inquiries . . . there being now no longer a doubt in regard to the success of your Indian policy, as applied to the Navajo and Mescalero Apache tribes, the latter, with unimportant exceptions having surrendered and gone upon the reservation at Bosque Redondo, and the former now being in the act of following their example, it becomes a question of much importance how the large number of Indians which will shortly be collected on the reservation is to be subsisted and clothed. At the rate the Navajos are now surrendering themselves, voluntarily, prisoners of war, there will be of that tribe alone between four and five thousand on the reservation by the beginning of May. If the Indian department should not take steps to relieve the military of the care of them by taking them under its control, the duty of furnishing the estimates for the requisite supplies will doubtless devolve upon you; and in regard to that question I will say, that the Navajos, owing to the hostile attitude they have maintained towards the government for the last five or six years past, have been deprived of the presents which have been distributed among them annually previous to the beginning of their hostilities, and they are consequently entirely destitute of clothing. A large supply will therefore be necessary to issue to them. I would suggest, however, as a matter of economy, that the rations be confined to flour, corn meal and corn, and fresh meat, either beef or mutton; salt and soap might be added. I would not advise the issue of coffee and sugar, for they are not prepared to make proper use of these articles, especially coffee. . . .

Collins believed that a new, permanent location should be found for the Navajos, and that they should be compensated for the land that would be taken away from them:

If the removal and location of the Navajos should be a permanent one, and it certainly should be, the government will doubt-less give them some compensation for the large and valuable district of country which they abandon and leave to be disposed of by the government. This compensation should be made in stock and other useful articles suited to their mode of life. The labor of teaching the Navajos and Apaches the business of farming will be light compared with most other wild Indians, for they are already well advanced in this knowledge, but the complete success of the enterprise will in a great measure depend upon the personal fitness and efficiency of the agents who may be placed in charge of them. They should be men of liberal and practical views, well acquainted with the modes of life of the Indians, and who are willing to devote their whole time and attention to the duties required of them. None should be appointed to the position of Indian agent who is not specially qualified, both by inclination and ability.

Kit Carson signed his name as an endorsement of the Collins letter: "I have read this letter, and fully concur in the views expressed by Colonel Collins." Governor Connelly added his endorsement below Carson's signature: "I have read the foregoing letter, written by Colonel J. L. Collins, late superintendent of Indian Affairs, and fully concur in the views therein expressed." [95]

The necessity for approval of an Indian policy was so urgent that Carleton sent Collins to Washington as his personal representative with a letter to General Lorenzo Thomas. In the letter Carleton told Thomas that by means of the subjugation of the Navajo tribe, the government had acquired a country "much larger in extent than the State of Ohio":

I have the honor to enclose herewith for the information of the War Department a letter dated March 5, 1864, from Colonel James L. Collins, the late Superintendent of Indian Affairs, to myself, suggesting what the government ought at once to do with reference to the captured Indians. Col. Collins' views are worthy of great weight. I beg to say that I fully concur in all that Colonel Collins has said. By the subjugation and colonization of the Navajo tribe, we gain for civilization their whole country, which is much larger in extent than the state of Ohio; and besides, being by far the best pastoral region between the two oceans, is said to abound in the precious as well as the useful metals. I beg to impress upon your mind, General, that the government should at once take some action for the immediate support and the prospective advancement of the Navajos. Although they have been forced by military power to leave their country, yet the government is so greatly the gainer by their giving it up that an annuity of at least one hundred and fifty thousand dollars should be given them in clothing, farming implements, stock, seeds, storehouses, mills and the like for ten years, when they will not only have become self sustaining, but will be the happiest and the most delightfully located pueblo of Indians in New Mexico, perhaps in the United States.

Carleton was already gravely concerned about feeding and clothing the Navajos:

The troops have toiled hard to overcome this formidable tribe, and doubtless the operations against them will be entirely closed by the end of next May. It is a little hard that the Indian department does not stand ready to receive and provide for the captives, so that our attention and energies may be turned to other portions of the department, where bands of Apaches are killing and robbing the people with seeming immunity. These Indians are upon my hands. They must be clothed and fed until they can clothe and feed themselves. I will not turn them loose again to war upon the people, and cannot see them perish either from nakedness or hunger.

In further explanation of the Bosque Redondo project, General Carleton wrote another letter from Santa Fe to General Thomas, on March 12, 1864, in which he enlarged somewhat upon the nature of the enterprise, and indicated the extent to which government assistance would be necessary:

I have been informed that there are now three thousand Navajos, men, women and children, who have surrendered at Fort Canby, and are about starting for the Bosque Redondo. These, with those now at that place, and en route thither, will make five thousand five hundred, without including the captive Mescalero Apaches. There will, doubtless, be more Navajos come in to Fort Canby — what are known as the *ricos* of the tribe; men who have stock, and will, doubtless, be able to subsist themselves upon that stock until we are better prepared to take care of them. Colonel Carson has been instructed to send in the poor and destitute first. The *ricos* will come in afterwards. Among the poor are nearly or quite all of the *ladrones*⁹⁶ and murderers, so that we have already in our hands the bad men of the tribe. An exact census will be taken of the *ricos*, and a statement made of the probable amount of their stock, which has hitherto been greatly exaggerated, in my opinion. When this is done, Colonel Carson will himself come in from the Navajo country, and go down to the Bosque Redondo to give the Indians the counsel they so much need just at this time, as to how to start their farms and to commence their new mode of life.

The Navajos who had held out against capture had been harassed until subdued:

You have, from time to time, been informed of every step which I have taken with reference to operations against the Indians in this country. I multiplied, as much as possible, the points of contact between our troops and themselves; and although no great battle has been fought, still, the persistent efforts of small parties, acting simultaneously over a large extent of country has destroyed a great many, and harassed the survivors until they have become thoroughly subdued. Now, when they have surrendered and are at our mercy, they must be taken care of; must be fed, clothed and instructed. This admits of neither discussion nor delay. These six thousand mouths must eat, and these six thousand bodies must be clothed.

Money would be needed to feed and clothe the Indians, Carleton wrote, but in the same letter he pointed out the values that would accrue to the government:

When it is considered what a magnificent pastoral and mineral country they have surrendered to us — a country whose value can hardly be estimated — the mere pittance, in comparison, which must be given at once to support them, sinks into insignificance, as a price for their natural heritage. They must have two millions of pounds of breadstuffs sent from the states. This can be done by installments . . . this amount will last them, with what we can buy here, until the crop comes off in 1865; when from that time forward, as far as food may go, they will, in my opinion, be self sustaining. . . .

Carleton asked for 4,000 head of butcher-cattle for his charges at the Bosque Redondo; for clothing for the women and children, for agricultural implements "to insure crops." ⁹⁷

To help educate the Navajos, Carleton recommended the immediate appointment of a supervisor, a supervisory assistant and other employes. Carleton's specifications required a genius for the place of assistant supervisor: "The Assistant Supervisor should be apt at accounts; practical as a man of business; of resources as a farmer and a mechanic; of patience, industry and temperance — one whose heart would be in his business, and who would believe that his time belonged to the government, and need not be spent mainly in 'grinding axes' elsewhere, at the expense of the United States." Carleton advocated passage of a law providing for reorganization of Indian management, and recommended that very few things should be left to chance or discretion:

If all this be set forth in the law . . . the whole plan will go into successful operation at once. If not set forth in the law, you may depend upon it, General, that, what with changes in superintendents, with diverse counsels, and diverse interests, and lack of fixedness of purpose and system, the Indians will not be properly cared for; and instead of becoming a happy, prosperous, and contented people, will become sad and desponding, and will soon lapse into idle and intemperate habits. You wish them to become a people by whom all can contemplate with pride and satisfaction, as proteges of the United States, a people who, in return for having given you their country, have been remembered and carefully provided for by a powerful Christian nation like ourselves. But unless you make, in the law, all arrangements here contemplated, you will find this interesting and intelligent race of Indians will fast diminish in numbers, until, within a few years only, not one of those who boasted the proud name of Navajo will be left to upbraid us for having taken their birthright and left them to perish.

Although he had conducted a harsh and brutal campaign against the Navajos, Carleton now pleaded eloquently for justice for them:

With other tribes whose lands we have acquired, ever since the pilgrims stepped on shore at Plymouth, this has been done too often. For pity's sake, if not moved by any other consideration, let us, as a great nation, for once treat the Indian as he deserves to be treated. It is due to ourselves, as well as to them, that this be done. Having this purpose in view, I am sure the lawmakers will not be ungenerous; nor will they be unmindful of all those essential points which, in changing a people from a nomadic to an agricultural condition of life, should be kept in view, in order to guard them against imposition, to protect them in their rights, to encourage them in their labors, and to provide for all their reasonable wants.

In a detached way, as if he had not conceived and directed the campaign against the Navajos and urged Kit Carson to execute it, Carleton now described their pitiful plight:

The exodus of this whole people, from the land of their fathers, is not only an interesting, but a touching sight. They have fought us gallantly for years on years. They have defended their mountains and their stupendous canyons with a heroism which any people might be proud to emulate. But, when at length they found it was their destiny, too, as it had been of their brethren, tribe after tribe, away back towards the rising of the sun, to give way to the insatiable progress of our race, they threw down their arms, and as brave men, entitled to our admiration and respect, have come to us with confidence in our magnanimity, and feeling that we are too powerful and too just a people to repay that confidence with meanness or neglect; feeling that for having sacrificed to us their beautiful country, their homes, the associations of their lives, the scenes rendered classic in their traditions, we will not dole out to them a miser's pittance in return for what they know to be, and what we know to be, a princely realm.

The Navajos, in Carleton's opinion, were no longer hostile. By rounding them up and impounding them, the military had finished its work, and Carleton was ready to wash his hands of them:

The War Department, General, has performed its whole duty in having brought these Navajo Indians into subjection and now, in my opinion, stands ready to transfer them to the Department of the Interior. Other tribes along the Gila and in Arizona are murdering our people and committing robberies almost every week. We certainly should not be embarrassed with the care of Indians no longer hostile. So that it follows that laws should be at once passed to provide for them, and the proper officers be sent out immediately to receive them. We certainly, as soldiers, have come to that point where our services cannot properly be required any longer with anything which concerns the Navajos, unless it be to station a guard in their midst for the preservation of order, and to protect them for a while from the nomads of the plains.[98]

Carleton's communications about the Navajos were referred to Commissioner of Indian Affairs William P. Dole. Dole conceded, in a letter written to Secretary of the Interior John P. Usher, on April 11, 1864, that the Navajos "forced from their mountain homes and located upon a tract of country entirely in a state of nature," should be fed and clothed by the government. Commissioner Dole, however, commented: "I feel constrained to say, however, that the spirit manifested in General Carleton's communication, so far as it has reference to the past or future action of the Indian Bureau, is manifestly unkind, and the references unfair." [99]

Having advised the War Department of the situation at Bosque Redondo, Carleton wrote on March 11, 1864, to Major Henry D. Wallen, commanding officer at Fort Sumner, instructing him to reduce the rations for the Navajos. Carleton was beginning to see that rounding up Navajos in their own country, and herding them across New Mexico to a place of confinement, was one thing; that maintaining them as prisoners was another.[100] In his letter to Major Wallen, Carleton instructed him to fix the rations at one pound of food per day per person:

I have heard that over five thousand of the Navajos have surrendered, and, within a few days, you will have over two thousand of this tribe; the other three thousand are about leaving Fort Canby. This question about sufficient food for them to support life, is one about which, as you may well suppose, I am very anxious. In conversing with Colonel Carson, Governor Connelly, and Major McFerran, on this point, I find it is their opinion that one pound of flour, or meal, or of meat, into soup, could be made to be enough, and is probably more nutriment per day than they have been accustomed to obtain. Counting big and little, it is believed that this would feed them. On this basis, one pound of food per day — that is to say, of flour, or of corn or of wheat, or of meat, made into soup or atole — I can barely see how they can be supported until we get provisions from the States, or their corn becomes ripe enough to pluck. The other day it occurred to me that it would not be well for you to sow much wheat; but I am told the wheat crop will mature much sooner than corn, and therefore submit the question entirely to your judgment as to how much of each you will plant. You will at once commence the system of issuing the pound. The Indians themselves must be informed of the necessity of the restriction. Unless this plan be adopted, and at once, ultimate suffering must ensue. Soup and atole are the most nutritious, and the best way in which the food should be prepared, to go a long way and at the same time be wholesome.

Optimistic over making a crop, General Carleton offered minute suggestions to Major Wallen about planting:

I am told the Navajos never plough. I am told that corn can be planted (so the ground be prepared for irrigation) in hills, and that if afterwards the intermediate grass be cut down, and the turf loosened, quite a good crop can be raised in that way. I have more anxiety about the length and capacity of your acequia than a little. If you only have water enough, you can plant wheat, corn, beans, English turnips, in this order, until the summer be far advanced. The Indian villages should be along the acequia and each family or band have their separate lot, so that all could be spading up ground and getting it ready at the same time. Your acequia should be at least six miles in length allowing that your land to be cultivated is one mile in width. If the land is narrower, the acequia should be longer. If you can get in six sections of crops, you can laugh at next winter. Working every hand every hour from morning until evening, you all will be surprised at what you will accomplish.... Being upon the ground, you will be the best judge of how best to employ your force. The troops I know will feel like lending a hand in so important a work.... With plenty of water and such a soil, I am sure you can raise a year's supply of bread this year.

The Mescalero Apaches, in the beginning of their captivity, were fairly well satisfied at Bosque Redondo. They were displeased, however, when the Navajos joined them there, according to a report sent to the Commissioner of Indian Affairs by Lorenzo Labadie, United States Indian Agent at Fort Sumner on Oct. 22, 1864. In Labadie's opinion, it had been a fatal mistake to settle Navajos in an Apache country. Referring to the difficulties between Apaches and Navajos on and off the reservation, Labadie expressed views entirely contrary to those of General Carleton, who believed that the two tribes could live together in peace and harmony. Describing the difficulties between Navajos and Apaches, which resulted in the killing of fifty-two Navajos in one day, Labadie wrote:

During the month of December last year a war party of one hundred and thirty Navajos passed near the reservation with 1,000 sheep. I followed them with twenty Apaches, for twenty-six miles, when we overtook the party, and after a fight of four hours, succeeded in retaking the stolen property, and leaving twelve dead Navajos on the field of battle, our only loss being one Apache mortally wounded. On the 4th day of January of this year the Navajos returned to avenge their loss. Taking advantage of the darkness of night, they approached within one mile of the post, and drove off sixty horses belonging to the Apaches, together with others belonging to the military department. At five o'clock in the morning, in a cold storm, almost insupportable, I again started with sixty Apaches, accompanied by Lieut. Newbold and fifteen mounted men. After following the trail nine miles we overtook the enemy, evidently awaiting our arrival, formed in a small valley to give us battle. We immediately attacked them, and fought from eleven o'clock until sundown, retaking all the stolen stock, except twenty-seven horses, a part of those not recovered had taken a different direction. There were one hundred and twenty Navajos in the fight, fifty-two of whom were left dead on the field, and others escaped wounded under the cover of darkness. The Mescaleros are ever prompt to serve the government, and when thus employed are as cheerful and obedient as regular soldiers.

The Mescaleros seemed to get along all right, according to Labadie, until the Navajos began to move in at the Bosque. From that time on, according to Labadie, the Navajos made life miserable for the Apaches:

During the last year all was contentment among the Mescaleros. They had no one to annoy them, and believed themselves sole proprietors of the reservation. They planted their crops, and were not molested; great interest was manifested by the tribe to live a civilized life; but since the arrival of the Navajos their ardor has been dampened. The Navajos are much more numerous, and never cease to threaten them when they recur to their former difficulties. During the summer many difficulties have arisen between the two tribes — the Apaches in defense of their fields and gardens, and the Navajos in endeavoring to destroy them. The commander of the post made use of every means to prevent these abuses, but without effect. They fought; Navajos were confined in the guardhouse; shots were sometimes fired at them by the guards, but all could not prevent them from stealing from the Apaches; in fact, their fields were, in some cases, completely destroyed; and to make matters still worse, as the corn commenced maturing, a worm destroyed great quantities, and between the Navajo Indians and the insect they left but little to harvest. The Mescaleros, after all their ill fortune in their corn fields, were, however, more fortunate with their gardens, of which they had one hundred acres under cultivation. . . . The Navajos and Apaches cannot agree, and it is impracticable to locate the two tribes together. I have witnessed the difficulties during the year and am satisfied that my presence and the proximity of the military alone prevented an open rupture long ago. I regard the attempt to permanently locate the Navajos in this valley as a fatal error. The land, wood and water are sufficient for the Mescalero and Jicarilla Apaches alone, who together will number about 3,000. To locate the Navajos, who number not less than 15,000 together with them must prove a failure. The Apaches and Navajos cannot ever agree. They are savages, and must remain so for many years. And if the military force should be removed in five or ten years, the old animosity would end in driving the weaker party from the reservation.[101]

The corn crop at Bosque Redondo, with which General Carleton expected to feed the Indians through the winter of 1864, and the spring of 1865, was a total failure. This was a major blow to Carleton's plans. He deferred sending the bad news on to Washington until Oct. 30, 1864, when he wrote from Santa Fe to advise Adjutant-General Thomas of the seriousness of the situation:

I have delayed making a formal report on the important matter of subsisting the Navajo and Apache Indians now on the Bosque Redondo reservation, until I could learn definitely the probable result of the harvest in this Territory. Everything at Bosque Redondo was a success this year except the corn crop. We had a field of nearly three thousand acres, which promised to mature finely, when, after it had tasselled, and the ears formed, it was attacked by what they call here the cut worm, or army worm, and the whole crop destroyed.

The truth of the matter was that by the fall of 1864 thousands of Navajos at the Bosque were in a fair way to die from starvation. It was almost impossible to obtain and transport food supplies for them from the Missouri River, almost the only available source of supply. New Mexico failed to produce sufficient grain in 1864 to take care of civilian requirements. Confronted with a situation that was rapidly reaching the desperation stage, Carleton wrote to Brigadier General Marcellus M. Crocker, Commanding Officer at Fort Sumner on Oct. 31, 1864, asking him to tell the Navajos to be "too proud to murmur." He suggested that Crocker show the Indians how to make dugouts as a protection against the cold of approaching winter. Carleton was hopeful that he might obtain authority to buy 4,000 sheep which would be sent to the Bosque from Fort Union, "to furnish wool to weave into blankets for the smaller children." Carleton was anxious that Crocker see to it that the carcass of a sheep was wisely butchered. He suggested soup as part of the food ration for the Navajos. He blamed crop failures on the elements:

The skins of sheep can be dressed for clothing, and the flesh issued for food; the whole animal, including what the butchers call the "head and pluck," must be issued. . . . The economy in the use of food in all things must be observed. The making of soups, which is by far the best way to cook what they have, must be inculcated as a religion. And let me observe that one pound of solid food made into nutritious soup — nutritious because well and thoroughly boiled, for each man, woman and child, per day —for a Frenchman—is more than he wants, and more than he gets, as a rule. . . . Tell the Navajos to be too proud to murmur at what cannot be helped. We could not foresee the total destruction of their corn crop, nor would we foresee that the frost and hail would come and destroy the other crops in the Territory— but tell them not to be discouraged; to work hard, every man and woman, to put in large fields next year, when if God smiles on our efforts, they will, at one bound, be forever placed beyond want and be independent; tell them not to believe ever that we are not their best friends.

The Navajos had Carleton's implied permission to forage for beef in Comanche country:

If the Navajos had the spirit with reference to the Comanches which they ought to have toward their hereditary enemies, a war party of 500 of the former could go out and get all the stock they wanted. It would add to the punishment which the Comanches deserve for their stock depredations and butcheries of this year.[102]

By midsummer of 1864, it was an open secret in military and official circles at Fort Sumner and Santa Fe, that things were in a bad way at Bosque Redondo. Almost nine thousand Navajos and Apaches, men, women and children, were confined and impounded in a place that offered no immediate hope for sustaining life for more than a few hundred people at the maximum. Supplies from Missouri river points, under ordinary circumstances, were hauled overland with difficulty and at enormous expense. During wartime, the task of getting supplies across the Plains offered tremendous obstacles. Bushwhackers and Indians were on the alert, day and night, to rob and loot supply trains. Getting supplies through from Fort Leavenworth to Fort Union to care for the military in New Mexico was difficult enough. Getting supplies through for thousands of Indians was an insuperable task.

As of December 31, 1864, a census taken by Captain Francis McCabe, 1st Cavalry, New Mexico Volunteers, showed that there were 8,354 Navajos at the Bosque, made up of 1,782 families. Their possessions included 3,038 horses, 143 mules, 6,962 sheep, 2,858 goats and 630 looms. In addition to the Navajos, there were 405 Mescalero Apaches and 20 Gila Apaches at the Bosque, with 14 Gila Apaches reported as captured and enroute.

By order of General Carleton a bulletin was issued by Assistant Adjutant General Cutler, at the year end of 1864, telling of the army's hardships and achievements in the war against the Indians, and of the predicament in which the Navajos found themselves:

The Navajos soon found they had no place of security from

such determined adversaries, and, being pressed on every hand by unexampled vigor, the spirit of the tribe was soon broken. Many were captured, and more voluntarily surrendered, when, in bands of fifty to one and two thousand, they commenced their pilgrimage to the Bosque Redondo, a place selected for them by the government, and situated upon the open plains east of the Rio Grande, and more than four hundred miles from their native valleys and mountains. The exodus of this whole people, men, women and children, with their flocks and herds, leaving forever the land of their fathers was an interesting but touching sight.

With the Navajos subdued to some extent at least, the troops campaigned against the Apaches in Arizona:

Then came the operations of the troops against the Apaches of Arizona. To those acquainted with the difficulties of campaigning in that distant country — formidable against the movement and supply of troops in every way in which a country can be formidable, whether considered on account of its deserts, its rugged and sterile mountains, its frequent and often impassable defiles, and, in widely extended regions, the scarcity of water and grass — the wonder will be that the troops were ever able to overtake the Indian at all. . . . The marches of the troops were long and sometimes repaid by but poor results. For example, on one expedition, under one of our most distinguished officers, the troops marched 1,200 miles and actually killed but one Indian. Oftentimes long scouts would be made, and not an Indian, or even the track of one, would be discovered.[103]

Although conditions at Bosque Redondo were discouraging in the later months of 1864, nevertheless General Carleton pushed his campaign against the Navajos with never ceasing vigilance and diligence. Herrera Grande and five other Navajo chiefs were brought to Santa Fe from Bosque Redondo in compliance with Carleton's order to General Crocker at Fort Sumner. Carleton talked to them on Feb. 15, 1865, in the presence of Governor Henry Connelly and Don Jose Manuel Gallegos, and through an interpreter instructed them:

They were to go out into the old Navajo country and tell the Navajos still remaining there that they must come in at once, and go to the reservation at Bosque Redondo; that this is the last warning they will have; that if they come in now, their stock shall remain as their own. But if, within five weeks from the time of the notice, they are not at Fort Wingate, the door will be shut, and we will fight them, the people will fight them, and the Utes will fight them, and they will be destroyed. In this case their blood will be on their own heads, not on ours, as they have had fair warning. These Navajos whom I send out as delegates with this warning are then to return to Santa Fe, and thence to the Bosque Redondo, without waiting for any others.

Chief Herrera Grande and his lieutenants went into Navajo country, interviewed Chief Manuelito, and attempted to persuade him to go to the Bosque and take his people with him. Manuelito answered:

That he could not go to the Bosque; that his God and his mother lived in the west and he would not leave them; that there was a tradition that his people should never cross the Rio Grande, the Rio San Juan, or the Rio Colorado; that he also could not pass three mountains, and particularly could not leave the Chusca Mountains, his native hills; that his intention was to remain; that he was there to suffer all the consequences of war or famine; that he had now nothing to lose but his life; and that they could come and take him whenever they pleased, but he would not move; that he had never done any wrong to the Americans or Mexicans; that he had never robbed, but had lived on his own resources; that if he were killed, innocent blood would be shed.

Dissatisfied with Manuelito's stand, Carleton sent a message to Major Julius C. Shaw, Commanding Officer at Fort Wingate, on March 23, 1865:

Try hard to get Manuelito. Have him securely ironed and carefully guarded. It will be a mercy to others whom he controls to capture or kill him at once. I prefer he should be captured. If he attempt to escape when again in our power, as he did from Fort Canby, he will be shot down.[104]

The year 1865 was the most disastrous for New Mexico within the memory and experience of any man then living in the Territory. Apparently no part of New Mexico enjoyed immunity from disaster. Heavy frosts nipped the buds and blossoms, and destroyed the fruit from one end of New Mexico to the other. Torrential hail and rain storms at one time, and devastating drouths at another, seemingly conspired to thwart man's efforts to produce the fruits of the earth. Locusts and grasshoppers descended on fields of wheat, corn and beans in the granary counties of Taos, Mora, Rio Arriba and San Miguel, devouring every stalk, branch and blossom. Crops of every kind were a total failure. The Rio Abajo country, from Peña Blanca on the north to Las Cruces on the south, a distance of over two hundred miles, resembled in appearance a Babylonic destruction. Spring time flood waters of the Rio Grande washed out overnight the river bottom wheat and corn fields of Bernalillo County, and threatened the lives of the people to such an extent that the entire population was forced to flee to the hills. From Los Lunas to Paraje, a distance up and down the Rio Grande more than 100 miles, and westward from Albuquerque to Fort Wingate, the grasshoppers and corn worms destroyed every leaf, branch and twig. The river settlements of Atrisco, Pajarito and Padillas, several miles south of Albuquerque, were almost entirely submerged. La Mesa and Sabinal, below Los Lunas, were surrounded by the combined flood waters of the Rio Grande, and the Rio Puerco. Flood conditions prevailed along the Rio Grande as far south as Las Cruces and Mesilla. Many people of the afflicted communities found themselves homeless and destitute as a result of the floods. Appeals were made to Santa Fe for help, and the Pueblo Indians, because of the knowledge that it was their custom to store up grain against the coming of the lean years, were asked for donations of foodstuffs. No doubt about it, there was no harvest of grain, fruits or vegetables in New Mexico in the year 1865. The Santa Fe *Gazette* of June 17 summed up the extent of the calamity by saying: "Properly to describe the misery created by frost, flood and other combinations of earth and sky this year, a man ought to write with tears instead of ink."

The disaster that overwhelmed most of New Mexico in 1865 did not spare the Bosque Redondo in the Pecos river country. The corn crop at the Bosque for 1865, planted with care and laboriously cultivated, and upon which Carleton had depended to feed the Indians through the fall and winter of that year, proved a total failure. This was a stunning blow for the entire project. The failure of the corn crop in 1864 had been tragic enough, but the 1865 failure was infinitely more serious because of the total crop failure throughout the Territory. Upon learning that a worm was threatening for the second consecutive year to destroy the corn crop at the Bosque, Carleton sent a letter to Major William McCleave, Commanding Officer at Fort Sumner, on July 18, 1865, urging him to exterminate the pest, if at all possible. Carleton offered such suggestions as occurred to him:

So much is at stake in this matter that I wish you would make the attempt to remove the worm from the ears of the corn, and let me know the result. The moth that lays the egg looks like a small butterfly; and if some plan could be had to destroy that, the evil would be attacked at the proper place. In Kansas, it is said that plates with molasses in them were placed on posts in corn fields, and at these the moths would come, when they could be destroyed. It would be well to try this experiment in three or four places. Of course in your extended farm, it would be impossible to carry it out effectually.

A bit panicky by the unexpected turn of events, and anticipating tragic consequences, Carleton wrote a long letter to Washington, explaining the situation:

The failure of the corn crop at Bosque Redondo this year was a visitation of God — I could not contend against it. It came, and now we must meet the consequences as best we may. The Indians cannot be turned loose, or even taken back to their country, without being obliged to war upon the people, as heretofore, or perish. . . . We must feed them where they are, at least until the harvest of next year. . . . The future of not only New Mexico, but of Arizona, depends on the determination and the ability of the general government to hold this formidable tribe of Navajos, now that it has been subdued and gotten in hand, until it can support itself. . . . You can hardly imagine, General, the great difficulties which have lain in the path leading toward the settlement of this nation. . . . Congress passed a bill appropriating one hundred thousand dollars toward clothing and getting them farming utensils, tools and the like. This was the first of July last, and as yet, not a yard of cloth, or a blanket, or a spade, or plough, has reached them. Now, cold weather is setting in, and I have thousands of women and children who need the protection of a blanket. It is said that the goods bought by this money left Leavenworth on October 1. With good luck they may be at Bosque Redondo by the tenth of December. All these things the Indians were told would be here long ago, and they have waited and hoped for them until now, when the winter is upon us, and they think we may be acting in bad faith. This has been very unfortunate. Add to this the complete destruction by the army worm of their crops, which they labored so hard to raise. Then, to fill the measure of their troubles, the failure of the crops elsewhere in their Territory obliges me to cut down their rations. . . . It is absolutely necessary that two thousand five hundred head of good cattle be bought in Kansas or Missouri and sent out at once. . . . Then, if we cannot get bread, we can give the Indians more meat, and at least keep them from perishing.

The Navajo prisoners, slowly starving to death, homesick and heartsick, many of them desperately ill, deserted the detested Bosque Redondo in droves in the late summer and fall of 1865.[105]

CHAPTER SIX

Martial Law

NEW MEXICO NEWSPAPERMEN endured their fair share of annoyance and vexation during the Civil War years. Some of them, on occasion, spent considerable time cursing and damning, in absentia, the horses and mules that had transported them to the Territory. Editors reminded their readers, from time to time, that New Mexico was a land of grasshoppers and

smallpox, of desolation and disillusionment, of famine and
pestilence. In pre-Civil War years mail service was suspended,
now and then, for periods of from ten days to six weeks, because of Indian uprisings. Stagecoach traffic was abandoned
entirely at the outbreak of the war. From 1861 until 1865
any mail that got through to New Mexico was forwarded to
Santa Fe, Albuquerque and Mesilla, the three principal post-
offices, through the military, at long time intervals. New
Mexico had no telegraph communication of any kind until
three years after the end of the war.[106]

New Mexico's population in 1860 was 93,516, including
40,000 Indians. The territory served by newspaper coverage
was vast, and most of it was inaccessible for all ordinary purposes.[107] But few newspapers were published in New Mexico
during the period between the American Occupation and the
Civil War. All publications were in Spanish, or in both English and Spanish. The most important papers of the war
years in the territory were the Santa Fe *New Mexican,* and the
Santa Fe *Gazette,* both weeklies. Both were forced to suspend
publication temporarily at times during the Civil War, because of "military necessity."[108] Both the *New Mexican* and
the *Gazette* changed political policy from time to time, before,
during and after the Civil War. For some months prior to
the war, the Santa Fe *Gazette* was pro-slavery. James L. Collins, founder of the *Gazette,* was indiscreet enough, while Superintendent of Indian Affairs in New Mexico, to write a
letter to Commissioner of Indian Affairs Greenwood during
the national political campaign of 1860, which later caused
him considerable embarrassment. The Collins letter, among
other things, advised Greenwood in confidence: "I hope to
God no such calamity will befall the country as the election
of Abraham Lincoln." That the *Gazette* was pro-slavery and
anti-Lincoln was demonstrated by an editorial published in
that paper on Feb. 2, 1861:

To attempt to subjugate the southern states looks very much
like an absurd project. The southern people will fight until the
last drop of blood shall have been shed, or until the invader shall

have been driven from the soil. The mercenary hosts from the north will meet on the battlefield men who will take up arms in defense of their liberties and altars, and who will not lay them down until all their rights shall have been vindicated, and their peaceable enjoyment secured for the future. It is most devoutly to be prayed that such a conflict will never take place; that such wisdom will prevail in Mr. Lincoln's counsels as will avert this collision and all its dreadful consequences. The party of which Mr. Lincoln is now the head has, in all conscience, been the author of enough injury to the human race, in so perverting the spirit of the government as to make it odious in the sight of so many of the states as to render secession necessary for the maintenance of rights sacred to them under the constitution of the confederation; we say in this they have done enough injury to our race without now adding to past iniquities the crimes of bloodshed and devastation.

Three weeks later, on Feb. 23, 1861, the day on which Texas seceded from the Union, the *Gazette* published an editorial on page 1, written in Spanish, addressed "To the People of New Mexico," warning of dire things to come, and urging them to be on guard to protect against invasion of their property rights, religion, laws and customs. The editorial was a frank and open appeal to New Mexicans of Spanish or Mexican ancestry, to align themselves with the Confederate cause. There were those in Santa Fe who suspected that Alexander M. Jackson (who had become Secretary of the Territory on Dec. 23, 1858), had either written or inspired both the editorial of Feb. 2, and the appeal to the Spanish speaking people of Feb. 23. It was well known that Jackson, while serving as Territorial Secretary, had been an active and open "advocate of rebellion."

The editorial published in the *Gazette* of Feb. 23, was also distributed as a broadside. Pointing out the possibilities if the "detestable principles of Black Republicanism" prevailed, the *Gazette's* front page editorial in part was as follows:

Political events of importance are now transpiring in the states, which sooner or later, for good or evil, will affect your destinies. The government of the Republic, in case there exists any, for the first time is passing into the hands of a party purely sectional in its origin, the principles and powers of which party abjure the constitution, appealing to a higher law which has neither the sanction of God nor man.... Fellow citizens, we put this paper before you that you may be upon your guard against any insidious design which the coming party may entertain against you, or their emissary officers who will soon be among you.... Their programme in this Territory will be commenced by an onslaught against your just legislation in regard to the protection of the property of your fellow citizens who possess African slaves, but they will not be satisfied with that; your holy religion, your civil rights, your social bands, your established laws, so well adapted to your condition, they will very soon dispatch with the same spirit of fanaticism which sees nothing inviolable which is not in conformity with the edicts of their infidelity towards God, and their intolerance toward man.... The detestable principles of Black Republicanism are not the principles of the American people.... After enjoying a power of short duration, this horde of infidels will be driven from the capital, and you as well as your fellow citizens of the states whose rights are menaced, will be left in peace and prosperity.[109]

The Rio Abajo Weekly *Press,* published in Albuquerque during most of the Civil War years, was a fairly well edited paper, although a bit shabby looking at times, while suffering from what its editor noted as a "lack of political pap." The Mesilla *Times,* published in the then important town of Mesilla, in the extreme southern part of New Mexico, was definitely pro-Southern before the Civil War, and until it suspended publication when Baylor returned to Texas after the Sibley debacle. No complete file of the *Times* is in existence today, insofar as known, to tell accurately the story of its fight to uphold and extend the doctrine of states' rights. From a review of copies of the paper now available, it is apparent that the editor of the *Times* was a fiery individual, with ability to write front page editorials which caused Mesilla Valley people to hurrah for Jeff Davis at mass meetings, and enthusiastically espouse the Southern cause.[110]

No doubt but that the Mesilla *Times,* in the early months of 1861, reflected the temper of most Mesilla Valley people. In many parts of the valley, particularly in the county seat of

Mesilla, there was a strong and persistent sentiment for the Confederacy. On March 16, 1861, a group of Southern sympathizers gathered in Mesilla (then a town of 2,420, according to the U. S. Census of 1860), and adopted resolutions declaring among other things that "the people of New Mexico would not recognize the present black administration," and that they "would resist any officers appointed to the Territory by said administration with whatever means in our power." [111] New Mexico's representative in Washington at the time was Delegate in Congress John S. Watts, a Union man. Observing with alarm the progress of events, Delegate Watts wrote to Major General H. W. Halleck, of the War Department, on March 23, 1861, pointing out the possibility that New Mexico might be attacked by Texas troops, with the result that "the valley of the Rio Grande would be desolated for 200 miles." Pleading for prompt help for "the oppressed people of New Mexico," Watts offered to sacrifice his own personal interests for the good of the country:

I have been twenty-six times across the plains; feel a deep interest in the rescue from destruction of the people of New Mexico, who have been my friends for many years, and if my services should be required I will leave my place here vacant, and without money and without price, aid all I can to forward the movement. I do not wish to command, but will go and aid the command or commandant all in my power if it should be thought best for me to do so.[112]

The Confederate "Territory of Arizona" (carved out of New Mexico and Arizona) with Mesilla as its capital, had been in existence *de jure,* insofar as the Congress of the Confederate States of America might be concerned, since March 10, 1861. That conditions in the new Confederate "Territory" were unstable, and disconcerting to its citizens, was evident from a letter written from "Mesilla, Ariz. Terr.", on June 6, 1861, to Dr. E. N. Covey,[113] by Samuel J. Jones, R. P. Kelley, James A. Lucas and L. S. Owings. Sam Jones and companions wanted Dr. Covey to explain to officials in Montgomery the conditions prevailing in the new territory. They were apprehensive that "ere twelve months, abolitionism will be preached among us without fear." The letter, reflecting apprehension of Confederate adherents in the Mesilla valley, was in part as follows:

You will confer a great favor on the citizens of this Territory by representing to the department at Montgomery our exposed condition, with which you are perfectly familiar. We desire above all things a Territorial organization by the Confederate States of America, the subjugation of all the Indian tribes, and the administration of law and justice. Should the Confederate Congress not deem it prudent to give us these, please ask that means be sent to this Territory to arm and equip one volunteer regiment to be kept in active service against the marauding savages. This would insure peace with the Indians, would strengthen and perpetuate that sympathy with the South which is now unanimous. All this may be done without any conflict with the U. S. troops now here, unless it should be desired by the government of the Confederate States of America. You will also please represent that most, if not all, the officers who are not Republicans or Abolitionists in the U. S. Army will resign, and the vacancies will be filled by those who are opposed to the South, leaving in our midst those directly opposed to the sentiments of the community, and between the marauding Indian and an opposition without protection and laws, it is fair to conclude that ere twelve months, abolitionism will be preached among us without fear, and hence opposition, and open contest for North and South. You will be able to explain this more fully, and by so doing will confer a lasting favor on the people of Arizona and render the Confederate States of America some service too.[114]

That "matters" in Mesilla were in a "deplorable condition," was declared by W. W. Mills, a Union sympathizer, of El Paso, some 40 miles to the south. Mills wrote from Mesilla on June 23, 1861 (four weeks before Baylor captured nearby Fort Fillmore), to Delegate Watts, then in Santa Fe, describing the situation as he observed it:

I assure you that I find matters here in a most deplorable condition. A disunion flag is now flying from the house in which I write, and this country is now as much in the possession of the enemy as Charleston is. All the officers at Fort Fillmore, except two, are avowedly with the South, and are only holding on to

their commissions in order to embarrass our government, and at
the proper time to turn over everything to the South, after the
manner of General Twiggs. The Mesilla Times is bitterly disunion, and threatens with death any one who refuses to acknowledge this usurpation. . . . The soldiers at Fillmore, in defiance of
the teachings of their officers, and the offer of gold from Hart, are
yet faithful, and, if a second lieutenant were to ask them to follow him, they would tear down the Confederate flag here, and
throw the Times office into the Rio Grande in one hour. . . .

The Santa Fe *Gazette* suspended publication on March 22,
1862, the day on which the Confederates captured New Mexico's capital city. Major C. L. Pyron, of Sibley's brigade, commanding Confederate troops in Santa Fe, sent a note to John
T. Russell, the *Gazette's* editor, which was brief and to the
point:

Santa Fe, New Mexico, March 22, 1862.
Mr. John T. Russell: Sir: — You deliver to the barrer the keys
of the printing of the Santa Fe Gazett.
C. L. Pyron, C.S.A.
Maj. Comd'g. Santa Fe.

Printers recruited from Pyron's command took over the
Gazette plant, and by March 23 had set up in type, and were
printing hundreds of copies of General Sibley's proclamation,
issued at Albuquerque on March 13, urging the inhabitants
of New Mexico to unite with the invaders. Editor Russell had
been deprived of the *Gazette* at a most inopportune time. Exciting things were taking place in Santa Fe. There had not
been so much commotion in the capital since Aug. 18, 1846,
fifteen years previous, the first day of the American Occupation. The Confederates were masters of Santa Fe. Men from
Texas and other southern states, walking and riding, lashing
at mules, hurrying up supply trains and ammunition wagons,
were on their way through Santa Fe to attack federal troops
known to be on the Santa Fe trail some place west of Fort
Union. Although deprived of his newspaper by the fortunes
of war, the Confederates allowed Editor Russell the freedom
of the city. In going about Santa Fe, Russell must have been
aware of the excitement among the people when it became

known that Hon. J. M. Gallegos, former Delegate in Congress, and Facundo Pino, a very prominent citizen of Santa Fe, had been arrested by the Texans, and were confined under military guard; and of the buzzing that followed the discovery by the Texans of valuable government supplies stored away to await delivery at an opportune time to the Navajo Indians. The supplies had been hidden by James L. Collins, Superintendent of Indian Affairs, in a place believed safe from discovery. "Some one betrayed the place of concealment," was the explanation heard on the street. The Texans confiscated the supplies and put them to good use without delay. There was talk too, which Russell might have heard, that some few Texans had gone into stores in Santa Fe, purchased trinkets and merchandise, and then walked out without paying; but such incidents were rare after the first few days of the occupation.

That Santa Fe had fallen into the hands of the Confederates seemed incredible to many, but it was not such a preposterous happening to those who had closely observed the trend of events in New Mexico. There were even those who put in writing just how they felt about the entire situation. Among those who wrote down his thoughts in the early months of the war was William Need.[115]

Contending that "intolerable conditions" had existed in New Mexico before and after the beginning of the war, Need wrote a personal letter to Secretary of War Simon Cameron, in Washington, composed "at intervals snatched from military duty as a sentinel on the watch tower," at Fort Fauntleroy, in western New Mexico. Written on Sept. 27, 1861, Need's letter was critical of men in public life in New Mexico and Arizona. He scolded about government policy in conducting military affairs in the field and at army posts. He accused the government of mismanagement in administration of affairs. Pontificating on many subjects of first importance at the time, Need's letter demonstrated an intelligent grasp of questions of current interest in the Southwest:

As an old printer, and soldier of the line in the grand Union

Army, I exercise the privilege of addressing you this communication. Having resided sufficiently long in New Mexico and Arizona to become measurably acquainted with the wants and wishes of the people ... of a country ... which ... is nearly four times as large as the state of Missouri, I feel that I can with some degree of safety and accuracy describe to you the present political condition and standing of the community. After the conquest of New Mexico in 1846 by the army of General Stephen W. Kearny, the people hereof have had a succession of military and civil governors, embracing General Kearny, Colonel Washington, Colonel Weightman, Colonel John Munroe, Colonel Garland, Major Bonneville, Colonel Fauntleroy and Colonel W. W. Loring, besides Governors Calhoun, Lane, Meriwether, and Rencher. I am not aware that any of these gentlemen, comprising a list of high sounding names, ever distinguished themselves by any signal abilities or left their impress upon the statutes or improved the pecuniary condition of the inhabitants, their manners or morals. There are no visible monuments in the Territory, or gilded marks of progress or improvement to denote their deeds as warriors or acquirements as civilians.... The country, stretching from the Kansas borders or Indian Territory west of the Arkansas, extends to the Colorado river west and to the Mexican line of Sonora on the south.

Officials of New Mexico had no time to administer affairs in Arizona, Need claimed, with the result that a group in Arizona had attempted to establish a separate sovereignty:

The governors of New Mexico somehow or other never have paid the slightest attention to the will or wishes or wants of the people of the district of Arizona, and hence the citizens of that expansive region, under the political teachings of Philemon T. Herbert, Judge Edward McGowan, Samuel J. Jones, Lieut. S. Mowry, Judge Lucas, Governor Owings, Granville H. Oury, Colonel Ewell (of the U.S. Army), and others, sought to erect, a little more than a year ago, a provisional government, embracing the region lying between La Mesilla, on the Rio Grande, and extending north to the Gila, west to the Colorado, and south to the Sonora line. Our country, stretching more than 1,000 miles along the Mexican frontier, requires a vigilant eye to be kept upon the machinations of the secession forces, who are now straining every nerve, using every device, pulling every cord with might and main to circumvent the supporters of our glorious Union, and incorporating the border states of Mexico, into the government of the Confederate States of the South.

The governors of New Mexico, Need contended, were listless and apathetic, secessionists at heart:

While all this is going on, or has been transpiring under their very eyes and noses, what have the governors of New Mexico been doing to avert the fatal catastrophe? Listless and apathetic, if not secessionists at heart, they are the next thing to them, and have remained as dormant and passive as old Mrs. Partington and her door mop. The time has arrived when a "Sir Forcible Feeble" policy will not answer for the region of the Rio Grande. . . . The restless eye of Jeff Davis is particularly bent on Arizona. That country was purchased by him of Santa Anna. I say by Davis, for it was by his influence in the Cabinet, the identical man who swayed the councils of President Pierce, who originated the measure and urged it forward until its final completion. He had an object of no ordinary consideration to accomplish . . . a grand scheme of intercommunication and territorial expansion more vast and complicated than was ever dreamed of by Napoleon Bonaparte in his balmiest days of pride and power. With an eye that never winked and a wing that never tired has Jeff Davis for more than ten years turned his thoughts and desires to the Mexican line for expansion. . . . His military prototypes and proteges, Ewell, Fauntleroy, Steen, Loring, Longstreet, Crittenden, Grayson, Rhett, Raynolds, and others, were placed here purposely to second and forward his ulterior designs.

Need was critical of the calibre of men sent to govern New Mexico:

A governor is necessarily thrown upon his own resources in assuming to govern the people of New Mexico. If he has paucity of intellect, no staid or fixed principles, no wise or comprehensive view of statesmanship, no ripe judgment, no iron will or determination to guide him, he will be a perfect cipher, a mere pumpkin head at the helm of affairs. I speak it more in sorrow than in anger when I say that the governing power in New Mexico, since it has been under the jurisdiction and subject to the American Union, has been anything than possessing a vigorous grasp and characterized by energy and ability. The numerous Indian wars, the disregard of law and open defiance of courts and legislative enactments, the murders and robberies which are perpetrated with impunity all over the country, the demoralization of the U. S. Army, and the abandonment of their duty and of the Union in solemn contravention of their oath of officers high on the roll of military fame have all measurably proceeded from want of vigor and decisive action on part of the executive head....

A Republican governor instead of "old Rencher" might have saved the day; "old fogy generals and governors" had "played the deuce" with the entire region:

Had a Republican governor been appointed for this Territory last May (instead of old Rencher, who is fit, perhaps, to govern Buncombe or Currituck counties in North Carolina), the robbing of government trains, the burning and surrendering of military posts, and the disgraceful surrender of old Lynde, superannuated and unfit for service, of a U. S. force of 750 men to 350 Texas cutthroats would never have occurred.... Old fogy generals and governors have played the deuce with this region. They have permitted the demoralization of the army and the people, the spread of faro and monte banks, the reign of lynch law and filibusterism, vice and crime to run riot, and virtue, liberty and intelligence to be overslaughed. There must be a change, a radical change, or the country is undone.... In the meantime, while the war is progressing, I desire to call your attention to the condition of things in this Territory. I have visited five forts — Buchanan, Breckinridge, McLane, Fillmore, and Fauntleroy — within the last six months — and at each of these military posts I have uniformly found the sutlers to be bold, open, avowed secessionists in favor of the Confederate States of the South, real, live, pure, adamantine Jeff Davis rebels ... sucking blood, charging about five prices for everything they have to sell to Union soldiers.

Private Need described Fort Fauntleroy, and expressed his views on Navajo Indian troubles:

Fort Fauntleroy is located about 140 miles west of Albuquerque, a town on the Rio Grande. It is far advanced in the Navajo country. The weather here at the present time is delightful, the air cool and bracing. The distance from here to old Fort Defiance (deserted) is about forty-five miles; from Fort McLane (burnt down or destroyed), about 120, nearly due south. The Navajos appear to be a peaceable, quiet, inoffensive sort of Indian, more sinned against than sinning, five times over, I venture to assert. White people here do a great many things in this country, and then lay it to the charge of the poor Indians. They get one pound of beef, perhaps, from the government, and are charged with twenty, one blanket, and are charged with six, one pound of tobacco and charged with ten, and so on ad infinitum.

The Indians were cuffed and kicked about, but, in Need's opinion, would react to justice and kindness:

They are kicked and cuffed about on all sides, and if they venture to complain or retaliate upon their oppressors or aggressors, a great hue and cry is raised about the encroachments of the terrible Navajos. All gammon, for the most part. Treated with justice and kindness, they will not be troublesome for the authorities of the United States. Col. Thomas Hart Benton, in his admirable speech delivered in the House of Representatives, at Washington, in the winter of 1854-1855 (see Congressional Globe), told the truth in a manly way about the Navajos and other Indian tribes of New Mexico. That speech will endure. It will "abide unshaken the test of human scrutiny, of talents and of time." If there be a just God, and all nature and revealed religion would imply there is, who rules above, He will yet right the wrongs to which the untutored savages of the forest have been subjected. They have been badly treated and deserve the commiseration and fostering care of the American people.

Need deplored the fact that the soldiers at Fort Fauntleroy did not observe the day of prayer requested by the President and Congress:

These rough notes ... may furnish you with a glimpse of the condition of public matters in this far distant region of the Union, and give you a slight idea how affairs are conducted and progressing in New Mexico and Arizona. ... Yesterday was the day set apart by the President and Congress of the United States as a day of prayer, fasting, and humiliation for the success of the American arms and the return of peace. It was not observed at this post. If the trumpet of the archangel were sounded tomorrow and I was summoned to appear before the throne of the Great Jehovah to testify, I would aver that the facts set forth in the foregoing rough notes are true. I have nothing further to say.

Need warned that there were "secessionists at heart" holding office in New Mexico, as well as in Washington:

There are a number of persons in this Territory, holding office, who are rank secessionists at heart, but pretend loyalty to the Union, to cloak their designs, and to keep their places on account of the salary; they are here, as in Washington, mighty cunning, but won't do to be trusted. They require weeding out.[116]

Because events of major importance overshadowed the minor during Civil War years, New Mexico newspaper men failed to cover in 1861 one of the biggest news stories in New Mexico's history — the trial and hanging of a woman for murder. Not a word was published by any newspaper in the Territory about the then celebrated case of the Territory of New Mexico against Paula Angel, who, charged with the murder of her late lover, Miguel Martín, was tried in the District Court of San Miguel County, before a jury of twelve men. Famed Judge Kirby Benedict was the trial judge. From the testimony developed at the trial it appeared that Paula Angel had permitted Miguel Martín to embrace her, and while submitting to the embrace had taken a butcher knife, which she had concealed about her person, and stabbed him to death. Paula Angel was defended by Attorney Spruce M. Baird (widely known as *"Colorado,"* because of his red beard). Addressing the jury alternately in English and Spanish, Judge Baird pleaded fervently for Paula's life. As Judge Benedict viewed the law of the case, the defendant was guilty of first degree murder, or not guilty of any crime. Kirby Benedict wrote instructions to that effect in his own handwriting, and delivered them to the jury. A bit reluctantly, it may be imagined, the jury returned a verdict finding Paula Angel guilty of murder in the first degree. Judge Benedict sentenced her to be hanged by the neck until dead, on April 26, 1861. The condemned woman was placed in solitary confinement to await the coming of the day on which she would pay the penalty for her misdeed. Each morning Sheriff Antonio Abad Herrera passed by her cell and spoke to her, always using the same words: "Paula! The judge sentenced you to be hanged, and I am going to hang you until you are dead, dead, dead." Each day the sheriff reminded Paula of the number of days yet remaining before the day for the hanging. Poor Paula

Angel grew weaker with each passing day, withering away miserably, almost before the eyes of the sheriff, but he was not a man who believed in pity. Unable to eat, and to sleep only fitfully, Paula's appearance resembled a sack of bones enveloped in flesh. On April 26, 1861, soon after daylight, Sheriff Herrera hitched a team of horses to a spring wagon, loaded Paula Angel into it, and started for the place he had selected for the execution, located near a country road to the northwest of Las Vegas, where there was a large shade tree, with limbs strong enough to accommodate a hanging. Hundreds of people gathered at the place, coming from town and countryside, from the ranches along the Mora and Sapello rivers, some even from far-off Pecos river villages.

Utilizing the wagon bed for a scaffold, Sheriff Herrera placed a rope around Paula's neck. The sheriff had not thought it necessary to tie Paula's arms behind her back, or to tie her knees together. He soon realized that Paula would not submit tamely to hanging. She kicked and squirmed, and fought against the execution to the extent possible in her weakened condition. The sheriff finally managed to tie his victim adequately, then looped the rope over a limb of the tree, and started to drive his team away.

A shudder ran through the crowd, as it appeared inevitable that in a matter of seconds Paula's neck would be broken, perhaps jerked from her body. Strong men grabbed the lines and held the horses' check rein, arguing meanwhile with the sheriff that the woman had already been sufficiently hanged to satisfy the law. Sheriff Herrera disagreed. He said that he was the sheriff of the county of San Miguel; that it was his duty to hang the woman and that he was going to hang her; that he would shoot the first man who attempted to interfere; that he had armed depuies in the crowd who would support him in the performance of his duty. Colonel J. D. Sena of Santa Fe, of the New Mexico Volunteers, addressed the people, urging them not to interfere with the processes of the law. The hanging proceeded. The sheriff made his return on the death warrant in Spanish, which translated read: "I, Antonio Abad Herrera, Sheriff of San Miguel County, New Mexico, do hereby make return on the within warrant; That on the 21st day of April 1861, by the authority in me vested, I did hang Paula Angel, all according to the law of the Territory and instructions of the court." [117]

Martial law, the bane of a newspaper's existence whether in time of peace or war, was in effect in New Mexico from Aug. 8, 1861, to July 4, 1865. During that time, New Mexico's administrative affairs were subject to, if not directed by, the military. The writ of habeas corpus was suspended. Civil courts had no jurisdiction in criminal cases except by consent of the army. But few civil cases were tried during the war years in territorial courts. If General Canby had continued as commander of the Department of New Mexico, martial law, in all probability, would have been abolished in the summer of 1862. But Canby had been succeeded by James H. Carleton, an officer who believed that the army was infinitely more capable of administering public affairs, in times of national emergency, than any other local or federal authority. As a result of Carleton's conviction, New Mexico was governed under the iron clamp of martial law for nearly four years.[118]

Judges of civil courts were restricted in the exercise of the functions of their office. Their jurisdiction was curtailed to conform to the army's views. Military courts took over practically all criminal work, and most of the civil cases. Indian agents, ordinarily working under the direction of the Commissioner of Indian Affairs, occupied a most peculiar situation. They had very little, if anything, to say about management of the Indians. General Carleton's attitude, and his interpretation of martial law, drew guarded fire from the press, the judiciary, and the Indian service. Discreetly worded editorials suggested that General Carleton's policies were not entirely popular with the masses of the people. Hope was expressed that other more important areas of activity might be found for General Carleton which would take him far away from New Mexico. The judiciary chafed under martial law for many months.

Finally, Judge Joseph G. Knapp, of the third judicial district, at Mesilla, challenged Carleton's authority under then existing circumstances, to continue to suppress the functioning of the courts. Dr. Michael Steck, an Indian agent in New Mexico since 1853, questioned Carleton's right to dictate Indian policy. Steck contended, among other things, that Carleton's policy in dealing with the Navajo Indians was fundamentally wrong, and would ultimately result in disaster for the entire tribe. Carleton ignored both Judge Knapp and Dr. Steck for many months, but finally undertook to defend himself in public addresses, and in the press. Both Judge Knapp and Superintendent Steck complained to Washington about the Carleton policy, by petition and in person. But Carleton's viewpoint prevailed at the War Department, and both Knapp and Steck were obliged to resign "for the good of the service."

Residents of the Mesilla Valley, in southern New Mexico, opposing what they considered unnecessary prolongation of martial law, adopted resolutions of opposition to Carleton's policy early in 1863. Attention was directed to the fact that "the Texans passed Fort Craig on their return from Santa Fe on April 25, 1862, and only stopped in the Mesilla Valley because of the neglect of Canby to follow them." The resolutions also pointed out that "the Confederates had abandoned all of their positions, and their whole power in New Mexico had been broken by July 4, 1862, and that by Sept. 26, 1862, the date of Carleton's order extending martial law as proclaimed by Canby, the last remnants of the invading army had reached San Antonio."

Tightening up the lines in a military way, instead of loosening them, Carleton issued an order requiring all persons to carry military passes when traveling from place to place in New Mexico. Judge Knapp contended that judges of courts of record should be exempt from this rule. Carleton decreed otherwise. Defying Carleton's order, Knapp left Mesilla for Santa Fe, without a pass, with the announced intention of attending a session of the Supreme Court commencing

Jan. 2, 1863. As Knapp probably anticipated, he was challenged by every military sentry encountered enroute, but managed to reach Santa Fe, fuming and sputtering with indignation. Taking his seat on the supreme bench, Judge Knapp related his experiences in open court, dwelling particularly on the difficulties he had been obliged to overcome in order to get to Santa Fe. Judge Knapp expressed the hope that in the future the person of the court, while on official business, might be free to come and go any place in the Territory. Six months later, on Aug. 1, 1863, Judge Knapp was arrested at Las Cruces, and confined there in the guardhouse until Aug. 7, "for failure to properly cooperate with the military." Knapp blamed Carleton for his arrest and detention.[119]

Judge Knapp wrote to Brig. Gen. West at Mesilla, on Dec. 24, 1863, saying that although horse thieves and Indians were not obliged to carry military passes, he had been prevented from going to Santa Fe, without one. He told West:

In my character as judge, I cannot and will not take a pass, and shall not call for one. When I desire to travel on private business I will cheerfully submit to any rule you may make, not inconsistent with the dignity of a man; but as a judge my duty not less than my rights prevent me from submitting to any rule or order which can in any manner lower the dignity of that office. If you insist on your terms, I place the responsibility of preventing the courts upon your hands.[120]

In his reply to Judge Knapp's letter, West stated his position:

Your loyalty nor your fidelity as a sworn officer of the government are not in the least questioned by me. The military usage is to allow no man to pass from post to post in this territory, without a permit, signed by competent military authority, with the oath of allegiance of the bearer attached thereto, and then it becomes his safeguard. . . . You cannot go from place to place within my command without the usual pass; this pass will be furnished you upon your application at these headquarters.

Upon receiving West's ultimatum, Judge Knapp had handbills printed by the Denver *News,* in Denver, Colorado (beyond Carleton's jurisdiction), protesting against the permit policy. The handbills were distributed in Mesilla, Albuquerque and Santa Fe, much to the annoyance of the military. Determined to get an official ruling on jurisdictional matters, Knapp wrote to Washington. His letter prompted General Halleck to write a letter to Carleton in Santa Fe on Feb. 4, 1864, calling his attention to the line of demarcation between military rule and the civil courts:

General: Judge Knapp, of New Mexico, in a communication to the Attorney General, has complained among other things that under your authority, military commissioners in your department have taken cognizance of and adjudicated upon actions of debt, trespass, etc., between persons not in the military service. I am directed by the Secretary of War to say that military commissions and military courts in your department have no jurisdiction of such cases, and that their decisions are entirely null and void. Moreover, the individual members may thus render themselves liable to punishment and damage. The practice, if it exists, should be immediately discontinued.[121]

Early in 1864, Knapp sought a showdown on the right of the military to compel members of the judiciary to carry military passes while on official business, by appealing directly to the Attorney General of the United States. The National *Intelligencer* of Feb. 26, 1864, carried several columns of the Knapp argument, one paragraph reading as follows:

It may be, and even has been objected, that I should submit more readily to the regulation requiring passports than any man in this community for the sake of example. That is a question of policy about which men may entertain different opinions. . . . If the commander of the United States forces in New Mexico may proclaim and continue martial law and rules in force in this Territory, compel obedience to them by the citizens for a year and a half after the necessity for the proclamation has ceased, he may continue it indefinitely, and thus pass the whole Territory under despotism at once. Under the orders as they exist, the Judges of courts, the members of the Legislature, the officers of the Territory, and counties, are obliged to get leave of the military to travel in the discharge of their official duties, and private citizens are equally hampered in the transaction of their private business.

A parallel cannot be found in the worst despotism of Europe.... It was reserved for the military commanders of New Mexico to set this example for the world. But I cannot and will not submit to it. The public interests demand my presence in Santa Fe; but public freedom and the liberty of the people in a greater degree require me to resist and oppose all attempts to trample down that freedom and liberty. As my oath of office requires me to "support and defend the Constitution of the United States against all enemies, foreign and domestic," and "bear true faith and allegiance to the same," I will religiously maintain and keep that oath, as well against those who would overthrow it while in the pay of the government as in the ranks of rebellion. The latter I will meet, if need be, with arms in my hands, the former, by the means pointed out by the laws.[122]

Attorney General Bates discussed the problem with President Lincoln, but the President declined to become involved in the controversy. The National *Intelligencer,* of Feb. 26, 1864, published the Attorney General's reply to Knapp, admitting inability to change the situation:

There seems to be a general and a growing disposition of the military, wherever stationed, to engross all power and to treat the civil government with contumely, as if the object were to bring it into contempt. I have delivered my opinion very plainly to the President, and I have reason to hope that he, in the main, concurs with me in believing that those arbitrary proceedings ought to be suppressed. I regret exceedingly the existence of the difficulties of which you so strongly complain, and would be glad to remove them, if it were in my power. But I have no control over the military authorities in New Mexico.

Willing to expose himself to the fire of the military, in order to hasten the return of the day when civil rights would be restored to the people, Judge Knapp convened the Dona Ana County grand jury in special session in Mesilla on June 10, 1864. With an eye on the courtroom door, through which the military might enter to arrest him, Knapp instructed the grand jurors on their duties. The grand jury report, in all probability inspired or written by Judge Knapp, was a recital for the record of the grievances of the people of the Mesilla Valley during the Civil War years. Copies of the report were sent to President Lincoln, and to the Secretary of War. In part the report said:

In the year 1861, this country was by order of Brevet Lieutenant Colonel Ed. R. S. Canby, of United States Army, directed to Major I. Lynde, a subordinate of his command, and dated Santa Fe, New Mexico, July 14, 1861, abandoned and surrendered to an insignificant handful of rebels, less than one-third of the federal forces; and the citizens of Dona Ana County were thus deserted by its military officers, and thereby were subjected to such restraints and oppressions as the enemy chose to impose. For temporarily acquiescing in order to preserve life, liberty and property, we have been stigmatized as disloyal, when it is well known that private citizens of the Mesilla Valley were the only ones who, unsolicited and unsupported, attacked the rebels and by force of arms, resisted the occupation of our Territory by the so-styled Confederate army; and in thus proving our devotion to our government, we were called upon to mourn the untimely deaths of some of our most valued citizens; and instead of receiving, as we merited, the support and countenance of the Federal troops in their reoccupation of the country under the command of Brigadier General James H. Carleton, we were treated as citizens of a conquered province.

Carleton's conduct of public affairs in the Mesilla Valley was severely criticized:

Instead of being protected in the rights secured to us, General Carleton through his subordinates, has imprisoned citizens, has fined and compelled them to submit to the performance of labor without conviction or trial; has taken away property without just compensation, and refused to restore it upon demand being made, or to pay for the same. Setting up courts of his own creation in our midst, he has compelled citizens to answer before them for offenses unknown to the law, and has prevented the courts established by law from discharging their duty. His subordinates have openly resisted the ministerial officers in the service of process issued by the civil courts and threatened them with death if they persisted in making service.[123]

To all intents and purposes, the Dona Ana County grand jury had indicted Carleton. The grand jury report received little attention at the time, being overshadowed by significant events of national importance. Contemporaneously, Abraham

Lincoln was being renominated for the Presidency at the Baltimore convention. Grant was in front of Petersburg. Robert E. Lee was reorganizing his armies in Virginia. Sherman was fighting his way through Georgia. A controversy in far off New Mexico, over martial law and military passes, was of no national significance.

The Dona Ana County grand jury report infuriated Carleton, however, as Knapp had probably anticipated. The Santa Fe *Gazette,* always partial to Carleton, accused Judge Knapp in an editorial on July 9, 1864, of having stage managed the grand jury attack:

We have seen in the New Mexican the presentment that was made by the grand jury to the court at the recent term held in Dona Ana County, in this Territory. That the precious document was put through the formality of having been sanctioned by the grand jury we have no reason to doubt. There, however, can be as little doubt of the fact that it was done by the procurement of Knapp, who sat upon the Bench, ermine soiled, in the court to which the presentment was made. The earmarks of the document are such as would fix its authorship on him, but he is, of course, too much of a knave to have left marks of his pen on the paper by which it would be identified.

After the Dona Ana County grand jury had criticized Carleton and his military rule, Judge Knapp left Mesilla for Santa Fe, again without a military pass, running the gauntlet of sentry challenge at every post on the way. Having finally reached Santa Fe with his tail feathers ruffled, Judge Knapp took his seat on the supreme court bench, on July 4, 1864. When the court convened Knapp cooperated in disposing of several matters of public interest, and then announced that he would not transact any other business "until the judges of New Mexico were freed from the tyranny of passport government." Exasperated by Knapp's conduct in Santa Fe, and smarting from the sting of the Dona Ana County grand jury report, Carleton complained to General Thomas in Washington:

The inevitable Judge Joseph G. Knapp, who has written so many letters to the War Department and so many scurrilous articles for the press against the officers serving in this department, claiming that New Mexico is under a military despotism, and that because I have established for the safety of the country against spies and traitors a system of passports which has long since been approved by the general-in-chief, that I have subverted the liberties of the people, and other claptrap of this sort, came here last week to sit as an associate justice. After the court was organized and had transacted some business which he, Knapp, wanted to have done, he got up and said he would do no more business until my order with reference to passports was rescinded unconditionally; and, so, the court stopped. The judge would not take a passport for Mesilla, 300 miles off, but started without one. As he might have known before he left, he was stopped at the first military post he came to. He then returned to this city, and says, so I understand, that he will proceed to Washington by the mail that takes this letter and have me ousted from my command.

Carleton believed that Knapp was "a compound of a knave and a fool, or else crazy":

I have written a letter to Chief Justice Kirby Benedict, to the attorney general, and to all the leading members of the bar, to say whether I have ever interfered with the courts, and if on the contrary I have not given them every help in my power. . . . It is believed here by many, and seriously, that Knapp is a compound of a knave and a fool, or else he is crazy. He has the unmitigated contempt of every respectable man in the country. I know that his being an abuser of myself forbids my saying this, but it is the truth. I regret that the itching to make himself a martyr, or to be notorious in some way, on the part of this man Knapp, has put the War Department to so much trouble.[124]

Attached to Carleton's report to Thomas were interesting letters signed by Chief Justice Kirby Benedict, attorneys R. H. Tompkins, M. Ashurst, Theodore D. Wheaton, and J. Houghton, and by Clerk of the Court Samuel Ellison, describing Knapp's conduct on July 4. The Santa Fe *Gazette*, describing the incident, said that upon leaving the court, Judge Knapp had "turned his stern end toward the bench." Benedict, the attorneys, and Clerk Ellison in their letters expressed the opinion that Carleton had not attempted to interfere with the processes of the courts in New Mexico.

Lawyer Tompkins said in his letter that Knapp had "balked like a mule in open court" and had stated from the bench "that for the sake of the liberty and freedom of the people of New Mexico he would stake his commission upon the result of the controversy over the military pass requirement; that it appeared from the conduct of General Carleton that he desired to break up the civil courts so that he could have the sole and absolute power in his hands." [125]

In order to explain and defend his position on permit requirements, Carleton issued an order on July 12, 1864, undoubtedly the result of Judge Knapp's action on the Supreme bench:

The condition of affairs in the Department of New Mexico, having reference to the proximity of Texas, and to the fact that Confederate spies have been hovering about our boundaries and prowling in our midst, where they have many friends and correspondents, of which we have positive proof, and considering the fact that the commander of the Confederate forces in Texas still claims this Territory and that of Arizona as belonging to his department, and still flaunts at the head of his orders and letters, "Headquarters Department of Texas, New Mexico, and Arizona," thereby making either a puerile and ridiculous vaunt, or indicating a standing claim to this country ... and considering the fact that bands of guerrillas and robbers, claiming to be Confederate troops, hover along the thoroughfares leading to New Mexico from the east, which bands doubtless have their emissaries in our midst to give information when the trains of our wealthy citizens start with funds for the purchase of goods in the States, so that these trains may be waylaid and robbed at the points of the road favorable to such enterprises, as has been recently done, it continues to be a military necessity that persons traveling through this department shall be provided with passports by which they can be identified and distinguished from spies and traitors and rebels.

Carleton contended it was but a slight inconvenience for those requiring passes to obtain them:

All civil magistrates and officers of civil courts, and all lawyers practicing in the country, and all officers of the United States, who have business in the department, as well as resident citizens not natives of New Mexico or Arizona, will, on application, be furnished with standing passports which they can exhibit when traveling whenever it becomes necessary to do so. Officers and soldiers and military employees will also be obliged to have such passports. . . . In times like these we must know who are our friends and who are our enemies. It is but a slight inconvenience to a good and loyal man to conform to these rules, and it may be the means of detecting the traitors who are still plotting to bring this beautiful country again under the cloud and the blight and the mildew which seems to overshadow as a pall and attach as a curse to every spot of our beloved land over which this cruel and causeless rebellion has had sway.[126]

Disappointed and perhaps humiliated because of indignities, real or imaginary, suffered at the hands of the military, Judge Knapp, on July 6, 1864, left Santa Fe for Washington. The journey required almost three weeks. Knapp complained to department heads in Washington and to acquaintances in the House and Senate of Carleton's conduct in New Mexico. The complaints were referred to the War Department. Within a short time Knapp was told that he had lost in his fight with Carleton; that President Lincoln had "accepted his resignation" as judge of the third judicial district of the Territory. The President appointed Sidney A. Hubbell to succeed him on Aug. 15, 1864. Knapp returned to Mesilla on Oct. 16, 1864, announcing to his friends that "henceforth he would be among the people, not as the administrator, but as the expounder of the law, and constitution." The Santa Fe *Gazette* of Sept. 10, 1864, published an editorial on Knapp's resignation, which undoubtedly had General Carleton's entire approval:

We are happy in being able to announce to the people of the Territory that the administration at Washington has relieved them from the presence in their midst of Knapp as an associate judge in New Mexico. His conduct while he occupied a seat on the bench here was such as to disgust all who admire honesty and probity in a judge, and his unofficial life brought him into a depth of contempt that men in official position seldom attain.[127]

CHAPTER SEVEN

Dr. Michael Steck

DURING CIVIL WAR YEARS in New Mexico, few men were in a position to defy, or even publicly question the wisdom of General Carleton's policies pertaining to the administration of affairs in the Territory. Martial law, synonymous with "Carleton law," was in effect throughout New Mexico from Aug. 8, 1861, until July 4, 1865. The War Department, almost with routine regularity, sustained Carleton's decisions. It was futile for a private citizen, or for a territorial or federal official, to challenge, or even criticize a Carleton decision. Among the handful of men with the will and courage to fight Carleton in the open on Indian policy, almost single handed, was Dr. Michael Steck, of Pennsylvania. A physician by profession, Dr. Steck had come to New Mexico in 1853 as an Indian agent for the Mescalero Apaches, and had served as Superintendent of Indian Affairs in the Territory during 1863 and 1864.

In the early days of Carleton's campaign against the Indians, Dr. Steck agreed with Carleton that the Apaches should be placed on a reservation, and that the Navajos should be compelled to accept and respect the army's discipline. As the campaign progressed, however, Steck was horrified by the fatalities suffered by the Indians as part of Carleton's policy of "surrender or die." Steck was particularly concerned about the Navajos. He was convinced that unless Carleton's hand could be stayed, the Navajos, as a tribal unit, would be wiped out, and those Navajos who might survive, and their offspring, would suffer lasting psychological injuries.

409

After ten years of labor as an Indian agent among the Mescalero Apaches and other tribes in the Territory, Dr. Steck succeeded James L. Collins as Superintendent of Indian Affairs for New Mexico. He took office on July 17, 1863, and established official headquarters in Santa Fe. Two months later, on Sept. 19, 1863, he reported on the situation in New Mexico to Commissioner of Indian Affairs W. P. Dole:

The condition of the Territory shows that it has not fully recovered from the effects of the Texas invasion. During the occupation by the insurgents all intercourse with many of the Indian tribes was entirely broken up. The military force was necessarily withdrawn from the frontiers to defend the Territory against the invaders, and the Indians were thus left without the controlling influence of its presence. This at once led to evil consequences, which still exist to a greater or less extent. The Navajos, occupying the western portion of the Territory, at the time I reached my post, were at war. A campaign against them was planned, and a force already in the field at that time under Colonel Kit Carson. This tribe is the most formidable of all with which we have to deal, and at no time since the acquisition of New Mexico, in 1847, has it, as an entirety, been at peace. Six treaties have been held with it, at different times, by officers of the government, all of which were broken before any ratification could be effected. The tribe is now in the hands of the military department. Whatever the causes of the war, it is too late to discuss them. The Indians, by their acts of wholesale destruction of life and property, and the general disregard they have exhibited of all former promises, have rendered themselves liable to severe punishment. The force now in the field, it is hoped, will be able to convey to them some practical lessons of the power of the government. It will be a difficult undertaking, however, as they are a powerful tribe, with an extensive, and in many places, inaccessible country. Until subdued by force, any treaty or offer of peace must prove of but little avail. These people are ingenious in the manufacture of blankets and other fabrics. They also cultivate wheat and corn quite extensively, and in these and other respects are far in advance of any tribe within the limits of this superintendency.

Steck told the Commissioner of the background of the Indians of New Mexico, and of their utter disregard for the sanctity of treaties:

The wandering tribes of New Mexico, numbering in the aggregate about 15,000, are so similar in habits — the resources of the country over which they wander so nearly the same, and their future wants so identical, that to speak of a policy suited to any particular one would be applicable to all. The course heretofore pursued regarding these tribes as nations, and treating them as such, is no longer the true or correct one. Not one of them is bound together by any general laws. All are divided into fragments, and these fragments of from ten to fifty men each, headed by some successful warrior, separately act without any consultation with the mass, and recognize in their war raids no law but that of individual caprice. There seems to be no distinguished or national chieftain among them capable of concentrating and leading an undivided tribe to battle, or inspiring their confidence and imparting council in time of peace. With the exception of the Pueblos (an amiable, happy and law abiding people), the condition will apply to every nation within the jurisdiction of this superintendency. I would, therefore, respectfully suggest the propriety of choosing for them suitable reservations, where military posts can be established of sufficient strength not only to command *their* respect, but at the same time prevent the encroachment of settlers and the consequent evils that always result from a free intercourse with the whites. Having made a suitable selection, the tribe should be kindly requested to settle. There will be found no difficulty in eliciting fair promises to locate, as a liberal supply of beef is, of itself, a great incentive to compliance, at least nominally. They will sign any paper presented, whether they understand its contents or not. The treaties heretofore held with them, as before observed, have in every instance been broken almost as soon as made, or before ratification could be effected within the usual time.

The Mescalero Apaches were becoming inured to reservation life, but their "barbarous superstitions" interfered with the process of reclamation:

The success attending the settlement of the Mescaleros last spring under the management of their agent and the active cooperation of General Carleton, commander of the military department, gives us a practical instance of the wisdom of this policy. The report of Agent Labadie shows that that portion of the tribe which came willingly upon the reserve have extensive and well cultivated fields of corn, and I have no doubt that by next spring the entire band, together with a part at least, of the Jicarillas, can be induced to follow this method of industrial pursuit. Under the immediate eye and supervision of the military and an efficient superintendent, or agent, many of their barbarous superstitions may be broken up — customs and superstitious rites that in their nature and effects must retard materially all advances toward civilization. Treated as a nation, they claim the right to adhere to these notions, and dignify them with the importance of laws. One of these superstitions demands the total destruction of the property of a deceased owner; another requires the removal of the huts (if but a few hundred yards) of a band upon the occasion of a death amongst them; and still another imposes the obligation of making feasts, a great number of which are observed, of the most extravagant kind, whenever a female arrives at a marriageable age, in honor of which event the parents will sacrifice all the property they possess, the ceremony being protracted from five to ten days with every demonstration of hilarity. With these and other rites of a like character, it is hardly necessary to say that no permanent radical changes can be effected.

Steck believed the Indians could be taught to think in the ways of the civilized man, but that eradication of the "wild religious superstitions," of the Indians was a prerequisite:

To teach them the necessity and beauty of economy, the value of property, and the true method of its accumulation, it is indispensably requisite that these wild religious superstitions should be eradicated; to accomplish which we must exercise a more potent influence than has yet been brought to bear — an influence that can only be felt and applied by means of the reservation system. . . . By making these large reservations, 200 miles apart, and so far from the white settlements as to preclude any interference, at least with the present inhabitants, we have an entire band collected, and thus avoid the necessity of treating with fragments of squads separately. This method will commend the system also for its economy. The fact that these people cannot obtain subsistence at certain seasons from game and other resources of the country, has so often been presented to your notice by my predecessor and the agents that I shall not dwell upon the point, but take it for granted that the department must be aware that, under pressing circumstances, the Indian is compelled to steal or starve. Hence the necessity for liberal supplies of food, and such a concentration of the tribes as will conduce to an easy and just distribution among them.

The white man's search for gold in the Apache country dislocated Indian life, and opened the gateway to eventual extermination:

Human nature exhibits itself as well in the Indian as in the Anglo-Saxon; supply the wants of either, and the disposition to revolt is suppressed or materially weakened. This was clearly shown by the Mescaleros and Gila Apaches from 1854 to 1860. Liberally supplied with goods during that period by their agents, they remained quiet and planted large breadths of corn. But for the discovery of gold mines in the immediate vicinity of their fields, which attracted a population not exactly, in disposition as well as in numbers, adapted to the best interests of the Indian, and the Texas invasion, they would at this time be at peace and comfortably situated. It may be urged that to locate and feed 12,000 Indians is an expensive method of treatment. It is susceptible of the clearest proof, however, that such a policy is not only the most philanthropic, but the most economical. It needs no prophetic eye to see that, in a few years, the Indians of New Mexico must be exterminated, unless the government interposes its benevolent hand to protect and support them.

With the oncoming tide of immigration, and the disappearance of the buffalo, deer and elk, Steck believed that the time had arrived for the government to intervene and protect the Indians:

The rich gold fields and other mineral wealth of the country cannot otherwise than draw hither a vast population, before which the buffalo, deer and elk will disappear, and for the support of which every available acre must necessarily be appropriated. Divested in this way of all their peculiar and former means of subsistence, and contending with a race, who under the circumstances, can feel no sympathy with them, the Indian must soon be swept from the face of the earth. If every redman were a Spartan, they would find it impossible to withstand this overpowering influx of immigration. Humanity and religion, therefore, demand of us that we interpose a barrier for their safety, and this can be effected only in the way we have been considering.

Steck pointed out that the government had spent and was spending vast sums of money to fight the Indians, and expressed the opinion that continuation of this policy spelled disaster for the red man:

That to supply the wants of the Indians of this department is a cheaper mode for their successful management to the government than to fight and subjugate them by force, and far more likely to give security to life and property, can be readily shown by facts and figures. I have the authority of officers in the army, whose positions and rank enable them to know, that the military establishments of this Territory, since its acquisition, has cost not less than $3,000,000 annually, independent of land warrant bounties. This expenditure, it may be contended, was necessary for a conquered country; but whether it was or not, the chastisement and subjection of the Indians have been the sole employment of the United States forces, among whom and for whom these large sums have been distributed. The military force, frequently numbering as high as 2,000 men, has at different times, fought every tribe in the Territory, and experience shows that we are now no nearer a permanent peace than when that consummation was first sought in 1848. Nor has this been owing to the want of able commanders, as we have always had, and still have, men of ability and experience in command of the department, and gallant and active officers and men in the field; but we must rather attribute it to the extent and nature of the country, which prevents or protracts operations, and to those constantly occurring demands from hunger and exposure which impel to acts of aggression, not to mention the incentives to retaliation so frequently elicited. The loss of life and property during the past three years shows a greater amount than that of any other three years in the history of the Territory since the treaty of Guadalupe Hidalgo.

As Steck saw it, the government would be obliged to find a home for the Indians, and feed them there, or adopt a policy of extermination:

The irresistible conclusion, then, is that we must either locate and feed these wild tribes, or hunt them in their fastnesses until they are exterminated. The latter course we have pursued up to the present, at an outlay of three millions annually to the government; the former, it is confidently believed, can be made the more effectual plan, at a cost of one twentieth the expenditures heretofore defrayed, and without loss of life or property.[128]

Convinced by General Carleton that the Navajo Indians

could be colonized, and anxious to be relieved as quickly as possible of the burden of either fighting them, or supporting them, the War Department gave assurance of its "hearty cooperation" to Carleton's Bosque Redondo project. The Commissioner of Indian Affairs accepted Carleton's recommendations, and reluctantly consented to the Bosque experiment. Secretary of War Stanton, wrote to Secretary of the Interior J. P. Usher on March 31, 1864:

The commander of the department of New Mexico reports that there are now at the Bosque Redondo 4,106 Navajo Indians, with strong probabilities that the remainder of the tribe will soon be collected at that place. General Carleton estimates the entire number of these Indians at 5,000, but it is believed that this is an under estimate, and that the tribe, when collected, will number at least seven thousand souls.

These Indians have been at war with the people of New Mexico (with short intervals of peace) for nearly two centuries, and if the plan of colonization now commenced can be successfully carried out, it will relieve the treasury from the large expenditures that have been necessary in carrying on military operations against them, and will do much for the settlement and prosperity of New Mexico. It is important for the success of this plan that measures should be taken at once to establish them fully in their determination to abandon their old homes and manner of living.

They are now dependents of the War Department, but there is no appropriation under the control of the department from which their wants can be supplied, except that the issue of subsistence is justified by necessity, and must be continued until the Interior Department is prepared to assume their control and relieve this department from the burden of maintaining them. It is important that this should be done as speedily as possible, and in this, and whatever else that may be necessary to insure the success of this plan, the War Department will give its hearty cooperation.

Secretary Stanton's letter was referred to Speaker Schuyler Colfax of the House of Representatives, by Secretary Usher, with a memorandum saying that William P. Dole had concurred with War Department conclusions, and was recommending an appropriation of $100,000 to enable furtherance of the colonization plan.

Commissioner Dole wrote to Secretary Usher on April 4, 1864, saying that he had discussed the Indian situation with General Canby, Carleton's predecessor as commander of the military in New Mexico:

Referring to the letter of the Secretary of War of the 31st ultimo, relative to the Navajo Indians at the Bosque Redondo, in New Mexico, I have the honor to state, that from information received from various sources, as well as from conferences held with General Canby, who has spent many years in that country, and is well acquainted with the habits and customs of said Indians, I learn that they are an agricultural and pastoral people, and that, if properly established at the new agency at Bosque Redondo, they will soon become self sustaining. I am not sufficiently acquainted with the location to be able to judge whether or not it is the best that could be found for them, but it is the opinion of the commandant of the military forces in New Mexico that the site is a proper one; and as the Indians are now nearly all held under military duress, at that point, I do not think it best to look further for a new home for them.[129]

Voicing strong opposition to Carleton's program to establish the Navajo Indians at Bosque Redondo, Dr. Michael Steck wrote letters to Commissioner of Indian Affairs William P. Dole, on May 28, and June 25, 1864, criticizing Carleton's scheme for transplanting the Navajo tribe on the Bosque Redondo. In view of later developments, his letter of May 28 was prophetic:

Friends of the policy of locating the Navajos on the Bosque Redondo have represented that most of the tribe are already removed, and that by the month of July the whole number will be brought in. The fact is that the tribe has not been subdued. A vast majority of the warriors are still in their own country, and those at Bosque Redondo are principally the poor who have willingly given themselves up under promises that they should be fed. The rich and powerful portion of them are still in their own country. . . . It may be argued that it would be an unnecessary expense to send back 4,500 paupers, now at Fort Sumner, to their own country; but, sir, if it does cost a few thousand dollars, it will cost ten times the amount to catch and remove the wealthy portion of the tribe to the Bosque, and years will elapse before it is accomplished. . . . If the Navajos are removed to the Bosque Redondo, which has already been set apart for the Apaches, difficulties and complications will constantly arise between these tribes, and also between them and the people of the Territory, whose best grazing is in that portion of the Territory.... The people of New Mexico are almost universally opposed to the location of the Navajos at Fort Sumner, or even in New Mexico, as they belong properly to the Territory of Arizona.

In his letter of June 25, Steck quoted facts and figures tending to prove that enormous sums of money would be required to carry out the Carleton policy. He cited the fact that Carleton had authorized purchases in the total amount of $510,000 for the Bosque Redondo enterprise for the three months commencing March 1 and ending June 1. Defending his actions and policies against Superintendent Steck's arguments, Gen. Carleton wrote to Secretary Usher on August 27, 1864, questioning Steck's motives, and contending his statements were misleading:

I have been furnished with copies of two letters written to William P. Dole, Commissioner of Indian Affairs, by Michael Steck. ... I have no disposition to have any controversy with Dr. Steck, nor do I wish to claim for the Indians anything that is not their just due, but truth and candor compel me to say that those letters are calculated greatly to mislead you with reference to the whole question.... Navajos now on the new reservation on the Pecos river comprise the principal chiefs and the most of the tribe, including nearly all the rich Indians. The fact is patent to every person in this country. The Indians on the reservation are the happiest people I have ever seen. They are industrious and look forward with ardent hopes to the time when they can raise enough to support themselves. In room of committing depredations, they have gone out and attacked Indians who were attempting to run off the herds of the people. This fact is of public notoriety.... The people are not opposed to the Indians being located at Bosque Redondo. We all know that such an idea has been started and written upon for effect. We hardly supposed that an officer of the government could sit down, and by such an array of misstatements endeavor to prejudice so high a public functionary as yourself against the only measure that can ever secure peace and prosperity to this impoverished country.... I do not believe that all told there are 1,000 Navajos left in their own country and these have fled away beyond the Little Colorado. You will perhaps sometime or other learn the motives which have induced these statements by Dr. Steck. It is a pity, when so much has been accomplished for the country, that any one should come forward with a studied effort to undo it all.[130]

Throughout the Civil War years, the War and Interior Departments in Washington were plagued by the cross fire in New Mexico between Carleton, of the military, and Steck, of the Indian service. The Commissioner of Indian Affairs was particularly concerned, but to a great extent he was powerless to exert influence because of the superior position occupied by the War Department in all matters, however remote, relating to the conduct of Indian affairs.

The current situation with reference to the Apaches and Navajos was related to the Commissioner of Indian Affairs by Superintendent Michael Steck in a letter written from Santa Fe on October 16, 1864:

> The Apaches are divided into two bands, the Jicarillas and Mescaleros — the first living in the northeast part of the Territory, and the latter in the southeast. About four hundred of the Mescaleros are now living upon the reservation set apart for them by the order of the Secretary of the Interior dated December 1, 1863, and have a large amount of land planted in corn, wheat and vegetables . . . the crops are a partial failure, yet I have no doubt that the Apaches upon the reservation will, from the proceeds of their farm, have sufficient grain to furnish them bread rations for some months. There has been much dissatisfaction among the Mescaleros upon the reservation, relative to the location of the Navajos upon their lands. Most of the tribe would undoubtedly now have been on the reservation if it had not been for this objection. They are, and for a century have been, inveterate enemies, and it is folly to suppose that they can agree upon the same reservation after having been induced to move but for this same objection, and a beginning been made to break up the roving disposition of the band. Unless a large military force is used to compel the Apaches to remove, they cannot be induced to do so while the Navajos are upon their lands.

Steck emphasized the immensity of the gap between the Apaches and the Navajos, a circumstance which Carleton had apparently entirely ignored:

The Apaches are so greatly in the minority at Bosque Redondo that the Navajos could in one hour annihilate them, and no doubt would find a pretext for doing so were it not for the military force at Fort Sumner, which holds them in check. Under the circumstances I shall not be surprised if, after the Apaches gather their crops, many of them desert and join the hostile portion of the tribe. They cannot coalesce, and future and continual difficulties must take place between the two tribes unless they are widely separated. If the Navajos should be located in their own country, the entire difficulty would be removed. . . .

As of the fall of 1864 the Navajos were still at war, still stealing sheep from the settlers:

About seven thousand of the tribe have surrendered themselves, and are now held as prisoners of war at Fort Sumner, on the Pecos River. The remainder of the tribe are still at war, and commit frequent and daring outrages; many thousand sheep have been stolen and driven off by them during the last few months. The tribe at large, as well as the prisoners held at Fort Sumner, are still in the hands of the military authorities, and, under the direction of General Carleton, an effort is being made to remove the whole tribe from their own country to the Pecos River, from four to five hundred miles east of their former homes. I have, from the commencement of the scheme to remove the tribe from their own country, protested against it, believing the plan to be impracticable, unless a large military force was employed, and a larger sum of money appropriated than I believe Congress will be willing to appropriate for one tribe of Indians.

Superintendent Steck argued that the Navajos should be placed on a large reservation in their own country and gradually obliged to make their own living. He regarded Carleton's choice of the Pecos River reservation for that purpose "most unfortunate," and suggested that the Navajos be taken to lands on the Little Colorado or the San Juan:

They might be so located, in their own country, as to be far removed from any road across the country, while at the Pecos River they are but a short distance from the general thoroughfare from Missouri and Kansas, to New Mexico, Arizona, and the state of Chihuahua, in the republic of Mexico. They have lands, in their own country, equally as good as those of the Pecos for farming purposes, from which together with their resources, such as making blankets, saddles and bridle bits, they will get along, as they have in the past, without assistance from the government, something they have demonstrated during periods of many years, at a time when the Spanish and Mexican governments were supposed to have authority over them. . . . It has been contended by some that they have no country suitable for farming. In answer to this, I would state that Colonel Kit Carson informed me that during the summer of 1863, when in command of the forces set against the tribe, he destroyed a great quantity of wheat and corn fields; that at one point, without moving his camp, he was seven day thus engaged, and at other places he was two, three and four days, destroying as fine fields of wheat and corn as the Territory produced.

Steck pleaded fervently for the return of the Navajos to their own orchards and fields:

More than half the Navajos are still at large, and only the poor and those unable to make a resistance have given themselves up. It will, therefore, be necessary to make another campaign to reduce them, at an immense cost to the government, double and perhaps ten times the amount it will take to remove those who are now held as prisoners back to their own country. Established there, the transportation of provisions would cost more, but the quantity required would be so much less that the cost would be trifling compared with the present expenses at the Pecos. If they will work at Bosque Redondo, it would be ridiculous to say that they would not work elsewhere; and if they can support themselves on the Pecos in a few years by their own labor, where they have no resources except what they produce, they certainly can where the natural resources of the country gives them a supply to last half the year, or more. I know the views I have expressed were opposed during the last session of Congress, and a law passed so as to enlarge the Apache reservation as to provide for the Navajos upon the same reserve. But feeling satisfied that the policy was ill advised, I consider it my duty to report fully my opinions with reference to it. If I differ with others, I would state that my opinions were formed only after a careful examination of the subject and consultation with the best authority in the Territory. Although we are told by friends of the scheme that the Indians are satisfied and happy at their new home, we know it is not the case, as they frequently make the inquiry when they are to be returned to their own country. Their former houses, their orchards, and fields have a charm not so easily forgotten. It is human nature, and if they are not sent back, or permitted to go, they will return stealthily, and in doing so, commit depredations upon our people, and thus keep up a state of insecurity for a generation to come.

Estimating that the cost of handling the Navajos under the military department for the next year would be two millions of dollars, Steck urged that the Navajos be returned at once to their own country and fed, at an annual cost of two hundred thousand dollars, until such time as they could plant their corn, and "the cactus and other fruits mature." Steck suggested the selection of a reservation in the country belonging to the tribe, "as proposed by General Canby in 1860." "This excellent officer and gentleman's proposition," Steck wrote, "was to build a military post on the Little Colorado, around which the Indians had already agreed to plant, and if his plans had not been broken up by the war, I have little doubt the Navajos would this day be at peace, and supporting themselves, instead of being an enormous tax upon the treasury."

Commissioner Dole studied the Steck report, and submitted his comments on it to Secretary of the Interior, J. P. Usher:

Superintendent Steck asserts, and he claims to have reliable authority for the statement, that not less than three millions of dollars have been annually expended since our acquisition of the Territory of New Mexico in maintaining its military organization, which, with the exception of repelling the Texas invasion of last year, have done nothing aside from occasional expeditions against the Navajos. It is also estimated that during the past three years not less than five hundred thousand sheep, and five thousand cattle, mules, and horses have been killed or stolen by the Indians. To this large account must also be added the lives of our citizens that have been sacrificed, the sufferings of others who have been carried into captivity, and the general insecurity which prevails throughout the Territory to such an extent that it is said there is not a single county that is absolutely secure. Surely a policy, or, I should rather say, a want of policy which is so enormously expensive as this, so fruitless of good results, and which promises so little for the future either in improving the condition of our own people or that of the Indians, ought to be abandoned at once and forever, and some system adopted from which better results may be reasonably anticipated.

Dole had given serious attention to the problems involved, and was anxious to have the Indians treated fairly:

I have heretofore urged the propriety of recognizing the right of the Indians to a qualified ownership of the soil, and treating with them for its extinction in such portions as may be required for the purposes of settlement, thereby providing a fund from which the Indians may derive such assistance as may be necessary, while acquiring a sufficient knowledge of the arts of civilization to enable them to provide for their own wants. I am still of the opinion that this is much the best policy to pursue towards the Indians in providing for their wants when located on reservations, for, in the first place, it is attended with the same expense whether we assign them a tract of land, and then, by direct appropriations, provide for their necessities, or treating with them for their claim to the territory we extinguish their title to such portions as we desire, they retaining the same tract that would otherwise be assigned to them, and receiving for the lands surrendered the moneys which must otherwise be appropriated to enable them to live; and secondly, it would preserve in the Indian his native pride and independence, since, instead of feeling that his freedom to roam at will had been restrained by arbitrary and resistless power, and he compelled to relinquish the homes and customs of his ancestors, he would realize that the change had been wrought by fair negotiations to which he was a party, and that, for the rights and privileges surrendered, he had received a fair equivalent.

The Commissioner asked cooperation in connection with the establishment of reservations for the Utes, Apaches and Navajos:

Whether the one method or the other shall be preferred, I think it perfectly evident that we shall be guilty of little less than criminal neglect if we longer delay the adoption of such measures as will result in the concentration of the Indians upon suitable reservations, and to this end I earnestly invite your cooperation in an endeavor to procure the passage of a joint resolution by Congress, at its approaching session, authorizing either the negotiation of treaties having for their object the establishing of the Indians upon three suitable reservations, of which one for the

Utahs shall be in the northern or northwestern portion of the Territory, one for the Apaches, in the southeastern, and one for the Navajos in the western, or empowering the President, by proclamation, to set apart suitable tracts for such reservations, and vesting title in the same in the respective tribes for which they are designed. As to the Pueblos, I believe they may safely be left, with temporary appropriations for their benefit, to the operation of the present Territorial and future state laws. If action such as or similar to that I have indicated can be had from Congress, I have the fullest confidence that in a very few years it will prove of inestimable value alike to the Indians and whites of New Mexico.[131]

Dr. Michael Steck's letter of October 16, 1864, to the Commissioner of Indian Affairs, contained no statement or argument that he had not previously submitted personally to General Carleton in Santa Fe. Carleton was quite familiar with Steck's contention that the Army's policy of managing the Indians, particularly the Navajos, was impractical, even visionary, and that it offered no possibility for success. Steck visited the Bosque Redondo in the fall of 1863, and examined the conditions under which the Navajos and Apaches were being detained. He returned to Santa Fe, and told General Carleton that the entire project, in his opinion, was headed for disaster; that the Indians were homesick; that many of them had died during the confinement, and that many others were dying from starvation and disease; that only a complete about-face and abandonment of Bosque Redondo, and the return of the Indians to their own country would prevent a tragedy of major importance.

Carleton stubbornly defended his position. He contended that the army was the only governmental facility adequately equipped to deal with Indians. Carleton closed his talk with Steck by politely suggesting that Steck keep his hands off Indian affairs until such time as the army requested his assistance. In reports to Washington, written after the interview, Carleton accused Steck of "meddling" and particularly of having promoted restlessness among the Navajos and Apaches by his visit, and by talks with individual Indians at the

Bosque. Among other things, Carleton blamed Steck for giving the Mescalero Apaches permission to leave the Bosque and go to their own country in order to make mescal.

In Washington, in the summer and fall of 1864, the Department of the Interior was in a dilemma over the Indian situation in New Mexico. The army recommended one plan for the Navajos, the Indian Service the direct opposite. Secretary Usher was confused and puzzled by the conflicting reports and varying contentions. Submitting his report for 1864, Secretary Usher explained:

The propriety of the removal of the Navajos of New Mexico and Arizona to the Bosque Redondo reservation has been a subject of much contrariety of opinion. This department upon the best information at its command, consented to their removal. As the reservation has been set apart, and a large sum of money expended by the military authorities there, great fickleness of purpose would be manifested in abandoning the enterprise before it shall have been fully and fairly tested. I am strongly inclined to the opinion, notwithstanding all that has been urged against it, that if the scheme receives a fair and just support, it will prove a success, and these Indians, so long foes of the government, will become its faithful supporters.

In his 1864 report, Commissioner Dole could see little in the way of hope for an early solution of the vexatious problems:

From a glance at the history of our relations with the Indians, it will appear that we have been governed by the course of events, rather than by the adoption of a well settled policy. The early settlers of the country everywhere met with a kind reception from the Indians, but as the settlements increased and extended their borders, it soon became manifest to the Indians that their hunting grounds were being invaded and their limits gradually restricted. Their feelings of hospitality were in time changed to sentiments of bitterest hostility, and that dark page of our national history, containing a recital of our numerous Indian wars, and the peculiarly bloody and barbarous scenes attending them, has been the result. As our borders have extended, and treaties have been negotiated with them from time to time, and uniformly, and in almost innumerable instances, they have been recognized as a separate and distinct people, possessing in a restricted sense the peculiarities and characteristics of distinct nations. . . . It was perhaps inevitable, owing to the peculiar character of the Indians, that they should retire as their country became occupied by the whites. Thus far they seem to form an exception among all people whose territories have been overrun and wrested from them by a foreign race; for while it has been found in all other instances that a people thus situated have gradually assimilated and become incorporated with, and, as it were absorbed by the superior nation, the Indians still adhere to their tribal organizations, and pertinaciously maintain their existence as distinct political communities.

Commissioner Dole realized that the government could pursue a policy of compulsion, or of negotiation:

There are two methods by which we may handle the Indians . . . first, by availing ourselves of our overwhelming numerical, physical and intellectual superiority, we may set apart a country for the use of the Indians, prescribe the laws by which they shall be governed, and the rules to be observed in the intercourse of the two races, and compel a conformity on the part of the Indians; or secondly, we may, as has been the almost universal practice of the government, after resorting to military force only so far as may be necessary in order to induce the Indians to negotiate, bring about understanding through the instrumentality of treaties to which they are parties, and as such, have yielded their assent. Fortunately, the immense disparity in the relative power and resources of the two races enables us to pursue either of these methods, and it is incumbent upon us to adopt that course, which, judged by past experience, is best calculated to produce the desired results, the security of our frontier settlements, and the ultimate reclamation and civilization, and consequently, the permanent welfare of the Indians. By the one course, it is contemplated that the independence of the Indians shall be entirely ignored, and that they shall be reduced to absolute subjection; by the other, that they shall not altogether be deprived of their sense of nationality and independence as a people. . . . The Indians of New Mexico, with but trifling exceptions, have been managed by the former policy. In New Mexico, from the time of its acquisition, and for a long period anterior thereto, military operations have been almost continuous. . . . I regret that I am unable to report any decided improvement in the condition of the Indians of New Mexico.

The government had expended an enormous sum of money in attempting to subdue the Indians of New Mexico, with little show of satisfactory results:

The care and control of the tribes in New Mexico have resulted in enormous expense to the government, although from the fact that military operations have been almost constant for a long period of time, that expense has been generally felt through the War Department rather than the Indian office; and yet, with all the expense attendant upon the management, we are unable to see very little improvement in their condition, whether we look for the development of a desire to abandon the nomadic life, and settle down to the arts of peace, or simply for a willingness to abandon their acts of hostility against the whites.

Referring to the differences of opinion between General Carleton and Superintendent Steck on Indian policy, Commissioner Dole discussed the alternatives in matters of authority and jurisdiction:

The subject of the Navajo Indians has been continually before the department, in one form or another, during the present year, as in the past . . . hence I do not deem it necessary to enter upon any lengthy discussion of the subject here. . . . The differences between Brigadier General Carleton and Superintendent Steck upon this subject are, of course, honestly entertained by both gentlemen. They have the same end in view — the pacification of the Indians, and arrangements for their permanent good — and it is to be regretted that there should be any difference as to the proper policy to be pursued. The Navajos have thus far been left to the military authorities during and since the campaign against them. The larger portion of them, subdued and captured, are, and have been for a long time, prisoners at the Bosque Redondo, in the eastern (having been brought from their homes in the western) portion of the Territory. This office and its agents have had, until recently, no means at their disposal with which to feed and care for these seven thousand Indians, leaving out of view entirely the question as to whether the policy of bringing them eastward was a good one or not. . . . If the policy of removing the whole tribe of Navajos from their own country to the Bosque Redondo is to be continued, and the War Department charged with the care and expense of managing them, this office is divested of all responsibility beyond the general interest in the subject. . . . If on the other hand, the views of Superintendent Steck are to be accepted and prevail, that the Navajos shall be placed upon a reservation in their own country, where they have always been able to subsist themselves, then an appropriation by Congress is a pressing matter. . . .

Escorted by soldiers from Fort Union, on Carleton's authority, Steck went to Bosque Redondo from Santa Fe, on November 25, 1864, in order to inspect once more the place of Indian confinement. Steck expressed himself as being shocked by the desperate and deplorable conditions he found at the Bosque. All Mescalero Apaches who were strong enough to travel, men, women and children, had run away from the Bosque and returned to their own country in the Sacramento Mountains, where they were trying to keep body and soul together by hunting and fishing. The Navajos at the Bosque were actually starving. Scores of Navajos had died since Steck's visit of the previous year. Syphilis, diphtheria, smallpox, pneumonia and malnutrition had done quickly what Carleton had attempted to do with bullets in the home-land of the Navajos. It would only be a question of time, in Steck's opinion, until not a Navajo man, woman or child would remain alive to tell the tragic story of the Bosque Redondo. The meat ration had been reduced to eight ounces daily for each Indian. Other provisions were either not available at all, or only on a starvation diet basis. Steck found that most of the Navajos, as a protest against their exile, had refused to work in the fields. Some, willing to work, were unable to do so because they were weak and ill. Navajos were evading sentinels and guards, and escaping from the Bosque at all hours of the day and night, desperate, disillusioned, homesick, hopeful to make their way on foot, back to their own country. They preferred death in the open on the way home to ignominious confinement at the Bosque.

Back in Santa Fe again, Steck told Carleton once more of the horrible situation that existed at Bosque Redondo. He pleaded once again for a change of heart and of policy. Carleton refused to deviate one inch from the plan of colonization he had adopted. Discouraged and disheartened, Steck wrote to officials and friends in Washington, without any appreciable result. In desperation, Steck went to Washington himself, tramped the streets, visited one department of government after another, pleading the justice of his cause. Washington officials were not entirely indifferent to Steck's appeals, but all of them were reluctant to interfere in New Mexico Indian affairs in war time. Men of high rank in the War Department were quick to point out the possibility that the Confederacy might use the Indians in New Mexico to further their military enterprises, with resultant detriment to the federal government. As a final argument, the military pointed out that General Carleton was on the ground in New Mexico, and that the War Department preferred to accept his recommendations and hold him personally responsible for matters involving the national security in New Mexico. If, in the interest of that security, a tribe of Indians was to be impounded during the war — well, that was war.

The time came, in the fall of 1864, when General Carleton was obliged to suspend to some extent the campaign against the Navajos and fight Plains Indians in the northeastern part of the Territory. The Kiowas and Comanches had caused trouble in New Mexico off and on for many years. Believing that the troops would remain in the Navajo country indefinitely, bands of the two Plains tribes attacked trains and murdered people at Walnut Creek in the summer of 1864. They also robbed the train of Ambrosio Armijo, an Albuquerque merchant, at Pawnee's Fork, and got away with much valuable merchandise. Not long after robbing the Armijo train, the Kiowas returned to Pawnee Rock and attacked Allison's train, killed and scalped five men, and carried off five small boys as captives. Determined to chastise the Plains Indians, Carleton on Oct. 22, 1864, ordered an expedition against the Kiowas and Comanches, placing Kit Carson in command. Carson was to cooperate with troops from near Fort Larned, commanded by Major General Blunt. Carleton's marching orders urged speed and action:

As the season is now getting late, every moment becomes more and more precious. Every officer and soldier must therefore do his utmost, not only to take the field promptly, but to accomplish all that can be accomplished in punishing these treacherous savages before the winter fairly sets in. They have wantonly and brutally murdered our people without cause, and robbed them of their property; and it is not proposed that they shall talk, and smoke, and patch up a peace, until they have, if possible, been punished for the atrocities they have already committed. To permit them to do this would be to invite further hostile acts from them as soon as the spring opens, and our citizens once more embark on their long journeys across the plains.[132]

Kit Carson reached Fort Bascom, the point agreed upon for troop concentration, on Nov. 10, 1864, with 14 officers and 321 enlisted men from Fort Union, Fort Sumner and Fort Bascom. Carson recruited 75 Ute and Jicarilla Apache scouts and fighters at Lucien B. Maxwell's ranch on the Rayado. The commissary being provided with rations for four weeks,[133] Carson left for Adobe Fort, 200 miles east of Fort Bascom, on the Canadian River, where he changed from wagon to pack mule transportation. On Nov. 24, while about 30 miles west of Adobe Fort, Carson's Indian scouts reported sight of the enemy. That night the troops marched 15 miles. Carson was up before dawn the next day, mounted his horse, and rode down the Canadian. By sun-up he was at the place where the Indians had abandoned their camp of 150 lodges, and gone in the direction of Adobe Fort, about four miles away. Almost before he knew what was happening, Carson found himself and his troops almost completely surrounded by not less than 1,000 Indian warriors, mounted on fine horses, whooping and yelling, firing their rifles from ambush and open country.

Although the Indians repeatedly charged Carson's command, his men valiantly stood their ground, and repeatedly repulsed the attackers. Two mountain howitzers, carried over mountain and plain on pack mules, and used under command of Lieutenant George H. Pettis, of Carleton's California Column, proved disastrous for the Indians. Once the howitzers found the range, the Indians were driven from the field in panic. Carson's troops burned the Kiowa village at Adobe

Fort and captured large stores of dried meat, berries, buffalo robes, powder and cooking utensils, together with a buggy and spring wagon, the property of "Sierrito," or Little Mountain, a Kiowa chief. Carson's report, modest as usual, told the story briefly:

Of the Indians which I engaged, the principal number were Kiowas, with a small number of Comanches, Apaches and Arapahoes; all of which were armed with rifles, and I must say that they acted with more daring and bravery than I have ever before witnessed. The engagement commenced about 8:30 o'clock a.m., and lasted, I may say, without intermission until sunset, during which I had 2 soldiers killed, ten wounded, 1 Indian killed, and five wounded, and a large number of horses wounded. It is impossible for me to form a correct estimate of the enemy's loss, but from the number I saw fall from their horses during the engagement, I cannot call its loss less than sixty in killed and wounded. I flatter myself that I have taught these Indians a severe lesson, and hereafter they will be more cautious about how they engage a force of civilized troops.

Because the horses were badly used up and broken down, Carson and his command returned to Fort Bascom the second day after the fighting.[134]

Still smarting from the chastisement administered to them by Kit Carson near Adobe Fort in 1864, the Plains Indians did not live up to the promises made to Carleton. They continued to attack trains, and Carleton issued an order, effective February 8, 1865, authorizing a soldier escort for two wagon trains each month between Fort Larned, Kansas, and Fort Union, New Mexico, the first escort to follow the Raton Mountain route, and the second to follow the Cimarron route, and to alternate thereafter. Eastbound merchants were instructed to assemble their wagons near Fort Union in order to obtain protection of the soldier escort. Carleton requested Kit Carson, then in Taos, to communicate with the Comanches and Kiowas, and explain his policy to them. In a letter written from Santa Fe to Carson on May 8, 1865, Carleton threatened a fight to the finish:

... If the Indians behave themselves, that is all the peace we want, and we shall not molest them; if they do not, we will fight them on sight and to the bitter end. The war is over now, and, if necessary, 10,000 men can be put into the field against them. Tell them this. It is a short speech, but it covers all the ground. You know, I don't believe much in smoking with Indians. When they fear us, they behave. They must be made to fear us or we can have no lasting peace. They must not think to stop the commerce of the plains, or must they imagine that we are going to keep escorts with trains. We do this now until we learn whether they will behave or not. If they will not, we will end the matter by a war which will remove all further necessity for escorts. . . .

Writing from Fort Bascom on Dec. 16, 1864, Kit Carson told Carleton of the news in the Plains country:

There are immense quantities of buffalo in two days' travel of the point at which I had the fight, and I think the Indians can be found there in large numbers. On the day of the fight, my men found in the lodges a number of women and children's dresses, bonnets and shoes, some of these I saw myself. I have been told since by Mexican traders that the Indians have in their possession five white women and two children. If we can take some of their women and children, I may be able to buy the white women and children from them.

Kit Carson, who seldom complained about anything or anybody, blamed Superintendent Michael Steck for permitting Mexican traders to go into the Kiowa country and sell them ammunition, which they used later to kill his men:

I would suggest that no more of these Mexican traders be allowed to go amongst these Indians. On the day of the fight, I destroyed a large amount of powder, lead, caps and the like, and I have no doubt that this and the very balls with which my men were killed and wounded were sold by these Mexicans not ten days before. We saw the tracks of three wagons going down the Canadian river, and you may be sure they belonged to these traders. But I blame the Mexicans not half so much as I do Mr. Steck, the superintendent of Indian affairs, who gave them the pass to go and trade, he knowing perfectly well at the time that we were at war with the Indians, and that the Mexicans would take what they could sell best, which was powder, and lead, and caps. Mr. Steck should have known better than to give passes to these men to trade, when every one knows that ammunition is all the Indians want at this time.[135]

Before the Adobe Fort fight, Dr. Steck lodged a strong protest with Carleton, urging him not to authorize the use of Navajo Indians to fight Kiowas and Comanches, or any other Indian tribe. Steck's letter of protest brought a sharp rebuke from Carleton. On Nov. 8, 1864, three weeks before the fight, Carleton virtually told Steck to mind his own business:

I have the honor to acknowledge the receipt of your communication of the 5th instant, and to say in reply that it has hitherto seemed to be my duty, when Indians murdered our people, and ran off with their stock, to punish the aggressors if I could. The responsibility of all the consequences which may follow my acts, it is expected, will rest where it rightly belongs — that is to say, upon myself. I was not aware until so informed by yourself that it was expected that investigations with reference to Indian hostilities upon our people were to be made through your office before a blow could be struck. It is, however, acknowledged that you should be informed when hostile demonstrations are to be made against Indians within your superintendency, and therefore copies of orders in such cases have been sent to you.

That Indian was set against Indian as a part of the military strategy, was disclosed by Carleton's letter to Steck:

Utes and Apaches have had authority to go against the Kiowas and Comanches with Colonel Carson, mainly because it was desirable, when so many conditions are forming between the various Indian tribes against the whites, to have the savages of the mountains committed on our side as against the Indians of the plains. This subject seemed to be the peculiar province of the military department, which is charged with the protection of the people. It may not be improper to inform you that I myself was in command of the troops at Albuquerque in 1856 when the Comanches and Kiowas visited that town. I gave them an ox and some flour and sugar and coffee and had a talk with them.

Carleton regretted existing differences of opinion, but absolved the military from all wrong:

It is to be regretted that from no cause on the part of the military, there has come to exist a state of affairs officially which seems to preclude the idea of much cordiality in consultation or in cooperation, but my earnest efforts shall continue and the whole of my ability be given to protect the persons and property of people residing within this department from Indian aggression, even though, unhappily, there be not such a condition of harmony between ourselves as public officers as might be desirable.[136]

That the bickering and quarreling between General Carleton and Superintendent Steck merited the serious attention of the government, was declared editorially by the Santa Fe *New Mexican* of November 18, 1864:

We are informed that General Carleton made known to Superintendent Steck in writing, that on account of a state of feeling toward him there could not be any cordial cooperation with him, in connection with the management of the Indian tribes in New Mexico. General Carleton and Dr. Steck cannot be useful in the same territory. Dr. Steck is a man of prudent and high character, and strict in all his official duties where not crowded out of his place by General Carleton with usurping and arbitrary acts, backing himself with military pretensions. When the General avows motives and puts them in practice which embarrass the public service and the Government's civil officers out here, what is to be done by the government?

Hopeful that he might demonstrate the effectiveness of civil negotiation when contrasted with military might, Dr. Steck wrote to General Carleton on March 15, 1865, asking permission to visit bands of Apaches in the Gila river country in southwestern New Mexico. Carleton answered Steck's letter immediately, not only refusing permission, but telling him, in so many words, to defer all missionary work until the army relinquished jurisdiction:

I have the honor to receive your letter of the 15th instant, stating, that you have received information that the Apache Indians, known as the Mimbres band of that tribe, desire peace; and that you propose to have a talk with them in their own country, and desire that I give you an escort as far as Fort West on the Gila River. . . . I have hitherto considered, and am still of the opinion, that when we are at war with a band of Indians, the military department of the government should and must manage all affairs connected with them until the war is ended; otherwise a superintendent or Indian agent might go and have talks and negotiate with them, when in the opinion of the military commander the proper time had come to prosecute hostilities with increased rigor;

and thus the two branches of the government might act with cross purposes. . . . These Indians are still in the hands of the military, and will be, until the military commander makes peace with them upon his own terms. . . . To have any person outside of the military go and hold talks with them would be productive of no good, and might lead to complications which should be avoided. . . . Until they are at peace, and returned to the reservation, the military will claim to manage them to the best of its ability, whether in making war or in making peace.

The time came, on May 1, 1865, when Michael Steck was obliged to resign as superintendent of Indian affairs in New Mexico, "for the good of the service." After resigning from the Indian Service by request, Steck prospected for gold at the Placers in Santa Fe County, and eventually became superintendent of the New Mexico Mining Co. there. Before resigning, however, Steck had the satisfaction of knowing that as a result in part of his efforts, the entire Indian situation in New Mexico would be explored and investigated by a Congressional Committee. The *Congressional News* of January 29, 1865, noted the adoption by the Congress of a joint resolution, sponsored by Senator Doolittle of Wisconsin, providing for the appointment of a committee of three senators and four members of the House, "to investigate the treatment of Indians by the civil and military authorities of the United States." [137]

A. B. Norton, who succeeded Michael Steck as Superintendent of Indian Affairs in New Mexico, adopted almost entirely the views that Steck had so persistently advocated about the Indians for so many months. In his annual report to the Commissioner of Indian Affairs of August 24, 1867, Norton deplored the fact that his 1866 report had been "mutilated and published by Commissioner Cooley in garbled and disjointed extracts," and complained that the opinions he had expressed concerning Indian policy had been "utterly ignored, and the policy of Mr. Graves, who never visited but one tribe of Indians in this Territory, substituted in their stead." Concerning the Navajo problem, Norton's 1867 report said:

With regard to the Navajos, former Commissioner Cooley recommended that the Bosque Redondo be decided upon as a permanent reservation for these Indians . . . and he prophesied that the reservation will be a success. I have thought otherwise and recommended to the contrary, and have prophesied that in the end it will prove a failure. In fact it has proven so already. The soil is cold, and the alkali in the water destroys it. The corn crop this year is a total failure. Last year 3,000 bushels only was raised on 3,000 acres, and year before last six thousand bushels; continually growing worse instead of better. The self sustaining properties of the soil are all gone. The Indians now dig up the mesquite root for wood, and carry it upon their galled and lacerated backs for 12 miles. The present agent now asserts there is a scarcity of fuel, and recommends an estimate for funds to furnish conveyance for wood for 8,000 Indians to be hauled or packed 12 miles. The wood for the garrison is hauled from 40 to 50 miles, at an expense of about $75,000 per year. The water is black and brackish, scarcely bearable to the taste, and said by the Indians to be unhealthy, because one-fourth of their population have been swept off by disease, which they attribute mainly to the effects of the water.[138]

Superintendent Norton was frankly critical of the Bosque Redondo as a site for an Indian reservation:

What a beautiful selection is this for a reservation! It has cost the government millions of dollars, and the sooner it is abandoned and the Indians removed the better. I have heard it suggested that there was a speculation at the bottom of it. To say the least, it was certainly a very unfortunate selection, and an enormous expense upon the government, costing, as I verily believe, from first to last, over $10,000,000. Think of it! Do you expect an Indian to be satisfied and contented, deprived of the common comforts of life, without which a white man would not be contented anywhere? Would any sensible man select a spot for a reservation of 8,000 Indians where the water is scarcely bearable; where the soil is poor and cold, and where the mesquite roots, 12 miles distant, are the only wood for the Indians to use? In the selection of a reservation you must have good wood, good soil, and good water; these are three essentials, without all or either of which every reservation must, in the end, prove a failure. This reservation has neither of these qualifications, which alone are calculated to give content and satisfaction to the human heart and mind.

The Indians were unhappy and dissatisfied at Bosque Redondo, in Norton's opinion, and kept there only by force:

Besides all this, I care not what any man say to the contrary, these Indians are all dissatisfied, and that dissatisfaction is universal. They remain there on the reservation today by force. Free them from military control and fear and they would leap therefrom as the bird from its open cage. They will never work there with any heart, and never have done so, and the idea of keeping these wild brutes of the forest, if you call them not human beings, subject to such torture is a disgrace to the age we live in and to the government we support. No matter how much these Indians may be taught the arts of peace, to cultivate the soil, and to manufacture; no matter how successful they may be in supporting and maintaining themselves; no matter how civilized and Christianized they may become, if they remain on this reservation they must always be held by force, and not from choice.

Norton pleaded for the release of the Navajos from their Bosque Redondo imprisonment, and their return to their own country where they could get a drink of good cool water, and where they could sustain life:

Oh! Let them go back, or take them back to where they can have good cool water to drink, wood plenty to keep them from freezing to death, and where the soil will produce something for them to eat, and place them, at some future day, in an independent and self sustaining position, honored among men, and an honor to the government we live under, for having raised them from their present condition to one far better. The removal of these Indians, however, is objected to because so much has already been expended there by the military for buildings, but let a proper selection be made, where buildings and materials are plenty and convenient, and the amount expended for fuel alone in two years at the Bosque would replace all the buildings. It may also be found desirable to keep up the post, and set apart this reservation for some smaller, and not agricultural, band of Indians. As to the cost of removal, these Indians can be removed at very little extra expense, if any more, than it costs to feed them, by giving them their entire ration in beef daily, which would cost no transportation, but be driven along and fed to them as they go. Where they shall be taken, is a question of the greatest importance.

Norton had no particular choice of a place to which the Navajos should be moved, but suggested the possibility, among others, of acquiring the Maxwell Land Grant,[139] a vast wilderness area in the mountains of northeastern New Mexico, with many small rivers and streams, and fine hunting, owned at the time by Lucien B. Maxwell:

In consideration of which I would most respectfully recommend that either they must be located in their own country on three or four reservations, because there is no sufficient spot of land there to place them all upon, or the purchase of the Maxwell Grant, 40 by 60 miles, at $250,000, or else take them south of Fort Stanton and east of the Sacramento mountains, between the mountains and Pecos, but next to the mountains for timber, and on the Rio Feliz or Rio Penasco for water. These are the only three suitable and desirable locations known to me at present, and it is for your department to decide which is the best and most desirable, or whether they shall be removed at all.

The last of the Mescalero Apaches had left the Bosque Redondo reservation by 1866, and were shifting for themselves, robbing and plundering the whites, according to Superintendent Norton:

Little is known of the Mescalero Apaches since they left the reservation of the Bosque Redondo, where the most of them had been located with the Navajos. They were unable to agree with the Navajos, and were therefore dissatisfied and left at night in a body, on the 3d of November, 1865, ever since which time they have been committing depredations upon the settlements, and some murders. When not in the mountains, south of Fort Stanton (their native country,) they range between that and Las Vegas in search of booty. Their agent, Lorenzo Labadie, says "they number about 525 souls," and that he has no doubt but that he can prevail on them to settle on a reservation which might be selected for them south of Fort Stanton, and to live at peace with the inhabitants, but he does not think they can ever be induced to return to the Bosque Redondo.[140]

During Civil War years, as in pre-war years, New Mexico political leaders were in sharp conflict when it came to the adoption of a concrete program for handling the "wild Indians." The Territory of New Mexico, as a political unit, had little to do with actual policy making. In the final analysis, this responsibility rested on the federal government. However, as was only natural, territorial leaders manifested an ever alert interest in everything that pertained to Indian affairs, insofar as they affected non-Indian settlers. There were many men in New Mexico who strongly supported Carleton's campaign to put the Indians in Bosque Redondo country, and were heartily in favor of keeping them there indefinitely under strict military supervision. Many others, perhaps a majority, were decidedly opposed to the establishment or maintenance of a reservation of any kind at Bosque Redondo. Some of this opposition undoubtedly developed because it was apparent that if the Indians were to be permitted to occupy large areas in the Pecos River country, non-Indian livestock raisers would be deprived of tremendously important grazing rights on hundreds of thousands of acres of public domain. Since time immemorial livestock owners had enjoyed the privilege of free grazing on public domain, and this privilege they did not propose to forfeit without a terrific struggle.

Citizens of New Mexico, directly concerned, fostered opposition to the Bosque Redondo project which soon reflected itself in the political sentiment of the day. Typical of the protests against the Bosque Redondo resettlement representative of grazing interests was the opinion expressed by Probate Judge Miguel Romero y Baca, of San Miguel County, at the time a stamping and grazing ground for vast herds of cattle and sheep. Writing from Las Vegas on June 23, 1864, Judge Baca, complaining of serious losses resulting from Indian depredations, argued the case for the white settlers:

For some time the people of this county have been bitterly complaining against the Navajo Indians, begging me to notify you of their discontent. Almost every citizen in this country is the owner of stock. I believe two-thirds of the stock, such as sheep, belongs to this county and the adjoining county of Mora, so that we have not been able this spring to find sufficient pasturage for our herds. The consequence has been that two-thirds of the brood this year has been lost for the want of suitable herding grounds, and a climate such as the Pecos River affords, and has supplied us with for twenty years. It is said now that six or eight thousand Indians are located upon the Pecos River, and that it is the intention to locate the whole tribe on that river with their stock of sheep, which will amount to at least two hundred thousand, with other animals. They must have room for this stock to pasture, so that the people of this county and others will be obliged to move their herds two hundred and fifty miles east; and the farther they go east, the less pasture they will find, especially the kind of pasturage needed for the lambing season.

Were the Indians to be preferred to the peaceful white citizens? This was the question Judge Baca asked:

The people complain, thinking it injustice to drive them away from their common pastures that have been theirs for many years. Is it just that the Indian shall be preferred to the peaceful white citizen? No, sir, this cannot be so. . . . These Indians have done so much damage; we have lost by them not less than five hundred thousand sheep in three years, yet we fear to lose much more. If they should revolt against the troops, who will suffer, but the people of this county? God forbid that these Indians should again be hostile; the property of this county would be lost, and many families fall into the hands of the savages. Not a single day that the people do not complain. They are against the location of the Navajos on the Pecos River; at this time it takes a regiment of troops to keep them at the Bosque, and if the whole tribe is removed, it will take not less than five regiments and a full battery of artillery to keep them on the reservation. We are now trying the experiment with those on the reservation, and about a month ago forty Apaches left the reservation and came to this county, and killed eleven persons and carried off seventy horses and mules. This shows that the military force is not sufficient to keep them quiet. It will be the same with the Navajos, who are very fond of sheep. If I have a herd of sheep and they mix with the herds of a Navajo, we would have trouble to separate them without exposing our lives.[141]

CHAPTER EIGHT

Carleton on the Defensive

IT WAS INEVITABLE that General James H. Carleton, Commander of the Department of New Mexico, would face a day of reckoning. During his several years of despotical control over affairs in the Territory, he had inaugurated and carried forward a program of violence against the Indians which had no precedent in recorded New Mexico history. His campaigns, violating many of the rules of civilized warfare, had brought tragedy and death to scores of Apaches and Navajos. Permanent traumatic and psychological injury had been inflicted on many individual Indians of both tribes, and upon the tribes as an entirety, as the result of the methods of pursuit and castigation adopted by the military. The Indians, ignorant of the white man's ways or objectives, had fought Carleton's soldiers desperately in defense of their lives and their way of life. Dragging their half starved and half naked families with them, Apache and Navajo alike had wandered about in the Indian country, living from day to day like frightened jack rabbits, looking in vain for a place of refuge; scurrying from place to place, almost from one rock to another, hiding day and night like hunted animals in canyon and mountain crevice, fearful of lighting a fire because the smoke would reveal their hiding place.

Not one Apache or Navajo in a hundred could speak a word of English. The government agents, who theoretically represented the Indians, had been powerless to help, silenced and subdued by the application of Carleton's autocratic policy,

440

which he attempted to defend and justify on the ground that the country was at war.

There were developments in the summer and fall of 1864 indicating that Carleton's reign in New Mexico was about over. Only two years previous, the people of the Territory had hailed him as a conquering hero, not so much because of his much heralded march from California to New Mexico to fight rebels, but because he had promised them protection from the Indians. When Carleton initiated the campaigns against the Apaches and Navajos, he was perhaps the most talked of man in the Territory. Public sentiment changed quickly when it appeared that he proposed to re-settle the Apaches and Navajos on public domain that had been considered by New Mexicans since time immemorial as their exclusive grazing lands.

The Santa Fe *New Mexican* of Oct. 31, 1864, fired the opening gun in the campaign to "get Carleton," by publishing an editorial attacking him from several directions. Considering the fact that martial law was still in effect in New Mexico, publication of the editorial was a bit hazardous, but the paper assumed the risk. With a view perhaps to discrediting Carleton politically with the national administration, the *New Mexican* charged that he had been "an original democrat from away down east in the State of Maine;" that he had been an ardent and enthusiastic supporter of General Geo. B. McClellan; that he had belittled President Lincoln; that he had pushed friends of Lincoln aside, and favored friends of McClellan in transactions involving bids and purchase contracts for army supplies in New Mexico. In an obvious attempt to stir up religious prejudice, the *New Mexican* charged that Carleton had behaved disrespectfully toward religion on the occasion when he had prevailed upon the Vicario of Santa Fe, during the absence of Bishop John B. Lamy, to sing a Te Deum in celebration of the army's successful campaign against the Navajos, and had then pointedly remained away from the service. The *New Mexican* charged editorially that Carleton had been unduly active politically; that he had used the influence and prestige of his office in attempting to have the Legislature adopt a resolution which he had inspired, lauding his military record, and urging that he be promoted to major general. The *New Mexican's* principal complaint against Carleton, however, was his mismanagement of the campaign against the Navajo Indians:

The deplorable condition of this Territory and the wants and starvation staring our people in the face, owing to the ruinous policy pursued by the political General commanding this department makes it the duty of every man capable of using a pen to wield it with all the mental vigor and power he possesses in behalf of this, our much abused, long suffering, down trodden community. In endeavoring to set the matter fairly before the public, we shall strive to avoid everything of a military or a personal nature, for we have too much patriotism and too much self respect either to deal in scurrilities or meddle with the plans of the government in chastising its enemies, whether they be rebels, Indians or copper-heads. . . . When we find the thimble-rigger politician using his official position and peddling out the immense patronage at his disposal to subserve his own personal purposes, to gratify his insane vanity, and his still crazier ambition, we feel that as public journalists we would be derelict in duty did we not speak frankly, fully and fearlessly on the questions now at issue, involving as they do, the lives, liberties, the fortunes of all New Mexico; no matter whether the party culpable wears the dress of a citizen, or struts the sidewalks with a feather in his hat, a sword at his side, or a star on his shoulder. . . . Probably the most brilliant feature of the pompous general is to be seen in his management of the Navajo Indians. For two hundred years there has been an hereditary feud between this most powerful tribe of Indians and the people of New Mexico. In defiance of this strong and deadly hostility, these savages, the scourge and terror of New Mexico, for two centuries, have been brought from their own country in the Territory of Arizona, by only the mere will of this one man, and placed upon the rich pasture lands of the Pecos by the thousands — a stench in the nostrils of the people. Whether this insane policy is to be attributed to the brain of an unscrupulous and designing politician or the visions of a depraved ambition, it is difficult to say. . . . Large bodies of troops were sent into the Navajo country last year, and days and weeks did they consume in destroying the abundant crops of the Indians. This might have been well enough had the evil results fallen upon the parties intended.

The *New Mexican* contended that Carleton tolerated no opposition to the Bosque Redondo project:

But instead of that, they are brought hundreds of miles through the settlements to the Bosque, and there fed at the expense of the government. Perhaps this peddling politician will figure out how much the government will gain by this as a financial operation. . . . The Navajos have heretofore subsisted and clothed themselves, asking no favors of the government. Colonel Sumner placed a fort in the heart of their country, and for several years, while under the command of Majors Kendrick and Backus, not a word of complaint was heard from any one. Why was not a similar policy inaugurated? Let the same number of troops required at the Bosque to keep the peace, be placed anywhere west of the Rio Grande to prevent the ingress and egress of marauding parties, and there would be no more trouble with the Navajos. They would subsist and clothe themselves, and cost the government practically nothing. But this was not to be so. Without stopping to enquire whether the lands on the Pecos had been ceded by the Comanches in whose country they are situated, without consulting any one as to the feasibility of the project — this irresponsible individual assumes the power of making New Mexico a poor house, an asylum, for the Indian paupers of Arizona, in order that his interests in the various gold mine claims in that Territory, in which it is believed he is deeply engaged, may be protected and enhanced in value. This Bosque reservation is the darling object, the pet scheme of the Commandant, and any one under his command, daring to breathe a doubt as to its practicability, would be subjected to such annoyances at his hands that he would soon find the Department too hot to hold him. . . . Carleton has gathered at the Bosque, "eight thousand Indians whose untutored minds, don't know enough to cover their behinds . . ." It was a sorry day for our Territory when this man Carleton first set foot within her borders. His visionary schemes prompted by the most inordinate vanity, his ambitious projects pointing ever to the accomplishment of his most unscrupulous designs for his personal aggrandizement, with their ruinous results have fallen like a funeral pall upon the hearts of our people. Starvation and desolation darken our doors and edict has gone forth from this petty despot, that the Indians shall be fed though the people starve.

Following up the full-dress attack of October 31, the *New Mexican* published a more restrained editorial on November

4, 1864, eulogizing Kit Carson's services in the field, and undertaking to give due credit to Carleton and all others who had participated in the campaign against the Navajos. Nevertheless the *New Mexican* restated its position with reference to Carleton's Navajo policy, emphasizing the business and economic phases, and ignoring anything relating to the humanitarian aspects of the questions involved:

The war upon the Navajos was necessary and was well executed by Colonel Kit Carson and his New Mexico regiment. General Carleton is entitled to the credit of having put in motion the means in his hands and so committed them to Carson that he was enabled to obtain great success against the ancient and treacherous tribe of Navajos. To him and his regiment of native New Mexicans, with the mixture of Americans who were with him, and his excellent American and Mexican officers, will ever belong in history the credit and fame of having brought to terms so many of the tribe of Navajos. Although the General did not go with the campaign, we are satisfied that while he remained in Santa Fe, he was awake to see that means and supplies were forwarded to those who were enduring all toil and risking constant danger so that they should be cheered and sustained midst their toils and dangers. None in the territory now wishes to see any of the advantages lost gained over the Navajos. All believe these should be kept.

While willing to give credit where credit was due, nevertheless the *New Mexican* complained that General Carleton in proposing to locate permanently not only New Mexico's Navajos, but also those from Arizona, on the Bosque Redondo, was sponsoring a project that would adversely affect the Territory's economy forever:

Who in New Mexico, when General Carleton was engaged in reducing the Navajos, thought that the General intended to bring all the Navajos from Arizona and put them as examples of "politeness and good order" upon New Mexican soil? . . . What preference has Arizona that she must be cleared of her Indians and New Mexico receive them? . . . General Sumner, when in command of this Department, gravely advised the government to turn New Mexico over to the Indian tribes, and based his argument upon the ground that the people of New Mexico were too vicious, ignorant, corrupt and unworthy to deserve the further attention of the government, and that the Indians should be permanently established here and the people disposed of. General Carleton is the first officer in authority who has dared to carry out the recommendations of his predecessor. In bringing the Indians from Arizona and putting them upon the Pecos River, he has begun the plan of General Sumner. He has not yet disposed of the citizens, but he does deprive them of their pasture grounds, upon the best portions of the Pecos, so that the Arizona Indians may enjoy them.

The *New Mexican* made it clear that it was for the white man, and advocated that the "thieving redskins" be ejected from Bosque Redondo and returned forthwith to their own land:

We are for the white man. We hold that the people, the farmers and stock growers, should not be crowded off their lands for the benefit of a pack of thieving redskins. And so far from advocating further importations, we urge the removal of those already at Bosque Redondo to their own land, and believe that the interests of the Territory demand it. Every day goes to show the injury the territory sustains from the policy now pursued. Instead of securing peace in the country, it has rendered life and property more unsafe than before colonization was carried out. The heavy premium on theft will soon ruin our stock growers. An Indian steals a herd of mules or flock of sheep, delivers himself up as a prisoner, and then the Department Commander confirms his title to the plunder, and the unfortunate loser must submit to the wrong. The theft is legalized and the thief goes rejoicing on his way to "Carleton's rich and verdant lands," there to be feasted until he recruits for another raid. This is one of the beauties of the importation policy.

Ordinarily Carleton pursued a policy of ignoring criticism. But the sledge-hammer attacks in the *New Mexican* provoked him to such an extent that he delivered a reply in person on Dec. 16, 1864, at a mass meeting of citizens in Las Cruces, a place far removed from the Navajo country, but only a short distance from Mesilla, the home of Judge Knapp. The Las Cruces speech, printed as a pamphlet, was distributed to friends and supporters in New Mexico, and copies found their way into friendly hands in Washington. Carleton's defense, in which he demonstrated once again extraordinary ability to write effective English, was perhaps the frankest and most explicit statement he ever made in justification of his war against the Navajo tribe. After sketching the current aspect of the war against the Navajos, Carleton said:

From time immemorial these Navajo Indians subsisted upon the flocks and herds of your fathers; had, times without number, even in one single hour, reduced whole families from comparative wealth to poverty. Their ravages had impoverished not only your country, but these barbarians had murdered your people; had slain your fathers — your brothers — your children; or had carried many of them into a horrible and hopeless captivity, until there was hardly a home in the land which was not filled with mourning and with hearts made desolate.

Your ancestors, under the Spanish government, made many campaigns against them, and many treaties of peace with them. But the Indians soon forgot the terror which had been inspired by the presence of the troops in their country, and soon forgot the obligations to which they had pledged themselves, in each successive treaty.

Then came other campaigns and other treaties, under the Mexican Republic, and you all know with what result, again, the Navajos forgot the punishment they had received, and over and over again, broke their treaties as of old.

After the annexation of New Mexico to the United States, by the Treaty of Guadalupe Hidalgo, the troops from the north commenced their campaigns, with as high hopes of a permanent success as your fathers had entertained. First Doniphan his, then Washington, then Sumner, then Bonneville, then Miles, then Canby, all of them our best men. It is true they gained many advantages, but concluded, each one his campaign, by the inevitable treaty. And what *now* was the result? You can all answer for me, because this brings matters down to your own times. Why, the treaties were broken, and, on some occasions, even before the troops had been entirely withdrawn from the Navajo country. Navajo faith, like Punic faith, became, at length, a scoff and a jeer. The Navajos themselves, from long experience in this matter, had learned to see that the prudent way to end a campaign against them, was to come in with a white flag and say they wanted peace; say that the murders and robberies had been committed by some of their young men; that this thing should not occur again; that if our people would only smoke and be friends, and make a treaty, *this time* it should be kept most sacredly!

Over, and over, and over again, this was done. Fellow citizens, is not all this the truth? I appeal to any one man of you all, if one single point, thus far stated, can be denied.

Well, now, in finding myself in command of the troops within your borders, it naturally occurred to me that, to cure this great evil from which your territory had been so long a prey, some new remedy had to be adopted. You know that I had lived among you for several years on a former occasion, and had had many opportunities, not only of learning somewhat of the geography of New Mexico, but of knowing some little of your Indian difficulties. When I came here this time, it not only became my professional business, but my bounden duty, not only to yourselves, but to the government, to devise *some* plan which might, with God's blessing, forever bring these troubles to an end. In a short time after my arrival, some eighteen of the Navajo chiefs came to see me, and said they wanted to make a treaty of peace. I told them it was unnecessary for us to go through with the *form* of making a treaty; that if their peoples committed no murders nor robberies on our people, there would be peace without a treaty. That we were not children to be beguiled any more by their promises; that we had learned not to believe those promises; and did not care to hear them. That hereafter we would judge of their sincerity solely by their acts. That if they committed any more murders and robberies, as surely as that the sun shone, so surely would the troops come, and, this time, make a war upon them which they would long remember.

They said they had never been refused the making of a treaty before, but returned to their own country, promising to do the best they could to keep their people from perpetrating any more acts of hostility. What was the result of these promises? Why in less than six weeks time, murders and robberies were committed on every hand. Finally the spring of 1863 came, when, having ascertained that a great many Navajos claimed to belong to a peace party, word was sent that all who did not wish to be exposed to the perils of war, must come in and go down to the Bosque Redondo, where they would be fed and cared for, until those who remained hostile should be subdued. That we could not discriminate between the innocent and the guilty unless this were done; that unless those who claimed to be our friends would thus separate themselves from our acknowledged enemies, we should be obliged to consider all we encountered as enemies, once the war began, when on themselves would rest the consequences, and not upon us. The reply they made was, that not a

Navajo would come in under such conditions. Word was again sent to them to consider the matter more maturely; that the peace party would have until the 20th of the following July, in which to make up their minds and come in; that the door should remain open until that day. Afterwards, it would be forever closed, and the war would begin in earnest. Still not one Navajo came. They did not believe we *were* in earnest, and on that day, as had been promised, the war began.

Carleton explained why he moved the Navajos from their own country:

Little by little, a few Navajos were captured here, a small band there, and, by and by, some began voluntarily to surrender, until we had on our hands quite a large number of prisoners. We could not feed them in the Navajo country — that was impossible. Nor had we troops to guard them there, even though we could have furnished them with subsistence. We could not, as Christians, kill them; we could not see them perish by starvation; we could not turn them loose, for the war itself was still raging, and we had nearly two hundred years of the making of treaties, which had been broken almost as soon as made. It was clearly seen that, even admitting it would have been good policy to place the captive Navajos upon a reservation in their own country, there could be found no one piece of irrigable and fertile land, large enough for such reservation within all its boundaries. Besides, the enormous cost of land transportation for stores, not only for the Indians, but for the large military establishment which would have to be kept up to guard them, could not and would not be incurred by the government, for the maintenance of any such a system, in a region so very distant from the source of supply. But such a plan was not admitted to be a good one, of itself, even when free from these fatal objections. For in that country, so familiar to every man, woman and child of the Navajo nation — so formidable from its huge mesas, its rugged mountains, its deep forests, its labyrinthine canons, ten times the number of troops now within this Department could not prevent the Indians, by ones and twos, from leaving such reservation whenever it should please them to do so. Thus the whole system would crumble away and fall through, as totally impracticable. What then, would have been the result? Why, still more murders, more robberies, then another war — and then what? Why, of course, another treaty; and so on forever, in that inevitable circle, which had become as fatal to the prosperity of New Mexico, as the shirt of Nessus to Hercules.[142]

Judge Joseph G. Knapp of Mesilla, long-time opponent of Carleton's policies, was quick to answer Carleton's Las Cruces speech, by writing a letter to the Santa Fe *New Mexican,* in which he said:

Your *policy,* as you have stated it in your pamphlet of December 16, 1864, ought not to have been accepted by any reasonable being. The Navajo chiefs came to treat with you in the fall of 1862. You said not a word to them about any reservation on the Pecos, at that time; on the contrary you told them they must remain at peace in their own country. Was the Bosque Grande an afterthought? You then waited until the spring of 1863 had come, although "in less than six weeks time," after your interview with the eighteen chiefs, "murders and robberies were committed on every hand," by these Navajos. You did nothing but wait some six months, permitting the people to be murdered and robbed; waiting until the peace party in the Navajo country had planted their crops — and in the meantime had not heard a word from you. You then sent them word that these peace men must leave their fields, their houses, gardens, their orchards, and their country itself, and voluntarily remove to the Pecos River where there were neither fields, houses, gardens, fruit trees, wood nor water fit to use, upon your naked promise that they should be "fed and cared for." This is their first information that they are to be removed from their own country. You send them word, but do not say whether it ever reached them. In a word, you specify nothing; you appoint no place of rendezvous; offer no means of conveyance or food for the journey, but require "these pagans," with their women and helpless children to "come in and go down to the Bosque," and crown the whole with a threat that unless they do as you command, they will be exposed to all the perils of war, and that you cannot "discriminate between the innocent and guilty." Do you, on calm reflection, on sober second thought, now believe that your "plan" was not rather calculated to alienate and sour the minds of those peace Indians, than to make them more friendly?

Judge Knapp charged that General Carleton had failed to cooperate with the Navajo "peace party":

On that fixed day, July 20, 1863, you close the door of peace forever. *You* do it, you do not even wait for orders from your superior officers, but you begin a war in earnest, letting it fall on the heads of all alike — on the helpless and innocent as well as the guilty. You send them a force composed of but one regiment of New Mexican volunteers. Your favorite column from California is not employed in that service. Thus you showed that in your own estimation the peace party composed nearly all of the entire nation, or that the Navajo was not after all, that "formidable" nation of savages you have been trying to make the government and people believe them to be. Those peace Indians, to the number of thousands, surrendered themselves up, stripped of everything. This you call "fulfilling their part of the compact." A compact implies an agreement between two or more persons, voluntarily entered into. You and these Navajos had made no compact. You refused to make one. You ordered and they obeyed, not assented to a proposition. You then tell us, you could not as a Christian kill these surrendered Indians — could not see them perish by starvation — a condition to which your "plan" reduced them. So you must feed them, and your "plan" put them at the Bosque Redondo, the most inconvenient spot you could have selected so far as economy is concerned, and it has fastened that enormous expense upon the government at this inopportune period, when it is struggling for existence.[143]

In a second "open letter," Judge Knapp contended that Carleton had no authority to begin a "war" against the Indians:

Soon after the command of the Department of New Mexico came into your possession, you declared war against the Apaches and Navajos; and planned your campaign against them. In this, you exceeded your powers and usurped those belonging to others. The constitution has given this authority to Congress. But, even, if the President of the United States may have this power in the first instance, of declaring war during the recess of Congress, to be approved afterwards, it does not follow from thence, that every Brigadier General is vested with it, without regard to any action of Congress on the subject. You cannot avoid this position by asserting that individual Indians had committed murders and robberies on the inhabitants, and that your acts, in declaring war against the entire nation or bands of Indians, were necessary for the protection of this Territory. Individuals are liable personally for their own acts, but the nation is not, unless that nation, in its supreme authority, assume the responsibility of the commission of the acts complained of. Apply this rule to these Indians, and how stands the case.

Cadette, for the Mescalero Apaches, and eighteen chiefs for the Navajo tribe, had assured Carleton of their peaceful intentions, according to Knapp:

Before you had matured your plans, in the fall of 1862, Cadette, the Mescalero Apache chief, under the guidance of the Indian agent, came to your quarters and assured you of the peaceful intention of his band of Mescaleros. So, too, eighteen of the Navajo chiefs, came to you and gave similar assurances of their peaceful intentions. But how did you meet these peaceful indications? Your domineering spirit displayed itself in telling them that you did not care to hear them; that you had planned a war against their nation and all Apaches and Navajos must go to the Bosque, if they wished to escape the perils of war; and that you should not discriminate between the innocent and the guilty. Cadette and his band of Apaches followed their agent in. The peaceful Navajos, seeing Colonel Carson in their country, and trusting to his word and promises, also surrendered themselves, and you have taken them to the Bosque as prisoners of war. Old men and women too decrepit to walk, little ones equally, yes more helpless, women and children, non combatants, and those not able to take care of themselves much less to fight, are all held as prisoners of war — persons who have voluntarily come in for their protection and food, are treated in the same manner as those taken with arms in their hands, if indeed, you have one such in your possession. Where do you find the rule for such conduct? Certainly not in any code of civilized warfare. That has been the rule of heathens and pagans, not Christians.[144]

Quite thoroughly convinced in his own mind that the California troops, in marching across the country from Los Angeles to the Rio Grande, had accomplished something extraordinary, and deserving of a high place in the history of the Civil War, General Carleton never overlooked an opportunity to direct attention to that performance. The Santa Fe *New Mexican* took occasion, from time to time, to belittle the march and Carleton's participation in it. The *Journal* of Wilmington, Calif., of Feb. 18, 1865, published an article which retold the story of the march, and eulogized Carleton's part in its accomplishment. The Santa Fe *Gazette* of May 1, 1865, copied the Wilmington *Journal's* article in full. The *New Mexican* published one paragraph of the eulogy, which read:

The planning and execution of the great and rapid march of General Carleton's command from the Pacific to the Rio Grande, will ever be remembered to his credit, as a skillful and persevering officer. They will illustrate his familiarity with desert travel, and his ability to overcome obstacles and difficulties which must have dismayed an officer of less force and experience.

The *New Mexican* then proceeded to pay its respects to the march and to Carleton personally:

We have seen this idea under various forms in the newspapers in the pay of General Carleton and heard it from his retainers until it would seem that they have either forgotten the facts, or have repeated the story so often that he and they have come to believe that it is true. This wonderful march, when stripped of all leather and prunella is simply this, no more, no less: General Carleton was from the month of October, 1861, to July following, in coming from Los Angeles to the Rio Grande, a distance by the road he traveled less than seven hundred miles, one hundred miles in a month, or three miles and a third in a day! Truly a wonderful "great and rapid march!" Renowned "credit of such a skillful and persevering officer!" More strange still, that one man chasing glory and fame could have spent so much time on such a road! Sherman is nowhere. Carleton is the hero of the war, after all, where rapid and unprecedented marches are to be made. And then such difficulties and obstacles. His column encountered between the two points eight rebel pickets, who drove back the whole column fifty miles to the Pima villages, where they entrenched themselves until the enemy leisurely moved off. He also heard tell of thousands of the enemy "over yonder," but he never came nearer them than he who chases a report. When all these facts are known, it is more than questionable whether these retainers are not trying to bring his administration into ridicule. . . . General Carleton had better set his invention to work out something new, or else stop writing for and editing newspapers.[145]

While the Santa Fe *New Mexican* prodded Carleton in its editorial columns, he was being subjected to an attack at the hands of some of his former comrades-in-arms in the southern part of the Territory. California Column veterans recently mustered out of the service, led by John M. Kerr, William Jones, Howard Morrison and John Collins, met in Mesilla, and arranged for the publication of "An Address to Our Late Commander, James H. Carleton." The "address" criticized Carleton's "tyrannical conduct," and demanded his removal as commander of the army in New Mexico. Copies were distributed throughout New Mexico and Arizona, and sent to California and Atlantic seaboard newspapers requesting publication. Carleton was grievously offended because of the adoption and circulation of the address. He had cherished the idea that the California Column, "to a man," held him in affection and esteem, and that none of them would ever criticize him publicly. The "address," belittling Carleton and contending that he was incompetent to administer military affairs in New Mexico, was in part as follows:

Three years ago, buoyant with hope and full of anticipation that we would be led against the common enemy of our country, we left our homes, all that was near and dear to us, sacrificing personal interests, and took up the line of march. Nothing of importance characterized that march until our arrival at Fort Yuma, on the Colorado River; at this point commenced the series of gross derelictions of duty, frauds, unwarranted delays, marches and countermarches without any progress, which facts, when they receive the awful sentence of history, will forever shroud the name of James H. Carleton, in the darkest obloquy and disgrace.

The discharged soldiers claimed that Carleton loitered on the march, and marked time in Tucson while rebels raided and plundered along the Rio Grande:

General James H. Carleton, while at Tucson, in Arizona Territory, knowing that the rebels were on the Rio Grande, plundering and robbing the citizens of that valley, for no good cause whatever, persistently delayed and refused to follow and punish them when fully within his power to do so, although both men and officers were clamorous to be led forward, and it is an indisputable fact that he never moved from that point towards the Rio Grande until he was positively informed the enemy had retired.

And on the arrival of the column on the Rio Grande, instead

of being, as we desired, sent against the hostile Indians who were murdering and robbing citizens and devastating the country, a large number of us were shut up in towns and compelled to do police duty over loyal citizens who heroically suffered from the common enemy, and who had, unsolicited and unsupported, taken up arms and resisted the occupation of the country by them.

General Carleton has established a military surveillance over these same citizens, imprisoned and brutally treated their judges, inaugurated martial law, established courts of his own creation, and compelled citizens to answer before them for offenses unknown to the laws, has fined and compelled citizens to labor without conviction or trial, has taken private property without just compensation, and has encouraged his subordinates in resisting ministerial officers in the service of process issued by the civil courts. These are but a few of the many outrages that have been perpetrated by General Carleton under the specious pretext of serving his country, during our stay in New Mexico, and while the citizens have been denied their rights, the soldiers too, have likewise suffered from his tyrannical conduct. We believe that the interests of the government which we volunteered to defend cannot be better served than by dispensing with the services of General Carleton. As an officer, he is incompetent — he is wanting in all those qualities which endear and adorn the citizen and characterize the true soldier.

Blaming Carleton for the discharge of California troops needed to protect New Mexico against Indian attacks, the Santa Fe *New Mexican* of Nov. 3, 1865, demanded his removal as Department Commander:

The people of New Mexico can now see, and we will soon feel the baneful results of Carleton's insane policy. We now, as before, ask that troops be sent here knowing that they are absolutely necessary to the safety and protection of our people, and we would further ask Major General Pope that a new commander be sent with the troops, and that General Carleton, "the brightest star in the constellation of American generals," be sent to some point where his greatness can develop itself, and not waste itself and run to seed, as it is destined to should he remain unappreciated in New Mexico.

The campaign to obtain Carleton's removal gained momentum in the summer and fall of 1865. New Mexico politicians, expert in the Machiavellistic art of accomplishing the removal of officials, maneuvered the Carleton fight into the Territorial Legislature of 1865-1866. The Legislature could do nothing directly about Carleton's removal, because he was a federal officer. The Legislature, however, could accelerate the movement by resorting to the time-honored New Mexico custom of adopting a memorial professing to reflect the sentiment of the people.

Routine legislative matters became of secondary importance in the session of 1865-1866 to the controversy over Carleton and his Navajo Indian policy. Gossip in legislative corridors was to the effect that members of both House and Council had been bribed to vote for or against a memorial antagonistic to Carleton. Discussed and debated for several days, the memorial was adopted on Jan. 21, 1866, by a vote of 9 to 2 in the Council, and 20 to 4 in the House. The memorial, addressed to President Andrew Johnson, urging Carleton's removal, and asking "that a more capable officer be sent to command the troops immediately," read in part as follows:

Your memorialists, the Council and House of Representatives of the Territory of New Mexico, most respectfully represent to your excellency and the War Department that Brevet Major General James H. Carleton, of the United States Volunteers, has commanded the troops in the Territory for more than three years, and that during this time, with all the means and resources necessarily in his hands, has failed entirely in reducing the Indians to subjection, or in giving peace and security to the inhabitants of the country; all this time keeping the forces under his command stationed at points that are never threatened by the hostile Indians, but which are lucrative for sutlers and speculators, and by a continued system of falsification unworthy of the character of an officer or soldier, has represented to the general government the contrary, and thus by pernicious management to our citizens and their interests, which is well known by the inhabitants of this Territory, has acquired credit and military position which he does not deserve.

The memorial charged that Carleton blamed the Mexican people for crimes actually committed by Indians:

Satisfied that the military administration has been a terrible calamity to the people of this Territory, and their interests, not only in not having discharged his duties in protecting our interests when threatened by the Indians, whose savage forays during the time above stated have been more frequent and have committed more murders and thefts than ever before in the same length of time, and when he has been informed of depredations having been committed by the Indians, he has denied the facts, charging the Mexican people of this country with the crime, thereby calumniating our people.

The pro-Carleton Santa Fe *Gazette* paid its respects to the Legislature on Jan. 27, 1866, publishing a single column, page length, black-bordered announcement in the style of an obituary notice, which was intended to serve as a memorial of the Legislature's alleged betrayal of the cause of James H. Carleton, a reproduction of which follows:

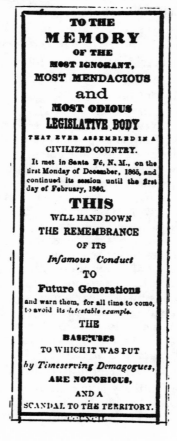

TO THE
MEMORY
OF THE
MOST IGNORANT,
MOST MENDACIOUS
and
MOST ODIOUS
LEGISLATIVE BODY
THAT EVER ASSEMBLED IN A
CIVILIZED COUNTRY.

It met in Santa Fé, N. M., on the first Monday of December, 1865, and continued its session until the first day of February, 1866.

THIS
WILL HAND DOWN
THE REMEMBRANCE
OF ITS
Infamous Conduct
TO
Future Generations
and warn them, for all time to come, to avoid its *detestable example.*
THE
BASE USES
TO WHICH IT WAS PUT
by Timeserving Demagogues,
ARE NOTORIOUS,
AND A
SCANDAL TO THE TERRITORY.

The Secretary of War, on Sept. 19, 1866, issued an order directing the Commander of the Department of Missouri to relieve General Carleton as commander of the Department of New Mexico. New Mexico politicians were quick to appropriate the credit for Carleton's removal. There was rejoicing in many parts of the Territory that the end of Carleton's reign was at hand, but it was only natural that sincere regret would be expressed in many places.

The Santa Fe *New Mexican* of Oct. 27, 1866, referring to the order for Carleton's removal, summed up the position of the anti-Carleton faction:

It thus appears that our territory will be relieved from the presence of this man Carleton, who has so long lorded it amongst us. For five years or more he has been in supreme command in New Mexico, and during that whole time has accomplished nothing for which he is entitled to the thanks or gratitude of our people, or the confidence of the War Department. He has, however, succeeded in gaining for himself the detestation and contempt of almost the entire population of our territory, as had been manifested in more than one way, public and private. The community at large will rejoice at his removal, and well they may, because with the means at his disposal, such as no commander ever had before, he has signally failed in giving peace and security to the country. As the legislature most truly remarked in its memorial praying for his removal, instead of placing troops where they were needed for protection of the settlements, he has stationed them where it would be most lucrative to speculators and favorites. As a military man his whole administration has been a most ignominious failure, and his removal from the chief command cannot but redound to the profit of the Territory.

James Henry Carleton's military career in New Mexico, after four years of high drama, had come to an end. He had arrived in the Territory on Aug. 7, 1862, in command of more than 1,500 California Volunteers, with instructions to accomplish three things: "To drive the Texans from New Mexico soil;" "to uphold the Union;" and "to see to it that the American flag flew from every fort and public building in the Territory." The Texans had returned to the south before he reached the Rio Grande in New Mexico. No doubt he had "upheld the Union," loyally and with the utmost strength. He had faithfully seen to it that the Stars and Stripes were respected on every foot of New Mexico soil. Fate decreed that the California troops were not to fire a single shot at the Confederates in New Mexico.

It was Carleton's misfortune to become commander of the Department of New Mexico at a most inopportune time. In almost any other theatre of the war he would probably have won honor and renown similar to that achieved elsewhere by major officers of his rank and experience. With hundreds of soldiers marking time, demanding action in the war, Carleton blundered into the campaign against the Apaches and Navajos, and conducted it with results that were disastrous to the Indians, and unfortunate for the government. No doubt but that Carleton was in authority in New Mexico at a time when unusual and extraordinary conditions prevailed. People blamed him for almost every adverse happening in the Territory between the times of his arrival and departure. When beef and flour sold for twenty dollars the hundred in 1864, the near starving civilian population blamed Carleton because he used government gold to outbid them in buying supplies for the army and the Indians. When the Indians raided the settlements, the people criticized Carleton for failure to prevent the raids, and for not following the raiders and killing them. When Carleton's troops shot and killed Apaches and Navajos, some New Mexico citizens called him a barbarian and a cold blooded murderer. When Carleton rounded up the Navajos, showing no mercy, and imprisoned them at Bosque Redondo, some New Mexico politicians accused him of high crimes and misdemeanors, not because of his treatment of the Indians, but because it was believed the Indians would be settled on public domain that had been used by the white settlers rent-free as grazing and breeding grounds since the days of the Spanish conquest.[146]

CHAPTER NINE

Navajos Released From Bondage

WITHIN FOUR MONTHS after General Carleton was relieved as commander of the Department of New Mexico, the War Department formally relinquished authority over the Navajo Indians and the Bosque Redondo project. Secretary of War U. S. Grant directed issuance of the order of relinquishment, effective Jan. 16, 1867. Although the War Department's order automatically restored custody of the Navajos to the Bureau of Indian Affairs of the Department of the Interior, it contained a reservation requiring the army to continue their subsistence until other arrangements could be completed.

The Santa Fe *New Mexican* viewed the relinquishment order as a point-blank repudiation of General Carleton's policy. In an editorial on Jan. 26, 1867, the *New Mexican* said that "this act but proves the oft repeated charge that the imbecile manner in which Bosque Redondo was being conducted by General Carleton was suicidal to the government." The Santa Fe *Gazette,* a consistent Carleton supporter, published an editorial on the same day signed by John T. Russell, Editor and Proprietor, which praised Carleton and lauded the Bosque Redondo project:

We have nothing but regrets to express in placing this order before our readers. We sincerely lament that General Grant should have regarded it his duty to make this change, at present, in the management of the Navajo Indians who have within the past three years been the scourge of New Mexico and a botheration to the government of the United States. In this step we plainly see the first move towards a return to the former condi-

459

tion of things, so far as the Navajos are concerned, in New Mexico, and that we are soon to begin to live over our past experiences. The few years of comparative peace that have just been enjoyed by New Mexico will in future years be looked upon as a bright spot in the annals of the Territory, and those who secured it will be regarded as the best friends she ever had.

The *Gazette's* "hopes had been blasted," according to Editor Russell:

The conception of the colonization policy for the Navajos was a piece of wise military foresight on the part of General Carleton, and its execution was marked by a boldness, independence, determination and success that is to him an honor living, and when in the course of time he shall be called to sleep the sleep that knows no waking, it will be an honor to his memory that will not be forgotten for generations to come, and will be pointed out to future chieftains as an example worthy of imitation by all those who may wish to become distinguished in their profession as Indian warriors. . . . We have confidence that General Grant has done what he conceived to be his duty in the premises, and although in doing so he may entail upon New Mexico untold evils, he has done so innocently and unintentionally. . . . As for us and the journal we have, in our poor way, conducted during the Navajo war, we have nothing for which to be sorry. We took an honest pride in looking upon the rapid strides that were being made towards the pacification and development of New Mexico, and if we are now called upon to record the fact that our hopes have been blasted, that our anticipations have not been fulfilled, we do it in sorrow and not in anger.

Preliminary to final relinquishment of control over the Navajo Indians, the War Department assigned Lieut. R. McDonald, of the Fifth Cavalry, then at Fort Sumner, to make a study of the entire Bosque project. McDonald, having completed his report on Nov. 12, 1867, recommended that the enterprise be abandoned and that the Navajos be removed to a more suitable location.

Although comprehensive and intelligently written, McDonald's report did not add anything to the information already available to the Commissioner of Indian Affairs. McDonald described the Bosque and its atmosphere:

The Indian farm is on the left bank of the Pecos, extending northwest by north, adjoining and above the post, in latitude 34° 19′ 45″ north, longitude 140° 19′ west magnetic declination (June 1866) 13° 45′ east, approximate altitude 5,500 feet. The valley declines to the southeast, forming the western limit of the dry Llano Estacado. The climate is very warm and dry; the air exhilarating and invigorating; unsurpassed for purity. Here are no marshes or sloughs, giving forth miasmatic exhalations; timber alone is wanting to realize the poet's dream of Arcady. Here one ought to attain, if ever, a patriarchal age. Frost, however, lingers in the lap of spring, too often destroying the early hopes of the ambitious gardener; indeed, few plants are safe until after the 25th of April. Again, the hoar king manifests his pleasure in early October, followed by a lengthened period of consecutive fine weather, winter being scarcely felt. Snow, indeed, may fall, and ice form, but under our ardent beam both evanescent as the morning shadows. Rain and timber are alone wanting to make this a second Paradise; bordering on the dry Llano Estacado, in no season does the rain falling exceed 10 inches, and during the six months of the summer scarcely any fell, the heat being very great.

McDonald used quite a few words to describe the poor land at the Bosque and the menace of alkali:

A rich alluvion, here and there belts of sand, and gravel and sand. Could a sufficient supply of water be obtained for irrigation there could be no question of its productiveness. Some portions of the farm exhibit on the surface a white efflorescence of an alkaline character, which, in combination with the river water, contains a principle highly destructive to the cereal forms of vegetative life. This kind of soil need not be cultivated, as thousands of acres of a better quality wait, since the dawn of creation, the hand of industry.

The irrigation system was inadequate and poorly constructed:

The present acequia, when charged to its full capacity, does not convey one-third of the volume required. It is about eight miles long, tapping the river six miles above the post, where a temporary dam is thrown across the river to enable the acequia to drain it during its low stages. Through winter the Pecos is a brackish, diminutive stream, but when the snows melt its volume swells, overflowing the valley, tearing and dragging everything with it in its headlong fury. Last winter this dam had been greatly strengthened and extended, and supposed by competent judges, sufficiently strong to resist the force of the current, which proved a fact; but during the periodic rise, unable to force the dam, it cut the left bank away to the extent of one hundred and twenty feet, forming a new channel nine feet deep at high water; the stream was so formidable that nothing could be done to prevent further injury until after the river had subsided. It was found, however, that there were no means at the post that could be diverted to this object; the crevasse in consequence, remaining open.

The Navajos hoed the ground, and planted seed corn, but the irrigation waters failed in the season of 1866-1867:

Farming operations commenced on the 16th of December; forty ploughs were set to work, Indians holding them, and by the 10th of March the whole farm was ploughed. Dividing the farm into ten acre fields, casting up borders, and digging acequias to convey into each water from the acequia madre, occupied until the 18th of April. The prevailing winds in spring blow from the west, conveying with them immense clouds of sand, which, had the acequias been dug earlier, would have entirely refilled them; hence this kind of labor cannot be done in the fall or winter. Corn planting commenced on the 19th of April, and was finished on the 24th of May, thus planting over one hundred acres per day in holes dug with hoes by Indians, three and a half by four feet apart, dropping six to eight grains in each hill. Towards the close of April the weather grew very cold, so that seed dropped in May appeared first. As soon as braird appeared irrigation commenced in earnest. One hundred and fifty Indians were daily employed for that purpose, and running the ploughs between the rows; but soon it became evident that unless the rainy season came to our relief our efforts would be fruitless. Some days no water could be obtained, owing to the crevasse; at all times the discharge was so diminutive that in the endeavor to do too much all was lost. The sky contained no moisture, no rain having fallen in May, and about .70 inch in June, .50 of which were the contents of a hail storm, which caused much injury to the growing crops. On the 30th of June I became convinced that should July indicate rain, resort should be had to replanting. After replanting 250 acres and no indication of rain I deemed further replanting inexcusable, the supply of water having entirely failed, and but .80 inch having fallen in July.

The corn fields were turned over to the Navajo chiefs when the white man's way of farming proved a failure:

To save the crops from complete destruction, they were turned over to the Navajo chiefs. The labor and seed used, in consequence of the dry season, and the impossibility to procure sufficient water, did not yield appreciable results. The Indians strove hard to aid the young corn in its struggle for existence. The awful Deity which presides over the laws of rains and storms refused to be propitiated, the inexorable cause could not be turned aside, and although the Navajos brought much labor to bear, economizing every spare drop of water, their efforts were crowned with little success. The endeavor to cultivate too much defeats itself; until a permanent dam is built and an acequia made of sufficient capacity dug, all efforts to cultivate the whole of the Indian farm under similar circumstances will, in the future, as hitherto, end in failure.

The Navajos were unhappy at the Bosque, and determined to leave, even at the cost of life itself:

A two years' experience, and an intimate knowledge of the views which the Navajos entertain with regard to the Bosque, convinces me that the Indian will never be contented here, and that the want of wood will compel him (in his struggle for life) to leave, even if he perish in the attempt. At no distant day the government will be compelled to seek a more suitable location for a permanent reservation.

Squaws and papooses helped to farm, using primitive methods:

In corn planting the Navajos do not disturb old ground, merely letting on water for a day or two; the squaws with hoes dig shallow holes, the papooses dropping the seed and covering it with a dash of the foot. In a similar manner they plant other varieties of seed. Should they have to break in a meadow they soften it sufficiently, then dig it up with heavy hoes three or four inches deep . . . when the young vines or shoots appear they go over the whole surface with a light hoe, and should there be no indication of rain, or it be found impracticable to irrigate by hand, they keep hoeing their patches every second day after sunset.

Three essentials for a successful operation, water, wood and grass, were lacking at the Bosque:

Any efforts to ameliorate the condition of the Navajos at the Bosque will have but a temporary effect, as the want of timber, both for building and fuel, will prove an inseparable barrier to the permanency of the Bosque as a permanent reservation. The Indians have told me time and again that unless the government provides them with a suitable location they will, by bands or collectively, make an effort to leave the Bosque, even if assured of perishing in the attempt. All that is requisite to make the Navajos a contented and useful people, the equal in every respect of the Pueblos, is their removal to a suitable location, where wood, water and grass abound.

The McDonald report was the death warrant, in advance, of General Carleton's grandiose scheme to convert Navajo Indians to the life of the Pueblo Indians, and to colonize them on the Pecos River. In Washington, General of Subsistence A. B. Eaton, in submitting McDonald's report to the Secretary of War, used the word "unfortunate," to describe Carleton's choice of a location for the rehabilitation of the Indians:

Respectfully returned to the Secretary of War with the remark that the general and detailed report of these very reliable papers, as well as the whole experience of the subsistence department in its efforts of several years to subsist and instruct in agricultural and stock pursuits of the Navajo and Apache Indians placed on the Bosque Redondo reservation, on the Pecos River in New Mexico, clearly indicate that the selection of that location as a place for the attempt to civilize these Indians was unfortunate, and that it ought not to be further continued, but that some more suitable location should be selected and the Indians transferred to it.

Although they did not suspect it, the day of deliverance of the Navajo Indians from their bondage at Bosque Redondo was almost at hand. The Congress passed an Act early in 1868, authorizing treaty making with Indian tribes. Commissioners were appointed to negotiate treaties. General William Tecumseh Sherman, nationally known because of his service on the Union side during the Civil War, accompanied by Colonel Samuel F. Tappan,[147] reached Fort Sumner, New Mexico, on May 28, 1868, with authority to negotiate a treaty with the Navajos.[148]

Two days after reaching Fort Sumner, Sherman sent a message by express rider to Fort Union, which was telegraphed from the nearest station in Colorado, to Senator John Brooks Henderson, Chairman of the Committee on Indian Affairs, in Washington, in which he said that the Navajos were unalterably opposed to any resettlement in Texas, or any place further east, and would not remain at the Bosque Redondo without the use of overwhelming military force. Having advised Senator Henderson of the attitude of the Navajos, Sherman and Tappan prepared a treaty, and submitted it to the Navajos for signature. The Navajo chiefs, aware of the great anxiety of their people to return to their own country, were willing to agree to any kind of a treaty that would allow them to leave the Bosque. By June 1, 1868, within three days after Sherman's arrival in Fort Sumner, a treaty had been drafted, accepted by both the government and the Indians, and executed with the usual solemn formalities. The treaty provided that the Navajos would be allowed to leave the Bosque Redondo at once and live on a reservation in their own country in northwestern New Mexico and northeastern Arizona. This provision, to the Navajos, was the all important, in fact the only important part of the entire treaty. The other provisions, for the moment, were merely incidental. In other provisions of the treaty, the Commissioner agreed on behalf of the government to make $150,000 available for rehabilitation of the tribe, to provide transportation to the reservation that had been agreed upon, to furnish 15,000 sheep and goats, and 500 cattle, to rebuild their livestock industry. Every Navajo was to receive an annual token payment of five dollars, and those engaging in agricultural or mechanical pursuits were promised an annual gift of ten dollars. If the head of a family wished to own land in severalty, he was promised a quarter section of land, with seeds and implements of the value of one hundred dollars the first year, and of the value of twenty-five dollars in each of the two succeeding years. On their part, the Navajos pledged themselves to send all children to school between the ages of six and thirteen years. In turn, the government promised to provide a teacher and schoolhouse for every thirty pupils.[149] When the Navajos signed the treaty of peace at Fort Sumner, the end of their exile was almost in sight. General Sherman notified Washington that the Navajos could be "put in motion" as soon as the money for their transportation could be made available. The Indians needed no prodding to get them in readiness for the homeward march.[150]

The news that a treaty had been signed, and that they would soon be free to return to their own country, spread among the Navajos at Bosque Redondo like blazing sparks in a New Mexico forest fire on a windswept day. There was joy in the hearts of the older men and women; perplexed elation evident in the faces of the younger people; suppressed excitement among the children. Within a matter of days the army was ready to escort the Navajos from the Pecos River to the Rio Grande, back to their beloved Chuska Mountains, back to what was to them the sublimely glorious country of the Canon de Chelle.

Seven thousand Navajo Indians started from Bosque Redondo for their home-land at dawn on June 15, 1868. Their departure was thrilling for them and an impressive and touching sight even for the hardened soldier. Major Charles Whiting, in command of four companies of United States cavalry, directed the expedition. The supply train consisted of more than 100 wagons. Five or six thousand head of livestock, salvaged by the Navajos from the wreck of their herds, trailed along. Barboncito, an energetic chief anxious to cooperate, was chosen as Major Whiting's interpreter. Needless to say, it was not necessary for any soldier to draw a sabre or point a gun in order to preserve order and discipline. Every Indian was on good behavior, from the most important chief down to the youngest papoose. The journey toward the Navajo country was necessarily slow and tedious. From 10 to 12 miles was considered a good day's travel. Twenty-one days after leaving the Bosque Redondo, the expedition reached the mouth of Tijeras Canyon twelve miles east of Albuquerque.

One Navajo became temporarily deranged at the first glimpse of Mount Taylor, a landmark in the Cebolleta Mountains, a hundred miles west of Albuquerque. He was quieted down when soldiers tied his hands to the end-gate of a wagon, and cautioned him to behave. Traveling onward toward Albuquerque, the home-going Navajos presented a never-to-be-forgotten spectacle, as they walked and rode in a procession more than ten miles long, scattered over the broad and beautiful mesa green with range grass from the Sandia Mountains almost to the banks of the Rio Grande.

The Navajos reached Albuqureque, one hundred fifty miles east of their own country, on Sunday, July 5, 1868. Free to wander about the plaza, they looked longingly at the fruits of the valley offered for sale, watermelons, cantaloupes, peaches, plums, grapes and pears. Few had money to buy the things they craved. For the grand entry into Albuquerque, the Navajo squaws had dressed in their finery, patched and faded red, yellow and green velvet skirts and blouses. Some of the men celebrated the occasion by wearing the silver ornaments they had managed to retain during their exile. The day's stop in Albuquerque was somewhat of a homecoming. Wandering about the plaza, the Navajos felt at ease for the first time since leaving Bosque Redondo. They were on the edge of their country again; thy could see far off the mountain ranges that guarded the gateway to their homeland. The new light of hope and courage apparent in the eyes of Navajo men was matched by the looks of wistful eagerness and renewed faith in the faces of homesick squaws. Some of the children now returning home, although born in the Navajo country, had no recollection of it. Many other children, born at the Bosque in exile, knew nothing of their homeland except through the medium of the mournful songs they had heard their mothers chant on the banks of the Pecos River.

The homeward-bound Navajos camped Sunday night on the east bank of the Rio Grande at Albuquerque. They slept fitfully and uneasily, anxiously awaiting the coming of the dawn. Some of them, unable to sleep, joined in singing age-

old songs in low voices, as wind-borne sparks from smoulder-
ing campfires flew upward toward skies they recognized as
friendly horizons of home. The Navajos started to ford the
Rio Grande at Albuquerque before daylight on July 6, 1868.
They traveled slowly, but steadily, westward, hour after hour
toward the land of their heart's desire. Three days out of Albuquerque, Chief Delgadito and four hundred men, women
and children, of the Sandoval branch of the tribe, dropped
out of the procession some miles west of the Rio Puerco, hoping to begin life anew in the country about Cubero and Cebolleta, which had been their home for generations before the
exodus.[151]

The Navajos, as a tribe, were back in their own home country by July 20, 1868. Their homecoming was tragic. Five
years before, they had been a proud and mighty people, almost entirely self-supporting. For years without number,
before the ill-fated Bosque Redondo expedition, they had
roamed about freely in a country of vast area — a strange,
weird looking country of desert-like wasteland, of rocky canyons, of dry washes, of great soil-eroded expanses, of high
mountains and towering pine trees, with the mighty Colorado
River many miles away to the west, and the Little Colorado
nearby. The Navajos had diligently tilled the stubborn soil
of their patched-up country, which reluctantly yielded meagre
harvests of corn and wheat, yet sufficient to provide the tribe
with its daily bread. They had been proud of their peach orchards, hidden away in the Canon de Chelle. The Navajo
men had been industrious enough, willing to work at tasks
which interested them. Some Navajo women, working on
crude looms, had woven artistic and valuable blankets. The
tribe as a whole had been vitally interested in livestock. They
were ambitious to own and raise horses. Some Navajos, bolder
than others, coveting their neighbors' goods, had raided the
settlements despite the warnings of their elders and returned
home with stolen livestock.

The Navajos had been warned repeatedly by the white man
of the coming of a day of reckoning. That day had now come

and gone. The tribe as a whole had paid a terrible penalty for the sins of the few. Hundreds of men, women and children, most of them guiltless of any punishable offense, had died from gunshot wounds, starvation and disease, at the hands of the white man. Those who escaped death suffered imprisonment for five long years in a country and under conditions they detested. But the Navajo, at long last, was home again. The surviving remnants of the tribe, and its individual members, could resume life where it and they had left off on that eventful day when General Carleton, exasperated by the wickedness of some among them, had started the Navajo war. As they looked about and began to pick up the broken threads of life and living, the Navajos were certain in their minds about one thing. It would be many a day before they would think about raiding the settlements again.[152]

The Navajo Indians were deprived of their liberty for five years by the order of a military commander in time of war, but this in itself was not something that would really shock the people of the Territory. "Peonage," a mild form of slavery, inherited from Spanish and Mexican rule, had been accepted and tolerated in New Mexico for generations. New Mexicans generally considered that it was not inconsistent with Christian doctrine to capture or otherwise acquire a likely looking Navajo or Apache, and reduce him or her to a lifetime of servitude. Once "reduced to service," as it was expressed in Spanish, and trained in the ways of the white man, the average Navajo or Apache made a good servant in field or home. Ute Indians, considered too wild and too hard to train, were never popular candidates for domestic service. As a result captured Utes had little commercial value. Although accepted and tolerated generally in New Mexico by the most prominent families, peonage never became an important public issue prior to the Civil War. However, some men of national stature believed that Abraham Lincoln's proclamation freeing the slaves had been intended to be all-embracing, and to include all peoples, regardless of whether they were white, black, red or brown. There were repercussions of some moment when it became generally known in the States that peonage existed in New Mexico. Fire-eating Charles Sumner, of Massachusetts, delivered a vitriolic speech in the Congress, bitterly condemning peonage. He criticized Governor Henry Connelly and General Carleton for allowing it to continue. Sumner's criticism prompted the publication of an open letter in the Santa Fe *Gazette* of February 2, 1867, defending Connelly and Carleton, and accusing J. Francisco Chaves, then New Mexico's Delegate in Congress, of duplicity in dealing with the question. The letter said, among other things:

General Carleton and Governor Connelly and those who have cooperated with them in New Mexico, have uniformly and persistently done all they could have done to break up the trade in Indian captives, and if they have not done as much as you gentlemen of the east think they should have done, you ought to take into consideration the difficulties of the circumstances by which they were surrounded.

Delegate Chaves' family, it was charged, had held people as peons:

J. Francisco Chaves' immediate family, that of his mother, with whom he stays while at home in this Territory, has beyond the shadow of a doubt the most numerous lot of Mexican peons and Indian slaves of any one family in New Mexico. This assertion we make as an indisputable fact and have no apprehensions that any attempt will be made to controvert it. Outside of this, his connections by close degrees of consanguinity, are the largest holders of this species of property in the country and exert an almost insurmountable influence in behalf of its perpetuation.

On March 2, 1867, the Congress passed an act entitled, "An Act to Abolish and Forever Prohibit the System of Peonage in the Territory of New Mexico and Elsewhere." The act was all-embracing, and provided severe penalties for violations. It specifically declared that all laws, resolutions, orders, regulations, usages or customs, then or previously in effect in New Mexico, purporting to tolerate or permit peonage, should be and were null and void; and prohibited the voluntary or involuntary service or labor of any persons as peons, in liquidation of any debt or obligation. Governor Robert B. Mitchell issued a proclamation on April 14, 1867, based on the act of March 2, which in effect "freed the peons of New Mexico," insofar as a proclamation could be expected to accomplish such an objective.

The enactment of the law of March 2, 1867, and Governor Mitchell's proclamation of April 14, 1867, did little more than call the attention of the people of New Mexico to a practice which they had never considered immoral or illegal. Very few peons or Indian slaves gained their freedom as the result of the act of 1867, or the governor's proclamation. The peonage and slavery problem slumbered on until July 27, 1868, when the Congress adopted Joint Resolution No. 65, providing as follows:

Be it resolved by the Senate and House of Representatives of the United States of America in Congress assembled, that Lieutenant General W. T. Sherman be, and is hereby authorized and requested to use the most efficient means his judgment will approve to reclaim from peonage the women and children of the Navajo Indians, now held in slavery in the Territory adjoining their homes and the reservation on which the Navajo Indians have been confined.

The adoption of the Congressional Resolution resulted in much scurrying around in New Mexico. Many families in Santa Fe and elsewhere in the Territory, "employed" Indian men, women and children as household servants, sheepherders, agricultural laborers and the like. It was generally understood that such Indians were peons. In order to carry out the positive instructions given to him from Washington to break up peonage in New Mexico by prosecuting those guilty of the practice, the United States District Attorney subpoenaed three hundred witnesses from Santa Fe, Taos and Rio Arriba Counties to appear before the United States grand jury. No indictments were returned. Those who "employed" peons declined to testify. The grand jurors themselves owned Indian servants, and were not sympathetic to the investigation.

The Santa Fe *New Mexican* of August 6, 1868, argued the case for the people of New Mexico:

It should be known, first, that most of the Navajos, men, women and children, scattered over our territory, are those who, during past years of war between their tribe and the whites, and Indians hostile to them were captured, and by one means and another, passed into the families of our citizens. At first these people may have been regarded in the light of peons, perhaps of slaves, but it is certain that, as soon as Congress and the Legislature of this Territory passed laws abolishing both peonage and every other class of slavery in the Territories, these people became free, and there are few, if any, of them, who do not know that they are, and have been since the passage of those laws, at liberty to go wheresoever they may have pleased. The Navajos are a savage and barbarous people. These captives from this tribe have now for years lived among civilized people; have learned the language of the country, have become christianized — all being Catholics; their habits have become those of the civilized race among whom they dwell, and not one in fifty of them desire to leave their civilized life for a renewal of the barbarous and uncivilized life of their tribes. They prefer a life among our people to one among their own. They are free — they may hire to any person whom they may please to serve; but it is certain, that, constituted as they are, most if not all of those who come under the classification of "Navajo captives," prefer to remain in homes where they have so long been domesticated, and where they possess the advantages not only of religion, but of civilized life. These they cannot possess if they are returned to their nation. It becomes then a serious question of humanity, whether those Navajos who are now voluntarily living among our people, upon the terms and in the manner named, shall be forced back upon savage life against their will, and only, because their tribe desires their return, or whether, by voluntary action they shall remain as they are, the objects of care by the church, and civil protection by the Territory.

From St. Louis, General Sherman on August 14, 1868, ordered the army to begin an immediate investigation into the peonage in New Mexico, supplementing the order with a letter on September 8 addressed to Major General George W. Getty, then commanding the District of New Mexico. Sherman advised Getty to consult with the District Attorney of New Mexico, and urged that he recommend that the Navajos do likewise. Among other things, Sherman told Getty:

Convey to the Navajos themselves the substance of the law, and of our purpose to execute it in a spirit of fairness to them and in justice to the women and children affected. If they as a tribe, or any of them in their private capacities, wish to search for missing women and children supposed to be held in bondage, you may permit them to make search and provide for it out of the moneys held by you on account of the Navajo nation. In like manner, if you know or learn of the whereabouts of such women or children, or if any officer of your command obtain such knowledge, you or they may act in the nature of guardian to such women or children till they make election to remain where they are or to rejoin their tribe, in which case you may provide for their removal.[153]

Although freed from imprisonment on the Pecos River, and permitted to return and occupy their own country, the problems of the Navajos were greater in number and of greater magnitude than ever before. Some men in the Indian service, with first-hand knowledge of Indian affairs, carried on the fight that had been led on their behalf by Dr. Michael Steck, one time Indian Service official in New Mexico. Prominent among those who fought valiantly on the side of the Indians during this period was Indian Agent John Ward, who had served at various agencies in New Mexico for several years. Critical of methods employed by the government in dealing with Indians, Agent Ward, then in Santa Fe, wrote an open letter to members of the Congressional Committee on Indian Affairs on Dec. 4, 1868.

Agent Ward explained how the army had gained control of Indian affairs, and how it had engaged in war against the Indians, and made peace with them without the advice or consent of any Indian agent, or the head of any Indian commission, bureau or department. There was still much talk in the late sixties, according to Ward, to the effect that extermination of the Indians offered the only possible solution of the problem:

Many, we regret to say, are of the opinion, and freely express it, that extermination is the only remedy, but this is all bombast. It will hardly do to talk about it. There has already been too much talk about extermination, a subject which should not even be listened to by any sensible man. We do not hesitate in saying, that it cannot be done. It is a false notion, a humbug to even think of it. . . . No more treaties should be made with wild Indians. The government should take entire charge of them, and act with them as a father with his children. Comparatively speaking, the Indians are but children and it is as ridiculous to make treaties with them as it would be to make them with so many school boys. You must be their sole guardian, instead of their common equal, and treat them accordingly. Ten minutes after an Indian makes his mark upon the paper containing a treaty which he has made with you, he is ready to break it, and it cannot be otherwise. The whole thing is "Greek" to him. What effect can these mere declarations have upon a wild and uncultivated mind, upon a savage? And yet the government will go into these treaties with the same formality and solemnity as if it were entering into it with one of the most enlightened nations of the globe. And what is more astonishing to us, is not that the Indians should break a treaty, but that a civilized and educated nation like ours, should expect the Indians to keep it sacred.

Ward believed that the power of an Indian chief was nominal rather than actual:

The very chief who signs a treaty knows but little about it, and as to the entire tribe, they know less. Many chiefs are self constituted, and their power and influence over their people are not near as great as many are led to believe. The power of the Indian chiefs of the present day is nominal rather than otherwise. This is certainly the case with the wild tribes of New Mexico and Arizona. It should be borne in mind also that many of the Indian interpreters are not able to convey correctly to the minds of the Indians everything contained in a treaty. No matter how well disposed they may be to do so, the want of proper and adequate words and sentences will prevent them from doing so. By the time the interpretation reaches the Indians it has lost much of its force and effect, particularly if it has to go through more than one interpreter. Nor is there any doubt that some interpreters will introduce their own notions and opinions in the interpretation rather than to express those of the Indians. For the most part the only clause of a treaty that is ordinarily understood by an Indian is the one containing a provision for the amount of gifts the Indians are to receive. The prevailing idea with most wild Indians in making a treaty is that the government is obligating itself to pay the Indians a certain amount to get them to keep the peace. Thus it is, that many of the Indians receive their presents more as a matter of course than as a bounty from the government. And the moment the government fails to comply with the gift clause, the Indians feel that they have been deceived, which in effect the government does in every such failure. The inevitable result is discontent, and perhaps a resort to depredations, with a war to crown the performance.[154]

Getting down to cases, Agent John Ward referred to the failure of the Army in its relation to the Navajo war:

Let us take the Navajo Indians. Did not the military declare war against them and carry on such war until they were subjugated, as it is called, and afterwards placed them on a reservation selected by the military and keep them there for six years, entirely under their control and management, without any one preventing them from doing what they thought proper with the Indians, or for them? And did not the military themselves, again remove them back to their own country after having expended several millions of dollars, according to their own official reports, and after six years of experiment? And now, where is the honest and unbiased man, knowing anything about the circumstances, that can point to the least particle of benefit or improvement that these Indians of the Territory received from all this? What better trial or evidence does any one need to demonstrate the fact that the only remedy to mitigate the Indian troubles, and to better the Indian's condition is not to be found in turning them over to the military? We think none. With very few exceptions the military man is very apt to have an inability to take care of the Indians; his schooling is against it, and his profession is entirely different from that of any other class of men. Anything properly in their line of duty, they will take hold of with zeal and energy — their fame and reputation are at stake.

That a deep seated antagonism existed between soldiers and Indians, was declared by Agent Ward:

But, when outside of their military duty, soldiers are compelled to be constantly surrounded and annoyed "by a set of cowardly, lousy, dirty, stinking Indians," as the soldiers call them — and the result can easily be imagined. The feeling between the soldier and the Indian is naturally antagonistic and it will never be otherwise. Equally notorious is the fact that the closer situated they are, and the more frequent intercourse the Indians have with the military, the less fear and respect they have for the soldier. . . . Strange as it may appear, it is nevertheless, a notorious fact that the only way an Indian can call the special attention of the government to his wants is by committing robberies and murders. The mere fact of an Indian being peaceably and well disposed is of itself sufficient cause for him to be neglected and entirely disregarded. This has been fully demonstrated by the neglected condition of the peaceful and deserving Moqui Indians and the Pueblos of New Mexico, who although they have never cost the government one cent for military expeditions during the last twenty-two years which they have been under our government, yet nothing is done toward elevating them from their present dormant and sorrowful condition. . . .

As a result of the methods that had been pursued for years in driving the Indians, "from pillar to post," Ward gave it as his opinion that the Indians of New Mexico had become "wearied, bewildered and infuriated." He declared that it was up to Congress to find a place for the wild Indian tribes to live:

Congress must find a place for the wild Indian tribes to live. This is a serious matter; the Indian must have a place to live on, and Congress must procure it for him. . . . You gentlemen of Congress have allowed the Indian to be driven from "pillar to post" and to be harassed almost at pleasure, until he has become wearied, bewildered, and infuriated. . . . The present system of appointing and removing Indian agents is neither wise nor just. You often make Indian agents out of men entirely incompetent, and you remove them without even an investigation. As far as New Mexico is concerned the changes of superintendents and Indian Agents have come to be a perfect farce; so much so, that in reality the name of the "Indian Department," alone exists. . . . It has become notorious that you do not even allow men time enough to become properly acquainted with their duties, nor with the Indians under their charge, before you turn them out of office, upon the least pretext and in many cases without any. In some instances the agents know nothing about their removal until their successors present themselves to take charge of the office. . . . Indian matters must be concentrated in one department, instead of being, as they are now, divided between the war department and the Interior, which cannot but operate very badly, and we may say detrimentally, both to the interest of the public and the Indians generally. This is more apt to be the case when the departments act independently of each other, if not against each other, which through various causes, is very frequently the case. . . . We most respectfully say to every member of Congress for the honor and credit of our nation at large, and for the sake of all that is good, do, go to work, in earnest, and take hold of this costly, troublesome and bloody Indian question. . . . The whole of the western frontier is "boiling over" in regard to our Indian troubles.[155]

A government which should have manifested a deep seated and abiding interest, and made extraordinary efforts to right the wrongs inflicted by the Bosque Redondo confinement, failed to extend adequate help to the Navajo Indians in their efforts at resettlement. How they lived, what they had done to rehabilitate themselves by the year 1877, nine years after they had been returned from Bosque Redondo, was told by Indian Agent Alex. G. Irvine, in a report to the Commissioner of Indian Affairs in Washington, written from Fort Defiance, Arizona, on Sept. 1, 1877. Navajo chiefs, according to Irvine, caused most of the trouble at the Fort Defiance agency:

The number of the tribe cannot be given with any certainty, and is estimated at from 12,000 to 15,000. . . . The Navajos are a pastoral people, and depend almost entirely upon their flocks of sheep and goats for their subsistence. The character of the country in which they live prevents them from being anything else. The nearest approach to a permanent house is what is known as the hogan. A frame is first built of pinon poles, which is covered with sod and earth; an opening is left in the side of a door, and immediately over the door is an opening to allow the smoke to escape; when the whole is finished it very much resembles a charcoal pit, and serves for a house while living and a grave when dead. Those built for winter are much more substantial than the summer hogan, which is little more than a brush shelter. Owing to the scarcity of water and grass it sometimes becomes necessary to move about from place to place; their families have no permanent abode, and they build a shelter every night wherever they may happen to be. At times the hardest herding falls upon the children. Corn and wheat are planted upon every available piece of land upon the whole reservation, and peaches and melons are raised in considerable quantities in the Canon de Chelle. Wool is the principal article for sale and exchange, 200,000 pounds being sold by them this year. Next in order come the Navajo blankets; large quantities find their way to southern Utah in exchange for horses. The blankets are made by hand, and are close, rather hard, and for camping out and saddle have no superiors, and are to be found in use all over the southwest. Next in order come sheep and goatskins, of which large quantities are annually sold. The sheep industry I consider as of the most importance to the Navajos, and should be encouraged by all means, and the possession of horses discouraged; and if I were to make any recommendation at all on the subject, it would be to allow no horses to be held by any Indian. In their hands they are a power for mischief, and no good ever comes of their possession by them. The horses are used for riding, not work. At first, it might seem arbitrary, but would cause the Indians to remain where they were placed, and be under better control.

Agent Irvine reported that whiskey was being sold to the Navajos in large quantities, that there was no law to restrict or prohibit the sale of intoxicating liquor:

Whiskey is sold to the Navajos in large quantities at all the settlements around the reservation. The United States statutes should be amended so as to punish any who sell whiskey to Indians, either on or off the reservation.... The only difficulty we have with the Navajos at the present time is the opposition that comes from the council of chiefs, not from the Navajos themselves. They are under the lead of Manuelito, who has been a disturber ever since the Navajos were placed upon the present reservation. The council is composed of 26 chiefs or headmen, and they consider every pound of supplies and all the annuities as under their control and for their personal benefit. I have done much during the two years past to do away with that idea, but they are very tenacious and still hold out. I can truly say that the 26 chiefs have given me all the trouble I have had at this agency, and they will do the same with any other agent....[156]

By the year 1884, the Navajos had been away from Bosque Redondo for sixteen years and had settled down to a way of life in which today was an indefinite extension of tomorrow.

Writing to the Commissioner of Indian Affairs on September 3, 1884, John H. Bowman, agent for the Navajos, described the reservation, its people, and their manner of living. Agent Bowman estimated that there was a Navajo population in that year of 17,000, but conceded that it was difficult to make a reliable census. The Navajo reservation was a place of confusion, according to Bowman, with Indians going and coming in and out of New Mexico, Arizona and Utah, the women and children herding the sheep; the men trailing scrubby horses, in which they took great pride and interest, and used as a substitute for money. Bowman was not enthusiastic about the reservation:

This reservation is about my ideal of a desert; and although very large, it might have been much larger without covering any land of the least value. It is merely a space on the map of so many degrees and parallels. Three-fourths of it is about as valuable for stock grazing as that many acres of blue sky. As there are no running streams it can only be irrigated by buckets. Nearly all the water is bad, alkali. The valleys are composed of sand formed by wash and erosions; no soil worthy of the name; about three-fourths of the entire tract is covered by rock and barren mesas. Where springs of water do exist the water has usually found a channel through the debris under the surface and is lost there. Still these Indians manage to eke out an existence. They are patient and industrious workers. Nearly every family has a small patch of corn somewhere, and although they may move their camp every month in the year, they always manage to put in a little crop and return at intervals to cultivate it. Corn, mutton and goat flesh is their chief food. There is no game or fish on the reservation. They generally exchange their wool and pelts for calico, flour, sugar, coffee and leather. The men wear calico pants and shirts in the summer, and the same costume, with the addition of a blanket, in the winter, and the greater part of them live at an elevation of more than 7,000 feet.... Their luxuries are flour, coffee and sugar. The leather produced from their animals they use to make saddles, leggings and soles for their sheepskin moccasins. They live in miserable huts, generally made of stone or brush, very low, with one whole side left entirely open for the smoke to escape through. They usually manage to build all their residences as far as possible from both wood and water. Why I do not know. They make a great many blankets, only a few are experts at it. They sell the good ones, keep the common ones for their own use. They card their own wool, spin it into yarn with a stick, and weave with a frame made of four rough poles tied together at the corners. These Indians, unlike most other tribes, share the work about equally with the squaws. They do not consider it disgraceful to labor and are very good workers.[157]

The Irvine report of 1877, and the Bowman report of 1884, were typical of the annual reports submitted to Washington since 1868, almost down to the present day. Notwithstanding the optimistic tenor reflected in some of the reports, there are those who hold that the plight of the Navajos today is not greatly different from their plight on that glad day in 1868 when General Sherman freed them from bondage at Bosque Redondo. And there are those who will argue, with much to sustain their views, that the plight of the Navajo today is infinitely worse than it was on that fateful day in 1846 when General Kearny, acting for the government of the United States of America, assumed responsibility for the welfare of the Indians of New Mexico.

NOTES AND PROFILES

[1] Born in Las Padillas, Bernalillo County, Mexico (now New Mexico), on June 27, 1833, Jose Francisco Chaves was a member of one of New Mexico's wealthiest and most influential families. He was the son of Don Mariano Chaves, one time New Mexico governor under Mexican rule, and of a daughter of Don Pedro Perea, of Bernalillo. Jose Francisco Chaves attended St. Louis University, St. Louis, Mo., and studied medicine in the New York College of Physicians and Surgeons. After the death of Mariano Chaves, his widow married Dr. Henry Connelly, New Mexico's Civil War governor. When the First Regiment of New Mexico Volunteers was organized, Gov. Connelly gave a major's commission to his stepson. When Kit Carson was appointed Colonel of the Regiment, after Col. Ceran St.Vrain resigned, Major Chaves was promoted to lieutenant colonel. Col. Chaves took part with New Mexico troops in the battle of Valverde on Feb. 21, 1862. In 1863 Chaves was stationed at Fort Wingate and was active in fighting against the Navajos. When Arizona became a Territory, Chaves commanded the troops escorting the first Governor and other officials to Fort Whipple. Chaves and Gen. Carleton, Commander of the Department of New Mexico, differed on military and political matters, and Chaves resigned from the army. Going into public life Chaves was elected Delegate in Congress from New Mexico for the 39th (March 4, 1865-March 3, 1867), 40th and 41st congress, and was president of the Council in the New Mexico legislature for eight sessions. After the Civil War Chaves studied law and became District Attorney of the Second Judicial District, 1875-1877, in which position he gained fame for the vigor of prosecutions in

criminal cases. Prominent for decades in the rough and tumble of New Mexico politics, Chaves was shot and killed in an isolated cabin near Cedar Vale, Pinos Wells, present Torrance County, New Mexico, on the night of Nov. 26, 1904. The talk at the time was that "higher ups" in New Mexico politics had obtained a pardon for a life-termer in the territorial penitentiary, and promised him immunity from prosecution in exchange for an agreement to kill Chaves. Interment was in the National Cemetery in Santa Fe. The 1905 legislature authorized a reward of $2,500 for the arrest and conviction of the persons who assassinated Col. Chaves, "and for the arrest of the accomplices," but the reward was never claimed. The identity of the murderer remains a mystery to this day. The legislature of 1905 appropriated $1,000 for a bronze bust to perpetuate the memory of Jose Francisco Chaves. George Washington Armijo, a grandson of Jose Francisco Chaves, was born in Peralta, Valencia County, New Mexico. on March 16, 1877, Armijo died in Santa Fe Feb. 16, 1947. In 1898 Armijo was a member of Col. Theodore Roosevelt's famed "Rough Riders." From 1900 to 1947 Armijo held public office in New Mexico almost continuously. For decades he was a vital, colorful, picturesque figure in New Mexico politics. See H.J.R. 1947, N.M. Legislature.

2 Carleton sketched his military career, when testifying before a committee investigating Indian Affairs in Santa Fe on July 3, 1865, "I was appointed a second lieutenant in the United States first dragoons Oct. 18, 1839. In the spring of 1841, I was sent to Fort Gibson, in the Cherokee nation. Saw more or less of the Cherokees, Creeks and Seminoles from that time until the spring of 1842. Then I went to Council Bluffs, now in Iowa, where I became acquainted with the Pottawatomies. In the fall of 1843, I went to Fort Leavenworth, then near the Delawares, Kickapoos and Shawnees. In 1844 I was one of the armed expedition to visit the four bands of the Pawnees on the Platte river. These were the Grand Pawnees, the Republican Pawnees, the Pawnees Tepage and the Loup Pawnees. With these we held councils. They were supposed to number—all told—about 12,000 people. Thence we visited and held council with the Ottoes and Missourias at Belleview; and thence visited and held councils with the Iowas and Sacs and Foxes, then living on the west bank of the Missouri river, a little south of Jeffrey's Point. In the spring and summer of 1845 I went with General Kearney in his expedition to the Rocky Mountains. We held councils with the Ogallalla and Brule bands of Sioux, at Scott's Bluffs, and at Fort Laramie and Dodge Pole Creek; with the Cheyennes between that point and where Denver City now stands; and with a band of the Comanches below Bent's Fort, on the Arkansas. After the Mexican War, I was stationed at Fort Leavenworth again, from the fall of 1851, except six months which I spent at Fort Kearny, above the Pawnee villages, and at Fort Laramie. In the spring of 1853, I went to New Mexico, when there were opportunities to see something of the Apaches, Utes, Navajos and Pueblo Indians. In 1857 I left New Mexico, and in 1858, went to California, where I was stationed at Fort Tejon, within twelve miles of an Indian reservation. In 1859 I went across the desert to the Mountain Meadows in Utah. In this long march I saw a good many Pah-Utes (Water Utes). In 1860, made a campaign against them having my headquarters on the Mojave River. In 1862 came to the Maricopa and Pima villages on the Gila, and to the Papago villages at San Xavier de Bac, in Arizona. Then I came to New Mexico again. All the experiences I have had of Indian affairs has been afforded by what I have been able to observe of them in the service named; during much of which I only occupied the position of a subaltern, and was not called upon by official obligation or duty to be more than a casual observer of their character, habits, numbers and the like." See Rep. Com. Ind. Affairs, 1867, p. 435. Although military duties demanded first attention, nevertheless Carleton found time during the years of army life to write about things which interested him outside of the military sphere. In 1844, when he was "one of the armed expedition to visit the four bands of Pawnees on the Platte River," Carleton wrote a series of articles for the "Spirit of the Times, a Chronicle of

the *Turf, Agriculture, Field, Sports, Literature* and the *Stage,*" published in New York City, captioned "Prairie Log Book, or Rough Notes of a Dragoon Campaign to the Pawnee Villages in 1844," beginning with the issue of September 14, 1844, and ending April 12, 1845; and wrote a second series, "Farther West; or Rough Notes of the Dragoon Campaign to the Rocky Mountains in 1845," for the issues beginning June 14, 1845, and ending November 21 1846. See "Spirit of the Times," Vol. XIV, No. 29; Vol. XV, No. 7; Vol. XV, No. 16, and XVI, No. 39. Also see "The Prairie Logbooks, Dragoon Campaigning to the Pawnee Villages in 1844, and to the Rocky Mountains in 1845, by J. Henry Carleton"; The Caxton Club, Chicago, 1943. As a captain in the First Regiment of Dragoons, Carleton was in the battle of Buena Vista, in the Mexican War, fought beginning on Feb. 23, 1847, and wrote a book descriptive of the fighting, which was quite widely distributed and accepted at the time as authentic and definitive. See "The Battle of Buena Vista, with the operations of the Army of Occupation for one month," by James Henry Carleton, Harper & Brothers, Publishers, 82 Cliff Street, New York, July 4, 1848. Of the battle itself, Carleton wrote: "In our country's history, it stands beside that of Trenton, Saratoga, Niagara and New Orleans; but in many respects it much surpasses them all. Of the numerous triumphs of our arms, it is by far the greatest; as a proof of American valor, it shines forth immeasurably the most glorious. . . . The Battle of Buena Vista will probably be regarded as the greatest fought on this continent; and it may be doubted if there can be found one that surpasses it in the history of any nation or of any age." James Henry Carleton's son, Henry Guy Carleton, who inherited his father's literary ability, was born at Fort Union, New Mexico, June 21, 1856, was a student at Santa Clara College, California, from 1865 to 1870, became a Cavalry officer in the United States Army, Oct. 21, 1873, served in Miles' campaign against the Kiowas and Arapahoes in Texas in 1874 and 1875. He resigned from the army in 1876 to devote his time to journalism and literature, and worked on the New Orleans *Times,* Chicago *Tribune,* and New York *Times,* and for a time was literary editor of *Life.* In 1881 he gave up journalism and thereafter devoted all of his time to the drama, writing a number of plays between that year and his death in New Jersey in 1910, among them, the *Pembertons, The Lion's Mouth, A Gilded Fool.*

3 Rio Abajo *Press,* April 21, 1863. Carleton left Albuquerque on Dec. 14, 1853, with a detachment of dragoons for a ten day reconnaissance. He travelled south along the villages of the Rio Grande, thence east to the ruins of Abo, Quarai and Gran Quivira, north to Manzano, east through Tijeras Canyon to the point of the beginning. Carleton described the trip in "Diary of an Excursion to the ruins of Abo, Quarai, and Gran Quivira, in New Mexico, under the command of Major James Henry Carleton, U.S.A.," published in the 9th Annual Report of the Smithsonian Institution, pp. 296-316. Lieut. J. J. Abert of the U. S. Topographical Corps traveled through much of the same country in 1847. Abert's report was published in Ex. Doc. 41, 30th Cong., 1st Sess.

In 1866 when attempts were being made to have Carleton removed as Department Commander, quotations from the Smithsonian report were used to discredit him. The Santa Fe *New Mexican* of December 9, 1864, published selections from the report, and called his descriptions of the people in the villages "insolent" and "insulting," saying: "We have lately seen a book called 'El Gringo,' written by a former Secretary of this Territory, about this people and country. He speaks of arriving at a certain town, where he saw a pig tied up in a corner. He then tells the world the pig was the most respectable inhabitant in town. Carleton's remarks about the people are in substance no better."

4 See Book A of Deeds, page 195, records of Santa Fe County, New Mexico. New Mexico had a "slave" law between Feb. 3, 1859 and Dec. 10, 1861. The Legislature of 1861 repealed the act of 1859, entitled "An Act Providing for

the Protection of Slave Property in this Territory." The 1859 law contained 30 sections. One section specifically provided that the act did not in any manner "apply to relations between masters and servants contracted in this Territory, but the word 'slave' shall apply only to the African race." Briefly, the law provided: Marriage between slaves and white persons was prohibited and declared void; emancipation of slaves within the Territory was "totally prohibited." No slave was permitted to go from the premises of his owner or master after sunset or before sunrise without a written pass. Any person claiming a slave could file a writ of replevin in court, as for other personal property, and the case prosecuted to judgment. Any person holding a slave entitled to freedom was liable to a penalty of from $500 to $2,000. Any slave attempting rape upon a white woman, if convicted, was subject to a sentence of death. No slave, free negro or mulatto was permitted to give evidence in court against a free white person, but one slave might be a competent witness against another slave. Any slave owner convicted of cruel and inhuman treatment of a slave was liable to imprisonment for a term not exceeding one year, and a fine of not more than $1,000. If any slave was convicted of any crime or misdemeanor for which the penalty assigned by law was in all or in part for a sum of money, the court, in passing sentence, might in its discretion, substitute for such fine corporal punishment by branding or stripes. Any slave who conducted himself in a disorderly manner in a public place, or who talked insolently, or made signs to or about any free white person, might be arrested, taken before a justice of the peace, and punished, if convicted, by the constable giving the slave any number of stripes upon his bare back not exceeding thirty-nine. Runaway slaves, if apprehended, were to be detained by the Sheriff of the county of apprehension, and advertised as lost or stolen. If the slave was not claimed within a specified time, he was to be sold to the highest and best bidder, and the sale price, if not claimed by the true owner, was to be paid to the Territorial Treasurer. Any free person, who played cards or other games of skill or chance with a slave, was subject to a fine of not to exceed $100 or by imprisonment up to 3 months, or by both such fine and imprisonment.

5 Santa Fe *Gazette*, May 19, 1866. While apparently not squeamish about ordering Apaches and Navajos shot and killed, under conditions he described as "declared war," Carleton would not condone cruelty to Indians in civilian life. He wrote a sharply worded letter to Judge Joseph G. Knapp, at Fort Barclay (near the present town of Watrous), on Dec. 9, 1862, directing his attention to the horrible murder of a Ute Indian at Taos: "I learned a week since that an Indian of the Utah tribe was in Taos recently, where certain parties are said to have gotten him drunk, then to have saturated some parts of his garments with spirits of turpentine and set fire to the clothing thus saturated. From the effect of this burning the Indian is said to have died. The Utah tribe to which he belonged is said to be very much incensed at this inhuman outrage, and to threaten to be avenged. As one of the United States officers in New Mexico, and as one whose particular calling is to see justice done, I trust I have but to call your attention to this alleged crime to awaken your zeal in the cause of justice and humanity. In many years experience in affairs connected with Indians, I think it never has been my lot to have heard of such horrible barbarity on the part of white men toward Indians." Rep. Com. Indian Affairs, 1867. In contrast with Carleton's attitude in connection with the burning of the Ute Indian at Taos, there is to be cited Carleton's apparent indifference to the manner in which Magnus Colorado, an Apache chief, was treated in 1863, while held as a prisoner of war in the Mimbres river country. Judge Joseph G. Knapp, of Mesilla, claimed that Magnus Colorado had been scandalously treated, and killed under circumstances which could not be justified by a civilized people.

6 Santa Fe *Gazette*, Aug. 13, 1864.

7 OR Series I, Vol. XV, p. 576.

8 Lorenzo Labadie died at Puerto de Luna, on the Pecos river, on Aug. 10, 1904, at the age of eighty years.

9 Rep. Com. Ind. Affairs, 1862.

10 See Rep. Com. Ind. Affairs, 1862. At the time of his death in 1869, the Santa Fe *Gazette* referred to James L. Collins as "the oldest American citizen in New Mexico, and the bravest." Collins was born in Crab Orchard, Kentucky, Feb. 1, 1800, and emigrated to Booneville, southwestern Missouri, in 1819. He made in 1826 his first trip across the plains to Santa Fe, using pack animals, wagons and teams being then unknown to the Santa Fe trade. Collins went from Santa Fe to Chihuahua in 1828, and engaged in the mercantile business there from that time until 1846. When the Mexican War began, he left Chihuahua, and thereafter made his home in Santa Fe. During and after the Mexican War he rendered valuable patriotic services to the United States and to New Mexico. He accompanied Col. John M. Washington on an expedition into the Navajo country in 1849. In 1852 Collins established the Santa Fe *Weekly Gazette,* which he published until 1858. He was appointed Superintendent of Indian Affairs in New Mexico by President Buchanan, and reappointed by President Lincoln. During the Civil War he took an active part in military affairs, from Valverde to Pigeon's Ranch. The Santa Fe *Gazette* of June 12, 1869, said: "To the counsel and guidance of James L. Collins more than to anything else is to be attributed the destruction of the Texas supply train at Johnson's ranch on the day of the battle of Glorieta. The destruction of this train crippled Sibley's forces more than all the battles that were fought during that, to our people, memorable invasion." He was appointed Receiver of the land office and custodian of United States funds at Santa Fe, on May 16, 1866. On Sunday, June 6, 1869, Collins was found dead in the office of the depository, with a bullet hole through his heart. Robbers had stolen from the vault $100,000, which was to have been used to pay troops. On June 9th $65,000 of the stolen money was found in a brewery adjacent to the depository. The government filed suit to recover from his bondsmen, Hamilton G. Fant, of Georgetown, D. C., William Craig, of Colorado, John S. Watts, of Santa Fe, Vincent St. Vrain, of Mora, and William W. Mills, of El Paso, Texas. Judgment for $38,593.35 was rendered against them. Pending an appeal to the supreme court a claim was filed for reimbursement through Congressional act. The claim was considered by the Committee on the Judiciary in the House, and finally was allowed on March 3, 1873. The committee reported that its members were satisfied, after thorough investigation, "that said Collins was an excellent officer; that he had always borne a high character for integrity, patriotism, and courage; that he was well advanced in years—over sixty; that he was reasonably well off, of good habits—lived simply and cheaply; that he was thoroughly devoted to the proper discharge of his every duty," and in the opinion of the committee, "was wickedly and cruelly murdered while bravely attempting to defend the property of the United States against unknown thieves and robbers." See Report No. 104, 43rd Congress, 1st Session, H. of R.

11 Rep. Com. Ind. Affairs, 1862, p. 252.

12 OR Series I, Vol. XV, p. 579.

13 Rep. on Cond. Indian Affairs, 1867, p. 100.

14 McCleave and Pishon returned to their respective posts, at Fort Fillmore and Fort Franklin on Dec. 29, 1862, without having encountered the Mescaleros. McCleave had trailed them into their usual haunts in Dog Canon and beyond in the Sacramento Mountains. Numerous trails into the mountains pointed the way they had gone, but McCleave did not catch up with them. Pishon, scouting in the Guadalupe Mountains, visited nine different *ranchos,* but failed to see the sign of an Indian. Pishon reported to General West from Ojo del Martin that his men were "disappointed, but none so much as

myself, in not getting a fight out of the redskins." OR Series I, Vol. L, part 2, p. 267.

15 Known as Fort Breckenridge (Arizona) until Carleton changed the name to Stanford, in honor of California's governor, Leland Stanford, on May 14, 1862.

16 Rep. Cond. Ind. Tribes, 1867. To help along Carson's campaign against the Mescalero Apaches, and to discourage Kiowas and Comanches from coming into the Pecos River country, General Carleton established Fort Sumner, some 75 miles north and east of Fort Stanton. He notified the War Department on Nov. 9, 1862, of the establishment of Fort Sumner: "By establishing Fort Sumner, at the Bosque Redondo, I shut up the door through which the Kiowas and Comanches have hitherto entered New Mexico, and cut off a great thoroughfare northward of the Mescaleros. Another very important consideration in establishing this post was to open a portion of the country where good grass is found all winter for our worn out animals to keep them from perishing. We could not buy enough hay to subsist them even if we had the money. The saving on hay alone, this winter, will more than build the post in the spring. During the winter the troops will live in tents or under canvas."

17 Padre Taladrid, successor to famed Padre Jose Antonio Martinez as pastor of the Catholic Church in Taos, enlisted in the militia at Taos on Aug. 13, 1861.

18 Three soldiers accused of killing Dr. Whitlock were taken to Albuquerque and surrendered to the civil authorities. They were to be tried for murder before Judge Sidney A. Hubbell, in the Second Judicial District Court. A few days before the trial was to begin, the doors of the Bernalillo County Jail were forced open in the night time. By daylight the liberated prisoners were well on their way to Chihuahua, Mexico. The jail delivery had been arranged by members of Company H. See Las Vegas *Gazette*, June 23, 1877.

19 Round thicket, or forest.

20 Rio Abajo Weekly, Feb. 4, 1863. Notwithstanding Carson's assurance, Carleton wrote to the Commanding Officer at Fort Sumner on April 10, 1863, enclosing a copy of a report made by Major Arthur Morrison, of the New Mexico Volunteers, concerning "a dreadful massacre of a party of Mexicans, on the plains west of Fort Stanton." Carleton admonished Captain Joseph Undergraff, the commander at Fort Stanton: "Thus you will see the remainder of that tribe, still at large, are as hostile as ever. This will admonish you to be doubly on your guard against the clandestine departure of any of those now at the Bosque Redondo. Should any of the men of those Mescaleros now at Bosque Redondo attempt to escape, after their promises to me to remain quietly there, you will be sure to cause them to be shot. If they give you much trouble in this respect, seize every animal they have and have all of them sent to Fort Union, and disarm all the men, even of their bows and arrows.... You will be sure to have slain every Mescalero Indian who may be met with at large in the vicinity of your post. No woman or child of the tribe will be injured, but such will be sent as prisoners to Fort Sumner.... These are the orders. Be sure they are executed. Rep. Cond. Ind. Affairs, 1867, p. 100.

21 OR Series I, Vol. L, part 2, p. 275.

22 OR Series I, Vol. XV, p. 670.

23 General West wrote from Mesilla on Jan. 30, 1863, to Don Jose Maria Uranga, Prefect of El Paso (now Juarez), advising him that he proposed to conduct vigorous warfare against Apaches "infesting the country lying east and west of the Rio Grande, and north of the boundary of Mexican territory,"

and asking him to solicit the cooperation of the Governor of Chihuahua. West told Uranga that in some part of Chihuahua, "particularly Janos, the Apache Indians were courted, their ill-gotten booty found a market, and their necessities for ammunition were supplied through the cupidity of traders." West also wrote to Sonora's governor, Ignacio Pesqueira, advising that the American military was attempting to subjugate the Apaches inhabiting the country bounded by the Rio Grande and Gila rivers, the Mexican line, and the Santa Cruz and San Pedro valleys, and warned him to be on the lookout for atrocities committed by Apaches driven from the United States into Mexico. OR Series I, Vol. L, part 2, p. 300.

24 Spanish for Red Sleeve.

25 Whatever the facts, the story of the killing of Mangus Colorado was not a pretty one, even in a day when the Apaches were on the loose. There were those who contended that Chief Mangus was "inveigled into protective custody." Be that as it may, it is certain that he was arrested by Captain E. D. Shirland, First Cavalry, California Volunteers, and a detachment of 20 men, near Pinos Altos, on Jan. 17, 1863, and escorted to Fort McLane, where he was confined. After being questioned by army officers, and lectured on the personal responsibility that he should assume because of the atrocities committed by his tribe, he was told that he would be obliged to spend the remainder of his days as a prisoner in the hands of the United States authorities, but assured that his family would be permitted to join him, and that he and his family would be well treated. Chief Mangus Colorado was warned, according to the official report, that "upon making any attempt to escape, his life would be the immediate forfeit." A sergeant and three privates of Company A, California Volunteers, went on duty at midnight as relief guards. Mangus was shot and killed at 1 o'clock on the morning of Jan. 19. The guardsmen awakened Gen. West to tell him the story, and he reported that the Chief had made three attempts to escape between midnight and 1 o'clock, and added: "Even with a murderous Indian, whose life was clearly forfeited by all laws, either human or divine, the good faith of the U. S. military authorities was in no way compromised." Under the arrangement by which Mangus Colorado was taken into custody, he was supposed to have been returned to his tribe at an appointed time and place. On this phase of the incident, West reported: "His detention prevented this, and being apprehensive that his people would scatter, alarmed at his absence, I decided to pursue and punish them." In the "pursuit," Captain Shirland's troops killed nine of the unsuspecting Gilas and wounded many more. Captain William McCleave, First Cavalry, California Column, went from Fort McLane to the Pinos Altos mining country on Jan. 19. A party of Mangus Colorado's band approached. The soldiers were ordered to attack them, killed eleven Indians, and wounded one, the widow of the late Mangus Colorado. On Jan. 29, 1863, the Gila Apaches attacked two hunting parties of Company A, Fifth Infantry, California Volunteers, at the Pinos Altos mines, killing Private William Hussey, and wounding Sergeant T. B. Sitton. When the smoke cleared away, it was found that the soldier-hunters had killed 20 Apaches and wounded 15. In a twenty minute skirmish near Fort West, on March 22, Captain McCleave's company killed 25 Apaches. OR Series I, Vol. XV, p. 229; and Series I, Vol. L, part 2, p. 296.

26 OR Series I, Vol. XV, p. 670.

27 Fort West was established as a temporary post on Feb. 1, 1863.

28 Mangus Colorado had roamed up and down the Mimbres and the Gila rivers, and in and about the mountains in that country off and on for many years. Gen. Kearny had a talk with him near the Copper Mines, in present Grant County, New Mexico, on Oct. 19, 1846, according to Capt. A. R. Johnson's journal, Ex. Doc. 41, p. 579: "The general gave Red Sleeve and two

other chiefs papers to show he had talked with them, and that they had promised perpetual friendship with the Americans. They seemed all anxious to conciliate the Americans. . . . Trading mules with the Apaches is dull work. The Apaches came to us this morning. Red Sleeve came with fifteen or twenty other persons—some women; they ride small but fine horses. The high roads leading from the mountain to Sonora and California show whence they came; they are partly clothed like the Spaniards, with wide drawers, moccasins, and leggings to the knee; they carry a knife frequently in the right legging, on the outside; their moccasins have turned up square toes; their hair is long, and mostly they have no headdress; some have hats, some have fantastic helmets; they have some guns, but are mostly armed with lances and bows and arrows. . . . Just as we were leaving camp today, an old Apache chief came in and harangued the General thus: 'You have taken Santa Fe, let us go on and take Chihuahua and Sonora; we will go with you. You fight for the soil, we fight for the plunder; so we will agree perfectly'."

29 Rep. Cond. Ind. Tribes, 1867, p. 105.

30 Ibid, p. 106.

31 Fort Fauntleroy, in its heyday was "the light of the desert, and there the wilderness bloomed like a rose, with a large stream flowing past the station house door," according to the Rio Abajo *Press,* Albuquerque, of March 15, 1864, but in that year (1864) its adobe buildings were "a mass of ruins, standing in all the majesty of decayed glory, having historical interest, in that they had witnessed the treaties made and broken by the Navajos, and the easy confidence and sublime gullibility of the credulous white man."

Located at the foot of Mount Taylor, near the present village of San Rafael, three miles south of Grants, Valencia County, New Mexico, alongside a great spring known in the old days as *Ojo del Gallo* (Chicken Spring), Fort Fauntleroy was named for Colonel Thomas T. Fauntleroy, a Virginian who fought Indians in New Mexico and Utah for several years, beginning in 1855. Fauntleroy resigned his commission in the Union Army at the beginning of the Civil War, and fought with the Confederacy. When Fauntleroy "went south," the name of the fort was changed to Fort Lyon, and changed again in 1863 to Fort Wingate, in memory of Captain Benjamin Wingate, mortally wounded at the Battle of Valverde on Feb. 21, 1862. Fort Wingate (once Fort Fauntleroy) was abandoned in 1868 and a new Fort Wingate was built eleven miles east of present Gallup, McKinley County, New Mexico, near *Ojo del Oso* (Bear Spring). Gallup, New Mexico, in the heart of the Navajo, Hopi and Zuni Indian country, and which, under ordinary circumstances might be expected to have been given an appropriate Indian name, was named after David Leeds Gallup, a New Englander. Gallup was born in Mystic, Conn., Dec. 19, 1842, the son of Russell Gallup, seventh in a straight line from Captain John Gallup, sea captain and Indian fighter, who emigrated from England to Boston in 1630. David Gallup, in 1880, was paymaster at a construction camp on the Atlantic & Pacific Railway (now a part of the A. T. & S. F. Ry. Co.). The town, which sprung up at the construction camp, was named for him. Gallup later served as cashier for the railroad company in Albuquerque, and eventually became the Santa Fe Company's first auditor in Boston. In the latter years of his life, David Leeds Gallup was known as "The Grand Old Man of the Santa Fe Railroad."

32 Rep. Cond. Ind. Tribes, 1867, p. 314 et seq., OR Series I, Vol. 4, p. 71. Captain Nicholas Hoydt, 1st Cav. N. M. Volunteers, was killed on May 16, 1866, by the accidental discharge of his own pistol, near Cubero, while enroute from Fort Wingate to Albuquerque with 17 Navajo prisoners. Santa Fe *Gazette,* May 26, 1866.

33 Rep. Cond. of Indian Tribes, 1867, pp. 330-332.

34 In the fall and winter of 1863 the Navajos harrassed the New Mexico troops at Fort Wingate. Carleton wrote a scolding letter to Chaves, criticizing

him for allowing officers to go "on leave" to Cubero, some twenty miles away. Carleton said: "Shall the Indians always get the best of Fort Wingate troops? I see that officers from your post go to Cubero. They have no duties there. Send me an abstract of all officers who have been absent from your command since Oct. 31, 1863. Stop half of their pay when absent. Every train going from Fort Wingate to Fort Canby will be escorted efficiently, and the escort will be commanded by an officer.... The escort to each train should have spies on ahead, on the flanks, and in the rear, to prevent surprise."

35 Receiving word of Union victories at Gettysburg and Vicksburg while at Los Pinos, Carleton ordered salutes fired at every fort in New Mexico. As part of the celebration at Fort Union, 30 short term prisoners were released from the guard house, and "fire balls were thrown in the plaza."

36 Rio Abajo *Press,* June 30, 1862.

37 Rio Abajo *Press,* Nov. 10, 1863.

38 Among New Mexico Indians scalping seemed to be practiced only by the Utes. The American soldiers were of the opinion that "Apaches didn't scalp," a belief which found support in the absence of evidence of scalping in the Indian fighting in southeastern and southwestern New Mexico. Some evidence that the Utahs scalped Navajos was contained in Supt. Michael Steck's report of August 11, 1863, which said that "the Utes during the last ten days killed thirty Navajos, captured and brought in sixty children of both sexes, captured thirty horses, and two thousand sheep; four Utahs came in with three scalps." While the Navajos did not scalp they had an equally effective method of killing. They shot an intended victim with bow and arrow, and then bashed his head in with a rock.

39 Rev. Anselm Weber, a Franciscan, described the Navajo country in 1910 as part of the foreword to his monumental work, "An Ethnologic Dictionary of the Navajo Language." Fr. Weber's description may be accepted as authentic today. There can be but little doubt that the topography and atmosphere of today are for all practical purposes identical with those of 1863: "The greater part of the Navajo country is a bare and barren desert. It is traversed by a range of mountains from northwest to southeast. The northwestern end of this range is called the Luckachukai (white reed patches) mountains, the central part is called the Tunicha (large water) range, and the southeastern end the Chuska (white spruce) range. The higher regions are covered with a splendid growth of white pine. At a lower level the pinon predominates, and still lower the slopes are covered with forests of red cedar and juniper. Patches of scrub oak are to be found everywhere on the mountains, while in the canons cottonwoods, box elder, aspen, alder, walnut, peach, and a few other species of trees, thrive. Besides the main range of mountains, there are a few isolated groups, for instance, the Carrizos (mountain surrounded by mountains) in the northeast, and the Black Mountains in the west. The mountains are cut up and reft by deep gorged, tortuously winding canons, through which the rain, falling on the mountains, is drained out into the valleys. There are no live rivers in the Navajo country, except the San Juan in the northeast, and the Colorado, in the southwest. On the reservation, a few uncertain creeks, springs and floods from the canons, must be depended upon for irrigation. In some localities there are signs of abundant underground water. The annual rainfall averages from 10 to 14 inches and is usually confined to two short seasons, in the spring and in the fall. The greater part of this falls between the latter part of July and the forepart of September. The spring rains are not reliable, and both seasons are separated by about three months of absolute drouth. The altitude averages from 4,000 feet in the lower regions to 6,000 and 7,000 in the higher parts, while the mountain tops are 9,000 and 10,000 feet. Owing to this high altitude, the nights are cool and pleasant all year round, the winters are long

and cold, and the season for maturing crops is short. The spring is usually very stormy, with high southwestern winds, and the summer is very hot, although it is always pleasant in the shade, and the heat cools off rapidly after sunset.... The valleys of the Navaho country, on first sight, present the appearance of broad, rolling wastes, covered in some places by sagebrush, cactus, yucca, greasewood and bunches of grass. The valleys as a rule, are destitute of trees, except where irrigation is practiced, or where a sufficient amount of underground water is near enough to the surface. In such places, cottonwoods and other trees thrive well, as also fruit trees, grains and vegetables."

Born in New Salem, Mich., Nov. 10, 1862, Rev. Anselm Weber, O.F.M., died in Rochester, Minn., on March 8, 1921. A brilliant student at Franciscan schools, Father Weber was ordained to the priesthood on Dec. 28, 1889. He came to New Mexico on Oct. 7, 1898, but moved soon to a place in the Navajo country subsequently named St. Michaels, Arizona, just beyond the New Mexico line. Father Weber on many occasions demonstrated his friendship for the Navajos. A prolific writer, with an amazing zest for sustained work, Father Weber compiled in 1910 a dictionary of the Navajo language, and supervised compilation of "A Vocabulary of the Navajo Language," published in 1912. During the early 1900's, when the Navajos threatened from time to time to start a war against the American government, the army invariably sent Gen. Hugh L. Scott to pacify them. Scott almost as invariably stopped at St. Michaels, and invited Father Weber to accompany him as interpreter and friend of the Navajos. For details of the life of Father Weber, see "Rev. Anselm Weber, O.F.M.", by Rev. Leopold Ostermann, in "The Franciscan Missions of the Southwest," for 1922, St. Michaels, Ariz.

40 OR Series I, Vol. XXVI, part 1, pp. 233-234.

41 Ibid, p. 235. On Aug. 19, 1863, Carson reported the death of "the brave and lamented Major Joseph Cummings, who fell, shot through the abdomen by a concealed Indian." When General Carleton later established a fort at Cooke's Spring, at the mouth of Cooke's Canyon, in southwestern New Mexico, "on the main road from Mesilla to Tucson," he named it in memory of Major Cummings. Fort Cummings was abandoned in 1873 and the troops were moved to Fort Selden. For an interesting account of Fort Cummings, see "Annals of Old Fort Cummings, New Mexico, 1867-8," by William Thornton Parker, M.D., Northampton, Mass., 1916.

42 Ibid, p. 727.

43 Ibid, p. 728.

44 Santa Fe *Gazette*, Jan. 21, 1865.

45 Rep. Com. Ind. Affairs, 1863, p. 110. The initial consignment of 51 Navajo prisoners was delivered at Bosque Redondo on Sept. 4, 1863, by Lieut. Thomas Holmes, of the First New Mexico Volunteers. The prisoners were taken first to Fort Wingate, then to Fort Union, where they were confined for a time, and finally to the Bosque.

46 Rep. Cond. Indian Tribes, 1867, pp. 247-255. For Carson's letters to Carleton covering operations against the Navajos for the period July 7 to Aug. 19, 1863, see OR Series I, Vol. XXVI, part 1, pp. 232-238. For a detailed, day by day, report of operations against Indians in New Mexico for the year 1863, with statistics of property taken by and from Indians, see same volume, pp. 23-34. For report of Captain Rafael Chacon, First New Mexico Cavalry, see same volume, pp. 257-259.

47 OR Series L, Vol. XXXIV, part 1, p. 73—Rio Abajo *Press*, Feb. 10, 1864.

48 OR Series L, Vol. XXIV, part 1, p. 73. The destruction of their peach trees was an act of vandalism for which the Navajos never forgave Kit Carson or the American government. The peach trees in the Canon de Chelle, located

in a country where any kind of a fruit tree was a rarity, were considered by the Navajos to be priceless possessions.

James Conklin, a resident of New Mexico since 1825, testified in Santa Fe on July 4, 1865, that the Navajo tribe had in 1860 between 1,000 and 1,200 peach trees "in the mouth of the Chelly, nothing but peaches." These peach trees were cut down and destroyed by Kit Carson's soldiers in 1863-1864. See Rep. Com. Ind. Afrs., 1867, p. 336. To this day the Navajo prefers a peach to any other fruit. It is not an uncommon sight for a Navajo to go into a trader's post on the reservation, buy a can of peaches, open it with a jack-knife, and eat the entire contents. The peach of the Navajo Indians was referred to as early as 1865 by Dr. Jonathan Letterman, an early day surgeon, stationed at various army posts in New Mexico for many years. Letterman wrote one of the first reports on the tribe, subsequent to the American Occupation, a document which influenced Navajo policy in the government. Letterman wrote that the Navajos were ignorant of their origin; that they had no government worthy of the name; that any man with a few head of horses and sheep was a "head man"; that the Navajos had exaggerated ideas of their own importance, and were kept in check only by fear of the military; that they had many superstitious customs, wore almost any kind of clothing from coat and pantaloons imported from the States, to the blanket, wearing nothing but the breechcloth in summer, and went about in a cotton shirt and moccasins in below zero weather; he told how the Navajo women dressed, and how they wore their hair; what the Navajos used for food, and how they prepared it. The Navajos, according to Letterman's report, ran an estimated 200,000 sheep in 1854, had a great many horses, but did not pay any particular attention to breeding. The women did the spinning and weaving, dominated family life to a considerable extent, owned and controlled their own property. Letterman said that the Navajos had some rifles in 1855, but the bow, arrow and spear were the weapons in general use; that they were hospitable and generous, treacherous, but not cruel; were addicted to raiding the settlements and stealing property, and carrying men, women and children into slavery; that they had no religion; that their songs, chants and tribal dances were meaningless. Concerning the peach in the Navajo country, Letterman wrote: "The only fruit cultivated is the peach, and this is only found in the Canon de Chelly and a few small canons adjoining. We have seen some fine specimens of this fruit brought in from that canon, but it can seldom be ripe, as the only mode of transporting in vogue among the people is by means of buckskin bags on horses. During August and September hundreds of Indians are collected in *Canon de Chelly,* living on corn and peaches until the crops are exhausted."

The "Letterman Letter," published in the Tenth Annual Report of the Smithsonian Institution in 1856, Mis. Doc. No. 73 of the 34th Congress, 1st Sess., was written by Dr. Letterman after a stay of many months on the Navajo reservation. He acknowledged assistance in preparation by Major Kendrick, then commanding officer at Fort Defiance. (In the report the author's name is given as "Jona. Letherman.") Jonathan Letterman had a most extraordinary career in the United States Army, the details of which would justify an entire volume. On Nov. 24, 1947, he was nominated as the "all time, all American medical officer," by Dr. Paul R. Hawley, then medical chief of the U.S. Veterans' Administration (*Time,* Nov. 24, 1947, pp. 64-65). Born in Canonsburg, Washington County, Penna., on Dec. 11, 1824, son of an eminent physician and surgeon of western Pennsylvania, Jonathan Letterman was graduated from Jefferson College in 1845, and from Jefferson Medical College, Philadelphia, in March, 1849. Appointed an assistant surgeon in the army on June 29, 1849, he served in campaigns against the Seminole Indians in Florida, until March, 1853, when he was transferred and served briefly at Fort Ripley, Minn. Letterman came to New Mexico from Fort Leavenworth, Kansas, in 1854, served at Fort Union under Col. W. W. Loring, and at Fort Defiance, under Major Henry Lane Kendrick. While in New Mexico, Letterman served for a time with Major James H. Carleton, then in command of dragoons at Albuquerque, and accompanied him in 1860 on an expedition against the Pah Ute Indians in California. At the outbreak of the Civil War, Letterman accompanied California troops to New York. On June 19, 1862, he was appointed medical chief of the Army of the Potomac, and began at once the work of revolutionizing the army medical service, placing it under the supervision of army surgeons instead of the quartermaster corps. He discontinued the use of civilian doctors and nurses on battlefields, reorganized the ambulance service, established field hospitals, was credited with saving the lives of thousands of wounded soldiers. Letterman's system in its entirety was adopted by the Army of the Potomac in general orders issued by General McClellan on Aug. 2, 1862, and subsequently provided the framework for future military medical organization in the United States. Several countries in Europe, notably Germany, adopted the Letterman plan. Its great value and efficiency were demonstrated at Antietam, at Chancellorville, in the Wilderness, and especially at Gettysburg, where 14,000 wounded men were carried off the battlefield within a few hours after they had fallen. On October 1, 1863, Letterman was married to Mary Diggs, of Maryland, daughter of Harriett Carroll Diggs, who was a granddaughter of Charles Carroll, of Carrollton, and related to the Lees of Virginia. Thomas A. Scott, president of the Pennsylvania Railroad, interested in prospecting for oil in southern California, induced Letterman to resign from the army on Dec. 22, 1864, to take an executive position with an oil company, and he went to Los Angeles to live. Unhappy in the oil venture, Letterman resigned and went to San Francisco in 1867, and held various posts of public honor and trust until his death in that city on March 15, 1872, at the age of 48 years. Funeral services were held in St. Mary's Cathedral in San Francisco, with burial in nearby Lone Mountain cemetery. Dr. Letterman's body was later removed to Washington, D. C., and buried in Arlington cemetery. The great Letterman General Hospital in San Francisco is a monument to his memory. See "Memoir of Jonathan Letterman, M.D., by Brevet Lieutenant Colonel Bennett A. Clements," G. P. Putnam's Sons, New York, 1883, a reprint from the Journal of the Military Service Institution, Vol. IV, No. 15, Sept., 1883. Dr. Letterman's daughters, Catherine and Madeline Letterman, now in their eighties, are residents of Albuquerque, New Mexico. A medical man with Letterman's genius for organization, knowledge of medicine and surgery, and zeal for providing hospitalization, is desperately needed on the Navajo reservation today, where Letterman served nearly a hundred years ago as a frontier assistant army surgeon. Because of age-old belief in the magic of their medical men, most Navajos accept hospitalization only as a last resort. Hospitals and doctors are pitifully few, and separated by great distances from the *hogans* scattered over the reservation. Many Navajo patients are brought to reservation hospitals in a dying condition, after the tribal medicine men have done their worst. In many instances, after taking one look at a patient, doctors in the Navajo country signal their helpers: "Get another coffin ready—this patient is going to die soon."

Twenty-five years after Dr. Letterman wrote his report for the Smithsonian Institution, Dr. Washington Matthews, a young medical doctor, was appointed assistant army surgeon at Fort Defiance, the same post at which Letterman had served in 1854. Becoming interested in the Navajos and their ceremonies, Washington Matthews read and pondered over the Letterman report on the Navajos. He compared and contrasted Letterman's findings with his own observations. He listened to every Navajo willing to talk of the individual Navajos, the tribe and tribal background. As a result of his studies, Matthews felt justified in contradicting Letterman's findings that the Navajos knew nothing of their origin or history—that their lack of tradition was surprising —that they knew little or nothing of their tribal religion—that "their singing was but a succession of grunts and anything but agreeable." Dr. Matthews related the story of how he came to disagree with Letterman's theories, saying that the Navajos had a song for almost every situation in life; that they composed according to established rules; that their compositions abounded in poetic figures of speech; that the men were talented composers and singers, but asserted that the women were songless. See "Songs of the Navajos," by Washington Matthews, October, 1896, in "Land of Sunshine," Los Angeles, a magazine edited by Charles Fletcher Lummis, a versatile and enthusiastic writer on southwestern lore. For a scholarly evaluation of the writings of Lummis, see "Charles Lummis, American Hidalgo," Dr. James J. Walsh, *Commonweal* (N. Y.), Dec. 19, 1928. In "The Land of Sunshine" for November, 1896, Lummis published "Songs of the Navajos," by John Comfort Fillmore, giving a musician's opinion on Navajo chants. Fillmore wrote the article after Dr. Matthews had furnished him with phonographic records of "Slayer of the Alien Gods" and "Child of the Waters" in order that he might study and compare them with songs of other American Indian tribes.

Born in Dublin, Ireland, July 17, 1843, Washington Matthews studied medicine at the University of Iowa, from which he was graduated in 1864. Dr. Matthews was stationed in the early eighties at Fort Wingate, New Mexico, and Fort Defiance, Arizona. Among his best known works are *Navajo Silversmiths,* 1883; *Navajo Weavers,* 1884; *The Mountain Chant, a Navajo Ceremony,* 1887; and the monumental *The Night Chant, a Navajo Ceremony,* 1902. He died in Washington, D.C., in 1905.

Since the days of Letterman and Matthews, countless articles, monographs and books have been published on the Navajo Indian, covering almost every conceivable subject relating to tribe, brain and personality, superstitions, religious beliefs, blanket weaving, silversmithing, horse raising, sheep growing and wool production. Scores of eminent scientists have studied the Navajo and his characteristics. The Federal government has sponsored many expeditions and published hundreds of official reports of their findings. To undertake to catalog the books, monographs, reports and articles on the Navajo would be foreign to this work. Outstanding in any category, however, is the book, "Navajo Weaving," by Charles Avery Amsden, Fine Arts Press, Santa Ana, Cal., in cooperation with Southwest Museum, Los Angeles, 1934. Born in Forest City, Iowa, Aug. 18, 1899, Amsden died in Monrovia, Cal., March 3, 1941. Taken by his parents to Farmington, New Mexico, on the edge of the Navajo reservation when a child in arms, Amsden grew up in the Navajo country, and absorbed its authentic color and atmosphere. He showed an aptitude in boyhood for work in archaeology, and accomplished much of importance in that field in his short life. For Amsden's biography and a list of his publications see "The Master Key," Southwest Museum, Los Angeles, Cal., May, 1941. For a comparatively recent important book on the psychological and cultural aspects of the Navajo tribe, see "The Navaho," by Dr. Clyde Kluckhon and Dr. Dorothea Leighton, Harvard U. Press, 1947.

[49] Ibid, p. 77.

[50] Ibid, p. 71. Carleton's statement that Carson had passed through the Canon de Chelle was quickly challenged. It was claimed by those purporting to know that the only troops to march *through* the canon, were those commanded by Capt. A. B. Carey, of the 13th U.S. Infantry, and Capt. A. H. Pfeiffer, of the 1st N.M. Cavalry.

[51] Ibid, p. 76.

[52] OR Series L, Vol. XXXIV, Part 1, p. 119.

[53] In testimony given before an investigating committee at Fort Union, on June 20, 1865, Capt. Asa B. Carey told of his experiences in attempting to convince the Navajos they ought to go to the Bosque Redondo: "In the campaign of 1863 it was estimated that two hundred Indians were killed, their sheep and cattle were also captured; the sheep were issued to the troops as provisions, the horses sold and proceeds turned over to the company, making a company fund, some were used for cavalry purposes, some used up and some died. In the last campaign, probably not over two hundred and fifty were killed and wounded. All the property they had was captured or surrendered; the captured sheep issued to the troops as part of the meat ration. . . . About

five hundred were taken to the Bosque in small squads by force. The remainder went voluntarily. It required a great deal of talk to convince them that the Bosque was the best place for them. The distance was about three hundred and fifty miles. At one time I had about three thousand Navajos at Fort Canby, who were just ready to go when there came in a Mexican and a Zuni Indian, who told them that the purpose was to get them down there and kill or poison them. I had considerable difficulty in disabusing their minds and persuading them to go. During this time considerable mortality attended them, some one hundred and fifty died. They are very superstitious and would constantly inquire what we wanted them to go to the Bosque for if they were going to be put to death when they got there." Rep. Cond. Ind. Tribes, 1867, p. 345.

⁵⁴ Testifying that he had been stationed at Fort Sumner since May 22, 1863, Captain Henry B. Bristol submitted the figures on Navajos at Bosque Redondo, on June 27, 1865. Bristol said: "When I came here there was but one Navajo Indian here. He was taken from a Mexican who offered him for sale for ten dollars; so that all of them have been brought here since I came here. They came at different times. Total number brought here, 8,474; of these there were men 2,325; of women 2,710; of children, 3,164; infants at the breast, 275. At the last count, on April 30, 1865, there were present 7,169. The difference in numbers is accounted for by deaths not reported, and absence of those who were hunting. . . . When the Indians came here, as a general thing, they were very much impoverished and in tatters. I never saw anything like it. Now, they are much better clothed, because the pelts of sheep slaughtered by the government were given to the poorer classes of the Indians, and their women have made the wool into blankets, and they are now much better clothed. The hides also have been used by them to make soles for their moccasins." Rep. Cond. Ind. Tribes, 1865, pp. 343-344.

⁵⁵ OR Series L, Vol. XXXIV, part 1, p. 71.

⁵⁶ OR Series I, Vol. XLI, part 2, p. 674.

⁵⁷ Emil Fritz marched into New Mexico with the California Column in 1862. After the Civil War he engaged in business in Lincoln. His estate was involved in the so-called Lincoln County War, as the result of litigation over the method of distributing the proceeds of a $10,000 life insurance policy. The fight over the insurance money led indirectly to the killing of A. A. McSween, one of the principal actors in the bloody drama in Lincoln.

⁵⁸ OR Series I, Vol. XLVIII, part 2, p. 1266.

⁵⁹ OR Series I, Vol. L, part 1.

⁶⁰ OR Series I, Vol. L, part 1, p. 942.

⁶¹ OR Series I, Vol. L, part 1, p. 1108.

⁶² OR Series X, Vol. XV, p. 599.

⁶³ Of more than ordinary historical interest is the case of the United States vs. Simeon Hart, 6 Wallace, pp. 770-773, 18 L. Ed. 914, 73 U.S. 914, involving jurisdiction of New Mexico courts over real estate situated in Texas, argued in the Supreme Court of the United States on March 24, decided on March 30, 1868. The Congress enacted a statute on July 17, 1862, which subjected to seizure and confiscation the property of any person within the states or territories of the United States engaged in armed rebellion against the government of the United States, or aiding and abetting such rebellion after public warning by the President of the United States. A libel was filed in the district court of the United States' for the third judicial district of the territory of New Mexico, seizing real estate belonging to Simeon Hart, situated in the town of Franklin (now El Paso), Texas. The New Mexico district court entered its

decree condemning the property in Texas and ordering it sold. The supreme court of New Mexico reversed the district court of the third judicial district, a decision sustained by the Supreme Court of the United States, which held that the statutes involved conferred no jurisdiction on the district court of New Mexico in proceedings against real estate in Texas. The opinion in the Hart case disposed of appeals taken by the United States in two other cases, against Josiah F. Crosby, Henry S. Gillett and John S. Gillett, involving the right of New Mexico courts to decree the sale of real estate in Texas declared confiscated by the federal government. Attempts by federal officers to confiscate property, either in Texas or New Mexico, were vigorously opposed by residents of Mesilla and Franklin (El Paso), Texas. Abraham Cutler, of Kansas, who announced that he had "no friends to punish, or friends to protect," in carrying out his official duties, was appointed United States Marshal for New Mexico in 1863. Cutler and United States District Attorney T. D. Wheaton attempted to carry out confiscation orders issued on Jan. 2, 1864, by the Attorney General of the United States. Marshal Cutler soon discovered that it was useless to confiscate wagon trains owned by persons suspected of having cooperated with the Confederacy. Because of fear of reprisal no one would bid when confiscated property was offered at public sale; the government had no storage facilities; and livestock was difficult to handle, because while in the custody of the marshal it "ate its head off." It was different with real estate, which could be bid in at public sale, and title conveyed to dummy purchasers. Entire pages of the Santa Fe *Gazette* for week after week contained nothing but legal notices, giving dates and places for the sale of confiscated real estate, most of it ordered sold under decrees of the third judicial district court at Mesilla, New Mexico. The federal government was especially anxious to confiscate and sell the real estate of Simeon Hart and James W. Magoffin, in El Paso County, Texas, both of whom had been very active and influential in affairs pertaining to the Confederacy in the southwest during the war years. The legal notice for the sale of the Magoffin properties was published in the Santa Fe *Gazette* of Sept. 2, 1865. General Carleton opposed the policy of attempting to have federal officials in New Mexico confiscate property in Texas, claiming that the confiscations were illegal because New Mexico courts had no jurisdiction over property in Texas, a contention which was upheld by the Supreme Court of the United States. See Santa Fe *Gazette*, Jan. 13, 1865.

64 OR Series I, Vol. XV, p. 599-601.

65 OR Series I, Vol. XV, p. 666.

66 OR Series I, Vol. XV, p. 918. A personal letter of unusual interest signed "John R. Baylor," date unknown, was found in the ransacked office of the Tucson Post, by a California soldier and handed to Major D. Fergusson, of the First Cavalry California Volunteers, who reported the find to Lieut. Col. Drum in San Francisco in a letter written from Tucson on Oct. 4, 1862. Probably written from Mesilla, in January or early February, 1862, the text of the letter follows: "Dear Theodore: I write this letter in hopes that it may reach you by some good luck. I am, as you may know, in command of this Territory as civil and military governor, having come up in last July with 375 men—thrashed and took prisoners all the troops at Fort Fillmore, 700 in number, and have held the country until the arrival of General Sibley with 4,000 Texans, who are now enroute for Fort Craig, where Colonel Canby is, with 1,200 regulars and 2,800 greasers, all of whom will get used up in no time when the fight comes off. I take it for granted that you are with us. So far Mr. Lincoln is not making much headway in suppressing the rebellion. He has got himself thrashed at every fight from Manassas to Mesilla, and today we dare them to attack us at any point. I have only to say that I would be glad to see you with us, and the way is open. Sister is with me at Galveston (sic) who is Captain Wharton now and quartermaster. She wrote to you, but I have had no chance to send the letter. She was well by last letter from

San Antonio. Our family are all in the rebellion. I am (sic) and when the Union is restored by force of arms it will be when there is not a battalion of Southern men left to fight. I rely on your coming to me, for I can now aid you and give you a position; and bring with you in your own way all who want to fight for Dixie's Land." OR Series I, Vol. L, part 2, p. 152.

67 OR Series I, Vol. L, part 2, p. 434.

68 OR Series 4, Vol. 2, p. 960.

69 Ibid, p. 1036.

70 New Mex. Sess. Laws, 1860-61, p. 16.

71 Rio Abajo *Press,* April 21, 1863.

72 Santa Fe *Gazette,* July 27, 1867. Milton B. Duffield, Arizona's first United States Marshal, resigned on Nov. 25, 1865. He presented a claim against the United States for $5,356.00 for extraordinary expenses, alleging that he was "induced to resign by the insufficiency of his $600 per annum salary," and "the want of harmony between him and other government officials of the Territory; that from the first election in the Territory his course was considered obnoxious by opposing active and unforgiven rebels who were striving to guide and control the Territory, and that he was persecuted by malicious suits for discharging his official duties in accordance with the spirit as well as the letter of the laws." Duffield's claim was disallowed. See Rep. Com. on Claims No. 23, Senate, 40th Cong., 2nd Sess., Jan. 30, 1868.

73 There was excitement concerning a gold discovery as Carleton's soldiers reached Fort Yuma. Rich placer fields were reported to have been found "between the Colorado and Gila rivers, and about thirty miles from their junction." The gold was reported to be of "fine quality, and in coarse grains." Most of the panning for gold was done by Mexican men and women. One woman was reported to have panned $100 in gold in one day. However, there were drawbacks to the gold rush. Water at the diggings cost twenty-five to forty cents a barrel. Many people died of hunger and thirst in attempting to reach the gold fields. There were in 1862 from 600 to 800 people from Sonora, Mexico, and about 200 Americans in the gold fields, described as being 40 x 20 miles in area. Taking notice of the gold rush, the Apache Indians drew a line beyond which people should not go, but this only made the gold seekers more anxious to go beyond that line, figuring that the Indians knew where rich ore could be found. The gold fever spread to California. The clipper bark E. A. Rawlings, from San Francisco, loaded with gold seekers and freight, sailed via Cape St. Lucas on the Gulf of California, to the mouth of the Colorado, and reshipped thence up the Colorado to Fort Yuma. See *Daily Alta California,* May 20, 1862.

74 OR Series III, Vol. III, p. 798.

75 OR Series I, Vol. XV, p. 670.

76 Rep. Com. Ind. Affairs, 1867.

77 "Captain" Joseph Reddeford Walker was one of the most colorful characters in the west. Wherever and whenever adventure beckoned, Joe Walker responded. Born in Knoxville, Tenn., in 1798, Walker went to Jackson County, Mo., in 1818 and began a career as a guide which only ended by his death in Ignacio valley, Contra Costa County, Cal., on Oct. 27, 1876. Walker guided Captain Bonneville's expedition to the Rocky Mountains in 1832, conducted a party from Great Salt Lake to California in 1833, discovered "Walker's Pass" in 1834. In and out of New Mexico and Arizona during Civil War years, Walker went to Contra Costa County, Cal., after the war.

78 Gen. James H. Carleton established Fort Whipple, near present day Prescott in 1863, to accelerate development of the Arizona gold fields. The new

fort was named in memory of Brig. Gen. Amiel W. Whipple, "who fell in the Battle of Chancellorville," and who, as a First Lieutenant of Topographical Engineers in 1853, explored the road leading from Albuquerque through "the country of the new gold fields" (which road was called Whipple Route). Carleton ordered a board of officers headed by Major Edward B. Willis to select the exact site for the post, which was intended to accommodate 2 companies of infantry and a company of cavalry. See Abajo *Press,* Albuquerque, Nov. 3, 1863. After the establishment of Fort Whipple mail was sent to Mesilla, thence to Tucson, thence to Whipple, pending the improvement of the road west from Albuquerque.

Of peculiar interest is the fact that the trustees of the Walnut Grove Mining Company filed a claim against the government in 1889 for $292,000, alleging that the company had been invited by the Arizona territorial government in 1864 to develop the Bully Bueno mine, 17 miles from Prescott, "the capital of Arizona," and that the enterprise had been destroyed by the Apache Indians. The federal government was responsible, according to the claimants, because of a letter written by Gen. Carleton in Santa Fe on July 11, 1864, to George H. Vickroy, of Philadelphia, which read: "In answer to your verbal question as to the safety of carrying on mining operations hereafter in Arizona, I will say I have already inaugurated a campaign against the Apache Indians that will result in their complete subjugation, and should you induce friends in the east to join you in erecting a quartz mill in the newly discovered gold regions near Fort Whipple, the enterprise will be fully protected by the military. I am well assured that building a quartz mill there, and developing some one of the rich mines, will result in such benefit to the government as to amply compensate for the protection given." The claim was approved by a committee of the House of Representatives on March 26, 1890. The committee blamed Carleton: "Your committee calls the attention of Congress to the fact that at the time this enterprise was undertaken the Territory of Arizona had been but recently organized, and the great desire and anxiety of the inhabitants of the sparsely settled country and the officers of the Territory, civil and military, was expressed in its favor; that the mines were known to be fabulously rich, and, as it was confidently believed, that the introduction and successful prosecution of such an enterprise would induce a large emigration, rapid growth, and development of the country . . . at this time the Territory was under martial law; General Carleton, then in command, exercised supreme control over the whole country, and was the recognized authority there. He made war and peace with the Indian tribes, built military posts and forts, and carried on the whole machinery of the civil and military government, and every act of his was endorsed by the general government, and while thus exercising supreme control, he announced officially that he had inaugurated a campaign against the Apache Indians that would result in their complete subjugation, and this enterprise should be fully protected by the military. . . . But instead of protecting this property, as he promised to do, and which he had a perfect right to do, the Indians were permitted to kill the employes and to destroy the property . . ." See Report No. 1083, H.R. 51st Cong., 1st Sess.

For a comprehensive summary of post Civil War Apache troubles in the sixties and seventies, see "Peace with the Apaches of New Mexico and Arizona," by Vincent Colyer, a member of the Board of Indian Commissioners, 1871, Washington, 1872. On October 6, 1871, Colyer wrote an interesting letter from Camp Whipple, near Prescott, telling of an encounter with a newspaper publisher: "Mr. Merriam, the editor of the 'Arizona Miner,' and several other gentlemen, called to invite me to address in public meeting the citizens of Prescott on the Indian question. I read to Mr. Merriam his editorials, published before my arrival, wherein he called me a 'cold blooded scoundrel,' 'red handed assassin,' and the like, and had said: 'Colyer will soon be here. . . . We ought, in justice to our murdered dead, to dump the old devil into the shaft of some mine, and pile rocks upon him until he is dead. A rascal who comes here to thwart the efforts of the military and citizens to conquer a peace from our savage foe, deserves to be stoned to death, like the treacherous, black hearted dog that he is.' I told Merriam I had no hankering for that kind of 'mining.' The gentlemen present assured me that they would protect me with their rifles and revolvers.... I was unable to see sufficient reasons for addressing a public meeting in which I should have to be protected with rifles and revolvers, and I respectfully declined to speak. Mr. Merriam gave me a beautiful specimen of gold quartz, and I thought we had parted pretty good friends; but three days after he published an editorial containing several gross calumnies, and abusing me worse than ever."

79 Rep. Cond. Indian Tribes, 1867.

80 Rep. Cond. Ind. Tribes, 1867, pp. 136-137.

81 Rep. Cond. Ind. Tribes, 1867, p. 140.

82 OR Series I, Vol. XLVIII, part 2, pp. 1150-1151.

83 James Rood Doolittle was born in Hampton, Washington County, N. Y., on Jan. 3, 1815, attended Middlebury Academy and Geneva (later Hobart) college, from which he was graduated in 1834. Doolittle studied law, practiced in Rochester, removed to Wisconsin in 1851, was elected judge of the first judicial circuit of that state in 1853, elected to the United States senate in 1857, serving until 1869. While in the Senate Dootlittle served as chairman of the committee on Indian affairs. Retiring from the Senate in 1869, Doolittle lived in Racine, Wis., became one of the first trustees of the University of Chicago, served as president one year, and taught in its law school for many years.

84 On June 9, 1865, President Andrew Johnson issued a statement from the Executive Mansion saying that he had been advised by the Secretary of the Interior that Indians in New Mexico had been seized and reduced to slavery. The President ordered the heads of the various departments in Washington to notify thir agents and employes to "discontinue the practice and to take all lawful means to suppress it." James Harlan, Secretary of the Interior, instructed Commissioner of Indian Affairs William P. Dole to obey the President's order. Dole in turn notified Felipe Delgado, superintendent of Indian Affairs in Santa Fe, and Delgado published a notice warning against purchasing or trading in Indian captives, "as the transaction would be essentially in violation of the law and against the spirit of liberty and our system of government." Santa Fe *Gazette,* Aug. 5, 1865.

85 The office of Provost Marshal at all army posts in New Mexico, excepting Fort Sumner, near Bosque Redondo, was discontinued on July 4, 1865. All provost records were ordered to be boxed up and sent to Santa Fe. Carleton's order said, among other things: "The security of life and property, except as against Indians, and responsibility of good order, rest, henceforth, with the civil authorities of New Mexico." Explaining the reasons for martial law, the Santa Fe *Gazette* said on July 22, 1865: "The state of war that then existed and the great vigilance which the safety of the country required on the part of the military, rendered the enforcement of this law necessary. Besides this, there was not a judicial officer higher than a probate judge in the Territory from March until August, 1862, a period of five months.... For several years before the Rebellion began, the people of Mesilla, then called Arizona, had established a provisional government in that region, and recognized the laws of that government only as binding upon them. They wanted the establishment of a territorial government and refused to acknowledge the laws of New Mexico." The "passport system," which Carleton enforced for some three years incident to maintenance of martial law, was ordered abolished as of July 22, 1865. The Santa Fe *Gazette* announced, by Carleton's permission, that passports would no longer be required in New Mexico, "because the army of the so called Confederate States, which was operating in Texas

under the command of Lieut. General Kirby Smith, has surrendered to the United States."

86 Report, Condition of the Indian Tribes, 1867.

87 Rep. Com. Ind. Affairs, 1867, p. 435.

88 Ibid.

89 Rep. Cond. Ind. Tribes, 1867, p. 326. Col. James L. Collins, former super-intendent of Indian Affairs in New Mexico, testified before the committee in Santa Fe on the peonage problem and gave it as his estimate that about 2,000 Indians were held captive in the Territory in 1865. Collins said: "They are held and treated as slaves, but become amalgamated with the Mexicans and lose their identity."

90 Supra, p. 438.

91 Supra, p. 486. Many witnesses testified before the Doolittle Committee in Santa Fe besides General Carleton, Judge Kirby Benedict and Padre Martinez, and gave testimony of unusual interest; among them were: Henry Connelly, the then governor of the Territory, Major Samuel Allison, Major Griner, Major H. M. Enos, Colonel Willis, of the army, Dr. Louis Kennon, Percy Ayers, James M. Giddings, Surveyor General John A. Clark, John Conklin. For their testimony see Rep. Cond. Ind. Tribes, 1867.

92 Santa Fe *New Mexican,* January 1, 1866.

93 Report of Commissioner of Indian Affairs for 1866, pp. 131, 136. Graves' report, particularly that part referring to peonage, was considered by the United States Senate of January 13, 1865. See Congressional Globe of that date and Santa Fe New Mexican, January 26, 1867.

94 Rep. Com. Ind. Affairs, 1866, p. 136.

95 When the first Navajo prisoners were delivered at Bosque Redondo, there were no supplies there for their subsistence, no clothing for them to wear, no tools for them to work with. In order to remedy this situation, Carson and Connelly on March 5, 1864, signed joint approval of a requisition expected to fill immediate needs. Among the items ordered were the following: 100 pieces of red standing; 15,000 yards unbleached domestic, wide and heavy; 5,000 yards blue or other dark calico; 3,000 yards brown drills, cotton, 3,000 blue denims; 5,000 pairs Mackinaw blankets; 2,000 Mexican blankets (for old women and children), 50 dozen spools thread, No. 12 to 20; 50 dozen cotton handkerchiefs; 100 dozen hickory shirts; 15 dozen flannel shirts; 10M needles, coarse numbers, paint, looking glasses, beads, butcher knives, scissors, hatchets, axes, pickaxes, stout hoes (at least 300), spades, long handled shovels, ploughs (12 breaking up and 12 small), 50 hand corn mills, 20 spinning wheels, brass ornaments for women and children, brass wire, a good supply of colored yarn, bright colors, awls, 12 sets shoemakers' tools, 6 sets blacksmith tools, 50 trowels, files, rasps, iron arrow points, fish hooks, lines, pipes in abundance, plenty tobacco, garden seeds of all kinds, hammers, nails, assorted, some saws, chisels and other common carpenters' tools, 2 sets saddlers' tools, 6 anvils, 6 vises, a good quantity of sole leather, worsted tapes of bright colors (a good supply), some cheap ribbons, a good supply of strong linen thread, of assorted colors; buttons in abundance, the more fancy the style the better. See Appropriations for Navajo Indians, Ex. Doc. 70, 38th Cong., 1st Session, H.R.

96 Thieves.

97 Carleton's requirements of beef for the Indians at Bosque Redondo marked the beginning of the New Mexico cattle trade on an extensive scale. By 1865, John Simpson Chisum, of Paris, Texas, was in New Mexico and had staked out a ranch at Bosque Grande, on the Pecos river, a few miles south

of Bosque Redondo. The army purchased thousands of cattle from Chisum to feed the soldiers at Fort Sumner and the Indians at Bosque Redondo. Army contracts for beef started Chisum on the way to become New Mexico's first cattle king after the American Occupation.

98 Ex. Doc. 70, 38th Congress, 1st Session, H. of R.

99 Rep. Com. Ind. Affairs, 1864, p. 212.

100 Writing in the "Land of Sunshine," more than fifty years ago, Dr. Washington Matthews, authority on the Navajo, gave a description of the Navajo country that is authentic today: "If you stand on the northern brow of the Carrizo mountains, about seven miles west of the boundary line between New Mexico and Arizona, you will behold an extensive panorama; to the west you will see the red deserts of Arizona; to the northwest, some dark, pine-clad summits in Utah; to the northeast, the great white peaks of Colorado, clad in eternal snow; and to the east, the tawny valley of the Chaco, the dry mesas and plains of New Mexico. Between you and the Colorado mountains lies a dreary, sage-covered land. In its lowest level, some 15 miles away, you can, with your field glass, discern the cottonwood groves which mark the course of the San Juan River as it flows on its way to the Colorado of the west. The view is grand but desolate. The sides of the Carrizo mountains are dark with pine and spruce; the comparatively level summit is nearly destitute of timber; but is green with a short and not very luxuriant growth of grass. You stand not on a range of mountains, but on a somewhat circular mountain mass, not more than 12 miles in diameter in any direction. Pastora peak, 9,420 feet above sea level, is the highest point. He who stands and gazes on the lesser eminences that immediately surround it, will recognize the Navajo name for this group—Dsilnaodsil, Mountain Surrounded by Mountains. Carrizo is Spanish for reed and was applied to these mountains by the Mexicans probably by mistake. The Reed mountain of the Navajos is the Lokachokai, the mountainous plateau which lies immediately south of the Carrizo. Lokachokai signifies great white arrow grass, and is the equivalent of the Spanish *carrizo*. In May, beautiful clear streams pour down the sides of the Carrizo, but a few weeks later, the rocky beds are bare. Again, during the brief summer rains, the waer flows at times to be absorbed by the sands at the base of the mountains; but when autumn comes all is dry again. During the season when the plains and mesas below afford scant food for the Navajos' sheep, some flocks are driven to the mountain pastures, and this pasturage is about the only economic use of the mountains. Game is scarce. When you have ridden over the Navajo country in every direction, you will probably conclude that, as a financial speculation, you would not take the whole tract as a gift and pay taxes on it." See "Seeking the Lost Adam," by Dr. Washington Matthews, Land of Sunshine, edited by Chas. F. Lummis, Los Angeles, Feb. 1899.

101 Rep. Com. Ind. Affairs, 1864, p. 202.

102 Rep. Com. Ind. Affairs, 1867. Carleton's suggestion that the Navajos might go out and steal beef cattle from the Comanches was not an extraordinary one. The custom of the day was to pit "Indian against Indian," whenever it appeared necessary or desirable. The background of the "Comanche trade" of the sixties was described in a report made in 1867 by A. B. Norton, Superintendent of Indian Affairs for New Mexico, to the Commissioner in Washington: "Last year on my arrival here I found that an unrestrained commerce was being carried on between the Comanches and the Mexicans, and that thousands of cattle stolen by the Comanches from the people of Texas were being traded for by Mexicans having trade permits from General Carleton and from my predecessor; in fact, the Territory was filled with Texas cattle. Believing it very unjust to the citizens of a neighboring state to encourage such a trade, and in order to stop it, I immediately issued an order forbidding anyone to trade with these Indians unless he had a license duly approved by the Commissioner of Indian Affairs in Washington. General Carleton acted in concert with me in suppressing this traffic. It was stopped

until former Commissioner Cooley granted licenses to four different citizens, and on those licenses and those granted or sublet by some of the parties holding them, I am informed that hundreds of these Mexicans are again trading with the Comanches, and matters are as bad as ever." Superintendent Norton explained how Texans were being robbed to increase the cattle herds in New Mexico: "Texas cattle bartered by these traders **are being scattered all over this** Territory. When no cattle or horses are found in the Comanche camp by the Mexican traders, they lend the Indians their pistols and horses and remain at the camp until the Comanches have time to go to Texas and return, and get the stock they desire. What a disgrace that our government should permit this plundering of the people on the frontiers of Texas by the Comanches to be encouraged by her own citizens giving to the Indians a market for their booty! But how can it be stopped? I would respectfully recommend that no more licenses be issued, and that those already issued be revoked, and that an agency be established at Fort Bascom, with an appropriation of $10,000 for goods for the Indians, and that one trader only be appointed, that shall be under the control of the agent, who must see, be instructed, and held responsible that Texas stolen cattle and horses are not traded for under any circumstances, and that orders be issued to the commandants of the different posts to send out scouts, seize and confiscate the stock of every unlicensed trader caught in that region. The establishment of this agency would exert a salutary and beneficial influence over the Indians, and prevent to a great extent the illicit commerce above alluded to. Agent Lorenzo Labadie, who was sent, in obedience to your instructions, to demand the return of Rudolph Fischer, and all other white captives held by the Comanches, and without ransom, has not yet returned. He has already been absent over six weeks, and I begin to be solicitous for his safety." Rep. Com. Ind. Affairs, 1867, p. 195. Lorenzo Labadie made a report to Norton on Aug. 28, 1867, advising him that he had left on May 1 of that year for the Comanche country, in company with six men, whom he had sent in different directions, to assemble all the Comanches he could find, notifying him that he, Labadie, would meet them at a place, called Quataque, "near the State of Texas, east of New Mexico." Labadie said: "After my long and dangerous journey, I accomplished my object. I got together over seven hundred lodges of the Comanches and Kiowas.... Unfortunately the principal chiefs were absent at the time; some were in Texas; some were in Old Mexico, and others at Fort Sumner after the Navajos; so that two thirds of the Indians were absent.... I demanded of them the delivery of Rudolph Fischer, and all white captives of the United States held by them, and without ransom. My claims surprised the Indians... but they finally said they would return at the full of the moon next October, and deliver up all captives, and also make a permanent treaty of peace. In speaking with the Indians in regard to the war they had been making against Texas they told me they were induced to do so by the military officers of the government, who told them to do all the damage they could against Texas, because Texas was fighting against our government, and that up to the present time they were not aware that peace had been established with our government, until I informed them of that fact; but hereafter they promised me that they would cease to commit depredations against that state.... The Comanches and Kiowas, in my opinion, are good Indians. They look upon the officers of the government with respect. These Indians appear very rich; they live in a country full of buffaloes and mustang horses. They have about 15,000 horses and 300 or 400 mules. They raise much of their own stock, and they now have more than 1,000 cows. They also have Texas cattle without number, and almost every day bring in more. Their country is large and fruitful; almost all kinds of wild fruit can be found; grass is abundant, but the wood is scarce. These Indians are of good heart, and desire to live at peace with our government. At no time have most of them seen an agent. They know nothing about the government distributing annually presents among the Indians.... At our first meeting I found many of the Indians very drunk, and almost uncontrollable." **Rep. Com. Indian Affairs, 1867, p. 214.**

103 Rep. on the Cond. Ind. Tribes, 1867, p. 265.

104 Chief Manuelito defied the army and evaded capture for almost fifteen months after Carleton's ultimatum to get him dead or alive. The army almost captured him at Ojo del Malpais, 75 miles west of old Fort Canby, on July 29, 1865. Manuelito fled at the approach of the soldiers, leaving his campfire burning. This time the soldiers took possession of 18 horses, Navajo blankets, saddles, mounted bridles and belts, which the chief left behind in his sudden get away. Finally Manuelito left his hiding place near the head waters of the Little Colorado, and went to Fort Wingate, where he surrendered on Sept. 1, 1866, together with 23 members of his band, mostly relatives, and a few horses and mules. Wounded several weeks before in a skirmish with soldiers, Manuelito had lost, almost entirely, the use of his left arm. Up to the day of his surrender, Manuelito had repeatedly declared that he would suffer death rather than go to the reservation at Bosque Redondo. Probably his wounded arm, which required medical attention, rather than starvation, finally compelled Manuelito to change his mind. Captain E. Butler and cavalrymen at Fort Wingate had given Manuelito no time to rest, or to provide himself or his band with necessaries of life. The captured chief was taken to Santa Fe, and then to the Bosque. At the time of his capture the Santa Fe *Gazette* commented: "Manuelito was the most stubborn of all the Navajo chiefs, and was the most difficult to be brought to terms." When word got about that Manuelito had surrendered, other last-ditch leaders of the tribe decided to give up the fight. Chief Barboncito, with a band of 21, left the *Cañon de Chelle* and surrendered near Fort Wingate on Nov. 7, 1866, followed soon after by 43 other stragglers. Barboncito and the 64 prisoners were taken to the Bosque. On Nov. 28, 1866, another band of 138 men, women and children, came in to Fort Wingate from the Little Colorado country, and surrendered, together with their 400 sheep and goats and 60 horses.

On Feb. 25, 1886, almost eighteen years after General Sherman made a treaty with the Navajos at Bosque Redondo, and permitted them to return to their own country, Chief Manuelito, in reminiscent mood, talked before a council of Navajos and government officials at Fort Defiance, Arizona. Through an interpreter, Manuelito told the story of the Navajo exodus of 1863, and of the confinement of the tribe at the Bosque. Manuelito was one of the most resourceful and intelligent of the Navajos. His recital of events, beginning with a time shortly before the American Occupation of 1846, and General Sherman's treaty talks with the tribe in 1868, is of great historical value and interest, demonstrating the almost total inadequacy of conception on the part of the Navajos of the might of the United States: "You have already heard some of the history of the Navajo tribe. When our fathers lived they heard that the Americans were coming across the great river westward. . . . We heard of the guns and powder and lead—first flint locks, then percussion caps, and now repeating rifles. We first saw the Americans at Cottonwood Wash. We had wars with the Mexicans and the Pueblos. We captured mules from the Mexicans, and had many mules. The Americans came to trade with us. When the Americans first came we had a big dance, and they danced with our women. We also traded. The Americans went back to Santa Fe, which the Mexicans then held. Afterwards we heard that the Mexicans had disarmed them and made them prisoners. That is how the Mexican war began. Had the Mexicans let the Americans alone they would not have been defeated by the Americans. Then there were many soldiers at Santa Fe, and the Mexican governor was driven away. They did not kill the governor. Therefore we like the Americans. The Americans fight fair and we like them. Then the soldiers built the fort here, and gave us an agent who advised us to behave well. He told us to live peaceably with the whites; to keep our promises. They wrote down the promises, so that we would always remember them. From that on we had sheep and horses. We had lots of horses and felt good; we had a fight with the Americans, and were whipped. At that time we thought we had a big country, extending over a great deal of land. We fought for that country because we did not want to lose it, but we made a mistake. We lost nearly everything, but we had some beads left, and with them we thought we were rich. I have always advised the young men to avoid war. The American nation is too powerful for us to fight. When we had a fight for a few days we felt fresh, but in a short time we were worn out, and the soldiers starved us out. Then the Americans gave us something to eat, and we came in from the mountains and went to Texas. We were there a few years; many of our people died from the climate. Then we became good friends with the white people. The Comanches wanted us to fight, but we would not join them. One day the soldiers went after the Comanches. I and the soldiers charged on the Comanches, but the Comanches drove us back, and I was left alone to fight them; so the white men came in twelve days to talk with us, as our people were dying off. People from Washington held a council with us. He explained how the whites punished those who disobeyed the law. We promised to obey the laws if we were permitted to get back to our own country. We promised to keep the treaty you read to us today. We promised four times to do so. We all said 'yes' to the treaty, and he gave us good advice. He was General Sherman. We told him we would try to re-member what he said. He said: 'I want all you people to look at me.' He stood up for us to see him. He said if we would do right we could look people in the face. Then he said: 'My children, I will send you back to your homes.' The nights and days were long before it came time for us to go to our homes. The day before we were to start we went a little way towards home, because we were so anxious to start. We came back and the Americans gave us a little stock to start with and we thanked them for that. We told the drivers to whip up the mules, we were in such a hurry. When we saw the top of the mountain from Albuquerque we wondered if it was our mountain, and we felt like talking to the ground, we loved it so, and some of the old men and women cried with joy when they reached their homes." Ex. Doc. 263, H. of R., 49th Cong., 1st Sess., p. 14.

105 The total population of Navajos at the Bosque Redondo as of Dec. 31, 1864, was 8,354. An accurate census of the Navajos and their property as of that date, prepared under the personal supervision of Captain Francis Mc-Cabe, of the First New Mexico Volunteer Cavalry, was submitted to Carleton at Santa Fe, on Jan. 7, 1865. The number of "Lodges" (crude living quarters) reported was 1,276. Other figures were as follows: Families, 1,782; males from 50 to 80 years of age, 300; males from 18 to 50 years, 2,129; males from 5 to 18 years, 1,525; male infants, 134; females from 50 to 80 years of age, 373; fe-males from 18 to 50 years of age, 2,187; females from 5 to 18 years of age, 1,418; female infants, 288. The Navajos had at Bosque Redondo, according to McCabe's census, the following livestock and personal property: Horses, 3,038, mules, 143, sheep, 6,962, goats, 2,757, looms, 630. Accompanying the McCabe report was an interesting letter giving McCabe's understanding of the origin and history of the Navajos, and the location of Bosque Redondo, "in the southeast from Fort Union, and 165 miles east-southeast from Santa Fe, in a valley of the Pecos River, a stream which rises in the mountains near Santa Fe, having its source in a region of almost perpetual snows, and flow-ing downward toward the outspreading plains, has its volume increased by several small tributaries, until at this point (Fort Sumner), the depth and width of the stream is very considerable, furnishing an inexhaustible supply of water for irrigation and all necessary purposes." McCabe's report told of the industry of the Navajos, their horses and sheep, of their marriage cus-toms, and relative past and present conditions. The names of the principal chiefs of Bosque Redondo in 1864, according to Capt. McCabe, were Herrera Grande, Ganado Blanco, Delgadito Grande, Delgadito Chiquito, Barbon, El Chino, El Iuhador, El Largo, Ganada Mucho. Quoting Delgadito on one sub-ject, McCabe said that he was "reliable, intelligent, and can write his signa-ture legibly." OR Series I, Vol. XLVIII, pp. 522-529.

106 The telegraph reached Santa Fe on July 8, 1868, over a line built from Denver via Fort Union. Acting Governor H. H. Heath sent the first official telegram from Santa Fe on July 8, 1868: "His Excellency, Andrew Johnson, President of the United States, Washington, D. C. — Sir: The capital of New Mexico sends to you, and through you to the world, her greetings over the first telegraphic line erected in the Territory. Its completion is another advanced step of an enlightened age, bringing an old into instantaneous communication with newer though more advanced sections of our blessed Union, and with mankind in all civilized lands." President Johnson sent a gracious reply to Heath on July 9, 1868: "I thank you for your kind greeting and congratulate you that the capital of New Mexico is in telegraphic communication with the nation. May the wires serve to render yet more indissoluble the bond that unites the people of your Territory with their fellow citizens of the States." With telegraph service now available, the Weekly *New Mexican* became the Daily *New Mexican*. Vol. 1, No. 1 of the Daily *New Mexican* was published on July 9, 1868. The publishers of the *New Mexican*, Manderfield & Tucker, in a box on page 1 of the first daily, announced that the paper would support U. S. Grant for president, but would not be "entirely a political paper." Although Santa Fe had the telegraph in 1868, it had no railroad connection until 1880. Stage lines tried desperately to maintain schedules and to render service to shippers. The *New Mexican* of July 29, 1868, reported that merchandise shipped from New York City to Spiegelberg Bros. had reached Santa Fe on July 27, 1868, in the record breaking time of forty days.

107 Until Arizona was established as a territory of the United States in 1863, New Mexico occupied an area of approximately 250,000 square miles (about 155,137,480 acres), measuring roughly 422 miles from north to south, and 664 miles from east to west.

108 The federal government owned and operated a printing plant in Santa Fe prior to 1849, as part of the plan of the American Occupation. The government sold the press and type in 1849 to "General" Oliver P. Hovey, who then started the week Santa Fe *Republican*, printed in English and Spanish, with a claimed subscription list of 700 at $5.00 a year. The second printing plant brought to the Territory after the Occupation was hauled across the plains to Albuquerque in 1853, and operated by R. H. Weightman, for a time Delegate in Congress. Weightman published *Amigo del Paiz* in Albuquerque for a few weeks, then moved the plant to Santa Fe, where he sold it to Judge Spruce M. Baird, who had represented Texas in keeping alive its claim to New Mexico as far west as the Rio Grande. In 1857 Baird rented the plant to Don Miguel E. Pino, who published a paper called *El Democrata*, which supported Baird's campaign for election to Congress. Baird was defeated and he sold the plant in 1858 to J. L. Collins, who thereupon established the Santa Fe *Gazette*. A Kentuckian, Collins had lived in New Mexico since 1825, and was superintendent of Indian Affairs for New Mexico for several years.

109 The Santa Fe *Gazette*, reversing its policy, became a supporter of the Union cause shortly after the war began. It was generally understood in Santa Fe that Gen. James H. Carleton became a part owner of the *Gazette* in 1863. J. H. Holmes, Secretary of the Territory, and publisher of the Santa Fe *Republican*, was arrested on or about Aug. 1, 1861, on order of Gen. E. R. S. Canby, accused of "giving information valuable to the enemy." Upon trial before a court martial in Santa Fe, Holmes was found guilty of "giving aid and comfort to the enemy." He was sentenced to two years in prison, but the sentence was suspended on assurance that he would reform his editorial conduct. However Canby ordered the *Republican* to suspend publication indefinitely "to prevent giving contraband information." See Santa Fe *Gazette*, Nov. 2, 1867. Canby proclaimed martial law for New Mexico on Aug. 8, 1861, some ten days after Baylor and his Texas Riflemen captured several hundred

Union troops at San Augustine Pass, 17 miles east of Mesilla, and took possession of nearby Fort Fillmore.

110 Only a meager description of the Mesilla *Times* plant has survived. A young soldier of the California Column referred to it incidentally in a letter written to his parents, published in the *Daily Alta California* of Nov. 1, 1862: "We have splendid quarters here at Mesilla, occupying the buildings of the Overland Mail Company. There is a printing office here, where once was published the treasonable sheet, 'The Mesilla Times.' It is an old outfit, imported here from Illinois, a regular one horse concern."

111 OR Series I, Vol. 4, p. 39.

112 OR Series I, Vol. 9, p. 650. John Sebrie Watts was born in Boone County, Kentucky, Jan. 19, 1816, died in Bloomington, Monroe County, Indiana, June 11, 1876. Educated at Indiana University at Bloomington, he was admitted to the Indiana Bar, served in the Indiana legislature in 1846 and 1847, was an associate justice of the Supreme Court of New Mexico, from 1851 to 1854. He practiced law in Santa Fe from 1854 until elected Delegate in Congress, where he served from March 4, 1861 to March 3, 1863. On July 11, 1868, President Johnson appointed Watts Chief Justice of the Supreme Court of New Mexico, from which position he resigned in 1869. Watts then resumed the practice of law in Santa Fe. He returned to his former home in Indiana a few months before his death.

113 Born in Maryland, Covey had been an Assistant Surgeon in the United States Army, stationed at Cubero, New Mexico. He resigned June 1, 1861 to accept a commission as Surgeon in the Confederate Army, in which he served until 1865, dying in 1867.

114 OR Series I, Vol. L, part 1, p. 501.

115 William Need probably drifted into New Mexico from Missouri. It is known that he was promoted to sergeant major of the First New Mexico Volunteers on or about July 1, 1863. He was one of the first men to enlist in the New Mexico Territorial militia after the call for volunteers. After being made sergeant major, Need served as clerk for adjutants and quartermasters.

116 OR Series I, Vol. L, part 1, pp. 635-641.

117 Insofar as known Paula Angel was the only woman ever hanged in New Mexico. The writer is indebted to Hon. Luis Armijo, of Las Vegas, for many years judge of the Fourth Judicial District, for the story of the hanging. Judge Armijo's grandmother, Senora Peregrina Apodaca de Armijo, told him about the hanging when he was a small boy, almost sixty years ago. He retained the story in his memory all during the intervening years, but had never been able to verify it to his satisfaction until, while browsing recently among old papers in the San Miguel County Courthouse, he discovered the file of original papers in the case. Taking the names, dates and other data from the papers, and recalling what his grandmother had told him so many years before, Judge Armijo pieced together a strange and interesting story of New Mexico during Civil War years.

118 Upon his arrival in Dona Ana County, New Mexico, in August, 1862, Carleton was advised that no legitimate government had existed in the country for many months. On Sept. 18, 1862, Col. J. R. West, then in "La Mesa, Arizona," following instructions from Carleton, appointed civil officers for the eighth precinct of Dona Ana County, naming Eugenio Mora, as Alcalde, Juan Zenobia Cadena, *mayorodomo de las aguas* (chief of irrigation waters), and Jose de la luz Jiron, as constable, to hold office at his pleasure. West instructed Alcalde Mora that his duties were to arrest, and send to Mesilla for trial by the military authorities all persons charged with crimes by the laws of New

Mexico punishable by sentences greater than twenty dollars or forty days in jail; appeals were to be taken to a military commission instead of to the district court. Such an arrangement was to continue until civil authority was replaced by the military. OR Series I, Vol. L, part 2, p. 105.

[119] Santa Fe *New Mexican*, Jan. 13, 1865.

[120] Rio Abajo Weekly *Press*, April 12, 1864.

[121] OR Series L, Vol. XXXIV, part 2, p. 245. After observing the "passport war" for some months, the Rio Abajo *Press* at Albuquerque commented editorially that "Knapp either had martial law on the brain," or was "afflicted with incurable copperheadism."

[122] Rio Abajo Weekly *Press*, April 5, 1864.

[123] Santa Fe *New Mexican*, July 1, 1864.

[124] OR Series I, Vol. XLI, part 2, p. 111.

[125] Ibid, p. 114. Joseph Gillette Knapp, colorful character during New Mexico's Civil War years, was born at Moravia, Cayuga County, New York, in 1805, and died in Limona, Florida, July 2, 1888. He attended the Academy in Cazenovia, Madison County, New York, and after being graduated, was ordained a Methodist minister. He preached the gospel for about one year, and then united with the Episcopal church and attended the college at Geneva, New York, and the Theological Seminary at New York City, after which he was appointed a missionary to the Six Nations at Green Bay, Wisconsin, laboring there for several years. In 1838, Knapp moved to Madison, Wisconsin, where he lived for more than 20 years. For a time he was editor and proprietor of the Wisconsin *Inquirer,* the first paper published at Madison; then he became Superintendent of Public Property for the Territory of Wisconsin, during which time he studied law, was admitted to the Wisconsin Bar, and became prominent in practice in Dane County, Wisconsin. In 1861 he was appointed a judge of the New Mexico Territorial Supreme Court, and assigned to the third judicial district, with headquarters at Mesilla. Judge Knapp arrived in New Mexico at a time when the country around Mesilla, for miles in every direction, was seething over Civil War difficulties. For a detailed history of Judge Knapp's life, see *Wisconsin State Journal*, Madison, Wis., July 18, 1888.

[126] OR Series I, Vol. XLI, part 2, p. 169. Carleton quoted General U. S. Grant on passports, as follows: "In a department like that of New Mexico and Arizona, of great geographical extent and a sparse population, mostly strangers to each other, with a small military force mostly at isolated and remote stations and with numerous spies and traitors scattered throughout the country, measures of military police somewhat stringent in their character are sometimes necessary to preserve peace and good order. No good and loyal citizen can object to them. All such can comply with the rule without inconvenience or loss of dignity. I mention in this connection that I myself and the officers of my staff in Washington and St. Louis have been required to procure passports from our inferior officers, the provost marshals, for our identification, to enable us to pass the guards in the streets and public roads. In times of war and public danger, this is a proper and necessary measure of military policy, and no officer, military or civil, no matter what his rank, can object to it in places where the public safety requires its adoption." Ibid, p. 169.

[127] When Judge Knapp left Mesilla for "the states" on June 15, 1865, on account of Mrs. Knapp's illness, Carleton issued an unsolicited order to the commanders of all military posts in New Mexico, instructing them to tender any possible courtesy or assistance to the Knapps on their journey.

[128] Rep. Com. Ind. Affairs, 1863, pp. 105-109.

129 Ex. Doc. 65, 38th Cong., 1st Session, H. R.

130 OR Series I, Vol. XLI, part 2, p. 723.

131 Rep. Com. Ind. Affairs, 1863.

132 Santa Fe *Gazette*, Oct. 29, 1864.

133 Both Carleton and Carson had expected to enlist Navajo Indians from Bosque Redondo to help defeat the Plains Indians. A number of Navajos were willing to enlist, but it was decided not to use them because of strong protests made by the Utes, who were willing to fight with Apaches, but not with the Navajos. See letter from Carson to Carleton, OR Series L, Vol. XLI, p. 99, dated Oct. 18, 1864.

134 The Comanche chief, Sheer-kea-na-kwangh, appeared at Fort Bascom on Jan. 21, 1865, carrying a flag of truce, and asked for a treaty of peace. Carleton went to Fort Bascom from Santa Fe. He agreed upon a temporary arrangement with the Comanche chief who promised that no trains would be robbed on the Plains until treaty terms could be agreed upon. Reluctant to compromise with the Comanches by "talks," Carleton was anxious at the same time to halt train robberies on the plains. He was even more anxious to have Kit Carson return to the Navajo country without delay and resume his campaign against the Navajos, which had dragged during his absence fighting Comanches and Kiowas.

135 OR Series I, Vol. XLI, p. 943. Trading by civilians with the Indians of New Mexico was entirely prohibited by proclamation issued by Governor Robt. B. Mitchell in Santa Fe, on September 12, 1867.

136 OR Series L. Vol. XLI, part 4, p. 496.

137 Dr. Michael Steck, son of John and Elizabeth Steck, was born in Hughesville, Lycoming County, Pennsylvania, October 6, 1818. He died on a farm to which he had retired, five miles from Winchester, Frederick County, Virginia, on October 6, 1883. In Pennsylvania, prior to 1759, the Stecks were staunch Lutherans. Eight of them in the male line became Lutheran ministers. Michael Steck was inclined in his youth to study for the church, but studied medicine instead. Graduated from Jefferson Medical College in 1844, Steck practiced medicine for several years in Mifflinville, Pennsylvania. Because of his wife's failing health, he accepted an appointment from President Fillmore as Indian Agent for the Mescalero Apaches in southeastern New Mexico. President Buchanan subsequently appointed him superintendent of Indian Affairs for New Mexico. Steck became involved in a bitter controversy with General Carleton over his Navajo Indian policy. Steck stood his ground with courage and fortitude in the face of Carleton's overwhelming advantage as commander of the military forces in New Mexico, and during the period the Territory was under martial law. Although no longer in the Indian service, Steck saw the day come in 1868 when, through General William T. Sherman, the Navajo Indians were released from their Bosque Redondo bondage, and returned to their own country. After "retiring" from the Indian service during his quarrel with Carleton, Steck engaged in gold mining in New Mexico in partnership with Stephen B. Elkins, later United States Senator from West Virginia, Chairman of the Republican National Committee when J. G. Blaine ran for president, and Secretary of War in President Benjamin Harrison's cabinet. Making a small fortune in New Mexico gold mining enterprises, Dr. Steck returned to Hughesville, Pennsylvania, and with a part of his fortune built the finest house there. It is still standing. He invested his remaining funds with promoters of the Williamsport and North Branch railroad, which connected for many years with the Pennsylvania and Reading railroad on the west branch of the Susquehanna River, and with the Lehigh railroad on the North Branch. Steck endorsed promissory notes for promoters and investors

and eventually lost his entire fortune, including "the finest house in Hughesville." Buried in the cemetery in Winchester, Virginia, the Navajo Indians could well afford to erect a monument over Steck's grave, dedicated to the memory of a man who was a staunch friend during the years of their exile on the banks of the Pecos River in New Mexico.

138 There was a makeshift hospital for the Indians at Fort Sumner. On Sept. 6, 1866, Assistant Surgeon M. Hilary, M.R.C.S., Ireland, reported to Col. Theo. E. Dodd, Agent at Fort Sumner for the Navajos, advising him that during the six months period, Jan. 1, 1866 to August 31, 1866, the hospital had treated 235 cases of syphilis. Describing the hospital facilities, and prevailing health conditions, Dr. Hilary wrote: "The hospital building is a regular tumble down concern; even rain comes through the roof—in fact I may say the place is only fit to keep pigs in. So, having an idea of what it is, you may see the necessity of a speedy change to a more suitable one. If the military puts up a building according to the plan forwarded to them six months ago, I think we will have something like a hospital. You can see from my report the vast preponderance of syphilis over every other disease, and which will always be the case as long as so many soldiers are around here, because the Indian women have not the slightest idea of virtue, and are bought and sold by their own people like cattle. . . . I would recommend you try to keep the women as far from the fort as possible; to build a good substantial hospital; to employ a first class physician (and you had better have a good one or none at all)." See Rep. Com. Ind. Affairs, 1866, p. 150.

139 For the history of this fabulous property, see *Maxwell Land Grant, a New Mexico Item,* by William A. Keleher, Rydal Press, Santa Fe, 1943. At the price of $250,000 suggested by Norton, which would have been accepted by the owner at the time, the grant would have cost the government about 35¢ an acre, and provided an ideal place for the Navajos. Gold, coal, timber and other resources on the grant would have made the Navajos an immensely wealthy tribe.

140 See Rep. Com. Ind. Affairs, 1867. The Mescaleros were finally settled on the Mescalero Indian reservation, in their own country, not far from Fort Stanton, in southeastern New Mexico, where they remain today as a tribal unit.

141 Rep. Com. Indian Affairs, 1864, p. 215.

142 Santa Fe *Gazette,* Jan. 21, 1865.

143 *New Mexican,* Feb. 3, 1865.

144 *New Mexican,* April 7, 1865.

145 Santa Fe *New Mexican,* May 12, 1865. On June 6, 1868, the Santa Fe *Gazette* took a dig at the *New Mexican:* "Since 1860, the *Gazette* suspended but once, and that was in consequence of the occupation of Santa Fe by the Texans in 1862. Since the beginning of 1862, what is now the *New Mexican,* has been suspended twice, once suppressed by military authority for publishing contraband information useful to the enemies of the country, and once for inability to exist longer."

146 After being relieved of his command in New Mexico, Carleton went to Washington, and from there to Eastport, Maine, on what proved to be his last visit to his native state. On June 1, 1867, Carleton was confirmed as a major general by the United States Senate. A year later, June 1, 1868, he was assigned to the command of troops in San Antonio, Texas, where he died of pneumonia on Jan. 3, 1873. Posts of the Grand Army of the Republic in New Mexico and elsewhere adopted resolutions of regret.

Sophia Garland Wolfe Carleton, wife of James H. Carleton, acquired property in Albuquerque, in 1854, consisting of twelve buildings, corrals and other improvements, which she rented to the United States Army at a monthly rental of $125.00 for use as shops, stables, storehouses and a hospital. Under direction of Captain H. M. Enos, Assistant Quartermaster at Albuquerque, the Carleton buildings were destroyed by fire on March 2, 1862. On Sept. 12, 1862, a board of survey composed of Colonel C. Carson, Captain H. R. Selden and Lieut. A. L. Anderson met at Albuquerque and assessed the damage done to the Carleton property at $8,600. On Nov. 15, 1862, Carleton wrote from Santa Fe to Senator Milton S. Latham, of California, then in Washington, requesting his assistance in getting a bill through the Congress authorizing reimbursement for the property loss sustained in Albuquerque. Carleton said: "The loss of this property and of some real estate which I had bought for my children in Texas, and which was long since confiscated by the rebels, takes everything I had in the world. I now have only my commission, after twenty odd years hard work, and if I should die tomorrow my children would be beggars." OR Series I, Vol. L, p. 225. A bill for relief was introduced in Congress on Feb. 21, 1863. See Report No. 441, 42d Congress, 3rd session, H. R. On March 4, 1884, nearly eleven years after Carleton's death, the committee on War Claims of the House of Representatives reported: "The town of Albuquerque was the theater of military operations; the enemy were in possession; the destruction of the property was the result of an overruling military necessity; the damage resulting from its destruction was inevitably and unavoidably incidental to its operations; and there is no obligation to make recompense. The hardship to the individual is heavy to be borne, but if the rule is to be established that the government is to make good all destruction of property consequent upon war we shall break down and destroy the government in our effort to care for the individual." See Report No. 926, N. R., 48th Congress, 1st Session. The Carleton claim was eventually revived in the House in the name of Eva Moore, Henry Carleton and Maude Carleton, children of General Carleton, deceased, and allowed on March 16, 1890. See Rep. No. 879, H. R., 51st Congress, 1st Session. The Carleton property in Albuquerque was located between the San Felipe Church and the Rio Grande. The land on which the structures were located up to 1862 is now subdivided. Dora Ann Drive is one of the principal streets in the subdivision. For a record of the conveyances to and from the Carletons, see Book A, pp. 128-129, and Book B, pp. 8 and 9, records of Bernalillo County.

147 Tappan recruited Union troops at Central City and Black Hawk, Colo., and fought with them against Confederates at Pigeon's Ranch, near present Glorieta, New Mexico, on March 28, 1862. Sherman and Tappan negotiated treaties in 1868, before coming to New Mexico, with the Cheyennes, Arapahoes, Kiowas, Comanches and Crows. See Gen. Sherman's report on the treaties written in St. Louis as of Nov. 1, 1868, published in full in Santa Fe *Gazette,* Dec. 26, 1868. It is believed that Sherman had not been in New Mexico previously. At the beginning of the Mexican War in 1846 Sherman, then a lieutenant, accompanied troops shipped around the Horn to California, where he served as an adjutant to General Kearny.

148 See Maj. Gen. John Pope's report on New Mexico Indian Affairs, submitted to Gen. Sherman, written at Fort Union, New Mexico, dated Aug. 11, 1866, published in part in Santa Fe *Gazette,* Jan. 5, 1867.

149 By actual survey, the Navajos were given 4,500,000 acres of land under the treaty of 1868. By executive orders of Oct. 29, 1878, Jan. 6, 1880, and at various times thereafter, the original reservation was substantially enlarged. The total area of the Navajo reservation today is approximately 16,000,000 acres, embracing 25,000 square miles. It is 195 miles straight across from the east boundary in New Mexico to the west boundary in Arizona. The Navajo reservation is half as big as the State of Pennsylvania—half as big as England with its 51,000 square miles. (See p. 205, Interior Department Appropriation Bill for 1947.) The treaty between the government and the Navajo tribe of Indians, concluded at Fort Sumner, on June 1, 1868, is a document of absorb-

ing interest even today, more than eighty years after its execution. By and with the advice of the Senate, as provided in a resolution of July 25, 1868, Andrew Johnson, President of the United States, signed the treaty in Washington on Aug. 12, 1868, thus making it final and official. The treaty was signed at Fort Sumner by General Sherman and Colonel Tappan on behalf of the United States, and by a council of twelve Navajos and seventeen sub-chiefs. Barboncito, chief of the Navajos at Bosque Redondo, was the first man to sign for the Council. Every Indian signatory signed by mark. Not one could write his name. Among those who "signed" were men with such outlandish names as Muerto de Hombre, Ganado Mucho, Muchachos Muchos, Cabares Colorados, all, however, descriptive of and identifying the owner of the name, a custom still prevalent among the tribe. Article 2 of the treaty fixed the country, partly in New Mexico, partly in Arizona, to which the Navajos should go after their exile on the Pecos River. The land to belong to them was roughly described as being bounded on the north by the 37th degree of north latitude, south by an east and west line passing through the site of old Fort Defiance, in *Canon Bonito*, east by the parallel of longitude, which, if prolonged south, would pass through old Fort Lyon, or the *Ojo-de-oso* (Bear Spring,) and west by a parallel of longitude about 109° 30' west of Greenwich provided it embraced the outlet of the Canon de Chelly, and the entire canon itself. A present-day timber cruise indicates that in the mountainous parts of the land there are some twenty-two billion feet of standing timber. Vast areas of the original treaty land are ideal for grazing of live-stock, but many thousands of acres of land acquired under the original treaty, and subsequent grants, are of little or no value.

150 General Sherman testified on Jan. 6, 1874, concerning New Mexico's fitness for statehood before the Committee on Military Affairs of the House of Representatives in Washington. Sherman displayed a map of New Mexico, and declared that "ownership of the Territory was not worth the cost of defense." Sherman explained: "The Eighth Cavalry is in New Mexico, another of those delightful lands acquired from Old Mexico at the end of our Mexican War. We have got it, and we have got to take care of it, unless you can prevail on Mexico to take it back. The highest point occupied by our troops is Fort Garland, in what is called the San Juan valley. To the westward of it is Fort Wingate, a post that is necessary in connection with the Navajo Indians; Fort Union, to the east, where the mail road comes into New Mexico. Down the valley you have Fort Bayard, Fort McRae and Fort Craig. To the right and left in the lower valley, you have Fort Stanton and Fort Cummings—we call it Tularosa; so that regiment covers substantially the whole of New Mexico, protecting the native population against the Indians, the protecting the Indians as against the native population. Between them there is, and has been for three hundred years—longer than this country has been settled—a war, and the soldiers have to catch the knocks of both. As long as that condition of affairs lasts you will have to keep a regiment of cavalry there. If we should disband the Eighth Cavalry tomorrow, we would have to replace it within three weeks, or else acknowledge that we are incompetent to defend our own territory. It is not worth the cost of defense, but that is not our business." See Testimony of Sherman, 44th Congress, 1st Session, Report 503. In August, 1878, ten years after he had negotiated the Navajo treaty at Fort Sumner, Sherman inspected Fort Union and Fort Marcy in New Mexico. See Las Vegas *Gazette,* Aug. 24, 1878.

151 By Aug. 5, 1868, Cubero people accused the recently returned Navajos of stealing livestock. The government had failed to provide the Navajos with the necessaries of life, forcing them to steal or starve. See Santa Fe *New Mexican,* July 10, 1868, August 10, 1868.

152 The Navajo treaty, signed at Fort Sumner, as with most government-Indian treaties at the time, was not a generous one. There was no provision to compensate the Navajos for the irreparable damage they had sustained in connection with capture and confinement. The treaty signed by the Navajo

chiefs, at the request of Gen. Sherman and Col. Tappan, was to them just one more puzzling bit of paper. In a general way, the government has faithfully carried out, over the years, the thirteen-paragraph treaty drawn up by Sherman and Tappan. The government, however, has failed miserably in its attempts to carry out Article 6 of the treaty, under which it promised to educate all Navajo children between the ages of six and sixteen; and to provide a school house and teacher for every thirty children of that age who could be induced or compelled to attend school, the teacher to reside among the Indians. Regardless of the why or wherefore, the government has not educated the Navajos. Eighty odd years after the treaty of 1868 only five per cent of the Navajos can read and write the English language. A bare eight per cent may be able to speak English. When the treaty was signed at Fort Sumner in 1868, the Navajo population was 9,000, according to the best information then available. As of 1951 the population was estimated at 65,546, divided as follows: Arizona, 39,087 (Apache County, 19,744, Coconino County, 7,549, Navajo County, 11,794); New Mexico, 24,090 (McKinley County, 13,192, San Juan County, 10,898); Utah (San Juan County 2,369). Problems incident to marriage and family life are the source of much concern to those sincerely interested in the Navajo. Peyote, shipped in great quantities from Oklahoma and elsewhere, not a narcotic, perhaps, but nevertheless a prolific source of trouble of various types and of varying degrees of seriousness and magnitude, is penetrating the Navajo country. The use of peyote by the Navajos is being encouraged by neighboring Ute Indians, ancient enemies, through the efforts of their peyote "priests." The peyote group on the Navajo reservation, anxious to get control of affairs in which they are particularly interested, backs candidates for election to the Navajo Council, causes no end of trouble to officials and other groups of Navajos not interested in peyote. The pitiful and pitiable condition of the Navajo today, in the opinion of the writer, may be charged primarily to the government's failure to educate the Indians according to the treaty of 1868. As a result of that failure, the Navajo had no vote as an American citizen, until 1948, when the federal court in New Mexico signed a mandatory decree granting them the right of franchise, whether on or off the reservation. As a direct result of their inability to vote, the Navajo has never had any political influence, or prestige, in New Mexico, Arizona or in the nation. The Navajo has suffered tremendously from lack of continuity of policy. The fate of the Navajo, since 1868, has been in the hands of a commissioner of Indian Affairs. Some commissioners have been incapable, stupid, eccentric. Other commissioners have been honest and able men.

153 Santa Fe *New Mexican*, Sept. 26, 1868.

154 See Las Vegas *Gazette*, March 1, 1873.

155 Ibid.

156 Report of Com. Ind. Affairs, 1877.

157 In the year 1896, almost thirty years after General Sherman freed the Navajos from their Bosque Redondo bondage, the official census gave them a population on the reservation in New Mexico and Arizona of 20,500, of whom it was estimated that 1,000 wore citizen's dress in part, 250 Navajos could read, and that there were 500 more who could carry on an ordinary conversation in English. Rep. Com. Ind. Affairs, 1897, p. 598.

SOURCES

Ex. Doc. 41, 30th Cong., 1st Sess.
H.R. Ex. Doc. 65, 38th Cong., 1st Sess.

H.R. Ex. Doc. 70, 38th Cong., 1st Sess.
H.R. Ex. Doc. 263, 49th Cong., 1st Sess., p. 14.
H.R. Mis. Doc. 73, 34th Cong., 1st Sess.
H.R. No. 104, 43rd Cong., 1st Sess.
H.R. Rep. No. 441, 42nd Cong., 3rd Sess.
H.R. Rep. No. 503, 44th Cong., 1st Sess.
H.R. Rep. 879, 51st Cong., 1st Sess.
H.R. Rep. 926, 48th Cong., 1st Sess.

Official Reports —
    Series I,
        Vol.   4, pp. 39, 71.
                9, p. 650.
              XV, pp. 229, 576, 670.
            XXVI, Part 1, pp. 23 to 728, at random.
             XLI, Part 1, p. 943.
             XLI, Part 2, pp. 111 to 723, at random.
         XLVIII, Part 1, pp. 522-529.
         XLVIII, Part 2, pp. 1150, 1151, 1266.
                L, Part 1, pp. 501, 635-641.
                L, Part 2, pp. 105, 225, 267, 275, 296, 300.

    Series X,
        Vol. XV, p. 579.

    Serie L,
        Vol. XLI, p. 99.
             XLI, Part 4, p. 496.
           XXXIV, Part 1, pp. 71 to 119, at random.
           XXXIV, Part 2, p. 245.

Reports Commissioner of Indian Affairs, 1862, 1863, 1864, 1865, 1866, 1867, 1877, 1884, 1897.

REFERENCES

"Annals of Old Fort Cummings, New Mexico, 1867-8," by William Thornton Parker, Northampton, Mass., 1916.
"The Battle of Buena Vista, With the Operations of the Army of Occupation for One Month," James H. Carleton, 1848.
"The Franciscan Missions of the Southwest," 1922, St. Michael's, Arizona.
Journal of the Military Service Institution, Vol. IV, No. 15, Sept., 1883.
"Maxwell Land Grant, a New Mexico Item," by W. A. Keleher, Santa Fe, 1943.
"The Navaho," by Dr. Clyde Kluckhon and Dr. Dorothea Leighton, Harvard U. Press, 1947.

NEWSPAPERS AND PERIODICALS

Daily Alta California, Nov. 1, 1862.

Land of Sunshine, Los Angeles, Oct., Nov., 1896; Feb., 1899.

Las Vegas Gazette, June 23, 1867; June 6, Dec. 4, 1868; March 1, 1873; July 10, Aug. 12, 1876; June 30, 1877; Aug. 24, 1878.

National Intelligencer, Feb. 26, 1864.

Rio Abajo Press, Albuquerque, June 30, 1862; Feb. 4, April 21, July 7, Nov. 10, Dec. 8, 1863; Feb. 10, April 5, 12, 1864.

Santa Fe Gazette, Feb. 2, 23, 1861; Aug. 13, Oct. 29, 1864; Jan. 21, May 1, June 21, July 22, Aug. 5, Sept. 2, 1865; May 19, 26, 1866, Jan. 27, 1866; Jan. 5, 26, Feb. 2, Nov. 2, 1867; Dec. 26, 1868; June 21, 1869.

Santa Fe New Mexican, May 27, July 1-9, Oct. 31, Nov. 4, 18, Dec. 9, 1864; Jan. 13, Feb. 3, April 7, May 12, Nov. 3, 1865; Jan. 1, 1866; Jan. 26, 1867; July 10, 27, Aug. 6, 10, Sept. 26, 1868.

Wilmington Journal, Feb. 18, 1865.

Wisconsin State Journal, July 18, 1888.

INDEX

513